The Gun Digest Book Of

TRAP & SKEET SHOOTING

2ND EDITION

By Art Blatt

DBI BOOKS, INC.

Staff

SENIOR EDITOR
Harold A. Murtz

EDITORIAL ASSISTANT
Jamie L. McCoy

COVER PHOTOGRAPHY
John Hanusin

MANAGING EDITOR
Pamela J. Johnson

PUBLISHER
Sheldon L. Factor

About Our Covers

Trap and Skeet shooters the world over will instantly recognize the familiar lines of our two cover guns — the Remington Model 870 TC Trap and Model 11-87 Premier Skeet autoloader.

The upper gun, the slide-action Model 870 TC Trap, is legendary for its reliable action, smooth handling and great overall quality. It gives the target shooter the same dependable pump action that has made the Model 870 the choice of more than 4 million shotgunners worldwide.

The TC Trap offers the shooter a choice of either standard trap stock or the Monte Carlo, both featuring tournament-grade cut checkering and durable satin finish. It's available with a 2¾-inch chamber, ventilated rib barrel and with Trap Full or Rem Choke choke tube.

Below it is the newer autoloading Model 11-87 Premier Skeet, designed for the balance, pointability and soft recoil target shooters need. It has a stainless steel magazine tube that resists rust and corrosion. The extractor, firing pin spring, heat-treated piston and seal are engineered to give extremely reliable maintenance-free operation through thousands of rounds.

The stock and forend are carved from select American walnut, have tournament-grade cut checkering and a satin finish.

The 11-87 Premier Skeet is available in 12-gauge only with 2¾-inch chamber and 26-inch ventilated rib barrel, with either fixed Skeet choke or Rem Choke choke tubes.

Featured with these great shotguns are Remington's Premier Rem-Lite target shotshells designed to reduce recoil. That's a great asset in long tournaments where shoulder fatigue can affect concentration. Remington's Premier Duplex target loads contain two shot sizes in each shell — No. 7½ and No. 8. Where competition targets vary in range and angle, the smaller No. 8s help improve patterns; the heavier No. 7½s help to break targets at longer ranges. Both loads should help the competition shooter smoke more targets.

Photo by John Hanusin.

ACKNOWLEDGEMENTS

IT TAKES MORE than a single person to put together all the information required to produce a book of this kind. I'm deeply indebted to the following people who helped in this project.

My personal thanks to: David Bopp, ATA; Dick Dietz, Remington Arms; Phil Murray, Mike Bussard, Federal Cartridge Co.; Bob Sheridan, ACTIV Ammunition; Bob Oxsen, Fiocchi Ammunition; Frank Kodl, *Shotgun Sports* magazine; Bonnie Nash, *Trap & Field* magazine; Ed Sowers, and the personnel at various gun clubs throughout the western United States.

Contents

Foreword

IN THIS BOOK, the author has presented a comprehensive view of the shotgun sports of trap and Skeet. The book is much more than a mere instruction manual of shooting techniques, although a vast quantity of valuable information concerning practical applications of shooting methodolgy is included. Primarily, this is a compendium of information that is essential to a complete understanding of aerial target shooting.

Beginning with a brief history of the sport of shooting flying targets as practiced in days long gone by, the development of trap and Skeet as formal competitive shooting events is traced from humble origins to contemporary World Championship Tournaments. A thorough knowledge of the background of any sport enhances enjoyment of that sport by both participants and spectators alike. Since trap and Skeet are spectator sports, especially for families of competitors, reading of many parts of this book will be most helpful in making trap and Skeet more interesting to those who only watch and wait.

For novices, or those who are only contemplating entry into the world of trap and Skeet, there is a wealth of information to be found in this book that will serve as a much needed confidence booster. Not only is the tyro told what to do when first starting out, but also why things should be done in a certain way. Such subjects as safe gun handling, range etiquette, gun mounting, swing and lead, foot and body position, as well as basic rules are covered in great detail.

It is hoped that even advanced or expert trap and Skeet shooters will benefit from many of the small but important points that are brought to light. Perhaps much of the information contained in this book will be "old stuff" to experienced shooters, but there is bound to be much that is new—or at least represents a slightly different viewpoint. Even the most knowledgeable among us can frequently learn more by simply being exposed to ideas that act as a reinforcement to concepts that have perhaps been submerged by time.

It would be highly (and improperly) presumptuous to claim that this book contains all there is to know about these fascinating shooting games. No one knows it all, not even the greatest of champions—a fact that most top shooters will freely admit. However, this book does offer to dedicated shotgunners a source of information gleaned from interviews with experts, extensive research into the literature of the sports, and many years of personal experience in competitive shooting.

For the first time, as far as is known, the complete rules of trap and Skeet are here included in a book about these shooting sports. The importance of a thorough understanding of rules and regulations cannot be over-emphasized. A competitor who has a solid background in the proper conduct of an event will exhibit an air of confidence that can only be beneficial to his scores. Not only will a knowledgeable shooter avoid costly or embarrassing mistakes, but he will also be able to stand up for his rights with authority on those occasions when a question arises during the course of a competitive event. Knowing the rules will also enable a competitor to realize some of the problems and responsibilities that confront the organizers of tournaments.

There is one thing this book is guaranteed not to do. Reading a book cannot make a shooter a champion overnight. Only one thing can do that—practice. Constant, consistent practice is the secret of successful shotgunning. Though there is no substitute for years of experience, knowledge gained through reading, if conscientiously applied, can speed up a shooter's progress toward a hard-won championship. And that is the purpose of this book—to help clay bird enthusiasts achieve their goals in the world of trap and Skeet.

1

Early Shotgunning History

DO YOU REMEMBER the first time you took a rock in hand and tossed it at a fast-flying bird? Your efforts seemed very futile, right? The odds of coldcocking flying prey seemed astronomical. Well, you can imagine the consternation of baseball player Dave Winfield, left fielder for the New York Yankees, when, while playing in Toronto, Canada in 1983, he made a routine throw back to the infield and either a seagull entered the flight path of the ball or the ball strayed into the flight path of the unfortunate gull. Anyway, it was a tie, and the gull tumbled to the ball field, deader than the proverbial mackerel. So incensed were the spectators that the Canadian version of the SPCA filed charges against Mr. Winfield, claiming he did it on purpose. Cool heads eventually prevailed and all charges against Winfield were subsequently dismissed. The death was ruled "accidental." As much money as Dave Winfield makes — in the vicinity of $2 million a year — if he *could* hit *any* flying object with a hand-thrown baseball on a guaranteed basis, I think he could probably make money performing that kind of exhibition. The point is obvious — to hit a high, fast-flying object with a hand-propelled projectile takes a great deal more luck than the average person could muster in a lifetime.

Since man's earliest beginnings, he quickly realized that his best chance to capture flying prey was when they were on the ground. Man's skills and knowledge leaned toward traps, nets and careful stalking techniques that made him successful in his quest for food. But when the bird took flight, man was defeated. Sharpened rocks, stones and spears were man's earliest hunting devices on ground animals, but all were worthless against flighted prey.

Then came the bow and arrow which greatly fortified man's hunting equipment — again on ground animals. A few expert archers were able to occasionally bag a

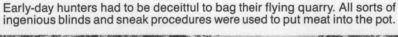

Early-day hunters had to be deceitful to bag their flying quarry. All sorts of ingenious blinds and sneak procedures were used to put meat into the pot.

This is a French artist's conception of a successful hunter downing a brace of game birds. Notice the hunting dog ready to make the retrieve and a non-shooting accomplice who appears to be holding a live decoy for reasons unknown.

flying bird or two after mastering lead, windage and the smallish target area. Somewhere along the way, ancient hunters armed with crude slings attempted to load up the pouch with a number of smaller pebbles rather than the usual single projectile. It would seem that this was the first "scattergun," though that is really stretching the point.

With the advent of firearms in the 14th century, historians might have believed that by using firearms man could take all types of game afoot or aflight. Not so. The early matchlocks were slow to ignite, difficult to aim and clumsy to hold. The word "balance" was not yet invented when it came to early-day firearms. At best, they were a little better than early Chinese hand cannons. To illustrate how difficult it was to use a matchlock rifle, let's pretend you are reading the operating instructions from the owner's manual. Step One: Pour a proper charge of blackpowder down the barrel. Fine, but what is proper charge? There were no reloading manuals from Sierra, Speer or Hornady in those days, so the rifleman had to make a risky guess. Often, his mistake led to his demise. Eventually, by word of mouth, proper charges were not only developed, but recorded for others' knowledge. Next, hopefully a round ball, slightly smaller than the inside bore diameter of the barrel, was rammed home on top of the powder charge. (Patched balls didn't make their appearance for a couple more centuries.) After the barrel work, a smaller charge of priming powder was placed into a pan located above a small hole at the breech section of the barrel. Then came the hard part. A smoldering piece of cord, or the "match" in matchlock, was touched to the priming powder in the pan. The priming powder ignited, traveled through the flash hole and set off the main charge in the barrel. The burning of the main charge created rapidly expanding gases which, in turn, forced the ball down the barrel and out the muzzle. So, as one can see, the entire operation was neither speedy nor effective — but it was a start!

The early matchlocks were extremely heavy, often weighing upward of 25 pounds. They were designed to be shot from the "hip" position as the butt end of the stock left something to be desired for both comfort and steadiness. In the event the rifleman missed with the first shot, rapid reloading was out of the question. No, the matchlock was not an effective firearm on high-flying targets.

About a century later, the wheellock replaced the matchlock. It was basically a matchlock rifle, but instead of using a burning string, it used a device not unlike a Zippo lighter to produce a spark from a special piece of flint stone and iron. The wheellock was really a transitional firearm; the flintlock was the preferred action of the 17th and 18th centuries. Not only did the flintlock increase reloading speed and reliability, but gunmakers and designers were making special "fowling pieces," which incorporated shorter barrels, better balance and more reliable ignition systems.

The blunderbuss was a unique shotgun. It proved to be more scary in appearance than performance. The belled mouth gave the impression that it would spread its payload over a much wider range than its traditional shotgun counterpart. However, the belled mouth did nothing to improve the gun's pattern; it was only an aid in loading, much like using a funnel to pour water into a small bottle.

Even though the flintlock ignition system was reliable, hunters still preferred to shoot birds on the ground rather than in the air. Taking shots at flying birds seemed foolish, considering the great abundance of game. It was not uncommon to harvest eight to 10 birds with one shot when "sluicing 'em." Market hunters, farmers and men who had to put meat on the table really weren't looking to become "sportsmen," their job was to fill meat pots! Besides, reloading time between shots averaged at least 40 seconds for a dexterous shooter, and by then any winged prey, no matter how slow, would be well out of range.

It wasn't until the double-barrel flintlock shotgun came along that wingshooting showed any degree of success. Guns were shortened and lightened and stocks redesigned — all helped the hunter, but none of these changes brought as much success as the two-barreled scattergun. Anyone who has used a double-barrel shotgun — be it a side-by-side or over/under — can attest to the brain's uncanny ability to make corrections after the first shot is missed. Even fair to middlin' nimrods make about 80 percent of the their follow-up shots, while experienced hunters probably enjoy a 92 to 95 percentage of second-shot "kills."

One of the more serious problems hunters experienced was inclement weather. If even a single drop of water found its way into the priming pan of a flintlock shotgun, that charge was voided and a new charge of priming powder had to be poured into the pan. With the invention of percussion caps around 1830, a shooter could load and fire his shotgun during a rain or snow storm.

Equally as important, the use of percussion caps eliminated some of the iron work on the right side of the gun, thereby reducing excess weight. Percussion guns were lighter, much faster to reload, produced a faster lock time by nearly 50 percent over the flintlock, and many "experts" claimed the percussion shotguns were not only state-of-the-art, but would be "the" guns for generations to come. Those soothsayers were proved wrong a few decades later with the invention of the breech-loaded shotshell.

The forerunner to the brass shotshell was the pinfire cartridge, the brainchild of a trio of French gunsmiths — Houiller, LePage and LeFaucheux — around 1840. The pinfire cartridge helped develop the breech-loading, or break-action, shotguns. You couldn't have one without the other. Thus, after nearly 500 years of gun development, a practical and efficient tool for hunting winged prey was finally invented — and perfected.

By the end of the American Civil War, self-contained handgun, rifle and shotgun cartridges were commonplace. For a half-century, from about 1830 to 1880, shotguns and ammunition enjoyed a far greater advancement than what was seen in the preceding half-millennium.

You may be wondering why all this verbiage about early-day gun and ammunition development? Well, if it weren't for those advancements, we wouldn't have trap and Skeet shooting as we know it today. Who knows, perhaps "caseless" ammunition will soon be with us, or shotguns that are really nothing more than sophisticated "airguns." Only time will tell and I wouldn't bet

Market hunters in the late 1860s harvested huge amounts of waterfowl, thanks to the self-contained shotshell. This successful hunter employed a 10-gauge Parker double-barrel shotgun to "bring home the bacon."

against seeing more radical gun and ammunition changes in our lifetime.

Anytime there is a gathering of two or more shooters, you're sure to find either a match, a bet or some sort of competition. Such is human nature. Early-day spear carriers helped develop javelin matches, and longbow archers pitted their skills against each other as part of English jousts and shooting events. The English are credited for establishing semi-formal shooting rules in competition live-game shooting, according to most journals. One of Britain's first "named" shooting events was called "popinjay" shooting. An old English name for parrot, popinjay enjoyed great success with affluent English gentlemen. Both live and stuffed birds were used as targets. The live ones were tethered to a pole by a long line tied to the bird's leg. The lassoed bird could flap its wings and fly for a short distance before it was brought to an abrupt halt — a very difficult target for the gunner. Often, if the bird survived five such volleys, its life was spared and it was released back into the wild. Perhaps the British expression "good show" can be traced back to these early shooting events.

Pigeons, all kinds and species, were, and still are, the favorite target at many shooting matches. These

This early-day sink box was an effective floating blind that enabled waterfowl hunters to invade the duck's lair without being detected.

Scull, sneak or punt boats were used to bring the shooter as close to a flock of water-nesting birds as possible. Often, large-bore shotguns — up to 4 bore — were used to slaughter vast numbers of birds with a single salvo.

birds are rather small, usually weighing about 1-pound, are tough to bring to earth, and fly both fast and erratically. But more importantly, these birds are predictable. They can be expected to do certain things under certain conditions. When released from ground traps, especially those equipped with air-blast systems, they will almost always rise vertically before making a flap into the wind. Experienced shooters know this and will always take note of wind direction just before mounting their "pigeon" gun.

In the shooting sport of columbare, instead of ground boxes, a pigeon thrower launches the bird into the wind which makes the pigeon fly even more erratically. Popular in both Spain and Latin America, columbare shooting is one of the most difficult of the live-bird shooting sports. The contestant stands at the edge of a large circle, usually 100 meters in diameter. In from the shooter is a "thrower" who takes the pigeon in hand, and like a baseball pitcher, tosses the bird over a wire suspended 10 feet above the ground in front of the

shooter. When the bird clears this barrier, the contestant is allowed to shoot twice. The bird must fall within the 100-meter circle to be scored. Any bird that falls outside the chalked circle is scored "lost." Columbare is a difficult game for the shotgunner, but come to think of it, the pigeon isn't exactly enjoying himself!

Trapshooting

The term "trapshooting" was coined by the English to describe shooting events in which targets (live birds) were kept in traps (spring-loaded boxes or cages). Near the end of the 18th century, 1793 in fact, an old English publication titled *Sporting Magazine* featured an article stating that trapshooting was a fairly well-established sport, tracing its roots back as early as 1750 or so.

Early trapshooting equipment was simple, rather crude, but nevertheless effective. There was no one dominant type of trap at the time. Sometimes the traps were merely holes in the ground, covered with planks. Attached to each plank was a long cord, and at the com-

The Cock of the Woods

WINCHESTER

FACTORY LOADED SHOTGUN SHELLS

NUBLACK   NEW RIVAL   LEADER   REPEATER

WINCHESTER REPEATING ARMS CO. NEW HAVEN CONN.

shooting. Once the competitors toed the line, all merriment stopped and serious competition started. Often, large sums of money were wagered — like today — and small fortunes were often won or lost in a shower of feathers.

Another famous early-day English shooting club was Notting Hill. This club drew its membership from only the more affluent hunters, unlike the Hornsey House which allowed the more common folks to join. The "Hill" boasted inhouse servants, an elaborate clubhouse, a superb dining room and bar and offered social affairs such as dances and banquets that included wives and lady friends. Verily, those were the days when shooting was socially acceptable to the gentry.

As shooters became more proficient, new rules and variations of the game were encouraged to make trapshooting more challenging. Around 1832, an English shooting club called the "High Hats" was formed and featured a set of special trapshooting rules. Shooters placed a live bird under a hat placed at their feet. On a signal from a referee, the shooter reached down to pick up his hat — releasing the bird — and had to place it back on top of his head before taking the shot. This extra time gave the bird a much better chance of getting away, thus providing a more sporting proposition.

By the middle of the 19th century, trap clubs had sprung up all over England, throughout the British empire, in fact. There were many accounts of trap shoots in India, Africa and other British colonies. The only difference was the type of indigenous birds and traps used from one country to the next. The Union Jack was the unofficial flag of trapshooting.

By the middle of the 19th century, America discovered trapshooting. Because hunting and shooting were a natural way of life in the "colonies," trap was an instant hit. Some accounts report live pigeon shoots taking place on the East coast as early as 1825. The first official and documented records of such events are found in the journals of the Sportsman's Club of Cincinnati, Ohio. They reported that in 1840, the Long Island Gun Club was established along with a companion organization called the New York Sportsman's Club. These three gun clubs formed the foundation of trapshooting. There were countless inter-club challenges, and all three boasted some of the finest wingshots in the country. Shooting events were held at least once each month and travel between the three clubs was a social gathering.

As in most shooting sports where live game is the target, strong objections against the killing of thousands of pigeons were raised. The inhumane slaughter of pigeons in the name of "sport shooting" was de-

mand "pull," a servant gave the cord a sharp tug, uncovering the hole and freeing the bird. Often, however, the bird was content to stay in the hole, forcing the servant to toss dirt at the bird to encourage flight. Top hats of the day were also often used as traps. They, too, had a cord attachment which tipped them over and allowed the bird to escape. There were other countless ingenious devices employed as traps to hold birds until the shooter asked for them to be released.

The English are great record keepers and preservers of information and events. The first shooting club established in England in 1810, was called the Hornsey Wood House Pigeon Club. A day of shooting led to more than just shooting — it was a major social event for members and their guests. The wealthy members brought their servants to set up tents and prepare food and drink — in great abundance. Eventually, some spoilsport would interrupt the day's eat and gab fest to announce that the traps were loaded and it was time to set down drink, hoist fowling pieces and have a go at cried, and as the movement took hold, legislation was introduced in every state where there was a sanctioned pigeon shooting gun club. Arguments on both sides lasted for nearly 30 years without any official ruling.

Live bird target shooting met its end outside of the Congressional hearing rooms. With the untimely demise of the passenger pigeon in the populated areas of the East coast, combined with preservationists' outcries, trapshooters were constantly seeking substitute airborne targets to replace live pigeons. Another factor that led to the demise of pigeon shooting was the unpredictable flight of the birds. Large sums of money were being wagered on shooting events, and the flight of the pigeon was being challenged. Some birds flew more erratically than others and thus were easier or harder to hit. As a result, many protests and insults were exchanged between contestants. Some claimed the birds were being "drugged" or put into a light sleep just before they were released. In fact, there were so many squabbles, arguments and charges of "fowl" play that trapshooting almost self-destructed. Around 1860, dedicated searches for inanimate targets were conducted. The handwriting was on the wall for live pigeon targets.

At the end of the American Civil War, Charles Portlock of Boston introduced glass balls as targets. Mr. Portlock served on various sailing ships in his youth and probably remembered seeing the Japanese "float balls" used on fishing nets. The Portlock glass balls were about 2½ inches in diameter and were available in various colors, green and clear were the shooters' preferences. These inanimate objects were propelled from a launching device consisting of a cup sitting atop of a compressed spring. When the spring was released, the ball was thrown into the air. Not a very imaginative beginning. Within a short time, however, feathers were glued to the outside of the balls. Then, when the balls were smashed, the feathers fluttered to earth, increasing the live-bird realism. The next step was to load feathers inside the balls, which greatly increased the shooters' enthusiasm. Some balls were loaded with blackpowder, which, when struck with a shot swarm, would explode or give off a bright flash. These targets pleased the audiences.

Glass balls did have some shortcomings. Their hardness was inconsistent. One ball could take a full shot charge squarely, shudder in mid-flight and continue downrange, seemingly unscathed. Others would break as they were propelled out of the launch. The next biggest problem was cleanup and housekeeping. At a larger shoot, there would often be a ton or more of broken glass to be cleaned up. Trenches had to be dug and workers were often cut on the glass shards strewn hither and yon. Despite the glass ball's obvious problems, shooting them remained in vogue for over 40 years, and many exhibition shooters used them well into the 20th century for dramatic special effects.

Clay targets came on the shooting scene around 1870. However, the baked clay targets were, like glass balls, difficult to produce with consistent hardness. Some were as soft as goop, others like dinner plates, and still others couldn't be broken with a blow from a hammer. Myriad targets made of wood, rubber, cardboard, and anything that was available were tried, and all failed.

Two men, one English and the other American, can be called the grandfathers of the clay target. Around 1880, George Ligowsky of Cincinnati, Ohio overcame most of the unpleasantness surrounding the original clay target with his secret recipe. At about the same time, the Englishman, McCaskey, introduced his target made from pitch and river silt. This combination produced the sturdiness and brittleness needed for the "perfect" target. With few chemical changes, this is the same target used today. Pitch is the main ingredient.

Using Ligowsky's targets and special launching machines, trapshooting spread across the United States like wildfire. "Clay" targets flew consistently and presented targets to all shooters equally. There was no bird "doping," and trapshooting matches became more competitive. For a decade and a half, clay target shooting grew to such proportions that the National Gun Association decided to hold its first annual national trapshooting tournament. The site chosen was New Orleans, Louisiana, and the year was 1885. This first shoot was somewhat less than a huge success, but it was held nonetheless. Five years later, the Interstate Association of Trapshooters was formed in Long Island, New York. The association promoted, sponsored and conducted both live bird and clay target events along the Eastern seaboard. They also held what many regard as the first Grand American Tournament in 1900.

The American Trapshooting Association was created in 1900 to act as a governing body for trapshoots and trapshooters. This group, however, was made up of representatives from firearms and ammunition manufacturers, which led to many abuses of power. As a result of much ill will, the Amateur Trapshooting Association was formed in 1924 and remains today as the guiding light of trapshoots and its membership. The ATA's annual bash, the Grand American Tournament, is held in late August every year with over 20,000 trapshooters in attendance for the week's festivities.

Trapshooting underwent dramatic, yet slow changes during the first 80 years or so of its evolution. However, since 1924 there have been only a few rule changes; the game has basically remained the same for over 6 decades.

Skeet Shooting

Hot on the heels of trapshooting and waiting in the wings backstage to make its entrance was another shooting game — Skeet. Skeet shooting, the new kid on the block, didn't become popular until the mid-1930s.

A New Sport FOR Shotgun Shooters

Hunting & Fishing and National Sportsman Magazines combine in introducing to their readers a new sport. Every man who owns a shotgun should get into this new game. Twelve months of open season for the wing shooters who take up this big, practical, fascinating and economical shooting game.

Hunting & Fishing, and *National Sportsman* magazines announced a contest in February, 1926 to select a name for a new shooting game. Mrs. Gertrude Hurlbutt from Dayton, Montana won $100 by suggesting the name "Skeet."

Skeet heritage can be traced back to Massachusetts dog kennel owner C.E. Davies. In 1915, Davies' son Henry and companion William H. Foster scratched out a layout in a horse pasture that was initially called "shooting around the clock." The same guns and traps used in trapshooting were employed. A circle of approximately 25 yards in diameter was used with 12 stations marked off, like those on a clock's face. The trap was located at 12 o'clock, and it threw targets over the 6 o'clock position. Shooters fired two shots from each station, 1 through 11, and completed the round by taking three shots from the middle of the circle. It was an exciting new shooting concept, and for many years, neighbors, friends, friends of friends and other shooting enthusiasts made their own backyard shooting fields. The name "Skeet" wasn't invented until many years later.

As one could imagine, this type of field would not support spectators due to its 360-degree shooting arc. Visitors either had to stand directly behind the shooters and move with them, or position themselves beyond the range of falling shot pellets. The absence of an audience did not seem to bother the Davies clan, but their neighbor who raised chickens objected to his birds being peppered with shot pellets and slapped the Davies with a lawsuit to stop the shooting. Their "newfangled shooting business threatened," Davies unknowingly solved both problems by cutting the shooting circle in half, placing a second trap at 6 o'clock and shooting from one side of the half circle away from his neighbor's chicken coops. This new layout allowed spectators to view this unique shooting game with zeal and enthusiasm and kept falling shot well away from his neighbor's chickens. Thus, "Skeet" shooting was born, just because a neighbor became a little chicken manure!

Davies' friend Foster was the assistant editor of the *National Sportsman* magazine and wrote an article on "Shooting 'Round the Clock" in the November, 1920 issue. After 4 years of publicity in various other shooting periodicals, scores of inquiries beset these publications asking for assistance in setting up "clock" fields. In 1926, Foster wrote up a set of rules for the sport and published them in the February issue. The magazine also sponsored a contest to "name the game," offering a huge $100 prize for the winning entry. From over 10,000 entries, Mrs. Gertrude Hurlbutt of Dayton, Montana proposed an old Scandinavian word for shooting called "Skeet." It was short, snappy, and easy to say and remember. Thus Skeet became an officially-named shooting sport. Then the game moved along like gangbusters.

Skeet needed a governing body, and the likely candidate was the *National Sportsman.* The power of the press was in evidence. The magazine could provide communication with the readership, and in return, every time a new member was solicited, a new subscription was added. It was an ideal marriage for both the shooters and the publication. Finally in 1935, the National Skeet Shooting Association was formed by the *National Sportsman.* Its first sanctioned tournament was held in 1935 in Cleveland, Ohio. With the beginning of World War II, Skeet was placed on hold among civilian shooters due to absence of arms and ammunition. Immediately following the cessation of hostilities in 1945, the publishing firm severed all relations with the NSSA, and the association emerged as an independent organization.

Both trap and Skeet shooting were originally devised as shooting games to hone shooting skills and lessen off-season boredom. Soon, however, both sports began to stand on their own two legs, four if you please, and have drawn adherents who simply shoot for the pure fun of it, not to merely sharpen their hunting skills. In fact, there are thousands of registered Skeet and trap shooters who have never set foot in a hunting field, never killed a wild game bird, nor ever raised a ribbed barrel over a pointing dog. Skeet and trapshooting are addictive shooting sports enjoyed by hundreds of thousands of American shooters.

2

The History of Targets and Traps

TO BECOME A proficient wing shot, it takes thousands of rounds of ammunition to develop the skill necessary to become consistent at downing either game birds or fast-flying clay targets. There's no such thing as a "natural" shooter. It takes excellent hand-to-eye coordination, which can be learned, along with the dedication to put in long hours of sustained practice. Not only does practice help teach us the fundamentals of shooting, but it keeps us in peak shape for maximum performance.

During the reign of muzzle-loading shotguns, it was difficult to get in much practice due to the slow reloading process. It often took upward of 1 or 2 minutes to reload either a flintlock or percussion shotgun. And, double-barreled models almost doubled the time frame. It wasn't until breech-loading shotguns were invented that truly "outstanding" wing shots were developed. Why? Self-contained ammunition could be carried in vast quantities and shotguns could be reloaded as fast as the break-action guns of today.

By the turn of the century, live bird shooting was becoming less popular for various reasons. Live pigeons were becoming short in supply, and those birds that were raised in captivity demanded big prices. The average shooter was being priced out of the market—almost like today. Thus entry lists were drastically reduced. There were hues and cries from groups wishing to spare the slaughter of pigeons and they voiced their objections to governmental agencies—or anyone else who would listen. They had a huge following, enough so that live pigeon shooting died a natural death at the hands of its originators—not from outside pressure groups. After nearly one-half century of pigeon shooting, all the pitfalls took its toll and inanimate target shooting became vogue.

Glass Ball Targets

The first American targets that attempted to replace live birds were those glass balls offered by Charles Portlock of Boston, Massachusetts. The English also used glass balls as early as 1860, but by 1866, the U.S. shooters accepted glass balls as their "standard" target. Some historians claim Portlock got his idea from the Japanese who used glass balls as fishing net floats. Others claim that Portlock got the idea from "witch balls," glass spheres ranging in diameter from 1 to 6 inches and filled with dried flower petals or feathers to help keep evil spirits at bay. After all, in the mid-19th century, Boston was reknown for being in the heart of "witch country." Regardless of their origin, glass balls were used for nearly 50 years, even with their limitations.

The original theory was sound—glass was easily breakable and transportable, and materials were cheap. On the other side of the coin there were inherent problems. They were expensive to produce. Each half had to be either hand formed from a mould or hand blown to form a hollow sphere. Manufacturing methods of the day couldn't produce large quantities of targets with consistent wall thickness. Some glass balls would shatter when struck with a single pellet; others couldn't be broken from the kick of a proverbial mule. Another major problem was the flight of the glass targets. Their naturally high arcs and large surface area made them susceptible to wind deflection, even when gusts were as low as 15 mph. Another major problem was the disposal of large amounts of broken glass. Even though the obvious solution was to bury it, there was the cost factor involved.

Although glass balls were sturdy and strong enough to withstand the forces of inertia created by the throwing devices of the day, everything considered, glass balls were not thrown very high, far or fast. In fact, they were quite easy to hit in the air, even by less-than-accomplished wing shots. Purdey, the famous English shotgun maker is credited with the first widespread throwing device used by American shooters. There is, however, one discrepancy in honoring Purdey, as these devices were clearly marked "Purdy," without the letter "e." This crude device was simply a single wooden bar, hinged near the middle to a vertical stand. A round cup, approximately 3 inches in diameter, one end cra-

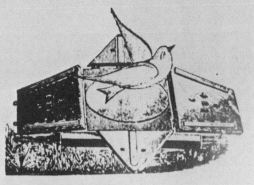

This early English sheet metal pigeon trap flipped open when a locking pin was removed by pulling a long cord leading to the shooting line. Birds were given a boost skyward by a spring-loaded plate on the floor of the trap.

In the beginning, glass balls were made with a smooth outer surface and were quite thin and easy to break. Often they were filled with feathers or leaves which would float to earth when a ball was broken by shotgun pellets.

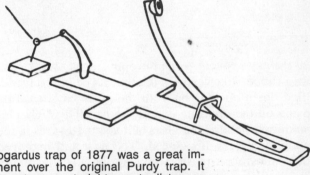

The Bogardus trap of 1877 was a great improvement over the original Purdy trap. It threw targets more straightaway to distances up to 35 yards. Captain Bogardus also marketed his own roughened glass balls.

(Below) Later glass balls had patterned surfaces to promote breakage and resist ricochets. Balls were made in a variety of colors to increase visibility.

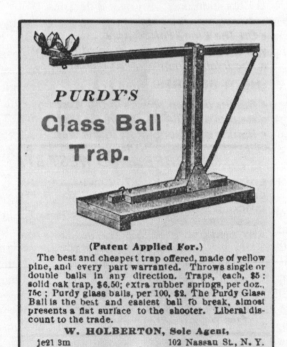

America's first glass ball trap was imported from England in 1866. Reportedly made by the famous English gunmaker, it was not very powerful, and threw targets almost straight into the air.

(Left) One of the most popular glass ball targets was developed in 1876 by Ira A. Paine, a renowned exhibition shooter of the period. Paine's balls were filled with chicken and guinea feathers that scattered spectacularly when a ball was shattered. They were widely advertised in sporting journals.

Improved models of the Bogardus trap threw targets farther and faster, and could be turned to change the direction of flight. Card's rotating trap of 1889 could also throw doubles.

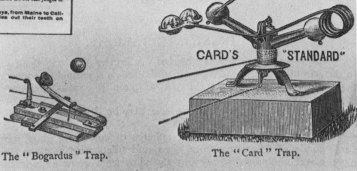

The "Bogardus" Trap.

The "Card" Trap.

dled the glass sphere while the opposite end was rigged with a rubber-like cord. To operate the device, a loader pulled down on the end with the glass ball, creating tension on the opposite end of the bar. This light tension only propelled the glass ball about 10 yards in the air and at a very low speed. The new and improved model substituted a steel coil spring for the rubber band, but it too hardly provided a challenge for experienced gunners. If nothing else, though, the Purdy trap could lay claim to being first!

Historians log that the first American glass ball shoot was held in 1867 in Boston's Beacon Park with the Purdy trap exclusively, but only because it was the only trap available. In spite of its target-throwing limitation, it lasted for a full decade until the famous Captain Adam H. Bogardus invented his own trap. The Bogardus Trap could propel either single or doubles targets at a distance and speed tripling that of the older Purdy model. The principle Bogardus used to design his trap was similar to the rudimentary Purdy's, except better. More flexible materials were incorporated into the trap along with a locking notch, which could hold the trap in a cocked position and be remotely released with a tug on the attached cord.

The Bogardus trap was universally accepted, not because of a lack of competition, as there were over 3 dozen patents for other glass ball throwing devices issued at that time, but because of Bogardus himself. The good Captain was widely known as a terrific wingshot and experienced market hunter. He made his living shooting a shotgun when hordes of winged prey filled the sky. However, when the game thinned out, so did

his income. He had vision and immediately took up the exhibition sport of glass ball shooting. Bogardus toured the country with his shotguns, traps and glass balls and gave exhibitions, challenging all comers. Often his bets ranged into four figures, sometimes even five, and he rarely lost. Old Cap made a handsome living beating the local "hot-hammers" for over 2 decades.

While he was racking up an impressive string of shooting victories, he was constantly promoting his trap and glass ball business as well. At virtually every location, he sold at a tremendous profit a generous supply of traps and his patented Bogardus "rough glass balls," manufactured exclusively for him by Palmer O'Neil & Company of Pittsburgh, Pennsylvania. The price for a Bogardus trap was $6 and his glass balls were marketed at $11 per thousand. The spheres were packed in sawdust-filled wooden barrels at 300 count. Most were made of clear glass, although colors such as red, green and blue were tried. Nearly all had a distinctive design or pattern on the outside face to make them break easier and prevent ricochets. For over 2 decades, all the glass ball makers offered a horde of designs, each one better than the last and far better than their competitor's wares. Very few have survived, and those that did are in the hands of collectors or museums.

Bogardus did have one major competitor, Ira A. Paine, whose glass balls were filled with chicken or guinea feathers. When a Paine target was shattered, an explosion of 300 feathers burst in the air and slowly fluttered to earth. It was quite a sight and the nearest visual effect to live bird shooting available at the time. Old-time live bird shooters demanded Paine glass balls

The "Steel Passenger Pigeon" was an attempt to emulate a bird's flight by rapidly pulling a metal "pigeon" along wires stretched between two chain-driven reels. Needless to say, it enjoyed only limited acceptance.

just to revive the bygone days. Depending on where one could "get a deal," the Paine targets cost nearly 25 percent more than nonfilled-feathered balls, but they enjoyed a brief period of acceptance prior to the adoption of standard clay targets.

Paine sought less expensive ways to manufacture his "feathered orbs." One was to glue feathers to the outside surface. This seemed to make sense, and it gave a good visual effect to the shooter before he took his shot. However, the 200-plus feathers attached to the outside surface slowed the target's flight and arc by nearly 40 percent, thus making the target too easy to hit. It did not survive very long.

Anyone who had an idea for a new target jumped on the bandwagon. There were literally hundreds of designs, types, shapes, and kinds of materials used. One of the more ingenious ideas was the Powell Patent Puff Balls, which initially seemed to be a good replacement for the glass ball. It was made of coarse, hard paper and filled with fine sawdust. The paper ball was perforated so that the dust particles would escape when hit by shot pellets—even a single pellet would cause quite a burst. These balls contained no explosives or hazardous materials, thereby leaving no waste on the target range. In fact, if the target was not too badly torn or shot up, it could be reused. These puff balls were compatible with the day's launching devices and survived for quite a few years after 1867.

Another target was made from manure. Its claim to fame was that it was biodegradable and turned to fertilizer when it rained. Side benefits were that it eliminated the mountains of broken glass and helped restore pastures to their natural beauty. However, American gunners were more interested in target performance than ecological benefits, and it just never caught on.

Another challenger to the glass ball throne was Colonel Fletcher's Bell-Metal ball that clanged loudly when struck by a shot charge. As most shooters are partially deaf from years of shooting, not all competitors could "hear" the results of their shots. Arguments ensued and much ill will was caused by the Colonel's invention. Besides, it was too heavy to be thrown a reasonable distance. Its only redeeming quality was that it was virtually indestructible, and therefore, reusable. Some inventors attempted to market targets made of pottery clay but these targets were scorned by shooters. There were several would-be makers who produced targets that gave off a large puff of smoke when struck. Unquestionably, the most popular of these was one that not only produced a large puff of smoke, but a brilliant flash accompanied by a loud bang. Impressive as it seemed, it did not survive. Even cardboard disks with rubber balloon centers were tried with no success. None of the glass ball substitutes were accepted by American trapshooters, and the reason was quite simple.

Near the end of the glass ball era two target systems that are worth mentioning emerged, even though they did not last very long. The first was dubbed the "steel passenger pigeon," a metal bird that was manually pulled along a cable stretched between two tall poles. Covered with a blue, chalky powder, the birds, when struck by even a single pellet, gave off a puff of blue smoke, usually far behind the speeding target. It was a bit baffling to shooters to see the target continue downrange when obviously it had been smacked dead center. The other serious drawbacks of the steel pigeon were its predictable flight path and slowness "awing."

The other clever target was named the "gyro pigeon," which looked like the blade of a modern electric

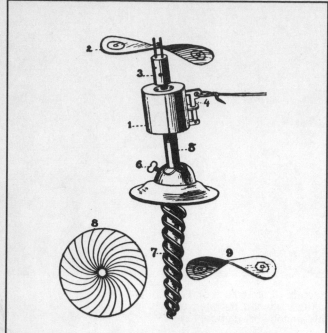

Bussey's Gyro Trap of 1872 was powered by a coil spring and launched with a strong, propelling upward spin. The "propeller" target was reusable by repainting its all-white surface.

fan. It was powered by a coil spring and was launched from a spiraling center post that gave it a strong, propelling upward spin. Like the propeller on an airplane, it rose up and out upon release. This target was reusable by merely repainting its all-white surface. Scoring was determined by the number of pellets that struck its body. This system is still used somewhat in England and is called the ZZ target, probably short for zig-zag.

And speaking of England, around 1870 there was a creative target system called the Jones Snipe Throwing Trap. This technique made use of a powerful catapult to launch a large metal bird-shaped target in irregular, undulating flight often to a distance between 50 to 60 yards downrange. When the iron snipe was struck, it gave off a light puff of blue smoke. Some versions were equipped with rubber balloons to provide sound effects when hit. Because the Jones "bird" had to be retrieved after each sortie to be repaired and repainted, it was less than ideal, unless a large supply of birds were at hand.

Back in the colonies, G.F. Kolb Company of Philadelphia manufactured and sold Belcher's Patent Paper Bird. This was simply a wire ball to which a stiff paper cutout of a bird was attached. The ball could be used in a standard glass ball thrower, and the targets were repairable by simply counting and marking the existing holes or replacing the paper bird silhoutte. But, like the Jones snipe, shooters did not like to wait for targets to be repaired. So much for the Belcher Bird.

Trapshooters were used to the sights and sounds of glass ball shooting. The tinkling of shattered glass falling to the ground had a certain sound and ring to it that the alternative targets could not duplicate. The glass balls being struck squarely with a heavy load of buckshot caused just the right amount of graphic impact, not too little and not overpowering—visually just right. Also, shooters had become used to the trajectory, speed and visual flight of the glass ball targets. Glass balls traveled rather slowly, around 30 feet per second, which gave even novice shooters an excellent opportunity to break at least 50 percent of the targets thrown the first time out. Success breeds success, and glass ball shooters were numbered in legions, not thousands.

The crème de la crème among glass ball shooters from the 1870s to the turn of the century were Bogardus, Paine and Doc Carver. This trio often shot and broke phenomenal numbers of targets in a measured amount of time. Bogardus once shattered 5000 glass balls in an incredible 500 minutes, which averaged 10 per minute, or one every 6 seconds for 8 hours and 20 minutes without a break. And he loaded his own gun to boot! Many shooters fired at 1000 targets in 90 minutes during those heydays of exhibition shooting with many shooters averaging over a 90 percent hit ratio.

After about a decade of fast and furious shooting at glass balls, the majority of shooters demanded a newer and tougher target. Hit percentages were rapidly climbing to near perfect scores and boredom among the top guns was setting in. Something had to be done about revising and revitalizing target shooting. A new type of target that would fly faster and better emulate a live bird would be the answer to the shooter's demands. The new target must also have a semi-predictable flight path regardless of the climatic conditions, and to assure profits to the local gun club, they must be easily transportable and resist breakage under normal handling. Sounded like a big order to fill, but it was satisfied eventually by the composition pitch and silt targets.

Clay Targets

The first practical improvement over glass balls was developed by two men almost simultaneously, yet independent of each other. George Ligowsky, of Cincinnati, Ohio supposedly got the idea for his saucer-shaped, spinning clay target while watching small boys skipping clam shells across a lake. Whether the Englishman McCaskey had a similar inspiration isn't known, but what we know today as a "clay pigeon" appeared on both sides of the Atlantic ocean in the same year—1880. History records that Ligowsky experimented with about 40 different disk designs before perfecting the dome-shaped saucer he finally patented.

Prototype clay pigeons, oddly enough, were made of clay. Ligowsky's birds were baked in cast iron moulds heated in a long, narrow furnace and moved along in assembly-line fashion. After baking, the red clay targets were removed to a brick kiln to be fired again.

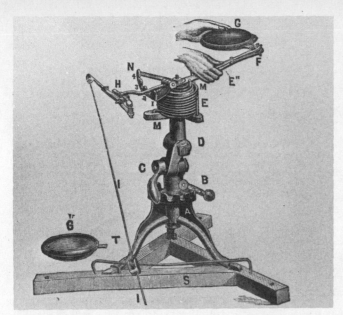

Clay pigeons, invented by George Ligowsky in 1880, quickly supplanted glass balls as the standard inanimate target of trapshooters. Ligowsky also developed and marketed the first trap machine for launching the new targets.

The "Peoria Blackbird" target and trap was first sold by Fred Kimble of Peoria, Illinois, in 1884. "Blackbird" targets had two ears that were clasped by the trap to insure consistent flight.

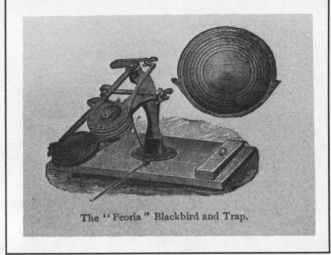

The "Peoria" Blackbird and Trap.

Temperatures, however, of both kiln and baking furnace were impossible to control accurately enough to produce a consistently hard target. Some were quite soft, while others resisted breakage to the point that they rang like a bell when hit by pellets. Most shooters agreed that clay targets were almost impossible to break. Obviously some material other than clay would have to be developed if "clay" pigeons were to be universally accepted as replacements for glass balls.

The obvious problem, of course, was to produce a target that was not easily broken in transit from factory to range, and that could withstand initial thrust of the trap. Even with these conditions satisfied, targets had to be brittle enough to break easily when struck by a single pellet. Time has proven that these were, indeed, tough criteria to meet, but hundreds of hunters, shooters, inventors, gunsmiths and tinkerers devoted a lot of time and energy perfecting clay targets during the 1880s.

Exotic formulas for target materials included such substances as coal tar (asphalt), plaster of paris, sand, cinders, gypsum, various pottery clays, sawdust, colluloid (a then newly-discovered plastic), common dirt and silt from river bottoms.

Fred Kimble, a one-time market hunter from Peoria, Illinois was credited in 1884 with the first composition saucer-shaped target. Identified as the Peoria Blackbird, it was made of river silt and plaster of paris and, according to reports of the period, seemed to work reasonably well. Kimble's formula was strikingly similar to the Kimber composition ball target developed in 1881. Note the coincidental similarity of these two men's names. Because they knew each other, it is likely that Kimber gave his formula to Fred Kimble.

Al Bandel, an enterprising Kentuckian, promoted a target made mostly of tar. The bird, called the Lark, performed fairly well in cold weather, but sagged into a useless blob that could neither be set in motion properly nor broken in flight on a warm day.

Metal target disks were devised and tried with limited success. The idea of reuse was of primary consideration. The Parkersburg Tin Target was supposed to release a wire ring when hit that would cause the target to fall quickly to the ground. It must not have worked as advertised for it was only on the market for a year or so. A similar target was invented by W.T. Best and distributed by the Champion Tin Target Co. of Chicago, Illinois. The Best bird had a large flange that dropped when struck by a shot stream. Interfering with its aerodynamics, the flange caused the disk to flop to the ground like a wounded bird. Many flanged targets refused to behave properly, however, often sailing on their way with no evidence of a fair hit. Needless to say, shooters didn't take too kindly to this, and Mr. Best was soon out of the Tin Bird business.

The Lafayette Target Company of Lafayette, Indiana made a clay bird chock full of feathers that showered down when hit. One can only wonder how this target flew with its extra payload. Not too well, apparently, since it was only made for a short time in the late 1880s.

The Blue Rock Paper Pigeon was one of the most awesome targets offered during that long-ago era of experimentation. Invented by Charles Franzmann and made of pasteboard, it was covered with a layer of fulminate of mercury, then given an outer coat of sand and

From day one to the present, clay targets and their instruments for catapulting them have changed little in design — none in principle. These targets and machines are more than 100 years old.

(Below) The standard asphalt pitch and ground lime target has a diameter of 4.25 inches, height is 1 1/16 inches and weight 3.5 ounces. Targets are available in a wide range of color schemes from all-white to jet black. Fluorescent green and orange are the most popular on the West coast.

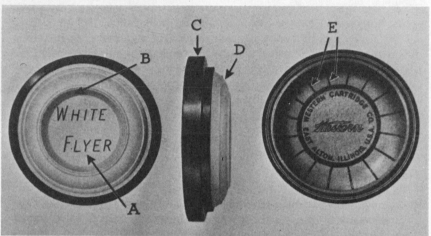

REMINGTON TRAP & SKEET EQUIPMENT

The Blue Rock Pigeon.

The "Blue Rock" clay pigeon was the first successful target without any projections for the trap to grip. Thin in the center with a sturdy rim, it was the forerunner to today's clay birds.

(Right) "Blue Rock" brand clay pigeons as made today by Remington are considerably different in shape from Fred Kimble's original 1887 model. Design principles remain the same, however.

glue to add necessary weight. When struck by shot, it exploded, releasing a cloud of smoke. The inventor claimed it wasn't dangerous to handle or transport. Either the shooters of the time didn't believe the advertising or the paper pigeon did not perform as advertised, because this brilliant design died an almost instant death. The mere thought of hauling a barrel containing 500 of these explosive devices over a bumpy road is not only chilling, it's apt to ruin your whole day.

Inventors, seeking the ultimate inanimate target even after a multitude of designs had been tried and found mostly wanting, discovered that the solution to the problem of "clay" bird material lay in a combination of asphalt and silt, or asphalt and gypsum. The proper recipe, when mixed in correct proportions, gave a flying target the desired properties of transportability and fragility. Curiously, the first disk-shaped targets marketed in England by McCaskey were made from tar (pitch) and river silt.

By the end of the 19th century, after the dust had settled, two brands of clay targets became the accepted leaders—White Flyer and Blue Rock. White Flyer was made by Western Trap & Target Company, which eventually became Western Cartridge Company and later was absorbed by Winchester Firearms Company. The Blue Rock (named after the famous English pigeon) was manufactured by both the Chamberlin Cartridge and Target Company and the Cleveland Target Company, both located in Cleveland, Ohio. Eventually the two companies merged, were purchased by Remington Arms, and were moved to Findlay, Ohio where Blue Rock targets are still manufactured.

There were some interesting and most unusual monikers attached to flying-disk targets during their development. The English, for some inexplicable reason, called them "spheres." In America, they were referred to as inanimate targets, asphalts, flying disks, traps, blackbirds, baked birds, muds, soil disks, river bottoms, clay birds and clay pigeons. The last two names stuck and, even though not made of clay for about 100 years, we still call them by those anachronistic names.

By 1900, clay targets had evolved into roughly the same size, shape and composition that are used today. Modern clay birds are made of pitch (asphalt tar) and ground limestone or gypsum, and size and weight have been standardized. Today's bird is $4^1/4$ inches in diameter, $1^1/16$ inches in height and weighs $3^1/2$ ounces. They're a far cry from glass balls, but they aren't too far removed from designs that were first introduced a century ago.

Modern-day clay pigeons are entirely satisfactory as aerial targets, yet finding ways to improve them are still underway. White Flyer has added dimples to their newly-designed dome, while Blue Rock and a few other independent manufacturers are constantly working up a new brew, which will hopefully enable shooters to break bigger scores.

A novel method of producing targets was developed some 25 years ago and, for a time, appeared to be a most practical idea. The system relied on a quick-freezing machine to make ice targets. The freezer, containing a mould in the shape of a regulation clay pigeon was installed next to the trap. Water injected into the mould was instantly frozen into a target that could be placed immediately into the trap. A continuous freezing process produced targets as fast as a commercial freezer can make ice cubes. Colored targets were easily made by adding dye of the desired hue into the water before moulding. Ice seemed to be an ideal material for targets, because there was no debris left on the range and there were no problems with transportation or storage, plus irrigating the trap field reduced maintenance. Unfortunately, the cost of delivering ice targets to the trap was higher than the cost of clay pigeons. Someday, perhaps, ice targets will be revived in a system that will be competitive with current practices. The concept is basically quite sound.

In recent years, the Environmental Protection Agency has conducted toxic surveys and quite a few gun clubs around the country are being investigated because of the somewhat-toxic qualities of target materials. There have been a few gun clubs—Lordship in particular—that have been closed down by the U.S. government because of the large buildup of lead pellets in the water where ducks and geese feed.

Improved Traps

As better targets were conceived, vastly-improved traps were also being produced. A simple catapult is adequate for launching a glass ball down range, but a disk target requires a different sort of trap machine. A clay target must have a certain amount of spin when thrown to give it the stability necessary for consistent flight and breakage. Today's clay targets are made of a harder substance than those made at the turn of the century, yet today's targets break easier than those of yesteryear. Why is this, you might ask? Because of the fast spin applied to the aerial clay target. When the shot hits it, the momentum of the target helps to break the bird in pieces. Targets that are propelled from a trap with too little spin will be punctured by shot pellets and will raise some dust, but no piece large enough to be scored will come off the main body. And to make matters even more difficult, almost 90 percent of all targets sold today are painted in various colors to improve visibility. The paint, although quite thin and watery, still helps keep the target together even if hit by only a few pellets. It is amazing how many targets lying in the field have pellet holes in them without even the smallest scoring chip broken off.

Prototype clay targets had a small "tongue" on the rim that fit into a clamp on the trap arm to hold the target in place and aid in spinning it as it left the trap. This tongue was either moulded into the lip of the clay

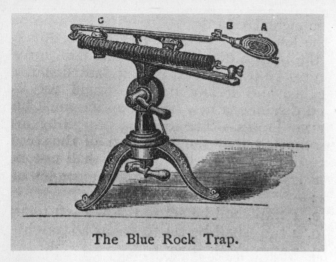

The Blue Rock Trap.

"Blue Rock" traps had a simple clip, attached to the trap arm by a pivot, to control the target as it was being launched. Introduced in 1887, this trap, with improvements, lasted well into the 20th century.

bird or was made of cardboard and glued to the target. Later developments in both birds and traps showed that the tongue was unnecessary and perfectly-round targets were used thereafter.

The granddaddy of the first successful clay pigeon trap machine, and the most widely used, was patented and manufactured by the Ligowsky Clay Pigeon Company. Although similar in principle to later traps, it differed in one major respect. As in more modern versions, it consisted of an arm that was drawn back against the tension of a coil spring and held by a notch on the main frame. A tug on a rope activated a release mechanism that allowed the arm to fly forward, sending a target spinning on its path downrange. The clay bird, however, was held in place by a clamp on the end of the arm that clipped onto the aforementioned tongue. There was no other support for the target. Because the clamp was subject to slippage, especially in wet weather, performance of Ligowsky's trap was sometimes unpredictable. Thus it wasn't long until a better trap was invented.

Fred Kimble's Blackbird trap was designed to throw his patented Blackbird clay pigeon which had two projections on its rim, diametrically opposed. Targets were held on the end of the trap's throwing arm by a clip that partially encircled the rim of the bird, holding it tightly enough to keep it in place as the arm flew forward. Kimble's system was a distinct improvement over Ligowsky's. Patented in 1884, the Blackbird enjoyed a very short life, as it was rendered obsolete by the 1887 introduction of the Blue Rock trap and clay pigeon.

Virtually identical to today's clay target, the Blue Rock pigeon was perfectly round, with no projections on its rim. The Blue Rock trap held a clay bird in a clip that was pivoted on the end of the throwing arm. Action of the pivot reduced initial shock, and thus lessened the chance of the bird being broken as it was launched from the trap. An improved version of the Blue Rock trap, first sold in 1889, had a more positive method of holding the target—much the same that is used in many modern traps.

On the other side of the Atlantic, an English trap called the Highflyer had a tray mounted on the end of the throwing arm that was only a bit wider than the target bird. As the trap arm moved forward under force from a heavy coil spring, the bird slid forward along the edge of the tray spinning the target. A variation of this principle has been used on many traps and is still found on traps currently in use.

One testy problem virtually all disc-throwing traps encountered was the ability to launch two targets simultaneously. Some traps produced in the glass-ball era could throw doubles and at various angles, so it didn't take long for someone to make a workable, multiple trap for clay birds. The first one that had any degree of success was the Davenport Revolving Clay Pigeon Trap introduced in 1884 by A.F. Martin of Davenport, New York. It could throw both singles and doubles, but had to be handloaded as are many of today's machines.

Labor factors became important to trap clubs even back in the late 1890s. The Magau Trap, made in 1887 by the Chamberlin Company of Cleveland, Ohio, was the first practical automatic trap to see widespread use.

Odd-looking though it was, the Magau trap was the first successful automatic target launcher. An extremely complicated machine, it was difficult to operate and maintain.

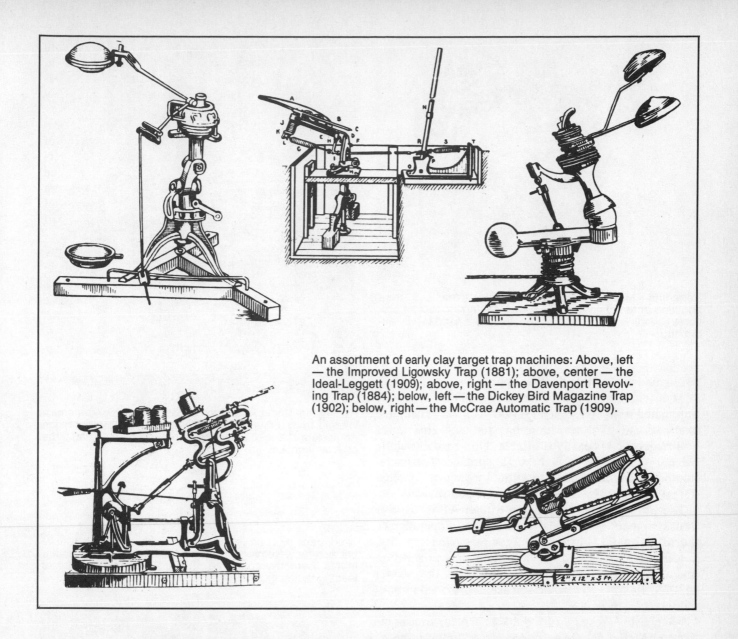

An assortment of early clay target trap machines: Above, left — the Improved Ligowsky Trap (1881); above, center — the Ideal-Leggett (1909); above, right — the Davenport Revolving Trap (1884); below, left — the Dickey Bird Magazine Trap (1902); below, right — the McCrae Automatic Trap (1909).

It was a highly-complicated apparatus, in which speed and direction of delivery were controlled by an operator who powered the machine by pedaling a bicycle sprocket connected by a chain to the operating mechanism. Clever as this device was, it had many obvious flaws and was soon supplanted by an electrically-powered trap that was remotely controlled.

One name not lost in the annals of early trap machines was the Dickey Bird Automatic Trap. It was first marketed in 1905 by W.S. Dickey of Kansas City, Missouri. It was simple in operation and could throw singles or doubles at the will of the operator at precisely-prescribed angles. It was in general use for many years, and ranks as one of the more successful traps of its era. One is on display at the ATA museum in Vandalia, Ohio.

The forerunner to the Western Trap was invented by A.M. McCrae of Lamar, Missouri. He sold the patent rights to his automatic trap in 1909 to the Western Car-

tridge Company of East Alton, Illinois. Marketed under the Western name, McCrae's trap was the ancestor of a long line of Winchester-Western traps that have proven popular over the years.

A clever design with foot pedals to control angle targets was the Champion Trap devised in 1914 by H.W. Vietmeyer of Indianapolis, Indiana. It was not fully automatic, loaded by the trap boy for each delivery of a target, but it was exceedingly simple in construction and easy to operate. It could be operated mechanically, or electrically by remote control. After 1916, an improved model called the Black Diamond was made by the Black Products Company of Chicago, Illinois. An offshoot of the Black Diamond is still being used worldwide.

By the end of WWII and with the building of many new trapshooting facilities, manufacturers of trap equipment were able to modernize many of their products. Much of today's sophisticated trap machinery

Remington Model 4100 is adaptable for either U.S. trapshooting or Modified Clay Pigeon. Auto-angling feature prevents "reading" of targets by shooters. The 4100 is fully automatic.

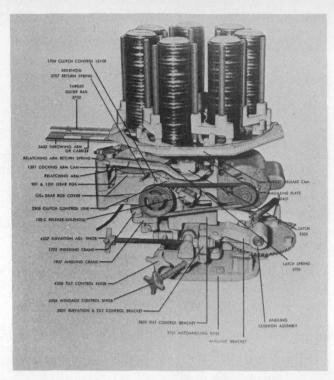

Remington Model A100T for trapshooting offers automatic loading from a magazine for completely remote operation. Angles are changed at random to prevent memorizing target path sequences.

Skeet traps must be reliable and throw targets with consistent accuracy. Remington Model M200S meets both requirements. Remotely controlled, it needs attention only for reloading the magazine.

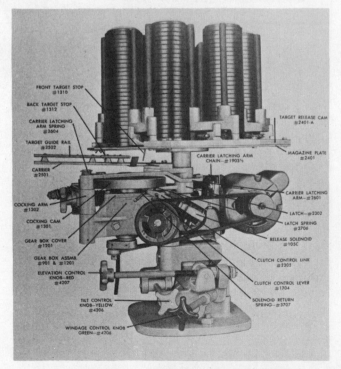

originated during this post-war period.

The Remington Model 4100 is typical of present-day automated traps. Designed for both U.S. and simulated International-style trapshooting, its magazine holds 154 targets and is easily refillable. Non-readable angle selection is offered in eight angle spreads. The magazine is easily detachable to allow loading of doubles. Target release is by remote electronic control.

The ultra-popular Remington Model A100T is also in use on many trap fields. It is similar in operation to the Model 4100, but has a larger magazine capacity, holding 203 targets in seven columns. A companion machine adapted for Skeet shooting is the Model M200S. Remote electronic release is provided in both models.

Winchester-Western's Model V1577A for trapshooting and Model V1574A for Skeet are found in many clay bird shooting installations. Like the Remington traps, these operate automatically, requiring only periodic manual loading of their magazines.

International Trapshooting requires a highly-specialized trap machine and Winchester offers their Model V1583A, which is a modification of Model V1582A, a regulation trap for U.S. trapshooting. Model V1583A has a provision for interrupted vertical motion, plus increased power for throwing 75-yard targets as required in ISU (International Shooting Union) regulations. Smaller diameter International targets are easily accommodated in the 190-target magazine. The trap is also adaptable for shooting ATA Modified Clay Pigeon.

Remington's Wonder Trap is a less expensive machine for both trap and Skeet shooting. A manual unit, it requires the services of an attendant for both cocking and loading. Wonder traps are used by many smaller clubs all over the country. Target release may be either operated mechanically or electrically.

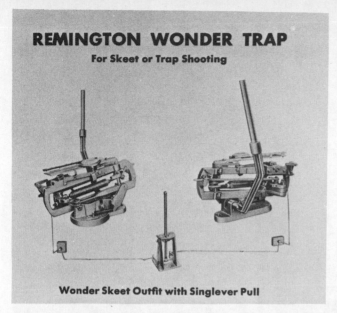

REMINGTON WONDER TRAP

For Skeet or Trap Shooting

Wonder Skeet Outfit with Singlever Pull

(Above) The Remington "Wonder Trap" may be used for both trap and Skeet shooting. Completely manual in operation, it requires the services of a trap attendant for cocking and loading.

(Right) Electric regulation trap from Western holds targets in a rotary magazine. Angles are changed at random by an interruptor gearbox powered by a separate electric motor.

(Below) Western's Autoloading Model V1583A is intended for use in International Trap. It throws targets farther and faster than traps designed for U.S. trapshooting.

Western

AUTOLOADING REGULATION TRAP V1582A
(MODEL "U")

AUTOLOADING INTERNATIONAL TRAP V1583A
(MODEL "US" – ILLUSTRATED)

There are probably tens of thousands of clay target shooters who have fired at targets launched by the Remington Expert trap machine. A simple single-loading trap, it may be installed permanently or is portable for informal shooting sessions. A slightly more sophisticated trap designed for permanent installation is Remington's Blue Rock model, especially suited for small clubs and private shooting areas. It may be used for both Skeet and straight trap and is manually loaded and released. The Blue Rock has a tray-type carrier that allows the throwing of doubles. Both units are ideal for moving games such as Quail Walk that use several traps in various locations along a trail.

Both Remington and Winchester have had their mar-

ket share of the clay target launching machines cut into by an upstart from Sweden—The Beomat Clay Target Launcher. The Beomat was developed by two shooters from Sweden disgusted with existing launching machines. They took matters into their own hands and built a machine that eliminated target breakage, had large target capacity, was super-simple in design and virtually maintenance free. A tall order. Because neither of these Swedish engineers had any previous experience with clay target throwers, they were not encumbered by traditional manufacturing techniques or design ideas. By 1971, a pair of prototypes were set up at a local gun club just outside the city of Karlstad, Sweden. The snowball had started to roll.

Today, there are thousands of these marvelous machines in operation all over the U.S. They have simply performed as advertised—a rare feat today. The Model MS700 holds 700 clay targets and is designed for both American and International Skeet. An additional 700 targets can be added with a special turret, which allows a gun club attendee to load enough targets at a single filling to shoot 55 full rounds of Skeet. It takes about 5 minutes to convert the Model MS700 from Interna-

(Above) This French-built LaPorte can hold 360 targets and recycles automatically within 2 seconds after launching.

(Right) This is Beomat's top-of-the-line model that has a magazine capable of accommodating 700 targets. It is primarily a high-volume trap or Skeet machine that requires little maintenance.

(Above) The Kromson A-350 is a new target launching machine that features a completely vertical magazine that holds up to 350 targets. A rugged design, this machine is at the leading edge of technology.

tional to American Skeet, and vice versa. The Model MS400 is similar in design to the MS700 except it holds a more modest 400 clay targets. The workhorse of the Beomat lineup is the Model MJT400. This is the machine found in many American gun club's traphouses. It is especially popular in practice fields because it has a 400-target capacity, exceptional reliability, and needs very little maintenance. Beomat also offers specialized trap machines for Continental Trap (the Model MT400), which has a 400-target capacity, the Model SS85, an 85-target capacity Skeet machine, along with the Model SOT40, a super-tough device designed exclusively for International trapshooting. This machine must throw a slightly smaller target nearly 50 percent farther than what is prescribed for American trapshooting.

Beomat has also perfected a voice-activated system called Voicemaster that consists of five microphones and a central control unit. A unique feature of the Voicemaster is its special electronic circuit which is insensitive to all mechanical sounds, such as the loading and unloading of guns, shooting or extraneous noises. It only recognizes human voices, which guarantees that only the shooter's command will release a target.

One of the world's largest manufacturers of both target launching equipment and clay targets is the French firm LaPorte S.A. This old-line company has been in business for over 6 decades and claims to have manufactured more than 1000 million clay targets—that's a bunch! Their target design and shape is a wee bit different than what U.S. shooters are used to seeing, but like our American target makers, colors range from black to white with virtually every other color available.

Their trap machine lineup is equally impressive with their top-of-the-line Model 2001. It is loaded with 720 targets along with a spring tension oscillator that makes it possible to vary the speed of the target both horizontally and vertically, producing totally unpredictable target angles. The LaPorte Model American Trap 185 has a magazine capacity of 250 or 400 targets. The factory claims that this entirely-automatic machine incorporates a controlling device that makes it impossible to predict the flight of the next target, like our "interrupter." The Model 185 will also run on two heavy-duty 12-volt batteries, which makes it an ideal "back-up" system for gun clubs which do not have electricity, but want to use automatic traps. LaPorte also makes comparable machines for Skeet fields along with remote- and delayed-timing mechanisms.

Hoppes, the famous gun solvent maker also offers a lightweight, inexpensive, series of portable traps as do Outers and Trius. Basically, all these units are similar

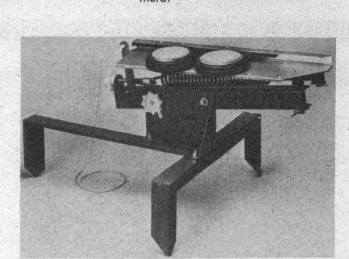

(Left) Hand target throwers are perfect for teaching beginners the fundamentals of Skeet and trapshooting.

(Left) This English-made hand thrower is about as simple as a sundial — yet effective and a practiced operator can toss targets 50 yards or more.

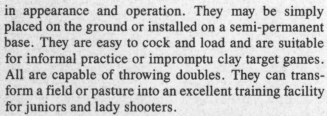

The hand target thrower, this one by Remington, is ideal for informal practice. Easily portable, hand traps are quite inexpensive, yet capable of excellent performance. There are a number of brands and styles on the market.

(Right) Outer's "Mini Grand" trap features an adjustable throwing arm for a variety of patterns at different speeds. It may be used anywhere, and is perfect for casual clay bird shooting.

in appearance and operation. They may be simply placed on the ground or installed on a semi-permanent base. They are easy to cock and load and are suitable for informal practice or impromptu clay target games. All are capable of throwing doubles. They can transform a field or pasture into an excellent training facility for juniors and lady shooters.

Hand traps are the simplest of all and the least expensive. Many makes are stocked by most sporting goods stores and gun shops. Hand target throwers are perfect for teaching beginners the fundamentals of Skeet and trapshooting, as well as providing excellent practice for hunters honing their pre-season skills. With just a minimum amount of practice—and getting the hang of it— the thrower can regulate the speed and flight of the bird from slow and easy to a screaming hard angle. The hand trap should not be overlooked as an excellent teaching tool.

A full catalog and description of all available clay target throwing machines is beyond the scope of this book, but this is a brief summary of the variety from which a shotgunner may choose. There is also a large selection of clay targets, all of standard size and weight, with slightly different forms and colors. Manufacturers of clay pigeons all have their own ideas about construction, and it's up to the individual shooters to pick the one that meets their needs and performs best.

Today's clay targets of whatever manufacture are as nearly impeccable in design, materials and consistency as one could wish, but that level of perfection was not achieved overnight. It is the result of nearly a century of refinement and development and represents the combined efforts of innumerable people, most of whom are not mentioned in written records. Trap and Skeet shooters owe them all a big "thank you," because without their pioneering work, our shooting sports would not be as enjoyable as they are today.

Trap machines available to scattergun aficionados today range from simple hand throwers to those marvels of sophistication and mechanical ingenuity that are used for International trapshooting. We've come a long way from Purdy's glass-ball throwing machine. It would seem that perfection has been achieved in the development of trapshooting equipment, but who knows what the future might bring? Every time we seem to have gone as far as possible in any given field, someone invariably pops up with an improved model. Unbelievable as it might be, improved trapshooting equipment is probably on the way even now. And, if I were a betting man (which I am), I'd bet the farm that frozen water targets will reappear in the not-too-distant future. Any takers?

3

Clay Target Shooting Games

TRAP AND SKEET are the overwhelming choices for clay target shooting. Yet, there are unlimited variations of both of these basic games enjoyed by thousands of shotgun enthusiasts. There are unquestionably more clay targets smashed to smithereens by shooters firing under casual conditions than by those partaking in regimented, registered clay target events. And trap and Skeet are not alone . . . there's International Skeet, International Trap and the Johnny Come Lately — Sporting Clays.

If we were to classify clay target sport shooting, we would have to break it into two categories — formal (registered shooting with strict rules) and informal (fun, with no restrictions or rules). The oldest formal shotgunning game is trap, then comes Skeet, and more recently, Sporting Clays, a revised "Hunter's Clays," a long-time favorite of British shotgunners. Trap is broken into two different games and governing bodies. The first is the Amateur Trapshooting Association, which sanctions and rules over three trapshooting events — 16-Yard Singles, Handicap and Doubles. The second

trap competition is International Trap and is governed in the United States by the National Rifle Association. International Trap is often referred to as Bunker, or Trench, shooting. Skeet, too, has both domestic and international versions. The domestic version is ruled by the National Skeet Shooting Association and the International by the NRA.

Both international versions of trap and Skeet are not nearly as popular as American Trap or Skeet for various reasons. International Trap fields are complex and expensive to build, are difficult to operate and maintain, and there are not enough facilities in the U.S. to arouse new shooters' interests. Both international shooting games are in the Olympics, World Games, and the Pan-American games. During the 1960s and 1970s, American shooters didn't take a back seat to any nation. Sporting Clays has its own ruling order, the USSCA which is located in Houston, Texas and was established in May of 1985. Although relatively new, the USSCA has set forth rules and guidelines for both gun clubs and shooters and boasts a membership of more

Organized trapshooting is a hustle-bustle game because often hundreds of competitors shoot at hundreds of targets, often over a 7- to 10-day period. If it's shooting you want, then trap is your game!

than 100 gun club affiliates in the U.S., Canada and Dominican Republic. Robert Davis presides over the USSCA, as of this writing.

American Trap

Shooters stand behind a hidden trap inside a trap house no less than 16 yards away. The trap house itself is about 8 feet square by 6 feet deep; approximately half of it is below ground.

On the shooter's command, a referee/scorer releases the target remotely by pressing a button on an electrical cord attached to a target launching machine. The flying

target is launched at an unknown angle because the launching machine oscillates back and forth. To prevent shooters from figuring out the exact arc of the machine, an interrupter, built into all trap machines, breaks up any particular oscillating pattern. The shooter, therefore, is never exactly sure where the target will be thrown, only that it should fly within a 44-degree arc from the trap. It could fly between 22 degrees to the left of the trap center and 22 degrees to the right. These angles were chosen, of course, to simulate the flight pattern of a wild bird rising ahead of a hunter and away from the source of apparent danger. A clay pigeon leaves the trap at approximately 41 miles per hour on a low trajectory that keeps it airborne for about 50 yards. The target must have a trajectory that starts its curve 10 feet from the trap so it will rise between 8 to 12 feet, and land no less than 48 yards and no more than 52 yards from the trap.

This large height-adjustment spread is to compensate for various types of weather. In calm air, most clubs set the target height at 9½ feet. However, on a windy day with a predominant head wind, the target will be set lower so it still travels its legal distance without being raised by the head wind, which would slow it down drastically and cause it to fall short of its intended distance. Conversely, if a tail wind persists, most gun clubs or target-setting committees will initially set the target's flight close to the 12-foot height limit to keep it in the air long enough to reach its legal destination. In other words, a head wind will raise the target and cause it to fall short of its 50-yard mark. A tail wind will lower the target also causing it to fall short of its 50-yard mark.

If wind shift causes the targets to fall too far or too short, a shooter on any squad can at any time request

(Left) Like any hand-eye coordination sport, trapshooting cannot be learned overnight. The shooter must go out on the field, shoot, make mistakes, and then, after a few thousand targets, he will get the "hang of it."

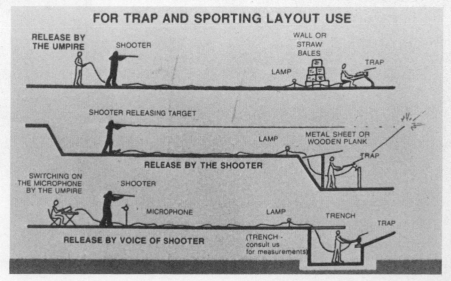

Whenever setting up a trap machine, safety is the first consideration, especially when the target launcher and operator are in front of the shooter.

FOR TRAP AND SPORTING LAYOUT USE

RELEASE BY THE UMPIRE · SHOOTER · WALL OR STRAW BALES · LAMP · TRAP

SHOOTER RELEASING TARGET · LAMP · METAL SHEET OR WOODEN PLANK · TRAP

RELEASE BY THE SHOOTER

SWITCHING ON THE MICROPHONE BY THE UMPIRE · SHOOTER · MICROPHONE · LAMP · TRENCH · TRAP

RELEASE BY VOICE OF SHOOTER · (TRENCH - consult us for measurements)

A.T.A. DEFINITIVE TRAP FIELD

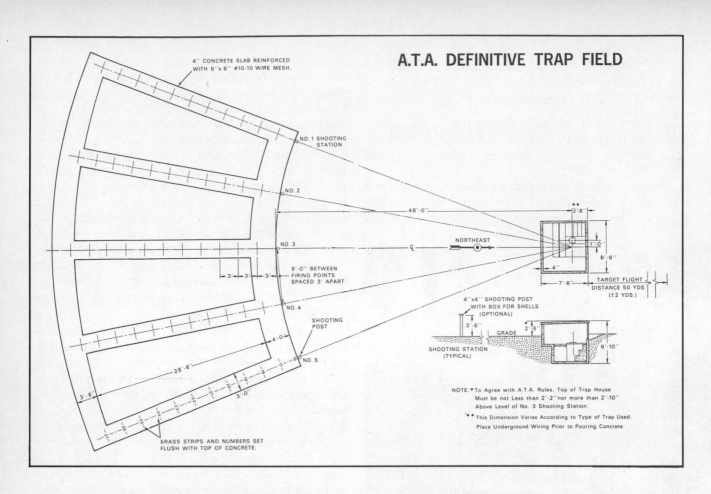

4" CONCRETE SLAB REINFORCED WITH 6"x 6" #10-10 WIRE MESH.

NO.1 SHOOTING STATION

NO. 2

48'-0"

2'-6"

NORTHEAST

1'-0"

8'-6"

NO. 3

9'-0" BETWEEN FIRING POINTS SPACED 3' APART.

3'- 3'-

4"

7'-6"

TARGET FLIGHT DISTANCE 50 YDS. (±2 YDS.)

NO. 4

SHOOTING POST

4"x4" SHOOTING POST WITH BOX FOR SHELLS (OPTIONAL)

4'-0"

NO. 5

3'-6"

GRADE

2'-6"

28'-6"

3'-0"

SHOOTING STATION (TYPICAL)

6'-10"

3'-6"

BRASS STRIPS AND NUMBERS SET FLUSH WITH TOP OF CONCRETE.

NOTE: * To Agree with A.T.A. Rules, Top of Trap House Must be not Less than 2'-2" nor more than 2'-10" Above Level of No. 3 Shooting Station.

** This Dimension Varies According to Type of Trap Used. Place Underground Wiring Prior to Pouring Concrete.

TRAP FIELD - SHOT FALL ZONE

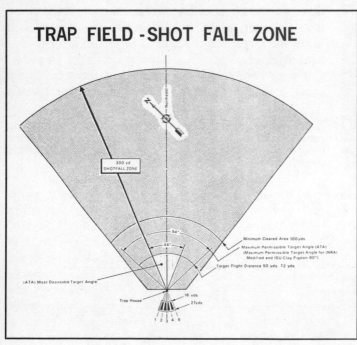

300 yd SHOTFALL ZONE

94°

44°

Minimum Cleared Area 100 yds.

Maximum Permissible Target Angle (ATA) (Maximum Permissible Target Angle for (NRA) Modified and (ISU Clay Pigeon-90°)

Target Flight Distance 50 yds. ±2 yds.

(ATA) Most Desireable Target Angle

Trap House

16 yds

27yds

1 2 3 4 5

A trapshoot is in progress showing spectators displaying various degrees of interest. Both trap and Skeet are good spectator sports because action is fast and results immediately apparent.

that the targets be reset to legal height and distance. All too often, shooters accept improperly-set targets or those that have been drastically changed by climatic conditions. It is a mistake to shoot at them. It's similar to accepting bad pulls—they do not have to be taken. They can be refused by the shooter. However, if the shooter accepts the illegal targets or poorly-timed pulls, his score stands.

The most popular American trap game is 16-Yard Singles. Here, participants stand 16 yards behind the trap house. Shooters are classified by their previous scores and a running average. There are usually five classes in larger Singles events, although the ATA rule book lists guidelines for four or even three classes. In Handicap events, however, shooters are moved back from the trap house according to their demonstrated abilities, up to a maximum of 27 yards for the most adept scattergunners. Because most targets are broken between 30 and 35 yards from the gun when firing from the 16-yard line, it's obvious that shooting from a 27-yard handicap position requires more than a little skill and quickness.

Both Singles and Handicap trap are shot from five stations, the center one being directly behind the trap house. The other stations are spaced 3 yards apart on both sides in an arc so that all five positions are equidistant from the trap. Positions are numbered, One through Five, starting from the left. Each participant fires five shots from each station (post), making a total of 25 shots per "round," which is the number of shells in a box. Older shooters refer to stations as "posts," which comes from trapshooting's earlier days when a wooden stand with a small platform on top was located in front of each shooting station. The shooter usually placed his box of shotgun shells on this "post," providing easy access to his ammunition.

Whenever possible, five shooters comprise a squad. A shooter may fire a round alone, but it is more common to have enough competitors to form a squad of five. In that case, each shooter moves one station to the right after each string of five shots has been fired in rotation by all squad members for a total of 125 shots (5×25). Each station presents a different view of the target, which can be anywhere from straight ahead to sharp right or left.

A hit is claimed when any part of the target, no matter how small, separates from the main body of the disk. A direct hit at fairly close range literally pulverizes a clay bird into a cloud of black smoke. There is no question of a hit or miss in that case, but when a single pellet chips off only a small piece of the target, an occasional argument ensues. That is when the referee earns his or her pay—if any. The official arbiter's decision on trap and Skeet fields is final. Only poor sports will dispute the judgment of a referee. As with a baseball umpire, even if he's wrong—he's right! There is no other way to run a competitive event. Someone must be in charge at all times, not only to interpret rules, but to see that matters are handled fairly and safely.

Unfortunately, there are a few shooters who take advantage of the rules and intimidate the puller/referee. At a typical registered trapshoot around the U.S., trap pullers and setters are usually teenagers. Most of them have had little briefing about the rules they are supposed to enforce. Therefore, when they call a target "lost" because they didn't see a visible piece, some shooters will challenge this decision. If the shooter is backed by one or two of his squad mates, the young referee will usually change the score from "lost" to "dead" and initial the score sheet.

It is a difficult situation to police. I have been on countless rounds in which I felt I missed a target, only to have a fellow squad member tell the referee he saw a piece fly off and the target should be declared "dead." That is not unusual because of the differences in viewing angles between shooters and puller/referee.

Trapshooting is a simple game. After taking his place at the designated station, a shooter shoulders his gun with his cheek tight against the stock comb and his eye sighted straight down the barrel rib. He points the muzzle where the bird will emerge from the trap house and calls "Pull!" The bird, released electronically by the puller, comes out of the house only an instant after the call is made. The shooter tracks the target with both gun and body, then, slightly accelerating his swing, passes the target and pulls the trigger. If track and lead are correct and swing and follow-through smooth, the target will break. Sounds easy enough, doesn't it? It really isn't quite that simple. Even experts miss every now and again, and it often takes years of practice to get good enough to break 21 or 22 out of 25 birds. Rank beginners frequently shoot several boxes of shells before ever scoring on a clay target. But, as with all sports, the challenge is there and most shooters are hooked once they try. Otherwise, why would they keep coming back for more?

Although trapshooting was originally an off-season training game to retain or improve one's hunting skills, it is still an excellent practice vehicle for the upland game hunter. However, there are some differences between practice and actual shooting that should be noted. In trap, the gunner shoulders his gun and is ready to fire before the bird is seen. He knows where the target will first appear and when it will pop out of the trap. Swing, timing and lead improve with practice, but field conditions are not quite the same. A clay pigeon starts off fast and then slows down, while a game bird takes off slowly and then speeds up. In spite of existing differences, however, a good clay bird shooter will probably be a better wingshot in the field than a shooter who has trouble with trap.

Trap Doubles

Trap Doubles is the most difficult of all three trapshooting games. Two clay targets are released at the same time on separate courses. One bird goes to the extreme left, the other to the far right. Even though the shooter knows the paths the targets will take, it's not easy to break them both before they hit the ground. The usual method is to break the most straightaway bird first, then swing smoothly over to take the second target. Doubles is nowhere near as popular as Singles or Handicap trap because it's more difficult to master and requires the shooter to own and use a shotgun capable of firing two shots in rapid order. Over 93 percent of Doubles shooters use an over/under gun with the balance made up of autoloaders and very few pump actions. Side-by-sides are virtually extinct on today's trap line.

Trapshooting newcomers are reluctant to shoot Doubles because of the widely-held opinion that bringing down two targets in rapid succession is far too difficult. This argument doesn't quite hold water, however, when considering that in Skeet, two targets are in the air simultaneously and flying in two different directions. Skeet shooters handle this awkward situation without questioning its possibility or apparent difficulty. As with any new undertaking, shooting Doubles with a reasonable degree of success takes quite a bit of practice, more so than either Singles or Handicap shooting. There are quite a few American trapshooters who maintain a Doubles average well above a normal shooter's Singles average. Yes, Doubles shooting can be mastered, but only by those who annually shoot upward of 5000 targets.

To spice up early-day shooting, Doubles was introduced into tournaments in 1911. The purpose was to allow more field-shooting practice in which two or more birds might rise at the same time. The value of such training for taking doubles in the field should be perfectly obvious. Mastering the art of Doubles is not easy, but far from impossible. It is certainly a more exciting and challenging alternative to Singles.

Handicap Trap

During trapshooting's early days, all contestants competed against each other on a head-to-head basis. Soon, the best shooters were always winning. The result was that if certain shooters were scheduled to appear at a particular trapshoot, other contestants would not enter the field. Attendance dropped drastically, enough so that the Amateur Trapshooting Association decided that a new rule was needed to make trapshooting equal for all entrants. Handicap Trap was inaugurated for the same reasons that handicaps are utilized in other sports such as golf and bowling. By giving a less skillful participant an even chance, or perhaps a bit of an edge, competition is more equal. In trapshooting, distance is the basis for making all shooters as equal as possible. Trap handicaps begin at 17 yards. Distance up to 27 yards is added as skill increases. Handicap

yards are added for good shooters until their advantage in overall scores disappears. The ATA determines shooter's individual handicaps based on past performance in both registered and unregistered events. Unfortunately, over the past decade or two, the 27-yard shooters across the nation have dominated Handicap Trap. These shooters are the best and their averages show it. There have been various verbal attempts to add further handicaps to the 27-yard shooters, though no hard, fast rules or laws have been invoked.

There's been clamor among ATA members and officials to increase the maximum yardage from 27 to 30 (the maximum yardage was changed from 25 to 27 in the middle 1950s). This would put extreme hardship on most gun clubs where space and layout prevent increased yardage. Many think that this 3-yard increase would only be a temporary solution because this same class of outstanding "guns" would get the new yardage "down pat" after a couple of seasons and their scores would suffer little. Finally, the proposed 30-yard rule isn't really penalizing the shooter, but taxing the gun and ammunition well past its effective range. Other proposals claim the amount of shot should be reduced from $1^1/8$ ounces to 1-ounce loads. Again, this is penalizing the equipment, not the shooter. As of today, there are no new rules or worthwhile suggestions to placate the general membership, and those two handfuls of shooters will continue to dominate Handicap Trap.

International Trap

International Trap has many names and few U.S. followers. It's also called International Clay Pigeon, Olympic Trap, Bunker or Trench shooting. International Trap is a difficult game to master and unquestionably, in my opinion, the most difficult of all the formal clay target games. It is entirely different from American Trap in that the field layout is more elaborate (and more expensive), and the traps are housed in a structure with a roof at ground level—the same height as the shooting stations. A ditch, known as the "Olympic Trench," is dug into the ground ahead of the trap line to allow target clearance. There are 15 traps—three for each shooting station spaced 1-meter apart. The center trap throws targets within 15 degrees to the right or left of the straightaway setting. The left trap covers an area straight forward to 45 degrees to the right and the right trap releases targets from dead ahead to 45 degrees to the left. Ten meters from the trap, each preset machine angles clay birds upward from 1 to 4 meters above ground.

In tournaments, each of the 15 traps in the bunker are reset in a different location each day. In case you're wondering, International Trap machines do not oscillate horizontally or vertically, but remain in a fixed position for a given day. Shooting stations are located 15 meters to the rear of the centers of the traps in a straight line—not an arc as in American Trap.

International trapshooting is often called "Bunker" or "Trench" due to the layout of the 15 traps underground. Each trap is set daily to throw a set target, and during the course of a 200-target program, each contestant fires at the exact type of targets as his competition.

Trap selection is random, controlled by an electronic device that is independent of all human input. When the shot is called and the control button pressed by the puller, a trap, directed solely by the electronic "brain," releases a target in an unknown direction. At the end of a 100-, 200- or even 300-target race, every shooter will have received the same combination of birds. Now, that's what I call fair! Just another reason why International Trap is perhaps the finest clay target game played today. International Trap birds also fly faster and farther than American Trap birds, and the minimum distance covered by an International target is 77 meters.

Unlike American Trap, there are six shooters to a squad—five are on the line while one is walking from Station Five back to Station One. Stations are changed after each man on the line has fired at one bird. Two shots are allowed at each bird. A bird is "dead" if hit by one or both shots. Many gunners always shoot twice to keep their two-shot rhythm. This two-shot sequence keeps the top-notch competitor sharp and prevents "lulling," which can happen to a shooter if he starts to break too many targets with the first shot. That may sound strange, but if a shooter does well and makes most of his "breaks" with the first shot, human nature takes over and the all-important back-up shot is not only unneeded, but ignored. Then, if the shooter misses his first shot, his reflexes have been drastically slowed, and though the second shot is taken, it is usually too late to hit the target. That is "lulling." Twenty-five targets constitute a single event.

Special ammunition plays a big part in the shooter's overall performance. Once shooters get "locked in" to using a certain brand, dram equivalent and size of shot, switching ammunition can and has proved to be disastrous. There are no restrictions on the "power" of the shell because any dram equivalent is permissible. There are two restrictions regarding the size and amount of shot—No. 7½ and 1¼ ounces is the legal allowable maximum. Most of the American shooters I've talked to prefer 3¼ drams and 1¼ ounces of No. 7½ shot for the first barrel and 3¾ drams and 1¼ ounces of No. 7½ shot for the second barrel. Both of these loads are about on par with what the average hunter uses for ducks and pheasants. How would you like to shoot a couple hundred shells with this wallop in a single day? It's not pleasant, which is why most International Trap events are held over a 3-day span.

Most major events consist of a 200-target race shot over 2 or 3 days, depending on the sponsoring club's facilities, with 75 targets on the first and second days and 50 on the final day. In comparison, it is not unusual to find most American trap clubs hosting 300 or more

International-type trapshooting does not have as large a following in the U.S. as ATA trap, due to the gun club's resistance to install more fields — and with each field requiring 15 traps, it's an economical disaster.

targets in a single day. Who says a shotgun's recoil isn't an influencing factor?

Due to the high cost of building an International Trap field, as well as the increased cost of each individual round, there is not much interest in the U.S. in this activity.

In comparison, this type of trapshooting is *the* game in Europe and especially Italy. Shooters on the other side of the pond are sponsored by many of the larger industrial firms, and the ranges are more like country clubs where members are required to join and pay annual dues, just for the privilege to pop primers over the trench.

the country, although most of them too small to truly be international. The 1984 Olympic facility Prado de Tiro near Los Angeles, California is probably the finest shooting facility on this continent and is equipped with both International Trap and Skeet fields.

International Trap is gaining in popularity, simply because a few more new fields are being built. This sport, however, will surely never enjoy the mass appeal American Trap does for economic reasons. The fields are expensive to install and shooting costs are usually 50 percent higher than American Trap. Shooting two shells at each target is also becoming very expensive.

Spectators love to watch International Trap because

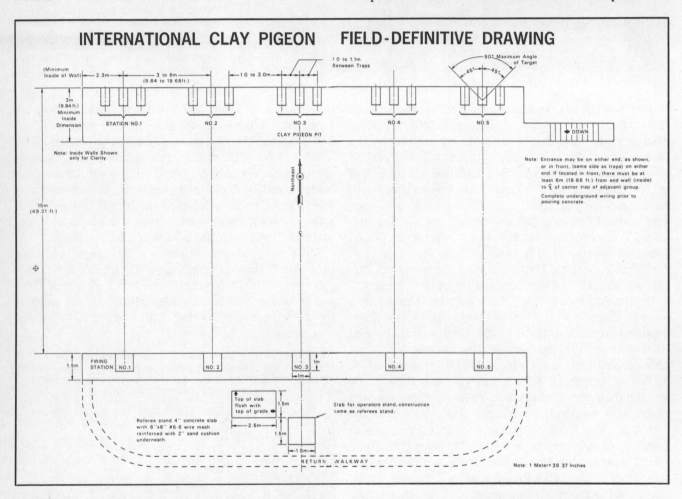

INTERNATIONAL CLAY PIGEON   FIELD-DEFINITIVE DRAWING

Recently in the U.S., more shooters have become involved in this highly-sophisticated sport, thanks to sponsorship by the NRA and the efforts of the U.S. Army Marksmanship Training Unit (USAMTU) in Fort Benning, Georgia. The U.S. Air Force has also resumed its shooting program at Lackland Air Force Base in San Antonio, Texas.

There are only about a dozen International Trap facilities in North America. The first two were built on military bases in Fort Benning, Georgia and San Antonio, Texas. The first private International Trap field was built at the Hamilton Gun Club in Vinemount, Ontario, Canada. A few more clubs are scattered around

the action is fast and furious and the shooters are constantly moving from one post to another. The best, or worst, depending on your point of view as a shooter or spectator, is when a shooter misses a target and a blast from an air horn chills the air for all to hear. If I were seriously shooting, I'd change the rules and have the referee muffle a simple "lost," instead of that intimidating and embarrassing fog horn.

Modified Clay Pigeon

No longer seen in formal ATA competitions, Modified Clay Pigeon shooting was devised three decades ago to encourage trapshooters to train for and enter In-

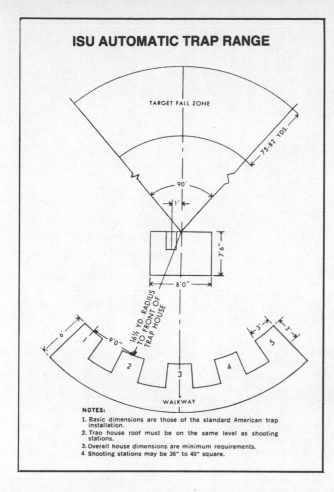

ISU AUTOMATIC TRAP RANGE

TARGET FALL ZONE

75-82 YDS.

90°

1'

7'6"

8'0"

16½ YD. RADIUS TO FRONT OF TRAP HOUSE

WALKWAY

1 2 3 4 5

9'0"

6'

3' 3'

NOTES:
1. Basic dimensions are those of the standard American trap installation.
2. Trap house roof must be on the same level as shooting stations.
3. Overall house dimensions are minimum requirements.
4. Shooting stations may be 36" to 40" square.

ternational Trap tournaments and solve the lack of shooting facilities problem. The game is known by several other names such as NRA Modified Clay Pigeon, NRA International Clay Pigeon, UIT Automatic Trap, and ISU Automatic Trap.

In Modified Clay Pigeon, trap houses used in American Trap are acceptable as long as the roof is no more than 34 inches above Station Three. A single Winchester trap modified to move both vertically and horizontally within limits prescribed for International Trap competition is used. The trap may be fired either mechanically or electrically and loaded automatically or by hand. Targets are released randomly and like International Trap, the shooter has no inkling of where the bird may fly. The target leaves the arm of the trap machine in excess of 60 mph. Therefore, if the shooter hesitates, due to indecision or a slow functioning shotgun, he can kiss the target goodbye, especially on a "grass-cutting" 1-meter bird.

Modified Clay Pigeon rules closely follow International Trap's in that six shooters comprise a squad, each shooter moves over one station after each shot, 25 targets make up a round and two shots may be fired at each target. In club events, it is not unusual for some of these rules to be altered slightly as local conditions dictate, but as long as the regulation trap is used, these programs are excellent practice for "big time" Interna-

tional Trap. A few gun clubs still have "wobble-trap" events, but Modified International Trapshooting has gone the way of the dinosaur. Pity, too, because those who shot this game found it challenging, exciting and totally unpredictable. Probably the reason for its demise was that perfect, even near perfect, scores were virtually impossible, even for the finest shotgun shooters. Unfortunately, American trap and Skeet shooters prefer easy games that maintain high year-end averages. It seems as though peer pressure is applied through personal averages instead of the number of wins in the scorebook, regardless of the scores.

Skeet

The only similarity between Skeet and trapshooting is that both use shotguns and clay targets. Field layout is distinctly different—traps that throw the targets are set up uniquely and shooting angles are not all alike. Not to say that trapshooting experience is not transferable to the Skeet field. Gun mounting techniques, swing and lead are much the same, although some differences in shooting methods and equipment have been introduced since Skeet first became popular in the 1920s.

American Skeet, to differentiate it from International Skeet, is shot on a field that is approximately semi-circular with eight shooting stations. Two traps are used—one mounted in an elevated position at the left of the field in the "high house," the other at the right of the layout in the "low house." Trap houses are 40 yards apart and targets are thrown in a consistent flight path from each house. Target paths from the two houses cross 6 yards from shooting Station Eight, which is midway between the two houses. Shooting Stations One through Seven are on a 21-yard radius arc, the center being at the target crossing point, 6 yards in front of Station Eight.

Like a round of trap, a round of Skeet consists of 25 shots. Each competitor fires at two targets from each station, one from the high house and one from the low. Doubles, in which targets are launched from both houses simultaneously, are shot from Stations One, Two, Six and Seven. Though there are five shooters in a full Skeet squad, one to five may play in practice sessions.

Skeet rules often seem complicated to beginners, but following through a round of Skeet should clarify procedures. All squad members gather at Station One and the first shooter steps into firing position. First, he shoots at a target from the high house and then one from the low, calling "Pull!" for each target. He then stays at Station One and shoots doubles — targets released from both houses at the same time. When all squad members have shot, they move to Station Two, where the same sequence is repeated. At Station Three, singles *only* are shot — high house first, then low house. Singles are shot in turn from Stations Four and

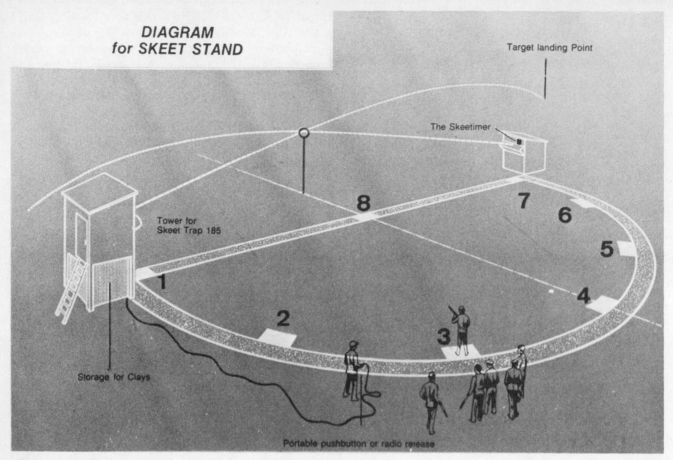

DIAGRAM
for SKEET STAND

Target landing Point

The Skeetimer

8

7

6

5

4

Tower for
Skeet Trap 185

1

2

3

Storage for Clays

Portable pushbutton or radio release

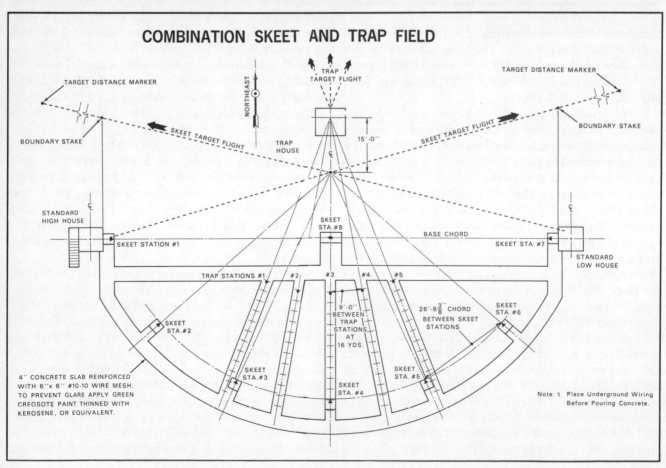

COMBINATION SKEET AND TRAP FIELD

TARGET DISTANCE MARKER

TARGET DISTANCE MARKER

NORTHEAST

TRAP TARGET FLIGHT

SKEET TARGET FLIGHT

SKEET TARGET FLIGHT

TRAP HOUSE

BOUNDARY STAKE

BOUNDARY STAKE

15'-0''

STANDARD HIGH HOUSE

SKEET STA. #8

BASE CHORD

SKEET STATION #1

SKEET STA. #7

STANDARD LOW HOUSE

TRAP STATIONS #1   #2   #3   #4   #5

SKEET STA.#2

9'-0'' BETWEEN TRAP STATIONS AT 16 YDS.

26'-8 3/8'' CHORD BETWEEN SKEET STATIONS

SKEET STA.#6

SKEET STA.#3

SKEET STA.#5

SKEET STA. #4

4'' CONCRETE SLAB REINFORCED WITH 6''x 6'' #10-10 WIRE MESH. TO PREVENT GLARE APPLY GREEN CREOSOTE PAINT THINNED WITH KEROSENE, OR EQUIVALENT.

Note: 1. Place Underground Wiring Before Pouring Concrete.

SKEET FIELD-SHOT FALL ZONE

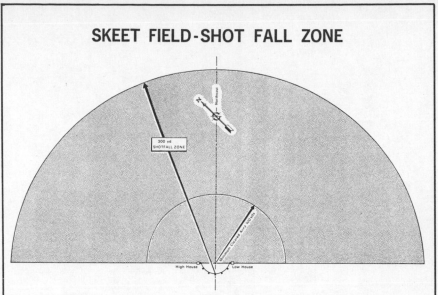

MULTIPLE SKEET FIELD LAYOUT

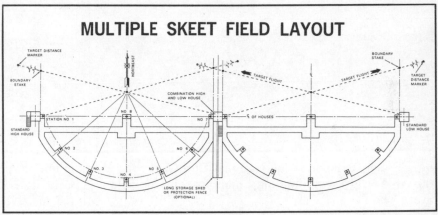

Five. At Stations Six and Seven, both singles and doubles are fired upon, repeating Stations One and Two procedures, except that targets from the low house are shot first. At Station Eight, each squad member shoots at the high-house target in turn, then at the low-house target. The total shots thus far is 24. Shot number 25 is the "optional" shot, and is fired from the low house at Station Eight if no shots have previously been missed. If a shooter misses anywhere along the line, his optional shot must be taken as a repeat of the shot that was missed. This may be a bit confusing to the Skeet newcomer, but after shooting a couple of rounds, it all begins to make sense and things fall into place quite nicely.

Most newcomers are confused about the "optional" target. By definition alone, Skeet rules dictate when and where you must fire your 25th shot depending on whether or not the shooter is "straight" or has missed a target. Where does the word "optional" fit in? Like trapshooting, a few early-day terms carry over. When Skeet shooting began, it was a very social game, and it would often take hours to complete a single round. One reason Skeet shooting was so slow was because the

shooters choose where they wanted to shoot their 25th shot. It wasn't until the late 1950s that the rule governing singles and doubles shooting was changed. Before that, all shooters shot singles from Stations One through Seven. Then, they returned to Station One to shoot doubles, then Station Two for more doubles, then on to Stations Six and Seven to complete the doubles, and then they eventually shot Station Eight. As you can see, this strolling around the field twice really slowed down the pace, and it would typically take 40 to 60 minutes for a five-man squad to finish.

Skeet offers a greater variety of shooting angles than trap and more closely simulates hunting conditions, with both incoming and departing birds represented. Near overhead shots from Station Eight are similar to those that might be encountered when shooting from a duck blind and over a set of decoys. Other shots duplicate crossing shots, and other angles are similar to a covey of quail on the rise. For field-shooting practice, Skeet is an excellent trainer, but only if the shooter approaches the target with the shotgun unmounted.

The National Skeet Shooting Association is the sanctioning body for Skeet with headquarters in San Anto-

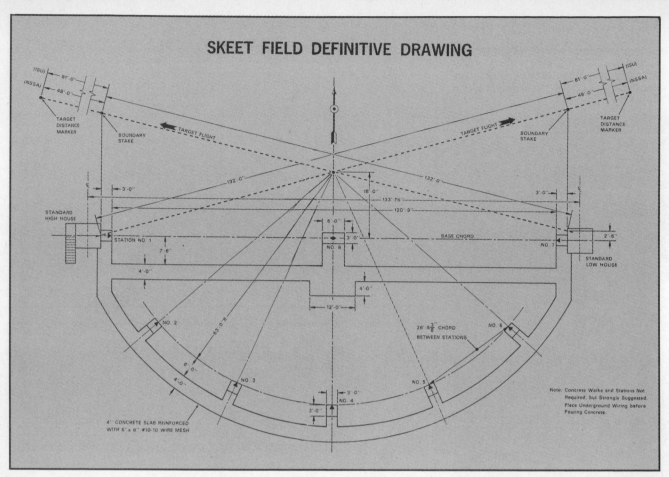

SKEET FIELD DEFINITIVE DRAWING

nio, Texas. Its home is the National Gun Club where the All-World Skeet Shooting Championships are held every year.

Skeet newcomers use a 12-gauge shotgun, although there are events scheduled in most tournaments for 410, 28- and 20-gauge categories. Scoring with smaller-bored guns is naturally more difficult because of reduced pattern density and shot load. Skeet with a 410 is a true experts game! Like trapshooting, there are various classes in each gauge plus special entries such as two- and five-man teams, two-in-a-family, etc. Skeet is not nearly as formal as trapshooting, and there seems to be more levity during a registered NSSA shoot than a typical ATA event.

International Skeet

Although Skeet was invented in the U.S., the rest of the world didn't like the way we slowly, but surely, made the game easier. International Skeet then, more popular in Europe than here, is simply the original version of the American game. The International field layout is the same, but there are some major differences in rules and procedures. Shooters are required to hold the gun at hip level when calling for a target. After the target appears, the gun must be raised to the shoulder before firing. If a shooter calls for a target and raises his gun off his hip and onto his shoulder before the target is presented, a "lost" target is declared. This rule puts a

premium on speed and mounting techniques. The targets fly faster from an International Skeet trap, required to travel 72 yards, as opposed to 60 yards in American Skeet. To withstand the added stress of being launched at a higher velocity, International birds are made from a harder material — and so are a little tougher to break.

The target speed makes bringing the gun up quickly and precisely from its "low" position tricky and somewhat unpleasant. It can best be described as semi-controlled snapshooting. Therefore, International Skeet guns and ammunition are quite a bit different from those used in American Skeet.

For openers, the dominant type of gun used in International Skeet is the over/under because it is more reliable than autoloaders or pump-action repeaters, and it's faster between shots. Granted, there are some shotgun virtuosos who can make multiple shots from a pump gun sound like one roaring boom, but even exhibition shooters like John Satterwhite who use pump guns in their act, switch back to the over/under for serious International target work.

Shotgun stock dimensions are also quite different from those found on domestic Skeet guns. As a rule, there is considerably more pitch and drop at the comb and heel. Unless the gun is mounted perfectly every time in swift, fluid-like motions, the shooter doesn't stand a chance against these ultra-fast targets. Fast and correct gun mounting techniques are the single most important part in learning how to shoot International Skeet — at least successfully.

Also, the gun chokes are virtually wide open and many are really "chokeless." The Tula-type choke is the predominant favorite among shooters worldwide because it helps create a garden hose-like pattern at relatively short range. Contributing to the shooter's need to have a quick-opening pattern is special ammunition made by both Federal and Winchester. Federal's T-122 has no shot protector built into the wad column and is loaded with 1¹/₈ ounces of No. 9 shot with a muzzle velocity approaching 1200 fps. The T-123 cartridge is loaded with 1¹/₈ ounces of No. 10 shot (slightly smaller) and exits the muzzle 100 fps faster, at 1300. Both shells are loaded with soft shot, which has a tendency to spread the pattern more than shells loaded with hard shot.

Winchester's International Skeet loads are "hot" and record about 1330 fps, pushing ¹/₈-ounce of No. 9¹/₂-size shot. And, like Federal, Winchester's International loads don't have a built-in shot protector and use card and fiber filler wads and an umbrella-type over powder wad.

Quite a few proponents of International Skeet claim that their game is closer to duplicating similar shots taken in the field, but I doubt this. Most of the upland game bird hunters I have seen rarely carry the gun butt at their hip, but elevated quite a bit higher and thrust away from their bodies for fast and smooth mounting.

Another major difference between domestic and International Skeet is in target launching times. As of the late 1950s, the American Skeet target is launched immediately after a shooter calls, "Pull!" In International Skeet, there may be a delay of up to 3 seconds before a bird emerges from the house. Target presentation is different in International Skeet because the optional shot is eliminated. Shots are as follows.

Station:
One — one single (high house), plus one pair of doubles.
Two — two singles (1H, 1L), plus one pair of doubles.
Three — two singles (1H, 1L), plus one pair of doubles.
Four — two singles (1H, 1L), no doubles.
Five — two singles (1H, 1L), plus one pair of doubles.
Six — two singles (1H, 1L), plus one pair of doubles.
Seven — no singles, only one pair of doubles.
Eight — two singles, (1H, 1L), no doubles.

There are also several loading and gun handling rules that are not the same as in American Skeet. American Skeet shooters may have difficulty switching to the International sport, but to compete in other countries or in World Championship events, a bit of concentrated effort to make the transition could be highly rewarding.

Instead of the U.S. becoming the global governing body, the ISU is the worldwide controlling group for International Skeet. In the United States, though, the NRA is the guiding organization.

International Skeet is a scheduled event in the Olympic Games and other World Championship programs, but it has never attracted much of a following in America. Although equipment used is not as complex as for International Trap, altering range machinery to reproduce target velocities essential to International competition is an added expense. Many gun clubs are reluctant to spend money to equip Skeet fields for International shooting only. Some clubs have tried to promote International Skeet shooting by "cranking up" the mainspring on target launching machines to throw a faster target, but shooter interest just wasn't there. Like Grand Prix automobile racing is to the Europeans, stock car and the Indy is to the Americans. Each have their own set of followers, and although one group respects and admires the other, neither really wants to compete on the other's courses.

Sporting Clays

There's never been a clay target shooting game to come down the pike with so much initial publicity and glamour; the *Wall Street Journal* even ran an article about it. It is not uncommon to find similar stories and articles about Sporting Clays in local newspapers even

All Sporting Clays courses demand that the contestant start out with a "low gun," unlike trap and Skeet in which a mounted gun is permitted. (Photo courtesy of *The Houston Post.*)

Sporting Clays "towers" are extremely popular and are designed to duplicate waterfowl coming into a spread of decoys usually from behind the shooter. (Photo courtesy of *The Houston Post*.)

though regular trap and Skeet shoots are written about less frequently. Why this craze?

Well, first of all, Sporting Clays appeals to the majority of shotgun shooters — that is the hunter. This shotgunning sport simulates game bird hunting and originated in England more than 60 years ago. It's immensely popular in Europe and regularly scheduled shoots draw upward of 400 competitors.

Sporting Clays was introduced in the U.S. by the Orvis Company, well-known for its shooting school and hunting and shooting supplies, and Orvis' key employee, Bryan Balinski. Balinski set up a formal Sporting Clays shooting course in Houston, Texas in 1983 called the Orvis Cup Classic. That event was the forerunner to what we know today. There were more than 200 scheduled tournaments in 1988.

Every target put in the air during a Sporting Clays event simulates a typical hunting situation. In fact, there are so many different "posts" or "stations," so to speak, that if the average hunter/shooter encounters them, he or she will probably pass up the shot. However, when coming across one of these nearly impossible shots, the contestant had better shoot anyway, or a "lost" will be called.

Target launching machines are routinely set in blind locations, out of view of the contestant. Therefore, the "hunter" must use his other senses as well to discover not only the flight of the target, but when the trap is tripped. Both eyes and ears are perked at all times because shooting situations are as imaginative as the course director conjures.

The terrain varies from one gun club to the next, so there is no "standard" course layout. One gun club can have as few as five shooting stations, whereas another may have eight. The number of "birds" per round may vary, depending on the whim of the director.

Using a Sporting Clays coach is recommended for novice shooters because they will help neophytes learn faster how to shoot effectively and safely. (Photo courtesy of *The Houston Post*.)

(Right) This Sporting Clays station can accommodate up to three shooters and often six targets are released simultaneously for some fast and furious shooting.

(Below) The Sporting Clays trap is positioned in a blind location, unknown to the shooter. It could easily duplicate a wildly-flushing cock pheasant. (Photo courtesy of *The Houston Post.*)

(Left) Clay target machines set up in the back of a station wagon provide mobility for a minimum amount of effort and can provide shooters with an informal game of Sporting Clays.

(Above) As a rule, most Sporting Clays courses use all-white targets because they are the easiest to see against various dark backgrounds. I wonder what color targets are used in Alaska in the winter?

This non-standard shooting course may well be a two-edged sword. After continually shooting a local course, a shooter more or less gets locked into his home court. The more he shoots, the more his proficiency and confidence increases at that course. Most gun club managers alter a course by moving traps, shooting singles instead of doubles, etc. The point is that once a shooter learns and more or less masters the idiosyncrasies of his "home field," his mastery will be for naught on a new and strange setup.

There are those who claim that good shotgun handling will win overall, regardless of the course or layout, and the best shooters will eventually come to the top like cream in milk. This is true in the long run, but Sporting Clays tournaments are generally no more than 200-target events and local shooters have a decided advantage over "foreigners," even if the course changes. General background, weather, wind conditions and off-field activities will usually favor the hometown heroes.

The USSCA recently recognized this problem and started sanctioning and scheduling courses around the U.S., sort of like a series of Grand Prix events. The multi-course concept should eliminate past problems except in cases in which shooters have the time, money and wherewithal to "practice" at each gun club prior to the scheduled event.

Sporting Clays shooting is currently a very enjoyable pastime. It is certainly more fun than registered trap or Skeet shooting, if missing targets is one's idea of fun. The few courses that I've shot make hitting targets as difficult as it is practical without it being impossible for shooters to break scores that are mentally demoralizing. I have witnessed first-time shooters score 10 to 15 out of 50 with second attempts nearly doubling their initial scores. A Sporting Clays contestant who breaks 70 to 75 percent of his targets is considered an exceptional shooter.

Shooting into a gully is to duplicate flushing quail or perhaps a running bunny. This Sporting Clays station calls for the hunter to be in a sitting position.

Most Sporting Clays courses depend on manually-operated target launching machines for two reasons — lack of electricity and ease of moving from one location to another.

Star Shot

Frankly, most clay target shooting games are boring to watch unless you're a contestant. One reason national TV rarely shows trap and Skeet shooting is because it is difficult, in fact, virtually impossible to graphically illustrate what is happening. In trapshooting, it is hard to record results unless the camera zooms in on the clay target, and then the shooter is out of the picture. The shooting perspective is simply not recordable by traditional camera angles. Skeet is somewhat easier because the shooter and target are fairly close to each other. Unless the target is "smoked," or broken,

This celebrity Star Shoot was composed of (left to right) trapshooting's all-American Frank Little, ex-Pittsburg Steeler quarterback Terry Bradshaw, the announcer, TV celebrity John James and perennial trapshooting champion Dan Bonillas.

though, it is difficult to determine through the eyes of a camera if a target is hit or missed, especially if only a chip or two is knocked off.

Another problem shooters are always striving to overcome is the public image of shooting; specifically, the image of shooters using guns. Archery is considered socially acceptable, yet I'd say that from the advent of the stick and string, archers have killed more people than riflemen through the decades.

Star Shot is a terrific clay target shooting game specifically designed to show action, both in live and recorded images. It has been on cable TV for almost 6 months at the time of this writing. Many sports, movie and TV celebrities have competed against trap and Skeet shooting's elite. Football players like Terry Bradshaw and Mark Malone, TV personalities John James and Bo Hopkins, along with trapshooting stars Frank Little, Dan Bonillas and Frank Kodl are regular attendees.

Other Games

Many shooters do not care for formal shooting. As alternatives to regulation competition there are games that can be played with the equipment already in place on standard trap and Skeet fields. With these novelty games, shooters can practice in a more relaxed atmosphere.

There are countless types of clay target shooting games, two trapshooting variations being **Rabbit Run** and **Quail Walk**. In Rabbit Run, the throwing trap is set to cast targets as close to the ground as possible. A shooter either stands on the trap house or immediately behind it and fires down at the target, much the same way one might shoot at a rabbit flushed from under foot. Each round usually consists of 25 shots. Quail Walk (or Grouse Walk) may be played with either one or two shots per target or arranged for shooting dou-

bles. The shooter starts at Station Three and walks steadily toward the trap house. The puller releases the target anywhere along the route once the shooter calls "ready," but he must keep moving until the bird appears. If a trap field is superimposed on a Skeet field, as is many times the case, further variety may be added by using all three trap machines. A more realistic Quail Walk involves special traps arranged on either side of a trail laid out through brushy country. As the shooter progresses along the trail, birds are released sporadically, simulating the rise of live birds. This type of Quail Walk provides many of the challenges of an actual hunting situation, and it takes a most skilled and alert shooter to break 25 straight.

"Shooting Down the Line" is a popular shooting game where the first shooter fires at the target; if he misses, the next shooter down the line shoots until the target is broken, eliminating the preceding shooters from the meet.

Sporting Clays, being endorsed by the National Shooting Sports Foundation, is gaining interest and popularity all over the country. (Photo courtesy of *The Houston Post*.)

Two-man teams are exceedingly popular, especially at turkey shoots. The **Buddy Shoot,** sometimes called Protection Trap or Back-Up Trap, consists of two shooters standing shoulder-to-shoulder at a single station, usually firing from the 27-yard line. Both assume the ready position, and when the target is launched, the person on the left fires first. If he misses, his partner shoots and the results are scored. If the first shooter hits the target, his partner does not shoot. If, however, his partner should shoot after the first shooter hits the target, it is scored as a miss. This is a game with a lot of hot and heavy action and participants must really keep on their toes. With two gunners on each target, scores are generally high, and it requires more than the usual amount of concentration to win. A Buddy Shoot usually consists of 10 pairs of targets and two birds per station with shooters alternating "who goes first?"

Another trapshooting standby is **Annie Oakley**, sometimes referred to as a Shooting Down The Line, or even Custer's Last Stand. As many shooters as can safely line up shoulder-to-shoulder on the 27-yard line may participate. Each competitor is assigned a number drawn by lot, and the shooters line up in numerical order. Shooter No. 1 calls for the target; if he hits it, he is credited. If No. 1 misses, shooter No. 2 shoots. If No. 2 hits the target, No. 1 is eliminated, but if No. 2 shoots at a bird that No. 1 has already hit, then he is out of the

"Buddy Shoots" are very popular, fun shooting games. Two-person teams take positions to shoot at 27-yard targets. A hit is scored if the target is broken either by the first man who shoots and breaks the target, or, if he should miss, his "buddy," who shoots and breaks the target.

For more shooting fun, two-person teams compete against each other for high-gun laurels on the Duck Tower.

game. If both shooters miss, player No. 3 shoots. If player No. 3 hits the target, then shooters one and two are eliminated. If No. 3 misses, shooter No. 4 fires. Some clubs "crank up the targets," which keeps a bird in the air long enough for five, six or seven shooters to have a chance to break it before it hits the ground. The game progresses this way until there is only one shooter left. When 30 to 35 contestants assemble for this game, things can get wild and woolly. This is obviously not a game for rank beginners because a great deal of discipline is needed for the sake of everyone's safety.

A real crowd pleaser is **Follow the Leader**, a game with a lot of laughs and a lot of moans, too. It may be played either on a trap or Skeet field, but preferably on a layout with both. Shooters draw a number at random. Player No. 1 selects the game — Skeet, trap or a combination of both, such as a Skeet and trap bird released at the same time. Any possible shot may be chosen by the leader. If No. 1 makes his shot, all players must attempt to duplicate his success. One-handed shots, shooting from the hip and so on, may be allowed to add difficulty. Follow the Leader may be run as an elimination contest or scores may be kept. In the former, he who misses is out. In the latter, high score wins.

This Sporting Clays course boasts a specially-built "Duck Tower" that stands almost 60-feet high. Both Singles and Doubles are thrown from this unique shooting setup. (Photo courtesy of *The Houston Post*.)

Perhaps the oldest of all informal shotgun games, but one that is still popular in many parts of the country is **Turkey Shoot**. Today's shoots are often named incorrectly, as live turkeys are not the target, but often the winning prize. Obviously, these shoots are annually conducted by most trap and Skeet clubs prior to Thanksgiving and Christmas. The trophy is usually a cleaned, wrapped and frozen turkey. Unlike our forefathers, if we can't win a turkey at a trap or Skeet shoot, there's always the supermarket, and who's to know the difference!

The Skeet field provides more of a variety of games than regular trapshooting. Perhaps the most enjoyable and challenging is **Doubles At All Stations**. As the name implies, double targets are shot at each of the eight stations, which increases the difficulty. Because only 16 shells are expended, other combinations of shooting positions may be included to make a total of 25 shots. However, most clubs prefer to make this event a "miss and out." That is, if you miss a target, you're out of the match. Very few shooters can shoot the entire field and go straight. It is a very informal game and rules can be changed along the way. Because it's all for fun, records are not ordinarily kept. With a little imagination, innumerable games can be staged for the Skeet field. Shooters should remember, however, that safety must always be given prime consideration when deviating from a normal, established shooting scheme.

One of the more difficult shotgunning games is **Crazy Quail,** which uses a trap in a pit below ground that is mounted on a central pedestal with a seat for the operator. Because the trap and seat rotate 360 degrees, targets may be sent in any direction — even toward the shooter. The target may be delayed for up to 10 seconds after a competitor calls "Pull!," which adds to the element of surprise. The shooter may not, for safety reasons, turn and fire at an incoming target after it passes him. Gunners may stand anywhere from 16 to 20 yards from the trap, depending on specified handicaps. Crazy Quail rules are quite flexible and are frequently formulated on the spot by the competitors. One or two shots at each bird is usually what shooters agree on. This is a shoot strictly for fun and there is no sanctioning organization, nor are records usually kept.

Waterfowl hunters enjoy **Duck Tower**, which is another game without rigid rules. Typically, a trap is situated at some convenient height above the shooter's station — usually a man-made tower, but the side of a sloping hill will do. The idea is to present targets flying at angles similar to a duck flying over a blind. Shooting procedures follow local rules and don't conform to a fixed pattern. The original purpose of the Duck Tower game was to provide practice before duck hunting season, but it is so enjoyable that many who shoot it never go anywhere near a duck blind.

Now defunct, but one of the most challenging Duck Tower setups was the King Tower at Aqua Sierra Gun Club in Chatsworth, California. What made this field so difficult was the height of the tower, which was 100 feet above the shooter, and the trap itself, which oscillated and released targets anywhere within a 30-degree arc. By the time the shooter "got on the target," it was usually 45 to 50 yards downrange. Hitting 60 to 70 percent of these targets was considered a good score. But wait, that's not all the King Tower field offered. When the shooter called "Pull," a second target was launched from a hill approximately 70 yards in front of the shooter. After firing at the first target, the shooter fired at the second, the incomer from the hill. By the time the incoming target was within shooting range, it was traveling very slowly, and gravity would bring it down sharply just before it hit the ground. The shot looked amazingly simple, yet shooters who missed it were the majority, and moaning, grumbling and complaining were the norm. The 25th shot (optional) was a repeat of the first miss — usually target number one! There were very few straights posted and the only two shooters who ever broke perfect scores with 410s were Clark Gable and Roy Rogers. Aqua Sierra Gun Club was "the" club where the stars shot. Each weekend would find Gary Cooper, Jackie Cooper, Frank Ferguson, Bob Sweeney, Andy Devine, Robert Taylor and other notables shooting trap, Skeet, King Tower or a host of other shotgunning games — all great shots.

There are many games devised for clay target shooting — too many to list, in fact. Shotgunners can think up their own games with a gun, a trap, a few boxes of shells and a wide open space. Safety should always be considered first, though. People, livestock and property should be out of the way before a shot is ever fired. There are few sports that are as individually challenging as clay target games.

4

Competitive Shooting Records

SOMEONE ONCE SAID, "records are made to be broken." Unlike some other sports, notably baseball, where virtually countless categories of noteworthy accomplishments are enshrined, shooting sports are much simpler. The target is either hit or missed — nothing more, nothing less. Shooters or statisticians do not have a separate scoring category for targets. Targets that have been "smoked" or broken, are scored.

Therefore, when we speak of shooting records, we are referring to outstanding performances by exceptionally

This is an early self-operated trap machine. Doffing his top hat, and shotgun "at ready," the shooter never knew which direction the pigeon was going to fly, which made this scenario very exciting.

talented trap and Skeet shooters — the best of the best. Exemplary accomplishments by champion shooters form the basis of this chapter. It should be noted, however, that there are other kinds of records.

All shooters should keep their own records as a testimonial to personal progress as skills are gained through both competition and practice. Clubs and sponsoring organizations keep records to award prizes or compute handicaps. National and international groups, as exemplified by the Amateur Trapshooting Association, National Skeet Shooting Association, National Rifle Association, and International Shooting Union, keep records of individual and team scores to classify shooters by their proven abilities. A distinction should be made between records of unique performances and records that are assembled for other purposes.

Today, fewer reports are written about shotgunners and their accomplishments as in the early days of live bird trapshooting. When trapshooting began, consistent rules had not yet been established, and there were no sanctioning organizations to regulate competition. Only a handful of shooting clubs existed, and most contests were merely friendly matches hosted by owners of large estates. These gatherings were primarily social events, with shooting only one of the many diversions for the guests. Pigeon traps were often located near country inns, where local residents of "lesser social status" could also shoot while enjoying the pleasures of food and drink offered by the establishment. Innkeepers usually presented winners of such informal matches with medals, cups or merchandise.

Often, shooting matches took on international overtones, with individuals and teams from Britain pitted against shooters from other countries — notably France. In addition to shooting trapped birds, it was quite common to hold contests in which participants fired from fixed stations at game driven toward them by beaters. Winners in driven game matches were determined by the total number of birds bagged in a given time frame. Rules were extremely variable. Alternate shots were taken when necessary to give each contestant an equal opportunity.

The Coast Pigeon (Blue Rock).

The lowly Coast Pigeon was the first successful target used for trapshooting. In fact, if it weren't for this bird, trap and Skeet shooting might not be around today. Small in body and quick starting, these English-bred birds proved to be a challenge for the finest wing shots in the early 19th century.

Doc Carver (above) was one of the leading exhibition shooters in the late 19th century. The rivalry between "Doc" and Captain Bogardus (left) was legendary and was extensively covered by the press. Their shooting exploits were closely followed by their fans around the world.

More often than not though, the shooting turned into a free-for-all, with every man for himself.

A highly-detailed written account of a driven game match in the early 19th century between six-man teams from France and England involving 3 days of shooting in southern France was recorded many years after the event. Total bag at the end of the contest was 2200 birds. The winning French team also bagged a wager of 10,000 pounds sterling — a veritable fortune in those times.

The use of fundamental flintlock and percussion fowling pieces of the period precluded high percentage scores. Downing only half of the birds released from the traps was considered a major accomplishment. To improve scores, larger, specialized guns were devised expressly for trapshooting and used at pigeon clubs everywhere. "Pigeon guns" were shorter than field guns and frequently carried no ramrod or other heavy furniture.

Huge, clumsy, single-barreled shotguns as large as 4-bore were regularly used at the traps in the early days of the percussion era. The diameter of the 4-gauge barrel was just under 1-inch, while, in comparison, a 12-gauge tube measures slightly less than 3/4-inch. Shot strings from a 4-bore contained about twice the number of pellets propelled from a "normal" 12-bore. Despite the advantage of enormous shot loads, the winner of the Crinden Medal at the "Old Hats" club in July, 1821 killed only 32 out of 60 birds. Though this score is not terribly impressive by today's standards, it was obviously better than typical scores of the time.

Shooters took every advantage as more and more big-bore shotguns were seen on pigeon fields. Many sportsmen felt rules should be made to ban them, in fairness to all concerned. Ultimately, the 12-gauge was accepted as the standard pigeon gun, and shot charges were generally

C. W. FLOYD
1902

M. DIEFENDORFER
1903

R. D. GUPTILL
1904

R. R. BARBER
1905

(Above) This quartet of early 20th-century trapshooters were pioneers in the clay target era. C.W. Floyd was the last live champion in 1902. Diefendorfer, Guptill and Barber were the Grand American all-clay target champions in 1903, 1904 and 1905, respectively.

(Above) Trapshooting, even in its earliest days, appealed to the distaff shooters. Many a woman dressed in Victorian-style clothes dominated trapshoots that were once thought as "for men only."

(Right) Early photo of Remington Gun Club in Lordship, Connecticut. This club was closed in 1986 due to EPA "lead-shot" sanctions. Lordship, as it was referred to, was the host of countless Skeet shooting records.

limited to 1¼ ounces. Those criteria have remained more or less in effect until today, although 10-gauge guns were used for a time in the United States toward the end of the 1800s. Elimination of big-bore shotguns from pigeon fields caused an immediate drop in match scores, but improvements were rapidly adapted to standard 12-gauge guns, which caused a steady rise in "dead bird" counts.

Unquestionably, the advent of lightweight, well-balanced, breech-loading shotguns improved live pigeon shooting scores dramatically. In the 1830s, downing 50 out of 100 birds was a prodigious feat of marksmanship, but by 1870, scores of 75 to 80 became rather commonplace. By the end of that decade, top shooters often scored 100 percent.

Most matches then, like today, were based on 100 targets — either live bird or clay. The name of the first man ever to kill 100 healthy, well-launched pigeons in a straight run will probably never be known. Most written accounts of shooting events that took place over a century ago are no longer available. Moreover, it is likely that even such a momentous achievement as 100 straight was not reported in any contemporary journal. The first man known to have accomplished this feat was Captain Adam H. Bogardus. On October 21, 1869, only a year after taking up the sport, Captain Bogardus killed 100 birds straight in a well-documented shoot in St. Louis, Missouri. In the same year, he downed 500 pigeons in 528 minutes to win a $1000 purse.

In a notable match held in New York on November 12, 1891, E.D. Fulford scored 100 to his opponent's 99. On October 12, 1894 J.A.R. Elliott duplicated Fulford's effort by defeating the world-renowned marksman, "Doc" Carver, who chalked up a losing 99x100.

The many variables in live pigeon shooting made com-

parative score listing an exercise in futility. Flight patterns of birds were affected by weather conditions, the length of time in close captivity, the type of trap used, their level of excitement due to noise and other factors, their age and general health, and so on. Distance from shooter to the trap was inconsistent, particularly in the earlier matches, varying from as little as 10 to as many as 35 yards, or in some cases even longer. Ammunition differences also had a greater influence on scores than it does today. Most competitive shooters consider equipment only a 10 percent factor of success — or failure.

One cannot state that live pigeon shooting records on a given day might be more difficult than 100 straight on another day in another locale. Only after the invention of reliable inanimate targets did comparative scores become relevant.

The era of glass ball shooting, which largely replaced live pigeon contests between 1866 and 1885, inspired

(Left) The American ammunition makers in the 1930s exploited the efforts of their customers with huge banners and placards praising both the shooters and ammo and/or guns for long runs, major event winners, etc.

(Below) This vintage drawing depicts an early-day Skeet field — virtually unchanged since its inception in 1926. Skeet shooting records, however, in the past 60-plus years have been "upped" virtually every year due to better shooters, ammunition, equipment and guns, and because the old records are there to be broken.

shooters to set some records that may never be broken. Glass balls flew neither very far nor very fast. Their trajectory was a high, looping arc, with the ball slowing appreciably near the apex of its path. Glass balls were so much easier to hit than live birds that scores took a giant leap upward — especially for expert scattergunners. Bogardus, Carver, Paine, Mitchell, Kimble and Stubbs — to mention a few — were able to break glass baubles with monotonous regularity. Because of this, shooting matches turned into endurance contests, with strings of 100 targets being commonplace.

Bogardus, Paine and Carver regularly astounded their spectators by breaking 1000 balls in less than 90 minutes. In Lincoln, Illinois on a hot, sultry Fourth of July in 1879, Bogardus set an all-time record by breaking 5000 glass balls in 500 minutes. In this grueling marathon, he averaged one shot every 6 seconds for 8 hours and 20 minutes. Actually, his pace was slightly faster than this because he missed 156 targets. So, in breaking 5000 balls, he actually fired 5156 shots in 20 minutes less than the allotted time. Stress and strain on the vocal cords alone —

(Right) Skeet shooting boomed after World War II because many ex-servicemen were exposed to this fascinating shooting sport while in the service.

(Below) The trophy room at the ATA headquarters in Vandalia, Ohio. These sterling silver trophies are personal reminders of the top shooters' accomplishments.

A Gallery of Greats

Shooting records are made by shooters. This gallery of yesterday's and today's greatest trap and Skeet shooters have helped mold competitive shooting into a great spectator sport.

Joe Hiestand

Mercer Tennille

Vic Reinders

Phil Miller

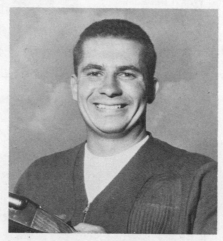
Johnny Sternberger

Bueford Bailey

Rudy Etchen

Britt Robinson

Ned Lilly

Lela Hall Frank

Gene Sears

Hiram Bradley

C.E. Barnhart

Roger Smith

Arnold Riegger

Dan Bonillas

Susan Nattrass

Punkin Flock

Larry Gravestock

Robert Stack

William Hay Rogers

Claude Purbaugh

Don Slavich

Ricky Pope

Frank Ferguson

D. Lee Braun

Frank Little

Leo Harrison

Ray Stafford

(Above) The great Dan Orlich being inducted into trapshooting's Hall of Fame. Orlich once held over 100 ATA records, but like the sands of time, they are being eroded one grain at a time by today's newest "hot hammers."

(Left) During the late 1950s and through the early 1970s, these two shooters, Dan Orlich (left) and Tom Frye (right) dominated trapshooting's amateur and professional categories. Many of Orlich's records still stand and may never be broken. Frye once shot over 100,000 2-inchx2-inch wooden blocks and missed only six!

shouting "Pull!" — is more than most men could survive. Assuming that he shouldered a shotgun that weighed approximately 8 pounds, he picked up over 20 tons of dead weight. That he could even move after this ordeal is mute testimony to his great physical and mental strength.

Early-day record keeping wasn't the most accurate by any stretch of the imagination. To illustrate, some authorities assert that Bogardus shot his 5000 glass balls in New York City, not Lincoln, Illinois, in 1877, not 1879. Because there aren't any contemporary newspaper reports to confirm the site, we have a choice of what to believe.

Never satisfied with his personal shooting records, 1-year later Captain Bogardus announced his intention of breaking 6000 glass targets in 2 consecutive days. Two sets of barrels, one 10-gauge and one 12-gauge set, were used on his W&C Scott shotgun. Shells were loaded with 4 drams equivalent of Dittmar powder in the 10-gauge and 3 1/2 drams equivalent in the 12-gauge, each getting 1 1/2 ounces of LeRoy tin-coated No. 6 shot. Barrels were frequently cooled by immersing them in water during the course of the event.

By the end of the first day, 3000 targets had been broken without a miss! On the second day, shooting continued apace, although the Captain sported bandages on his blis-

tered left hand and right thumb, made raw by cocking the exposed hammers of his shotgun. His very first miss came on ball number 5681. After that, Bogardus missed 12 more targets, so to complete the intended total of 6000, he fired 6013 shots.

It is unlikely that Bogardus' run of 5680 consecutive hits will ever be duplicated. Shooting events of this nature no longer arouse the interest they did 100 years ago, and such a phenomenal run against modern clay targets would appear an impossibility. However, when a challenge is presented, someone always steps up to accept it. For anyone aspiring to shotgun immortality, the record is there to be broken — step right up!

Only a handful of women were trapshooters in the 1880s, but it was beginning to be recognized that the sport was not merely a man's province. The first woman trapshooter of note, and certainly the most famous, was Annie Oakley. Her shooting and riding exploits in Buffalo Bill's Wild West show won spectators' hearts all over the world. Much of her shooting was pure showman(woman)ship, and did not require any extraordinary skill. The same must be said, incidentally, of most of the male shooters in Wild West shows of the time. Audiences were notably naive and easily dazzled by show business stunts into believing that rather easy trick shooting was marvelous.

Theatrical gimmicks aside, there is no doubt that Annie Oakley was indeed an exceptional shooter. Perhaps her greatest performance with a shotgun was in 1885 when she broke 4772 out of 5000 glass balls thrown from a trap at 15 yards rise. Not many present-day scattergunners of either sex could guarantee to equal, much less better her accomplishment.

The handwriting on the wall for glass ball shooting as a popular pastime declined rapidly after the mid-1880s. Newly-developed "clay" targets and improved traps to throw them doomed "glass balls" to extinction. Exhibition shooters continued to use them for some time, but by the end of the 19th century glass ball tournaments were largely a thing of the past. Clay targets flew farther and faster than glass balls, and as a result, scores plummeted as shooters grappled with technique changes. It was many years before the long runs common to glass ball shooting were matched — and some never were.

The first nationally-sanctioned trapshooting tournament in which clay targets were used exclusively was held in Chicago in May, 1884. Sponsored by the Ligowsky Clay Pigeon Company, it was billed as the First National Inanimate Clay Target Tourney. It was a team shoot, with five men to a team. Each entrant shot at 10 single birds at 18 yards rise and five doubles at 15 yards. A prize of $750 was offered to the winning team, with a $250 diamond badge for the high scorer. For some unknown reason, despite widespread publicity, only a handful of shooters attended the meet. Because the country's top shooters were not present, the tournament failed as a true national championship event. Unfortunately the winners names and scores are not mentioned in any records the author can find. This was, however, without question, the first all-clay target tournament of nationwide significance.

The first national clay pigeon championship of the National Gun Association was held in New Orleans on February 11-16, 1885. Unlike the Chicago tournament of the previous year, the New Orleans competition was well attended by many of the nation's top shooters, including such big names as Captain Bogardus, Doc Carver, J.A.R. Elliott, Al Bandle, Frank Chamberlain and Captain Stubbs. This meet was quite successful; Doc Carver took

This is one record that will be very difficult to top. This five-man squad, captained by 85-year-old George West (second from the right) had a combined age of 393 years. They wanted to break more targets than their combined age and did it handily, scoring 413x500.

D. Lee Braun and Grant Ilseng combined to shoot well over 1 million trap and Skeet targets between them. Both have been inducted into the Hall of Fame.

top honors with no misses. The New Orleans tournament, because of the class of competition, is generally considered the first true national clay target championship.

Shooting exhibitions with emphasis on sheer endurance had not entirely gone out of fashion yet in 1885, when Doc Carver announced that he would break 60,000 clay targets in 6 days. In his hometown of New Haven, Connecticut, he started his shooting marathon on a Monday, and by Thursday evening, had fired at 64,880 targets, breaking 60,616 for an average of 93.42 percent. That record has never been broken or equalled, nor is it likely to be. If it wasn't so well documented, Carver's feat would be totally unbelievable.

Around 1887, trapshooting zoomed in popularity. Championship tournaments sprang up all over the country, but because there was no governing body, most were not true "National Championships." Meets sponsored by the National Gun Association came closest to being legitimate contests to determine the best shooters of the year, and it was the Association's successor — the Interstate Manufacturers' and Dealers' Association — that promoted the first Grand American Handicap in March, 1893 in Dexter Park, New York. This organization underwent several name changes finally settling on the Amateur Trapshooting Association (ATA) — today's sponsor of the Grand American tournament held annually in Vandalia, Ohio each August.

The Grand American Handicap of 1893 was a live pigeon shoot, as were all succeeding annual events until 1900, when clay targets were added to the program. R.A. Welch topped 20 other entrants to capture the 1893 title with a score of 23x25. By 1900, the Grand's entry list had grown to 224, and scores had improved significantly. The winner of the live bird event was H.D. Bates, who went 25 straight and then added 34 more to his string in a lengthy shoot-off. The first Grand American Clay Target Champion was Rolla O. (Pop) Heikes, who shot 94 out of 100 targets at 16 yards.

By 1903, clay targets had replaced live birds at the Grand American. Martin Diefenderfer was the first All-Clay Champion, scoring 94x100. The first man to win the Handicap race with 100 straight was Riley Thompson in 1910, which wasn't repeated for 16 years, when C.A. Young took the title.

Dan Bonillas (right) holds the majority of trapshooting records. Gun club owner Gerald Eubanks of Redlands, California awards Bonillas with ammunition for his recent shooting exploits.

This quintet of trapshooting legends, (left to right) Vic Reinders, Bob Allen, Rudy Etchen, Bueford Bailey, and Dan Orlich, have done as much to promote trap and Skeet shooting as the number of personal records they have set.

(Above) This all-California squad composed of (left to right) Carl Thacker, Jimmy Poindexter, Maynard Henry, Curt King and Bill Harrison combined to hold over 200 major trapshooting titles between them.

(Left) Hortense Wood (left) and Nadine Ljutic during the 1960s were "the" women to try and beat on the trapshooting circuit. Both have retired, but their records still stand.

The Grand American attracts the nation's finest shooters. It has grown so large that today over 20,000 individual entries are received from aspiring champions for all events. Over 4000 shooters participated in 1988.

Even though Skeet was introduced to the American shooting public in 1926, it wasn't until August 16, 1935 that the first national championship tournament was held in Cleveland, Ohio. There were 113 participants in the 12-gauge event, which was not a bad turnout for such a comparatively new sport. Trapshooting was still king of the shotgun clay target games though, indicated by the 600-plus competitors in the 1935 Grand American Handicap.

The late 1930s were Skeet's golden years, and this great shotgun game steadily increased in popularity until the onset of WWII. Wartime shortages of guns, ammunition and other equipment virtually put an end to Skeet for civilians. The Armed Forces, however, used Skeet as a valuable training aid, and thousands of young GIs were introduced to the sport.

Skeet and the Army/Air Force joined hands as part of a broad gunnery program for all aircrew members. When the servicemen came home after the war, many wanted to continue Skeet shooting. As a result, there was a tremendous nationwide resurgence of interest in Skeet shooting activities. The National Skeet Shooting Association, dormant during the war, was reorganized in 1946.

What we now call modern Skeet shooting may have begun in 1947, under the aegis of the rejuvenated NSSA. Rules and procedures were changed slightly from those of pre-war days, so there was not a common basis for pre- and post-war records. In 1954, the rules again underwent modification to such an extent that records from then on occupy a special niche in Skeet history. For record purposes, there are three separate periods to consider: 1933-1947, 1947-1954, and 1954 to the present.

Shooting records have been kept for both individuals and teams for all gauges, but those that are of greatest interest are the high, overall achievements and long runs during registered competition. At the NSSA World Skeet Championships, only two 650x650 scores have ever been recorded. Based on 250 12-gauge targets, 100 20-gauge, 100 28-gauge, 100 410-bore and 100 doubles, Richard Boss of Grand Island, New York broke his "perfect" in

(Left) In 1964, Carl Thacker (left) was the oldest man on the 27-yard line and Jimmy Poindexter (right) was the youngest.

(Below) A Skeet shooting legend of the 1960s was Pete Candy of Los Angeles, California. The owner of many long-run Skeet records, Candy was one of the most consistent and stalwart performers ever to shoulder a Skeet gun. A believer in Winchester Model 12s and 42s, Candy was lightning smooth stroking these pump guns in Doubles.

July, 1982 in Savannah, Georgia. The very next year, Phil Murray duplicated this miraculous feat at the World Shoot in San Antonio, Texas.

The longest shoot-off in the history of Skeet was in 1983 between Wayne Mayes and Phil Murray for the World 12-gauge Championship. This terrific duo went 42 rounds of regular Skeet (1050 targets straight) and then shot four rounds of doubles from Station Four only (an additional 100 targets) for a total of 1150 targets. With that type of shooting, it was a pity that one of those superior Skeet shooters had to lose . . . and it wasn't Wayne Mayes.

There have been a total of 10 550x550 scores recorded in the NSSA World Skeet Shoots. This world-class championship is now 51 years old. The very first "550" was in 1976 by Charlie Parks of Bellevue, Ohio.

The typical Skeet shoot is 100 targets for each of the four guns with the optimum score of 400x400. It wasn't until 1967 that Kenny Barnes of Bakersfield, California saw a perfect "400." Since Barnes broke this seemingly insurmountable barrier, over 90 perfect 400s have been posted on score boards around the country.

In 1987, a total of 2802 100 straights were shot in 12-gauge registered competition by 1309 shooters. What follows is a list of long runs through the summer of 1987, when this was written.

Long Run Records Through 1987

Men

Event	Record Holder	State	Year	Record
12-gauge	Mike Schmidt, Jr.	MN	1983	1766 straight
20-gauge	Chip Youngblood	FL	1981-82	1620 straight
28-gauge	Wayne Mayes	TN	1985	1257 straight
410-bore	Wayne Mayes	TN	1986-87	448 straight
Doubles	Wayne Mayes	TN	1983-84	522 straight

Women

Event	Record Holder	State	Year	Record
12-gauge	Valerie Johnson	TX	1976-77	766 straight
20-gauge	Lori Desatoff	CA	1981-82	801 straight
28-gauge	Lori Desatoff	CA	1986-87	388 straight
410-bore	Connie Place	FL	1977	194 straight
Doubles	Lori Desatoff	CA	1985	223 straight

5

Today's Competition Shotgun

WITHOUT A DOUBT, the shotgun is the most important piece of equipment the competitive shooter owns. He or she can get by without proper shooting clothes, shoes or other attire. Even ammunition can be slightly different than what is preferred. But the shotgun must be like an old friend, a soft pair of gloves or a well-worn pair of hunting boots. The manipulation and handling of it must be purely a reflex action so that the shooter can concentrate on the problem at hand—hitting the target.

A few decades ago, there were no official competition shooting "classes" and each shooter shot against another, regardless of ability, with high score overall declared the winner.

To accomplish this and eliminate mechanical hindrances and distractions, the shotgun must come close to being perfectly fitted, balanced and suited for the shooter. In other words, the shotgun must work with the shooter—not against him. While it isn't usually possible for a shooter, particularly a beginner, to get proper gun fit the first time, he should conscientiously study and experiment with several guns. In a comparatively short time, he'll find one that suits both his pocketbook and shooting needs.

After that determination has been made, let me say forcefully that when you find this gun and shoot it with comfort and satisfaction, keep it, guard it and don't—even if you fall into a mild shooting slump—alter it! If you don't stick with any suitable gun for at least 10,000 shots, you can't possibly learn the gun's idiosyncrasies. This familiarization process requires a great deal of shooting and time—not to mention expense—but, suddenly you'll develop a rapport that will blossom into a relationship that will withstand the sands of time.

All too often a newcomer to clay target shooting blindly purchases a trap or Skeet gun without investigation or testfiring. How can the neophyte try a shotgun before buying one? Borrow or rent it. Many gun clubs offer gun rental privileges, and for a few bucks a prospective buyer can shoot quite a few different makes and models for minimal cost. Or, he can introduce himself to shooters at a local gun club and tell them that he wants to "rent" their gun to ascertain if that particular make and model is suitable for him. Most often, experienced shooters will "rent" their guns, providing the rentee uses only factory ammunition. Never shoot reloads in a borrowed shotgun!

On Sundays at a fairly active gun club, you should find at least 20 to 30 different makes and models of either trap or Skeet guns in the gun racks. A word of caution, though, is to never pick up a gun from a rack without first receiving the owner's permission. Simple courtesy goes a long way toward kindling new friendships.

There are seven basic types of shotgun actions—the autoloader, pump, over/under, single barrel, side-by-side, lever action and bolt action—however, only the first four are generally found on today's trap and Skeet fields. The latter three are either too slow to manipulate or are obsolete, as with the lever action. The classic side-by-side is rarely found in the hands of the competitive shooter because of its wide sighting plane. The over/under offers the same mechanical advantage as the side-by-side, but with a narrower view down the barrels.

58

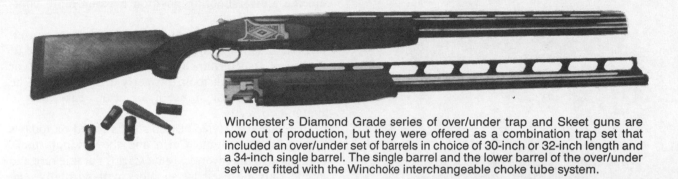

Winchester's Diamond Grade series of over/under trap and Skeet guns are now out of production, but they were offered as a combination trap set that included an over/under set of barrels in choice of 30-inch or 32-inch length and a 34-inch single barrel. The single barrel and the lower barrel of the over/under set were fitted with the Winchoke interchangeable choke tube system.

The type of shotgun chosen is based strictly on personal preference—not cost. Each action has its strengths and weaknesses, and it will require some diligent study plus intelligent advice to make the right decision. We'll go into greater detail later in this chapter and fully describe each of the proven and popular types of shotgun actions.

Is it necessary to own an expensive gun to shoot well? No, but it is necessary to own a gun of good quality and workmanship. A poorly-made shotgun cannot withstand the vigorous demands of trap and Skeet shooting. Consider that the average American hunter could conceivably—during an active and productive bird-hunting season—shoot a case or two of ammunition (1000 shells). Over 20 years, the hunter could fire 20,000 rounds from his gun. An active trap or Skeet shooter will consume a similar amount of ammunition in 6 to 10 months! Get the point? Quality competition shotguns can withstand this rugged use and still be ready for more.

Weight and balance of the competition shotgun are extremely important. I believe that the average male shooter should be able to handle a 9- to 10-pound trap gun. If strong enough, adding more weight will significantly reduce "felt" recoil and help the shooter develop a smoother style.

Bulk and weight help the shotgun "stick" on the target when properly pointed and tend to eliminate muzzle flip or whip, which is the cause of many missed targets, especially when shooting trap and Skeet Doubles. A lightweight gun (anything under 8 pounds) that handles "too fast," is apt to overrun the target and cause the shooter to make "herky-jerky" movements. Like most competitive events, a smooth style has better results. Skeet guns, too, should be heavier than their field-model counterparts, for the same reasons.

With a competitive shotgun, balance is most important. Gun writers usually describe a gun's balance as its mid-way point. On most break-open actions (single barrels, over/unders), it is usually at or near the hinge pin or where the barrels and receiver join. On single-barrel repeaters (pumps and autoloaders) the balance is where the barrel couples to the receiver.

And yet, balance is subjective. Five different shooters can pick up the same gun and all emphatically state that the gun's "balance" is different. The reason is hand placement. A shotgun is only "balanced" if the shooter places his hands an equal distance from the physical balance point of the shotgun. As a rule, the "master" hand—the one on the grip—is fairly inflexible because the index finger must be able to reach the trigger while the rest of the hand is around the grip. Therefore, the "off" hand—the one supporting the front of the shotgun—must be slid forward or back to "balance" the shotgun. We shall go into greater detail in another chapter.

"Fit" is an ambiguous three-letter word. Does the shotgun "fit" the shooter, or does the shooter "fit" the shotgun? There are two theories, both extremes. The majority of custom stockmakers will emphatically state that the factory-manufactured gunstocks will not properly fit anybody! On the other side of the coin are those preceptors who blindly oppose any alterations or modifications to a factory-installed gunstock for fear of diminishing a gun's value. To both of these hypotheses I say hogwash!

First, let's take a moment to understand how one "sights" a shotgun. Unlike rifles or handguns equipped with either mechanical or optical sights used to line up on the target, the shotgun must be "pointed" instead of "sighted." Virtually all competition shotguns are equipped with two metal or plastic sights called "beads." The front bead is near the muzzle, the rear is usually situated about halfway between the muzzle and the back of the barrel. The relative position between these two sighting beads determines the shotgun's vertical point of shot impact. If the barrel is true and straight—meaning the shot swarm (charge) impacts at 40 yards downrange to the corresponding line of sight—the two beads should appear superimposed, or, in other words, will form a figure "8." The rear bead, which is the smaller of the two, should appear perfectly placed within the diameter of the larger front bead. If there is a visual gap between the two, the shot charge will be slightly above the line of sight in proportion to the amount of space between the two beads.

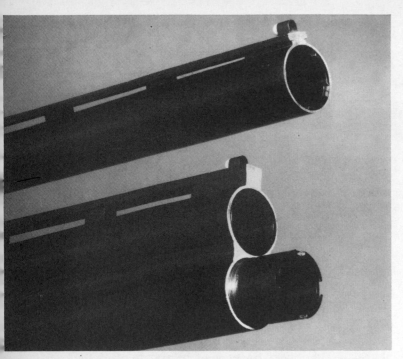

Browning's Invector screw-in choke system is made of stainless steel and available in five choke constrictions—Full, Improved Modified, Modified, Improved Cylinder and Skeet. These tubes are ultra-thin and thus do not bulge the barrel area at the muzzle.

Therefore, the shooter's master eye is actually the shotgun's rear sight. And, like pistol or rifle shooting, if the sights are not properly lined up on the mark, the target will be missed. Unlike pistols and rifles though, the shotgun has three sights—the two beads mounted on the barrel and the shooter's master eye. To the beginning shooter, it might appear more difficult to align and control three sights over the customary two, but that isn't so. This three-sight theorem is not used to sight on the target, but to determine and establish proper stock fit. I must digress for a moment and clarify the use of shotgun sights. To become a proficient trap, Skeet or field shooter, one must look past the sights at the ultimate target while looking down the barrel. The shotgun's sighting beads only align the shooter's eye and head in the proper shooting position—nothing more, nothing less!

There's only one proper way to mount a shotgun and it cannot be stressed strongly enough: Always bring the shotgun up with both hands to the face and cheek. *Never* bring the shotgun to the shoulder and tilt the head down to the top of the stock. To determine how a shotgun "fits," the shooter must first learn how to "mount" a shotgun.

I have listened to hundreds of trap and Skeet shooters complain about improperly-fitted stocks. But when these same distressed shooters were asked to mount their guns, no less than 50 percent mounted them incorrectly. After a few minutes of instruction on how to properly bring the gun up to the face, the gun, much to their wonderment fits much better. As a result, fewer

targets were missed, felt recoil was greatly reduced and the entire shooting position became more comfortable.

The obvious point is that in order to evaluate a product, one must first understand how to properly use it. Therefore, to determine if a factory-made gunstock, or even a custom gunstock, properly fits a shooter, he must first learn how to use it, or in this case, how to mount it correctly.

There are two styles of trap stocks found on today's trap guns—the Monte Carlo and the straight stock. There is also the reverse Monte Carlo, but it is rare and should only be used by shooters with virtually "no neck." (More on this unusual stock design a little later.) Some shotgun makers offer their stocks in both configurations. So that you can better understand what your choices are, and how they may benefit you, let's now go into greater detail. Unfortunately, the overwhelming majority of trap guns are equipped with a Monte Carlo stock. Why is that unfortunate? Most shooters believe that the Monte Carlo stock design "looks" like a genuine trap stock, without taking into account whether a straight stock might fit them better. The only major difference between the Monte Carlo and the straight stock design is the drop at the heel. Both stocks usually have the same comb height, which is simply the positioning of the butt (recoil pad) against the shoulder. The Monte Carlo-style buttstock places the top of the recoil pad lower on the shoulder than the straight stock. For all intents, a straight stock may have the same comb height, but the relative position of the butt is approximately on the same line as the comb or the top of the stock.

Which one is best for you? It depends primarily on your physical dimensions. "Long-necked" shooters are usually more comfortable with a Monte Carlo stock, while "bull-necked" shooters get along just fine with straight stocks. Measurements are taken from the shooter's "formed" pocket in his shoulder to his cheekbone. The greater the distance, the more drop required in the Monte Carlo stock at the rear. Finally, in the reverse Monte Carlo, the top of the butt is placed above the top of the comb, which allows short-necked shooters to place their heads in comfortable positions. A wealth of information regarding stock fit is discussed in a later chapter.

The following sub-chapters look in detail at the various types of trap and Skeet guns currently available and hopefully point out their strengths and weaknesses. For over a decade, the "combo" has been the "in" gun on the trapshooting circuit. As in any sport, the participants secretly desire to own and use a specialized piece of equipment. Trapshooters are no different, but for either economic or traditional reasons, there are other types of actions still seen on the trap fields.

The trap gun combo is simply an over/under shotgun with two barrel assemblies—a single barrel and an over/under set. Perhaps it is the other way around though, because the single barrel appeared on the trap fields around the turn of the century—long before the "stack barrel" was popularized by Browning's Superposed and Remington's Model 32, both of which appeared in the early 1930s.

For almost 75 years, the single-barreled trap gun was definitely a status symbol. Then, as today, they were more expensive than pumps or autoloaders. They were, and still are, a single-purpose tool designed expressly for competitive clay target trapshooting, and shooters who used them were considered "rich" by other people's standards. Even today, single-barreled trap guns, for the most part, are "handmade" with limited sales and are more expensive than pumps and autoloaders made on a production line. Great names in shotgun manufacturing produced thousands of single-barreled trap guns . . . Parker, Ithaca, LeFever, L.C. Smith, and Baker were some of the more popular American products. The English custom gunmakers also pro-

duced quite a few single-barreled trap guns for the affluent "colonists" with Greener, Purdey and Woodward being the major contributors.

Unquestionably, the single-barreled trap gun is the most dependable and strongest shotgun action ever built. It has changed little in design and concept from guns of yore. Typically, they are all based on a simple break-open type action, although various types of locking systems are employed. Because the single-barreled trap gun only has one objective—to fire a single shot without bothersome magazines to facilitate follow-up shots—it is the epitome of rugged simplicity.

Today's hot setup for trapshooting are the combo guns from a pair of Italian manufacturers—Perazzi and Beretta—along with Krieghoff's Model K80. The Perazzi was first imported into the U.S. in the early 1970s. It was, pardon the pun, an instant hit! During that time, there was only one American-made single-barreled trap gun—the Ithaca Single Barrel—which was expensive, well over $1500 for a plain-Jane ver-

This unusual photo has captured the target, the shot swarm and the wad, all in mid-air. Quite a lucky shot for the cameraman, but not for the target—it was smoked!

sion. The engraved and gold inlaid Model 5E carried a price tag about the same as a new, low-end Ford or Chevrolet. Therefore, when the Perazzi Comp I infiltrated the American trap fields with a retail price tag of about $800—often discounted to $600 to stimulate sales—American shooters went head over heels for this "spaghetti gun."

Close on Perazzi's heels, another popular import, Browning's BT-99 made in Japan and blessed with a retail price of $275, became a chosen favorite for new trapshooters. The BT-99 didn't compete with the Perazzi, but instead chipped away at the lower-end market then dominated by Remington's Models 870 and 1100, along with Winchester's Model 12. In fact, the BT-99's success "helped" take the Model 12 out of production and off the market.

Skeet guns have made a remarkable change in the past 25 years. The venerable Winchester Model 12 equipped with a Cutts Compensator on the muzzle was the hot setup until the mid-1960s. Remington's Models 870, 878, 58 and 11-48 were favored arms of some Skeeters until the introduction of the Model 1100 in 1963. The most popular stack-barrel Skeet gun was the Belgian-made Browning—preferably in Lightning grade. The Krieghoff Model 32 came on the American shooting scene in the late 1950s, and a few cherished Remington Model 32s were available at exorbitant prices.

When Remington introduced their fabulous Model 1100 in 1963, this sweet-shooting, light-recoiling, gas-operated autoloader put thousands of pseudo-Skeet guns into shooter's hands. The Model 1100 dominated the Skeet fields and made a pretty good dent in trap fields to boot. It wasn't long before Remington realized they had a highly acceptable competition shotgun at a reasonable price, which still holds true today, although it appears as though Remington's newest sensation—the Model 11-87—will supercede the venerable Model 1100.

The "stack barrel" is the "in" gun for Skeet shooters, and like trapshooting's combo set, the over/under is a prestige shooting tool. Browning, Perazzi, Rottweil, Krieghoff, Beretta and K-80s are widely used despite their initial cost, which is higher than pumps and autoloaders. There always seems to be a quality firearms buyer because none of the aforementioned firms are exactly begging for business and each year prices seem to increase.

The over/under is the overwhelming favorite in part because it combines many important features into a single gun. The stack-barrel configuration enables the shooter to utilize the advantages of twin tubes while peering down a single sighting plane, which is narrower than the side-by-side's. Nearly all of today's over/unders offer a single selective trigger mechanism. Interestingly, some of the Russian shooters have shied away from single triggers in favor of the older-style

double-trigger abomination, the excuse being reliabilty. Perhaps the Russians can't make a competition shotgun with a reliable single trigger mechanism—funny, the rest of the free world can!

The major over/under makers equip their guns with selective automatic ejectors that propel fired shells out of the chamber when the shotgun is scissored open. Some shooters disable this feature, claiming it's easier to pull the empty hulls from the gun's chamber than to pick them up off the ground. If this is a problem, here's a little tip. Instead of operating the opening tang lever with your thumb and forefinger, slide your hand up on

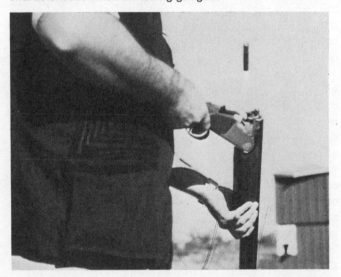

Briley tubes are custom fitted to the Rottweil and are available through Paxton Arms. During the past decade, both Skeet champions and novices have switched over to this shooting system in the search for consistent gun handling characteristics when switching gauges.

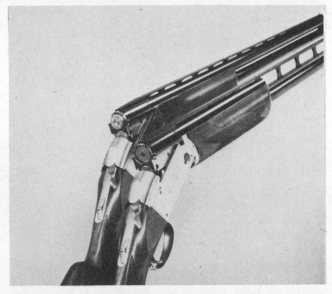

The combo concept is both beneficial to shoot and expensive to own. Most all major trap gun manufacturers offer these two-barrel, one-receiver ensembles.

the back of the receiver and set the opening lever inside the palm of your hand. Swing the lever to the right and extend your fingers over the top of the receiver to form a "cage" to catch the empty hulls. Try it, it works!

The use of insert tubes which quickly convert a 12-gauge shotgun into a four-gauge Skeet gun ensemble is another major reason for the stack barrel's popularity. This is a practical and economical way to shoot all "four guns" (12-, 20-, 28-gauge and 410 bore) during a Skeet program.

Since the mid-1950s, Skeet gun insert tubes have changed from a novelty item into the most popular multi-gauge Skeet shooting setup today. The tubes are full-length barrel inserts that enable one to shoot the three smaller gauges—20, 28 and 410 bore—in one common 12-gauge over/under shotgun. Actually, inserts are mini-barrels that fit inside and are supported by the existing 12-gauge barrel. Some of the tubes on the market today are made entirely of anodized aluminum, in other cases, the barrel portion of the tubes are made out of anodized aluminum and the chamber area out of stainless steel or titanium.

Tube systems offer unique advantages over the four-gauge gun sets and over/unders equipped with four sets of barrels. Consistency, the name of the game in Skeet, is just one of the direct results of using a tube set. The shooter becomes familiar with one stock, one trigger and one "feel" because he can shoot all four gauges with the same gun; he doesn't have to adapt to different conditions when switching gauges. Most insert tube makers carefully match the weights of the different diameter tubes, and add weight to the original shotgun, generally around the forend.

Some shooters quibble and claim the same feel and weight can be adjusted by using a four-barrel set. What then does the tube concept have over the four-barrel ensemble? Economics for one, because tube inserts are less expensive than barrel assemblies. Second, there is the weight factor. Over the past decade, shooters have taken a serious look at the theory and mechanics behind Skeet shooting. Most now agree that a heavier gun can yield higher scores than the lighter autos, pumps and four-barrel sets popular a couple of decades ago. Tubes add an average of 14 ounces to a gun, which create a new "standard" Skeet gun weight. Today, all types of barrel and gun weights are very popular, as Skeeters are adding weight to their lighter guns to get that "tube set feel."

Why the trend toward heavier Skeet guns? "Automatic" follow-through for one. A heavier gun is harder to stop after the trigger is pulled, which gives the shooter a slight hedge against stopping his swing. The added weight also creates a smoother, more consistent follow-through, and felt recoil is noticeably reduced.

American Skeet, as we know it, is shot with the gun already mounted. It is only natural that heavier guns evolved since the 1950s. Back then the gun had to be off the shoulder on the call and the shooting style called for quick gun movements and snap-shooting techniques. Today, Skeet requires more deliberate actions for consistency and to knock out those big scores.

Recoil, both "felt" and "free" has long been recognized as a "consistency killer." New recoil reduction devices are some of the most sought-after items on the Skeet gun aftermarket. Because overall weight and recoil are directly related, the tube set's built-in weight tames much of the recoil of an over/under scattergun. Barrel weight, especially out near the muzzle, helps reduce muzzle rise during recoil, which is critical when shooting Doubles.

There are more pros and cons regarding tube sets, but I believe a tubed gun can improve most shooters' consistency, which in turn raises scores and averages noticeably. One thing is for sure, because of its benefits, the tube system is no longer a novelty; it's here to stay.

What are the differences between a "competition" gun and a standard field or hunting gun? Actually, very little in outward appearance, but the emphasis is on quality materials, precise fitting of parts (both metal-to-metal and wood-to-metal), and nuances that transform a run-of-the-mill scattergun into a skillfully-prepared shooting tool.

Trap and Skeet fields are the shotgun manufacturer's "proving grounds" and their customers the product testers. If a shotgun has an inherent weakness such as a poorly-designed part, you can be sure that competition shooters will find the gun's inbred faults. A shotgun hawked by a maker with Trap or Skeet in its name had better be able to withstand the vigorous use and punishment dished out by competition shooters. If it can't, word will get around quickly, and it will soon be off the market for lack of sales. The most important criteria in a competition-grade shotgun is the 10-letter word "dependable."

Dependable is defined as, "to trust or rely." If a shotgun breaks down early, say within a couple thousand shots, it will have a stigma attached that is virtually impossible to overcome. Shooters will tolerate small inconveniences as part of the game, but not repeated "annoyances." These same shooters are usually meticulous about keeping their equipment in top-notch condition. Experience has taught them that cleanliness contributes immensely to dependability. If they don't keep their equipment in prime operating condition, they shoulder most of the blame for equipment failures. If an isolated problem occurs regularly that costs a shooter even a single target, then that shotgun will be abandoned—for good reason. Competitive shooters should only be concerned with their target's flight—not the equipment between their hands.

Following is an encapsulated description of today's trap and Skeet guns to help you determine which shotgun is best for you.

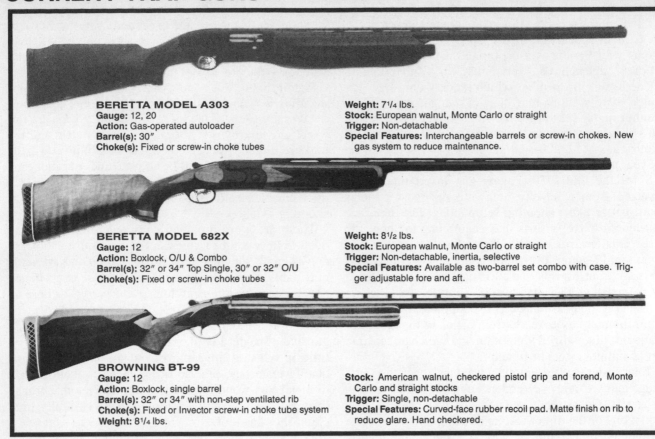

BERETTA MODEL A303
Gauge: 12, 20
Action: Gas-operated autoloader
Barrel(s): 30"
Choke(s): Fixed or screw-in choke tubes

Weight: 7¼ lbs.
Stock: European walnut, Monte Carlo or straight
Trigger: Non-detachable
Special Features: Interchangeable barrels or screw-in chokes. New gas system to reduce maintenance.

BERETTA MODEL 682X
Gauge: 12
Action: Boxlock, O/U & Combo
Barrel(s): 32" or 34" Top Single, 30" or 32" O/U
Choke(s): Fixed or screw-in choke tubes

Weight: 8½ lbs.
Stock: European walnut, Monte Carlo or straight
Trigger: Non-detachable, inertia, selective
Special Features: Available as two-barrel set combo with case. Trigger adjustable fore and aft.

BROWNING BT-99
Gauge: 12
Action: Boxlock, single barrel
Barrel(s): 32" or 34" with non-step ventilated rib
Choke(s): Fixed or Invector screw-in choke tube system
Weight: 8¼ lbs.

Stock: American walnut, checkered pistol grip and forend, Monte Carlo and straight stocks
Trigger: Single, non-detachable
Special Features: Curved-face rubber recoil pad. Matte finish on rib to reduce glare. Hand checkered.

BERETTA

The world's oldest firearms manufacturer is Beretta. More than 4 centuries of fine craftsmanship stand behind every Beretta shotgun made today. Although Bartolomeo Beretta had been a noted cannon maker early in the 16th century, the company that now bears that illustrious name was founded in 1680 by Pietro Beretta for the purpose of making all types of firearms. It has been under family management ever since.

From Gardone Val Trompia in northern Italy, Beretta expanded overseas to Accokeek, Maryland, headquarters for Beretta U.S.A. Though the American market is serviced by the Maryland facility, traditional old-world standards of excellence have remained the same.

Competition shotguns by Beretta have won more gold, silver and bronze medals than any other make. Trapshooters all over the world choose Beretta first. The current Beretta catalog lists three models specifically designed for trapshooting.

The Model A303 Competition Trap Gun is a gas-operated shotgun. Gas-action autoloaders are preferred by many shooters because the gas system absorbs a lot of the recoil shock. The A303 has a wide, grooved forend, and a handsome walnut stock fitted with a thick, recoil-absorbing butt pad. The barrel is topped by a wide, floating, ventilated rib. Two fluorescent bead sights are provided, one at the front, one mid-rib. Monte Carlo stocks on A303 models are adjustable for drop by a cleverly-designed stock bolt which allows for

changes to fit individual requirements. The forend and pistol grip are hand-checkered in a handsome, yet utilitarian, pattern. Barrels are available in 30- and 32-inch lengths with either a fixed choke barrel or multichoke interchangeable choke tubes. Tubes are made in Full, Improved Modified, Modified and Improved Cylinder constrictions. Receivers are forged alloy to help hold overall weight down to just over 7 pounds.

The flagship of the Beretta lineup is the Model 682 Competition Trap Gun, a boxlock over/under with interchangeable 30- or 32-inch barrels choked Improved Modified and Full. An alternate single barrel, the Mono Trap, has a high, ventilated rib in place of the top barrel. The Mono Trap barrel is made in 32- and 34-inch lengths in Full choke only for maximum effective range in Handicap Trapshooting. Also available is the more conventional Top Single barrel in 32- or 34-inch lengths, and like all Beretta trap guns, the buyer can choose between fixed choke barrels or screw-in chokes. The 682 has premium-grade walnut with a hand-checkered pistol grip and forend. A wide choice of stock dimensions may be supplied to discriminating clay birders, assuring a perfect stock fit. Beretta 682 receivers are finished in black chrome, triggers are gold plated and the gun is delivered in a beautiful, fitted case. A thick, curved buttpad is standard, ejectors are automatic, and a single selective trigger is fitted, along with a manual safety. Rebounding hammers and floating firing pins are at the heart of the 682's action.

BROWNING CITORI
Gauge: 12
Action: Boxlock, O/U
Barrel(s): 30″ or 32″ with non-step ventilated rib

Choke(s): Invector screw-in choke tube system
Weight: 8½ lbs.
Stock: American walnut, checkered pistol grip and forend, Monte Carlo and straight stocks
Trigger: Single selective, non-detachable
Special Features: Curved-face rubber recoil pad. Matte finish on rib to reduce glare. Automatic ejectors.

BROWNING SUPERPOSED
Gauge: 12 (Field version shown)
Action: O/U, boxlock
Barrel(s): 30″, ventilated rib

Choke(s): Full & Full, Full & Imp. Mod., or Full & Mod.
Weight: 8 lbs.
Stock: European walnut with special trap dimensions
Trigger: Single selective
Special Features: Basically a custom-made gun with many options available; silvered, engraved receiver.

ITHACA SINGLE-BARREL TRAP MODEL 5E
Gauge: 12
Action: Single barrel, boxlock
Barrel(s): 32″ or 34″ ventilated rib

Choke(s): Fixed, Full only
Weight: 8 lbs.
Stock: Exhibition-grade American walnut, hand checkered and carved
Trigger: Non-detachable, hand-honed to 3½ lbs. of let-off
Special Features: Special order only. Profusely engraved and all handmade. Gold inlays. Dollar Grade also available.

An upgraded Model 682 with beautiful engraving on the receiver and luscious wood for the stock and forend is the Model 687 EELL. Combos and Top Single models are available in a wide range of chokes, barrel lengths, and stock dimensions. Whether one prefers an autoloader, over/under, mono gun or Top Single, Beretta has a model for all with an impressive laundry list of 40 model variations.

BROWNING

The Browning name and shotguns have been synonymous for longer than most of us can remember. Brownings are well represented on all trap and Skeet fields. Current trapshooting models are the BT-99, Citori and Superposed.

The BT-99 single barrel has a wide, beavertail forend that tapers to the rear, along with either a straight stock or Monte Carlo. The receiver is machined from a solid steel block, and all internal parts are hand-fitted. Barrels are available in 32- and 34-inch lengths, choked Full, Improved Modified or with the Invector system. There are four variations of the BT-99, conventional or Monte Carlo stock and 32- or 34-inch barrels. All Browning trap guns are equipped with a curved face Pachmayr rubber recoil pad with a white line spacer. Average weight, for all BT-99s depending on the wood density, is approximately 8½ pounds. The balance point, however, is slightly behind the hinge pin, which makes the BT-99 slightly "butt heavy."

An over/under gun that has become almost standard equipment on many American trap fields is Browning's Citori model. The Standard 12 has either 30- or 32-inch barrels, and all models are fitted with the Invector choke system. A high-post, floating target rib tops all Citori trap gun barrels, which raises the sighting plane and keeps recoil low and away from the shooter's face.

A single selective trigger may be set to fire either barrel by a mechanism incorporated in the tang-mounted safety-lever. Pushing the safety to the right causes the under barrel to fire first; a shift to the left allows the over barrel to lead off the sequence. When the trigger is pulled again, a second shot follows from the other barrel. All Citori guns are fitted with automatic ejectors and stocks are Monte Carlo style, finely checkered in the grip area and capped with a thick, curved, recoil-absorbing buttpad. The forends are of the broad, beavertail variety with finger grooves and checkering on the lower surfaces. The 32-inch version weighs 8 pounds, 10 ounces, while the 30-incher is 2 ounces lighter. Five grades of finish varying in wood and engraving quality are offered.

Browning's top shotgun is their Superposed model. It is available with a long list of options that allow a buyer to have a truly custom-built gun. Because of the variables that may be specified by a purchaser, it's virtually impossible to adequately describe all of this superb shotgun's features. The Superposed, in whatever configuration, is one of the world's finest firearms. Addi-

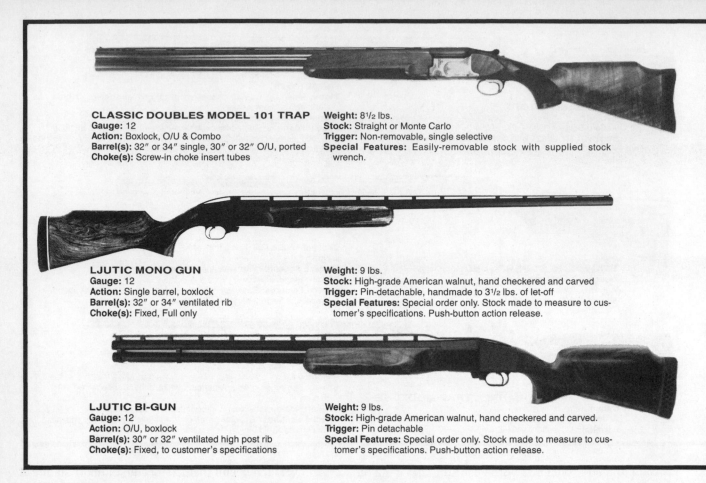

CLASSIC DOUBLES MODEL 101 TRAP
Gauge: 12
Action: Boxlock, O/U & Combo
Barrel(s): 32″ or 34″ single, 30″ or 32″ O/U, ported
Choke(s): Screw-in choke insert tubes
Weight: 8½ lbs.
Stock: Straight or Monte Carlo
Trigger: Non-removable, single selective
Special Features: Easily-removable stock with supplied stock wrench.

LJUTIC MONO GUN
Gauge: 12
Action: Single barrel, boxlock
Barrel(s): 32″ or 34″ ventilated rib
Choke(s): Fixed, Full only
Weight: 9 lbs.
Stock: High-grade American walnut, hand checkered and carved
Trigger: Pin-detachable, handmade to 3½ lbs. of let-off
Special Features: Special order only. Stock made to measure to customer's specifications. Push-button action release.

LJUTIC BI-GUN
Gauge: 12
Action: O/U, boxlock
Barrel(s): 30″ or 32″ ventilated high post rib
Choke(s): Fixed, to customer's specifications
Weight: 9 lbs.
Stock: High-grade American walnut, hand checkered and carved.
Trigger: Pin detachable
Special Features: Special order only. Stock made to measure to customer's specifications. Push-button action release.

tional information may be obtained from Browning.

Browning BT-99, BPS (pump) and Citori model trap guns are now available with Invector interchangeable choke tubes which screw completely into specially-threaded muzzles so they are invisible when viewed from the side. A special wrench needed for their insertion and removal is supplied with the units. Tubes choked Extra Full, Full, Improved Modified and Modified are normally supplied with trap guns, although other chokes are available on request. The Invector system allows a shooter to alter his gun's pattern without purchasing extra barrels.

CLASSIC DOUBLES INTERNATIONAL

The venerable Model 101 is currently marketed by Classic Doubles because Winchester went out of the shotgun business. The new lineup of Model 101 trap guns is impressive with 14 variations ranging from 32- and 34-inch single-barrel models, 30- or 32-inch over/under examples, and cased combo sets. Monte Carlo and straight stock designs are available and all versions are equipped with screw-in choke tubes.

Classic Doubles International trap guns boast some highly-desirable features — elongated forcing cones, which reduce felt recoil and often contribute to improved pattern performance; single selective, inertia-operated triggers adjustable for let-off weight; and highly-polished nitrated frames accented by stylish en-

graving patterns.

The stocks and forends are carved from semi-fancy American walnut, and are fine-line checkered and protected with a low-luster satin finish. Each stock is pre-drilled to accommodate a recoil reducer. A factory-supplied, T-shaped, oversized Allen wrench quickly separates the stock from the receiver. A curved-face recoil pad is standard on both stock designs. The barrels are made from chrome molybdenum and both the chamber and inside are chrome-lined to prevent rust buildup often caused by shooting plastic-cased ammunition.

All barrel assemblies are topped with tapered, high-profile, ventilated ribs that help draw the shooter's eye to the target. Twin beads are also standard and all barrels are ported to help prevent excessive muzzle rise, especially when shooting doubles targets.

The gold-plated trigger blade is set back in the trigger guard, which is a blessing for shooters with short fingers. The Model 101s have an excellent "feel," are properly balanced and tip the scales between 8½ and 9 pounds, depending on model and barrel length. These are quality trap guns and should be able to withstand vigorous use for generations.

ITHACA

Ithaca shotguns have been held in high esteem since 1880. Ithaca guns are "built," rather than "mass pro-

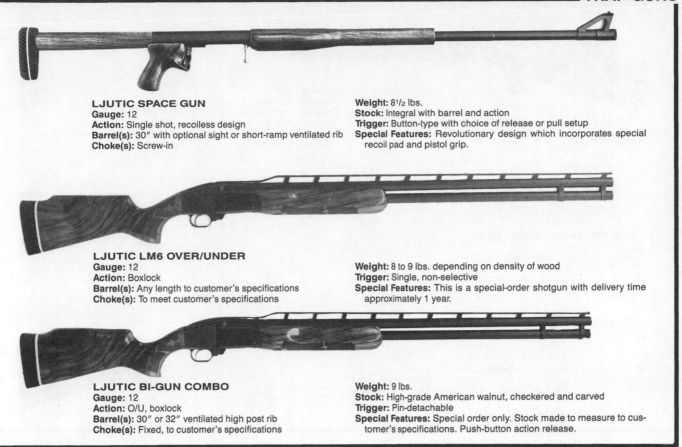

LJUTIC SPACE GUN
Gauge: 12
Action: Single shot, recoiless design
Barrel(s): 30″ with optional sight or short-ramp ventilated rib
Choke(s): Screw-in

Weight: 8½ lbs.
Stock: Integral with barrel and action
Trigger: Button-type with choice of release or pull setup
Special Features: Revolutionary design which incorporates special recoil pad and pistol grip.

LJUTIC LM6 OVER/UNDER
Gauge: 12
Action: Boxlock
Barrel(s): Any length to customer's specifications
Choke(s): To meet customer's specifications

Weight: 8 to 9 lbs. depending on density of wood
Trigger: Single, non-selective
Special Features: This is a special-order shotgun with delivery time approximately 1 year.

LJUTIC BI-GUN COMBO
Gauge: 12
Action: O/U, boxlock
Barrel(s): 30″ or 32″ ventilated high post rib
Choke(s): Fixed, to customer's specifications

Weight: 9 lbs.
Stock: High-grade American walnut, checkered and carved
Trigger: Pin-detachable
Special Features: Special order only. Stock made to measure to customer's specifications. Push-button action release.

duced"—parts are precision machined, but final assembly is accomplished by hand fitting and finishing.

Ithaca's single-barreled trap gun is hand built and available only by special order because a dozen or less are produced each year. Fit and finish of both wood and metal are carefully done by master craftsmen. Wood is specially-selected, figured walnut, and the receiver is highly engraved and inlaid. Either 32- or 34-inch barrels are supplied in Full choke. It weighs about 8½ pounds. The "regular" Single Barrel Trap gun known as the Custom Trap Grade sells for $7,176. An even finer version with more elaborate engraving and inlays of precious metals is called the Dollar Grade and costs an even 10 grand! Even the trigger is gold plated and hand-checkered for a more positive finger grip. The Model 37 Trap gun has been discontinued.

LJUTIC

Known throughout the world as innovators in shotgun design is Ljutic Industries. Ljutic guns are engineered for target shooters, with models for both trap and Skeet. Functional simplicity is the cornerstone of their design philosophy, which results in reliable guns with outstanding accuracy. All Ljutics are custom made to the buyer's specifications.

The Ljutic Mono-Gun, a single shot for trapshooting, is a break-action with the action opener a button form on the front of the trigger guard. The removable trigger assembly contains both trigger and hammer mechanisms. A 34-inch barrel is standard, with either a regular vent rib or a high Olympic rib giving a 35½-inch sighting plane. Choke is optional. Though stocks are made strictly to customer specifications, they typically feature a high Monte Carlo cheekpiece with a rather slim wrist, cut low for easy hand hold.

The Ljutic Bi-Gun over/under model is based on an action similar to the Mono-Gun except it's modified to fire two barrels instead of one. Over/under barrels are 32 inches, and are joined only at the breech and muzzle for maximum cooling. Other barrel lengths and choke selections are available. A Bi-Gun Combo is also made and is supplied with two trigger units — one for single shot, and one for double-barreled use.

By far, the Space Gun is the most revolutionary firearm in Ljutic's "armamentarium." The Space Gun has a truly futuristic design and might feel right at home on the set of *Star Wars*. Incorporating a recoil-absorbing mechanism, the Space Gun is said to be nearly recoilless. The Space Gun has no stock in the conventional sense, but rather a straight backward extension of the barrel and action unit, culminating in a simple shoulder pad. The standard barrel is 30 inches, Full choked. Both a plain front sight and a raised rib sight are available, and either regular pull or release triggers offered. It weighs about 8½ pounds. As with other Ljutic guns, numerous options provide the buyer with a truly cus-

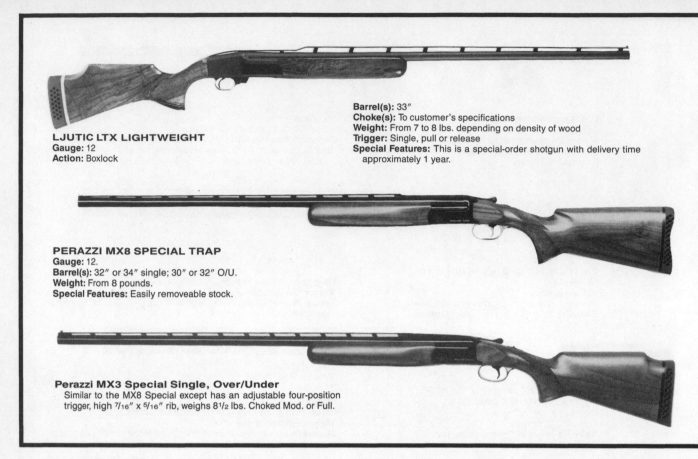

LJUTIC LTX LIGHTWEIGHT
Gauge: 12
Action: Boxlock

Barrel(s): 33″
Choke(s): To customer's specifications
Weight: From 7 to 8 lbs. depending on density of wood
Trigger: Single, pull or release
Special Features: This is a special-order shotgun with delivery time approximately 1 year.

PERAZZI MX8 SPECIAL TRAP
Gauge: 12.
Barrel(s): 32″ or 34″ single; 30″ or 32″ O/U.
Weight: From 8 pounds.
Special Features: Easily removeable stock.

Perazzi MX3 Special Single, Over/Under
Similar to the MX8 Special except has an adjustable four-position trigger, high 7/16″ x 5/16″ rib, weighs 8-1/2 lbs. Choked Mod. or Full.

tom-built shotgun. All Ljutic models are designed specifically for the buyer.

PERAZZI

More than 10 years ago, most American trapshooters thought Perazzi was a misspelling for a tasty Italian pie. Danielle Perazzi, a dynamic promoter of the shotguns that bear his name, "owns" the trap gun market, figuratively speaking. A few years ago, at the 1981 Grand American Tournament, a survey of all the gun marques being used was taken and nearly 40 percent of the shooters were using Perazzis! Today, that figure is a tad higher, which is truly incredible.

Danielle Perazzi keeps close tabs on the market like any successful entrepreneur and announces annual models like auto manufacturers. The original Comp I and MT-6 in its original striped receiver version are long gone. Today's lineup is staggering — as are the suggested retail prices.

The old standby MX-8 and DB-81 combos and the Mirage are still with us. A recent entrant is the TMX series and the MX-3 and MX-3 Special models. Virtually every stock configuration type, rib height, and barrel arrangement is available from Perazzi from plain-Jane grades to near-museum quality engraving and gold embellishments. Some models have fixed trigger assemblies, whereas most competition-grade guns boast removable trigger groups. This feature Perazzi helped initiate and is a desirable characteristic on a trap gun. If

a trigger spring or hammer should break unexpectedly, a replacement trigger assembly can be quickly exchanged. With input from Dan Bonillas, the Perazzi Model DB-81 shotgun (so named for this great California-based trapshooter) has all the features and design qualities of a truly great trap gun. It is a combo and uses a common receiver with two barrel sets. Twin trigger assemblies are part of the set and all are housed in a well-designed, compartmentalized hard case.

The newest MX-3 Special series of trap guns has a different receiver design than the MX-8 and MX-8 Special models and should become very popular. Screw-in chokes are available on some versions. The laundry list of Perazzi options is absolutely staggering. The newest Perazzi brochure is a wealth of information and worth having. Perazzi U.S.A. is the importer.

REMINGTON

Remington has a full lineup of shotguns for the target shooter. A slick new pump gun, a semi-auto, and an over/under combo is on the way.

The Model 870 pump action is only made for trapshooting in the 870TC. The TC has a special sear, trigger and hammer assembly designed specifically with the trapshooter in mind to improve lock time and smooth out the trigger pull. A ventilated rib lies along the top of a 30-inch Full-choked barrel in the standard configuration. The barrel is over-bored to help reduce recoil and the forcing cone has been tapered to produce

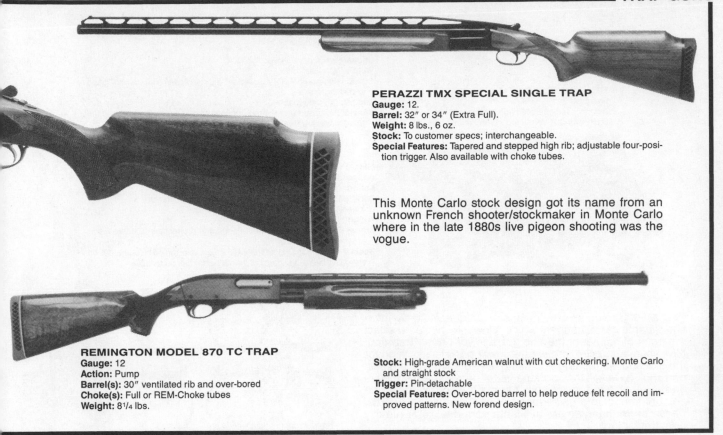

PERAZZI TMX SPECIAL SINGLE TRAP
Gauge: 12.
Barrel: 32″ or 34″ (Extra Full).
Weight: 8 lbs., 6 oz.
Stock: To customer specs; interchangeable.
Special Features: Tapered and stepped high rib; adjustable four-position trigger. Also available with choke tubes.

This Monte Carlo stock design got its name from an unknown French shooter/stockmaker in Monte Carlo where in the late 1880s live pigeon shooting was the vogue.

REMINGTON MODEL 870 TC TRAP
Gauge: 12
Action: Pump
Barrel(s): 30″ ventilated rib and over-bored
Choke(s): Full or REM-Choke tubes
Weight: 8¼ lbs.

Stock: High-grade American walnut with cut checkering. Monte Carlo and straight stock
Trigger: Pin-detachable
Special Features: Over-bored barrel to help reduce felt recoil and improved patterns. New forend design.

better patterns. REM-Choke barrels are also available and are supplied with three choke tubes and a special spanner-type wrench. The REM-Choke tubes fit flush with the end of the muzzle. Model 870 receivers are machined from solid bars of ordnance steel for maximum strength and durability. Twin action bars eliminate binding and twisting so second shots come as fast as a shooter can pump and pull the trigger. A cross-bolt safety is located at the rear of the trigger guard. High-comb stocks for the 870TC are solid American walnut with cut checkering, and have a 1-inch thick, recoil-absorbing buttpad. It weighs about 7¾ pounds.

Remington's Model 1100 has become a veritable legend in the world of shotgunning. More Model 1100s have been made than any other shotgun model. One version, the 1100 Trap, is made for trapshooting. The Model 1100 is a gas-operated semi-automatic that self-adjusts to the load being fired. Because of the energy absorbed in the gas action, recoil of the Model 1100 is more of a soft push than a jarring jolt. Model 1100 trap guns are supplied with a broad vent rib and either straight or Monte Carlo high-combed stock with a trap-style recoil pad. The standard barrel is 30 inches, choked Full, but optional barrels are available in 28- and 30-inch Modified, plus 28- and 34-inch Full. A left-handed model is made for southpaw shooters. Remington Model 1100 trap guns weigh a tad under 8 pounds in most configurations.

The newest offering from Remington is their gas-operated Model 11-87. This gun looks and handles like its daddy — the 1100 — but there have been substantial internal changes which greatly improved the reliability and durability of this self-shucker. The unique gas system is said to be self-cleaning along with a stainless steel magazine tube to resist rust and corrosion. There's also a newly-designed extractor, firing pin spring, specially heat-treated gas piston and piston seal. And, like its pump-action counterpart — the 870 TC — it boasts over-bored barrels and screw-in REM Choke tubes. This is a fine shooting scattergun — one that every trapshooter should take a long look at.

ROTTWEIL

Shotguns from Rottweil, made in West Germany, were imported until recently by Dynamit Nobel-RWS, but have apparently been dropped from the line. They were the first choice of many leading trapshooters. Rottweil's standard trap gun is the Montreal model with the receiver milled from a solid block of special gun steel to insure rigidity and longevity. All action parts are contained within the quickly removable trigger group. Coil springs, used throughout, are guided by telescoping sleeves that keep the springs in line and dirt out. The firing pins are of the rebounding type that retract automatically after firing, eliminating the possibility of interfering with opening the gun. They are also identical in dimension and fully interchangeable. The ejectors are selective and automatic and a sliding

REMINGTON MODEL 11-87 TRAP
Gauge: 12
Action: Gas-operated autoloader
Barrel(s): 30″ ventilated rib and over-bored

Choke(s): Full or Improved Modified
Weight: 8¼ lbs.
Stock: High-grade American walnut with cut checkering. Monte Carlo and straight stock
Trigger: Pin-detachable
Special Features: Over-bored barrel to help reduce felt recoil and improve patterns. New self-cleaning gas system.

SHOTGUNS OF ULM K-80
Gauge: 12
Action: O/U Combo
Barrel(s): 30″ or 32″ O/U with 32″ or 34″ single barrel
Choke(s): Fixed or screw-in models available
Weight: 8 lbs.
Stock: European walnut. Hand finished and checkered. Monte Carlo or straight stock
Special Features: O/U barrels are adjustable for point of impact by changing barrel hangers. Unsingle barrel dial adjustable.

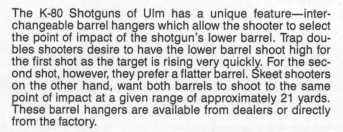

The K-80 Shotguns of Ulm has a unique feature—interchangeable barrel hangers which allow the shooter to select the point of impact of the shotgun's lower barrel. Trap doubles shooters desire to have the lower barrel shoot high for the first shot as the target is rising very quickly. For the second shot, however, they prefer a flatter barrel. Skeet shooters on the other hand, want both barrels to shoot to the same point of impact at a given range of approximately 21 yards. These barrel hangers are available from dealers or directly from the factory.

safety, positioned on the top tang, deactivates the trigger. Selected fine-grain walnut is used for the high-combed stock and forend, both of which are hand-checkered. The forend is a broad beavertail with fluted grooves for better grip. A satin oil wood finish is applied for an elegant appearance. Barrels are 30 inches and choked Improved Modified and Full. Cross-hatch machining of the vent rib assures minimum reflection from the top surface. The white plastic front sight is encased in a metal sleeve, while a central metal bead is located midway along the rib. Average weight of the Rottweil Montreal is about 8 pounds, 2 ounces.

Rottweil's Model 72 AAT (Adjustable American Trap) is designed specifically for American trapshooting. Its moniker reflects the unique point of impact adjustment on the shotgun, which is its principal feature. Infinite changes in impact points may be made by using a collar that surrounds the barrel at the muzzle. A wedge machined into the top of the collar rides against an opposing wedge on the lower front end of the extremely heavy and rigid top rib. When loosened with a special wrench, the barrel collar slides back and forth on the barrel, creating more or less pressure against the rib, which actually bends the barrel and changes the point of impact. Two single barrels are available — a 32-inch, choked Improved Modified and a 34-inch choked Full. Double-barreled units are 32 inches, choked Improved Modified and Full. Three different

fully interchangeable trigger groups are made for the AAT — regular Pull/Pull, Release/Release, and Release/Pull — which should satisfy any trapshooter, regardless of his trigger preference. AAT Monte Carlo stocks are of select French walnut with a satin oil finish, and fine hand engraving on the pistol grip and fluted beavertail forend. A thick, double-ventilated recoil pad is fitted. Unfinished stocks and forends are also available for those who wish to create a truly custom-fitted gun. Weight of the Rottweil AAT, in both single and double configurations, is about 8½ pounds.

Unfortunately, both of these fine Rottweil guns have been recently discontinued (at least in the U.S.), but you may be able to find left-over stock at some dealers.

SHOTGUNS OF ULM (KRIEGHOFF)

Distributed in the U.S. by Dieter Krieghoff of Shotguns of Ulm, the Model K-80 Trap gun is made in the ancient arms-making city of Ulm, West Germany. The K-80 is a boxlock with a machined steel frame. Barrels are locked to the frame by a massive top lockplate that slides over the rear of the barrels. Frames are finished in hard satin nickel, but blued models may be specially ordered. Single selective triggers are used, the selector button located ahead of the trigger in the trigger guard. The trigger is adjustable fore and aft to allow alteration of length of pull for varying conditions. Standard double barrels are made in both 30- and 32-inch lengths,

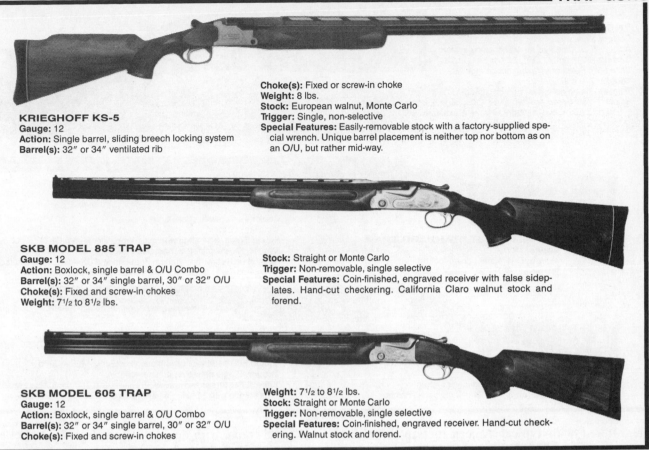

KRIEGHOFF KS-5
Gauge: 12
Action: Single barrel, sliding breech locking system
Barrel(s): 32″ or 34″ ventilated rib

Choke(s): Fixed or screw-in choke
Weight: 8 lbs.
Stock: European walnut, Monte Carlo
Trigger: Single, non-selective
Special Features: Easily-removable stock with a factory-supplied special wrench. Unique barrel placement is neither top nor bottom as on an O/U, but rather mid-way.

SKB MODEL 885 TRAP
Gauge: 12
Action: Boxlock, single barrel & O/U Combo
Barrel(s): 32″ or 34″ single barrel, 30″ or 32″ O/U
Choke(s): Fixed and screw-in chokes
Weight: 7¹/₂ to 8¹/₂ lbs.

Stock: Straight or Monte Carlo
Trigger: Non-removable, single selective
Special Features: Coin-finished, engraved receiver with false sideplates. Hand-cut checkering. California Claro walnut stock and forend.

SKB MODEL 605 TRAP
Gauge: 12
Action: Boxlock, single barrel & O/U Combo
Barrel(s): 32″ or 34″ single barrel, 30″ or 32″ O/U
Choke(s): Fixed and screw-in chokes

Weight: 7¹/₂ to 8¹/₂ lbs.
Stock: Straight or Monte Carlo
Trigger: Non-removable, single selective
Special Features: Coin-finished, engraved receiver. Hand-cut checkering. Walnut stock and forend.

choked Improved Modified and Full. Single trap barrels may be ordered as conventional top units or as an Unsingle with a sturdy high-post rib in place of the top barrel.

Single barrels are made in 32- or 34-inch lengths and are Full choked. Bottom barrels of the double units are free-floating, solidly joined only at the breech end. A ring spacer is fitted between barrels at the muzzle. Spacers of six different thicknesses are provided to easily change the point of impact spread between the two barrels. Point of impact may also be altered on the Unsingle barrel by a easily loosened screw adjustment located between the barrel and the rib at the muzzle. A wide adjustment is afforded, ranging from 7 inches low to 35 inches high at 40 yards. Stocks are either straight trap or Monte Carlo of select-grade European walnut. Forends are offered in several shapes to suit individual tastes and needs, and both forend and pistol grip are meticulously hand-checkered. A palm swell is incorporated on each side of the pistol grip to accommodate both right- and left-handed shooters. Stocks are fitted with a Pachmayr Pigeon recoil pad. Interestingly, stocks may be detached from the K-80 without removing the buttplate by using a special long screwdriver supplied with the gun. The K-80, fitted with 30-inch tubes, weighs about 8¹/₂ pounds. For the complete trapshooter, Shotguns of Ulm offers a trap combo consisting of the K-80 over/under with 30- or 32-inch bar-

rels, together with a 32- or 34-inch conventional single or Unsingle barrel delivered in a handsome, fitted case. Because there are so many small variations that may be built into a K-80, it is impossible to list them all here. Questions about optional equipment or alterations can be answered by contacting the importer.

SKB

Once a household name across American trap and Skeet fields, SKB pulled out of the American market in 1981. They have returned though with a selection of models, gauges, grades, versions, and options that is staggering. Remember, SKB never went out of the gun-making business in Japan, they simply left our shores and concentrated on sales in Australia and other parts of the Western hemisphere. All of SKB's over/unders share like features — the modified Kersten locking system, boxlock action, single-step ventilated rib barrels, screw-in choke tubes, automatic ejectors, single selective triggers, checkered walnut stocks and forends with white line spacer grip caps and curved face rubber recoil pads. The top of the trap gun line is the Model 885, available as an over/under, a single barrel or mated together in a combo set. This shotgun is magnificently engraved, hand-checkered at 32 lines per inch and has highly-figured American walnut furniture. The false sideplates add distinction and continuity to the graceful receiver. Both Monte Carlo or straight stock designs

SKB MODEL 505
Gauge: 12
Action: O/U, modified Kersten locking system
Barrel(s): 30″ or 32″ O/U, 32″ or 34″ single
Choke(s): Fixed or screw-in choke models
Weight: 7¾ lbs.
Trigger: Single selective, non-detachable
Special Features: Available as O/U, single barrel or two-barrel combo. Automatic ejectors. Hand checkered walnut stock and forend.

VALMET 412ST STANDARD TRAP
Gauge: 12
Action: O/U, sliding cover lockup
Barrel(s): 32″ or 34″ single barrel combo

Choke(s): Screw-in choke tubes
Weight: 7½ lbs.
Stock: European walnut with cut checkering. Monte Carlo
Trigger: Single selective, non-detachable
Special Features: Two grades, Premium and Standard. Also available as combo with 30″ or 32″ over/under barrels with fitted case.

VALMET 412ST OVER/UNDER PREMIUM TRAP
Gauge: 12
Action: O/U, sliding cover lockup
Barrel(s): 32″ or 34″ single barrel combo

Choke(s): Screw-in choke tubes
Weight: 7½ lbs.
Stock: European walnut with cut checkering. Monte Carlo
Trigger: Single selective, non-detachable
Special Features: Two grades, Premium and Standard. Also available as combo with 34″ single barrel with fitted case.

are offered with typical American trap dimensions. Like the Model 885, the two lower grades — Models 605 and 505 — are mechanically the same gun as the 885, but without the false sideplates, less or no engraving and straight-grained walnut. But, like the Model 885, they are available as combos, single barrels or over/unders. It seems that whatever the customer wants, SKB will oblige! SKB also offers custom guns at fairly reasonable prices. They list a Model 8000 that boasts gold inlays, carved engraving, Circassian-quality wood and impeccable checkering. Other custom features include detachable trigger mechanisms, boxlock or sideplate variations and stocks made-to-measure.

A pair of gas-operated autoloaders — Models 1900 and 3000 — are available in trap configuration, both equipped with 30-inch barrels and screw-in chokes. They weigh approximately 7 pounds, 4 ounces and Monte Carlo stocks are standard equipment. Both the forend and pistol grip feature hand-cut checkering — a rare commodity today. According to SKB, in 1981, a New Zealander shot at 2264 targets in a single hour with the Model 1900 to set a new record for *The Guiness Book of World Records*. That is a lot of abuse to heap on any shotgun.

VALMET

Built in Finland, Valmet shotguns are distributed in the U.S. by Stoeger Industries. Their trap gun, known as the Model 412ST Trap, is based on a time-proven

all-steel frame with double-locking lugs for barrel attachment. Both 30- and 32-inch over/under barrels are topped by a wide rib with a centerline groove and are equipped with stainless steel choke tube inserts. Chrome alloy steel is used to forge barrels by cold hammering. A single selective trigger is used, with a barrel selector button built into the upper part of the mechanical trigger mechanism. This allows the second barrel to fire even if the first chamber is empty. Indicator buttons near the rear of the top-mounted tang safety give both visual and tactile evidence as to which barrel was fired. Two-piece firing pins are an exclusive Valmet feature which greatly reduce breakage. The safety and ejectors are automatic; the safety is set by opening the action and the ejectors give smooth, positive extraction. All external metal is finished in a high-gloss deep blue and overall weight is about 8 pounds. Combo sets are also available with 30-inch over/under barrels and a 32- or 34-inch single barrel, or a 32-inch over/under with a matching 32- or 34-inch single barrel set. All barrels are equipped with screw-in choke tubes. The two versions available are Premium and Standard, the only major differences being in the metal finish of the receiver (satin chrome on the Premium, blue on the Standard) and the fanciness of the wood. Valmet's Model 412ST is a well-made, sturdy trap gun with many exclusive features at a modest price.

WEATHERBY

Weatherby guns have a long established reputation

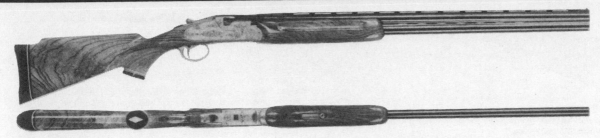

WEATHERBY ATHENA
Gauge: 12
Action: Boxlock, single barrel & O/U Combo
Barrel(s): 32″ or 34″ single barrel, 30″ or 32″ O/U
Choke(s): Fixed and screw-in chokes
Weight: 7½ to 8½ lbs.

Stock: Straight or Monte Carlo
Trigger: Non-removable, single selective
Special Features: Coin-finished, engraved receiver with false side-plates. Hand-cut checkering. California Claro walnut stock and forend.

WEATHERBY ORION O/U SHOTGUN
Gauge: 12 (Field version pictured)
Action: Boxlock.
Barrel(s): 30″ or 32″
Weight: 8-8½ lbs.

Stock: American walnut, checkered pistol grip and forend. Rubber recoil pad.
Special Features: Selective auto ejectors, single selective mechanical trigger. Top tang safety, Greener cross-bolt. Introduced 1982. Imported from Japan by Weatherby.

for fine fit and finish, as well as outstanding performance. Their trap guns are no exception, being both handsome and functional.

Weatherby's Orion and Athena Model over/unders are offered with 30-inch barrels choked Full and Modified or Full and Improved Modified. The hand-fitted monobloc and receiver are machined from high-strength steel and finely polished for smooth functioning. The strong boxlock design uses a modified Kersten-type cross-bolt locking system, and special sears maintain hammer engagement to prevent doubling and avoid accidental discharge. Selective automatic ejectors kick out only fired shells and simply raise unfired shells for easy extraction. The slide-type safety is located conveniently on the upper tang. A single selective trigger allows instant barrel choice for the first shot by pressing the marked selector button on the trigger blade. A mechanical switchover automatically allows the second barrel to be fired in the event of a misfire, since recoil is not required to set the trigger. An adjustment may be made, however, that will permit recoil-induced switchover if desired. The Orion's stock and forend are of Claro walnut, are hand-checkered, and have a thick recoil pad and rosewood pistol grip cap. Orion owners can choose between a high-combed straight stock or a Monte Carlo. All external metal is deeply blued. A wide, ventilated rib with both front and center bead sights provides a perfect sighting plane. The ribs between barrels are also ventilated for extra cooling. The Orion weighs about 8 pounds.

Weatherby's Athena is essentially the same as the Orion, but with a few extra touches for beauty, not utility. Specially-selected, highly-figured Claro walnut is used for the stock and forend. Sideplates are appended to the frame for more graceful lines, and both frame and plates are engraved in a graceful scroll pattern. Receiver, sideplates, trigger guard and locking lever are bright coin finished and the barrels are blued. A gold trigger completes the panoply of color. Both the Orion and Athena are made by SKB especially for Weatherby. This highly-respected firm pulled out of the American shotgun market a few years ago, but is now back under the Weatherby banner.

A single-barrel trap version is also available. Based on the Athena chassis, both 32- and 34-inch barrels are offered, each equipped with a Monte Carlo stock. Full, Improved Modified and Modified chokes are available. It weighs 8 to 8½ pounds. If this gorgeous single barrel is mated to an over/under, it should make a dazzling combo.

That concludes the lineup of trap guns available today. There may be a few we've missed due to publication deadlines, and to those manufacturers, we offer our apologies. We couldn't include suggested retail prices because of the constant fluctuation, but all the aforementioned manufacturers and importers have complete literature and current list prices for all their products. For their addresses see the Manufacturer's Directory, which is located in the Appendix at the back of this book.

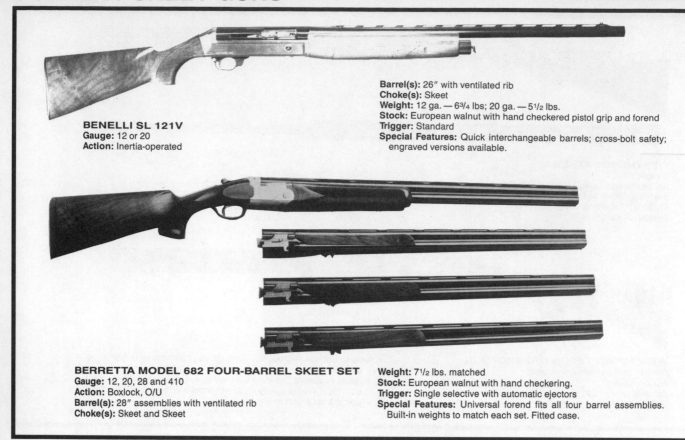

BENELLI SL 121V
Gauge: 12 or 20
Action: Inertia-operated

Barrel(s): 26″ with ventilated rib
Choke(s): Skeet
Weight: 12 ga. — 6¾ lbs; 20 ga. — 5½ lbs.
Stock: European walnut with hand checkered pistol grip and forend
Trigger: Standard
Special Features: Quick interchangeable barrels; cross-bolt safety; engraved versions available.

BERRETTA MODEL 682 FOUR-BARREL SKEET SET
Gauge: 12, 20, 28 and 410
Action: Boxlock, O/U
Barrel(s): 28″ assemblies with ventilated rib
Choke(s): Skeet and Skeet

Weight: 7½ lbs. matched
Stock: European walnut with hand checkering.
Trigger: Single selective with automatic ejectors
Special Features: Universal forend fits all four barrel assemblies. Built-in weights to match each set. Fitted case.

What is a Skeet gun and is it different than a field-grade shotgun? In actual performance, probably not. Due to the nature of the game, Skeet guns have stock dimensions virtually identical to field guns. Then what are the special ingredients that separate a Skeet gun from a field gun? Dependability and price.

To assure long-term dependability, a manufacturer must take extra measures to guarantee that his product will withstand the vigorous use of competitive Skeet. Skeet guns do not have the heat build-up problem incurred by trap guns, but they do digest the same number of rounds fired year after year. Because there is more time between shots, Skeet guns are less susceptible to heat-related problems than trap guns.

A Skeet newcomer can start nicely with any field-grade shotgun equipped with an open-choked barrel — Cylinder bore, Improved Cylinder or Skeet. If the novice already owns a shotgun — pump or autoloader — and optional barrels are available, it would be wise to buy one of these three chokes in order to be fairly well-equipped to begin learning the game. Then, if the "bug" bites him, as it has thousands of field shooters, he can choose a pure "Skeet" gun to satisfy his wants and wallet.

BENELLI

Although not specifically designed as a Skeet gun, the Model SL 121V with 26-inch barrel and choked Im-proved Cylinder does a pretty fair job of powdering clay birds. Excellent balance combined with exceptionally short feed time makes the Benelli a good Skeet gun, especially when shooting Doubles. The gun's inertia unlocking system greatly reduces felt recoil. The Model SL 121V weighs a shade under 7 pounds. The Benelli might be an excellent choice for the occasional Skeet shooter who needs a fine field gun as well. An interchangeable barrel with a tighter choke makes the gun a winner against both clay birds and wildfowl.

BERETTA

Beretta, the world's oldest established firearms manufacturer, has an enduring reputation for fine craftsmanship, as seen in their Skeet guns. Their product line for Skeet shooters is comprised of an autoloader and two over/unders.

The Beretta Model A303 Competition Skeet, made in both 12- and 20-gauge, is a gas-action autoloader with excellent balance, "swing" and pointability. The barrels have a high ventilated rib with fluorescent front and mid-rib sights. A 26-inch barrel choked Skeet or a 28-incher with interchangeable Multichoke tubes is offered. The receiver is of forged high-strength alloy engraved with simple floral motifs. The stock is made of select walnut with hand-checkering on the pistol grip and forend. The stock has Beretta's unique adjustable stock-drop system controlled by an eccentric washer

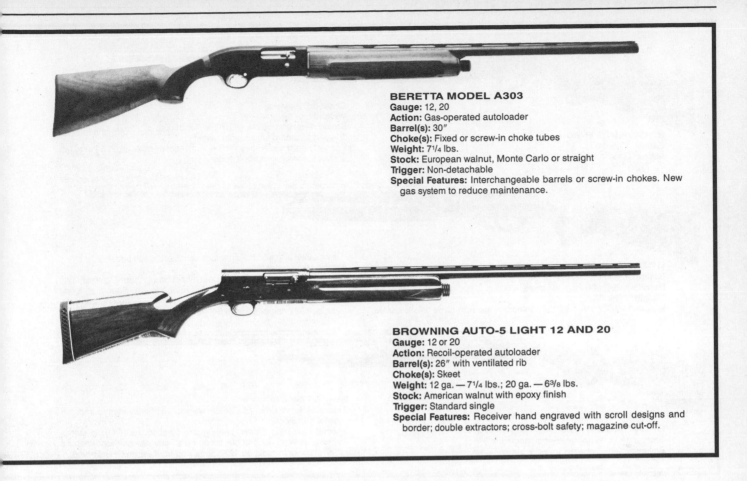

BERETTA MODEL A303
Gauge: 12, 20
Action: Gas-operated autoloader
Barrel(s): 30″
Choke(s): Fixed or screw-in choke tubes
Weight: 7¼ lbs.
Stock: European walnut, Monte Carlo or straight
Trigger: Non-detachable
Special Features: Interchangeable barrels or screw-in chokes. New gas system to reduce maintenance.

BROWNING AUTO-5 LIGHT 12 AND 20
Gauge: 12 or 20
Action: Recoil-operated autoloader
Barrel(s): 26″ with ventilated rib
Choke(s): Skeet
Weight: 12 ga. — 7¼ lbs.; 20 ga. — 6⅜ lbs.
Stock: American walnut with epoxy finish
Trigger: Standard single
Special Features: Receiver hand engraved with scroll designs and border; double extractors; cross-bolt safety; magazine cut-off.

under the head of the stock bolt. All external metal is deeply blued and a gold trigger adds a decorative touch.

There is a delicate balance in the Model 682 over/under Competition Skeet gun that makes it swing and track targets easily on American and International fields. It is perfectly suited for Skeet tubes, allowing a shooter to change gauges quickly and easily. Stock and forend are hand-checkered premium-grade walnut, and the receiver is steel, forged and hardened for lasting strength, with light hand engraving. The action is a low-profile boxlock with single selective trigger and automatic ejectors. Twelve-gauge barrels may be either 26 or 28 inches, choked Skeet and Skeet with a wide ventilated rib. The Model 682 Skeet weighs about 7½ pounds.

The Model 682 is also available in 20-, 28-gauge and 410 bore, along with a four-barrel Skeet set. Both the four-barrel set and smaller gauges are only available in 28-inch barrels.

The higher grade 687EELL is also available as a magnificent four-barrel Skeet set cherished by its owners and admired by its competitors.

Beretta was one of the first major gunmaking companies to jump on the Sporting Clays market. They offer four different models — the 686, a nicely-engraved version of the Model 682; the 682, of course; the Model 687; and a sporter version of the Model A303.

All three over/unders sport 28-inch barrels with screw-in chokes.

BROWNING

The senior citizen of Browning's Skeet gun lineup is the doughty Auto-5. This recoil-operated autoloader, invented by the legendary John M. Browning, has been in production far longer than any other current design. Over 2½ million Auto-5s are in the hands of sportsmen all over the world. Though primarily a field gun, there is also a Skeet version with screw-in Invector choke tubes that holds its own in competition. With a 26- or 28-inch barrel, choked for Skeet, the gun is a reliable clay bird buster. The Auto-5's long sighting plane is one key to its success. Beginning at the squared-off rear of the receiver and continuing along a low vent rib, the shooter's eye follows naturally to the target. Recoil is minimized because much of the force is taken up in moving a rather large mass to the rear during the operating cycle. Appearance of the Auto-5 is enhanced by tasteful hand engraving on the receiver, plus a highly-polished and deeply-blued finish on all external metal. A most desirable feature is that the breech remains open after the last shot is fired, making reloading quick and easy. More "modern" Skeet guns may come along, but the old Auto-5 seems destined to go on forever.

The B-80 is a gas-operated shotgun built with the old-fashioned Browning attention to detail. In appear-

BROWNING B-80
Gauge: 12 or 20
Action: Gas-operated autoloader
Barrel(s): 26″ with ventilated rib

Choke(s): Skeet
Weight: 6¹/₂ lbs.
Stock: American walnut with high-gloss finish
Trigger: Standard single, gold plated
Special Features: Non-reflective, matte finished metal; ventilated rib; steel receiver; cross-bolt safety.

BROWNING A-500 AUTO SHOTGUN
Gauge: 12 only.
Barrel(s): 26″ with Invector choke tubes.
Weight: 7 lbs., 7 oz.
Stock: 14¹/₄″ x 1¹/₂″ x 2¹/₂″; select walnut with gloss finish; check-ered pistol grip and forend; black ventilated recoil pad.
Sights: Metal bead front.
Special Features: Uses a short-recoil action with four-lug rotary bolt and composite and coil spring buffering system. Shoots all loads without adjustment. Has a magazine cut-off, Invector chokes. Introduced 1987. Imported from Belgium by Browning.

BROWNING BPS PUMP SHOTGUN
Gauge: 12 or 20 gauge, 5-shot magazine.
Barrel(s): 24″, 26″, 28″ Invector choke tubes.

Weight: 7 lbs. 8 oz.
Stock: 14¹/₄″x1¹/₂″x2¹/₂″. Select walnut, semi-beavertail forend, full pistol grip stock.
Special Features: Bottom feeding and ejection, receiver top safety, high post vent. rib. Double action bars eliminate binding. Vent. rib barrels only. Introduced 1977. Imported from Japan by Browning.

ance, the B-80 resembles the Auto-5 with its squared-off receiver. The rear of the B-80 is not perfectly square, but it does have a contour that attracts the shooter's eye and speeds up the sighting process. With a rib fitted atop a 26- or 28-inch Invector barrel, lining up on a flying clay bird is fast and sure. Recoil of the B-80 is much softer than might be expected because of the energy absorbed when operating the gas-action system. Trigger action is crisp and positive and a cross-bolt safety is immediately at hand in front of the trigger guard. B-80 wood is of select walnut with cut checkering on the pistol grip and the underside of the forend. The gun is made in both 12- and 20-gauge. The receiver is cold forged and machined from high-grade steel, or aluminum alloy in the case of the Superlight version. Barrels are drilled and bored from nickel-chromium-molybdenum steel bars and internally chrome-plated for longevity. The B-80 weighs a bit less than 7 pounds in the 12-gauge Superlight, and about 8 pounds in the standard model.

A near Auto-5 look-alike is Browning's newest entry — the A-500. Whereas the Auto-5 is a "long-recoil" operated autoloader and the B-80 is a gas-operated self-shucker, the Model A-500 is a combination of both, classified as a "short-recoil" operated mechanism. Its overall appearance comes from both of these fine Browning scatterguns. Internally, the boys from Bel-

gium have significantly reduced the number of working parts to a few more than a sundial. It is only available in 12 bore, but with 26- or 28-inch barrels and, of course, the Invector choke system.

Though not a true Skeet gun because of its Modified choke barrel, Browning offers a true reproduction of the fabled Winchester Model 12 in a 26-inch barreled 20-gauge. It is available in grades I and V with AAA walnut and gold inlays on the receiver. Both guns are magnificent in appearance and cry out to be tried.

The BPS, another Browning pump, is available in 12- and 20-gauge with both 26- and 28-inch barrels equipped with the Invector choke system. The 12-gauge weighs approximately 7¹/₂ pounds, while the 20 bore is about ¹/₂-pound less.

The Citori over/under is Browning's premier Skeet gun. Available in all gauges — 12, 20, 28 and 410 bore — the Citori meets all Skeet shooters needs. Both 26- and 28-inch barrels, choked Skeet and Skeet, are available in all gauges. Overall weights vary from 6 pounds, 9 ounces in the 26-inch 410 to 8 pounds, 2 ounces in the 28-inch 12-gauge. A high post target rib is standard on all barrels. Skeet Citoris have all-steel receivers, single selective triggers, and automatic ejectors. A sliding safety is located on the top tang, conveniently positioned for quick and easy operation. At least four grades of finish are offered, with other details available

BROWNING CITORI
Gauge: 12, 20, 28 and 410 bore
Action: Boxlock, O/U
Barrel(s): 28″ low ventilated rib

Choke(s): Skeet & Skeet
Weight: 7 1/2 lbs.
Stock: American walnut with cut checkering. Recoil pad standard
Trigger: Non-detachable, single selective
Special Features: Available as single gun in any of the four gauges or as a four-barrel set with fitted case.

BROWNING SUPERPOSED
Gauge: 12, 20, 28 and 410 bore
Action: Boxlock, O/U
Barrel(s): 28″ low ventilated rib

Choke(s): Skeet & Skeet
Weight: 7 1/2 lbs.
Stock: European walnut with hand-cut checkering. Recoil pad standard
Trigger: Non-detachable, single selective
Special Features: Available as single gun in any of the four gauges or as a four-barrel set with fitted case. Various grades.

CLASSIC DOUBLES MODEL 101 SKEET
Gauge: 12, 20, 28 and 410 bore
Action: Boxlock
Barrel(s): 27 1/2″ for all gauges, with porting
Choke(s): Screw-in choke insert tubes for 12-gauge, all others Skeet
Weight: 6 1/2 to 7 1/2 lbs. depending on model and gauge

Stock: Standard
Trigger: Non-removable, single selective
Special Features: Easily-removable stock with supplied stock wrench. Available in 12- or 20-gauge frames and as a four-barrel set on 12-gauge frame.

on request. Each Citori is delivered in a fitted luggage case.

The Citori is also available as a four-barrel Skeet set based on the 12-gauge action. And, resurrecting an idea from the past, the Citori is offered as a three-barrel set (20, 28 and 410) on a slimmer 20-gauge frame.

For more affluent Skeet shooters, Browning offers the Superposed series of over/unders. Made in Belgium, the Superposed is available in all gauges and a wide variety of finishes. This is truly a custom gun, with more options than can possibly be listed here. Anyone interested in this superb shotgun should contact Browning for complete information. Prices are high, ranging from about $5000 to more than $18,000 for complete sets, but the quality is outstanding.

CLASSIC DOUBLES INTERNATIONAL

A trio of Model 101s are offered which should satisfy any Skeet shooting enthusiast. The three versions (12-gauge, 20-gauge and four-barrel set) share many common features. Barrel lengths are set at 27 1/2 inches, all barrels are equipped with low-profile, tapered, ventilated ribs adorned with twin sighting beads and the guns have single, selective, mechanical triggers. Also, the Skeet guns' barrels are vented, which according to the factory, helps reduce muzzle flip. The jury is still out regarding the validity of this claim.

All 101 Skeet guns are equipped with mechanical triggers. Most over/unders are designed with inertia triggers, especially trap and field models. Because the Model 101 Skeet gun is available in a four-barrel set (12-, 20-, 28-gauge and 410 bore), Skeet loads in 28-gauge and 410 bore do not generate enough recoil to make an inertia-operated trigger unit function properly.

The 12-gauge version weighs about 7 1/4 pounds and is equipped with screw-in chokes. The smaller-framed 20-gauge weighs about 6 1/2 pounds and both barrels are choked Skeet. The elegant four-barrel set is selectively weighted so that regardless of the barrel assembly attached, the overall weight is 7 1/2 pounds. All eight tubes are bored Skeet.

Both buttstock and forend are made from selected, semi-fancy American walnut. Nicely finished in a fine-line checkering design, the dull, matte finish is a welcome relief from more common high-gloss glaze. Stock dimensions for the three models are the same — length of pull 14 1/4 inches; drop at heel 2 1/8 inches; drop at comb 1 3/8 inches. These are pretty standard proportions and will suit most American Skeet shooters.

Classic Doubles International has recognized the need for a special Model 101 Sporter for the Sporting Clays enthusiast. They offer a 12-gauge version, with

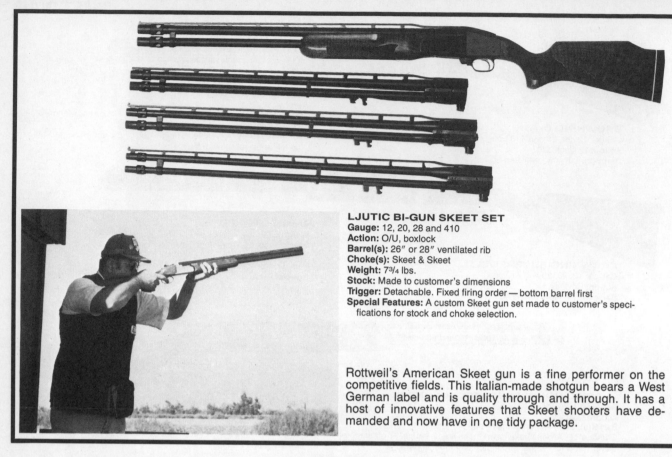

LJUTIC BI-GUN SKEET SET
Gauge: 12, 20, 28 and 410
Action: O/U, boxlock
Barrel(s): 26" or 28" ventilated rib
Choke(s): Skeet & Skeet
Weight: 7¾ lbs.
Stock: Made to customer's dimensions
Trigger: Detachable. Fixed firing order — bottom barrel first
Special Features: A custom Skeet gun set made to customer's specifications for stock and choke selection.

Rottweil's American Skeet gun is a fine performer on the competitive fields. This Italian-made shotgun bears a West German label and is quality through and through. It has a host of innovative features that Skeet shooters have demanded and now have in one tidy package.

six screw-in chokes, in two barrel lengths — 28 or 30 inches. There's even a two-barrel set available. Length of pull is 14½ inches, drop at the comb 1½ inches, and drop at the heel 2⅛ inches.

LJUTIC

Known as an innovator in shotgun design, Ljutic makes one gun specifically for Skeet. Ljutic's Bi-Gun Skeet is an over/under with separated barrels, milled vent rib and a host of options. Their patented "Paternator" chokes are made integral with the barrel. Sets are offered with matched barrels in 12, 20, 28 and 410 gauges. The Bi-Gun has a unique opening button located just ahead of the trigger guard. As with the Bi-Matic, the Bi-Gun is strictly custom made. Buyers may choose from a long list of options that satisfy the most discriminating shooter.

PERAZZI

The Perazzi lineup of shotguns has been primarily aimed at the trapshooter, but in the past few years, these magnificent shotguns have slowly, but surely, infiltrated American Skeet fields. The MX-3 Special and the Mirage are Skeet guns built to satisfy the most demanding needs of competition shooters. They are both available as single guns or as a four-barrel Skeet gun set. Both feature removable trigger assemblies and are equipped with V-type hammer springs. Both models sport a low-rib design and the furniture is European

walnut. One innovative feature on both is the adjustable trigger, which is on a track and can be moved fore or aft in any of four lockable positions. This is a blessing for shooters with small or extra-large hands.

A few of the more important features on both of the aforementioned models are: a single selective inertia-operated trigger; the action-opening top lever with positive opening stop; an easily removable stock; and a built-in adjustment for wood-to-metal and metal-to-metal play on the forend. The last feature is worth some elaboration and exemplifies this great gunmaking firm's foresight. All the new Perazzi shotguns are equipped with a means to adjust and compensate for wear in the critical area between the forend iron and the forend. The shock of firing tens of thousands of shells causes the forend wood to separate from the iron, which can seriously distract the shooter and be annoying because of the loosened grip. This aggravation has been eliminated by fitting two rods through the back of the forend iron, which screw into the locking bolts inside the forend. Any looseness between the forend and forend iron can be reduced by tightening these screws. To prevent further loosening, a special flat spring which rests against the catch bolt in the forend iron takes up any metal-to-metal play.

There are three major differences between the Mirage and MX-3 Special models. The Mirage has better grade walnut, the barrels on the Mirage are ported out near the muzzle to help reduce muzzle flip, and the Mi-

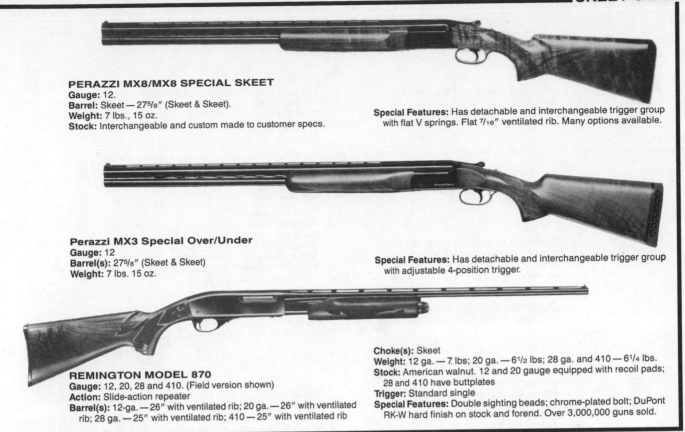

PERAZZI MX8/MX8 SPECIAL SKEET
Gauge: 12.
Barrel: Skeet — 27⁵/₈″ (Skeet & Skeet).
Weight: 7 lbs., 15 oz.
Stock: Interchangeable and custom made to customer specs.

Special Features: Has detachable and interchangeable trigger group with flat V springs. Flat 7/16″ ventilated rib. Many options available.

Perazzi MX3 Special Over/Under
Gauge: 12
Barrel(s): 27⁵/₈″ (Skeet & Skeet)
Weight: 7 lbs. 15 oz.

Special Features: Has detachable and interchangeable trigger group with adjustable 4-position trigger.

REMINGTON MODEL 870
Gauge: 12, 20, 28 and 410. (Field version shown)
Action: Slide-action repeater
Barrel(s): 12-ga. — 26″ with ventilated rib; 20 ga. — 26″ with ventilated rib; 28 ga. — 25″ with ventilated rib; 410 — 25″ with ventilated rib

Choke(s): Skeet
Weight: 12 ga. — 7 lbs; 20 ga. — 6½ lbs; 28 ga. and 410 — 6¼ lbs.
Stock: American walnut. 12 and 20 gauge equipped with recoil pads; 28 and 410 have buttplates
Trigger: Standard single
Special Features: Double sighting beads; chrome-plated bolt; DuPont RK-W hard finish on stock and forend. Over 3,000,000 guns sold.

rage fires the bottom barrel first, the MX-3 the top barrel first. There are two schools of thought about this, which is why Perazzi offers both versions. Some shooters claim that firing the bottom barrel first provides a lesser amount of initial recoil, which in turn helps reduce muzzle rise between shots. Proponents of the top barrel firing first claim the very same advantage, yet the laws of physics have proven that firing the under barrel provides a closer bore axis and recoil is, in fact, more of a straight line in nature. I personally vote for firing the under barrel first in any doubles gun.

REMINGTON

For more than 30 years, Remington's Model 870 has been a leader in the field of pump-action shotguns. It is the most popular pump gun in history, with over 3 million sold. Rugged dependability is the keystone of the Model 870 design. The receiver is machined from a solid billet of ordnance steel and vibra-honed for smoothness. Double-action slide bars eliminate binding and twisting that could interfere with consistent feeding. The barrels have a wide ventilated top rib with both front and mid sights. Model 870 Skeet guns are made in 12, 20, 28 and 410. The 12- and 20-gauge are available with 26-inch, Skeet-choked barrels; the 28-gauge and 410 barrels are 1-inch shorter.

Remington's Model 1100 is America's most popular

shotgun. Its fine handling qualities and low recoil have endeared it to shooters everywhere, but it is especially appreciated on the Skeet field. The 1100 is built to last, having a receiver and barrel cut from single blocks of ordnance steel. The Skeet model is made in all four gauges with 25- and 26-inch barrels choked for Skeet. Multi-event Skeet shooters will appreciate the weight equalizer kits because they give 20- and 28-gauge and 410 bore guns the same weight and feel as the larger 12-gauge. Model 1100 stocks are made of American walnut with impressed checkering on the pistol grip and forend.

ROTTWEIL

The Rottweil American Skeet was designed from the ground up with emphasis on strength, endurance and simplicity. With its superb balance and elegant classic appearance, the Rottweil AS 72 has all the qualities American Skeet shooters demand. The gun is designed to make use of American barrel tube sets for conversion of the 12-gauge to smaller bores. The 12-gauge barrels are 26³/₄ inches, bored Skeet and Skeet. The barrel rib is specially machined to eliminate glare, and it mounts a white plastic front sight housed in a durable metal sleeve, along with a metal mid-rib bead. The stock is select French walnut with a satin oil finish and hand-checkered on both pistol grip and forend. A double-

REMINGTON MODEL 11-87
Gauge: 12
Action: Gas-operated, semi-automatic
Barrel(s): 26″ or 28″ with ventilated rib
Choke(s): Fixed and screw-in REM-Choke tubes
Weight: 7½ lbs.
Special Features: New and improved gas system for fewer break-downs, self-cleaning.

REMINGTON MODEL 1100
Gauge: 12, 20, 28 and 410 bore
Action: Gas-operated autoloader
Barrel(s): 26″ ventilated rib, 25″ 28-gauge & 410 bore
Choke(s): Skeet
Weight: 7½ lbs.
Stock: Select American walnut
Trigger: Special competition model
Special Features: Polyurethane finish on stock and forend. Twin barrel beads. Engraved receiver.

ROTTWEIL 72 AMERICAN SKEET
Gauge: 12
Action: O/U, boxlock
Barrel(s): 28″ with ventilated rib
Choke(s): Fixed, Skeet & Skeet
Weight: 7¾ lbs.
Stock: European walnut. Hand checkered pistol grip and forend
Trigger: Single selective, detachable
Special Features: Available with Briley set of 20-, 28-gauge and 410 bore insert tubes. Fitted case. Satin finish, engraved receiver.

ventilated recoil pad is also fitted. The action has rebounding locks and automatic ejectors, and the firing pins are spring mounted to retract after firing, preventing damage to firing pin noses and possible interference with the loading cycle. Easily-removable trigger groups contain the hammers and coil springs are used throughout. The receiver is lightly engraved and sandblasted to avoid reflections. Weight of the Rottweil American Skeet gun is about 7½ pounds. Rottweils are imported by Dynamit Nobel-RWS, Inc. Rottweil guns were recently discontinued (at least in the United States), but you may be able to find left-over stock at some dealers.

RUGER

The Ruger Red Label available in both 12- and 20-gauge is a light over/under that weighs less than 7 pounds in the 20-gauge and only ½-pound more in the 12 bore. The Red Label offers Skeet barrels in both 26- and 28-inches in 20-gauge, and 26 inches in 12-gauge. The Red Label has a combination automatic safety and barrel selector, and the stock is made of American walnut with cut checkering on the pistol grip and forend. The Red Label is a strong, well-made shotgun, crafted in the finest Ruger tradition.

SHOTGUNS OF ULM

K-80 Skeet guns from Shotguns of Ulm have light-weight receivers and are hard nickel-plated with a satin gray finish. The locking mechanism consists of a massive top-locking plate that moves over the rear of the high-pivoted barrels. The mechanically-activated single trigger has the barrel selector located just ahead of it in the trigger guard. The position of the trigger is adjustable fore and aft, making it possible to make small changes in the effective length of pull. Standard vent rib barrels are 28 inches, choked Skeet and Skeet. The K-80 stock is select European walnut with hand-checkering on the palm swell pistol grip and on the forend. The stock may be removed without taking off the buttplate through use of a special, long screwdriver supplied with the gun. The K-80 is specifically designed to use barrel insert tubes, and tube sets are available in 20- and 28-gauge and 410 bore. The K-80, with its rugged dependability and excellent shooting characteristics, is rapidly becoming one of the world's leading Skeet guns. Four-barrel Skeet sets are available in 12, 20, 28 gauges and 410 bore. The K-80 is quite possibly the most popular over/under on today's Skeet fields and for good reason. A survey taken showed K-80 owners claim to have fewer malfunctions and breakdowns than any other Skeet gun now available. The guns are very simple, contain far fewer parts than most over/unders and have outstanding workmanship. Although certainly not cheap, these guns will last the typical Skeet shooter a lifetime and could be passed down through genera-

RUGER RED LABEL
Gauge: 12 and 20
Action: O/U, boxlock
Barrel(s): 28″ ventilated rib
Choke(s): Skeet & Skeet

Weight: 7¼ lbs.
Stock: American walnut with rubber recoil pad. Cut checkering
Trigger: Single selective, non-detachable
Special Features: Innovative design. Low center of gravity. Extra large pistol grip, 28 lines-per-inch checkering.

SHOTGUNS OF ULM K-80
Gauge: 12 or four-barrel Skeet set
Action: O/U with sliding breech lock
Barrel(s): 28″ with ventilated rib
Choke(s): Fixed, Skeet & Skeet
Weight: 8 lbs.

Stock: High-grade European with skip-line checkering
Trigger: Single selective, non-detachable, barrel selector forward of trigger blade
Special Features: Available as 12-gauge with insert tubes or as a four-barrel set. Premier Skeet gun. Fitted luggage-type hard case.

tions. They can take a lot of abuse.

SKB

This old-line Japanese firm has been in business since the mid-1850s. Once a great supplier of trap and Skeet guns to American shooters, SKB abandoned the U.S. market for greener pastures in 1981. They are now back with a staggering array of guns that should satisfy the needs and pocketbooks of any shooter — tyro or pro.

Three grades of over/unders are available — the Models 885, 605 and 505. All share common features as previously described in the trap gun section. Each model offers guns separately in 12, 20 and 28 gauges along with a sweet handling 410 bore. Additionally, SKB makes two three-barrel sets in 20, 28 and 410 in versions 885 and 505. Both sets are housed in a handsome all-aluminum gun case with a fitted-foam interior. These three-barrel sets are based on a 20-gauge size action and weigh a lightweight 6 pounds, 3 ounces. The length of pull is 14⅛ inches, drop at the comb is 1½ inches and drop at the heel is 2³⁄₁₆ inches. Both versions are equipped with a Skeet-style rubber ventilated recoil pad. The 20-gauge barrels are equipped with screw-in chokes, while the 28 and 410 barrels are bored Skeet and Skeet. SKB offers a Sporting Clays model close to Skeet stock specifications with 28-inch flat rib barrels equipped with screw-in chokes. If all

that doesn't satisfy you, two barrel combo sets are available in 12, 20 and 28 410 in all three grades. Whew!

VALMET

Built in Finland, Valmet's Skeet gun, the Model 412ST, is an over/under available in both 12- and 20-gauge. The 12-gauge barrels are only available in 28-inch lengths. All Valmet barrels are equipped with stainless steel screw-in choke tubes sized for Skeet dimensions. These barrels are made from pre-drilled blanks with final dimensioning on the cold hammering machine taking place in one single operation. The chamber and the bore are forged simultaneously for dimensional accuracy. Barrels are chrome alloy steel, while receivers are chrome molybdenum steel alloy. A single selective trigger also houses the barrel selector. The second barrel will fire even if the first barrel is empty. An automatic tang safety is provided, along with two indicator buttons located immediately behind the safety that give both visual and tactile indication of which barrel has been fired. The center screw of the safety may be tightened to change the safety to manual operation if desired. Weight of the Model 412ST is about 7½ pounds. Stock dimensions are just what most American Skeet shooters prefer — 14⅛-inch pull, 1½-inch drop at the comb and 2⅛-inch drop at the heel. Premium, semi-fancy grade walnut is used and 22-line

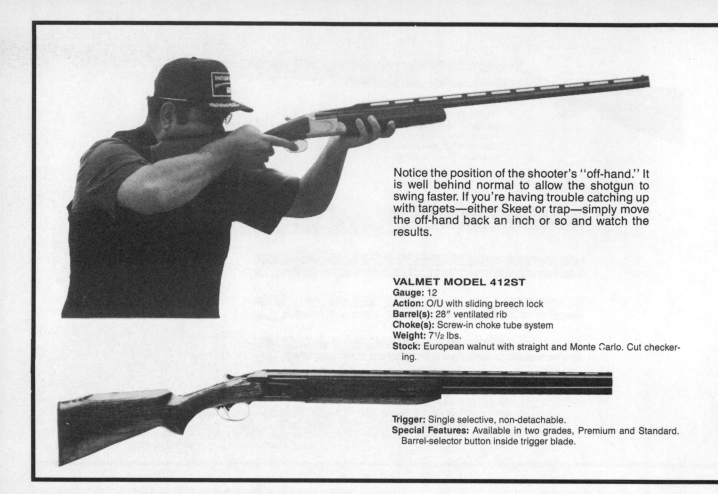

Notice the position of the shooter's "off-hand." It is well behind normal to allow the shotgun to swing faster. If you're having trouble catching up with targets—either Skeet or trap—simply move the off-hand back an inch or so and watch the results.

VALMET MODEL 412ST
Gauge: 12
Action: O/U with sliding breech lock
Barrel(s): 28″ ventilated rib
Choke(s): Screw-in choke tube system
Weight: 7¹/₂ lbs.
Stock: European walnut with straight and Monte Carlo. Cut checkering.

Trigger: Single selective, non-detachable.
Special Features: Available in two grades, Premium and Standard. Barrel-selector button inside trigger blade.

checkering is amply applied to both the pistol grip and forend. Two versions — Premium and Standard — are offered with the only difference being in the metal finish (satin-chrome receiver on the Premium, blued receiver on the Standard) and wood selection.

WEATHERBY

Weatherby offers two shotguns expressly designed for Skeet shooting — the Athena and Orion over/unders.

The gas-operated Model 82 autoloader has been a mainstay in the Weatherby lineup of shotguns for nearly a decade. Its gas-operated system absorbs much of the recoil, giving a softer shooting action. Weatherby has devised a floating gas piston that eliminates alignment, drag and friction wear problems found on some other autoloaders. A disconnect system is incorporated that prevents accidental firing of a shell unless the bolt is fully closed. Stocks and forends of the Model 82 are made of select Claro walnut protected with a durable high-gloss finish. Rosewood pistol grip caps add a touch of elegance. Ample fine-line hand-checkering is provided on the pistol grip and forend. Receivers are scroll engraved and finished in a luster blue. The Model 82 was dropped from the line recently, but you should still be able to find them at some dealers.

The Orion over/under is a strong boxlock design using time-proven Kersten cross-bolt locks. The mono-bloc and receiver are machined from high-strength steel and jewelled to a highly-polished finish for smooth functioning. Selective automatic ejectors kick out only fired hulls, while slightly raising unfired shells for easy removal. The safety is a traditional slide-type conveniently located on the top tang. The single selective trigger also allows instant barrel selection for the first shot by pressing the selector button on the trigger blade. A mechanical switchover automatically allows the second barrel to fire in case of a misfire, since recoil is not required to set the trigger. However, an adjustment will permit changeover to a recoil switchover if desired. The Claro walnut stock and forend are meticulously fitted to the action and the barrels and protected with a durable high-gloss finish. Distinctive hand-checkering, recoil pad and rosewood pistol grip cap are accents to an elegant firearm. The chrome moly barrels and receiver are deep blued in a lustrous finish. Available in both 12- and 20-gauge, the Orion is fitted with 26-inch barrels in both gauges. Barrels are topped by a broad ventilated rib, and vents are also machined into the interbarrel ribs for added cooling. The Orion weighs 7¹/₂ pounds in 12-gauge, 1 pound less in the 20-gauge.

The Athena model shares all the features of the Orion, except that it has ornamental sideplates, extensive engraving and better quality wood in the stock and

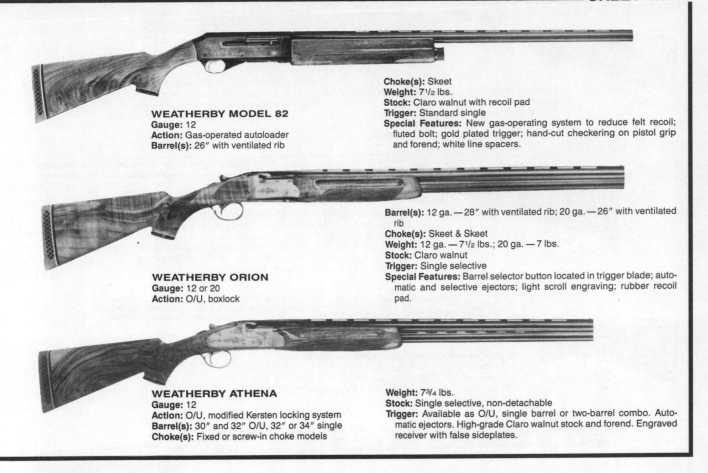

WEATHERBY MODEL 82
Gauge: 12
Action: Gas-operated autoloader
Barrel(s): 26″ with ventilated rib

Choke(s): Skeet
Weight: 7½ lbs.
Stock: Claro walnut with recoil pad
Trigger: Standard single
Special Features: New gas-operating system to reduce felt recoil; fluted bolt; gold plated trigger; hand-cut checkering on pistol grip and forend; white line spacers.

WEATHERBY ORION
Gauge: 12 or 20
Action: O/U, boxlock

Barrel(s): 12 ga. — 28″ with ventilated rib; 20 ga. — 26″ with ventilated rib
Choke(s): Skeet & Skeet
Weight: 12 ga. — 7½ lbs.; 20 ga. — 7 lbs.
Stock: Claro walnut
Trigger: Single selective
Special Features: Barrel selector button located in trigger blade; automatic and selective ejectors; light scroll engraving; rubber recoil pad.

WEATHERBY ATHENA
Gauge: 12
Action: O/U, modified Kersten locking system
Barrel(s): 30″ and 32″ O/U, 32″ or 34″ single
Choke(s): Fixed or screw-in choke models

Weight: 7¾ lbs.
Stock: Single selective, non-detachable
Trigger: Available as O/U, single barrel or two-barrel combo. Automatic ejectors. High-grade Claro walnut stock and forend. Engraved receiver with false sideplates.

forend. Receiver, sideplates, locking lever and trigger guard are finished in a rich, silver gray color that complements the deep blue of the barrels. Both of these quality stack-barrel shotguns are made by the respected Japanese firm of SKB expressly for Weatherby.

All the guns mentioned so far are called "Skeet" guns by the manufacturer, and yet, there are many models of field-grade shotguns made by Mossberg, Winchester (U.S.R.A.), Franchi and others that could qualify nicely as Skeet guns on an interim basis. All of them should be seriously considered by tyros.

Skeet shooting's golden era was the 1930s, when it was as elegant as playing polo. It was a shooting game for well-known personalities and unlike many of today's big-name "closet" shooters, movie stars like Clark Gable, Roy Rogers, Gary Cooper and others made it publicly known they "liked guns" and liked to shoot them.

Great American gunmakers during that time period made special Skeet guns. Winchester's Model 21 side-by-side was a favorite arm for many "name" Skeet shooters. The Model 21 Skeet guns were specially bored and the barrels marked "Skeet 1, Skeet 2" or "Skeet In, Skeet Out." The Model 21 was available in any gauge from 12 through 410 bore, and even the 16-gauge Skeet model was very popular though there were no 16-gauge events.

Iver Johnson, a popular handgun maker, joined the Skeet bandwagon in the 1930s and introduced a sleek, straight-grip, shot-barreled side-by-side appropriately named the "Skeeter." Not many of those guns were produced and few are seen today outside the hands of gun collectors.

Marlin's Model 90 over/under came on the scene a few years later and was chambered in 12- and 20-gauge plus 410 bore. It was one of the first American-made over/under shotguns which used spring-loaded strikers instead of the traditional internal hammers.

Possibly the most popular Skeet gun despite its short-lived career was Remington's Model 32. In production for less than a decade, it was big, heavy, clumsy, had poor triggers, and would often "double." Yet in spite of that, Skeet shooting champions preferred it. Alex Kerr shot one for many years as did a host of other champions.

At the start of WWII, Remington was forced to discontinue all "sporting" gun production and concentrate on the war effort. After the war, they sold all their tooling for the Model 32 to the old-time German gunmaking firm of Krieghoff. By the late 1950s, Krieghoff got their guns into production and started to ship these "new" Remington over/unders to the U.S., calling them the Krieghoff Model 32. The rest is history.

CURRENT SPORTING CLAYS GUNS

BERETTA MODEL 682 SPORTING CLAYS
Gauge: 12
Action: Boxlock, O/U
Barrel(s): 28″ or 30″, ventilated rib
Choke(s): Screw-in choke tube system
Weight: 7¾ lbs.
Stock: Oil-finished European walnut with cut checkering
Trigger: Non-detachable, single selective
Special Features: Designed specifically for American-style Sporting Clays. Low flat rib design. Satin-chrome receiver.

BROWNING CITORI GTI SPORTING CLAYS
Similar to the Citori Hunting except has semi-pistol grip with slightly grooved, semi-beavertail forend, satin-finish stock, radiused rubber butt pad. Has three interchangeable trigger shoes, trigger has three length of pull adjustments. Wide 13mm vent. rib, 28″ or 30″ barrels with Imp. Cyl. Invector choke tubes. Ventilated side ribs.

BROWNING SPECIAL SPORTING CLAYS
Similar to the GTI except has full pistol grip stock with palm swell, gloss finish, 28″, 30″ or 32″ barrels with fixed Imp. Cyl. & Mod. chokes; high post tapered rib. Also available as 28″ and 30″ two-barrel set.

CLASSIC DOUBLES MODEL 101 SPORTER
Gauge: 12
Action: Boxlock, O/U
Barrel(s): 28″ or 30″, ventilated and ported
Choke(s): Screw-in choke insert tubes
Weight: 7½ lbs.
Stock: Standard
Trigger: Non-removable, single selective
Special Features: Easily-removable stock with supplied stock wrench. Two-barrel combo available with 28″ and 30″ lengths.

The Sporting Clays shooting game is still fairly new on this side of the Atlantic and, therefore, most gunmakers haven't yet jumped on the bandwagon with separate models to fill this ever-growing niche. It may take a few years, but shooter interest will probably grow to the point that nearly every major maker/importer will have a "Sporting Clays" or "Sporter" model in their product line.

Like other clay target games, Sporting Clays is a specialized sport best played with a shotgun designed just for the purpose. Whereas trap and Skeet guns have built-in lead, a Clays gun should be designed to shoot exactly where it's pointed — not above or below — because the shooter shoots at a lot of ground-level targets, crossing birds, and those coming and going. In short, the targets present a real mixed bag of shooting opportunities and the shooter needs to hit exactly what he's looking at.

Basically, the Clays gun should have field-gun stock dimensions with the drop at the comb at 1½ inches (or lower) and drop at the heel 2¼ inches (or lower) — the most popular and workable dimensions for the majority of shooters. Also, there generally is not a Monte Carlo comb

Thus far, only one shotshell manufacturer has brought out special packaging for Sporting Clays — Federal Cartridge, which has converted its T122 loading *without* a plastic shotcup wad to a Sporting Clays motif. Some shooters think the absence of a shotcup produces quicker-opening patterns.

KRIEGHOFF K-80 SPORTING CLAYS O/U
Gauge: 12, 2¾″ chambers
Barrel: 28″ or 30″ with choke tubes
Weight: About 8 lbs.

Stock: #3 Sporting stock designed for gun-down shooting
Special Features: Choice of standard or lightweight receiver with satin nickel finish and classic scroll engraving. Selective mechanical trigger adjustable for position. Choice of tapered flat, 8mm parallel flat, or step-tapered barrel. Free floating barrels.

LAURONA SILHOUETTE 300 SPORTING CLAYS
Gauge: 12, 2¾″ chambers
Barrel: 28″ (Multichoke tubes, flush-type or knurled)

Weight: 7 lbs., 4 oz.
Stock: 14⅜″ × 1⅜″ × 2½″. European walnut with full pistol grip, beavertail forend. Rubber butt pad.
Special Features: Selective single trigger, automatic selective ejectors, automatic safety.

PERAZZI MX3 SPECIAL SPORTING
Gauge: 12, 2¾″ chambers
Barrel: 27⅝″ (Cyl. & Cyl.)
Weight: 7 lbs.
Stock: Made to customer specs; interchangeable.

Special Features: Detachable four-position trigger assembly, flat rib.

PERAZZI MIRAGE SPECIAL SPORTING O/U
Gauge: 12, 2¾″ chambers
Barrel: 27⅝″, 28⅜″
Weight: 7 lbs., 12 oz.
Stock: To customer specs; interchangeable
Special Features: Has adjustable four-position trigger; flat 7/16″ × 5/16″ vent. rib. Many options available.

on Clays guns, though it can be used.

Some shooters start out at the challenging game with 25- or 26-inch barreled Skeet guns, but soon learn that 28- or even 30-inch tubes work better because the increased length promotes a smoother swing and doesn't seem to cut down on timing — it's still quick to get on target.

As for choking, the way to go is with choke tubes. Which ones to use depends a great deal on the course being fired. As in golf, some courses play "long" and others "short." Since there is not a set course design, the shooter may need more or less choke depending on the particular course.

Since this game requires a lot of shooting, it's a good idea to use some sort of rubber recoil pad or solid buttpad. However, some experimentation will be necessary to find the pad design and material that suits your shooting style best. Some pads catch on clothing during the mount, and this can be disastrous to scores. A rubber pad with a hard rubber or plastic insert at the top (heel) to help prevent snagging on a shirt or jacket seems to work best.

Krieghoff incorporates this type of pad on their K-80 Sporting Clays gun, as do other manufacturers. Ported barrels are also seen on Clays guns to help reduce recoil, and the full pistol grip is usually in evidence for the same reason.

Some shooters can successfully negotiate a Sporting Clays course with a gun with double triggers, but most can't. A good field shooter who is used to this system can do with it, but most use a single trigger, which is the way the factory guns are equipped for American shooters. European shooters are more accustomed to double triggers, however. Though you can use any kind of rib, the flat tapered rib is the one that is most popular and widely used on Sporting Clays fields for the simple reason that it works the best.

As for the action type, the over/under is the predominant gun used more from a reliability standpoint than anything else. This is not to say that a pump or auto won't be appropriate, but the stack-barrel is nearly as trouble free these days as an anvil, and that's hard to beat. Automatic and pump-action shotguns can be used for this game.

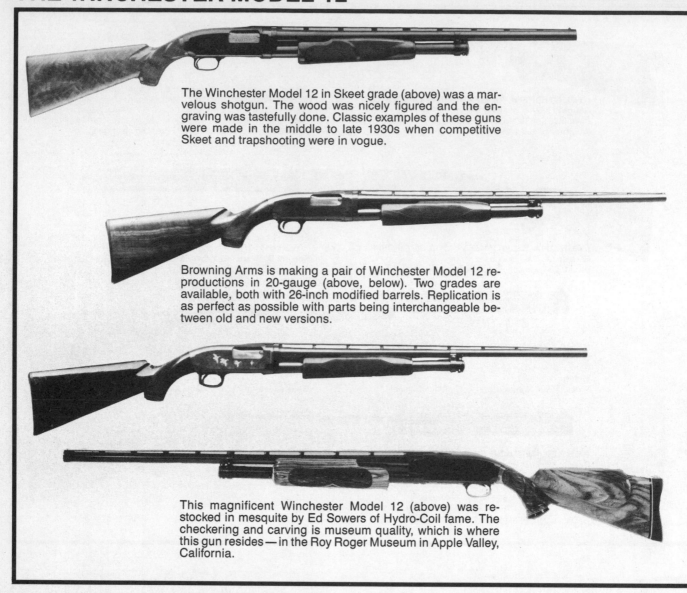

The Winchester Model 12 in Skeet grade (above) was a marvelous shotgun. The wood was nicely figured and the engraving was tastefully done. Classic examples of these guns were made in the middle to late 1930s when competitive Skeet and trapshooting were in vogue.

Browning Arms is making a pair of Winchester Model 12 reproductions in 20-gauge (above, below). Two grades are available, both with 26-inch modified barrels. Replication is as perfect as possible with parts being interchangeable between old and new versions.

This magnificent Winchester Model 12 (above) was restocked in mesquite by Ed Sowers of Hydro-Coil fame. The checkering and carving is museum quality, which is where this gun resides — in the Roy Roger Museum in Apple Valley, California.

Any book written about shotguns must have a special section devoted to the venerable Winchester Model 12. This revered veteran has probably gathered more trap and Skeet shooting honors than any other model shotgun ever produced. There's no way to know this for sure, but I doubt I'll hear many disagreements. There's probably not a trapshooter today who at one time or another hasn't either owned or tried to shoot the winningest Winchester of all time. There's a certain ingredient — call it style, balance or feel — that sets this old "pumper" apart from today's sophisticated trap and Skeet guns.

One of the all-time great classic-style shotguns, the Winchester Model 12's appearance was often emulated by other manufacturers. Even Winchester, after discontinuing production of the Model 12 in the early 1970s, hyped their new autoloader — the Super X-1 — as having handling characteristics like the Model 12. In fact, the Super X-1's receiver profile closely followed the smooth, flowing lines of the Model 12. Even though

the Model 12 has been out of production for more than 10 years, with over 2 million guns produced, there is still an overwhelming number found on today's trap and Skeet fields. Yes, there are still a few "diehards" who fondly shuck their doubles on the Skeet range.

Not long after I became a registered trapshooter in 1960, my search for a trap gun was limited to relatively few choices. There was only one single-barrel trap gun in production — the Ithaca — but that was well out of my financial reach. The Browning Broadway and discontinued Remington Model 32 were just not my cup of tea. Of the other two acceptable pump guns — Remington's Model 870 and the ancient Model 31 — neither suited my fancy at that time. Therefore, by process of elimination, the Winchester Model 12 was the logical choice — and it was a good one at that.

In 1960, a trap-grade Model 12 had a list price of $203.50. There were no "deals" in those days because consumers were protected by the Fair Trade Act and retail prices were rigidly enforced. The Model 12 had a

Another example of Pachmayr engraving on a Winchester Model 12. This is considered 100 percent coverage and the time on the receiver alone totals almost 200 hours of tedious workmanship.

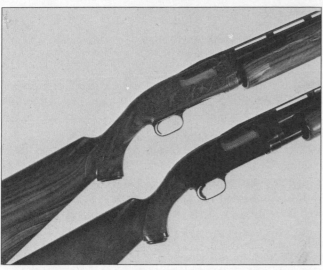

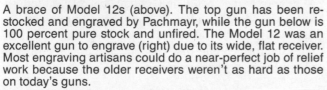

A brace of Model 12s (above). The top gun has been re-stocked and engraved by Pachmayr, while the gun below is 100 percent pure stock and unfired. The Model 12 was an excellent gun to engrave (right) due to its wide, flat receiver. Most engraving artisans could do a near-perfect job of relief work because the older receivers weren't as hard as those on today's guns.

30-inch ventilated rib barrel, nicely-figured walnut stock and forend with hand-cut checkering. Finally I was a trapshooter after spending nearly 3 years floundering and getting bloody on southern California Skeet fields. I, like many fellow shooters, "paid my dues" and watched some of the greatest Skeet and trapshooters routinely pocket my entry and option money.

Some of the greatest champions have used, and are still using, the Winchester Model 12. Arnold Riegger from Washington shot one for many years, and it was used when he bought it. Anyone who had the privilege of watching Riegger take his old Model 12 out for a Doubles event will recall how smoothly he and that old Model 12 ground up targets. It was like watching Toscanini conduct the Philharmonic orchestra.

The Poindexter brothers, Chuck, Tom and Jim, have all shot Model 12s during their illustrious careers. Another west coast trapshooter, Phil Ross, can still be seen using his Model 12 with a plastic Hydro-Coil stock that is only a decade or so younger than he.

Ross's phenomenal scores and yearly averages attest to the gun's ability to break targets in the hands of a competent shooter.

Thinking back to the 1960s, Peter Candy and William Hay Rogers come to mind, both Skeet shooting whiz-bangs who used the old "corn-sheller." Rummaging through old-time Skeet and trap magazines, it was graphically proven that the Winchester Model 12 was the "fair-haired boy" of the trap and Skeet fields until the early 1970s. There are numerous stories about Joe Devers, perhaps the greatest all-round shotgun shooter ever, who took his Model 12 to Europe and made a mockery out of live pigeon shooting.

During the mid-1970s, the European imports made their lasting impression and infiltrated both the pocket-books and hands of the American shooters. The hey-days of the Winchester Model 12 were obviously numbered and Winchester retired the venerable veteran twice—first in 1964 and again in 1979. Once "King of the Hill," the King is now dead. Long live the King!

Since the introduction of the Remington Model 870 in 1949, Remington has manufactured over 3.5 million Model 870s . . . that's over 50 percent more than the fabled Winchester Model 12, whose production days go back to 1912!

The Remington Model 870 is more than simply a shotgun model. It was Remington's "master" model, which was the forerunner of a host of other Remington shotguns and rifles. Its introduction was also the beginning of new production methods pioneered by Remington which enabled the Bridgeport, Connecticut company to offer quality shotguns and rifles to the shooting masses at low retail prices by using then-revolutionary computer tape-controlled tooling machines.

With the introduction of the Model 870, Remington had to "axe" the slick-shooting Model 31. Like the Winchester Model 12, the Remington Model 31 was doomed to the graveyard because it, too, was virtually handmade and the receiver was machined from a single chunk of tempered steel. Virtually every part was hand fitted and even in the early 1950s, the labor bill was too high for Remington to make a profit.

So, the Model 870 was not only called the "31 killer," but, in reality, this simplistic shotgun should be credited as the forefather of Remington's Models 58, 878, 1100, 760, 742, 11-87 and a few others I've probably forgotten. This shotgun's success was based on durability, simplicity and probably most importantly, affordability! In 1950, the Remington Model 870 AP grade listed for $69.95, while Winchester's Model 12 cost twice that amount.

The general shooting public has certainly accepted the Model 870. In 1974, 25 years after its inception, the 2 millionth 870 came off the production line. Four years later, the 3 millionth Model 870 exited the Remington plant. There have been many notable trap and Skeet shooters who have favored the Model 870 during their shooting careers. Two of the greatest are Skeet's Bill Rogers and trap's Rudy Etchen.

Not only has Remington's Model 870 proved highly successful, but it spawned a good many "knock-offs," thanks to its super-simple design. The old Weatherby Model Patrician pump-action shotgun had many internal parts very similar in design to the venerable 870. When the 870 was first introduced, all other pump shotguns only had a single action bar—the Winchester Model 12, the Ithaca Model 37 and the Remington Model 31. Shooters of these slide-action guns complained that the single bar caused the forend to twist and often bind against the side of the barrel. The 870's twin-action bars eliminated this problem. The way the 870's barrel extension fit inside the receiver prevented the mating of these two important parts from self-destructing like the Model 12 and Model 37. This barrel extension precluded the possibility of headspacing problems. The bolt and carrier from the 870's boiler room was so simple and effective it caused other gun

1950: Introduced in 12-, 16- and 20-gauge, standard and ADL Deluxe versions. Skeet versions in 12- and 20-gauge. Trap versions in standard and "TC" grades.

1955: Addition of Model 870 Magnum, 3-inch chambers, 12-gauge only.

1959: Addition of 12-gauge deer gun version with slug barrel and rifle sights.

1962: Introduction of "Brushmaster" 12-gauge Deer Gun with 20-inch slug barrel, rifle sights and rubber recoil pad.

1963: Model 870 consolidated to one basic Deluxe grade for all field models.

1968: Addition of recoil pads as standard equipment on all Model 870 12-, 16- and 20-gauge field models and 12- and 20-gauge Skeet models.

1969: Model 870 in 28-gauge and 410 bore field models with mahogany stocks introduced. Also, 28-gauge and 410 bore "Matched Pair" Skeet models and walnut stocks and hard, two-gun carrying case. Model 870 Brushmaster Deer Gun introduced in 20-gauge.

1970: Model 870 28-gauge and 410 bore Skeet guns offered individually in place of previous, combined "Matched Pair." Modified choke barrels added to Model 870 Magnum (3-inch chamber) shotguns in 12-gauge (30-inch barrel length) and 20-gauge (28-inch barrel length). White line spacers added at recoil pad or buttplate and pistol grip cap.

1971: Complete, mirror-image, left-hand Model 870s in 12- and 20-gauge announced in field, Magnum and Trap (12-gauge only) versions.

1972: New 20-gauge Lightweight Model 870 announced, with scaled-down receiver (28-gauge size) and mahogany stocks in both standard and Magnum field guns. Model 870 "All-American" fancy-grade trap gun introduced.

1974: Two millionth Model 870 came off the assembly line.

1976: Limited Edition Bicentennial Commemorative versions produced in 12-gauge Model 870 SA Skeet and Model 870 TB Trap.

1978: Model 870 "All-American" Trap gun discontinued. Model 870 trap gun line altered to include three grades of increasing quality—Models 870 TA, TB and TC. Introduction of Model 870 20-gauge Lightweight Deer Gun. Three millionth Model 870 produced.

1950s and 1960s

1957: 12-gauge 870 Magnum-AP, standard-grade pump action, Full choke, 3″ chambers

1969: Matched pair of 870 pump actions in 28 and 410 gauges with special carrying case

1969: 870 SA pump-action Skeet gun, small-bore version

1969: Match-Weight Skeet Cap for Remington 28 gauge and 410 bore

Early 1970s

1970: 12-gauge 870 Wingmaster, left-hand magnum pump action with ventilated rib

1970: 12-gauge 870 TB, left-hand pump action with Monte Carlo stock

1972: 20-gauge 870 Lightweight Magnum with ventilated rib

1972: Custom-built 870 Wingmaster with gold inlay

designers to say, "Gee, why didn't we think of that!"

Not only was—and is—the Remington Model 870 as trouble free as a sundial, knowledgeable shooters agree that 870 and 1100 barrels are straight, perfectly choked and rarely in need of "massaging" from barrelsmiths to make them as near perfect as possible. They throw consistently excellent patterns and the secret alloy that Remington uses keeps them in excellent condition for literally decades. There are documented cases on file at the Remington repair center in Ilion, New York that brag about the 870's longevity. Guns that have fired over 250,000 shells are still in good stead.

As a gun writer/tester, I have shot and evaluated virtually every trap and Skeet gun to come down the pike. During these evaluations, I've purchased a few of my favorites for tournament use. Currently, I own and shoot nine Model 870s—four Skeet guns, 410 bore, 28-, 20- and 12-gauge along with three Model 870 competition models and two 870 TCs. Ever since the 870 Competition Model was introduced in 1981, it has been my primary trap gun for both Singles and Handicap. I've maintained nearly a 98 percent Singles average on over 25,000 targets, a near 90 percent Handicap average from 27 yards and have earned over 30 honorary punches with it. All three of my Comps have been tuned and altered slightly so that each gun shoots and feels exactly like the other two. If something breaks down, and it has on rare occasion, I simply stroll back to my vehicle and grab another gun.

Having two or three of these Remington trap guns is inexpensive luxury. When found, these guns can be purchased for less than $400—sometimes even less. Why then, did Remington discontinue the Competition's production. Simply stated, lack of sales. For some inexplicable reason, American trapshooters demand that a pump-operated shotgun have the capability of follow-up shots—the 870 Competition is strictly single shot as the gas-operated mechanism fills the entire magazine tube. Also, as the gas-operated recoil-reducing system is exposed to operating gases, the internal system gets *very* dirty quickly. To keep the recoil-reduction system operating at factory specifications, the gun should be disassembled and thoroughly cleaned every 500 rounds—or less depending on atmospheric and ammunition variables. The average shooter though is lazy and doesn't want to spend that much time maintaining his shotgun. He wants to spend his recreational time shooting—or perhaps reloading—not cleaning.

In 1988, Remington really came up with a winner with their all-new 870 TC. Leaving the basic action and receiver alone, virtually everything else is new or redesigned. Starting from the rear, the buttstock boasts some of the most beautiful American walnut from the Missouri valley regions. The Monte Carlo was redesigned and its cut more streamlined and longer than earlier versions. The checkering on the pistol grip and forend is finely cut, 28 lines to the inch. The forend is a

direct copy—including the checkering pattern—of the defunct Competition model, which is approximately 1½-inches longer than the older version forends.

But Remington really did their homework with the new barrel concept. The new TC's barrels are over-bored, meaning they are larger in diameter than previous models and the forcing cone is less constrictive, which greatly reduces felt recoil. How, you might ask, does enlarging the forcing cone reduce felt recoil? Through a series of exhaustive scientific tests, it has been proven that nearly 85 percent of recoil in a shotgun barrel is generated when the shot charge and wad enter the forcing cone area. The other 15 percent is divided into two separate actions—when the shot charge and wad enter the choke and when the primer ignites the main powder charge.

Adding to the TC's originality is the addition of REM Choke tubes—Full, Extra Full and Super Full. These choke tubes are carefully matched to work only with these over-bored barrels and will not produce correct pattern percentages if installed in regular REM Choked barrels like those found on currently-manufactured Remington field and Skeet guns.

I don't know what else Remington can possibly do to improve the current crop of 870s. The Bridgeport people have taken an excellent design, improved it and offered it to the shooting public at a very affordable price. I guess that really says it all!

The Remington Model 870 is as trouble free as a sundial and ranks as one of the best domestic trap and Skeet guns ever made.

Early 1970s (cont.)

1972: Detailed right and left sides of the receiver of a 12-gauge 870 All American trap gun.

1972: This shield was attached to the side of the 870 All American trap gun and added a colorful touch to the blued receiver.

1974: 870 Wingmaster Ducks Unlimited Commemorative

Middle 1970s

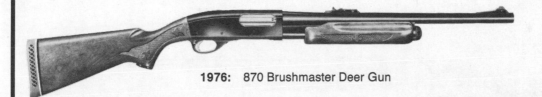

1976: 870 Brushmaster Deer Gun

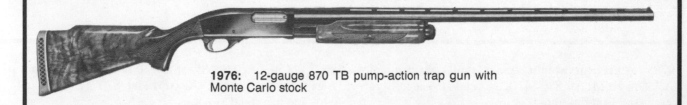

1976: 12-gauge 870 TB pump-action trap gun with Monte Carlo stock

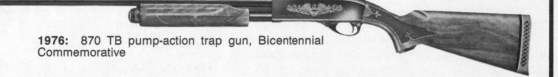

1976: 870 TB pump-action trap gun, Bicentennial Commemorative

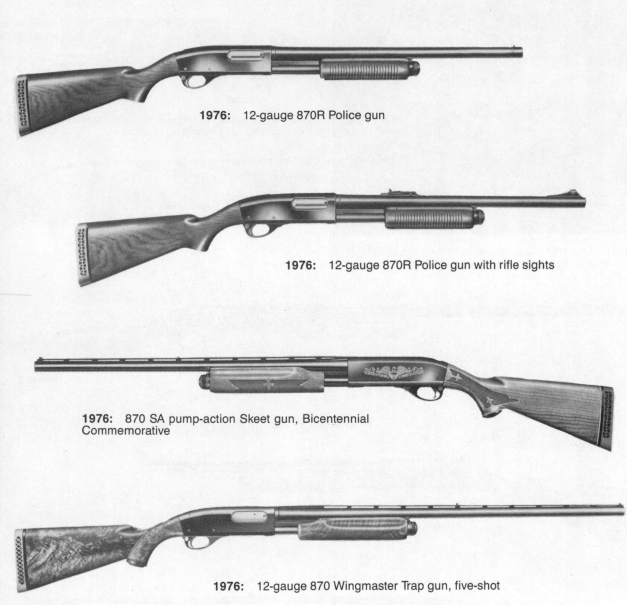

1976: 12-gauge 870R Police gun

1976: 12-gauge 870R Police gun with rifle sights

1976: 870 SA pump-action Skeet gun, Bicentennial Commemorative

1976: 12-gauge 870 Wingmaster Trap gun, five-shot

1979: American walnut stocks replaced mahogany stocks on all Model 870, 410, 28- and 20-gauge Lightweight field-model guns.

1980: New stock style for all Model 870 shotguns announced.

1981: Model 870 "Competition" Trap Gun with recoil-reducing gas piston built into magazine tube introduced. Single shot, non-repeating. Announcement of Model 870 "Limited" 20-gauge Lightweight with 23-inch barrel and 12½-inch length of pull for young and smaller-than-average adults.

1982: Model 870 SA Skeet in 410 bore, 28-, 20- and 12-gauge discontinued. Also Model 870 TB Trap in right- and left-hand versions.

1983: Model 870 12-gauge Magnum produced in special Ducks Unlimited Commemorative version. Addition of Model 870 left-hand 12-gauge Deer Gun. Addition of 28-inch, modified barrel to Model 870 20-gauge Lightweight Magnums.

1984: Introduction of Model 870 "Special Field" in 12- and 20-gauges with straight, "English-style" stock, no pistol grip and 21-inch ventilated rib bar-

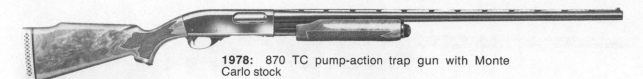

1978: 870 TC pump-action trap gun with Monte Carlo stock

Combining the recoil-reducing feature of the built-in gasport and piston of the Remington Model 870 along with the dependability of a pump-gun action, this single shot "repeater" is an outstanding gun for its reasonable retail price.

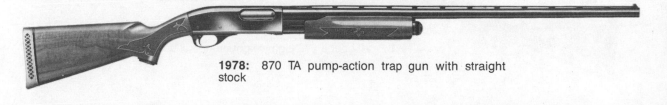

1978: 870 TA pump-action trap gun with straight stock

rels—Improved Cylinder, Modified and Full chokes. Name changed from Model 870 "Limited" 20-gauge Lightweight to Model 870 20-gauge Lightweight "Youth Gun" and barrel length changed from 23 to 21 inches.

1985: Model 870 "Special Purpose" Magnum introduced. New version of 12-gauge Model 870 specifically designed for waterfowling and turkey hunting. All exposed metal surfaces, both barrel and receiver given dull, non-glare, Parkerized finish. Blackened bolt. Stock given dull, non-glare, oil finish. Standard equipment includes 2-inch wide, padded carrying sling of "Cordura" nylon and Q.D. sling swivels. Three-inch chambers standard in 26- or 30-inch Full choke, ventilated rib barrels.

1986: Upgraded, restyled 12-gauge Model 870 now designated as "Wingmaster" announced. Stock includes raised-diamond cut checkering, low-gloss satin wood finish. Also includes ivory-bead "Bradley"-type front sight and mid-barrel metal bead. Three-inch chambers are standard. Choice of 26- or 28-inch barrels fitted with new REM Choke system of interchangeable choke tubes or regular 30-inch Full choke ventilated rib barrel. New REM Choke interchangeable

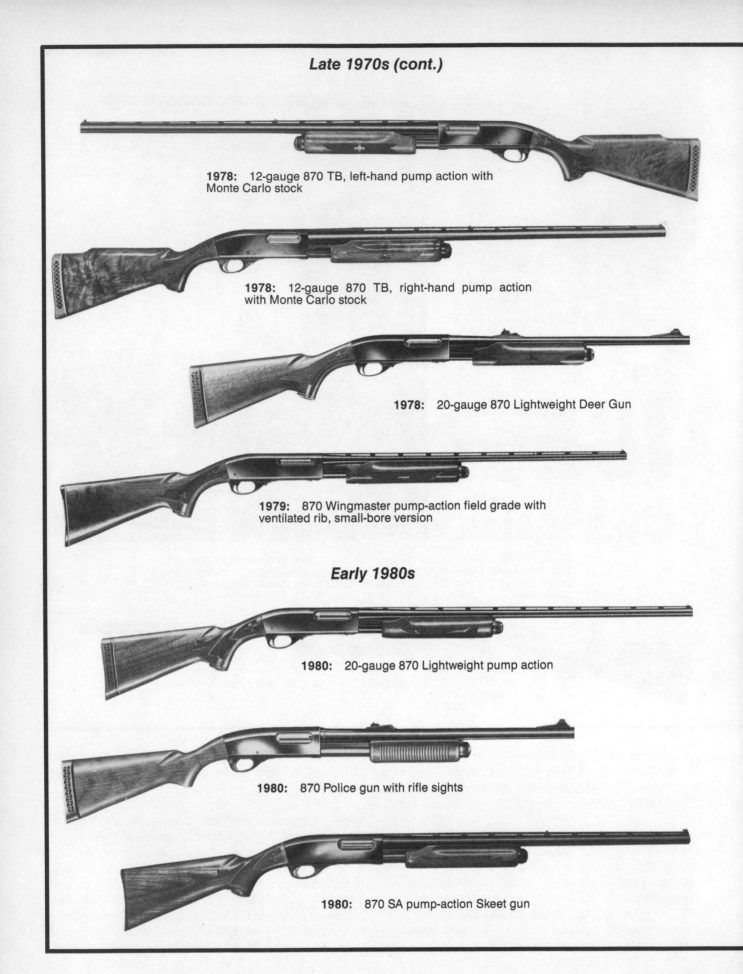

1978: 12-gauge 870 TB, left-hand pump action with Monte Carlo stock

1978: 12-gauge 870 TB, right-hand pump action with Monte Carlo stock

1978: 20-gauge 870 Lightweight Deer Gun

1979: 870 Wingmaster pump-action field grade with ventilated rib, small-bore version

Early 1980s

1980: 20-gauge 870 Lightweight pump action

1980: 870 Police gun with rifle sights

1980: 870 SA pump-action Skeet gun

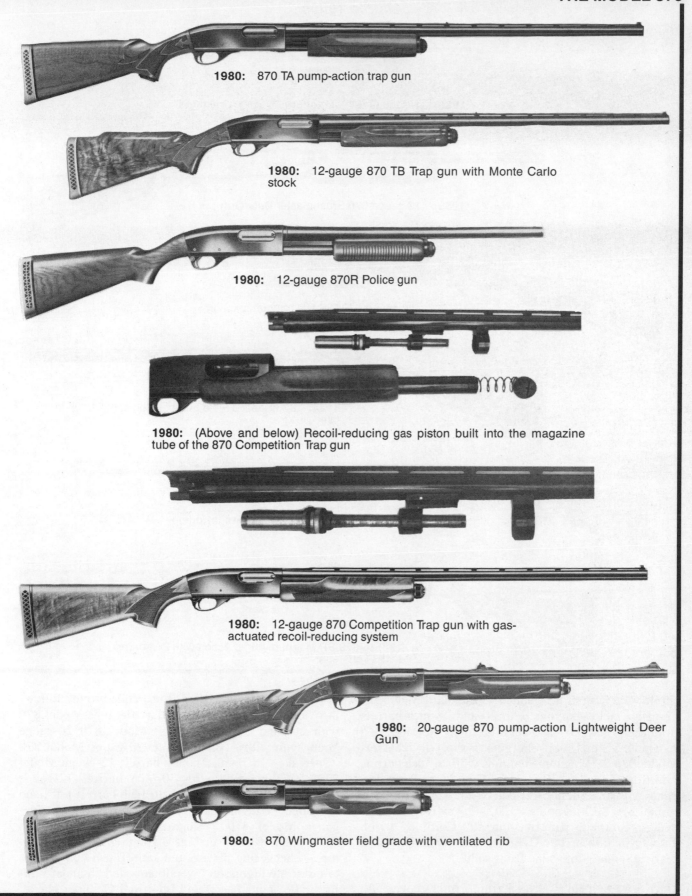

1980:   870 TA pump-action trap gun

1980:   12-gauge 870 TB Trap gun with Monte Carlo stock

1980:   12-gauge 870R Police gun

1980:   (Above and below) Recoil-reducing gas piston built into the magazine tube of the 870 Competition Trap gun

1980:   12-gauge 870 Competition Trap gun with gas-actuated recoil-reducing system

1980:   20-gauge 870 pump-action Lightweight Deer Gun

1980:   870 Wingmaster field grade with ventilated rib

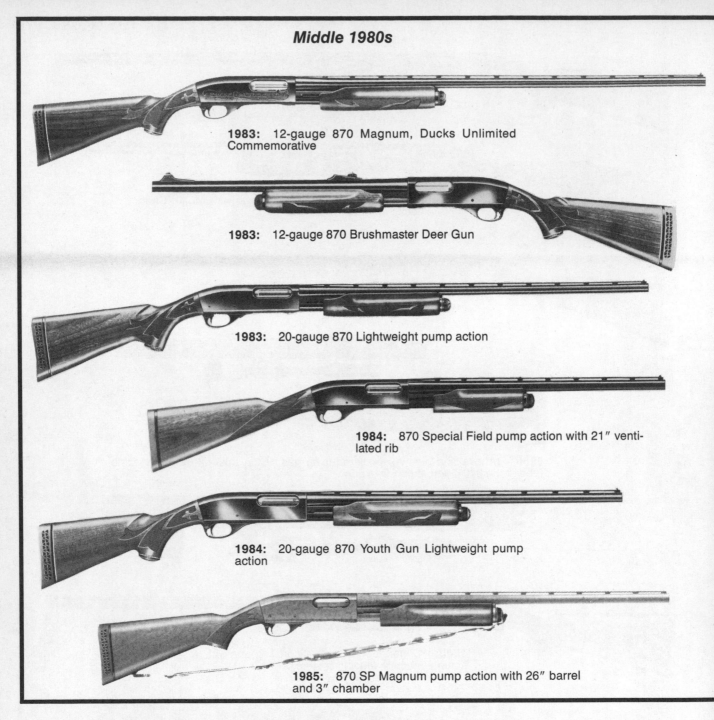

1983: 12-gauge 870 Magnum, Ducks Unlimited Commemorative

1983: 12-gauge 870 Brushmaster Deer Gun

1983: 20-gauge 870 Lightweight pump action

1984: 870 Special Field pump action with 21″ ventilated rib

1984: 20-gauge 870 Youth Gun Lightweight pump action

1985: 870 SP Magnum pump action with 26″ barrel and 3″ chamber

choke tube system also added to Standard Model 870 12-gauge field shotguns with 26 and 28-inch barrels. Both right- and left-hand versions of above. Model 870 12-gauge Special Field shotguns with 21-inch barrels. Model 870 SP Magnum shotguns with 26-inch barrels. Addition of Model 870 SP Deer Gun. Same Parkerized metal finish and non-reflective oil stock finish as Model 870 SP Magnums. Q.D. sling swivels and padded, camouflage pattern sling of "Cordura" nylon. Twenty-inch Improved Cylinder barrel with adjustable rear sight and white bead front sight.

1987: REM Choke system (three field chokes: Improved Cylinder, Modified, Full) added to the following Model 870 shotguns: regular 20-gauge Model 870 with 26- and 28-inch barrels; Model 870 20-gauge Youth Gun with 21-inch barrel; 20-gauge Model 870 "Special Field" with 21-inch barrel; 12-gauge Model 870 "Wingmaster" with 30-inch barrel; 12-gauge Model 870 SP Magnum with 30-inch barrel; left-hand 12-gauge "Wingmaster" with 28-inch barrel. Twelve-gauge Model 870 "Wingmaster" Deer Gun—both right- and left-hand versions—with upgraded stock features, checkering pattern and satin finish comparable to other "Wingmaster" versions added. Standard 20-inch rifle sights barrel and Improved Cylinder choke.

Late 1980s

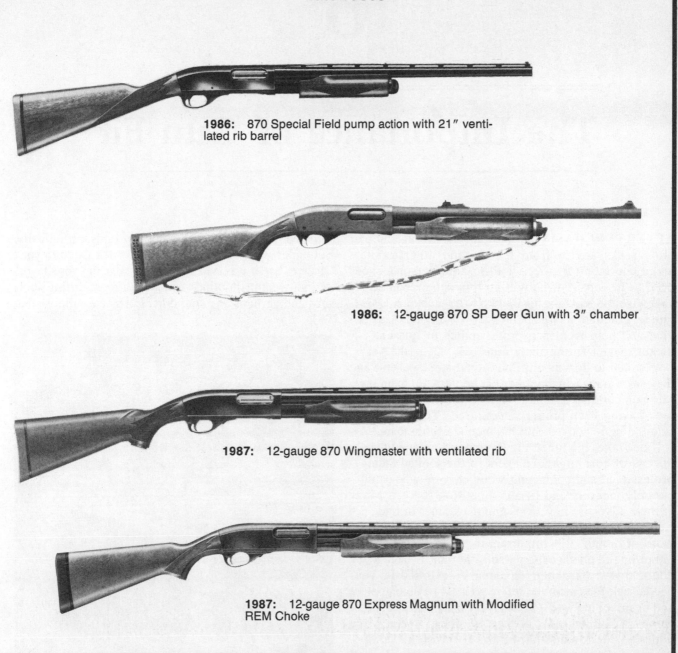

1986: 870 Special Field pump action with 21″ ventilated rib barrel

1986: 12-gauge 870 SP Deer Gun with 3″ chamber

1987: 12-gauge 870 Wingmaster with ventilated rib

1987: 12-gauge 870 Express Magnum with Modified REM Choke

Return of Model 870 TC Trap specification to the Model 870 line with REM Choke system, regular trap or Monte Carlo stock and 30-inch barrels with Bradley-type front bead. Model 870 "Express," a lower-priced, "no frills" version of standard Model 870 with 3-inch chambering, ventilated rib, 28-inch barrel and one—Modified—REM Choke insert introduced. The Model 870 "Express" retains all the well-established performance, dependability and durability features of regular Model 870s, but with fewer cosmetic features.

1988: Redesign of Model 870 TC Trap gun with new stock dimensions including competition-type forend for reduced felt recoil and fatigue. New, tournament-grade cut checkering. Thirty-inch barrels over-bored with three trap REM Choke inserts specially designed for optimum patterns with over-bored barrels: Trap Full, Trap Extra-Full and Trap Super-Full. (Note: The design and dimensions of these three trap chokes are matched to over-bore trap barrels. They will not provide comparable performance with regular shotgun barrels but they will provide non-typical patterns.) The Model 870 TC Trap is also supplied with 30-inch over-bored, fixed Full choke barrels. The Model 870 combo, a no frills Model 870 "Express" with an extra 20-inch rifle sights deer barrel was also introduced.

6

The Importance of Gun Fit

AFTER PURCHASING a shotgun, the average shooter often seeks advice from friends and other shooters about the gun's fit. Yet, if this same person's shoes need to be repaired, he will go to a shoe repair store. Likewise, he will take his ill auto to a mechanic. Unfortunately though, a large percentage of shooters seek advice and help from non-professionals or quasi-stockmakers when fitting their gunstock. Over the years, I've talked to dozens of professional stockmakers, and they say a staggering number of shooters tell them their ideas on building a stock to fit their dimensions without ever having been properly measured. That may seem astounding to you . . . but it's inconceivable to me!

If one takes the time to investigate, there are literally dozens of custom stockmakers in the United States—professional and competent wood carvers who can accurately measure and fit a competition shooter. Many of them advertise in various gun magazines or trade periodicals. Others don't advertise but depend solely on word-of-mouth. It is important to talk to a stockmaker either on the phone or in person, though. If there's any doubt that a particular stockmaker can satisfy your needs, ask for customer references. If he's competent and proud of his work, he'll gladly offer you a hatful of names. If he hesitates or says he doesn't want to be bothered, or resents that he has to prove his competency, take a pass and find another stockmaker who will comply with your wishes.

Finding and trusting a stockmaker isn't unlike finding a doctor, dentist or lawyer. You may not initially agree with his stock-fitting prescription, but the best stockmakers know what's best for you. As with any professional, as long as you're paying their prices, take their advice. You can be assured that when you occasionally need his services it will cost you some bucks, so choose wisely.

What is correct stock fit today, may be woefully wrong tomorrow, for many reasons. For example, let's assume you have a shotgun with a stock that seems to fit you perfectly. It is comfortable to shoot, you've shot some excellent scores with it, and you're 100 percent

satisfied with it both mechanically and aesthetically. But under what conditions was the stock fitted to you? Chances are it was when you were wearing your favorite lightweight shooting vest, with a loose-fitting sport shirt and perhaps an undershirt. Let's also suppose that

If the gun is fitted correctly to the shooter, a more natural and comfortable stance is automatically attained. Foot position, body balance and correct gun fit all contribute to consistent high scores.

at that time the length of pull was accurately measured at 14¼ inches. The drop at the comb was 1¼ inches and the drop at the Monte Carlo heel 1¾ inches—rather typical trap stock dimensions. (I hope Skeet shooters don't take offense, but these dimensions are only stated for comparisons which will be changed for various reasons, as you'll find out.)

Now for a little surprise. You're signed up, squadded and ready to go when suddenly a snow storm gathers and the temperature quickly drops 20 degrees. What do you do? The average shooter would naturally race back to the car, drag out a warm coat and trot back to the starting line. Warm, yes, but falsely prepared to shoot the best score of his career. Usually, this snugly-warm shooter will record a score from 10 to 12 percentage points less than his average. The beleaguered shooter will blame the weather for his sub-par performance, when actually the warm coat was the culprit. The thickness of the coat will increase the shotgun's length of pull between 1/2- to 1-inch, depending on the type of material and thickness of the padding. This extended stock dimension will dramatically change the gun's handling qualities. Yet, it wasn't noticed by the shooter because the coat made him warm and comfortable. So now we have a Catch 22 situation. Do shooters not wear a coat, brave the cold and attempt to shoot under these conditions—or vice versa?

Another cause of decreasing scores is weight. Many

of us gain or lose weight throughout our lives—some lose by diet, or illness and others gain by overeating or possibly illness. Regardless, whether physical structure adds or depletes weight, the body changes shape and dimensions. Two areas of change are extremely important to a shooter—the amount and thickness of the flesh, fat or muscle in the shoulder and chest area and below the master eye near the cheekbone.

It's virtually impossible to accurately measure how "thick" one's face is, or to weigh the amount of flesh and muscle in the shoulder "pocket" area, so another means for measurement is needed. In this instance, we'll use the shotgun stock as a reference tool. Once again, let's assume that you are shooting good scores with your gun. It's comfortable, and you've gained a great deal of confidence in it. Now is the time to accurately and precisely take the stock's physical measurements—the length of pull, drop at the heel and comb, pitch, and, if possible, cast-on or cast-off. Record these measurements on a slip of paper and set them aside. These important numbers can be preserved by taping them down to the inside of the recoil pad or buttplate. Or, you can scribe the dimensions directly on the back of the recoil pad. These dimensions, taken today, could be very important in determining and solving future shooting problems.

Now, 6 months down the shooting road, your scores are beginning to deteriorate. Shooting averages, instead of going up, are eroding. Why? If you have either lost or gained weight, your face and/or body no longer correctly fit the shotgun stock dimensions. Obviously, something has to be altered to put things back in their correct position. It is theoretically possible to add face

The old-fashioned methods of determining if a gunstock fits the shooter by placing it in the crook of the elbow using a measuring stick are neither accurate nor useful. Why? First, these methods do not take into consideration the shooter's natural style — does he "crawl" a stock, mount the gun with his head upright?, etc. If any stockmaker attempts to measure you using either method, find yourself a new stocksmith.

putty or body padding to compensate for weight loss, but how do you immediately remove ¹/₈-inch of extra flesh from your cheekbone or ¹/₂-inch of fleshy tissue from your shoulder pocket? Realistically, neither can be done, so, therefore, the gunstock must be altered to once again fit the semi-fixed dimensions. Usually, the stock comb must be lowered a little bit at a time, usually not more than ¹/₁₆-inch. The length of pull might have to be changed also, but pull length can be reduced in increments of ¹/₄-inch at a time until proper length has been determined by trial and error.

Top-notch shooters know how to adapt to and compensate for varying conditions—both physically and emotionally. For physical alterations, there are numerous mechanical means. We won't go into the emotional conditions here because they are covered in another chapter.

After shooting for awhile, we should realize and accept that all competitive shoots will not be held under ideal weather conditions. We'll encounter wind storms, rain, or fading light conditions, etc. throughout our shooting careers. Wind has the greatest influence on target flight. An incoming (head) wind will always cause the target to rise in a higher than normal arc. A trailing (tail) wind, conversely, will lower the target's normal flight path and force it to the ground faster than usual. For those few shooters who successfully shoot quicker than most of us, they will be able to fire at targets before the wind has any appreciable effect. During the initial 15 to 20 yards of the target's flight, it is not influenced by wind—it is still well under the influence of the momentum and speed produced by the trap machine. Most of us, however, will be shooting at targets influenced by the wind.

Let's assume that you have a properly-fitted gunstock and the shotgun's pattern prints a 50/50 percentage, i.e., half of the shot swarm is above a common sighting point and half below, and we are shooting trap in a head wind. Odds are that we will be attempting to break targets with only a half-pattern, which is really a handicap. It can be compared to attempting to hit targets with shells containing only ⁹/₁₆-ounce of shot (maximum shot charge is 1¹/₈ ounces for all 12-gauge competitive events). If the wind continues to consistently blow in a

A newcomer should not worry too much about stock fit until he first learns a basic shooting stance.

set direction, wouldn't it be nice to be able to change the gun's point of impact—immediately and easily?

To be a successful competitive shooter, we must learn how to properly adjust to all conditions. Until now, we've only highlighted and pointed out problems; now it is time to give some solutions.

Unquestionably, the dean of all stockmakers and one of the most respected in the world is Reinhart Fajen. Reinhart, now retired from actively pursuing the daily rigors of business life, still lives in Warsaw, Missouri. He has helped thousands of shotgun shooters with his unique ideas and innovative products; one of his very best products is the Fajen Try-Stock. Initially intended to be used by other stockmakers to accurately measure shooters, this fully-adjustable stock has proven to be a boon for hundreds of competitive trap and Skeet shooters. Remember earlier in this chapter when we discussed all the variables we will—or already have—encounter and wondered how to compensate for and correct them? In most cases, the Fajen Try-Stock allows shooters to make necessary "fitting" corrections to compensate for varying conditions, either physical or climatic. The following was written by Reinhart Fajen and provides excellent insight on correct shotgun stock fit.

The Fajen Try-Stock is certainly an usual looking apparatus, but that is because of its seemingly limitless adjustments and locking devices.

The position of the stock is too high on this shooter's shoulder which will cause him to absorb a greater amount of felt recoil because almost half of the stock is above contact with the shoulder.

The use of a try-gun stock enables the stock fitter and shooter to make adjustments on the field, under actual shooting conditions. This method will virtually guarantee that the shotgun will shoot exactly where the shooter is looking.

Most shotgun shooters cannot realize their ultimate shooting abilities if they are using guns that do not fit. They are continually forced to adjust themselves to the wrong dimensions in order to line up the beads and/or avoid recoil discomfort. Because they are not locked into a solid, comfortable shooting unit with their gun, they cannot concentrate entirely on the target. Even minor misalignments can have negative effects.

Some shooters can shoot accurately and comfortably with a gunstock right from the factory because the standard dimensions are close to their needs. Sometimes shooters can adjust with effort to the dimensions that are not quite right. Other shooters have the ability to take a shotgun with average dimensions, fire a few rounds, and be instinctively on target, learning to live with any uncomfortable recoil. Successful Skeet shooters are good at this and use a standard, average field-type stock. They do not depend on firm contact of the cheek to comb to line up with the target, and they learn to live with wherever the buttplate settles on their shoulder or chest. I think many of the better shooters could learn to shoot well from the hip without a buttstock. But, there are many shooters who do not have this natural ability and find it difficult to shoot accu-

rately and/or comfortably with a gun that does not fit properly.

Many shooters spend a lot of time and money trying different guns, or trading, in search of a gun that fits. The problem is that each shooter has his own combination of six or more important dimensions of a gunstock for a perfect fit. It is very unlikely a shooter will ever find that exact combination on any gun tried.

Trap and Skeet shooting are two shooting sports that require good gunstock fit for accuracy and freedom from recoil pain or discomfort. Painful recoil causes flinching and missed targets and can also take the pleasure out of shooting. It is very satisfying to shoot a shotgun and comfortably control recoil with a gunstock that fits properly.

Trapshooters especially must have a stock that fits for both accuracy and freedom from discomfort or pain at the shoulder, chest, cheek, cheekbone, or top of the middle finger of the trigger hand. Even a slight misfit at any of several points can develop into pain after a few rounds of 25 targets. It is important that the buttstock fit the shooter properly and comfortably so that complete attention can be given to the target.

A gunstock fits if the shooter can automatically, by

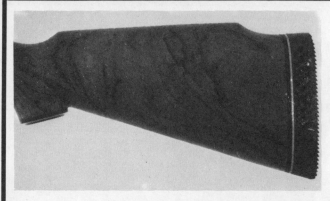

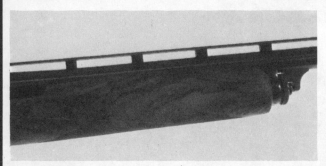

(Above and below) This stock for a Remington Model 31 is the author's "pet pumpgun" and was made by Pachmayr Gun Works from a piece of lightly-grained English walnut. Not only was the stock custom fitted, but the forend was also carefully proportioned to provide proper balance and handling qualities.

(Right) Some shooters prefer to place the trigger blade at the first joint on the index finger. There's no right or wrong way on trigger finger placement — whatever is most comfortable is the best location.

(Above) Placement of the trigger finger is an integral part of proper gun fit. Some shooter's prefer to place the fleshy pad of the finger, the most sensitive part, against the trigger blade.

the feel of the comb against his cheek and cheekbone and the feel of the buttplate in the right spot, place the gun consistently in shooting position so the barrel points at precisely the same object the shooter is looking at. Also, the shooter must have complete uniform control of the trigger and recoil, and feel no discomfort. These should be the requirements for every shooter during every shotgun shooting activity. Undivided attention can then be given to the target without worrying about lining up sights or the effects of recoil.

A very practical and quick way to determine gun-stock fit is by using a "try-stock" by a trained analyst. A good try-stock has at least six easily-, quickly- and precisely-adjustable comb and butt dimensions:

1. Drop from line of sight to point of comb.
2. Drop to Monte Carlo.
3. Drop to heel (top of buttplate or recoil pad).
4. Length of pull.
5. Thickness of comb.
6. Angle of buttplate or pad against shoulder or chest.
7. Positive trigger hand locater.

Without a try-stock the process can be long, arduous,

expensive and frustrating. It is difficult for shooters to determine for themselves what stock features or dimensions are best, even with a try-stock.

It is important that the three basic stock dimensions are determined in the following order: (1.) Pull, or length of stock, is decided first, giving a base to determine (2.) drop at the heel and (3.) the angle of the buttplate against the shoulder or chest. Then comb height and thickness can be determined. The length of pull is measured from the center front of the trigger to the rear center of the buttplate. This is the procedure generally followed; however, it is more accurate to determine pull by measuring the distance from the rear of the trigger guard to the center of the buttplate, especially if the pull dimension is used on various gun models. The rear of the trigger guard determines where your trigger hand and finger are placed, and this determines the *length-fit* of the stock. The trigger location within the guard can vary as much as 1-inch without affecting the stock fit. As you can see, if pull is measured on one gun with the trigger at the rear of the bow, and this same pull dimension is used on a gun with its trigger 1-inch forward, the *effective pull*, or *stock fit*,

The shooter is "crawling" the stock, which places his head too far forward on the stock. This incorrect position also causes the shooter to peer up through the top portion of his shooting glasses instead of looking through the middle.

It is important that the shooter's head be fairly erect so that he looks through the center of the shooting glasses. Any other position places additional stress on the eyes.

would be 1-inch different between the two guns. A uniform statement of pull can be given as: *the distance from the center of the rear of the buttplate to the rear center of the trigger guard bow, plus a nominal 1/2-inch to the front/center of the trigger.* This would give the same *fit* dimensions on guns where the trigger location varies within the bow.

Proper length of pull is determined by the shooter's physical dimensions, and more importantly, the shooting stance. Most successful shooters use the heads-up position rather than crawling forward with the head tilted down or sideways. This stance can develop when lining up with sights on a gun where the comb is too high or too thick. If the shooter leans forward, pull must be longer to prevent recoil from bumping his thumb into the shooter's nose.

I recommend the head-erect shooting stance. This permits the shooter to more accurately judge speed and location of target. It is especially important for shooters who wear glasses. They can look at the target through the center of their lenses rather than through the edge at an angle, which distorts their view. If the head-erect stance is used, the shooter must pose in that position while setting the try-stock. In some instances, this requires special effort to change from the tilted-head position. A changed stance requires different stock dimensions.

A suitable length can be determined for shooters wearing thin clothing. If heavier clothing is worn, later in the year, shooters will simply swing the gun farther forward to clear added thickness when mounting the gun. This will have no effect on the sight picture if the stock has a level comb and the drop from line of sight is the same wherever it is cheeked.

A stock is long enough if recoil does not jam the thumb into the shooter's nose, and short enough if the gun can be consistently placed into shooting position smoothly and comfortably. This usually leaves room to choose a suitable stock length if a level comb is used. The level comb usually calls for a Monte Carlo-style buttstock.

The second determination should be drop at the heel and the angle of the buttplate/recoil pad against the shoulder area. The drop at the heel is the distance from the line of sight, or extension, to the rear of the sighting plane level, down to the top of the buttplate.

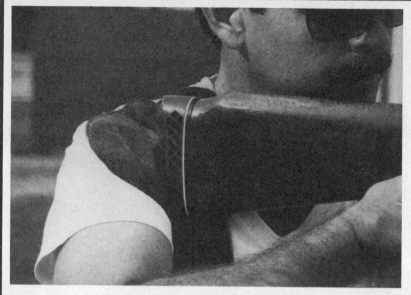

(Left) Placing the butt against the natural pocket formed at the shoulder when the arm is raised to approximately a 45-degree angle is the optimum position for proper gun fit and comfort.

(Below) A shooter's particular style often dictates stock dimensions. Remember that the most important part of stock fit is to make the stock fit you, not the other way around. One exception to this rule is if your shooting stance is totally wrong, then a new and proper stance should be learned *before* going through the expense of a new stock. A qualified stockmaker will determine if your stance is totally wrong, needs marginal improvement or is acceptable to breaking targets.

(Below) The Fajen Try-Stock allows positioning of the butt for pitch, toe-in or toe-out along with length of pull.

Location of the buttplate, or pad, is very important. Generally, recoil should be taken on the muscles in the shoulder and chest area. The buttplate should be placed so that the 2 or 3 inches in the center, or soft part of the recoil pad, fits solidly and squarely against this area. This avoids the hard top or bottom of the pad from punishing the shooter and helps put the buttplate consistently in the correct place. If contact of the butt is made on the shoulder, away from the chest, a curved trap-type pad is recommended for proper fit. If contact is made closer in on the chest, a flat Skeet-type pad may be called for or pads that are uniformly soft top to bottom may be used.

Generally, pitch should be between zero and 1½ inches down. This angle of the face of the buttplate, or recoil pad, should be square with the force of recoil thrust and parallel to the surface of the shoulder, or chest, where recoil is taken so that recoil is controlled comfortably and the gun remains in the same position against the shoulder before, during and after firing.

Excessive down pitch can cause the butt to slide upward off the shoulder from recoil and thus tighten against the cheekbone. Excessive up pitch makes it difficult to hold the butt up against the shoulder. Excessive up or down pitch leaves the gun out of shooting position for quick subsequent shots.

Special adjustments are called for by many shooters. Where the groove, or pocket, between the shoulder and chest is at an angle, the edge, or toe of the buttplate or recoil pad, may dig into the chest and prevent proper full contact with the center of the buttplate, or tend to cant the gun. Minor adjustments can be made by beveling the inside edge of the recoil pad or rounding off the bottom point of the recoil pad where it prevents proper fit. Most often, this is not adequate, so the toe only of the recoil pad must be turned away from fullness. This will also help prevent canting the gun in shooting position. This angle may be as much as 45 degrees off vertical to properly fit the groove between the shoulder and chest.

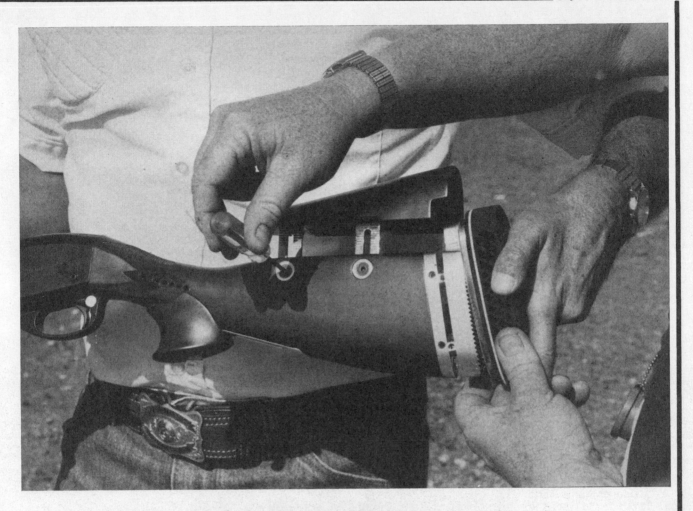

Adjustment to the try-stock comb is made by extending the removable comb upward and locking it in position with Allen screws. A similar procedure is used to fit other dimensions.

The proper trigger pull and drop of heel and position of the buttpad have now been determined and set on the try-stock. The next dimension to decide, and a most important one, is the drop of comb at the point of contact with the cheek and cheekbone.

The comb at the contact area should be a snug fit to the side of the cheek and under the cheekbone. The shooter can then, by feel, automatically and quickly line up with the sighting plane of the shotgun. With this firm contact, shooting position of the gun is always correct by feel without having to consciously line up with sights. This firm contact of the cheekbone with the top of the comb can result in bruising if the conventional-style stock, which slopes upward from the heel forward to the point of comb is used, or if the comb is too thick. With this type of stock, the pressure to the cheekbone will increase as recoil jolts the gun to the rear. It requires very few of these bumps to cause misses as well as pain and flinching with a common conclusion—"this model or brand of gun is not for me." The problem is

really the upward sloping comb and/or poor fit against the shoulder. If the comb is too thick, the shooter will be out of line with sights and will probably roll or cant the gun to be in line. This results in an uncomfortable, inaccurate shooting position. If the comb is too thin, there is no facial support for sight alignment with the front and rear bead on the shotgun.

For most shooters, the high Monte Carlo-type stock, with lower heel, permits the snug positive fit without recoil discomfort. The top of this stock is the same height at the point of comb, at the point of contact with the cheekbone, and at the Monte Carlo (the raised portion at the top rear). The comb tapers thinner toward the front and may slope downward slightly so that as the recoil pushes the gun toward the rear, pressure to the cheekbone actually lessens, and there is no danger of discomfort and no reason for flinching. Recoil will not jolt the gun back much independently in relation to the shooter if the butt fits solidly and squarely against the shooter's chest/shoulder area. There is more of a shove

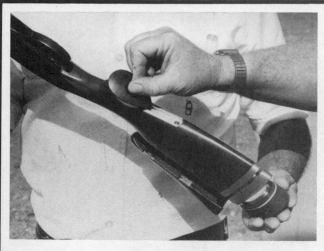

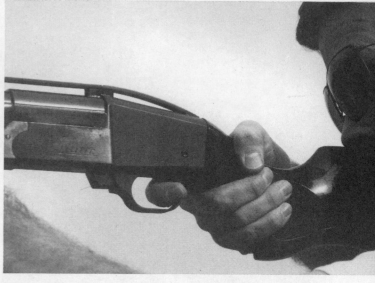

A unique feature of the Fajen Try-Stock is the adjustable pistol grip, which provides the stockmaker with a dimension from the inside of the pistol grip to the trigger.

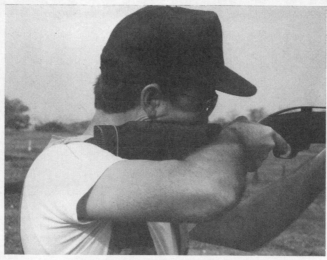

(Above) Notice that the shooter has a "death grip" on the shotgun and caused his master hand to encompass the pistol grip and place his trigger finger too far through the trigger guard.

(Right) If the sight picture for this shooter is correct, the stock is too high at the butt and a deeper Monte Carlo is needed to place the entire recoil pad in full contact with the shooter's shoulder.

moving the gun and the shooter back in unison. Consequently, there is no jarring or pain, and the gun stays in perfect shooting position for the next quick shot. The level comb also allows a variation in the horizontal point of contact of the cheekbone along with comb, without altering the sight picture. The comb on the try-stock can be made thicker or thinner to line the shooter's eye laterally with sights.

Accurate trigger control is very important for effective shooting. If the trigger is not pulled at the right instant, there is no hit. The shape and size of the pistol grip has a great deal to do with trigger control. Uniform trigger control can be had only if the trigger hand is in a uniform comfortable position on the grip of the gun for each shot. It is very difficult to uniformly grasp the grip of most guns that have a straight or half-moon shape far enough from the trigger so that Paul Bunyan himself would say, "It fits!" This shape and size permits the average shooter to place his hand anywhere from close to the trigger guard to an inch or more toward the rear. Unless the shooter consciously and care-fully places his hand in the same position each time, the trigger pull will be affected and a tight grip required to hold position. Several custom style grips are available that solve this problem. A more vertical grip, a thumb-hole type or the Etchen style with a locater lip or forward curve at the bottom front of the grip, will automatically place the trigger hand in exactly the same position each time for uniform trigger pull. This also aids in holding the gun firmly against the shoulder, which is necessary for better recoil control, without undue strain on the trigger hand. This positive location of the trigger hand also avoids bumping the rear of the trigger guard into the top of the middle finger. Incorporating the Wundhammer swell sometimes aids in a more comfortable positive grip. Some try-stocks have the adjustable Etchen-type grip and adjustable Wundhammer swell. Each can be set and recorded for further duplication.

With these vital dimensions established, the try-gun should be fired enough so that final fine adjustments can be made to suit the shooter. A few rounds at the trap

The advantage of a try-stock is its ability to lock the stock in any dimension and allow the shooter to "try" it on the firing line.

(Left) After testing the shotgun by shooting, the reshaped pistol grip may be rechecked and the entire stock refinished. This procedure will give the shooter a semi-custom stock at a price far less than a total restocking job.

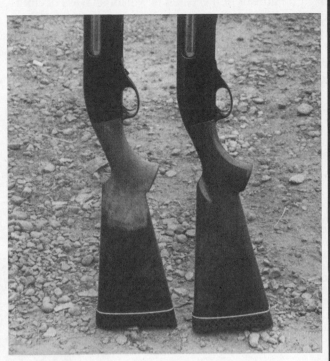

(Above) Grasping the pistol grip on a shotgun is like shaking hands with someone for the first time — it's all in the feel. Many of today's trap and Skeet guns have extra thick pistol grips designed that way by the factory. The shotgun on the left had the original pistol grip reshaped to better fit the shooter's hand. Some wood was removed from the wrist (the thinnest part) and the area in front of the comb was thinned to allow the hand to "get behind the gun." Any competent stockmaker can in short order reshape a pistol grip to better fit the shooter/customer.

line or Skeet field will help.

After the try-stock has been set to fit the shooter, the dimensions should be recorded so the existing stock can be altered or a new stock can be made to measure. A new stock is not always called for. Sometimes the existing stock on a gun can be altered to come closer to the ideal fit. Length of pull is usually easily lengthened by adding a recoil pad or spacers, and shortened by cutting off length. The comb can be thinned by removing wood and thickened or raised with a lace-on comb or by adding wood. An adjustable buttplate assembly can be installed for correct location against the muscle in the shoulder and chest area.

A gunstock with identical dimensions, according to the sighting plane, can be made for different types of guns, and the end result of hitting targets should be the same unless the guns do not shoot identically according to the sights. Shotgun sights are generally not easily adjustable, and shotguns of even the same model do not always shoot where the sights point. This can be confusing when one gun or barrel, according to the sights, shoots to the left and low at 25 yards and another shoots high and to the right. Making stocks of identical dimensions according to the sights would be a wasted effort in a case like this, and very disconcerting to a shooter using both guns. The center of your shot patterns can be determined by carefully shooting the gun at a spot or bullseye from a benchrest (recoil is usually noticed more when shooting from a benchrest so pad your shoulder). Before going through the expense of having a custom stock made, it should be determined that the point of impact is in line with the sights. Gunsmiths who specialize in this can bend single-barrel guns so that the shot pattern is in line with the sights. Some double guns have adjustments for this purpose.

Because a properly fitted stock against the shoulder area eliminates recoil pain, it would be best not to wear a shooting jacket with built-in shoulder padding. This added thickness tends to bunch up and distort proper fit to the shoulder when putting the gun in shooting position. So-called recoil eliminators would also probably not be needed.

Fajen's success with the try-gun stock has caused a great many trap and Skeet shooters to permanently replace their current stock with this unusual device—and for many good reasons. Earlier, we elaborated on different lengths of pull created by various layers of clothing. If a shooter wishes to shoot in a heavy, bulky jacket, the try-gun stock's existing length of pull can be shortened to proper length, ditto for angle or pitch. For shooters who drastically and quickly lose or gain weight that shows up in the cheek and cheekbone area,

ing more than the normal amount of clothing, etc.—and if you perform reasonably well with these different stock dimensions write them down. Don't trust your memory, make notes about why you made the changes and results. And, don't forget that when weather and shooting conditions revert to normal, re-adjust the stock to its original dimensions. An old-time shooting phrase sums up stock fit—"If it's hit, its history; if it's missed, it's a mystery!"

It is difficult for a seasoned competitor to change

Skeet shooting, for the most part, is a close-shooting game with targets rarely exceeding 25 yards. Gun fit is vitally important to World Class champions, but for the average Skeet shooter who wants to learn the game, most field-stocked shotguns are excellent "beginning" scatterguns.

the comb height and cast can also be altered easily and quickly with the try-stock.

The Fajen Try-Stock is a fiddler's delight, but its use can be overdone by a shooter lacking confidence in his particular shooting style. The try-stock cannot break more targets—only you can by shooting, shooting and more shooting. But, should shooting conditions vary, it can help you make necessary corrections. If you find that a certain set of dimensions work for you under certain shooting conditions—head wind, tail wind, wear-

timing or placement of the gun to the shoulder. Yet, if we are to compete—and hopefully win—we must learn how to adapt. How many times have you heard your shooting comrades say, "I know I was doing it wrong, but I just couldn't stop!" Nonsense. Bad habits can be broken easier than learning new techniques. Also remember that we compete because we enjoy our shooting sport, but if we are not shooting up to our potential most of the time, we are not enjoying ourselves. If we want to be aggravated, we can work weekends.

7

Trapshooting Fundamentals

POLLING THE TRAPSHOOTING wizards of today, they all agree on one point. Becoming the best trapshooter possible requires work, practice and dedication, not necessarily in that order. First, you must decide how much time, effort and money you want to put into your new shooting sport to achieve a level of competence. The more you shoot, both scheduled events and useful practice sessions, the more proficient you'll become. Please remember, the best any tutorial can do is explain the basics; converting these instructions into a form you can use is something you must do yourself.

The beginner should understand that there are many confusing aspects to trapshooting fundamentals. Trapshooting is divided into three separate divisions: 16-yard (Singles), Handicap and Doubles. The shooter's stance and gun mount are basically the same for all three events. There are a few nuances we will discover a bit later, but for now we can state that a proper stance and gun mount for 16-yard targets will work fine for Handicap or Doubles shooting. Gun mount and the proper shooting stance are broken into smaller sections for easier understanding.

There's no better way to enjoy a Sunday afternoon than to visit a local gun club and shoot a few rounds of trap with your buddies. A successful trapshooter must demonstrate "relaxed concentration" to consistently break good scores.

Advice from fellow shooters, classes, video tapes, audio cassettes, books, and photographs that illustrate or preach proper shooting form or define leads and timing don't mean anything until you can hit the target with regularity. The knack of making the shot charge and flying clay target meet at a given point is something that you can only learn by yourself. It's been stated over and over by many competition shooters that given a shotgun, enough ammunition and money, even a chimpanzee could eventually become a AA, 27-yard trapshooter or a AAA Skeet shooter with all four guns.

The Master Eye

Do you know which eye is your master eye? No? Do you know what a "master eye" is. Another no? Before we become too involved in gun mount and stance, we have to establish "eye dominance," or determine which eye is your "master eye." People are classified as right- or left-handed and the same holds true for eye dominance. Surprisingly, a large percentage of shooters do not know which eye is dominant. For right-handed shooters, the right eye is usually the "master," vice versa for southpaws. Unfortunately though, nature sometimes makes mistakes and righties are burdened with left-eye dominance.

Perhaps the easiest and fastest test to determine eye dominance is to make a circle with the index finger and tip of the thumb of your right hand. Pick a spot on the wall or any small object about 10 feet away. Keeping both eyes open, encircle the target with your handmade "O" and extend your hand approximately 12 to 15 inches from your face. After the target is centered, close your left eye. If the object remains in the circle, your right eye is dominant. If the object moves out of the circle, to the left, your left eye is dominant.

Neat test, huh? If you've discovered that your right eye is dominant and you're a right-handed shooter, all's well. The opposite holds true for lefties. But, if you've proven that your master side and master eye are 180 degrees opposed, some corrective measures must be taken before any shooting lessons begin. Novices may ask what the big deal is; they "shoot pool" or participate in many other hand-to-eye coordination games with both eyes open and never encounter any problems — why is trapshooting different? The problem is that shooters must sight down the barrel and pick up the flight of the target at the same time, which can only be done properly when both eyes work together. The master eye provides the shooter with a proper line of sight, while the "off" eye takes care of depth perception and peripheral vision. It's really more complicated than that simple explanation, and an optometrist could undoubtedly give a more detailed scientific explanation.

There are proven ways right-handed shooters can overcome having a left master eye. The obvious method is to completely cover the left eye with a patch or blacken out the left lens of the shooting glasses. Neither is recommended because eliminating one eye will cause the other to do double duty and nature will make the single eye provide depth perception, which is primarily the role of the "off" eye. A better way is to merely diffuse the left eye's vision by placing a small $3/4 \times 1^1/2$-inch strip of Scotch Magic Mending tape directly on the left lens of your shooting glasses. This will allow the left eye to "see out," but will reduce its dominance. Therefore, if only the right eye has clear vision of the target, it will artificially assume the role of the master.

An expensive way to compensate for "wrong" eye dominance is to have a special "cripple" stock made for the shotgun. The late John Amber, of *Gun Digest* fame, is one of the more notable shooters who used this unorthodox system for many years. Anyone who had butted shotguns with this fine gentleman knew that John was certainly not handicapping himself by using a crossover stock. Briefly, this stock has an acute bend in it slightly behind the wrist (grip) area. This enables the right-handed shooter to place his head and cheek in a traditional position, but the stock's "bend" is approximately the distance between the width of his eyeballs. Therefore, the shooter retains his right-hand dominance while peering down the barrel's rib with his left eye. These unusual stocks are only made by master stockmakers who can accurately select a stock blank with properly-structured grain that will withstand recoil without shattering after a few rounds are fired.

There are also auxiliary ribs which can be attached to the side of the shotgun barrel, which allow the shooter to sight down a second "railroad track." I've also seen mini-ribs glued, soldered or epoxied to a shotgun's main rib to provide a level shooting plane. Wherever there are shooters with handicaps, you'll find interesting ways to overcome these minor inconveniences.

In fact, the most ingenious method of overcoming "wrong-eye dominance" occurred in 1968 during a 500-target, 16-yard marathon in Walla Walla, Washington. I witnessed a remarkable degree of success by a shooter who overcame the dreaded wrong-eye syndrome. Throughout the 20 fields covered that day, this elderly gentleman shot the entire 500-target event by placing the shortened buttstock on his left shoulder, grasping the pistol grip on his ancient Winchester Model 12 with his right hand and placing his left cheek against the right side of the buttstock. In essence, he was shouldering the gun left-handed, but shooting right-handed, using his only "good" eye. He later explained to me that he lost his eye in an industrial accident only 18 months earlier and now attempted to shoot left-handed. But because he was nearly 60 years old, he couldn't successfully make the drastic changeover. Yet his score for the marathon was well into the 490s out of 500 and, as I recall, he won his class handily.

Gun Mount

There's an old adage that "form follows function." Form in trap or Skeet shooting is probably more important than in most other hand-and-eye coordinated sports. To attain and retain the proper shooting style, it must be cultivated early in the game because there's nothing more difficult than changing one's style after it has virtually become a habit. The other adage about "old dogs and new tricks" must be discarded, because if you have bad or improper form, you are hurting your chances of taking that nice big silver platter home to the house frau. If you seek professional advice, which I strongly suggest, take heed and make the physical changes to your stance.

Trapshooting instructors prefer to work with total neophytes rather than experienced shooters because they don't have to undo bad habits. That way they can start from page one and teach the new shooter the proper way to stand, how to shoulder the gun and about lead and the sight picture. There are only four physical points where the shooter is in contact with the shotgun — both hands, cheek and shoulder. Simply stated, gun mounting is the act of picking up the shotgun with both

Mounting Do's and Don'ts

(Top left) This is a modified form of a rifleman's position and the elevated right elbow places too much strain on the shooter's neck muscles. The nearly vertical left arm causes the left shoulder to droop and brings it too far forward thereby upsetting the shooter's balance.

(Bottom left) Here, the shooter's right arm is improperly positioned and the left arm is too high, which prevents the shooter from balancing the shotgun properly.

(Top right) This is the opposite extreme and the lowered right arm virtually eliminates the "pocket" formed at the shoulder when the arm is elevated to approximately 45 degrees.

(Bottom right) This is just about perfect arm position for most shooters. The right arm is held high enough to form a proper "pocket" in which to place the shotgun butt while the left arm is in balance to hold the shotgun. To check your own shooting style against these photos, stand in front of a mirror and compare your own arms' position.

(Left) It almost looks like somebody pulled the chair out from under this shooter. Many shooters over the years have used this type of aggressive stance. This stance is very fatiguing however, especially for a 200- to 300-target shooting day.

(Right) The shooter should stand fairly erect with his weight slightly forward. The left leg is slightly bent at the knee to keep the weight forward, allowing for a smooth swing of the upper torso in either direction.

hands, bringing it up to the cheek, and placing it against the shoulder. This seemingly uncomplicated maneuver has proven to be the downfall of many trapshooters before they really ever had a chance to become good shots. The biggest problem I've witnessed over the years is the way most tyros mount the shotgun.

Head Position

For inexplicable reasons, the most common mounting error is when the novice brings the gun to his shoulder and then cants his head against the stock. This incorrect mounting method creates the following problems. First, because the shooter's head is not level to the ground, his eyes are also at an unnatural "cant." None of us walk around with our heads tilted, yet too many competitors shoot in this most unnatural manner. Second, this position places undue stress and strain on the shoulder and neck muscles. In a very short time, these muscles will revolt by cramping and the obvious result will be "lost" targets. Proper stance, therefore, must be comfortable and within reasonable limits of total control of the shotgun through the various arcs of the target.

Body and Foot Stance

Stance and style vary greatly from one shooter to the next, and I've seen some exceptionally high scores recorded by shooters with strange-looking stances. One that especially comes to mind is that of a shooter from California named George Joseph who used to crouch so low that his right knee grazed the ground. George appeared as though he was "sneaking up on the targets." It worked for him, as he and his brother Bob cleaned up during the early and mid-1960s at West Coast trapshoots. But these shooters are exceptions to the rules of stance and body control and a new shooter should not copy one of these "off-beat" stances just to look like a seasoned competitor.

Foot position in relation to the anticipated flight of the target is also critical. The shooter must place his feet in a position that will enable him to twist his body — from the waist — to any comfortable position within a 45-degree arc in relation to the post on which he is standing. In Chapter 3, there is a chart showing the legal flight path of the trap target — about 22 degrees on either side of a straight line from the center post or Sta-

Pictured is a rifleman's stance which is too rigid, preventing the shooter from attacking a fast-flying angle target.

The shooter is standing "square" to the target and cannot move his upper torso to intercept an acute right-angle target. The shooter must position his feet, as well as the rest of his body, to track a target anywhere within a 44-degree arc of the station on which he is standing.

tion Three. Take another look at it now for a better understanding of "legal target flight path."

Following, or tracking, the target is not done by swinging the shotgun from the shoulders and arms, but by pivoting from the waist and flexing the lead knee. The shotgun, arms, neck, shoulders, head and eyes should be locked together as a single unit and move together when the shooter goes after the target. The lead leg should be slightly bent at the knee for flexibility of the upper body and control over changes needed for shotgun elevation. In other words, rotating from the waist controls the horizontal movements and the lead leg directs vertical adjustments. The flexed knee also provides proper front-to-rear stability because recoil will shove the shooter backward as soon as the shot is fired. The knee, therefore, also acts as a shock absorber, and as the upper body is jolted by the shotgun's recoil, the left knee is automatically straightened and the shooter's balance regained. Naturally, these two body parts must learn to work in perfect unison, but in time and after a few hours of introducing Mr. Waist to Mr. Knee, they'll go together like ham and eggs.

I've had numerous shooters ask how far apart they should spread their feet. This distance will vary because no two people are built alike. But as a guide, most shooters can hold their balance by spreading their heels about 9 to 12 inches. Wider stances seem to "lock up" a shooter, preventing a smooth approach to the target, and narrower stances tend to reduce the shooter's stability by creating a smaller angle of balance. The most important consideration, though, is comfort. If the above dimensions are not natural or comfortable, disregard them — but only if you are breaking good scores and not having serious shooting problems.

Have you ever noticed that today's shotgun magicians seem to have an almost nonchalant shooting style. They

Foot position is not dependent on what yardage line the shooter is standing on, but rather on what station, from One to Five.

This modified rifleman's stance with the elevated right elbow places too much strain on the shooter's neck and back muscles. In addition, the shooter's lead leg is not bent limiting his flexibility. His entire upper torso is too far forward, upsetting the shooter's balance.

always seem relaxed and under total body control — and they really are. They learned early in their careers that a proper and comfortable stance prevents fatigue and allows them to concentrate totally on the forthcoming target. Correct stance and gun placement will, with enough practice, become intuitive. Achieving this perfection usually happens after a few months of shooting. To paraphrase a psychoanalyst, "If a person performs a physical or mental act the same way 21 consecutive times, predicated by thinking about it, the 22nd occurrence will happen automatically, without thinking about it." Proper stance can quickly be learned and practiced, and in a short time, will become second nature.

Hand and Arm Position

Positioning the shooter's hands and arms in relation to the shotgun are also a part of proper stance and form. Let's first discuss the hands. The master hand — the one that grasps the pistol grip and manipulates the trigger — is the most important. Initially it should encircle the pistol grip firmly, and just before firing the shotgun, it should be squeezed tighter. The master hand controls the gun while the off-hand merely supports the front. There are those who preach and teach that the off-hand controls the gun while the other hand merely pulls the trigger. Tain't so! Taking a firm grip on the shotgun with the master hand keeps the buttstock locked in position against the shoulder and also helps to absorb a great deal of the gun's generated recoil through anticipation of firing.

Observe the finer trapshooters and note the way they take a large amount of recoil through the master hand — there's hardly any rearward movement of their shoulders when the shotgun is fired. Then observe some of

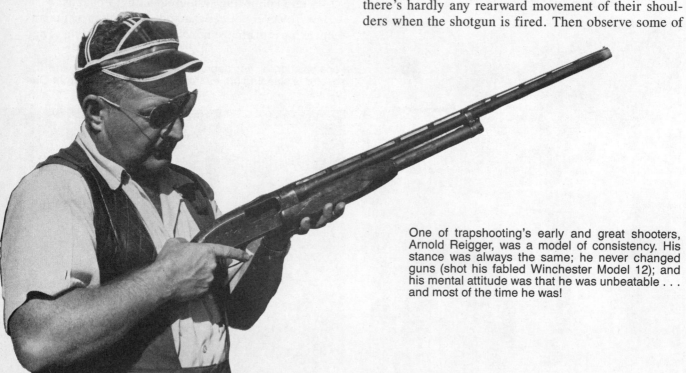

One of trapshooting's early and great shooters, Arnold Reigger, was a model of consistency. His stance was always the same; he never changed guns (shot his fabled Winchester Model 12); and his mental attitude was that he was unbeatable . . . and most of the time he was!

Off-hand Placement

Placement of the off-hand regulates the shotgun's balance point, thus if the hand is too far forward (top left and right), the shooter will have a tendency to swing the shotgun slower than normal. With the hand about midway on the forend (middle), a normal barrel swing can be obtained. If the shooter needs a faster swing to catch up with unusually fast flying targets, sliding the off-hand rearward (bottom left and right) will increase barrel speed.

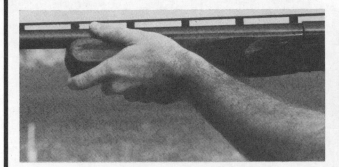 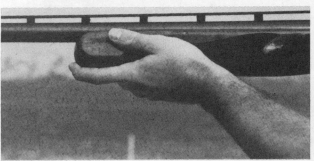

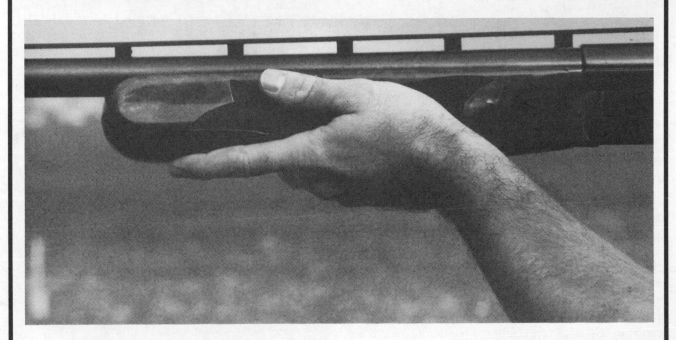

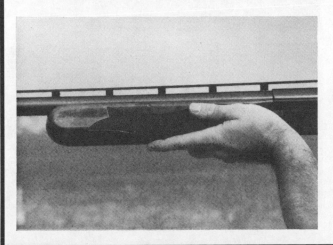 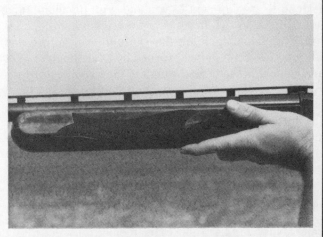

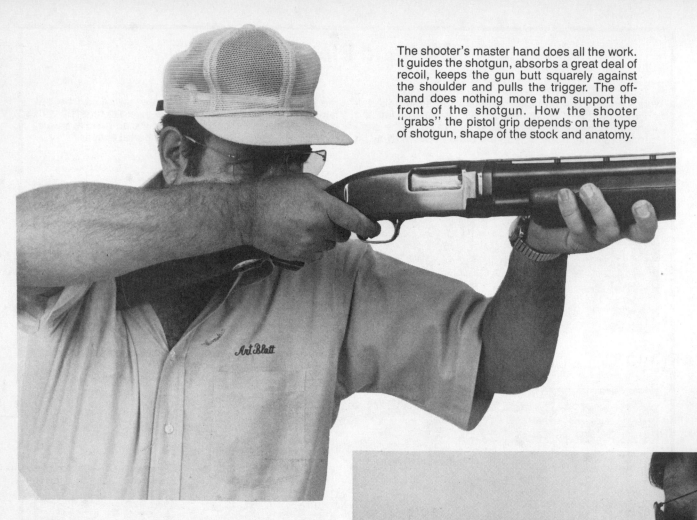

The shooter's master hand does all the work. It guides the shotgun, absorbs a great deal of recoil, keeps the gun butt squarely against the shoulder and pulls the trigger. The off-hand does nothing more than support the front of the shotgun. How the shooter "grabs" the pistol grip depends on the type of shotgun, shape of the stock and anatomy.

(Right) Some shooters, usually those who have had considerable handgun shooting experience, prefer to place the pad of the index finger on the trigger. This is the most sensitive part of the finger and provides the best "feel" for the trigger.

the newer shooters, they look like they're getting beat to death—and they literally are! Next time you're at the trap range, try this enlightening experiment. Step up to the line, load a shell in the chamber and mount the gun as if you're ready to call for a target, but don't. Instead, keep your trigger finger out of the trigger guard and ask a friend to step up next to you and with his thumb and index finger, have him squeeze the trigger at his discretion. Not knowing when the shotgun will go off, the full recoil effect will be absorbed by your shoulder. Not only does this scenario dramatize the full effects of recoil, but it helps establish the fact that the master hand does indeed absorb a great deal of the generated recoil.

What is the "proper" position of the trigger finger against the trigger blade? It is up to the shooter. I personally prefer to place the first pad, the most sensitive area of the index finger, against the trigger blade, prob-

(Right) Other shooters prefer to place the trigger blade in the index finger's first joint, which allows the hand to take a firmer hold on the pistol grip. Either method is correct; it is up to the shooter to determine what works best.

116

ably because of early handgun training. Some shooters place the trigger blade in the first joint. Again, it's a matter of personal preference. If one system doesn't work for you, try the other.

While discussing how to "activate" a trigger, I would like to take on a "sacred cow" among many shotgunners. All too often we read that shotgun triggers should be "slapped," which, by definition, means that the trigger finger should not touch the trigger until the instant of firing. The reasons given for this method are safety, overcoming heavy triggers and getting a quick response. Personally, I don't find any of these explanations valid. First, stationing the trigger finger away from the trigger until that sudden "moment of truth" is time-consuming and requires a complex series of instructions for the new shooter to learn. Like one of Parkinson's Laws, "More Complex — Sooner Dead," keep movements simple and straightforward. Second, regarding excessive trigger pull weights, there's no reason for any competitive trap or Skeet shooter to use a shotgun with an inordinately heavy trigger pull weight. What is considered "inordinate?" In the past decade, most quality competition guns were set at the factory to release at between 3½ and 5 pounds. Recently, however, many trap and Skeet guns have had their triggers "factory adjusted" to meet specifications and restrictions set forth by the insurance companies that carry the manufacturer's liability insurance. For some inexplicable reason, known only to these underwriters, they have forced shotgun makers to increase trigger pull weights to the point of being ridiculous. I've

Arm position is extremely important. Unless a shooter has some sort of physical handicap, the elbows should be approximately 45 degrees to the ground. This position will allow the shooter maximum comfort and natural movement of his upper torso.

(Right) This ex-rifle shooter is "locked up" and angled targets will give him fits. His left elbow is too high which impedes gun movement. He is trying to overcompensate for this deficiency by sliding his off-hand too far rearward. This is a good example of bad form.

(Left) This shooter has his elbow a bit too high, but the position of his off-hand, far forward, keeps his swing smooth, yet very deliberate.

117

Arm Position

Arm position when shooting trap is critical. (Top left) Here, both arms are raised too high which prevents the shooter from enjoying comfort and balance. All of these positions (top right, bottom left and right) tend to bind the shooter's arms and back muscles. Therefore, none are considered correct. Can you spot the errors?

recently tested "competition"-type trap and Skeet guns with trigger pulls in excess of 10 pounds, which is at least twice as heavy as they should be for needed sensitivity and quick response between shooter and shotgun.

On the other side of the coin, a trigger pull can be too light. Anything less than 3 pounds is not recommended because even the slight pressure of the shooter's natural tightening of the finger just before the shot is fired can prematurely release the trigger. Also, if the shotgun is dropped with a live shell in the chamber, an excessively-light trigger sear could slip off its precarious perch and allow the hammer to release to strike the firing pin. I've been able to "accidentally" fire a shotgun with a lightened trigger — releasing at 2 pounds — by first making certain that there was no live shell in the chamber, and then from a height of approximately 12 inches, dropping the buttstock onto a hard surface. This is a controlled test, of course, but nevertheless valid to determine if a shotgun's trigger pull is too light and unsafe under any conditions.

Correct arm and elbow position is subject to a shooter's needs and comfort. Generally though, the position of the elbows should be about 45 to 50 degrees relative to the horizontal plane of the shotgun. Some shooters prefer a "high" elbow, similar to the style prescribed by rifle shooters. In this position, a better-fitting pocket is formed at the shoulder in which to place the shotgun butt. The advantage of the "low" elbow is that it is more natural, thus comfortable, and is less tiring for the shooter over the long haul. I've also noticed that many shooters who develop a dreaded "cant" usually shoot with a high elbow, and lowering the elbow "straightens out" the "cant." Therefore, elbow position is a shooter's choice, and the new shooter should initially try each style and eventually settle on the elbow position that works best for him.

General Muzzle Position

One of the questions most often asked by beginners is where to hold the shotgun barrel in relation to the trap house. To answer that question, I must say that to become a skillful trapshooter, the tyro must first pick up the flight of the target as soon as it leaves the trap house and second, shoot at the target as close to the house as possible. The position of the gun, therefore, is critical to performing these two important criteria.

Where the muzzle is held over the house depends on eye usage. Two-eyed shooters can hold a "high" gun, or one that is over the top of the trap house roof. How high over depends on the flight of the target. For now, we'll simply classify a two-eyed shooter as one who should hold a "high" gun. If you are a one-eyed shooter you should hold a "low" gun, that is the muzzle starting position should be slightly below the top of the trap house roof. This "high" or "low" gun business may be a bit confusing, so let's take a deeper look

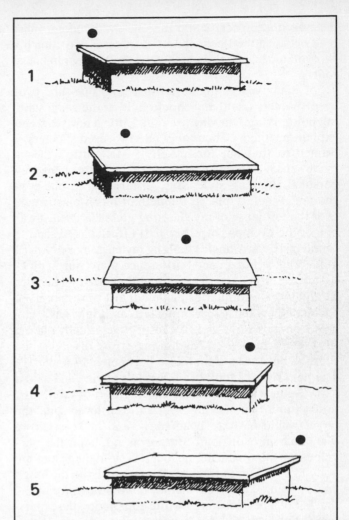

These are the correct points for a two-eyed trapshooter to hold his muzzle when calling for the target from Station One through Five. The amount of vertical hold above the house depends on the weather conditions and if the wind is affecting the flight of the targets. If the target is "flat," caused by a tail wind, 12 to 16 inches above the roof of the trap house is correct. If the wind is incoming however, it will raise the target very quickly and therefore the shooter should hold a higher gun — from 24 to 30 inches above the roof.

at the two terms. If $1 in the pocket is good, $2 are better. That is one way to describe the advantages of a two-eyed shooter over one who must only use one for sundry reasons. The two-eyed shooter subconsciously looks down the shotgun rib with his master eye while his "off" eye looks past the barrel down at the trap house, waiting for the target. The one-eyed shooter does not have this "bonus feature." Therefore, the one-eyed shooter must ask his good eye to perform both functions — look at the top of the trap house for the target *and* maintain correct sight alignment while peering down the shotgun's rib. Both tough jobs are quite a burdensome task for the one-eyed shooter.

So, with regard to muzzle position and the top of the trap house, the two-eyed shooter has the luxury of holding a "high" gun with a muzzle that is above the top of the trap house roof, while the one-eyed shooter must read between the lines, and in most cases, position his shotgun muzzle slightly below the top of the trap house roof.

For many years, I believed that both one- and two-eyed shooters could and should hold at the same starting point. After listening to Frank Little a few years ago explain his theory about one- and two-eyed shooters, I wanted to find out for myself if Mr. Little's theory made sense. As a two-eyed shooter, I did not change my personal shooting style. But, to turn into a one-eyed shooter, I merely placed a length of black plastic tape over the left lense of my shooting glasses. Then, I was one of the cyclops corp. My first effort was to shoot a round of 16-yard singles holding my customary "high" gun. What a monumental difference there was in picking up the flight and determining the speed and angle. Straightways and quarter angles didn't pose too many problems, but those screaming left- and right-angle targets from posts one and five respectively really did me in. I won't further embarrass myself by divulging the score — but it was somewhere between a 17 and a 19. The next round I took Frank Little's advice and held a "low" gun with the muzzle starting at roof level. One might think that starting with an even lower gun, the target would have a "head start" and make catch up that much more difficult. But, my mind, being the marvelous calculating machine that it is, told the rest of my body to speed up in tracking the target. Even the tough angles seemed more catchable. It would be nice to say that I shot a perfect 25x25 while completing the experiment, but I can't. I did however, prove to myself that the "low" gun principle works because I did shoot a respectable 23x25.

Muzzle Position for Singles and Handicap Shooting

Now, we can go through barrel placement post by post, which will be the same for Singles (16-yard) or Handicap shooting. Doubles will be discussed a little later. Again, we're going to explain gun position for a right-handed shooter; in most cases, lefties will have to mirror these instructions.

At Station One most right-handed shooters swing better to the left than to the right. Swinging "better" means that the movement of the shotgun and body is more natural due to the position of the arms and shoulders. Also, when the gun is moved to the left, the comb has a tendency to "stick" to the shooter's cheek because the master hand forces the stock to the face while moving the entire shotgun after the fleeting target.

Stand up and assume your shooting stance. Pretend you have your trap gun cradled between your hands and assume a mounted position with the gun shouldered, placing your right hand up to your cheek and your left hand out where you would hold up the front part of the shotgun. Then, visualize that you have called for your target and a sharp left angle appeared. Quickly go after

it. Did you notice that your right hand seemed to automatically press harder against your cheek? If it didn't, it should have, so try it a few more times. Then perform the same experiment pretending that you are going after a tougher right-angle target. This part of the experiment should illustrate the tendency for a right-handed shooter to pull the stock and comb away from his face and cheek — not by design, but due to muscular makeup. This body reaction is reflexive and is similar to backing away from somebody who's going to throw a punch at you. The point is that if we can understand what our body is going to do before it does it, the brain can make corrections to compensate.

Trap machines are supposed to be located dead center within the trap house, but quite often they aren't. The shooter can quickly determine the machine's position by watching the target's flight on the preceding squad. If a "straightaway" target from Station Three appears to be on a dead straight line with the 50-yard stake, the machine is properly located. The correct starting position of the gun barrel in relation to the trap house for Station One is about 18 inches above the left corner of the trap house. At Station Two, the muzzle should be aimed at a point halfway between the left corner and the center of the trap house. Usually, most shooters are taught to hold dead center on Station Three. I believe this is poor advice due to the flight of a straightaway target, which seems to come out of the house directly under the barrel. Therefore, the target's initial flight is obscured by the gun barrel. I recommend a hold slightly to the right of center, about 9 to 12 inches, which allows the shooter to quickly "read" a straightaway target. A left-handed shooter should hold to the left of center. At Station Four, the barrel should be pointed to a spot halfway between the right-hand corner and center as prescribed for Station Two, but closer to the outside edge of the trap house. At Station Five, the shooter should "cheat" even more by starting at a point 12 to 15 inches outside of the trap house's right-hand corner. A right-handed shooter should hold more to the right on posts three, four and five because of what we discussed earlier about why a right-handed shooter swings better to the left. "Favoring" the muzzle position on these posts helps the shooter catch up on those tougher, right-angle targets.

These muzzle starting positions are subject to change as wind conditions dictate. In the event of a head wind which will quickly elevate targets, the shooter should raise the muzzle and hold a "higher" gun. Depending on the velocity of the wind, a proper hold could range from 18 to 30 inches above the roof of the trap house. Conversely, should a trailing wind appear which drives the targets down, a "lower" gun mount would be in order, ranging from 6 inches below the roof line to 6 inches above it. If a cross wind has an apparent effect on the target's flight, the smart shooter will make gun positioning adjustments accordingly.

Proper Hold Positions

This five photo sequence illustrates the proper "hold" position for a right-handed shooter, post by post. The rubber pylon is used for reference. On Station 1 (top left) the muzzle should be aimed at the left corner of the trap house, about 18 inches high; on Station 2 (top right) approximately midway between dead center and the left edge of the trap house; on Station 3 (middle), dead center of the house, or slightly to the right of center if the shooter has a problem seeing the target emerge from under his barrel; on Station 4 (bottom left), approximately midway between center and the right edge of the trap house; on Station 5 (bottom right) hold to the outer edge of the trap house, or even farther out if you are having problems catching up to a hard right-angle target.

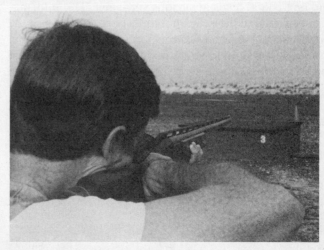

The better shooters can quickly pick up the direction of the target as it leaves the trap house, while others see it as a flashing blur. As soon as you can determine and chart the target's course, move the muzzle ahead of the target and pull the trigger, shooting as quickly as possible. Learn how to shoot fast without rushing the shot, don't attempt to become too fine in your pointing. The longer you wait on a target, the farther the target will travel so never hesitate or ride a target. If you acquire this bad habit, it'll be be very difficult to overcome. Also, the longer the target is in flight, the more subject it is to the whims of wind. The finest trapshooters shoot quickly at a target, usually within 17 to 20 yards from the trap house. Within this distance, even the strongest wind has little effect on the target, which is one reason all the top guns love to shoot big events on windy days.

Rarely will an instructor advise new shooters where to focus their eyes. Some shooters stare at the front sight like rifle and pistol shooters and some concentrate on the trap house. The preferred method is to look down the barrel while focusing on an area about 17 yards past the trap house, looking for the target. The end of the barrel will automatically be in your peripheral vision and the muzzle will be naturally guided to the target by your eyes. The one-eyed shooter must sight down the rib and wait for the target to appear before going after it as quickly as possible.

When shooting at moving targets, a "lead" is necessary to make the shot swarm and target arrive together. But how much lead? That is an impossible question for anyone other than the shooter to answer. Scientifically, we can compute the amount of lead necessary to hit a 50 mph target flying away at a 32-degree angle. Factoring in the velocity of the shot charge at 35 yards, our user-friendly home computer can tell us down to the 10th of an inch how much lead is necessary. But no two human brains compute the same, especially in open space. What appears to be 12 inches to one shooter may be 3 feet to another due to the speed of a shooter's swing. An accompanying chart defines both vertical and horizontal leads at various yardages. This information is predicated on the shotgun's barrel moving at the same visual speed as the target. Yet, under actual shooting conditions, some people move the gun faster than the apparent speed of the target, and some move

COMPUTED LEADS FOR TRAP SHOOTING

Station	Target Position	16 Yds. Lead (in.) Horiz.	Vert.	21 Yds. Lead (in.) Horiz.	Vert.	27 Yds. Lead (in.) Horiz.	Vert.
1	1	0	7	0	10	0	15
	2	10	7	13	10	17	15
	3	19	8	25	11	34	16
	4	27	10	36	13	48	17
	5	35	12	45	15	61	19
2	1	10	7	13	10	18	15
	2	0	7	0	10	0	15
	3	10	7	13	10	18	15
	4	19	8	25	11	34	16
	5	27	10	36	12	48	17
3	1	19	8	25	11	34	16
	2	10	7	13	10	18	15
	3	0	7	0	10	0	15
	4	10	7	13	10	18	15
	5	19	8	25	11	34	16
4	1	27	10	36	13	48	17
	2	19	8	25	11	34	16
	3	10	7	13	10	18	15
	4	0	7	0	10	0	15
	5	10	7	13	10	18	15
5	1	35	12	45	15	61	19
	2	27	10	36	13	48	17
	3	19	8	25	11	34	16
	4	10	7	13	10	18	15
	5	0	7	0	10	0	15

slower. Therefore, a shooter with a faster swing must reduce his "lead" as prescribed in the chart; conversely, a shooter with a slower swing must increase the prescribed amount of "lead."

Someone once said Skeet shooting was difficult to learn and easy to master, but nobody said trapshooting was easy to learn. Once proper leads are emblazoned on a shooter's mind, they're there forever, so don't fret if you're confused about leads and timing. They'll eventually come to you with practice, practice and more *practice*.

Muzzle Position for Doubles Shooting

In Doubles, the shooter is required to shoot at two targets thrown simultaneously while standing on the 16-yard line. As a rule, the "straightaway" target is shot at first and then the angled target. Sounds easy enough, doesn't it? Yet, Doubles is trapshooting's most difficult game for newcomers. Unlike Singles and Handicap, in which only one target and shot is required, Doubles demands specialized equipment. Single shot shotguns are obviously not recommended. Most Doubles shooters prefer over/under shotguns because of the availability of two different chokes and the over/under's high degree of reliability. Some Doubles contestants use autoloading shotguns, but that is frowned on by other shooters because of the shotgun's

VELOCITY AND TIME OF FLIGHT OF TARGETS AT VARIOUS DISTANCES FROM TRAP HOUSE

Distance	Velocity (fps)	Flight Time
0 yards	85 fps	—
20 yards	47 fps	1.0 seconds
25 yards	43 fps	1.3 seconds
30 yards	40 fps	1.7 seconds
50 yards	31 fps	3.4 seconds

ejection system. Unless the autoloader is altered so that it launches the empty hulls away from nearby shooters, the shooter using an autoloading gun not so equipped will often be asked to quit shooting on that particular squad—and rightly so. Being hit anywhere on the body with an ejected empty hull is very distracting and irritating. I don't recommend autoloaders for Doubles events for that reason.

I do not recommend that a trapshooting newcomer jump right into Doubles until he has become fairly proficient at both Singles and Handicap shooting. Shooting a poor score at Doubles tends to lower a shooter's confidence, and as a result, Singles and Handicap averages usually plummet. Learn one segment at a time before advancing to a more difficult challenge.

Someone once said that Doubles was nothing more than shooting two Singles targets. That's really oversimplifying a much more complex shooting game — complex because the two targets are not only shot differently but shot at with dissimilar techniques, chokes and often ammunition. No, shooting at ATA Doubles is not at all like shooting at two 16-yard Singles targets.

To be a good, consistent Doubles shooter, the newcomer must have acquired a particular shooting attribute — aggressiveness. An excellent 16-yard Singles shooter can be somewhat lethargic and still break high average scores. The same shooter can even be a bit deliberate and break big scores in Handicap events. But a nonaggressive shooter will not break big Doubles scores until he develops a forceful attitude toward his Singles and Handicap shooting. Only then, when he learns how to shoot the other two games with almost reckless abandon, will his Doubles shooting flourish.

The overwhelming majority of top Doubles shooters nationwide use over/under shotguns for at least three reasons. First, two barrels allow the shooter to custom choke his gun exclusively for the two targets because each target is shot at extremely different ranges. Second is reliability. Let's face it, we've all seen some terrible reloaded ammunition. Most of the time the hulls are swollen and have not been completely resized to original specifications. These reloads shoot and pattern well enough, but they usually will not cycle in autoloading shotguns. Though they almost always eject, they will not always load into the shotgun's chamber because they are simply oversized. Yet, these same shells can be forcefully inserted into over/under chambers with little effort. As an autoloading shotgun loads up with carbon in the gas system, the action has a tendency to slow down. If the buildup becomes too heavy for the mechanism to overcome, a failure to feed or eject becomes commonplace. In my opinion, unless the shooter meticulously maintains his autoloader, he will encounter problems on the Doubles fields that could easily cost him targets or a championship. And third, as the overwhelming majority of trapshooters today are opting and using "combo" sets, the back half of the shotgun has become an old, trusted friend. A quick switch of barrel assemblies allows the shooter to convert his combo into a Doubles gun.

Now that we've established the proper shootin' iron, let's determine what the best chokes are for shooting Doubles. First, we must find out how far away the targets are that we will be shooting at. If you're aggressive, especially on the first target, you could use a quarter choke (an English choke that's between our Improved Cylinder and Modified constrictions) or Modified choke for the first shot. The range of the first target will be approximately 14 to 16 yards from the trap (don't forget to add 16 yards from the trap to the shooter) for a "fast" shooter, a few yards farther for a more deliberate shooter. Ballistics experts might contend that these choke recommendations are a bit too "tight" and would be good for pheasants or mallards, but we are shooting at a target that only has a 1 1/2-inch high profile. Using a choke any more open than a quarter choke could allow the target to literally fly through the pattern unscathed.

RECOIL FACTOR WITH 30-34-INCH SHOTGUN BARRELS

3-DRAM, 1⅛-OUNCE		2¾-DRAM, 1⅛-OUNCE	
Weight Gun	Ft. Lbs. Recoil	Weight Gun	Ft. Lbs. Recoil
6.0 lbs.	20.2	6.0 lbs.	18.5
6.5 lbs.	18.6	6.5 lbs.	17.1
7.0 lbs.	17.3	7.0 lbs.	15.9
7.5 lbs.	16.1	7.5 lbs.	14.8
8.0 lbs.	15.1	8.0 lbs.	13.9
8.5 lbs.	14.2	8.5 lbs.	13.1
9.0 lbs.	13.4	9.0 lbs.	12.4
9.5 lbs.	12.7	9.5 lbs.	11.7

RECOIL FACTOR WITH 24-29-INCH SHOTGUN BARRELS

3-DRAM, 1⅛-OUNCE		2¾-DRAM, 1⅛-OUNCE	
Weight Gun	Ft. Lbs. Recoil	Weight Gun	Ft. Lbs. Recoil
6.0 lbs.	20.5	6.0 lbs.	18.9
6.5 lbs.	18.9	6.5 lbs.	17.4
7.0 lbs.	17.6	7.0 lbs.	16.2
7.5 lbs.	16.4	7.5 lbs.	15.1
8.0 lbs.	15.4	8.0 lbs.	14.1
8.5 lbs.	14.5	8.5 lbs.	13.3
9.0 lbs.	13.7	9.0 lbs.	12.6
9.5 lbs.	13.0	9.5 lbs.	11.9

The second shot is the one most shooters have problems with, simply because it is farther away. Therefore, you'll need a much tighter choke on the second shot unless you're super-fast and can get away with an Improved Modified instead of Full. The typical Doubles shooter fires at the second bird when it's approximately 43 to 45 yards downrange and fast shooters hammer it at slightly less than 40 yards. To recap, successful Doubles shooters use over/under shotguns choked Modified and Full or quarter choke and Full, or for the extremely fast shooter, quarter choke and Improved Modified. Interestingly, the better you become, you'll probably switch to using both barrels choked Full or tighter, which will produce those lovely-looking twin balls of smoke hanging in the air. But remember, chips count just as much as "ink balls." We score all targets — not grade them.

It would be so much easier if the ammunition makers and component manufacturers would get together and make one universal target load. Then we would not have 7½, 8, 8½ and 9 shot. We would not have "heavy" loads, "light" loads and more recently, "extra-lite" loads. All velocities would be the same and all shot would be of an unknown size, yet legal and generated recoil would be almost nonexistent. Like fishing lures designed to attract fishermen, not necessarily fish, I think we have too many different loads available today, which only muddies up the not too clear waters anyway. I don't think there is virtually any difference between a "heavy 8" or a light "7½" when at least five pellets have been placed on the target. It's doubtful that any shooter could distinguish the difference the way a target is broken with each of the dozen different legal trap loads available. My recommendation to the newcomer is to shoot one load for both shots in Doubles for one basic reason — don't add another variable to this tough game. If, after a reasonable amount of experience, you wish to use 8s, 8½s or even 9s on the first shot and 7½s or 8s on the second, go ahead. Odds are that after becoming more proficient in Doubles, you'll go back to using one load for both shots because then you'll realize the size of shot and dram equivalent isn't as important as consistently placing those five pellets on each target.

The straightaway target from posts one, two, four, and five should be shot first. At Station Three, the right-handed shooter should shoot the right bird first and the southpaw should shoot the left target first. In each case, the "easier" of the two targets is always shot at first. They are not exactly "gimmies," but they are at least 40 percent easier to break than the second target because four of the five are straightaways and 12 to 15

yards closer. At post three, the righty generally swings better from left to right because he tends to push the stock against his face and cheek, thus maintaining contact with the stock. The opposite holds true for the lefty.

Timing is the key ingredient to becoming a good Doubles shooter. Developing a rhythm and smooth style is paramount to timing. The first target should be shot as quickly as possible, enabling the shooter to take a crack at the second target while it is still rising. All super Doubles shooters are extremely aggressive and their timing between shots is anywhere from 30 to 50 percent faster than the average shooter's. That means they are shooting at targets that are still rising, and if the wind is blowing, the targets are still on course from the launching machine. The wind hasn't yet influenced the target's flight. Shooters who ride targets out, under these windy conditions, are at quite a disadvantage and it is not unlike shooting at confused hummingbirds.

The same rules apply to muzzle position, whether or not you're a one- or two-eyed shooter. Frank Little teaches one-eyed shooters to anticipate the first target, that is, to start their guns slightly ahead of seeing the target. This procedure could be detrimental if carried over to Singles and Handicap shooting. If you are a one-eyed jack and are not taking the first target fast enough, try this method. If it doesn't seem to help, I would advise against training yourself to anticipate targets.

For many years I never cared for shooting Doubles. Why? Because I didn't break good scores. My mentor was a California champion named Jimmy Poindexter. He gave me only one piece of advice that turned my Doubles shooting completely around. Jim said, "Attack the first target without caution. Don't hold yourself back to see if you broke the first target. That's what scorekeepers are for." Since this bit of sage advice was handed to me, by one who knows, my Doubles scores have risen nearly every year. The experts seem to agree that the key to breaking the second target with consistency is to shoot the first target as quickly as possible, which puts you in proper position to more easily break the second bird. And that is what I mean by timing.

8

Skeet Shooting Fundamentals

SHOOTERS WHO HAVE participated in both trap and Skeet agree that trapshooting is easier to learn but more difficult to master, vice versa for Skeet. The reason is the predictability of the Skeet target's flight. Initially, however, Skeet targets are more difficult because they scream across the horizon, illustrating their true speed, while trap targets seem much slower because they are always on a path away from you. The Skeet target can be intimidating, the trap target more friendly.

I tried clay target shooting for the first time in 1957 at the old Aqua Sierra Gun Club in Chatsworth, California. I had been invited by a friend who recently discovered Skeet shooting and asked me if I'd like to give it a try. I said yes and off we went. Armed with a well-used J.C. Higgins 12-gauge pump gun, complete with a Power-Pac hung on the muzzle, my first crack at clay targets was at Skeet — supposedly an easier game, or so I was told by the "experts." I recorded an embarrassing score of three out of 25. I was mentally shattered and quietly cursed my friend for talking me into participating. Ready to pack it up and call it a day after a single shooting "lesson," one of the club members asked me if I'd like to try trapshooting, because he noticed I didn't fare well on the Skeet range. Under any other circumstances I would have politely begged off, but the interested shooter was none other than Frank Ferguson — a long-time character actor in films and television. How could I refuse shooting with a "movie star!"

After attentively listening to Frank's mini-clinic on trapshooting, I shot a respectable 17x25, and from that point on, was smitten by clay target shooting. The point is that if you don't initially do well at either trap or Skeet, try the other. You'll quickly learn which one is best suited to your tastes and fits your "untrained" shooting style. You may switch to the other game later in your shooting career, but don't quit because of a poor beginning — we all had one!

The very best way to learn how to shoot Skeet is through the use of a qualified instructor. It's amazing how many shooters will squander money on guns and ammunition without dedicating some of that shooting budget to hiring an instructor.

Skeet, in my opinion, is easier to "master" than trap because the shooter knows in advance exactly where the target is going to fly. Also, after some experience, the shooter should be able to predict the exact spot to shoot and hopefully hit the target. Therefore, stance and gun placement are the keys to breaking Skeet targets with consistency.

Stance

Regardless of the station, the shooter should initially set up his stance to the approximate spot where he wants to break the target. After this is established by positioning the feet and body, twist the upper torso toward the trap house. Once the feet are positioned, they

(Right) Comfort and flexibility are the two important ingredients that make a good solid Skeet shooting stance. At each station (post) the shooter must fire at two totally different targets—an outgoer and an incomer. At Stations One, Two, Six and Seven, both of these targets are thrown simultaneously to make the game more interesting.

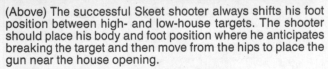

(Above) The successful Skeet shooter always shifts his foot position between high- and low-house targets. The shooter should place his body and foot position where he anticipates breaking the target and then move from the hips to place the gun near the house opening.

(Right) Remington's D. Lee Braun, probably the greatest Skeet instructor ever, was a staunch advocate of correct foot and body position. Braun demanded that all his students learn and master the basics of Skeet shooting positions, and that once learned — and used — high scores would be the result.

should not be moved until after the shot is taken. The shooter's feet must be repositioned for each upcoming target, regardless of which station he is standing on because the outgoing and incoming targets should be shot at different locations in relation to where the shooter is standing.

The shooter's stance must be comfortable, with the shotgun snuggled tightly to the shoulder and cheek. The left knee (for right-handed shooters) should be bent slightly more than when trapshooting because

Skeet is designed to be shot by five participants. Six may be allowed at some clubs, but the trap machines must be reloaded during the round. Most machines are equipped to accommodate only 135 targets. Shooting a "six-man" squad can cause a log jam for waiting squads, and therefore, its practice is felt to be inconsiderate.

Skeet shooters use a more pronounced and longer swing and arc.

Positioning the hands on the shotgun is very important because the "lead," or non-master hand, controls the speed of the shooter's swing. When the hands are properly balanced, the lead hand is an equal distance from the shotgun's center of balance — usually where the barrel(s) meet the receiver — in relation to the master hand. Because the master hand cannot easily be moved fore or aft as it must reach the trigger, the lead hand controls the shotgun's balance. Usually, the proper position of the off-hand is near the middle of the forend. If a Skeet shooter finds that he is swinging too slowly, he can simply slide his off-hand back a touch which will automatically increase the swing speed because the center of balance is altered and makes the gun "muzzle heavy." Conversely, moving the off-hand out — or forward — on the forend usually reduces muzzle speed.

Lead

Some well-intended Skeet instructors teach their students that the target should be broken where it crosses the middle stake on the Skeet field. Actually, though, top shooters rarely break targets at that spot. Both incoming and outgoing targets should be shot as close as possible. If you were in a duck blind, wouldn't you rather shoot at a fast-flying teal at 20 yards than 35? An African "white hunter" once told his client to sneak as close as possible and then slip up 10 yards closer! The old adage about waiting for a target to get downrange to make better use of the shotgun's pattern is poor advice. You should always shoot outgoing targets before they cross the middle stake and incoming targets after they cross it.

Nobody has ever broken a Skeet target by shooting behind it, so obviously "lead" is critical to doing well in this fun sport. There are three types of leads Skeet shooters employ. The first is a sustained lead, which the overwhelming majority of Skeet shooters use. Simply, the shooter tracks the target with the shotgun's muzzle at the same speed as the target is moving, and when the sight picture appears to be right, pulls the trigger and continues moving the muzzle after the shot for follow-through. The second type of lead is called swinging through. The shooter points the muzzle

(Left) The only way to break a moving target is by shooting in front of it. For all the millions of Skeet targets thrown over the years, *none* have ever been broken by shooting behind them. (Right) Skeet targets are shot at close range — rarely exceeding 21 yards and, when possible, even closer. The old tale about waiting on the target so that the shotgun's choke has a better opportunity to "open up" is misleading. You should always attempt to shoot outgoers before they reach the middle stake and incomers after they pass this mid-point. The closer the better!

slightly behind the target and subconsciously "whips" the muzzle past the target and pulls the trigger. I've asked successful Skeet shooters who use this method what leads they recommend for different targets, and they claim that all leads are the same, but the swinging-through motion of the gun at varying speeds provides the proper lead. This is a very difficult type of swing and lead technique to learn. The third type of lead is the spot-shooting technique in which the shooter aims at a spot he believes the target will fly to and shoots well in advance of the target getting there. Hopefully, the target will intercept the shot swarm. This style isn't as inefficient as one might think; in fact, on calm, windless days, spot shooters usually beat the pants off their competitors who are using either of the other two shooting styles. The spot shooter gets into trouble when the wind is blowing and the target's flight is both erratic and unpredictable.

As a Skeet shooter you have to select the type of lead

Most tournament Skeet shooters use a sustained lead by which they track the flying target with the shotgun's muzzle at the same speed as the target and when the lead seems about right, pull the trigger. If done properly, a puff of black smoke will fill the air!

which best suits your shooting style. Perhaps you might use a combination of all three kinds. Therefore, I won't prompt you on how to lead a target because this subject is wide open to conjecture. The actual amount of lead for each target is fixed and calculable, but what appears to be 2 feet at 20 yards to me, may look like 6 feet to you. Remember when you were a youngster and heaved rocks and stones at anything that moved? It probably didn't take you very long to realize that you had to throw well in front of your moving object to assure a hit. Nobody could explain how much to lead your target — only by trial and error did you learn.

Muzzle Position

To be a good, or great, Skeet shooter you must have fast reaction time. The key word is reaction, not reflex. Reflex is an automatic movement of the body like pulling back from a punch thrown at you. Countering that punch with a haymaker of your own is a reaction. Picking up the target's flight as soon as it leaves the trap house is important to shooting good scores. There are two places to initially look for the target — at the open window of the trap house, and down the gun barrel until it comes into view. But, under no circumstances should you ever shoot at a target when it isn't perfectly clear and sharp in your line of vision. The initial flight of the target will appear blurred because the eyes cannot focus on such a fast-moving object. Wait a fraction of a second until the target is recognizable and its relationship to the end of the barrel is in the proper perspective. Then pull the trigger, and if everything was done correctly, a black puff of smoke will appear in the sky!

All too often, Skeet newcomers mimic the shooting styles of champions, hoping that if they look good, they will shoot good. To a degree, this isn't totally a bad idea if the "imitatee" has good form and stance and a smooth, fluid swing. One of the problems that often crops up is how the tyro should mount the shotgun. When some of the world's greatest Skeet shooters started playing, the "dropped stock" was mandatory. By definition, dropped gun means the buttstock must be off the shoulder when the target is called for. A mounted gun means that the shooter is allowed to place the gun butt against his shoulder, cheek firmly touching the comb, and then call for the target. Even though the rules were subsequently changed in the mid-1950s, permitting a mounted gun, many old-timers continued to shoot in their accustomed manner. Newcomers who see these great shooters still using the dropped-stock method mimic them. By doing so, they place an additional burden on themselves because a mounted gun is not only legal, but it helps eliminate mounting problems so often encountered. My advice is to take full

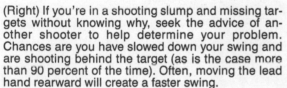

(Right) If you're in a shooting slump and missing targets without knowing why, seek the advice of another shooter to help determine your problem. Chances are you have slowed down your swing and are shooting behind the target (as is the case more than 90 percent of the time). Often, moving the lead hand rearward will create a faster swing.

(Left) Hold the muzzle slightly outside of the trap house, in line with the window. When the target emerges, simply raise the muzzle straight up and press the trigger. The target should disappear in a puff of black smoke.

While shooting an event, it's a good idea to keep your spare guns and parts close at hand. Should a gun break or malfunction, it's not nearly so traumatic to repair a gun on the field as it is to scurry back to your car and scratch around for parts.

Don't crowd your fellow shooter. Stand back for both safety reasons and good manners. But, don't go so far away that you delay the squad's rhythm while they're waiting for you to approach the shooting station.

Adding weight to the shotgun's barrel at the muzzle will smooth out a herky-jerky swing and also help to reduce muzzle rise between shots while firing at the elusive "doubles" targets.

Although the Skeet puller/scorer stands close to the shooter, remember to call for the target in a clear, crisp manner. Bad calls will create bad pulls and are, therefore, brought on by the shooter.

If you're "next-up," stand close enough to the shooter on the post so that you can watch the targets, and when it's your turn to shoot, all you have to do is take a few steps.

Here are two examples of bad on-field etiquette. (Above) The next shooter is crowding the person on the Skeet station. While waiting your turn to shoot, always stand behind the shooter, never off to one side. (Left) The previous shooter has left the shooting station and ambled over to pick up empty hulls. It is the responsibility of the shooter to pocket empty hulls before leaving the station. Many gun clubs will bar a shooter from competing for flagrant violation of this rule.

Never talk to squad mates while another is shooting. It can — and *will* — ruin the concentration of the shooter. The Skeet field is *not* the place to visit with your cronies.

Station Three high house can be a troublesome station, especially with the smaller gauges, as the angle of the target is more acute than what appears. There are no easy shots in Skeet; they are all hard until the target is broken, and then they can be called easy.

Skeet shooting rules allow you to shoulder and cheek the gun before calling for the bird. Some shooters prefer the older method of keeping the gun off the shoulder until the target is seen. It may appear effective, but actually isn't. Mount the gun like the shooter pictured below and then call for the target.

advantage of the rules set down by the NSSA, learn them, and more importantly, abide by them.

How many times have you heard shooters moan, "And that was an easy target I missed!" Are there really any "easy" targets on the Skeet field? Yes, the ones you break — all others are difficult. Some may be labeled easier than others, but until you can break every target from every station every time you shoot, you'll be better off believing they are all tough. For right-handed shooters, some targets are more difficult than others, as records prove. Right-handers seem to have the most difficult time with "high deuce," the outgoing target from Station Two. As explained in an earlier chapter, right-handed shooters do not swing to the right as effectively as to the left. Knowing, understanding and accepting this, the wise student will bear down a bit harder on this particular target and after many sessions of concentrated effort, will be able to turn this very difficult target into a confidence builder.

My method to overcome this target is a bit unconventional, but for me, very effective. I position the gun barrel parallel to the trap house. Then I deliberately move my head off the stock and look into the window. I call for the target and when I see it, track it with my head and eyes, and there waiting for me is my gun stock. In effect, I move my head and face into the gun while the target is moving. This unique method prevents me from pulling the gunstock away from my face, causing me to miss the target. Try it, it might work if you're having trouble belting the high deuce.

Station Eight is very intimidating to onlookers, and puts fear in newcomers' hearts. They can't imagine how they'll ever be able to hit a target that is so close and flying so fast. As any seasoned Skeet shooter will verify, the closer the target, the better the chance of hitting it. The tyro goes wrong when he places the gun's muzzle before calling for the target. If possible, stand directly behind the shooter ahead of you and watch the flight of the target — but don't watch the shooter's barrel. You'll see that the target clears the house rapidly and the flight path is consistent. For me, the best place to point the muzzle is about 18 inches outside and slightly below the window. This starting barrel position enables you to see the target clearly as it leaves the house, and placing the barrel outboard, cuts down on the distance the barrel must be moved to catch the target in flight. To hit the target, flip up the front end of the gun and pull the trigger. This technique works for high or low house Station Eight targets.

Skeet Versus Trap

To quote a hair-coloring commercial, Skeet shooters, like blonds, have more fun than trapshooters. This is evident by the way a Skeet shoot program is written — for the shooters. Many trapshoots, on the other hand, seem to be held for the benefit of the host club. At most major Skeet shoots, there are many concurrent events that add spice to the program such as two-man teams, husband and wife teams, two-in-a-family teams, five-man teams, zone teams, etc. The list is almost endless, and all help stimulate and promote Skeet shooting. Whereas major trapshoots employ five classes in Singles events (AA, A, B, C, D), Skeet events have eight classes (AAA, AA, A, B, C, D, E and N/C, or non-classified). Sharing the wealth among the rank and file has helped Skeet in the past 15 years or so increase both its membership and attendance at registered shoots faster than trapshooting.

Like trapshooting, shooting doubles is part of the game, but unlike trapshooting, the newcomer must learn how to shoot them almost immediately. Though it is possible to politely ask the puller to throw doubles targets during shooting practice — or two singles, one at a time from each house — you'll soon learn that shooting a pair in the air isn't all that difficult. As long as you shoot your outgoing target before it reaches the center stake, you will have plenty of time to pulverize the incomer. Like trap doubles, aggressiveness is the key to developing proper timing and rhythm. Doubles are shot from four stations — One, Two, Six and Seven, except in special events in which all stations except

(Right) During a regulation round of Skeet, doubles are shot from four stations — One, Two, Six and Seven. To an uninformed bystander, shooting at two targets in the air simultaneously seems an impossible task. Actually though, the shooter has plenty of time as long as he shoots the first target rather quickly.

(Below) For Station Eight low house, hold the muzzle approximately 18 inches outside the window and when the target emerges, bring the gun straight up, pull the trigger, and the target should literally explode.

Mastering Station Eight low house, to the newcomer, seems impossible. Yet, after learning proper barrel place-ment before the shot goes a long way toward taming this "trick" shot.

Eight are used. Some clubs use "doubles at all stations" to eliminate lengthy shootoffs. The problem with this type of tiebreaker is that competitors are not shooting the same game they previously participated in. It's like asking a bowler, who tied another kegler, to break a tie by shooting pool. Shooting doubles from all stations is an entirely different version of Skeet, and demands a great deal of practice because of the radically different leads, which are not similar to shooting singles targets.

Thanks to today's superior ammunition and improved shotguns, the "average" Skeet shooter must break every target thrown just to get into a shootoff. Every year at the Skeet world championships, perfect scores are recorded in every gauge, and it's not unusual to find a host of shooters who broke 550x550 targets. One hundred straights in doubles is commonplace. Being perfect nowadays only ties you with the best!

Skeet shooting tournaments often have separate events in which contestants must shoot shotguns smaller than the 12-gauge. There are four gun classifications — 12-gauge (all-bore where a contestant can shoot any shotgun in which the ammunition does not exceed 3 drams equivalent of powder and $1^1/8$ ounces of shot. A shooter using a smaller-gauge gun is doing so at his own risk.); 20-gauge, 28-gauge and 410 bore. Until a newcomer learns Skeet's demanding basics and can consistently shoot in the mid to high 90s with the 12-gauge, I advise him to stay away from the smaller-gauge games. It's very tempting to jump right in and enter 28-gauge and 410-bore events, but don't do it right away. Learn the 12-gauge first, then the 20-gauge and, ultimately, you'll taper down to the 410 bore.

Even though Skeet and trap are both clay target games, that's where the similarity ends. There is a big difference in the philosophy and personality of the two sports. Skeet, for the most part, is shot for fun, although recently there has been a renewed interest in

High Two is the most difficult shot for right-handed Skeet shooters. The person who is having difficulties breaking this bird with needed consistency is probably pulling his cheek away from the stock when going after the fast-flying target.

purses, options, giant jackpots, etc., designed to pique shooter interest. Trophies, awards, brassards, medals and other non-monetary rewards are what the Skeet shooters go after. The opposite holds true for trap-shooting, which from its inception, was designed as a cash award game. Therefore, a trapshooter's attitude toward his sport is different from the Skeet shooter's. Skeet participants shoot for fun, while the trapmen shoot for "blood." I don't mean to overgeneralize by

smoke the target, only chipped off a couple of pieces. Don't consider yourself lucky, but smart to stay in the game and finish the shot by following through.

Have you noticed the stake positioned in front of Station Eight? That 30-inch rod is a lead reference point. When standing at post four, the rod is perpendicular to you and your sustained lead should approximate that portion you see. At Stations Three and Five, your perspective is different and the bar appears to be about 24

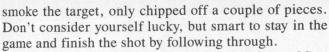

(Left) The 410-bore shotgun is often called the "fun gun" by top-notch Skeet shooters. However, by those who are not as proficient, the 410 is often referred to as an "idiot stick."

(Below) All Skeet shooting's fundamentals must be exercised when shooting the 410. Loaded with 1/2-ounce of shot, everything must be perfect to break the bird — there's little margin for error.

saying that Skeeters are a more gregarious group than trappers, but the atmosphere at major trapshoots is more austere than what I've witnessed at Skeet events over the years. Either of the two sports appeal to an individual's personality, and eventually, a newcomer to clay target shooting will comfortably settle into one or the other. Shooters who consistently partake in both games are rare.

If you are in a comfortable shooting position with stance and body facing where you intend to break the target, there will be times when it seems you hit the bird by accident because the sight picture was wrong, but your follow-through created by proper form made up for your mental miscalculation. Odds are you didn't

inches — which should be your sight picture for those stations. At Stations Two and Six, the bar appears to be about 1 1/2 feet long. At the corners of Stations One and Seven, 1/2-foot is all the lead you'll need to smoke the targets.

Skeet shooting demands excellent body control; trap-shooting doesn't require as much movement. Lost targets on the Skeet field can be attributed mostly to poor body position and stance. The best Skeet shooters use a pronounced body follow-through. A fluid motion using flexed knees and turning at the waist combined with upper body movement in conjunction with the arms and shoulders is proper form that results in high scores — most of the time!

9

Purses, Payoffs and Options

ONE MAJOR DIFFERENCE between Skeet and trap are the rewards. There has been a long dispute between trap and Skeet shooters about whether it is more enjoyable to shoot for money, trophies or just for the fun of it. So you can better understand and decipher a shoot program, the various types of purses and options will be discussed.

The first trophy a new shooter wins in competition becomes a prized possession throughout his life. Practically all winners in trap and Skeet tournaments receive trophies. Many years ago, I was on a Skeet squad with an elderly and obviously affluent gentleman who was attending his first registered Skeet shoot. In the late 1950s, it wasn't uncommon for the sponsoring gun club to put up enough trophies for shooters through Class D, 3rd place. You guessed it, the new shooter won that prestigious trophy, which stood at least 6½ inches. He beamed from ear to ear as though he had won the "Nationals." A few weeks later I saw him again at a local gun club and asked the condition of his trophy. He proudly stated that he had "built a room

around it" — a trophy room — and predicted that in a few years the room would be filled. He was right; that first trophy led to a distinguished Skeet shooting career which garnered over 150 trophies and awards.

There will always be converts to trap and Skeet, and their first trophies will have greater intrinsic value than any cash prize, and that's the way it should be. Trapshooters, however, have for generations preferred cash-pay events and many believe that this is what has kept trapshooting alive during both good and bad times. Skeet, on the other hand, has grown steadily and become firmly established in the shooting world as a trophy game. Time, however, brings many changes and

Most of the larger gun clubs reward shooters who break 100 straight with a pin commemorating the occasion. Sometimes a gun company will present pins and medals to shooters for exceptional shooting.

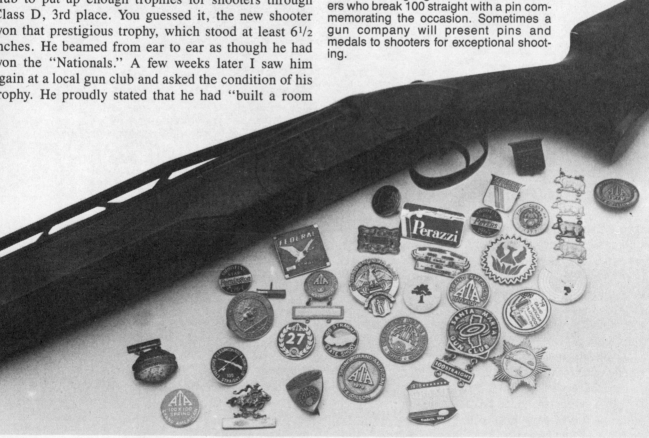

the majority of Skeet programs today have competitions for cash optionals, along with trophies and other awards.

Both trap and Skeet shooters who have attended tournaments for sport, recreation and friendly competition have won more trophies than they have use, or room, for. These same men and women, however, show an avid interest in the event-by-event payoff and will stand in line at the cashier's window to collect what they have won. Trap and Skeet shooting programs must appeal to new shooters as well as crusty campaigners to successfully draw a cross section of both trophy and money shooters.

Class Shooting

When trapshooting began, everyone competed together and the top scorers won. This method favored

87% and under	D

Four Classes

95% and over	A
92 - 94%	B
89 - 91%	C
88% and under	D

Three Classes

95% and over	A
91 - 94%	B
90% and under	C

Depending on where and when the shoot is held, usually only the largest tournaments maintain interest in all five classes. An average-sized tournament of 75 to 100 shooters usually calls for four-class competition,

Always check and verify your score at the main scoreboard. All too often, a shooter will miscalculate his score and get upset when he finds he missed making a major payoff. And, on rare occasions, simple addition errors will occur and it's the shooters' responsibility to make these errors known so they can be corrected. Once the shoot is over, it's virtually impossible to demand a recount.

the best, and shooters who could not protect their entry fees with their shooting abilities either withdrew from competition or entered "for targets only." After a few years of laboring under this system, tournament officials realized trapshooting could not grow under this one-class system. Thus the classification method based on registered target averages and known ability was created.

The standard system whereby trapshooters are classed in accordance with their known abilities and official 16-yard averages is shown below. These averages and classifications are recommended guidelines set down by the ATA.

Five Classes

97% and over	AA
94 - 96%	A
91 - 93%	B
88 - 90%	C

meaning four separate trophy and money divisions run concurrently on the same 100- or 200-target program. At most trapshoots, the class system works out to the satisfaction of all groups except in Class AA. The other classes generally have sufficient entries to make an interesting race, but the AA shooters sometimes have less to show for a perfect 100x100 score than a Class D entrant who barely shoots his average, yet wins his class.

For example, let's take a hypothetical case with 100 entries and five classes. Usually, the following occurs: AA entries-6, A entries-14, B entries-33, C entries-31 and D entries-16. Optional entries are refunded when there are less than five entries in any one class (entered for money). Obviously, in this example there are enough entries in each group for competition, but Class AA will have a dull event moneywise. Shooting by classes stimulates competition and creates action for trophies as well as money, for those who want it. Trap and Skeet tournaments could not have grown in size and shooter interest without the class system.

Yardage Handicaps

Since the advent of handicap trapshooting, four of the most important rule changes have been aimed at reducing the top-flight shooters' chances of maintaining anywhere near their 16-yard average in handicap shooting. (Recently, however, quite a few super-shooters have defeated these early rules with exceptional shooting exploits.) The changes in sequence were:

1. Elimination of plated shot in target loads.
2. Limitation of powder charge to 3-dram equivalent.
3. Reduction of shot load from 1¼ ounces to 1⅛ ounces.
4. Extension of the extreme yardage from 23 to 25 yards, and eventually to 27 yards.

The official ATA average books show that the shooter who can maintain a handicap average from 23 yards or farther, within 5 to 7 percent of his 16-yard average, is the exception rather than the rule. Shooting handicap targets from the long yardage positions (25 to 27 yards) is much different than singles from 16 yards. Some of the variables that must be considered are:

1. Greater leads, especially from extreme distances.
2. Longer distance of shot travel to target.
3. Reduced density of shot pattern.

Even in perfect weather, score sheets totalled for the squads standing back 23 yards in handicap events average 5 to 10 percent more "zeros" than when the same shooters shoot at 16-yard targets. Based on averages and the known-ability rule, top gunners in the 16-yard program can almost be named before shooting starts, but in handicaps, the folks who participate in the High Gun Money division invariably shoot well above their season's average.

New shooters must shoot at 1500 registered 16-yard or handicap targets before being issued their permanent handicap cards. Handicap committees tend to start male newcomers shooting at 22 yards and females at 19 yards.

Handicap shooting is a very healthy and growing segment of the trapshooting game. Most tournaments schedule more handicap events than either Singles or Doubles. At every state or zone shoot the yardage events usually bring out the largest entry lists of the entire shooting program. The three main handicap events at the Grand American attest to shooters' desires to play the money in the "reeeealy big" handicap events.

Shooters who wish to play the "options" and "purses" must do so at initial signup. Once an event has started, the shooter cannot play or withdraw his money. At some of the major trapshoots around the country, it's not uncommon to wager upward of $2,500 to pay for all events, purses and options.

```
 1  100%
 2  60-40
 3  50-30-20
 4  40-30-20-10
 5  30-25-20-15-10
 6  30-20-15-13-12-10
 7  25-20-15-13-12-10-5
 8  25-20-15-12-10-8-5-5
 9  22-18-15-12-10-8-6-5-4
10  22-18-14-11-10-8-5-5-4-3
11  20-16-13-10-9-7-6-6-5-4-4
12  20-16-13-10-9-7-6-5-5-4-3-2
13  17-14-12-10-8-7-6-6-5-5-4-3-3
14  18-15-12-10-9-7-6-5-5-4-3-2-2-2
15  16-13-11-8-7-7-6-6-5-5-4-4-3-3-2
16  16-14-11-9-8-7-6-5-5-4-3-3-3-2-2-2
17  15-13-10-8-8-7-6-5-5-4-4-3-3-3-2-2-2
18  15-13-10-8-8-7-6-5-5-4-3-3-3-2-2-2-2
19  14-12-9-8-7-6-6-5-5-4-4-3-3-3-3-2-2-2-2
20  14-12-9-8-7-7-6-5-5-4-3-3-3-2-2-2-2-2-2-2
21  14-12-9-8-7-6-6-5-5-4-3-3-2-2-2-2-2-2-2-2-2
22  13-11-9-8-7-6-5-5-5-4-3-3-3-2-2-2-2-2-2-2-2-2-2
23  13-11-9-8-7-6-5-5-4-4-3-3-2-2-2-2-2-2-2-2-2-2-2-2
24  12-10-9-8-7-6-5-4-3-3-3-3-3-3-3-2-2-2-2-2-2-2-2-2
25  12-10-9-8-7-6-5-4-3-3-3-3-3-3-2-2-2-2-2-2-2-2-2-2-2
26  11-10-9-8-7-6-5-4-3-3-3-3-2-2-2-2-2-2-2-2-2-2-2-2-2-2
27  11-10-9-8-7-6-5-4-3-3-2-2-2-2-2-2-2-2-2-2-2-2-2-2-2-2-2-2
28  10-9-8-7-6-5-4-3-3-3-3-3-3-3-3-3-2-2-2-2-2-2-2-2-2-2-2-2-2
29  10-9-8-7-6-5-4-3-3-3-3-3-3-3-2-2-2-2-2-2-2-2-2-2-2-2-2-2-2
30  10-9-8-7-6-5-4-3-3-3-3-3-3-2-2-2-2-2-2-2-2-2-2-2-2-1-1-1
31  10-9-8-7-6-5-4-3-3-3-3-3-2-2-2-2-2-2-2-2-2-2-2-2-2-2-1-1-1
32  10-9-8-7-6-5-4-3-3-3-3-2-2-2-2-2-2-2-2-2-2-2-2-2-2-2-1-1-1-1
33  10-9-8-7-6-5-4-3-3-3-2-2-2-2-2-2-2-2-2-2-2-2-2-2-2-1-1-1-1-1-1
34  10-9-8-7-6-5-4-3-3-2-2-2-2-2-2-2-2-2-2-2-2-2-2-2-1-1-1-1-1-1-1
35  10-9-8-7-6-5-4-3-2-2-2-2-2-2-2-2-2-2-2-2-2-2-2-1-1-1-1-1-1-1-1
36  10-9-8-7-6-5-4-3-2-2-2-2-2-2-2-2-2-2-2-2-2-2-1-1-1-1-1-1-1-1-1-1
37  10-9-8-7-6-5-4-2-2-2-2-2-2-2-2-2-2-2-2-2-2-1-1-1-1-1-1-1-1-1-1-1
38  10-9-8-7-6-5-4-2-2-2-2-2-2-2-2-2-2-2-2-2-1-1-1-1-1-1-1-1-1-1-1-1
39  10-9-8-7-6-5-4-2-2-2-2-2-2-2-2-2-2-2-2-1-1-1-1-1-1-1-1-1-1-1-1-1-1
40  10-9-8-7-6-5-4-2-2-2-2-2-2-2-2-2-2-2-1-1-1-1-1-1-1-1-1-1-1-1-1-1-1
41  10-9-8-7-6-5-4-3-2-2-2-2-2-2-2-2-2-2-1-1-1-1-1-1-1-1-1-1-1-1-1-1-1-1
42  10-9-8-7-6-5-4-3-2-2-2-2-2-2-2-2-2-1-1-1-1-1-1-1-1-1-1-1-1-1-1-1-1-1
43  10-9-8-7-6-5-4-3-2-2-2-2-2-2-2-2-1-1-1-1-1-1-1-1-1-1-1-1-1-1-1-1-1-1
44  10-9-8-7-6-5-4-3-2-2-2-2-2-2-2-1-1-1-1-1-1-1-1-1-1-1-1-1-1-1-1-1-1-1
45  10-9-8-7-6-5-4-3-2-2-2-2-2-2-1-1-1-1-1-1-1-1-1-1-1-1-1-1-1-1-1-1-1-1
    10-9-8-7-6-5-4-3-2-2-2-2-2-1-1-1-1-1-1-1-1-1-1-1-1-1-1-1-1-1-1-1-1
    10-9-8-7-6-5-4-3-2-2-2-2-2-1-1-1-1-1-1-1-1-1-1-1-1-1-1-1-1-1-1-1-1
    10-9-8-7-6-5-4-3-2-2-2-2-1-1-1-1-1-1-1-1-1-1-1-1-1-1-1-1-1-1-1-1-1
    10-9-8-7-6-5-4-3-2-2-2-1-1-1-1-1-1-1-1-1-1-1-1-1-1-1-1-1-1-1-1-1
    10-9-8-7-6-5-4-3-2-2-2-1-1-1-1-1-1-1-1-1-1-1-1-1-1-1-1-1-1-1-1-1
```

Trapshooting's long-yardage (25 to 27 yards) shooters over the long haul cannot expect as many cash payoffs as the short yardage (24 yards or less) shooters, especially during inclement weather, which takes its toll on the "back fencers."

This chart illustrates the Percentage System breakdown. The left-hand column indicates the number of places of "pays" and the rows of numbers for each payoff spot always equal 100 percent.

Percentage System

The method most widely used today for dividing the cash purses in trapshooting events is "Percentage," in which the top tied scores divide the proceeds. The system offers the shooter a chance to hit a lucky payoff — jackpot, so to speak — where a lone 25 straight in the optionals can result in a substantial payoff. There are numerous recorded payoffs in which a single "straight" on a particularly tough field (usually No. 1) paid a whopping $1,200 for a $2 entry. It is rare, but nevertheless has happened, and every shoot is capable of providing these bonanza payoffs.

Tournament shooters are a sporting crowd, and one of the best advertisements any program can have, when the shoot is concluded, is to have shooters talk about "lucky pay-spots" they lucked into. High-paying tournaments are never forgotten as evidenced by famous "Pot 'O Gold" shoots in the mid-1960s, in which trapshooters won as much as $10,000 for a 200-target handicap race.

There is a vast difference between "40-30-20-10 percent, High Gun," and "40-30-20-10 percent, Percentage (ties divide)." Therefore, the program must state explicitly what shoot management has in mind to avoid any possible misunderstandings at payoff time. On a single 25-target sub-event, if the program reads 40-30-20-10 percent, High Gun and four shooters break 25 straight, they win whatever money is in the pot, 25 percent each. When the program reads 40-30-20-10 percent, Percentage, everyone who breaks scores of 25, 24, 23, and 22 is assured of participating in the money division if they entered "for the money."

With 40-30-20-10 percent, Percentage, scores of 22 or higher in 25-bird sub-events pay off, and shooters who average 88 percent or better can expect to share in the money division when they "shoot their average" in a 25-bird sub-event. There are many variable sets of figures that can be used for percentage division; 40-30-20-10 percent is only used as a basis of illustration.

Changing the payoff figures to 50-30-20 percent gives 10 percent more to the high scores and limits the payoff from going below 23x25, or a 92-percent average. A 60-40 percent split does not pay scorers below 24x25, or a 96-percent average. To pay on scores as low as 21x25, the figures 30-25-20-15-10 are used. Any time there is not a 25x25 score among the shooters who entered the sub-event for money, the top pay goes to the 24s, and the payoff extends one score farther down the list.

High Gun System

The predominant payoff system is the High Gun method widely used to pay on the total score in handicap events, especially with the percentage points bro-

The first place a shooter must verify his score is on the field. If a mistake has been made, it's up to the shooter to straighten it out. Often, it will take the cooperation and verification of other squad mates to override a scorer's error.

ken down into much smaller units. For example, if 67 shooters enter an event for $5 each to be divided High Gun System on the total score, with one-money to each five entries, there are 14 High Gun "pays," scaled 18,15,12,10,9,7,6,5,5,4,3,2,2,2 percent, to divide the total $335 purse (67 entries at $5 each).

Percent/$335 Pot	Score	Pays
18/$60.30	98	$60.30
15/ 50.25	97	45.22
12/ 40.20	97	45.22
10/ 33.50	96	33.50
9/ 30.15	95	24.57
7/ 23.45	95	24.57
6/ 20.10	95	24.57
5/ 16.75	94	16.75
5/ 16.75	93	13.40
4/ 13.40	93	13.40
3/ 10.05	93	13.40
2/ 6.70	92	6.70
2/ 6.70	92	6.70
2/ 6.70	92	6.70

On the same basis, if there were 126 entries, $630 would be divided among the 26 High Guns scaled 11, 10,9,8,7,6,5,4,3,3,3,3,2,2,2,2,2,2,2,2,2,2,2,2,2,2 percent. This system of dividing the purse money on the total score satisfies most shooters in large or small handicap events because the yardage method of handicapping is the most equitable way devised so far to equalize shooters' abilities.

Increasing or decreasing the number of payoffs is easy when the gun club knows exactly what they want to do and the program clearly states it. When there are 100 entries in the High Gun options and the program reads, "one-money to each five shooters or fraction thereof," the first 20 High Guns participate in the money division using the following table: 14,12,9,8,7, 7,6,5,5,4,3,3,3,2,2,2,2,2,2,2 percent. When 100 entires are in the High Gun options and the program reads, "one-money to every seven entries or fraction thereof," the division, with 15 pays to the 15 High Guns, is 16,13,11,8,7,7,6,6,5,5,4,4,3,3,2 percent.

The Lewis Class System

This is strictly a luck-of-the-draw proposition. The Lewis Class System is only used for money or trophy

Scoreboard watching is a favorite pastime for trapshooters. Some shooters stand in front of the scoreboard for hours, pouring over the scores of their peers. Others never seek out the scoreboard and are often surprised when they find the score they "thought" they shot is indeed different from what the official results are.

division on total scores. It is widely favored in certain areas of the country and seldom is a program offered that does not include several Lewis Class options. Becoming popular on both coasts, the Lewis Class, nevertheless, is more popular east of the Rockies and west of the Alleghenys.

This betting system permits contestants to make long-shot bets on their scores. Many tournament shooters play the Lewis Class option, if nothing else. Because winning scores are not determined until after the shoot, it is similar to a lottery. Under this system, a shooter whose official classification is AA can emerge as a Class No. 3 winner because the number of targets broken designate the shooter's Lewis Class for that program.

A top-notch shooter can place a $5 or $10 "hedge" bet on himself and if he shoots poorly and is out of the optionals or purse, can still hit a lucky spot in the Lewis Class that will probably put him even for that event, or maybe even for the entire day. This bet is much like making an "any craps" insurance bet when a large sum of money is on the Pass Line on a crap table.

		100	Winner Class 1		90)	Rule 2 places all 90's in Class 4
		99			90	and they are winners of this
Class 1		98			90)	class.
Brackets repre-sent assign-ment of scores according to Rules 2 and 3.		98		Class 4	89	
		96			89	
		96			88	
			Horizontal lines represent division of all entries into classes according to Rule 1.		86	

Class 1
Brackets represent assignment of scores according to Rules 2 and 3.

{100, 99, 98, 98, 96, 96} **Winner Class 1**

Horizontal lines represent division of all entries into classes according to Rule 1.

Class 2
{95, 95, 94, 94, 93, 93, 93} **95's tie for Class 2**

Class 3
{92, 92, 92, 91, 91} Rule 2 places all 93's in Class 2 and therefore 92's tie for Class 3

Class 4
{90, 90, 90, 89, 89, 88, 86} Rule 2 places all 90's in Class 4 and they are winners of this class.

Class 5
{85, 85, 84, 80, 79, 75, 74, 70} Rule 3 places both 85's in Class 5 and they win this Class.

In case of ties, the winner may be decided by the toss of a coin, by the largest number of consecutive targets broken, etc. Where the Lewis System is used to divide money, the winnings are usually divided into equal parts.

The illustration above is an example of a Lewis Class payoff and breakdown sheet. The Lewis Class is a pure lottery and if a shooter's score falls in the right place, he'll take home a nice paycheck.

By the same reasoning, many low percentage shooters play the Lewis Class on the outside chance their score may "hit" where the Lewis pays, knowing well in advance that it is their only chance to have a "run for the money" under the average program offered.

Most veteran tournament shooters who long ago discarded any idea of participating regularly in optional entrance events, play the Lewis knowing they are making a small bet that will require some luck rather than pure shooting ability to walk up to the cashier's window and collect a few bucks for their day's efforts.

The Lewis Class System is variable and works in any program by stating how many shooters will make up a class, or if the entry will be divided into two, three, or four or more equal groups. To establish trophy or merchandise winners at a shoot where there are unknown and non-classified contestants, the Lewis Class System is at its best. Every contestant places in a class automatically by his score in that particular event, and long runs from either end of the event or within individual scores can be used to break ties.

At tournaments smaller than state or zone shoots in which there is no classification or handicap committee officiating, Lewis Class is widely accepted in Doubles events and the division is usually 50-30-20 percent High Gun in each Lewis Class group.

(Right) Both Lewis Class and Optionals are available at most of the major trapshoots around the country. The Lewis Class is virtually a "luck of the draw" event, while options only reward the shooter who breaks perfect or near-perfect scores.

PRELIMINARY DAYS
THURSDAY, AUGUST 11, 1983
Starting Time: 12:00 Noon
EVENT NO. 1 — HALL OF FAME SINGLES
100 TARGETS

Targets & Shooter Service $16.00
Shells (compulsory) $19.00
Maintenance Fund .... $ 1.00
Lewis Class Option — Five Classes
$10.00 on the 100 divided 20-20-20-20-20, high gun in each class.
Class Options —
$5.00 on each 50, divided 40-30-30%. $10.00 on total 100, divided one money for each five entries, high gun.
Trophies —
Trophy to Winner in each Class AA-A-B-C-D, Trophy to Lady, Trophy to Junior, Trophy to Veteran, Trophy to Industry.

EVENT NO. 2 — GEORGE S. McCARTY HANDICAP
100 TARGETS

Targets & Shooter Service $16.00
Shells (compulsory) $19.00
Maintenance Fund .... $ 1.00
Options — Open - - - - Purse—Yardage Group
$2.50 on each 25, divided 60-40%. $5.00 on each 50, divided 40-30-30%. $10.00 on total 100, divided one money for each five entries, in each yardage group, Grand American Point System. $1.00 on total 100, one money, divided high gun.
Lewis Class Option — Five Classes
$10.00 on the 100, divided 20-20-20-20-20, high gun in each class.
Trophies —
Trophy to Winner and Runner-up, Trophy to Lady, Trophy to Junior, Trophy to Veteran, Trophy to Industry.

FRIDAY, AUGUST 12, 1983
Starting Time: 10:00 A.M.
EVENT NO. 3 — ROBERT MUNSON SINGLES
100 TARGETS

Targets & Shooter Service $16.00
Shells (compulsory) $19.00
Maintenance Fund .... $ 1.00
Lewis Class Option — Five Classes
$10.00 on the 100, divided 20-20-20-20-20, high gun in each class.
Class Options —
$5.00 on each 50, divided 40-30-30%. $10.00 on total 100, divided one money for each five entries, high gun.
Trophies —
Trophy to Winner in each Class AA-A-B-C-D, Trophy to Lady, Trophy to Junior, Trophy to Veteran, Trophy to Industry.

EVENT NO. 4 — CHET HENDRICKSON HANDICAP
100 TARGETS

Targets & Shooter Service $16.00
Shells (compulsory) $19.00
Maintenance Fund .... $ 1.00

The Lewis Class System is based on final scores posted when the shoot is over. Every contestant has an equal chance to win, regardless of shooting ability or score. Prior to the shoot, management decides the number of classes, how many prizes will be in each class and publishes the class/payoff in the shoot program. If it is too difficult to forecast accurately, the program might state that "there will be one class for every 10 entries" or "one class for every 15 entries," and there will be "three winners in each class," etc.

At the shoot's end, the scores are listed numerically from highest to lowest. Then they are divided into as many groups as there are classes. For example, if there are 30 entries and five classes, there will be six scores in each class. The highest score in each class is the winner. Because there will be an odd number of entrants and tie scores on the dividing line between classes, several rules have been established.

1. When a "short" class is necessary, due to an odd number entry list, the short class or classes shall head the list.
2. When the line division falls in a number of tie scores, the contestants are assigned to the class in which the majority of the scores appear.
3. When an equal number of tie scores appear on either side of the dividing line, contestants shall be assigned to the head of the lower class.
4. When the original division is changed, due to tie scores, this change shall apply only to the classes directly affected and the original division shall continue in the other classes.

Let's take a shoot with a 100-target program, five Lewis Classes and 33 contestants. Because the short classes are placed first, six shooters will be in Classes No. 1 and No. 2 and seven shooters in Classes No. 3, No. 4 and No. 5. Final scores are arranged from highest to lowest and the lines drawn in between classes. In the event of tie scores, the winner may be decided by the toss of a coin or by the largest number of consecutive targets broken, long run from the front or back, etc. When the Lewis Class System is used to divide money, the winnings are usually divided equally.

The Rose System

One of the more equitable payoff systems is the Rose System that places a definite point value on every pay spot and totally eliminates any chance for a lucky payoff. A Rose program with points valued at "4,3,2,1, each 25," means scores of 25 are worth four points, 24s three points, 23s two points and 22s one point. At the conclusion of the event, all points won by the contestants who entered for money are totaled and this number divided into the amount of money available from entrance fees and added money to establish the value of a single point.

Therefore, if all pay scores totaled 200 points and

Virtually every gun club has an outside tote board that lists squads and fields. Because a typical trap field takes about 12 to 15 minutes to complete, a shooter can anticipate when and where he will be shooting. There's absolutely no excuse for not showing up on your appointed field on time.

there was $400 in the purse to be divided, each point would have a $2 cash value. A 25 straight would be worth $8, 24s $6, 23s $4 and even commons would earn $2 each. A variation of the Rose System on the 25 options is the Rose Accumulation Points. The point value is established at the conclusion of the program rather than on each 25-target sub-event. With this method, the cashier totals the points won on each event and a 100-straight score would be paid on the basis of having won 16 points when the points have a 4,3,2,1 value.

The beauty of the Rose System is that there is no limit to the point-value combination, and it is possible and logical to establish point value on the total score, rather than sub-events. A combination to bid for participation by all classes would appear in the program somewhat as follows:

Each class shoots for its own entrance and pro-rated added money.
    100 targets, 16 yards or All-Gauge Skeet
    Class AA points worth 3,2,1 — on total score
    Class A points worth 4,3,2,1 — on total score
    Class B points worth 4,3,2,1 — on total score
    Class C points worth 5,4,3,2,1 — on total score
    Class D points worth 6,5,4,3,2,1 — on total score.

Additional bookkeeping is required because it entails conducting five separate tournaments on the same 100 targets. Such a program would not add to the cashier's duties because it would entirely eliminate having to figure event pays, and payoffs on total scores could be quickly figured. An entry of 150 shooters, fairly evenly divided into classes, might show some merit in this plan, especially when there is every reason to believe scores will be high, and management feels that with each class shooting separately, the payoff should not be governed by luck, but by good scores.

The Rose System is as methodical as the multiplication table and eliminates lucky payoffs, which seems to be the only reason this paying on point value method has not been more widely accepted. Shooters seem to prefer some sort of "luck of the draw" aspect in shoot programs.

The Phil Miller System

Perhaps the best payoff to entry ratio system is the Phil Miller System, which has all the necessary ingredients to increase interest in purse competition at either 16-Yard Singles, Doubles targets or All-Gauge Skeet events. Also, the Miller System rewards shooters for firing scores well above their normal averages. The payoffs are higher percentage-wise than most other play-for-pay systems.

Example:
    50 targets, 16-Yard Singles or All-Gauge Skeet
    100 shooters, entry fee $5 = $500 purse

One of the "thankless" jobs at a competitive trap or Skeet shoot is recording and verifying scores. Often, the local "pro" will volunteer his time to do this job which should be provided for by the gun club.

Class AA shooters must break 50x50 to qualify.
Class A shooters must break 49x50 to qualify.
Class B shooters must break 48x50 to qualify.
Class C shooters must break 46x50 to qualify.
Class D shooters must break 45x50 to qualify.
Class E shooters must break 44x50 to qualify.

The cashier figures the payoff as follows:
2-**Class AA** shooters qualify
4-**Class A** shooters qualify
4-**Class B** shooters qualify
2-**Class C** shooters qualify
4-**Class D** shooters qualify
4-**Class E** shooters qualify

Recap: 20 shooters qualify for Purse Money Division — $25 to each shooter. If 40 shooters qualify for Purse Money Division, $12.50 goes to each shooter.

For a 100-target event, these are the recommended minimum scores to qualify for payoff in each class:

AA — 98 or better
A — 96 or better
B — 94 or better
C — 92 or better
D — 90 or better
E — 88 or better

For a 200-target event, these are the recommended minimum scores to qualify for payoff in each class:

Some of the larger trap and Skeet clubs can be intimidating because of their vast size. The shooting line at Tucson, Arizona is well over ¹/₂-mile long. One of the nicest clubs in the West, one of its virtues is that the shooting line is far enough away from the main walkway to eliminate distractions caused by non-shooters.

Gun clubs usually pride themselves on their cleanliness and make great efforts to keep debris and trash from entering the shooting fields. Scraps of paper flying about while attempting to shoot can be most disconcerting.

AA — 197x200 or better
A — 193x200 or better
B — 190x200 or better
C — 187x200 or better
D — 184x200 or better
E — 181x200 or better

These recommendations were established quite a few years ago, and noting that shooting averages nationwide have increased dramatically, these minimum qualifying scores may be a little low and could be raised by a target or two depending on club management. There are many proponents of the Miller system, which has several advantages over other options and purses.

1. Lower-class shooters have the advantage, and there are usually more of them partaking in any event than "hot hammers."
2. Each shooter bets on himself that he can shoot better than his average. If he does, he knows he'll earn a slice of the pie; if he doesn't, there's always tomorrow!
3. There's no dropping of targets for "place" bets, which virtually eliminates "sandbagging."

4. Purses are equal, regardless of the number of entries in each class, which favors the AA and A shooters because they are usually fewer in number. Any added money is divided equally among the winners.
5. The cashier's task is greatly reduced and this system is preferred by many gun club managers.

Added Money

Often, more aggressive gun clubs will earmark a portion of the entrance fee money as "Added Money." This is standard practice and the gun club guarantees that the money will be placed in the program as stated. Every well-operated club, therefore, should know the laid-in cost of their targets and run a preliminary cost audit on their entire tournament operation. (Target costs vary throughout the country because they are bulky and freight is expensive.) The following example will show how easily a club can overestimate the amount of money available to "add" to their shoot. In this case, club management wants to create an interesting handicap event and add all they possibly can over and above their target cost. They might figure 2 cents per target will be available for this purpose over operational and target costs.

Example:

100-target Handicap — $15 entry fee
targets trapped at $.06 each
$9 goes into High Gun Purse
$300 "added" to purse by gun club

At least 150 shooters were expected and the club planned to regain the added money from the sale of 15,000 or more targets. Bad weather, however, cut the entry list to 100 shooters, so the club overestimated their target income by one-third and added $100 more than their income from target sales permitted. Not a fatal loss, but in the wrong direction for a successful business.

Many tournaments do not have much added money in excess of any profit they might figure to derive from the sale of targets. Some additional added-money sources are:

1. At some state shoots the state association gives back a set portion of the fees charged at registered events to the shooters to create a substantial amount of added money for the state tournament.
2. Often, successful gun clubs, organized on a nonprofit basis, have more funds in their treasury than they need for operating expenses and return it to the shooters as added money to create interest in their own tournament.
3. Through ad sales in gun club programs from club supporters and local business firms added money is often collected.
4. When commercial operators of large gun clubs "beef up" their program with more added money than what they expect to show as profit on target sales, it is used as an advertising medium to draw tournament shooters who will travel long distances to attend major events in locations that have attractions other than shooting targets.

Guaranteed Purses

Most well-established annual tournaments have been built up to their current size through Guaranteed Purses. These clubs have experience that helps them prepare their program and realize the drawing power they can create so that they can accurately forecast attendance. Clubs without this experience should be aware that Guaranteed Purses pyramid the club's chances to win or lose money on the overall shoot.

Example:

100-target Handicap — $15 entry fee
$1500 guaranteed purse
$300 to High Gun
$200 to 2nd High Gun
$150 to 3rd High Gun
$100 to 4th High Gun
$75 to the next two High Guns
$50 to the next eight High Guns
$25 to the next eight High Guns

Using the same figures as the added money program described above, the club expects at least 150 entries. Instead of $.02 per target, which might normally be used for added money, they plan on $300. In this event, however, the $300 goes into a guarantee along with $9 from each entry, and the club has a fund of $1,650 against their $1,500 guarantee.

Most gun clubs state in their program that "All purse money collected in excess of the guarantee will be paid back to the shooters in additional cash purses at $25 each." In this instance, 166 entries at $9 each would be necessary before the gun club regained their guarantee from purse entrances.

On the other side of the coin, what would happen if the entry list dropped to 100 shooters? One hundred entries at $9, plus $200 (collected at $.02 per target on 10,000 targets) would create a fund of $1,100 against a guarantee of $1,500. The club has overextended itself and must dig up $400. Guaranteed Purses draw shooters, but have an added risk factor for the sponsoring gun club.

Wolf Options

Many major tournaments, especially those conducted throughout the West, offer a Wolf Option. It's usually offered to those who want to place an additional $35 optional on their ability to break big handicap scores. The Wolf Option is usually presented as follows:

Wolf Optionals on 200 Handicap
entry fee — $35
with $5 on each 50
with $5 on each 100
and $5 on total 200
Division 40-30-20-10 percent Percentage on each of seven events.

This adds an interesting feature and because the event is run concurrently with the regular program, it doesn't require additional expenditure for targets or ammunition. Some exceptional payoffs have resulted when a shooter happens to have the good fortune of turning in two excellent handicap scores back-to-back.

Ford Purses

O.N. Ford was one of trap's finest shooters and a great booster of the sport in the 1920s. He originated the Wolf Shoots, the Ford Purses and the Pacific International Trapshooting Association (PITA), all of which still exist.

Ford Purses call for an entry fee of $1 or $2 per event, usually optional, paid out on a winner-take-all basis. They run concurrently with the 25-target subevents and total scores in handicap programs, and pay off the lucky winners at long-shot odds. At the Grand American trapshooting tournament, a single Ford purse usually assures a shooter that his trip to Vandalia has been successful.

The official printed program should specify if there is a limit on the number of Ford purses one shooter can win, otherwise a lone 100 straight can claim all five Ford purses. Tie scores are shot off on the following 25 target sub-event, and the purses split between those still tied at the end of the fourth sub-event unless the program states "Ties on the first day's purses will carry over onto the next day's handicap events for shootoff." If reverse scores are used to break any ties, the program should definitely state that. Ties on the total score purse cause the purse to be split among those involved.

Shootoffs can produce some strange results. (Below) The author (left) and Walt Weaver had knotted at 299x300 in a 16-yard mini-marathon. At the start of the shootoff, the author lost his first target out of the house for a second place finish of 24x25 to Weaver's 25x25.

The original Ford Purse was for first-time winners to get $25 and repeat winners to be paid the entire accumulated amount except the original $25, which was held back to keep the purse alive in the name of its original donor. Repeat wins, however, in the same handicap occurred so infrequently that Ford Purses today are handled like above.

ATA Point System

A somewhat new method is the ATA Point System, which is a High-Gun system in which the more targets

(Above) Coming off a shootoff as the victor is a great accomplishment. Shootoffs are the culmination of any event and with the high degree of perfection found among today's shooters, shootoffs are extremely common.

Example:

If the program states that no shooter can win more than one event purse and the total score purse, and ties can be settled by the next sub-event, scores are divided between shooters. The following illustrates the working of five Ford Purses on a 100-target Handicap race. (Ford Purses on 16-yard events have proven unsuccessful because of the numerous 100 straights).

Shooter Scores by Sub-Event	Total Score	
25-25-23-22	95	winner, sub-event #1
25-24-25-21	93	winner, sub-event #3
25-25-22-25	97	winner, sub-event #2 and ½ total purse
25-24-24-24	97	½-total purse
24-22-23-25	94	½-sub-event #4
21-22-23-25	91	½-sub-event #4

the shooter breaks, the more he wins. One-money for each five entries means that one-fifth, or 20 percent, of the shooters will win. Low score in the money receives one point, the next higher score two points, etc. The difference between the first and second high scores is four points and the difference between second and third high scores three points instead of one. The total points awarded are divided into the total money to determine the value of each point. The amount the shooter receives will be the value of each point multiplied by his total number of points.

Optionals — 25s & 50s

I have yet to see a trapshooting program that hasn't offered the 25s and 50s options. So that they are thoroughly understood by new shooters, let's look closer at them and see if they're a "good buy."

The 25s option is usually a $2.50 bet per field and is split 60/40 percent on a percentage system. Simply, this means the highest score on each field will share the 60 percent portion of the pot and the second highest the 40 percent portion of the pot. For example, all entrants who shoot a 25 straight on Field No. 1 will share the 60 percent portion of the pot equally. All shooters who score a 24x25 on Field No. 1 will divvy up the 40 percent portion of the entry money. If there are no 25x25s recorded on Field No. 1 by any of the entrants, the next highest score (assuming someone shot a 24x25) moves up to the top spot, and of course a 23x25 moves up as well. As 100-target events are usually shot over two or four fields though, the 100 targets are divided into four separate 25-target sub-events, each "25 option" is an event within itself. Recently, however, I have noticed that many of the more active gun clubs have changed the percentages on the 25s from a 60/40 split to High Gun. This means that only the highest score on each sub-event shares in the prize. If there is a single 25 straight on Field No. 1, it takes the entire pot. The 24s don't pay.

The 50s option is similar to the 25s and is played on two 25s strung together. Some gun clubs offer two 50s options, based on Fields No. 1 and 2 and Fields No. 3 and No. 4. Recently, there has been a trend of offering three 50s options, with the middle Fields No. 2 and No. 3 making the third leg on the trio of 50s. Fifty straight in handicap, from any yardage, is difficult and therefore a 50 straight usually pays quite handsomely. There are many gun clubs, especially in the West, that offer another variation called "Perfect 50s." Anything less than a 50x50 is carried into the next handicap event. In 1986 at Miramar Gun Club in San Diego, California, one of the country's top guns broke a perfect 100x100 and took both the perfect 100 purse along with the three Perfect 50s to the tune of over $12,000! As you can see, these purses can add up very quickly. I have also witnessed many 50 straights that paid upward of $2,000 for a single event, especially at a large shoot where the weather made a mockery out of the scores. Regular 50s usually pay 50-30-20 percent Percentage system and are divided like the 25s option.

Traditionally, there's a purse bet based on the total 100 targets paid out one-money to each seven entries, or five entries, or whatever the host club decides. Therefore, if the program states there is a $10 purse and the payoff is based on "one-money for each seven" entries and there are 28 entries, the top four scores will share the $280 purse on a High Gun of 40, 30, 20 and 10 percent, or $112, $84, $56 and $28, respectively.

Calcuttas

Often called a "Special Event" or "Surprise from India," Calcuttas are widely used in golf events. Practically every country club sponsors one of these money-makers made up of enthusiastic players and buyers. Officially frowned upon by the ATA, Calcuttas nevertheless are an integral part of trapshooting and are wagering events that allow non-shooters to get into the act.

Each shooter entering the Calcutta usually pays a $10 entrance fee which enables him to have his name listed on a tote board. As his name is announced by an auctioneer, anybody in the audience, including the entrant, can make a cash bid for the shooter. Then the highest bidder claims his "horse." At the conclusion of the auction, all the money is totaled, including the shooters' entry fees, and placed in a giant Calcutta pot. Payoffs may be made either High Gun or Percentage system, and usually the auctioneer asks potential "buyers" how they want the pot to be split. A count of raised hands will dictate the type of payoff.

Regardless of the type of payoff — High Gun or Per-

Calcuttas are very big at most trapshoots. (Right) Before buying your "horse," it's a good idea to find out his track record. The best place to find that out is at the scoreboard. Picking a winner during a Calcutta is much like handicapping thoroughbreds with great emphasis on past performance.

The Calcutta board below lists all the shooters, their buyers and the amount that was bid on them. Calcutta pots can range from a few thousand dollars to amounts reaching six figures.

centage — the "buyer" usually receives 70 percent of his "horse" if he comes in and the shooter (horse) receives 30 percent of his share of the pot. If the shooter "buys" himself, he would, obviously, receive 100 percent of his share of the pot.

Let's say 100 shooters enter at $10 per entry fee for a beginning pot of $1,000. Their names are posted on a large blackboard. Adjacent to each shooter's name is a place for the buyer's name and the amount paid for the shooter. Often, the first offer made by the auctioneer is a "wild card." The highest bidder can select any name from the list. Sometimes, there will be two or even three "wild cards" offered depending on the number of "hot hammers" entered.

Now, let's say the total income from the auction is $5,000, which averages out to a $50 bid per shooter. Adding this to the entry fee of $1,000, there is now a grand total of $6,000 in the Calcutta pool. Most Calcuttas pay three places — 50 percent to the highest score, 30 percent to the first runner-up and 20 percent to the second runner-up. This is where the large difference between the High Gun and Percentage payoff systems comes into play. If the High Gun system is voted in the "bidders," the three highest scores — including ties — share the Calcutta pot. For example, let's assume a lone 99x100 and a pair of 98x100s are recorded. The 99 claims 50 percent of the pot and the pair of 98s take 30 and 20 percent and divide it equally, each receiving 25 percent of the Calcutta pool.

On the other hand, with the Percentage system invoked, the lone 99 still takes the top 50 percent, the 98s share 30 percent and any 97s divvy up the remaining 20 percent. With the Percentage system, more shooters have the opportunity to sneak into the payoff picture, but the amount of money in the pot is spread quite a bit thinner than in the High Gun system.

Now, let's go back to the $6,000 pot and see who gets what. As you recall, our first example was the High Gun system. Therefore, the lone 99 takes 50 percent of the $6,000 pot for a handsome $3,000 payoff. The buyer receives 70 percent of this amount — $2,100 — and the shooter receives 30 percent — $900. The two 98s take runner-up and third place, split it and receive 25 percent of the pot, or $1,500 per entrant. And, like the champion, the buyer and shooter must split the proceeds 70-30, respectively.

If the Percentage system is voted in, the single 99 score will not be affected, but the two 98s will share only in 30 percent of the pot, each receiving 15 percent, or $900, and the buyer/shooter receiving $630 and $270, respectively. Third place, or the 20 percent portion, is shared by the 97s, and if four 97s are produced, each is entitled to 5 percent of the pot or $300 each, and the buyer/shooter receives $210/$90. The Calcuttas add a lot of excitement to any large trapshoot. Their continued use, however, should not be encouraged and used no more than four times a year by the average gun club. Naturally, the Calcutta can be used for Skeet shooting events as well, in fact virtually any type of "sporting" event is more fun with a Calcutta.

If asked what keeps trapshooting alive and active, I believe the main reason is shooting for money. Being at the right place at the right time can reward the shooters with huge monetary payoffs. The other side of the financial coin is the amount of money invested to enter a single race and play all the purses and options. For example, at the 1988 Grand American Handicap Tournament, it costs shooters over $1,000 for targets and ammunition and to play all the options and purses for the week. That is quite a bit of money, but if one is a gambling man — and show me a true trapshooter who isn't — this would be the time and place to plunk down the cash. The number of entrants at the Grand American Handicap event, which is an activity in the Grand American Handicap Tournament, has averaged over 4000 shooters for the past 10 years — and remember, this is accomplished in a single day! It is the world's largest single-day shooting event.

Payoffs at the Grand range from fantastic to pitiful depending on the weather. With thousands of competitors playing the money, normally "excellent" handicap scores in the high 90s often net the shooter less than what he wagered. On the other hand, if poor weather prevails and the typical scores are sub-par, the few high scores may reap the benefits to the tune of $25,000 to $40,000 in total payoffs to a single shooter. Not exactly chicken feed!

"Playing the money" at the larger trapshoots is like playing $1 or nickel slot machines. The winner receives back in proportion to what he invests. Somewhat smaller in attendance, but still considered major shoots around the country are the various zone and state shoots, along with the mini-Grands such as the Spring Grand, Mid-Western Grand, Southern Grand, etc.

Many shooters — both trap and Skeet — can't handle the pressure of big-money shoots. These individuals like to enjoy themselves and shoot for "targets only." But don't kick yourself in the seat of your pants if you "accidentally" shoot a big score, and "if" you had played the money, you would have made out quite well. Someone once said that "hindsight is always 20/20," but in trap and Skeet events where cash is "on the barrelhead," you pay your money and you take your chances!

10

Overcoming Shooting Setbacks

THE PURPOSE of this chapter is to acquaint new shooters with a few pitfalls they'll encounter in both trap and Skeet shooting. The more you shoot, the more experience you'll gain. We all learn from experience and mistakes, but a wise man also learns from other people's mistakes.

Competitive trap and Skeet shooting is laced with setbacks that can be described as events, or a series of events, that oppose success. If you've been a clay target shooter for some time, you can undoubtedly rattle off any number of "happenings" that have led to the downfall of your shooting success. If, however, you've recently taken up trap or Skeet shooting, you may well be protected, so to speak, by the "beginner's luck" syndrome that allows many newcomers to say, "It's such an easy sport, how can anyone miss those clay targets?" Or, "With all those BBs in the air, you can't miss!"

These statements bring a wry smile to veteran shooters' faces. Newcomers can also invoke snickers if they make forecasts like, "I don't think it'll take much time

at all before I reach the 27-yard line," or, "The way I'm shooting now, I'm sure by the end of my first year I'll be able to hold a high 90s average in all four gauges."

You won't hear bold statements like those from experienced shooters' mouths because they've learned the hard way that "adversities" in trap and Skeet shooting are not to be taken lightly. Much like Murphy's Law, they can come into play ever so swiftly, making your attempts to shoot a good score all but impossible.

What are these misfortunes that can so drastically affect your shooting style? Unfortunately, there are quite a few; we'll discuss the more important ones. Keep in mind that our list is by no means complete. After reading this chapter, however, you should be able to correct some of the more common shooting obstacles that plague both new and old shooters.

Proper Gun Fit

Even though this subject is covered in detail in chapter 6, it must be mentioned here because improper gun

Successful competitive shooters learn how to quickly size up a different shooting situation than what they are accustomed to, make necessary corrections or alterations to their shooting style and then still go out and shoot good scores. The only difference between a good shooter and a great shooter is the ability to adapt to a given situation.

fit is trap and Skeet shooting's number one error. If you strive to be more than a once or twice a year shooter, you must become "as one" with your gun. If your scores are to improve, you must achieve consistent gun placement (mounting), proper gun fit, plus correct body and gun position in relation to the upcoming target.

An old adage claims, "The typical shotgun comes from the factory with stock dimensions to fit the average shooter." Guess what? There are no average shooters and it behooves each one of you to determine how your gun must be modified to fit you, not the other way around. Seek a professional's help and determine what the correct length of pull should be, find out if the comb is too high or too low, double check the relationship between the sight beads, rib and point of impact.

I have talked to many shooters more concerned with messing up a pretty piece of wood on their fine such-and-such tournament gun than having the stock fit them correctly. I believe they have their priorities mixed up. Your first and foremost objective should be to pulverize more targets, not preserve the good looks of a piece of wood. Too often, new shooters show off a cut of wood on their guns like it's a real work of art. Those same shooters will take their museum-quality pieces out on the firing line and tuck it in here or pull it there so they can see the target better, or position it a bit lower on

Take practice shooting seriously. If possible, make a Coke or cup of coffee wager with a squad mate to keep your mind firmly affixed on the task at hand. Also, the practice trap is the best place to "practice shootoffs." Use this practice time wisely.

their shoulders because "it breaks targets better that way."

Don't forget that the purpose of a trap or Skeet gun is to destroy clay targets. If you have a really fine piece of wood that doesn't fit you and you don't want it marred, buy another "using" stock for your gun and store the fancier wood. They don't give extra targets for good-looking guns.

Proper gun mounting is another "adversity" that takes its toll. One hard and fast rule . . . if it doesn't feel right, you can bet all the change in your pocket it isn't mounted correctly, and chances are, you'll miss that next target out of the trap house.

Your proven basic stance and barrel placement in relation to the target is yet another setback that can ruin some of your fun during a shoot. Re-read the section on stance and muzzle position in another chapter keeping in mind that the slightest deviation will have a profound effect on your ability to break clay targets effectively and effortlessly.

Bad Instruction

Here's a common scenario. A new shooter walks into a Skeet club, says he is a beginner and asks if there is anyone around who might give him a few pointers on shooting Skeet better. If you've ever seen this happen, you know what happens next.

A drove of unqualified "instructors" swoop down on this bedeviled novice like a flock of robins on a worm farm. What follows is a glossary of every shooting phrase ever heard — "you're shooting too high, too low; you're behind the target; you're in front of it, your stock is too short," — and on and on. Of course, the student is so confused by the end of his lesson that what little he thought he knew prior to the "everybody's a qualified instructor" experience has long since been modified or forgotten.

There is only one way to get qualified instruction — pay for professional help. How and where do you find it? Subscribe to or borrow magazines that deal with either trap or Skeet shooting. You'll find ads from various instructors around the country who give what they refer to as "clinics" at predetermined costs. If you want the best instruction available, clinics are the best way to go. Call the instructor who seems to best fit your needs and discuss his clinic requirements. Normally for a shooting expert to come to your area, a certain number of students must be guaranteed, etc. That is the Cadillac approach to receiving instruction.

There are currently a host of video tapes available that claim to help straighten out a veteran's problems or hold a tyro's hand through beginning stages of both trap and Skeet shooting. I have personally reviewed all the tapes available and a couple are excellent, a few good and many simply terrible. I suggest you preview a tape before you buy it, or at least have exchange privileges. The same holds true for cassette tapes — there's some

A new shooter is strongly advised to seek help from a professional instructor. A good one will charge and a poor one will give advice for free. You get what you pay for.

Listening to top guns will result in gathering important information that can only be learned first-hand. A wise man not only learns from his own mistakes, but from others as well.

fine material available as well as garbage; buyer beware.

If you're short on bucks or there are no clinics in your area, visit all the gun clubs around you and ask the club managers who they recommend for trap or Skeet lessons. Watch an actual lesson by each of the instructors and determine for yourself which one you like. If you have some difficulty coming up with names, borrow a year-end average book from one of the three clay target associations — National Skeet Shooting Association, Amateur Trapshooting Association or the Pacific International Trapshooting Association. Look for the shooter with the best overall average who lives in your area and ask him directly if he will instruct you. Keep in mind however, that the best shooters do not necessarily make qualified instructors. Some shooters just can't convey their techniques to others, even though they can consistently break big scores.

Switching Guns

Most top-notch trap and Skeet shooters agree that it takes at least a year to learn the nuances of a shotgun if you practice with it a lot and even longer if you practice infrequently. Plan on burning up a lot of shells with a new gun. It will take that long just to sort out the correct stock fit for your style of shooting and it will take awhile to discover which reload or factory round works best in your new gun.

After you test various guns and commit to shooting one, stay with it! If you shoot some bad scores, forget them, they aren't signals to change to another gun. It's mind boggling how many shooters frequently switch guns. Want some incentive? Look at the better shooters. Do they switch guns? Hardly ever. Stay with your gun through good scores and bad for at least 1 or 2 years before determining once and for all that you can't achieve your shooting goals with it. You should only switch to another gun if your physical dimensions radically change.

Barrel Patterning

If given a nickel for every shooter out of 100 who took the time to pattern a newly-acquired gun to determine what shotshell worked best and where and how it printed its pattern before buying it, you probably wouldn't end up with enough cash to buy a bag of beans. Yet, this is a very big problem in trap and Skeet.

How many times have you suspected that one load patterns better than another in your gun because you

Test your favorite shotgun's trigger pull weight at regular intervals. Triggers do vary from time to time and changes in the "go-switch" can play havoc with good scores. A good trigger pull scale isn't cheap, but they're well worth the $30 or so investment.

can see it pulverizing targets? On the other hand, you've probably shot some factory shells or reloads that seem to perform less efficiently. There are also probably times when you've shot and were convinced you were smack dab in the middle of each target, yet you only got a small piece of the bird. That's when doubt in your ability creeps in and you wonder whether your gun shoots where you point it.

Why shooters avoid the pattern board is a mystery to me. Believe me when I tell you the top bananas of the shooting sports know exactly what their shotgun will do at various ranges and with different loads and shot sizes. They don't leave anything to chance, which is another reason why they are on top of their game. A session at the pattern board will answer your questions, but failure to pattern your gun can lead to serious doubts about your loads, gun, ability — or all three. There's no quicker way to improve your scores than to determine what load (factory-new shells or reloads) performs best in your gun. The differences between various brands of shells and reloads and their patterning abilities in a gun can be dramatic.

After patterning your gun, you'll be able to determine if it shoots where you point it. If not, it is usually a simple matter for a competent gunsmith to alter the point of impact with a stock modification or choke work. It is a time-consuming task that will have you counting pellet holes in large pieces of paper until you're blue in the face. To do the job correctly, you'll have to fire a minimum of 10 rounds of each shell to establish which combination works best in your gun, but the rewards are worth the effort.

After you determine the right shell combination, you'll notice an increase in your ability to break clay targets at a trap or Skeet shoot or a weekend fun event. Taking time to pattern your gun will remove even more adversity from your clay target shooting efforts.

Flinching

It's safe to say that everyone has flinched at one time or another; an occasional flinch is something you can expect. Occasional flinching can be tolerated and when it happens, you can only hope to luck out and break the target anyway. But when that flinch becomes more frequent, it's truly an adversity that has to be quickly remedied or it just might destroy any and all shooting ability you've acquired.

Flinching, when it is epidemic, is horrible to see. As you may know, flinching is the body's reaction to the constant pounding of recoil produced every time the gun is fired. When flinching is bad, it can literally cause a shooter to abandon the clay target sports all together. Is flinching curable? Yes, in many cases it can be completely eliminated several ways.

Attacking the flinching problem is usually four-fold. First a shooter should try to use recoil devices in his stock or switch to an auto-loading shotgun with its somewhat drawn-out recoil curve. Custom barrel work from a competent gunsmith is yet another way to go. You can have the forcing cone of your chamber lengthened plus the entire barrel back-bored which will also reduce recoil. Another benefit of these modifications is that they should improve the patterning of your gun. Porting your barrel will also reduce recoil. Reloads should be seriously researched. A good 1-ounce load will recoil remarkably less than a regular 1⅛-ounce target load.

Finally, if all of the above fail to eliminate flinching, it's possibly time for a release trigger, or a trigger that fires the shell when it is released rather than pulled. The release trigger will probably go down in history as the one device that has cured the most flinching. However, it is something that should only be considered after all the above remedies have been tried.

Trap and Skeet shooters do not take a middle-of-the-road attitude toward release triggers — they either swear by them or at them! Those in favor claim their use has made them better shooters, extended their shooting careers, etc. Those opposed fear them for obvious safety reasons and say if they have to convert to release triggers, they will quit shooting.

For those not familiar with this type of mechanism, it is simply a standard pull trigger converted by a competent triggersmith to fire when released. The shooter first "sets" the trigger by pulling it rearward and holding it until he wants the gun to discharge, which he does by releasing the trigger. The better trigger experts can set up a release trigger much like a pull trigger, except in reverse. For example, a pull trigger that takes less than 3 pounds of pressure to cause the hammer to fall is considered a "fast" trigger. Conversely, a "fast" release trigger will "release," or cause the hammer to fall at the measured weight, different from what is necessary to "set" the trigger and "release" it. It typically takes 3 pounds of pressure to pull the trigger fully rearward, setting it at 1 to 1½ pounds of "release pressure" to make it fire. These poundages can easily be measured by a trigger scale.

Everyone has his or her own story regarding flinching and the use of release triggers. There are several different types of flinching. The "recoil" flinch occurs when the body can no longer accept and tolerate the pain from recoil and rebels by not allowing the trigger to be pulled. The "eye" flinch occurs when the target's flight path is not clearly defined. When the brain's computer reacts, the trigger is jerked to help "catch up" with the fleeing target. Another type of flinching is "emotional." This flinch is the most devastating because it strikes without warning. I was stricken with this "disease" for almost 3 months, but instead of laying off shooting for awhile, I kept right on shooting and my scores and averages plummeted.

Let's take a closer look at each type in greater detail. The recoil flinch is the most common among trap and Skeet shooters, especially for those "veterans" who shoot a lot of targets yearly. After countless thousands of rounds, the human body tries to stop the punishment it has been taking over the years. Most shooters claim recoil doesn't bother them. It doesn't until they start flinching, and then that statement doesn't hold water. Recoil-induced flinching cannot be prevented, but taking a few preventative precautions can help guard against its onset.

First, make sure the gun fits you properly. A poorly-fitted gunstock will cause excessive pain in the face, cheek, shoulder and chest areas. If even an occasional flinch raises its ugly head, it's time to take another precaution, which hopefully will become a prevention, by adding a recoil-reducing device to your shotgun. The best types are shock-absorbing styles that actually soak up a great amount of the recoil energy, preventing this kinetic energy from bombarding your body. Adding weight to the gun will also help reduce felt recoil because the recoil has to overcome the inertia of the heavier gun. I recommend that trap and Skeet guns weigh upward of 9½ to 10 pounds if the shooter has the strength and stamina to handle these heavyweights.

The eye flinch is solved more easily than the recoil flinch. The mind and eyes must work in perfect unison for the shooter to consistently break targets. Therefore,

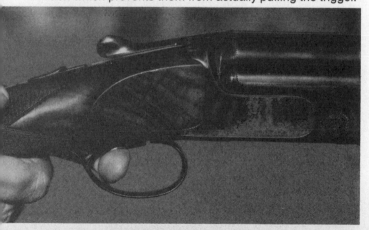

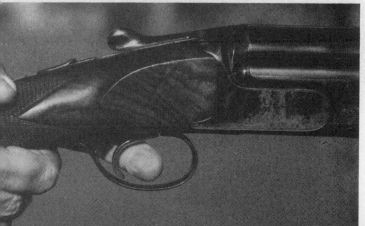

Many shooters use a release trigger in their trap guns. These "backward" triggers release the hammer when the trigger is released instead of pulled. Typically, trap shooters convert to the use of release triggers whenever they start to develop a flinch which prevents them from actually pulling the trigger.

if the eyes don't see the target when the brain expects it to, the shooter will make a desperate lunge at it well after the target is usually out of range. Often, the shooter cannot distinguish the direction of the "blur" coming out of the trap house, or worse, misreads the direction. Reading a target to be a quarter angle when actually it is a dead straightaway will surely cause the shooter to miss the target.

There are three proven methods to overcome the eye flinch. First, go have your eyes checked because you might need corrective glasses. If you already have prescription shooting glasses, have them checked too, because your prescription might need changing. If that doesn't cure your ills, gun position is next on the agenda.

If you are having problems distinguishing the "correct" flight of a target and carry a fairly high gun, lowering the muzzle to the top of the trap house roof, or even below it, will allow you to better "read" the beginning of the target's flight path and track the target with both your eyes and gun muzzle. If that doesn't work, bring the muzzle up about 3 feet above the top of the trap house, and instead of looking down the barrel, as most shooters do, focus your eyes and attention on the top of the trap house. This sighting system, which is often the most successful, does two things — it allows you to carry a high gun which eliminates a great deal of vertical barrel movement, and it allows the eyes to pick up the target earlier than normal, providing longer target "read time."

The emotional flinch is so sneaky that even experienced shooters don't know what's happened until it's too late. They generally will not admit that emotional stress, totally unrelated to competitive shooting, can cause disastrous problems overnight. Most of the time, shooters try to cure their problem by changing equipment, like converting to a release trigger, adding recoil devices, or even selling off a battery of proven guns and replacing them with a whole new set. All of these cure-alls are wrong; I know, I did them all.

During a 3-month "flinching" stretch in which I shot at over 3500 Singles and Handicap targets, I dropped over 4 percentage points off my Singles average and over 8 points off my Handicap average. I can tell horror stories, two in particular, about flinching that I wouldn't have thought possible. For more than 30 years of competitive shooting, I was proud of the fact that I *never* shot less than 90x100 in any Singles race, regardless of the weather or gun club, and didn't duck shoots to maintain an average. Palmdale California's Fin & Feather Gun Club is renowned for its windy conditions. Even though the wind was a brisk 20- to 25-knot crosswind, I entered the competition and came out with my lowest Singles score ever — 177x200.

The other exasperating experience occurred at the 1988 Spring Grand in Phoenix, Arizona. The weather was perfect; there was a light breeze and the sun was shining brightly. It was my third attempt using a release trigger, and I was down only one target in the first 95. I felt like I had overcome my flinching problem. Shooting from Post #1, I drew five consecutive hard left-angle targets. I couldn't release the trigger on any of the five birds. Each hit the ground without me ever firing a shot and was scored as a "lost" because of my flinch.

As my marital/divorce problems sorted themselves out, so did my scores. But at no time during this horrendous experience did I blame outside influences such as upcoming trials, property settlements, and all those other distasteful experiences on which I was about to embark.

Changing to a release trigger did not satisfactorily cure my flinching problem. Even after my mind settled down, I stuck with the release trigger. However, I found myself flinching at a higher rate than when I first started using it.

After much soul searching, I discovered why I was still flinching. Trap pullers being who they are, we must learn to overcome poor pulls by refusing them. Fast pulls are easier to turn down than slow ones in my experience with a pull trigger. However, when I used a release trigger, fast pulls literally "ate me up" and I jumped at the targets when I saw them. The slow pulls also caused me much consternation as I waited for the bird to emerge and then flinched going after it. My major problem with the release trigger was my inability to refuse bad pulls, thus I shot at everything that came out of the house, which resulted in poor scores and excessive flinching.

When I eventually went back to a pull trigger, the first thing I noticed about my shooting was my ability to turn down bad pulls and only shoot at targets that emerged on my command, not the trap puller's. I'm currently using a pull trigger, shooting decent scores again, and keeping an eye out for those guns I sold earlier.

Bad Weather

As both Skeet and trapshooting are outdoor sports, shooters are often shooting at the whim of Mother Nature. Therefore, to become a champion or earn the revered title of "consistent" competitor, one must shoot in all kinds of weather. It is rare that a trap or Skeet shoot is called off because of torrential downpours, hurricane-speed winds or sub-zero temperatures. Like show business, the game usually goes on, which makes these shooting sports both unique and challenging.

Neither Skeet nor trapshooting are seasonal sports, as both registered and fun shoots are held around the calendar in all parts of the country. Shoots are held in March in Montana, the shooters bundled up like Eskimos searching for seals. Conversely, trap and Skeet events are often scheduled in California and Arizona when the mercury tops 110 degrees! Shooter comfort has never been a criterion for scheduling an event!

The ability to shoot well in inclement weather is the mark of a champion. I won't forget one prime example that occurred when I was attending a trapshoot in Las Vegas, Nevada sponsored by the Mint Gun Club. It was February, when traditionally the weather is cold with a prevailing wind out of the north. Shooting conditions on that particular day were dreadful — bitter cold with temperatures hovering around the 40-degree mark, the wind was gusting from 10 to 30 knots, and to make matters completely sour, a light drizzle was falling.

Simply venturing out in this weather was a challenge — shooting in it an experience and shooting a good score preposterous. Everyone complained about the weather and accepted defeat before chambering a shell. Comments like, "Hope I can break an 80," or "Why bother!" were commonplace. Yet, a handful of half-frozen shooters looked at the rain-soaked flag and stood at attention with smiles on their faces. This was what they had come to Las Vegas for — bad weather!

A select group knew the odds were in their favor. Although Handicap trapshooting is theoretically the equalizer between average and outstanding trapshooters — because of the yardage differences — most 27-yard trapshooters maintain a higher Handicap average than the majority of short- or middle-yardage competitors. How did these superlative shooters get to the "back fence?" Not by ducking out of shoots held in bad weather. They learned not only how to cope with adversities, but to actually benefit from these normally-distracting circumstances.

But, back to the Las Vegas trapshoot. There were more than 175 squads of shooters signed up for the Handicap event. Normally, because of the large number of shooters, the Mint Gun Club would have to cut off entries due to time and space limitations. But, on this day bad weather made its mark. Squad after squad had "missing" shooters who pulled out of the event assuming they were beaten before they even started. They

went back to town for the luxury of a hotel suite and a toddy. Of the 800 shooters who originally signed up for the event, less than 700 "toed the line," and as anticipated, scores were very, very low. Normally "good-weather" shooters broke scores in the high 60s, low 70s, boasting that they weren't the lowest on their squads.

Positioned near the scoreboard, I noticed that once in awhile someone recorded a score of 90 or so and immediately the "gather arounders" shook their heads in dismay and moaned, "Don't know how he did it!" Suddenly, there was a roar of total amazement throughout the line. Somebody had shot a perfect 100x100! Incredible, yes indeed . . . surprising, not at all! The shooter was Dan Bonillas, trapshooter par excellence. Not only did he shatter 100 targets, but he did it from the maximum 27-yard handicap distance. No, the weather did not clear up suddenly when Bonillas shot, as scores by his squad mates proved. And it wasn't just a "lucky" day for him. His shooting records prove that when the weather is at its worst, Bonillas is at his best! He makes the weather work for him because he doesn't change his shooting style.

Most shooters perform miserably in foul weather because they believe they have to radically change their shooting styles or timing. This is a common mistake made by both newcomers and veteran shooters. Good competitive shooters learn how to cope and adapt their shooting styles to a particular shooting hazard . . . they don't drastically alter their timing, stance or gun mount; they stay with the style that made them great shooters. As a rural sage once said, "You dance with what you brung."

Can the average shooter learn how to cope with bad weather? Yes, but only by shooting in it. However, you have to prepare for it *before* you shoot, not after. If it's cold, don't wear every stitch of clothing you own — you may be warm on the inside but all those clothes will

If the gun club faces north, then early morning squads have the advantage of shooting in light overcast before the sun has much effect on the lighting conditions. Gray days usually produce highest shooting scores.

Learn how to shoot with a heavy shooting jacket before you need to put it on during an event. One of the keys to breaking good scores is comfort. Being cold is not comfortable, nor is shooting with too much clothing, which will affect the length of pull and sight picture.

Weather and wind are the greatest influences on a shooter's score. If shooting conditions are ideal, then the majority of shooters will fire scores well above their averages. But, if a cross-wind or inconsistent lighting conditions should rear their ugly heads, then scores will be lowered drastically.

togs or slip into a lightweight rain suit. A jacket only provides protection for the upper body, rain pants keep the legs dry and warm. A quality rain suit is expensive, usually running upward of $50 for a ventilated nylon version. It is probably the most expensive thing you'll ever wear considering the cost and the number of times it is worn. But when hundreds or thousands of dollars — or a championship — is at stake, a rain suit is an inexpensive insurance policy. Take it with you as religiously as you would ear plugs and ammunition.

Forecasting weather conditions is somewhat of a science — regardless of what local weathermen say on the evening news. If there's a storm predicted in the area you're going to shoot, take enough of the correct clothing to be able to dress as comfortably as possible, re-

hamper your shooting ability and drastically change your gun mount position. And such changes will virtually guarantee your failure for that given event. So, you should wear as little clothing as possible that will affect normal gun mount position. If you're accustomed to wearing a shooting vest and medium- to lightweight shirt, stay as close to those dimensions as possible because the more clothing you wear alters not only the length of the gun's pull, but also impedes the freedom of movement in your shoulder and chest muscles.

Depending on the gun club, a round of trap takes less than 12 minutes to complete on a single field. Skeet takes a bit longer, but experienced and fast shooters can complete a round in about the same amount of time. It's advisable, therefore, to keep a warm jacket nearby and slip into it between fields. That way, you'll be able to warm up between events and normalize your body temperature. Remember, the body has great resilience and can cope with bad weather better than the mind.

A rainstorm is usually no reason to cancel a shoot. You must either brave the elements in normal shooting

gardless of conditions. If you're away from home and packed extra shirts, gloves, rain gear, etc., don't leave them in the motel room! Too often I've seen shooters scurrying back to their rental cars only to find that their warm, lightweight, down jackets are resting on comfortable hangers inside motel room closets. Scratch one shoot fee!

Now that you're properly dressed, the wind is still blowing, and the rain is beating a tune on the metal roof of the clubhouse, it's time to take some mental precautions and evaluate the situation. If possible, go out on the shooting line and study the bird's flight — long before it's your turn to step to the line. There's nothing more demoralizing than to be surprised by the flight of the first bird out of the house, and 99 times out of 100, you'll miss it. If there's a tail wind, you can be certain the bird will be driven down long before it reaches the "setting stake." But, if you know that in advance, you're both mentally and physically prepared for its unorthodox flight.

Now you're keyed mentally and know in advance

what to expect. Instead of receiving a normal "regulation" target on your command, you're presented with a lower-flying "diver" that smashes into the ground somewhere between 10 and 15 yards short of the stake, depending on the intensity of the wind. But remember, unless the wind is of gale force or at least running 25 knots or more, the speed of the target will not increase. It is set — with properly-maintained trap machines — to leave the trap arm at about 40 mph. By the time the bird has traveled 40 yards or so, it has slowed down to 25 mph.

On the other hand, if a head wind is blowing, the target will rise drastically from the trap house. This type of ill wind will only have some effect on the target after it has traveled about half of its regularly prescribed distance. Therefore, the first half of the target's thrown arc is rarely affected by the wind's velocity or direction. It is during this flight time that the shooter must begin his millisecond calculations. If a shooter concentrates on the target when it first leaves the house, his mind will automatically make the necessary corrections to present a correct sight picture, with the result being a smashed target! And that, fellow shooters, is the name of the game!

Trap Pullers

I don't know of any other major sport in which a referee, umpire, field judge or any other official is called on to help or inadvertently hinder the contestants' performance. I've never seen a football back judge snap the ball to a quarterback, nor has anyone ever witnessed a hockey referee center the puck to Wayne Gretzky to shoot the winning goal. Not only must we as shooters learn how to control our own abilities, but we must learn how to synchronize our performances with those of nonshooters. Good shooters have reasons for missing a target — poor shooters have excuses. Unlike most other competitive sports in which money is involved, or at least semi-expensive trophies, shooting contestants are dependent on others' abilities to perform. Poorly-trained target pullers are the norm and that's what the shooter must learn to accept, tolerate and overcome. If one "blows his cool" over a trap puller's inconsistency, all he's done is greatly dilute his concentration on the target.

There are a few ways to prevent this from happening. Earlier it was suggested that shooters preview the targets before they shoot. At the same time, they should pay close attention to the trap puller's personality and timing. If quite a few targets are turned down by shooters on the squad being watched, you know in advance that the puller is either badly trained or just having a bad day. We all have bad days, so why not give that teenager the benefit of the doubt and allow him the same consideration.

The overwhelming majority of trap and Skeet help are youngsters, ranging in age from 10 to 18. These junior-age workers are usually paid minimum salary —

If the trap puller inadvertently "fast pulled" you, don't accept that target and don't shoot at it. There's nothing in the Skeet or trap shooting rules that says you must shoot at mis-pulled targets.

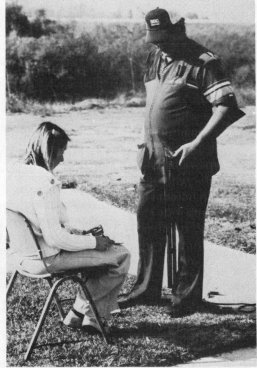

As a matter of practice, whenever passing by the puller/scorer, take a cursory glance at your scores while the sub-event is in progress. Any errors must be caught and changed at that time.

Another adversity is the trap personnel. Remember, these kids are human and will make mistakes both in pulling and setting of the targets. Remember, the shooter can refuse bad pulls and bad targets. Nobody pulls your trigger but you, so if you accept, shoot and miss a poorly set or miss-timed target, then it is your own fault.

in some instances less, depending on the gun club's management. Why? Simple economics. In any event, these kids are doing a job, not usually because they enjoy it, but because they have to work and earn a few bucks on their own. As a group, it's certain they would rather be off on a beach somewhere, enjoying themselves with their peers. Instead, they're constantly being scowled at and scolded and must take the abusive brunt of the inconsiderate shooter's personality.

While waiting for your turn to shoot, pre-check your upcoming field's targets and look for tell-tale signs of poorly-trained or inattentive trap help. If an unusually high percentage of targets is rejected by shooters, walk up to the field and determine whether the puller or shooter is at fault. Many shooters don't call for the target in a clear, decisive voice. Grunts and groans are fine for wrestlers, but clay bird shooters must develop sharp, distinctive "calls" for the target. If you can't hear the shooter's call for the target, odds are the trap puller can't either. On the other hand, if you can clearly hear the shooter's call and the puller doesn't respond quickly, you have a good idea who the culprit is. Another method to determine if there is a mental or mechanical problem with the puller is to politely ask him if you can test the "pull cord" before you shoot. You'll rarely be denied. If there's a delay or pause between the time you punch the button and when the bird is released, that field probably has a faulty cord or button that must be replaced. This happens quite frequently and any time the pullers are blamed for equipment failures, it's up to you to determine the source of slow pulls.

What is an inordinate number of "rejected" targets by shooters? First, we know there are five shooters on a squad and each fires at 25 targets for a total of 125 targets per field. If 10 percent of the targets are rejected — 12 to 13 — that means that each shooter, on an average, is turning down two to three per field. That is an objectionable and unacceptable number of shooter refusals.

Three to 5 percent is a tolerable and acceptable count.

After convincing yourself that the trap puller is not doing his job, there are some things you can do. First, talk to the puller and tell him your findings in a calm, orderly manner. If he apologizes and says he'll do better, go ahead and take your place on the field. Chances are you and your squad mates will receive excellent pulls and the problem will be quickly and easily solved. But, if your initial conversation with the puller isn't to your liking, then with the backing of your sqaud mates go to management or the range master and request a puller replacement. Most of the time, a heads-up range master will know which trap line personnel are going to create problems and which aren't. You'll rarely get a squawk when a "bad kid" is reported, yet, you'll probably get a bunch of static if the puller you "snitched on" has a proven track record with the range master.

We accept that bad weather can and probably will influence shooting. It also affects trap personnel. Whereas you have the opportunity to seek some relief from wind, rain or heat, the poor puller and trap setter usually have to work for long periods of time under these conditions with little or no break. No wonder shooters occasionally receive bad pulls for no apparent reason.

The most common excuse among competition shooters is "I shot a fast (or slow) pull." This alibi far exceeds whatever is currently in second place. Immediately, a shooting buddy sides with the griper and claims the same for his misses. There's no reference in any of the clay target shooting rule books that states the shooter must accept and shoot at a target that has been "fast" or "slow" pulled. It is the shooter's option to either take it or turn it down. Those in control will almost always refuse improper "pulls"; those who can't control their actions and thoughts seem to get stuck with all the "bad luck." Accepting and shooting at ill-timed calls and pulls is part of both trap and Skeet shooting games and one has to learn early on how to control these misfortunes. Here are some ideas on how to cut down on bad pulls:

1. Develop a sharp, distinctive call. Don't mumble, grunt or yell. It is better to make your call a tad louder than necessary than to make the trap puller strain his ears to hear you.

2. Become consistent in your call. Don't change it from one day to another. If you use the word "Pull," stay with it. If you prefer "Hup!" or "Pulit!" use the same call throughout your shooting career. Just because you once heard a 97 or better super shooter bellowing "Eeeeyooah!," it doesn't mean that his call is breaking the targets. Say whatever is comfortable for you, and over the years it'll become natural. To verify if your call is proper, ask a trap puller — either between stations or at the end of the round — if he can hear your call distinctly and clearly. If he can't, you can rest assured he'll tell you in no uncertain terms. This is one of the few times a trap puller can "get even" with a shooter, but in a nice way.

3. Don't get into an argument with trap personnel over scoring of targets. Remember that it is your responsibility to verify that they recorded what you shot. During a trap tournament, scores are called out after each post. Typically, the scorer/puller will simply say, "Change five, five, four, five, three" meaning shooters No. 1, No. 2 and No. 4 broke five out of five, shooter No. 3 broke four out of five and shooter No. 5 broke three out of five. If you have any questions about your score, the time to voice them is when you are changing stations. Afterward is too late! If you thought you broke five targets and the scorer/puller called out four, you'll have to have the backing of at least two squad mates to convince the scorer/puller that he made a mistake and needs to change your score. This rarely happens, but if you can't convince fellow squad members and the scorer that your score is incorrect, it will stand as originally stated. This is when you have to gather yourself together and control your emotions. If you can't or don't, you'll probably miss the next two targets because your thoughts will be back at the score sheet. Like baseball hits, they'll even out over the long haul and undoubtedly, somewhere down the shooting line, a scorer/puller will see a minute piece come off your target when you knew it was a "lost" target.

After reading this chapter, I'll bet you can add quite a few personal experiences to this tome. Remember though that if you can identify a potential problem before it happens, or recognize one that has already happened, you can make preparations to overcome it, or at least minimize it. It is always better to try and overcome a problem than to avoid it.

Night shooting is something every shooter will have to learn how to handle. At many of the larger trap and Skeet shoots, daytime is used to complete the events and night shooting is used to accommodate the shootoffs. Practice night shooting whenever possible.

11

Preparing for the Tournament

LIKE MOST SPORTS, trap and Skeet shooting have a fairly high rate of attrition. If you stay away from the competitive fields for a few months, there will be many new faces on the firing line when you come back. To these newer shooters we shall direct our comments; the "vets" will smile and nod their heads in agreement, as they, too, have paid their "dues" and experienced similar problems.

Tournament preparation should be a ritual whether

individual is eating himself up inside.

Why do people enjoy shooting registered trap or Skeet? Probably for the competition. If they were shooting strictly for fun, they would only shoot practice rounds where scores are meaningless and their names not listed on the club's scoreboard. We all strive for recognition through competition. If we win only because we are the only person in attendance, it would be meaningless.

Mental Attitude

Do you know what the difference is between 100 registered tournament targets and four rounds of practice? Nothing. There's no difference in the flight of the targets and the same guns and ammunition are used to shoot practice or tournament targets. The rules are the same — if you miss a target, a "0" is recorded on your

Preparing for a shooting tournament goes beyond checking out equipment. Many shooters consider guns and ammunition less than 10 percent of importance because everybody, for the most part, uses the same types of guns and ammunition.

it's your first, 11th or 77th tournament. And it demands the shooter's total concentration for success. If a business transaction entails a board meeting, a successful businessman will be well schooled and prepared in advance, right? Yet, all too many trap and Skeet shooters take their shooting too casually and hide behind the excuse, "I only do this for fun. If I want to work hard at something, I'll do it at my job." At best, that is pure nonsense. Show me a shooter who enjoys himself when he shoots a lousy score, and I'll wager that this same

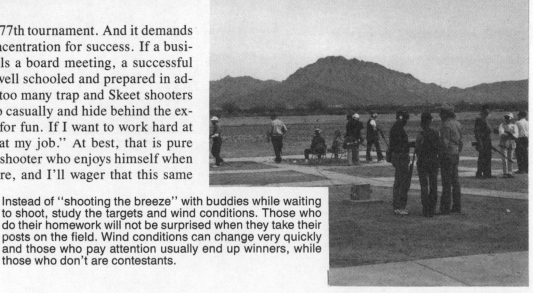

Instead of "shooting the breeze" with buddies while waiting to shoot, study the targets and wind conditions. Those who do their homework will not be surprised when they take their posts on the field. Wind conditions can change very quickly and those who pay attention usually end up winners, while those who don't are contestants.

Make certain you have enough time to prepare you and your equipment prior to the scheduled shoot. Arrive on the grounds early enough to lounge a bit and casually get ready — without haste. A calm attitude combined with relaxed concentration will help you break better scores and have a better time to boot!

score sheet, an "X" if you hit it. However, there is a difference in mental attitude and advance preparation.

Unlike most other sports, one of the basic reasons for trap and Skeet shooting's popularity is the lack of physical advantage of one person over another. Just because a super-strong male can benchpress 500 pounds doesn't mean he can shoot more accurately than a 13-year-old young lady. There's little correlation between physical strength and a winning attitude. There are a few exceptions, of course, such as when 500- or 1000-target marathons or time-consuming shootoffs occur, and one shooter's better physical condition lets him outlast "weaker" competitors. As a rule, however, physical condition is of little consequence as witnessed by shooters of both games, in all age groups, who come through as winners. Haven't we all envied and marveled at scores posted by sub-juniors and senior veterans?

Everything considered, most tournament shooters use virtually the same equipment — shotguns, ammunition and shooting techniques vary little. Like most sporting endeavors, the first 90 percent of a person's aptitude comes from learning the basics, using the equipment and perfecting a proprietary technique. The remaining 10 percent is mental preparedness. If a shooter can concentrate on perfecting the basics, a perfect 100x100 score will be the result.

Most other sports, especially those that feature "head-to-head" competition, can force opponents to make errors under normal conditions. Not so with trap or Skeet shooting. Each shooter pulls his own trigger and blunders in judgment are self-inflicted. Tennis has

two scoring rules that are unique — forced and unforced errors. Forced errors are caused when one player hits an unreturnable shot to his opponent. Unforced errors are those which, in the eyes of the scorer, should have been made and are classified as "easy." One of tennis's premier women players, Chris Everett, rarely makes an unforced error; she calmly stands on the baseline and returns every shot. In effect, she lets her opponent make all the mistakes. Her attitude toward tournament tennis play is "aggressive defense," thereby encouraging her opponent to make the mistakes en route to defeat.

Outwardly, competitive trap and Skeet shooting doesn't seem to inspire that type of play, yet inwardly, the better shooters understand and apply that psychology. Winning is striving for inner perfection and letting your opponents make the mistakes. Champions can only control their own games, not their opponents, and if they shoot their best — 100x100 — they've done their job. Perfect scores are commonplace at most of today's trap and Skeet shoots, but what exactly is "commonplace?" Literally translated, it means that more than 50 percent of the entrants break a perfect score. In the real world, that simply isn't true. At a 16-yard trapshoot or a 12-gauge Skeet event, if 100 competitors are shooting, four or five "straights" would be about par. Now that means only 4 or 5 percent of the shooters put it together. Hardly "commonplace" to those who didn't break them all!

I've interviewed dozens of shooters who have broke 'em all, and when asked how they did it, they say it was because of good mental and emotional control. A certain gun or brand of ammunition is rarely credited with a victory, but is often the accused culprit and excuse for failure. Actually, the shooter's mental attitude makes up that important "10 percent" to which we earlier alluded. Shooters who can control that all-important "10 percent factor" are the champions; those who cannot are participants.

Professional athletes, regardless of their particular sport, love to use the term "mental toughness," further described as two opposite meaning words — "relaxed concentration." Every successful competitor, prior to and during the shooting event, is "keyed-up" emotionally. Instead of allowing that pressure to play havoc on his nerves, the seasoned — and again, successful — shooter makes this mental condition work *for* him. How? Through desire and enthusiasm! Haven't we all scratched our heads after reading about the outstanding exploits of trap and Skeet champions shoot after shoot? How do they keep their interest levels high enough to consistently win? Again, it's an oversimplified case of mind over matter. They not only have a stronger desire to win, but in keeping with the tradition they have built among their fellow shooters, they are expected to win! And usually do.

The correct mental attitude goes hand-in-hand with a

many years. Back in the mid-1930s, a youngster drove past the ATA home grounds in Vandalia, Ohio while the Grand American Tournament was being conducted. Noting that a trapshooting event was being held, he wheeled his Model T pickup into the parking lot, signed up for the event, purchased his shells and went to work. After the smoke had cleared, guess whose name was at the top of the list? Right. Our farm boy, who used the only shotgun he ever owned — a field-grade Winchester Model 12 in 16-gauge! Obviously, nobody took the time to tell our hero that he didn't stand a ghost of a chance armed with a 16-gauge, field-grade shotgun, especially wearing bib overalls!

This wonderfully true story has been repeated numerous times, and it does have a moral. Equipment only contributes, it is not imperative to winning. At the same time, a shooter with properly-prepared and maintained equipment will have some beneficial peace of mind when standing on the firing line. There's nothing more distracting than subconsciously worrying about one's shotgun or ammunition. If, therefore, the shooter thoroughly cleans and oils his pet scattergun before the event and makes certain his ammunition is the best he can make — or buy — he has a winning attitude.

Close attention to other equipment is equally impor-

Arnold Riegger, a tremendous trap shooter during the 1950s, was able to master the difficult feat of total concentration. His secret was not to concentrate for the entire 100-target event, only for a brief period of 10 seconds at a time — 5 seconds before the target was released and the 5 seconds it took him to shoot and follow-through. Now that sounds easy, doesn't it?

Learn as much as possible about a new club before you shoot. This will help eliminate as many target-losing surprises as possible.

winning attitude. Hopefully, I've convinced you that mental preparation is 90 percent of a winning attitude. What's the other 10 percent? Most prominent clay target shooters agree that equipment makes up 10 percent of both games. We've all witnessed shooters who use "inferior" equipment and beat the pants off their competition armed with expensive guns and costly accessories.

A great story has circulated the Grand American for

tant. All trap and Skeet shooters should wear shooting glasses, both for protection and to improve eyesight. What happens if you accidentally drop a pair of glasses and crack a lens? If you don't carry a backup pair, the extra investment for a spare pair of glasses could prove to be an inexpensive insurance policy. The same backup policy holds true for any special accessories used and needed during a competitive event such as ear plugs or muffs and devices to hold ammunition such as

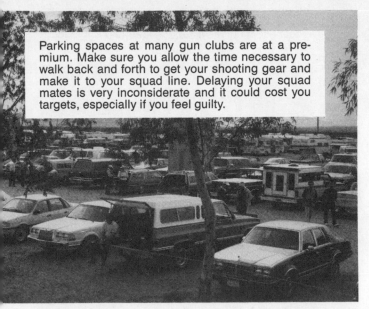

Parking spaces at many gun clubs are at a premium. Make sure you allow the time necessary to walk back and forth to get your shooting gear and make it to your squad line. Delaying your squad mates is very inconsiderate and it could cost you targets, especially if you feel guilty.

a pouch or holder. "Blinders," which attach to the sides of shooting glasses, are generally made from cardboard and can become badly disfigured by perspiration after a couple shoots. Is there a reserve set close by? Blinders prevent wind from entering the shooter's eyes and also help concentration by creating "tunnel vision."

Shooters must be prepared for all kinds of inclement weather. On hot, muggy days, perspiration can — and does — hinder many shooters. Sweat on shooting glasses is more than a hindrance, but a sweat band wrapped around the forehead will prevent perspiration from staining the glasses, allowing clear vision at all times. Another solution is to have your shooting glasses refit to stand off from your forehead and eyebrows.

Because of the nature of the game, trapshooting, more so than Skeet shooting, wreaks havoc with shotguns due to heat buildup. In trap, the time between shots is usually less than 1-minute as a typical fast-shooting five-member squad will run through a field in 12 to 15 minutes. This short amount of time between shots doesn't allow the gun to cool down and many shooters are victimized by heat waves coming off the top of the barrel. If this common problem affects your shooting, carry a water-soaked towel to artificially cool down the barrel between stations. I have done this for many years because heat waves bother me to the point of near hysteria.

Etiquette

How many times have you witnessed a friend or shooting acquaintance get into a heated discussion or even an argument while attending a shoot? Chances are that by the time Old Charley got to the line, he lost any chance of shooting a good score because he was still upset over his confrontation. Etiquette on and off the shooting field is just as important to know and learn as sight picture, gun placement and any other shooting "basic." How important is etiquette? Plenty, as it can

greatly influence your final score.

No one wants to associate with a poor sport or braggart, regardless of his vocation or avocation. Like any small group, and competitive trap and Skeet is considered a minor sport, the "word" quickly spreads like wildfire as to how a person handles himself on and off the field. One of the first rules a new shooter must learn is to let his score speak for itself. It is the only yardstick to measure a shooter's performance on any given day. Don't make up mundane excuses or place the blame on others for a bad day. Absorb the aches and pains of an "off" day and try to do better on the next outing.

There are many "no-nos" when shooting registered events; a few of the more serious violations are listed below.

1. **Tardiness.** There's nothing more irritating to fellow squad members than one member being late when your squad is called to the line. And there's little excuse for being late unless you just drove into the parking lot, jumped out of your car, grabbed your shells and shotgun and puffed up to your waiting field. This rarely happens and most of the late

This empty gun rack signifies that you either arrived at the shoot too early, or possibly too late. You'll have to check the surroundings to determine which one it is.

arrivals are inconsiderate individuals who were "tied up" chewing the fat with their cronies . . . while their squad mates were put on hold.

2. **Excuses.** I have heard literally hundreds of excuses from trap and Skeet shooters over the years, and none of them have ever been the real reason for their inability to break the targets. These evasions of the truth range from "fast or slow pulls," "bad ammunition" or other physical "defects," to more sophisticated morsels like, "I just wasn't ready for

163

(Above) It's always a good idea to verify what squad and position you're shooting. There's always the possibility of a mistake, or confusion, which would put you at the wrong field at the wrong time.

On- and off-field etiquette is as important to learn and practice as sight picture, gun control and other shooting techniques. Proper etiquette is demanded by ATA and NSSA rules.

TREAT EVERY GUN AS IF LOADED

KEEP MUZZLE POINTING SAFELY AT ALL TIMES

DO NOT LOAD GUN UNTIL READY TO SHOOT

MAKE SURE AMMO IS SAME GAUGE AS GUN

KEEP ACTION OF GUN OPEN WHEN NOT SHOOTING

(Left) If you perspire profusely during hot, muggy days, be certain that your shooting glasses fit properly and have them adjusted so that they stand away from the forehead and eyebrows. Perspiration will then merely fall off the face and not onto the glasses which could impair vision. If you can't see 'em, you can't hit 'em!

it'' or ''The pressure got to me.'' Some of these excuses may be valid and truthful — in your own mind — but your fellow shooters really don't want to hear them. They, too, have their own problems and don't care to offer a sympathetic ear. Keep your dirty laundry at home and don't hang it on the line.

3. Gripes. Complaints should always be directed to whoever can do something about your displeasure. If you have a complaint about the shooting field's condition, tell the gun club manager. Ditto for an excessive number of broken targets, inattentive trap help, parking lot conditions, etc. All of these problems can only be solved by the person in charge of the shoot, not by other shooters.

4. Talking. Verbal communication is important, but not on the competition fields. There are very few valid reasons to talk to fellow squad members on the field while a shoot is in progress. Not only does it disturb the person you are talking to, but others as well. Keep your on-the-field comments to yourself until you're off. And then, if possible, only after the final field is shot, unless they are important to the safety or well-being of a squad member. Some shooters do not like to talk even when walking between fields. Respect their wishes and hold your tongue until the 100th target is shot. Just because a fellow squad mate doesn't acknowledge your chitchat, doesn't mean he is a snob or doesn't like you, etc. Control your on- and off-field comments for the right time and place.

5. Advice. Don't give it unless asked. If you've never missed a target, you are the expert, but if you have missed a target somewhere along the long shooting road, you are not an expert unless solicited by a fellow shooter. Don't walk up to a buddy who had a bad field and tell him that he was shooting behind the targets. Don't you think he knows that? Of course he does. But, if you're the sage that you think you are, explain to him how not to shoot behind targets in three words or less. Can't be done, you say? OK, then pass this assignment.

Be ready to shoot when it is your turn! This sounds very simple, but it's amazing how many shooters have no idea when or where they are supposed to be. Some gun clubs have elaborate "message centers" informing the shooters which squads are shooting and on what fields. A little simple arithmetic will enable the shooter to figure where and when he will shoot.

6. Loud Talking. One of my personal peeves and certainly one of trap and Skeet's most vexing problems are bystanders who lean on the back fence and carry on a conversation with their cronies while another squad is on the field shooting. These inconsiderate shooters can and do cause a great deal of distraction, not only to those on the line but to the puller as well. Most shooters wear some form of hearing protection, but trap personnel don't and can't because they have to listen to the shooter's call for the target. All too often, fast or slow pulls are caused directly by distractions from the crowd that adversely affect the puller's concentration. Human nature being what it is, people have a tendency to listen to other's conversations while attempting to do their own task at hand. If you and a buddy are engrossed in telling or listening to an off-color joke, chances are the trap boy is listening as well. Trade places at that moment with the shooter who is about to call for his target and guess what kind of "pull" you'll receive. Be considerate of those at work.

7. Gun Handling. For almost 90 years of registered trap and Skeet tournaments, which represents countless millions of rounds of ammunition expended, there's never been a single recorded fatality. Why? Trap and Skeet shooters are a fanatical group of safety-conscious shooters who won't hesitate to "jump" a fellow shooter whenever there's a gun-handling violation. Not only are there specific and enforced rules regarding gun safety in both the ATA and NSSA guidelines, individual shooters, referees and trap personnel constantly watch those

Most major shooting events will have at least three gunsmiths on the grounds. There are smithys who specialize in triggers, ribs, recoil pads, etc. All of these on-the-premises services benefit the shooter. Large shoots can also become the shooter's supermarket as virtually everything in equipment and services are available —on the spot!

165

who break the rules. Even "bending" them can cause the culprit quite a bit of embarrassment. Never point a muzzle at another human being, unless, of course, you expect to be shot in return!

8. **Shooting Out Of Turn.** How could anyone paying attention possibly be guilty of this error? Strangely enough, it happens more often than one would expect. Generally, it happens in a trapshooting event and more times than not, when the shooter standing on Post #1 calls for a target that belongs to the shooter on Post #5. Losing the count between shots is easy to do, especially if one lets his mind wander. A sharp trap puller will usually realize the error, stop the squad from shooting, and tell the "out-of-turn" shooter it's not his shot. If a shooter shoots out of turn and hits the target, no score is recorded and the shooter in violation is not penalized — only ostracized!

9. **Stopping a Squad.** I've been on squads with shooters who deliberately interrupt the rhythm of the squad with all sorts of pretexts. Their objective is to cause deliberate dissension between them and others on the squad. Most of the time this ruse works and causes the "hot head" to lose his cool, costing him targets. Unless there are mitigating circumstances, like gun breakdowns, sudden sickness or such, stopping the flow and timing of a squad is demoralizing to the other shooters. Circumstances like not having enough shells to complete a round or asking a fellow shooter for an extra shell (due to firing at a broken target thus the shot must be retaken) shows a lack of preparation and consideration.

10. **Pulling Out.** Shooters pull out of a squad for many reasons, most of them legitimate. There are those though who leave a squad only to be found re-squadded later in the day, perhaps when the weather has improved. Many clubs have a surcharge equal to their entrance fee for those who practice this skulduggery. If a shooter must leave a shoot for valid reason such as ill health, sudden emergency or such, he should attempt to let his squad mates know in advance he cannot attend. The departing shooter should also tell the "squadder" (the person who makes up the squad sheets) he must leave the grounds and that his spot is open. The shoot cashier and squad-maker will attempt to fill this void. Less critical in Skeet than trap, shooting "short" greatly alters the rhythm and timing of a squad because of the nature of the game. Regardless, though, if one declines to shoot because of bad weather or unusually high scores already posted after officially entering an event, he is a classic example of a "fair-weather shooter."

These classic examples only scratch the surface of clay target "dont's." There are many more but space limits us to the most "popular" ones. Competitive shooters are a condescending lot and will forgive both new and veteran shooters an occasional violation. But those who don't heed advice and continue to make problems for fellow shooters will have a tough time scratching up a squad. I've seen cases in which a "problem shooter" enters an event and is squadded, but when his mates find his name on the score sheet, all pull out of the squad and form a new one! Now that's a message to be heeded. Competitive shooting is not a popularity contest, but attitude and conduct seriously affects those around you. Be thoughtful, courteous and enjoy yourself, but not at the expense of others.

Squadding

Picking squad mates is like choosing a wife — difficult, but not impossible. We are all affected by those around us and if we enjoy the company of certain individuals, we have a natural tendency to associate with them on and off the shooting field. Should this association be extended to the trap or Skeet squad? I feel it is a mistake to squad-up with close friends. Most shooters on a squad are cognizant of the other squad members' performances. It is natural to pay close attention to your targets and to those of others as well. You can accept a lost target better than your buddy, and his, "Gee, I'm sorry for Joe" attitude will ultimately adversely affect your friend's score. Deliberately squad yourself with associates — never close friends.

If you are a beginner, and probably in one of the lower classes, try to be placed on a squad of higher-classified shooters. Their shooting styles will positively influence your capabilities. Most higher-ranked (AA or A) trapshooters have developed a fast shooting rhythm which promotes better scores. Shooting with these "race cars" will bring out the best in you and you'll most likely shoot several points above your average. You may still be the low man on your squad in score, but you'll learn a valuable shooting lesson. Like frogs and ponds, 'tis better to be low man on a "big" squad than big man on a "low" squad. The novice and low-average shooters are plagued and characterized by poor timing and non-rhythmic shooting techniques. Trying to "keep up" with experienced and rhythmical shooters will automatically improve a new shooter's gun handling techniques and score. Therefore, poorer shooters will benefit from shooting with a better squad; conversely, a better shooter will suffer when "stuck" on a squad of slow-shooting novices.

Shootoffs

Shootoffs are an integral part of competitive trap and Skeet shooting. Not only do they determine the winners and losers of a certain event, this unique part of the game showcases shooters and either brings out the best or worst in all of us. There's a lot of pressure on those who participate in shootoffs, and the only way to overcome it, or at least learn how to cope with it, is to shoot. There's no other way to overcome sweaty palms, shaky hands or attacks of nervousness. Regardless of what is said in this chapter or other books, nothing effectively describes the inner feelings one gets when his name is called for a shootoff.

Shootoffs are mainly psychological and are not any more difficult than the main event — in fact, they're easier. After all, your score tied only a few others or maybe even a lone shooter. Therefore, you already beat most of the field, and overcoming a smaller hurdle (those involved in the shootoff with you) should be a snap. A positive attitude is the single most important aspect of winning a shootoff.

squad and there's been a long delay of a couple of hours or more, shoot a practice round to warm yourself up.

At the Grand American Tournament, along with many of the satellite "Grands" or most of the larger events, shootoffs may be held after dark and under the lights. If you haven't shot much under these conditions, you'll find night shooting is much more difficult. Again, the only way to learn how to shoot at night is to do it. Most gun clubs offer night shooting, so make it a point to learn how to shoot after dark, anticipating important after-hour shootoffs. Don't let night shooting bother you.

Butting heads with experienced shooters can literally "eat up" a new shooter. I've shot against one of America's top-notch high-average shooters who deliberately attempts to alter his competitor's timing and rhythm by

Picking a good squad is often more difficult than choosing a wife. Try to shoot with peers who have equal or better skills than you. The timing and rhythm of the squad will generally produce better scores than those who cannot maintain consistent timing.

Early in my shooting career, I was in a Skeet shootoff with a veteran shooter. This crafty virtuoso knew all the psychological tricks to keep me worried. When we went to Station One, I noticed he had a shell carrier with four full boxes of ammo neatly stacked. I asked him why he carried all that ammunition with him. He looked me coldly in the eye and said, "Sonny, I don't plan on missing any targets!" Scratch one shootoff as I blew High One and true to his word, my antagonist went straight!

Because shootoffs are usually summoned at the end of the shooting day, conditions are different from those found during the regular event. Lighting conditions are generally poorer and a late afternoon wind often comes up at many clubs. Be prepared for these changes. If, when you were shooting earlier, the sun was shining brightly but now is slowly setting, discard your sunglasses for clear lenses. Take a good look at the flight of the late afternoon targets, and if you shot on an early

changing his cadence and call. On one target he'll shout "Pull," the next "Hup," and perhaps another "Ugh." This is to make the other shooter worry about what the next "call" will sound like, instead of concentrating on his targets. All too often, this ruse works! Ignore this clever bit of shootoff strategy, though it's easier said than done for newcomers.

There are all kinds of "dirty tricks," and I've seen unscrupulous shooters "accidentally" discharge their guns just before calling for their first target in a shootoff, blaming nervousness, gun malfunction, etc. It was actually done deliberately to unnerve an opponent. Difficult to prove, but nevertheless commonplace around the country.

Another shootoff enigma is the jinx. Some years ago, my ex-wife, Marcie Blatt, was involved in at least a dozen shootoffs with a lady trapshooter named Irma Allison. On paper, their averages were about the same. Yet Irma had a jinx on Marcie so strong that when the

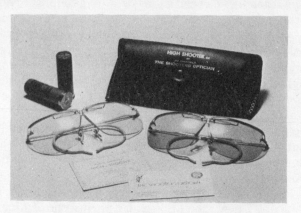

Most shootoffs are held at the end of the shooting day and lighting conditions are drastically reduced. The forewarned shooter will keep a spare set of clear-lens glasses to use for near-dusk or after-dark shooting conditions.

two locked horns, Marcie "knew" she was beaten before a shot was even fired. The law of averages never made itself known when these two butted heads and Irma always won!

Do you recall your first shootoff? Typically, everyone remembers their first shootoff, regardless if they won or lost. My first in trap was in 1961 during a Winter Chain shoot at the Kingsburg Gun Club in central California. I shot my first 100x100 in the 16-Yard Singles race, tying the venerable George Ross. The early 1960s were George Ross's "heydays," and a tougher competitor or more formidable foe couldn't be found. Going head-to-head against Mr. Ross at that time would

have made me a 100-to-1 longshot bet to beat him. The first field we both went straight. I then realized that he wasn't going to beat me, and regardless of the number of shots needed to be taken, I wasn't going to miss. It took three rounds (75x75) to defeat this great champion, and as a relative newcomer to the trap lines, I left the field 12 feet tall! Even the 10-inch "iron-man" trophy weighed 84 pounds and turned into solid gold to boot.

One of the most difficult shootoffs for a newcomer is in trap Doubles. The leadoff spot is the hardest position for shooters to learn because they don't have an opportunity to preview a pair of targets for a new post. They must "approximate" and "anticipate" the position of the target's flight. New shooters, unfortunately, when involved in a shootoff, and those who have never, or have rarely been squad leaders during a Doubles event, have a difficult time when thrust into the leadoff position for the first time. To avoid this traumatic experience, new shooters should occasionally sign up as squad leaders on a Doubles event to gain this invaluable experience.

Shootoffs are memorable occasions and can be fun. If you prepare ahead of time, you'll do well. Keep a positive attitude and above all, mind your own affairs and break targets the same way that put you in the shootoff in the first place. Winning a shootoff occurs when preparation meets opportunity.

Shooting Slumps

Shooting slumps are also part of both shooting games. When is a shooting slump a slump? It is difficult to categorize slumps because they are only measur-

Strange as it may seem, learning how to become a good winner is just as important as knowing how to be a gracious loser. Competitive shooting is a game of tomorrows . . . if you don't shoot well today, there's always tomorrow. There are only a handful of shooters who can make a living from these shooting sports, the rest of us participate for the enjoyment aspect.

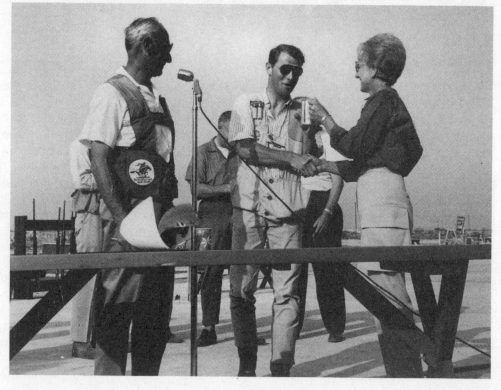

able in degrees. If a known AAA Skeet shooter "only" breaks a 98x100 in a 12-gauge event, is he in a slump? A minor one perhaps, but an occasional sub-par score doesn't make a shooting slump. We all have good and bad days, and our scores will fluctuate with the stars, biorhythms or the position of the moon in relation to Venus, etc. Shooting slumps are like baseball players going "oh for thutty." They cannot, however, be traced directly to luck, either good or bad. If a baseball player smacks a line drive directly at an infielder, he is "unlucky," yet still declared out. Golfers, too, can be both victims and beneficiaries of good and bad luck and their scores can reflect how that dame fortune smiles on them.

In trap and Skeet shooting there are hardly any "gray" areas. Near misses are still misses and unlike horseshoe pitching or hand grenade throwing, close doesn't count. Attempting to prevent a shooting slump takes a lot of mental preparation. I have never known any shooting champion who hasn't been affected by this bugaboo. It happens to the very best, so don't be discouraged if it happens to you. Expect it, and when it happens it won't hurt so much.

If your misses are fairly well distributed in terms of a specific target or station, improving your concentration is the only way to better your overall score. But, if you realize you're missing a particular target, say High Deuce on the Skeet field or a screaming right-angle from Post #5 on the trap field, you immediately classify that particular target as "difficult." There's actually no such thing as a "difficult" target — only that the shooter has acquired the difficulty. The main reason for missing a certain target is loss of proper shooting technique. For some unknown reason, a shooter cannot break a certain target under certain conditions, which leads to shooting slumps.

Worrying about a particular "problem" bird will cause you to miss "easy" targets and your level of confidence will soon be lowered, thus every target will suddenly seem "difficult." You will start flinching, lifting your head off the stock, or any number of disastrous things which will result in lost targets. Your confidence and poise will diminish and when attempting to regain these vital ingredients, you will make artificial corrections. Some shooters switch guns, install release triggers, alter stock dimensions, etc. These methods are extremes and should not be employed because they did not elevate you to your shooting status before the "slump" struck. What caused the slump and more importantly, how do you get out of it? Seek outside advice. There are many competent instructors who offer sound, expert counseling — at a price, of course. Remember, advice is only worth what you pay for it — if it's free, odds are it isn't worth listening to.

Most qualified shooting instructors agree that coaching a student back to the basics will get them out of a slump. Stance, body and head position, lead, timing and all the "learned" variables that the shooter either never knew or simply forgot are stressed. Like the forest and tree analogy, often shooters are too close to the problem and it takes an outsider with a keen and trained eye to spot the problem. Physical malfunctions lead to mental malfunctions which, in turn, are recorded on the score sheet.

Possibly the best method to eliminate a shooting slump is to quit shooting for awhile. All too often, shooters experiencing difficulties are practicing their mistakes instead of performing the basics, which reduces mistakes. Take a couple weeks or months off and try a new hobby; get shooting off your mind for awhile.

The "Granddaddy" of all trapshoots is the Grand American which is held in Vandalia, Ohio each August. Every trapshooter should attend at least one "Grand" to view the pageantry and vastness of this marvelous event.

When you return, you'll find that your level of enthusiasm is high, you'll enjoy kibitzing with shooting cronies and shooting will again be fun!

I can recall two separate occasions that I was unable to shoot registered ATA Singles events. After a 12-month absence, the first time out I miraculously broke a 100x100. On another occasion I was away from registered competition for nearly 2 years, and again the "Big Shooter In The Sky" rewarded my efforts with a 16-yard straight. Reflecting on those blessed events, I found my interest in trapshooting was piqued and my scores, just before semi-retirement, at their lowest ebb. Layoffs, for the most part, have proven beneficial for shooters mired in the midst of a slump.

We all want to become consistent shooters who can post average or above scores virtually every shoot. To become a proficient shooter, you must learn the basics the hard way because there are no shortcuts to success. But, you also must learn how to retain the basics while advancing forward. We all are guilty of letting previous knowledge slip through our fingers, which invites problems. Remembering is vital!

12

Ammunition and Shotgun Recoil

AT FIRST GLANCE at this chapter title, you might think the two aren't a logical pair, but actually, you can't have one without the other. A wide range of findings and recommendations regarding today's newest ammunition craze — "lite" loads, how you can nearly duplicate factory loads and an indepth look at recoil and its devastating effects — are discussed here.

Ammunition

In the past few years, ammunition makers such as Federal, Winchester and Remington have been marketing yet another line of target ammunition, all under the common "lite" moniker — "Ultra-Lite" from Federal, "Super-Lite" from Winchester and "Rem-Lite" from Remington. All three companies adhere to guidelines set down by SAAMI (Sporting Arms and Ammunition Manufacturers Institute) which state that no maker of guns or ammunition shall exceed safe and sane limits of velocity, payloads or chamber pressures. In most cases, ammunition is made so that it can be fired safely

(Above) Unquestionably, Federal Cartridge Co. has been an important contributor to the growth of trap and Skeet shooting. This is what the Federal plant looked like in the late 1920s. (Right) A portion of Federal's production floor during the early 1930s.

even in obsolete firearms, except for Damascus-barreled shotguns. If your 90-year-old 12-gauge Parker or Purdey has fluid steel barrels, you can safely fire today's low-brass ammunition without a second thought.

This built-in safety margin — measured in chamber pressure as 10,000 psi (pounds per square inch) — controls what manufacturers can safely develop. With the introduction of "lite" loads, which are simply $2^{1}/_{2}$- to $2^{5}/_{8}$-dram 12-gauge loads with $1^{1}/_{8}$ ounces of shot, the Big Three are going in the opposite direction of the "magnums."

Remember all the hyperbole a few years ago regarding the factory-inspired 1-ounce loads? Those loads were touted as the best thing for trap and Skeet shooters since the invention of smokeless powder and self-contained ammunition. Though that reduced payload ammo is still available, competition shooters are no fools and soon realized the $^{1}/_{8}$-ounce of shot is more important for breaking consistent high scores than the additional recoil the maximum payload develops over the 1-ounce shot charge.

Many trapshooters handload 1-ounce loads for their first shot at Doubles, and even a few more still use this load on 16-yard Singles targets. Not only are these "sub-load" shooters in the minority, but none of the top competitors use 1-ounce loads for any type of clay target competition shooting event — and not even for practice.

Then there are some diehards who maintain that the 1-ounce load is faster than the $1^{1}/_{8}$-ounce charge. They also claim the reduced recoil more than makes up for the $^{1}/_{8}$-ounce less shot swarm chasing the target. And finally, they believe that regardless of the shot size, powder charge, or amount of shot, there's always five pellets in the middle of every shotgun pattern, which should be applied to every target.

All three claims are not only valid, but unquestionably true; I have no arguments with 1-ounce shooters' rationale. I simply prefer to have my mind at ease when I miss a target, knowing that it was indeed me who missed the target and not worrying if I wasn't shooting maximum loads, would I still have missed? I am not an advocate of any additional distractions and prefer to keep trap and Skeet shooting as simple as possible. One of Parkinson's Laws, "More complex — sooner dead," certainly applies to allowing variables to sneak into one's mind when preparing for a registered shoot.

The new 12-gauge "lite" ammo approximates $2^{1}/_{2}$- to $2^{5}/_{8}$-dram loads charged with $1^{1}/_{8}$ ounces of shot. For example, Winchester's 1988 catalog lists all their 3-dram target loads at a velocity of 1200 fps and their $2^{3}/_{4}$-dram loads at 1145 fps. Their "Super-Lite" shell

This is what Federal Cartridge Co. looks like today. The leadership of Federal was provided by its founder, Charles L. Horn.

A Look At Federal Cartridge Company

The administration building at Federal-Hoffman, Inc.

Ballistic checks are an on-going part of the Federal production line. Thousands of shells are testfired every 24 hours to maintain the highest degree of consistency.

Federal employees are a pride-filled group of employees.

This is just one of the many high-speed Manhurin loading machines used by Federal.

Computer driven, driverless vehicles transfer finished goods and raw materials at Federal.

Primers are still visually inspected by a Federal employee even after a number of mechanical checks.

Federal Cartridge Co. offers special ammunition for all the shooting sports. Like all the major munitions makers, they thoroughly test and evaluate their ammunition before it hits the market.

Federal's newest sensation, Top Gun shotshell is a specially designed target load at a reduced price. For those who recall the older Federal "League" target loads, Top Gun is quite similar in price and performance.

Reloading Data "Lite" Ammunition

The following 12-gauge loading data will closely duplicate chamber pressure, velocity and felt recoil similar to "Lite" ammunition offered by Winchester, Remington and Federal.

Hull	Powder	Charge (grs.)	Primer	Wad	Pressure (psi)	Velocity (fps)
Win. AA	Green Dot	19.5	WIN 209	Pac. Versalite	7,000	1145
Win. AA	Green Dot	18.0	WIN 209	ACTIV T-32	7,600	1145
Win. AA	Sup-Lite	18.5	FED 209	WAA12SL	7,800	1145
ACTIV	Green Dot	22.5	WIN 209	WWAA12F1	6,500	1200
ACTIV	Red Dot	19.0	CCI 209	ACTIV L-29	6,600	1200
Fiocchi	Green Dot	21.5	CCI 209	Pac. Versalite	6,300	1145
Fiocchi	Unique	23.5	FIO 616	12S3	7,100	1200
Rem. Prem.	Green Dot	19.0	CCI 209M	Rem. TGT12	7,000	1145
Rem. Prem.	Green Dot	19.0	REM 209P	Win. WAA12	6,700	1145
Fed. Paper	Green Dot	20.5	FED 209	Windjammer	6,600	1145
Fed. Paper	Green Dot	19.5	FED 209	Pac. Versalite	6,900	1145
Fed. Gold	Green Dot	20.5	REM 209P	12S3	6,800	1145
Fed. Gold	Red Dot	18.0	FED 209	Windjammer	7,100	1090

Two of the newest kids on the ammunition block—ACTIV and Fiocchi. Both of these munitions makers offer a full range of target loads and usually at prices a bit lower than those published by the Big Three — Federal, Winchester and Remington.

No. W12SLAA, though, does not offer any information on dram equivalent or velocity, only the amount of shot (1$^1/_8$ ounces) and the sizes available (7$^1/_2$, 8, 8$^1/_2$ and 9). In fact, it is Winchester's only loading with No. 8$^1/_2$ shot. Winchester's AA200 is a shell designed specifically for 16-yard Singles shooting. It is available only in 2$^3/_4$-dram, 1$^1/_8$-ounce of No. 8 shot, and because of a slightly different wad design helps widen patterns in super-tight choked trap guns. Winchester's Skeet loads also feature special wad designs for wider patterns than those produced with regular shot cups. It seems the ammo makers have come full circle, beginning with wide-patterning shotgun shells. With the advent of plastic hulls and wads, patterns tightened considerably, and current ammunition provides a compromise between the two earlier versions.

Improved shooting scores can be directly credited to ammunition. If top shooters from early eras would have had today's plastic-based ammunition, there's no telling what kind of scores they could have racked up. For example, one of the all-time great Skeet shooters is Alex Kerr. This many-times world champion was considered a virtuoso with the 410 bore. And guess how many times Mr. Kerr broke a perfect 100x100 during 410 competition — none!

During the 1950s and early 1960s, an event-winning 410 score was generally in the mid-90s. An occasional 98 or 99 posted on the scoreboard always brought "oohs and ahhs" from the crowd. By the mid-1960s, Remington and Winchester developed all-plastic shells and wads for the revered "idiot stick," and scores skyrocketed. Perfect centuries were the norm, and shooting a 100x100 with the 410 only placed one in a shootoff.

Sometime around 1956, Remington conducted a series of exhaustive tests to determine whether it was possible to break a perfect 100x100 from the 27-yard line.

The details of the test were never announced, only the results. Because of the inherent qualities and performance of the paper-based shotshells with card and fiber wads and relatively soft shot, the report stated it was virtually impossible to hit every target with contemporary ammunition and guns. Also stated in the report was that the best score a shooter could hope to achieve was between 92 and 94 out of 100, under optimum shooting conditions.

The most conclusive tests, however, were conducted by shooters. Do you know who and when the first 100x100 was recorded in the ATA? Colonel Throckmorton broke the barrier in 1962 and just 2 weeks later, the great Dan Orlich duplicated the then-outstanding feat. What ammunition did those shooters use? You guessed it, the then-new plastic hulls with plastic wads. Incidentally, as this is written, Ray Stafford, the great Colorado trapshooter, broke his 24th 100 straight from 27 yards. Dan Bonillas from California is second with 23!

The "greats," whose shooting careers spanned between paper and plastic ammunition, agree that the new ammunition has resulted in consistently higher scores, and this isn't mere sour grapes. The current long runs in Skeet and trap are far above those from bygone eras, as are national averages. Blown patterns are virtually impossible with factory-loaded ammunition. The shotguns of today aren't that much different than guns of yore and, in my opinion, only contribute minutely to today's higher scores. With the exception of Ljutic's Space Gun and gas-operated autoloaders, every *type* of competitive shotgun currently available has been accessible for the past half-century. Single-barrel trap guns, over/unders, and pump actions have changed very little in either design or function. The technological advances in metallurgy have generally only hardened the steel of today and prevented parts from wearing out as quickly as older guns. As far as chokes and constrictions are concerned, old-time barrel makers and advanced barrelsmiths knew as much about patterns as today's experts. The ammunition has definitely made the difference . . . and it's getting better all the time with the exception of steel shot, but that is another story.

Major munitions makers present their trap and Skeet loads exclusively in plastic configurations — save Federal Cartridge Co. I'm certain Federal would like to eliminate that paper shell from their lineup, but shooters won't let them. There are those (myself included) who prefer this shell for a variety of reasons. First, their continued use does not cause a buildup of plastic in the chamber, nor does the shell contribute to barrel rust like the plastic versions do. Plastic hulls have a tendency to retain moisture and shooters who use fired plastic shells for "snap caps" would be wise to use the real McCoy, or at least switch to paper hulls to avoid a rust buildup in the shotgun's chamber. Second, the Federal paper target shells seem to shoot "softer." They don't have the sharp snap of plastic-based shells, putting forth a stout shove against the shoulder instead. And third, they have excellent reloading qualities for one or two refillings. Sure, a careful handloader can get six or seven reloads from a paper-tubed Federal, but they look ratty and do not present a tight, clean crimp, which is necessary for consistent shotshell performance.

Newcomers to the trap and Skeet market are those offerings from ACTIV and Fiocchi. ACTIV Industries makes the ACTIV hull via the Reiwelin Process, which produces an all-plastic hull with a steel reinforcement disk located inside the base head. A standard eight-point crimp is used along with an integral plastic base wad. ACTIV also makes a full line of proprietary plastic wads.

This hull is gaining in popularity among reloaders because there is no brass around the base head, which eliminates resizing. Shells run through reloading presses smoothly and effortlessly. Eliminating the traditional brass head also allows the company to shave some manufacturing costs. The ACTIV hull has been tested at chamber pressures around 11,000 psi without any signs of undue fatigue.

The hull is a composite of three separate units — the extruded tube, the perforated steel reinforcement platter and an injection molded head. Once the three units are co-mingled and assembled, it is virtually impossible to visually differentiate where the tube ends and the head begins. The end of the tube is sharply skived, which enables both the factory and handloader to place an excellent eight-point crimp that stays securely in place. Reloading life of the ACTIV is equal to, and perhaps better, than many of today's other plastic shells.

The other new kid on the block is Fiocchi. Initially this ammunition and components lineup was imported from Italy. Now, however, the ammunition is assembled and manufactured in the United States — Ozark, Missouri to be exact. Their array of 12-gauge ammunition includes 2^3/$_4$ and 3-dram loads in all three popular shot sizes — 7^1/$_2$, 8 and 9. Wads, primers and reloading data are starting to make their way into consumers hands. I shot this ammunition and found it completely satisfactory and without any ignition problems. Its tall brass base helps extraction from either a fixed breech action, a pump or an autoloader. So far, it has proven faultless except for its lack of a "homing" quality, whereby it makes corrections for a bad job of gun pointing. Only when a munitions maker unveils a new shotshell which automatically hunts out a target — like a heat-seeking missile — will they *own* the shotshell market. As long as there are at least a handful of ammo makers, shooters will benefit from their competitive instincts.

Recoil

According to Newton's Third Law of Physics, "For every action there is an opposite and equal reaction." Yes, but there are different ways to measure and determine recoil. "Felt" recoil is the slap or shove against your body when the shotshell is fired. "Free" recoil occurs when the shotgun, suspended as a pendulum, is fired and the amount of rearward thrust measured. Shooters are really concerned about felt recoil, regulated by many facets of both the shotgun and ammunition.

There are currently four methods that firearms manufacturers and aftermarket accessory people are using to attack the dreaded bugaboo — recoil.

First, there's the gas-operated shotguns which use a good deal of the burning powder gases to operate and cycle the shotgun's loading/unloading mechanism. The end result is more like a gentle shove than the short, violent jar caused by fixed-breech shotguns. A slight variation of this is the now-obsolete Remington Model 870 Competition, a manually-operated pump-action shotgun with a unique gas piston system which bled gases off the barrel through twin vents to operate a piston that went back and forth. It was not connected to an operating spring to operate the slide handle and bolt assembly. It operated in limbo, but seemed to reduce

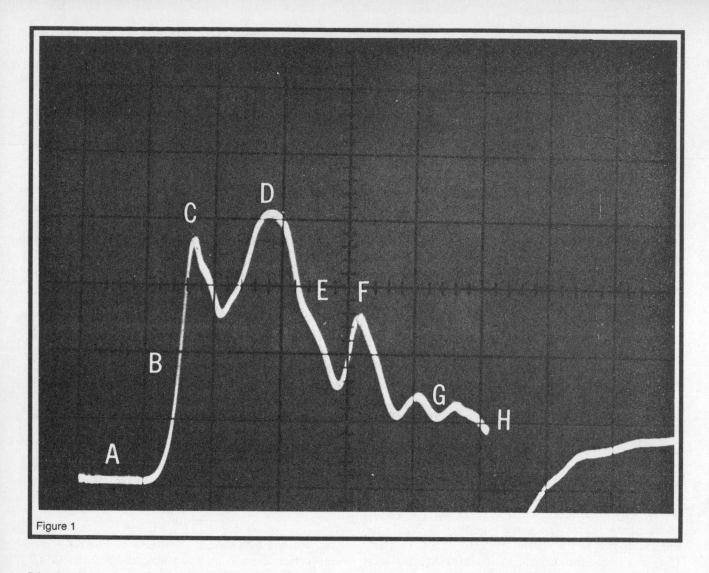

Figure 1

felt recoil by a considerable margin over a standard Model 870 pump gun.

Second, there're the "shock-absorber" type of devices usually installed on the buttstock which range from spring-loaded to air and/or oil-cushioned contrivances. Hydro-Coil and Soft-Touch are two examples. This type of device efficiently reduces apparent recoil because the recoiling shotgun slowly decelerates against the rear section of the stock. As deceleration slowly takes place, the apparent recoil force against the shoulder is greatly reduced.

Thirdly, barrels are often ported by introducing a complex series of holes near the end of the barrel, just behind the choke area. Many companies and independent gunsmiths such as Pro-Port and Jess Briley provide this service. Barrel porting and relieving the forcing cone inside the shotgun's barrel reduces pressures and results in lower recoil, but also reduces payload velocity. The same effect could be accomplished by reducing the powder charge of a handload.

Finally, other "gizmos" are installed within a buttstock, magazine tube or inside the unused barrel of an over/under. You'll recognize them by their brand names . . . Bear Trap, Edwards, etc. The "recoil reducers" work mostly because of the additional weight added to the shotgun.

For decades competitive shooters have been asking themselves and others if any of these devices actually work. Can any of them verifiably reduce recoil and take the unpleasantness out of trap and Skeet shooting? To determine if in fact these devices work, we must first understand recoil principles. Earlier I quoted Newton's Law about action and reaction. If the manufacturers of anti-recoil devices do not state that their gizmos and gadgets reduce felt recoil instead of free recoil, they are doing their customers a disservice. I've yet to see an advertisement state that the "Frazmataz Recoil Reducing System" reduced felt recoil, but virtually all claim their special "Rducrecoil" eliminates 80 percent of recoil, lessens muzzle jump by 50 percent, prevents "face slap," and so many other claims it's ludicrous. Unless one of these manufacturers can concoct a method to overcome physics, let's see a bit more "truth in advertising!"

Recoil is not a singular event, but a series of events that happen in a short time span — about 3 millisec-

RECOIL FACTOR WITH 30-34-INCH SHOTGUN BARRELS

3-DRAM, 1⅛-OUNCE		2¾-DRAM, 1⅛-OUNCE	
Weight Gun	Ft. Lbs. Recoil	Weight Gun	Ft. Lbs. Recoil
6.0 lbs.	20.2	6.0 lbs.	18.5
6.5 lbs.	18.6	6.5 lbs.	17.1
7.0 lbs.	17.3	7.0 lbs.	15.9
7.5 lbs.	16.1	7.5 lbs.	14.8
8.0 lbs.	15.1	8.0 lbs.	13.9
8.5 lbs.	14.2	8.5 lbs.	13.1
9.0 lbs.	13.4	9.0 lbs.	12.4
9.5 lbs.	12.7	9.5 lbs.	11.7

RECOIL FACTOR WITH 24-29-INCH SHOTGUN BARRELS

3-DRAM, 1⅛-OUNCE		2¾-DRAM, 1⅛-OUNCE	
Weight Gun	Ft. Lbs. Recoil	Weight Gun	Ft. Lbs. Recoil
6.0 lbs.	20.5	6.0 lbs.	18.9
6.5 lbs.	18.9	6.5 lbs.	17.4
7.0 lbs.	17.6	7.0 lbs.	16.2
7.5 lbs.	16.4	7.5 lbs.	15.1
8.0 lbs.	15.4	8.0 lbs.	14.1
8.5 lbs.	14.5	8.5 lbs.	13.3
9.0 lbs.	13.7	9.0 lbs.	12.6
9.5 lbs.	13.0	9.5 lbs.	11.9

— none of which are traced to gimmicks. But remember one important thing — anything done to the shotgun or ammunition is a compromise at best. For example, adding weight to the shotgun *will* reduce felt recoil because it helps absorb recoil within the instrument itself before it is forced on the body. On the other side of the coin, the additional weight of the shotgun may cause shooter fatigue or change the gun's balance, making it difficult for the shooter to catch up with the targets.

Shooting lighter recoiling loads, either the new "lite" loads currently offered or by mixing your own recipe, will push the standard 1⅛-ounce load along at approximately 1090 fps, or perhaps a tad slower. Many shooters may ask, "Can a shell that produces such a slow load velocity break the target at trapshooting distances?" Absolutely. In fact, these "slow" shells will probably break targets at farther distances than those 3-dram loads normally used. Why? Simply because a reduced powder charge tends not to "blow a pattern" and actually keeps the shot string intact at greater downrange distances. These "lite" loads also cause

This is Ralph Hoge, the inventor of the Hydro-Coil stock. This photo was taken at the site of the Aqua Sierra Gun Club owned then by Roy Rogers.

onds. The first measurable occurrence (see Figure 1) develops after the gunpowder is ignited (B), peak pressure reached and the shotshell crimp opened by the force of the wad and shot charge exiting the hull (C). The next and largest amount of generated recoil is when the wad and shot column are wedged into the forcing cone (D). This is the peak of recoil resistance. The next resistance point is when the shot and wad hit the choke area (F); everything from that point on is "recoilless".

By studying Figure 1 you'll be able to graph the various times and amount of recoil generated by a 2¾-dram shell loaded with 1⅛ ounces of shot fired in a shotgun weighing 9 pounds, 3 ounces. You'll understand that recoil is caused whenever a movable object (shot charge and wad) meets with some form of resistance. At its first occurrence, recoil registers at 175 pounds of energy. When the shot swarm and wad hit the forcing cone, greater resistance is encountered and the recoil energy climbs to a tad more than 200 pounds. At the choke area (constriction), the last point of resistance, recoil measures at 125 pounds of energy. As you can see, the recoil generated from a shotgun shell and barrel is subject to these three points of opposition.

These findings not only make sense, but more importantly, do not attempt to disprove physics, only verify facts. Someone once said that there are "facts" and there are "true facts." If a fact wasn't true in the first place, it would not be "fact" at all, but rather a lie. True?

So, how is recoil reduced? There are proven methods

much less shot deformation within the shell when all hell breaks loose within the barrel, as described above, and helps prevent "flyers" that quickly leave the main shot swarm. For those not familiar with a flyer, it is simply a single piece of shot not perfectly round. If it has a flat spot, it will not fly true and straight. Flyers can be caused in manufacture — although rarely — but most are developed when the shot swarm is sent down the barrel where it meets with the previously-described points of resistance.

Flyers are not all bad, however. In fact, munitions makers produce special loads for both field and Skeet shooting without a protective shot cup integral with the overpowder wad. When these shells are fired, flyers are manufactured within the shotgun barrel, which in turn enlarges the shot pattern, often greater than what is expected from a choked barrel. There are special "spreader" loads available that can produce Modified choke percentages from a Full choke barrel, an Improved Cylinder pattern from a Modified barrel, and so on through the choke spectrum.

Ballisticians, shooters, scientists and everyone remotely involved in shooting have attempted to overcome recoil. It is a subject so thoroughly dissected, researched and tested that even with all our high-tech equipment, there have been no new discoveries since the late 1950s. One of the most exhausting and informative tests was conducted by a group of dedicated shooters — not a white-coat set of scientists from a research university. No, this test was the brainchild of Ralph Hoge, inventor of the Hydro-Coil recoil-reducing system. All the expenditures were paid by Mr. Hoge because he was not backed by a major ammunition maker, nor did he receive funds via a federal grant. Hoge's accomplices were Ed Sowers, stockmaker for the Hydro-Coil, Kinky Carapalese, a Winchester pro, and Dr.

MEASURED FREE RECOIL 12-GAUGE AMMUNITION
1⅛-Ounce Loads

Gun Weight (lbs.)	1200 fps 3-Dram	1150 fps 2¾-Dram	1100 fps 2½-Dram
7.5	21.42	19.50	17.84
8.0	20.08	18.28	16.73
8.5	18.90	17.21	15.74
9.0	17.85	16.25	14.87
9.5	16.91	15.40	14.09
10.0	16.06	14.63	13.38

All figures measured in foot pounds of recoil energy

MEASURED FREE RECOIL 12-GAUGE AMMUNITION
1-Ounce Loads

Gun Weight (lbs.)	1150 fps 2¾-Dram
7.5	16.04
8.0	15.04
8.5	14.15
9.0	13.37
9.5	12.66
10.0	12.03

(Above) Hoge with Ed Sowers who is holding the specially equipped Ithaca trap gun that is wired to an awaiting oscilloscope to record recoil data.

(Left) Hoge, Sowers and Dr. Hutter are getting the "guinea pig" ready to record more findings. Notice the tube inserted into Hoge's windpipe to measure the effects of recoil on the heart and lungs.

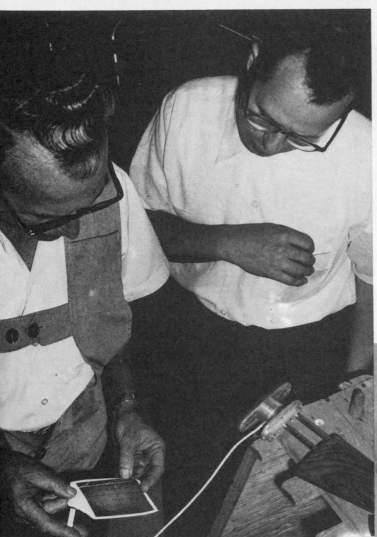

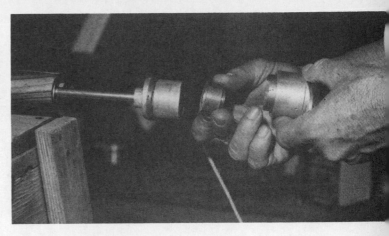

(Below) A special "thrust cell" developed by Ralph Hoge to measure recoil before it slammed against the shooter. These findings, compiled over a quarter century ago, are still valid and have been proven to be conclusive through other tests. (Above) Detail close-up of Hoge's "thrust cell."

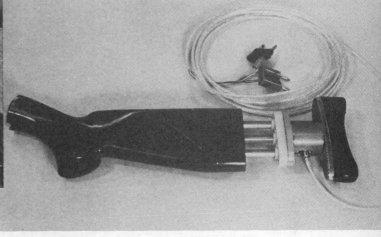

Hoge and Dr. Hutter examine the Polaroid print which accurately depicts recoil at various stages when the shotgun is fired.

C.G. Hutter.

This 1962 test was conducted at the now-defunct Aqua Sierra Gun Club in Chatsworth, California. Not only were the dramatic recoil effects recorded on an oscilloscope and captured on film, but through Dr. Hutter's findings, recoil effects on shooters' hearts and pulmonary systems were studied. To accurately measure the results of recoil on the shooter's body, a body probe had to be used. Hoge agreed to let Dr. Hutter insert a tube wired to the oscilloscope into his windpipe to record pulmonary pressure during recoil. Hoge also developed a special "thrust cell" which measured recoil in an unusual way. Instead of measuring and calculating recoil in fpe, the traditional method, his "thrust cell" recorded recoil, by using the oscilloscope, in actual pounds of force against the shooter.

One of the first facts established was that it takes 3 milliseconds between the ignition of the shotshell primer and the departure of the shot and wad from the barrel. Also, by using the "thrust cell," it was determined that a 12-gauge 2¾-dram Winchester trap load with 1⅛ ounces of No. 8 shot produced 200 pounds of recoil. A heavier field load (3¼ drams, 1¼ ounces of shot) conjured up a reading of 265 pounds of recoil. The test gun was a Model 12 equipped with a Hydro-Coil unit and measuring devices that raised the gun's normal weight from 8 pounds, 6 ounces to 9 pounds, 3 ounces. During these tests, the Hydro-Coil unit was made inoperable and an assistant held the shotgun against Hoge's shoulder and pulled the trigger.

The reason that another person held and fired the shotgun was to eliminate the human factor because all shooters learn to anticipate recoil. Just before pulling the trigger, the experienced shooter, ever so slightly, pushes the shotgun away and off his shoulder. Practiced shooters have also learned over the years and thousands of rounds of ammunition to absorb much of the recoil in their hands and arms, especially their master hand.

(Above and right) A fine electrical wire was placed across the primer to start the recording device — another wire was placed across the muzzle to stop the recording device.

This is the oscilloscope with the specially-mounted Polaroid camera to record the recoil-induced images. Even though this test equipment was developed a quarter century ago, it is still much in vogue today.

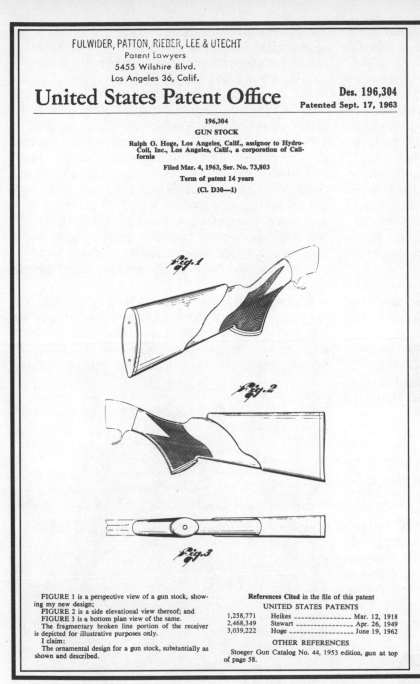

FULWIDER, PATTON, RIEBER, LEE & UTECHT
Patent Lawyers
5455 Wilshire Blvd.
Los Angeles 36, Calif.

United States Patent Office

Des. 196,304
Patented Sept. 17, 1963

196,304
GUN STOCK

Ralph O. Hoge, Los Angeles, Calif., assignor to Hydro-Coil, Inc., Los Angeles, Calif., a corporation of California

Filed Mar. 4, 1963, Ser. No. 73,803

Term of patent 14 years

(Cl. D30—1)

FIGURE 1 is a perspective view of a gun stock, showing my new design;
FIGURE 2 is a side elevational view thereof; and
FIGURE 3 is a bottom plan view of the same.
The fragmentary broken line portion of the receiver is depicted for illustrative purposes only.
I claim:
The ornamental design for a gun stock, substantially as shown and described.

References Cited in the file of this patent
UNITED STATES PATENTS

1,258,771	Heikes	Mar. 12, 1918
2,468,349	Stewart	Apr. 26, 1949
3,039,222	Hoge	June 19, 1962

OTHER REFERENCES
Stoeger Gun Catalog No. 44, 1953 edition, gun at top of page 58.

The U.S. Patent Office issued a patent on the Cycolac (plastic) Hydro-Coil stock in 1963 — the same year Winchester opted to place this device on their line of shotguns.
Unfortunately, the stock was ahead of its time as shooters for some reason did not trust plastic and demanded wood for gunstocks. Today, plastic rifle and shotgun stocks are not only accepted, but preferred because of their non-swelling and non-shrinking attributes.

Watch the backs of seasoned trap and Skeet shooters, especially at the rear of the shoulder where the shotgun is mounted. During recoil you'll note there is very little movement. Then look at a newcomer and observe the physical beating he is taking. Both shooters are absorbing the entire payload of recoil, but are taking it in different areas.

How many times have you heard and read in interviews with many of today's top shooters that "recoil doesn't bother me!" Their minds have subconsciously learned how to cope with recoil by using their entire body as a shock absorber. Like the phrase "practice makes perfect," after tens of thousands of rounds of fired ammunition, the shooter's subconscious takes over and finds a better way to cope with recoil.

A shooter's shotgun is a malicious mistress. On one end she serves him nicely and on the other, bites like a cornered rat. She discharges her duties well, but at a cost to the shooter in terms of punishment. The first time you fired a heavy-recoiling rifle or shotgun it probably wasn't a pleasant experience. Memorable yes, enjoyable no. Recall the impact against the shoulder and possible black and blue areas to the shoulder and face which appeared the next day.

Have you ever experienced dizziness, headaches or nausea while on the firing line or soon after a competitive event? If so, you probably blamed it on something you could relate to — an upset stomach from something you ate for breakfast, or your eyeglass prescription needs checking, etc. No one outwardly admits that recoil is really the problem. It just isn't macho to acknowledge that all that punishment you're subjected to is starting to take its toll.

Without going into all the medical jargon, the comprehensive tests led by Dr. Hutter proved beyond a shadow of a doubt that the effects of recoil place a serious strain on both the pulmonary and respiratory systems. In fact, if the peak strain is prolonged by a factor of five or more, the effects of recoil could put someone in shock or even a deep coma. It was further ascertained that the impact trauma of recoil damages the tissues directly behind the gunstock, especially on women. When this report was initially published in a national publication, many were concerned the results would scare off new shooters and many veterans would hang up their firearms and take up golf.

Well, like the warning labels on cigarettes, which don't stop many people from smoking, the report had little effect on the number of shooters who entered or quit competitive trap and Skeet shooting.

The test results were: **(1)** Recoil is a serious problem that should be dealt with the best way possible. **(2)** Some of the effects of recoil can be minimized by using special handloads and mechanical devices. **(3)** Recoil cannot be eliminated — only accommodated.

Recoil-Reducing Devices

From the Hydro-Coil tests of 1962, the measuring devices proved that the shock-absorbing quality of the Hydro-Coil unit reduced the 200 pounds of recoil energy created by a 2³/₄-dram Winchester shotshell loaded with 1¹/₈ ounces of shot to 40 pounds — quite a reduction. This type of shock absorber actually spreads out the effects of felt recoil perhaps better than any other type of mechanism. There are a host of devices that operate on the Hydro-Coil principle. **Soft Touch**, unfortunately, does not operate on air pressure, but a hydraulic cylinder instead. I found that this system re-

sponds slowly between shots. There's also the danger of an oil leak and because oil viscosity is at the mercy of ambient temperature, I would anticipate a slower response time in cold weather.

The **Carey Comb** is another shock absorber that boasts a split two-piece stock with a built-in hydraulic energy absorbing unit. The unit I shot was installed on a Winchester Model 12 which, in my opinion, changed the smooth-handling veteran into a muzzle-light, herky-herky shotgun. To better balance the gun, weight could be artificially added to the forward part of the gun. However, more weight would increase the shotgun's overall weight to somewhat more than 10 pounds. Not many shooters can handle that much weight for the long haul. Like the Soft Touch, an oil-filled hydraulic chamber is used, which I do not like for aforementioned reasons.

A knockoff from the original Hydro-Coil device is the **G-Squared** unit which operates on compressed air. This unit is available from a few specialized gunsmiths who make Hydro-Coil replicas and install the G-Squared shock absorber. It has two unique features.

(Above) Ed Sowers, of Hydro-Coil fame, checks and makes certain that every Hydro-Coil unit is fully inflated and operates perfectly before any gun leaves his shop in Sepulveda, California.

(Left) Sowers still makes stocks the old-fashioned way — he sands them! One of the last "old-time" custom stockmakers, Ed was one of the original designers of the Weatherby rifle stock.

In 1964, these four components made up a complete Hydro-Coil stock and forend and retailed for $80 — how many would you like to buy today at that price?

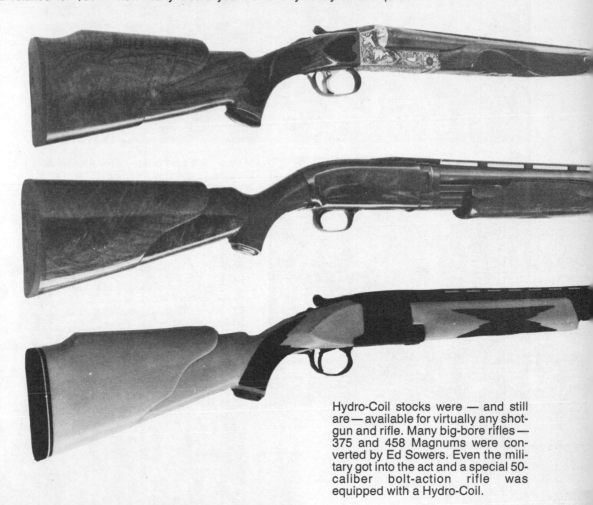

Hydro-Coil stocks were — and still are — available for virtually any shotgun and rifle. Many big-bore rifles — 375 and 458 Magnums were converted by Ed Sowers. Even the military got into the act and a special 50-caliber bolt-action rifle was equipped with a Hydro-Coil.

Part of the production facilities at Hydro-Coil in 1963.

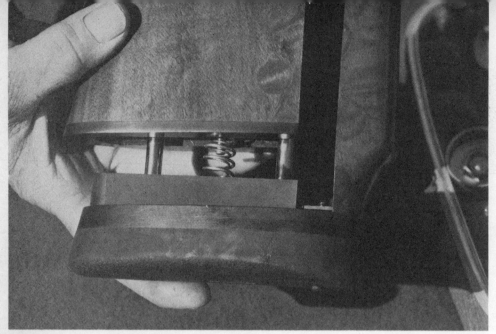

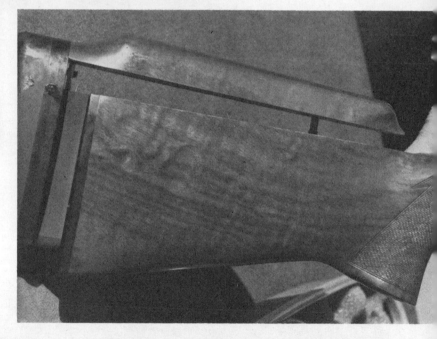

(Above, left and below) The Allison & Carey split comb is a combination of air and spring tension to operate the shock absorber. Conversion of an existing stock can only be done by the factory as there is a great amount of cutting and fitting required.

The first is the clever use of two adjustable posts, through which the length of pull of the buttstock can be adjusted, and second, is the air-filler valve which is accessible from the assembled stock by using an extension valve. This is an excellent unit and except for the original Hydro-Coil, comes in a close second for taming recoil.

Every few years a new wave of recoil reducers claim to reduce recoil to the point the claims start to be suspect. Most of these "flash-in-the-pan" devices last only a few months, cost anywhere from $39.95 to $99.95 (plus installation) and only add ½-pound or more in weight to the shotgun. This additional weight helps reduce felt recoil all by itself.

In my opinion, the so-called "porting" of a shotgun barrel is the least desirable of any process. First, the myriad arrangement of holes in the barrel does nothing to enhance the appearance of the shotgun. The holes are generally found slightly behind the choke area, where the least resistance is found. These "portholes" may help reduce muzzle flip — ever so slightly — but they create a different sound from the shotgun barrel. Therefore, if the shooter hears something different, he will naturally associate that with being better in per-

The Edwards Recoil reducer has been around for over a decade, so there must be enough satisfied shooters who have put their trust into this type of recoil reduction device.

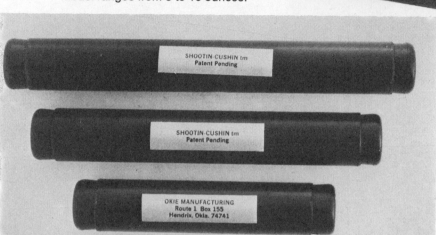

The Shootin-Cushin recoil reducer uses a special oil and a unique oil passage of the piston to create a true hydraulic action. The weight of each model ranges from 5 to 10 ounces.

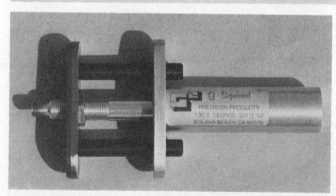

The G-Squared shock absorber is a simple affair that is installed in the end of the main section of the buttstock which is covered with a hollowed out comb.

(Above) The G-Squared recoil reducing device is air actuated and may be filled via an extension valve through the buttplate. This convenience eliminates the need to disassemble the two-piece stock for maintenance.

PATENTS FOR RECOIL REDUCING DEVICES

Devices to reduce recoil on shotguns and rifles aren't new. These six patents go back as far as 1892 and all seem to work quite nicely. Each is a variation on the same theme.

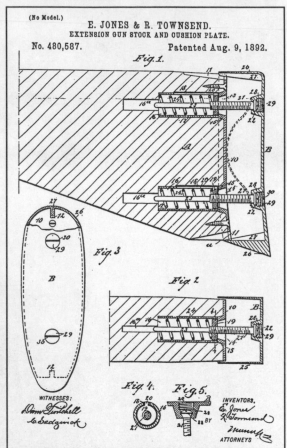

(No Model.)

E. JONES & R. TOWNSEND.
EXTENSION GUN STOCK AND CUSHION PLATE.
No. 480,587. Patented Aug. 9, 1892.

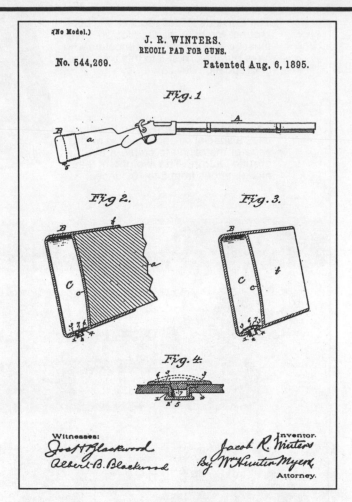

(No Model.)

J. R. WINTERS.
RECOIL PAD FOR GUNS.
No. 544,269. Patented Aug. 6, 1895.

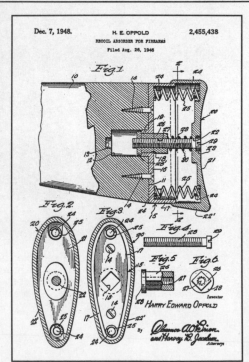

Dec. 7, 1948. H. E. OPPOLD 2,455,438
RECOIL ABSORBER FOR FIREARMS
Filed Aug. 26, 1946

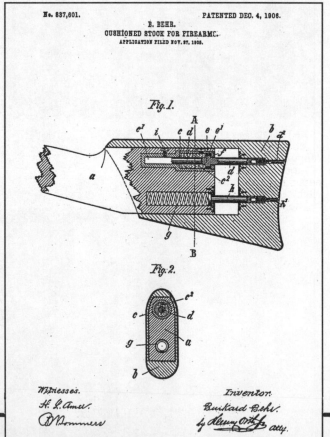

No. 837,601. PATENTED DEC. 4, 1906.
B. BEHR.
CUSHIONED STOCK FOR FIREARMS.
APPLICATION FILED NOV. 27, 1905.

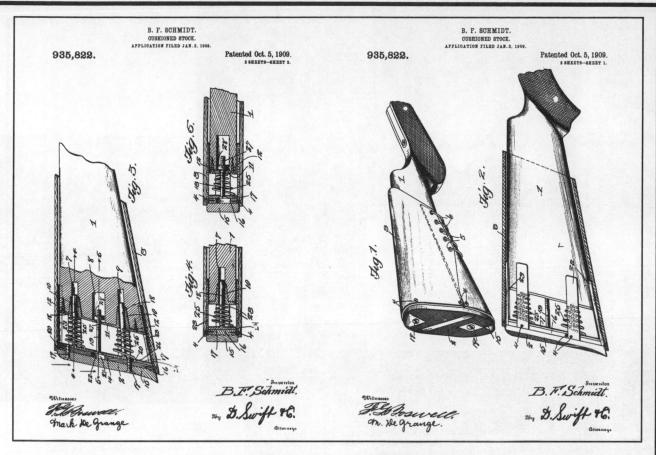

B. F. SCHMIDT.
CUSHIONED STOCK.
APPLICATION FILED JAN. 2, 1909.

935,822.

Patented Oct. 5, 1909.
2 SHEETS—SHEET 2.

B. F. SCHMIDT.
CUSHIONED STOCK.
APPLICATION FILED JAN. 2, 1909.

935,822.

Patented Oct. 5, 1909.
2 SHEETS—SHEET 1.

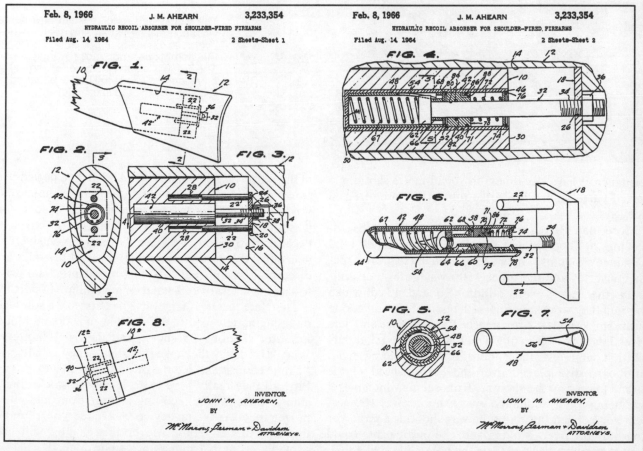

Feb. 8, 1966   J. M. AHEARN   3,233,354
HYDRAULIC RECOIL ABSORBER FOR SHOULDER-FIRED FIREARMS
Filed Aug. 14, 1964   2 Sheets-Sheet 1

Feb. 8, 1966   J. M. AHEARN   3,233,354
HYDRAULIC RECOIL ABSORBER FOR SHOULDER-FIRED FIREARMS
Filed Aug. 14, 1964   2 Sheets-Sheet 2

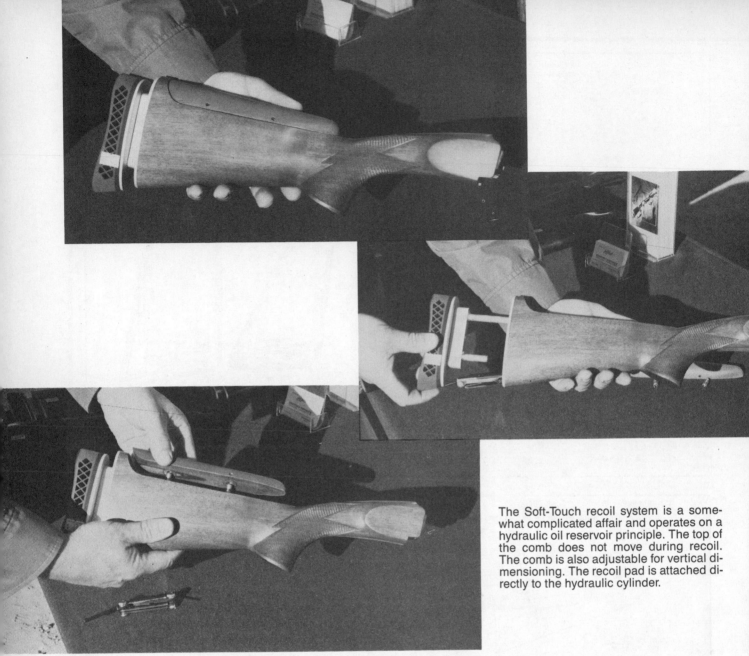

The Soft-Touch recoil system is a somewhat complicated affair and operates on a hydraulic oil reservoir principle. The top of the comb does not move during recoil. The comb is also adjustable for vertical dimensioning. The recoil pad is attached directly to the hydraulic cylinder.

formance. I have stood next to squad mates shooting a ported barrel and I don't like the extra noise directed sideways.

More than 10 years ago I was involved in a test involving 20 shooters and two Remington Model 1100 12-gauge shotguns. One had a ported barrel from a major converter and the other 1100 was pure stock. Initially, the testers were blindfolded and asked which shotgun they were shooting — the ported-barrel version or the stock model. After nearly 100 shots, the shooters agreed they were guessing which was which. Later during that same test, the blindfolds were removed and a cardboard disc placed over the barrel ahead of the forend to prevent the shooters from seeing which barrel was being used. Suddenly, every shooter was 100 percent correct determining if he was shooting a ported or non-ported barrel. Making sure the participants could not see past the disc and view the holes, I loaded a shell

in the ported version and fired. Ah ha! The ported version blew a small amount of tell-tale white smoke sideways — the non-ported barrel only blew smoke forward. That was how all the testers miraculously became clairvoyant. I have yet to see conclusive evidence that the porting of a shotgun barrel provides any discernible recoil-reducing qualities. Until I am privy to some new test data, I stand on my opinion of porting.

There are just too many variables to make a solid call on reducing felt recoil. We've all seen shooters bloodied after shooting 25 shots from their pet shotguns. When asked why they take that abuse, they usually say, "I'm used to it and it's the price I must pay to shoot." Pity, all they really have to do is change stock dimensions, shoot lighter-recoiling ammunition, and add a proven recoil-reducing device to take the "hurt" out of trap or Skeet shooting. Maybe this chapter will help convince them that something can be done!

13

Reloading—Is It Worthwhile?

RELOADING SHOTGUN SHELLS is an extension of shooting. The money saved by reloading enables shooters to shoot more on the same financial budget. As a shooter becomes more involved in competitive shooting, it is inevitable that the subject of reloading will crop up in conversation. More than 90 percent of active trap and Skeet shooters "roll their own."

The sight of all those empty shells that were scrupulously gathered, brought home, and are now residing in a large box or two is a temptation too hard to resist. Shooters often think "I have all these hulls sitting there, doing me no good. Why not reload them, save myself some money and put them back into action?" Why not, indeed?

Reloading "Costs"

There are excellent reloading tools on the market ranging from less than $100 to more than $500. Shot, powder, wads and primers are available at prices that seem to be a huge cost saver of finished ammo over what must be shelled out for factory fodder. But, before embarking on a shopping expedition for reloading gear, shooters should take a careful look at some of the reloading facts.

Those who handload ammunition for rifles and handguns generally have hopes of producing cartridges that are a bit better than factory loads. With careful planning and good reloading techniques, it is entirely possi-

Reloading shotshells will allow the average shooter to shoot more, which is what our shooting games are all about. On today's market, a box of factory ammunition sells for about $5 per box including tax. Reloaded ammunition costs about $3 per box for a tidy 40 percent savings, though there are other costs involved.

ble that a special combination of powder, primer and bullet can be found that will definitely give better performance. Certain guns shoot more accurately with ammo that has been "fine tuned" to their individual tastes. Special bullet sizes and shapes not offered by commercial ammunition sources may be utilized. Velocities may also be increased (or decreased) to meet the requirements of a particular shooting situation. In other words, leaving money out of the picture for the moment, it is quite feasible for a rifleman or pistolero to create a loaded round that is superior to factory ammo in one way or another. Does this same reasoning apply to reloading shotshells? Disappointingly, no.

The ultimate goals of the metallic rifle cartridge reloader are flat trajectory and pinpoint accuracy at ranges of 100 yards and farther. This requirement does not exist for shotshells. A shotshell used for trap or Skeet must deliver a pattern that covers a rather large area at target distances generally no farther than 50 yards. "Accuracy," in riflemen's terms, is meaningless applied to shotshells. *Accuracy in shotshells is defined*

wise restricted to No. 7½ shot or smaller.

Staying within the above-mentioned limitations of shot weight, shot size and powder charge, it is unlikely that a reloader can develop a load that performs better than factory ammunition. The opposite is more often the case because factories have development facilities and research capabilities far more elaborate than any reloader could possibly duplicate. Years of experience and the combined knowledge of a host of experts are behind every shotshell that leaves the assembly lines of any major ammunition manufacturer. A reloader who thinks he can put together a shotshell that will produce higher scores than factory shells on trap or Skeet fields is probably indulging in an ego-flattering fantasy.

A shotgun's test facility is the pattern board. If a shotgun is properly patterned and shoots to point of aim, scores will be made by the shooter, not the ammo used. The most meticulously-loaded shotshell in the history of the world cannot break a clay target unless the man holding the gun places the shot load in the path of the target. Fastidious reloading cannot improve

The first rule at any gun club is "If you want to keep your empty hulls, pocket them." Once the fired hulls hit the ground, the club claims them, for good reasons.

Over the years, the author has found that factory-loaded ammunition is the best to use for a number of reasons. First, it eliminates any mental distractions which can be caused by shooting reloads that do not equal the consistency and performance of factory fodder. Second, once-fired empty hulls can be sold to handloaders for a hefty $4 to $5 per hundred. This return on investment greatly reduces the cost of factory ammo making the few dollars savings per case questionable.

in terms of pattern size and density. Loading techniques undoubtedly affect patterns, but pattern size is largely a function of the gun and its barrel choking.

There are legal restrictions in the ATA and NSSA rule books regarding sizes of shot (nothing larger than No. 7½) and the ATA dram equivalent (3 dram). Competition trap and Skeet shooters have little or no choice about projectile weight or powder charge because the rules limit total shot weight to no more than 1⅛ ounces, and as previously mentioned, shot size is like-

scores, only practice. It takes years of hard, dedicated work and thousands of rounds of ammunition to become a proficient tournament shooter.

If I've convinced you that the above argument is true and that homemade shotshells are no better than factory ammo, why do competitive shooters spend large amounts of money for equipment and sit for countless hours at a bench year after year making thousands of shells? Most reloaders claim they're saving bags of money by recycling their ammo. There is no doubt that

Wooden loading blocks for shotshells are just as necessary as those used for metallic cartridge reloading. These are from the Stalwart Corporation and are available in 25 or 50 count and in 10-, 12- and 20-gauge size.

reloaded shells cost less than factory ammunition, but the actual savings may be somewhat lower than initially thought.

Depending on the area in which you live, it costs between 10 and 14 cents to reload a 12-gauge shotshell with $1^{1}/_{8}$ ounces of "hard" shot — not including the cost of the empty hull. For comparative purposes, let's say it costs $3 to reload a box of shells, or 12 cents per shell. On the surface, it seems that reloading is a pretty profitable enterprise, since a case of Winchester AA shells sells for about $80, or $4 a box. This adds up to a clear profit of $1 per box, or $20 a case. But, wait a minute! There is more to the economics of this business than meets the eye.

Let's say that instead of reloading all those shiny, once-fired hulls, the handloader sells them to another reloader. Empty plastic shells are about $4 per 100 on the open market, or $20 per case. The actual net cost of the factory ammo is not $80 per case, but $80 minus $20 for the empties, or $60 per case. Remember that the cost of the reloads was set at $60 per case, so the net savings drops to zero — a wash if empties are sold instead of reloaded. Hold on, the whole story still hasn't been told.

Now let's look at your investment in both equipment and inventory. Reloading paraphernalia is not exactly cheap. High-speed shotshell loaders range from about $300 to $500 or more with special accessories. A working inventory of powder, shot, primers and wads can eat up a lot of dollars and there are numerous little gadgets that make reloading life easier, but cost even more. Total investment in equipment and materials can quickly add up to $1000 or more. Amortized over a period of time, it will take a lot of reloading to recover this investment. What if the money tied up in reloading gear is placed in a high-yielding savings account? Interest will just about pay the remaining difference between reloads and factory ammo. Net financial gain from reloading? Virtually zeeeroe minus! And remember, we haven't said a word about the value of the time involved that might be spent more profitably.

Just like the old adage about the condemned man who just before the trap was to be sprung to hang him said, "You can't argue with facts," so much for the economics of reloading shotshells. It simply doesn't pay. In fact, it costs money. Even with special "deals" that are better than my examples, the best you can do is

break even. Then why, in the face of this fact, do experienced shooters reload their own ammunition? It is a good way to escape the pressures of modern society and spend a few hours now and then alone with your thoughts. There is also a certain satisfaction derived from making something with your hands that brings pleasure in return.

If reloading is mostly for pleasure, not profit, so be it! Nowhere is it written that all things must be done for financial gain. No man lives for money alone — or shouldn't. We shoot and reload for fun, that's reason enough.

Reloading Basics

I know I've just gored the sacred cow and eliminated your "reason" for reloading, which probably sounded something like, "By spending a few bucks on reloading equipment and components, I can save hundreds of dollars just in the next few months." Sorry about that, but now that the facts of reloading life are firmly in mind, let's get down to some of the basics. The key to quality reloading is consistency. Regardless of the load a shooter selects as standard, it must be consistent from one loading session to the next. Remember, no shotshell load will shoot around corners or dip in the middle of its flight path when the elusive claybird hits a chuckhole in the air. There will be times when targets are missed, especially on windy days, through no fault of the shooter. These things happen to us all, but there is no excuse for missing because of faulty reloads, which is where consistency comes into play. The shotshell and its charge of pellets must perform the same every time so the shooter knows exactly where the shot will go when the trigger is pulled.

Every handloader I've ever met, including myself decades ago, constantly searches for that "special" load usually made from a mishmash of components. I've listened to mind-boggling concoctions from, I thought, stable individuals who had some of the wierdest-sounding recipes imaginable. The most practical and easiest method of producing best-quality reloads is to follow factory recommendations. If you prefer a certain brand — be it Federal, Winchester, Remington, Activ or Fiocchi — stick with the factory components. If Federal Gold Medal hulls work best in your shotgun and reloading press, use only factory-manufactured or recommended components, including

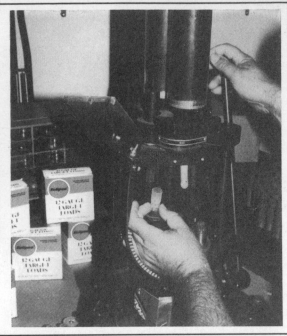

Whenever loading for a particular brand of hulls, always use matching components, i.e., Winchester hulls, wads, powder and primers; ditto for Remington and Federal, save for powder.

wads, shot and primers. If you lean toward Winchester AA hulls, you should achieve excellent results with Winchester components, ditto for the rest of the manufacturers. Every ammunition maker either makes proprietary components available or recommends others.

Shooters who reload and deviate from factory recommendations are not taking advantage of the factory's expertise and knowledge. Huge ammunition companies hire full-time ballisticians and use test equipment not available to the general public to both prove and disprove all types of shotshell loadings. Munitions makers have been successfully turning out millions of shotshells for decades with few, if any, problems. Can any reloader equal this record? No. So, instead of ignoring the advice on factory instruction sheets and developing your own "superloads," stick to the numbers supplied by the real experts. This doesn't mean that good reloads can't be made with mixed components and nonstandard loading techniques, though. But the amount of time, money and effort needed to work out all the nuances of your own reloads is likely to be greater than most shooters are willing to expend.

The selection of shot size has always been a vexing problem for shooters on the firing line. Now that you are making a custom-loaded shell, the same problem is carried over to the reloading bench. Assume that you have a batch of choice, clean, empty cases with matching components ready to load except for the shot. What size shot should be used, and how much? Some shooters use different loads for 16-yard Singles and Handicap trap, and yet another for Doubles. Is this sort of specialization necessary?

About a decade ago, there was quite a bit of conversation about 1-ounce trap and Skeet loads for 12-gauge shotguns. Proponents of the 1-ounce load claimed many advantages: reduced recoil, lower cost and better patterns. The first two claims are valid, the third is suspect. If governed by rules and regulations of both the ATA and NSSA, which allow 1 1/8 ounces of shot no larger than No. 7 1/2, why not play the game to the hilt? Why purposely handicap ourselves? The game is diffi-

One problem is where a shooter should put all 100 empty hulls during a registered shoot. The obvious solution is in some sort of pouch, bag or valise — there are dozens of commercial products available. This lightweight all-nylon model is handy.

cult enough without introducing artificial obstacles. The 1-ounce load may be great for upland game, but load all the shot you can legally use for claybirding.

Now that we've settled the quantity dispute (hopefully), what about shot sizes? A fabled white hunter was once asked by his client, "Why do you carry a 700 Nitro Express?" The professional replied, "Because they don't make an 800 Nitro Express!" The same

mum loads for both trap and Skeet: 3 drams equivalent with $1\frac{1}{8}$ ounces of No. $7\frac{1}{2}$ shot. The same load is equally effective for both trap and Skeet and using the same load for all events has certain advantages. For example, you get to know exactly what to expect from it, which should result in higher scores. Loading everything the same means you only have to buy one brand of wads, powder, primers and shot. Also, the reloading

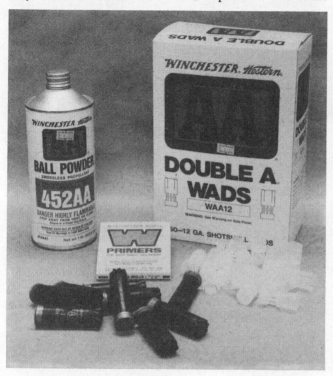

Whatever brand of hulls you are using, always use matching components whenever possible. Stay away from bargain-basement deals on "off" brands — stick to the big names.

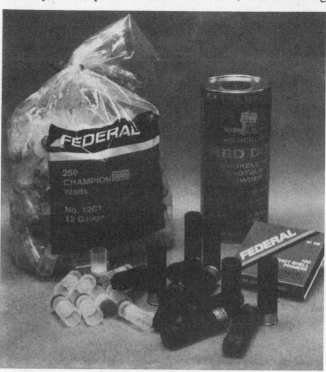

And, always adhere to manufacturers' reloading instructions. The munitions makers have all the skill, knowledge and equipment to determine the correct reloading data.

holds true for both trap and Skeet shooting — bigger is better in the long run. How many times have you hit a target that continues on its merry way, leaving a puff of dust in its wake? Usually when this happens, the shooter feels he made a mistake and either mispointed his gun or used the wrong load. But often, the culprit is the target. Ten years ago, practically all clay targets were left in their natural black color. Today, most target manufacturers and gun clubs offer colored targets painted in various hues of white, yellow, green, orange or red. A coat of paint on a target makes it harder to break — during manufacture, packaging, transportation and in the air. Today's harder targets have helped gun clubs reduce their operating costs by lowering breakage, and target manufacturers have eliminated a large portion of their protective packaging requirements. To overcome the target hardness problem, the largest size shot legally allowed (No. $7\frac{1}{2}$) should be used for both trap and Skeet. A single No. $7\frac{1}{2}$ pellet has 30 percent more energy at 40 yards than a single No. 8 pellet. It takes a good deal of energy to break today's targets.

Experience has taught me the value of using maxi-

equipment never has to be re-adjusted from one loading session to the next.

Reloading shotshells has a few major advantages. First, it offers a psychological edge to some shooters who think their "better" loads will improve their scores. If that helps them mentally, that is what we are striving for — a positive frame of mind. Second, there is a perceived notion of saving money and therefore having more shells to shoot. No doubt shooters who load a lot shoot a lot, which is probably the best reason for reloading. Gobs of ammunition means the shooter will practice a lot, and that's the true secret of successful tournament shotgunning.

Reloading Presses

Once you decide to reload, you must select a loading press that meets your personal needs. When picking a shotshell loading press, a reloader may choose a tool that produces handloads at rates from 10 to 20 per hour, up to 500 or more per hour. Prices range from a few dollars to $500 or more. Generally, the more expensive the press, the greater its production rate. Simpler tools are adequate for occasional shooters who load shells only now and then, but trap and Skeet shooters who burn up large volumes of ammo need a progressive press that turns out at least a couple hundred finished shells an hour. A careful reloader, using a modern progressive reloading tool, can produce reloaded shells second to none in quality. Single-station presses turn out good ammo, too, but it takes longer and the operator must be aware of the limitations of such equipment.

The simplest and least expensive press is the Lee Load-All II. The Load-All II will load plastic or paper shells with six- or eight-segment crimps. Dies are made of nylon, and shot and powder measures have built-in baffles. Each step of the loading process ends on a positive stop and there are no wad pressure adjustments. The press is supplied with a charge bar and 24 replaceable shot and powder bushings. Complete with load data, the Lee Load-All II is made for 12-, 16-, and 20-gauge. It is not a reloading press capable of even medium-speed production. It is, however, an excellent starter's tool, especially for the low cost of under $50 complete.

Bear brand loading presses come in several models, from the simple Bear Cat II to the semi-automatic Polar

The **Bear Glacier Bear** reloads up to 250 rounds per hour. The three-station loading sequence eliminates extra handling and the hinged charging assembly makes changing shot or powder and respective bushings fast and simple. It is available for 12 Magnum, 12 (2³/₄″ and 3″), 20 (2³/₄″ and 3″), 16, 28, 410 (2¹/₂″ and 3″) bore.

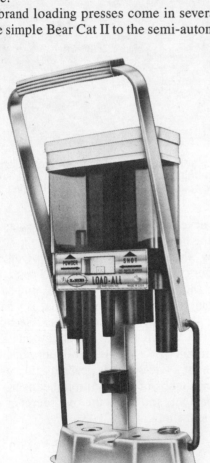

The **Lee Load-All II** has the same basic features as the tried and true Lee Load-All but comes with a redesigned base which allows for the addition of the optional primer feed. The base has a built-in primer catcher with a door in front for emptying. It is available for 12-, 16-, and 20-gauge.

The **MEC Sizemaster** is an inexpensive reloading press that features MEC's exclusive "Power Ring" that resizes the brass base on shotshells back to their original factory dimensions. It is available in 10-, 12-, 16-, 20-, and 28-gauge and 410 bore.

There are a host of aftermarket accessories that often enhance factory-designed equipment. This gizmo attaches to the low-cost MEC reloading presses and "kicks" out the completed shell so the handloader doesn't have to pull the finished shell from the holding plate.

Bear 600, which the company claims can produce up to 600 completed shells an hour. In the middle are the Honey and Glacier Bear models which are three- and six-station tools, respectively. All the Bears handle both paper and plastic cases and have a fully-adjustable wad pressure indicator. The high-end models are equipped with an automatic primer feeder.

MEC offers five models. The Sizemaster is a single-stage loading machine that resizes both steel or brass heads and high or low "brass." MEC's famous "E-Z Prime" automatic primer feeder is standard equipment as is their "Pro-Check," which reminds the operator of proper loading sequence. Available in all gauges from 10 through 410 bore, this is an excellent piece of equipment for the intermediate shooter/handloader.

The MEC 600 Jr. Mark 5 is a very popular reloading tool and one step up from the Sizemaster in both speed and features. The production rate is estimated at 250 shells per hour, depending on the operator's skill and experience.

Next up the MEC ladder is the MEC 650, a progressive tool that performs six functions at the pull of the operating lever. Standard features include an automatic primer feed and auto-cycle charging system to insure

This (right) is MEC's most popular reloading press — the **600 Jr. Mark 5.** The press is capable of reloading eight to 10 boxes of ammo per hour and is extremely rugged in design and manufacture. An excellent buy with many features found only on more expensive models.

E-Z-Pak (left) neatly stacks a full box of 12-gauge shotshells that enables the handloader to simply slip an empty shell box over the stack, tip it upside down, and voilá, a completely filled box of shells.

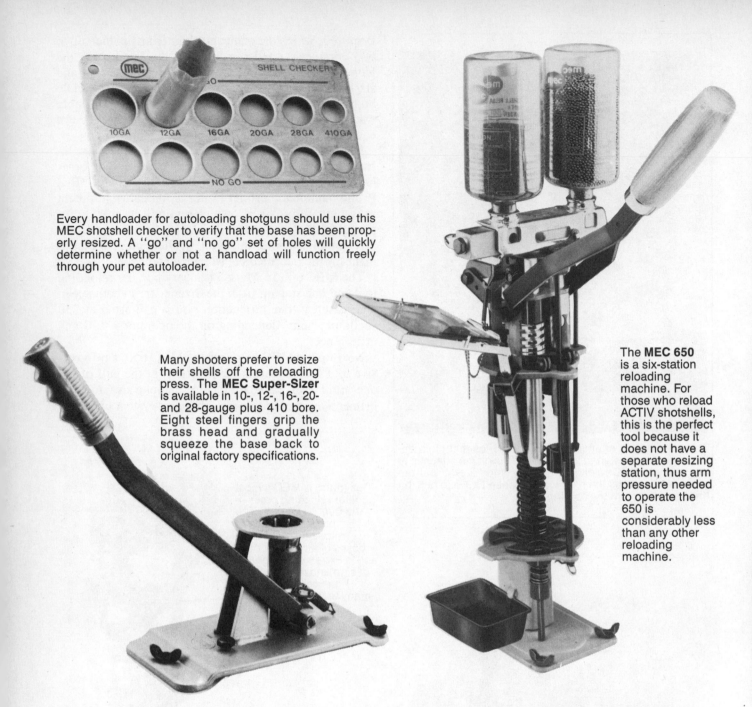

Every handloader for autoloading shotguns should use this MEC shotshell checker to verify that the base has been properly resized. A "go" and "no go" set of holes will quickly determine whether or not a handload will function freely through your pet autoloader.

Many shooters prefer to resize their shells off the reloading press. The **MEC Super-Sizer** is available in 10-, 12-, 16-, 20- and 28-gauge plus 410 bore. Eight steel fingers grip the brass head and gradually squeeze the base back to original factory specifications.

The **MEC 650** is a six-station reloading machine. For those who reload ACTIV shotshells, this is the perfect tool because it does not have a separate resizing station, thus arm pressure needed to operate the 650 is considerably less than any other reloading machine.

that no powder is dropped until the empty hull is in proper position. The 650 has three crimping stations (most presses have two, or even one) which gradually taper, close and finally crimp the reloaded shell. This tapered hull assures reliability when fed into autoloading shotguns. The Model 650 does not resize the hull as an integral operation, instead it can be done as a separate operation.

The famous MEC Grabber is the company's top of the line and most popular model. It is fully progressive and has all the features of the Model 650 except it *does* resize shells by its patented "Power Ring" collet system, which returns each shell to original factory specifications. It is available in 12-, 16-, 20-, 28-gauge and 410 bore. Like any reloading press, speed depends on

the operator, but the Grabber should be able to exceed one case per hour.

If you have an additional $610 lying around that you don't know what to do with, you can always upgrade a Grabber to the MEC Hustler, which is basically the same tool except that elbow grease is replaced with a built-in hydraulic system. It features toe-touch control that allows continuous action or stops at any stage within the cycle, fully controlled by the operator. Two cases per hour (1000 shells) isn't out of the question with this high-speed Hustler.

Hornady, or Pacific to us old-timers, offers a trio of time-proven units. The Hornady Model 105 is a simplified version of the more popular Model 155. It is available in three gauges only — 12, 16 or 20 — and is aimed

The **Hustler** is MEC's top-of-the-line reloading press. Basically the Grabber model with a hydraulic assist attached to it, electronics eliminate the need for a manually-operated handle. It turns the reloading chore into an evening of fun.

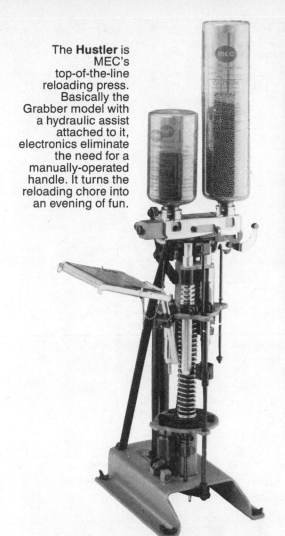

The heart of MEC's perfect recrimps is its Spindex crimp starter that rotates automatically and realigns itself on the original crimp of the shotshell. Two versions are available — six- and eight-point crimps.

The **MEC Model 8567 Grabber** (right) is a six-station reloading press that produces a completed shotshell on the completion of every upstroke. It boasts three-position crimping that challenges the looks of a factory shell.

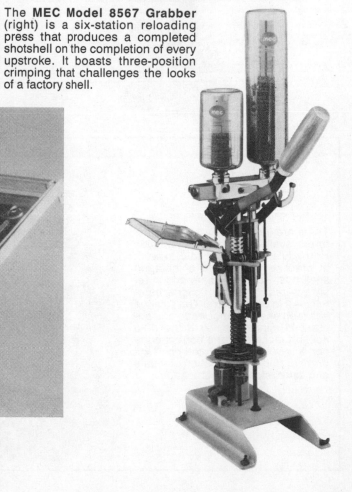

MEC's **E-Z Prime** accommodates a whole tray of shotshell primers in the reserve and then feeds them one at a time into the priming ram. It is a super simple, yet totally effective, design.

197

The **Hornady Model 105,** available for 12-, 16-, or 20-gauge, is a simplified version of the DL-155. All operations are the same as the more expensive loaders, but this model was designed to lower costs for beginning reloaders.

The **Hornady 155** sizes the head and rim of cases before loading and the rest of the case after loading. It loads over 200 shells per hour and turns out a shell that functions in all types of actions. It is available for 12- or 20-gauge.

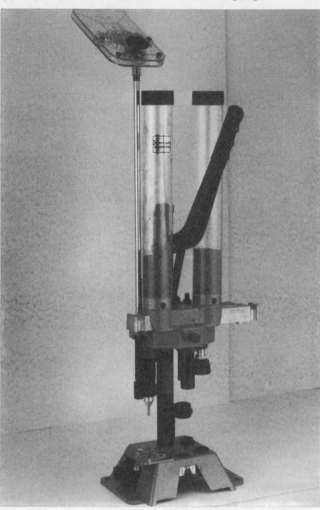

There are quite a few wad manufacturers available to the handloader. Hornady's Versalite is said to work in practically any type of shotgun shell hull. But, to be safe and sure, always read the instructions carefully—if in doubt, pass! The savings between one maker of wads and another is minuscule, so if the data doesn't include all the correct components you have on hand *don't improvise!* Stick to instructions for safe and sane reloading techniques.

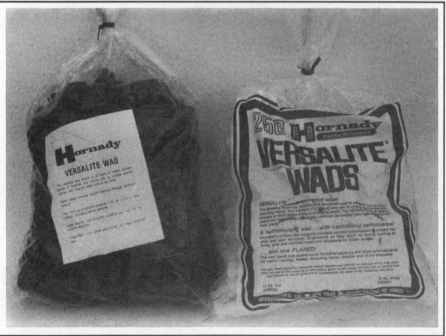

at the beginning handloader and does not have features like an automatic primer feed, wad feed, etc. The Model 155 is a multi-station press that sizes case rims and heads before loading, the rest of the case after. Capable of loading over 200 shells per hour, it is available with an automatic primer feed and all gauges are available from 12-gauge through 410 bore, as well as 3-inch magnum lengths.

The Hornady Model 366 is a progressive tool with an automatic turntable and swing-out wad guide plus many other high-production features. Eight shells move around the turntable, and eight different operations are performed at each stroke of the operating lever. After loading, the finished shell is ejected. All the operator does is place an empty hull on the shell plate and insert a wad into the machine; pulling the handle does the rest. About 500 to 600 shells per hour may be loaded with ease on this press. There are separate shut-off controls for powder and shot and it is available in 12-, 20-, 28-gauge and 410 bore. The Model 366 has been in production since the early 1970s and is popular among trap and Skeet shooters because of its high production and relatively low cost.

The **Ponsness-Warren Du-O-Matic 375,** a single-stage tool, requires only four moves to produce a loaded shell and does not need a crimp starter for paper cases. It is available for 12-, 16-, 20-, 28-gauge and 410 bore.

The **Ponsness-Warren Size-O-Matic 800** (below) is a progressive reloading tool which produces a reloaded shell with every pull of the handle — 500 to 1000 per hour. It handles both paper and plastic shells, new or fired, and is available for 12-, 20-, 28-gauge and 410 bore.

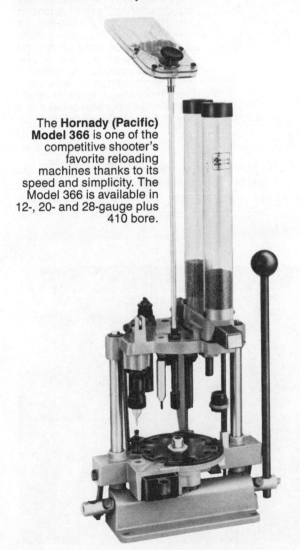

The **Hornady (Pacific) Model 366** is one of the competitive shooter's favorite reloading machines thanks to its speed and simplicity. The Model 366 is available in 12-, 20- and 28-gauge plus 410 bore.

The Ponsness-Warren Du-O-Matic Model 375 is a single-stage press that requires only four moves to produce a loaded shell. It is made for 12-, 16-, 20- and 28-gauge and 410 and will hold two sets of dies on a common head. In effect, a Skeet shooter/handloader could equip two machines for all four shells (12, 20, 28 and 410) for less than about $520 retail. Like all P-W machines, the cycled hull is encased in a stainless steel capsule throughout the entire loading cycle. Not only is the shell resized before components are fed into it, but it remains sized throughout the entire operation. A special version of the Model 375 is available in 10-gauge — just the ticket for long-yard trapshooters (just kidding).

Many handloaders consider Ponsness-Warren's Model 800C the Rolls Royce of reloading machines. The Size-O-Matic of today is not the same press produced during the reign of the original Idaho crew. There are some significant improvements and also some disturbing redesigns that, in my opinion, are far inferior to the original concept. All shells remain in one of eight sizing dies permanently affixed to the die cylinder, which automatically indexes to position the shells for each operation. A carrier receives and positions the wads for seating. Cyclic rate is extremely fast when everything is in time and 500 shells per hour produced by a single operator is a snap. Most production down time is caused by loading the shot and powder hoppers. Double-length tubes are available and highly recommended. The P-W Model 800C (C stands for convertible) is available in 12-, 20-, 28-gauge and 410 bore. It is also the most expensive shotshell reloading press on the American market but many users feel it's worth the price of admission.

There are many used machines on the market made by companies that are out of business. Lyman made many models, as did Redding and Texan. You may run across some "great deals" on these machines, but remember, if you break a major part, odds are you won't be able to get replacements. I advise against buying used reloading equipment, especially from makers who are out of business.

Whatever happened to this ingenious device? It enabled the handloader to "x-ray" a loaded shell to check its contents by beaming an ultra-strong light against the side of the plastic hull which allowed a view of the shell's contents. Often, a loaded shell might appear to look good from the outside, when in reality there could be a wad twisted or a short drop of powder or shot.

This is one of the handiest gadgets any serious reloader could install on his equipment. It is an AC-powered counter which attaches to virtually any type of manually-operated reloading press. Each time the handle is pulled, it makes contact with a spring-loaded micro switch which increases the counter by one.

Semi-autoloading shotguns present the shooter who wants to capture his empty hulls with a serious problem. Shell catchers are available for practically all popular brands and models of shotguns. There are clip-on models, bolt-on versions and a rubber band around the action will even get the job done in a pinch.

Another item of concern is powder and shot bushings. Do not take for granted what a particular bushing is supposed to do — verify it by weighing a sample charge. This holds true for both powder and shot. All too often, a bushing throws too light charges and operators reams them out to increase the "drops," especially with used bushings. New bushings should also be verified for accuracy — if they don't throw a powder charge to plus or minus $1/10$th of a grain of powder, take it back to the dealer for an exchange. Unfortunately, bushing makers will not release exact specifications that can be measured with two sets of micrometers — one for the inside dimension and the other for overall length.

There are very few accessories trap and Skeet shooters/handloaders initially need. In fact, there are very few worthwhile accessories on the market, though a few are noteworthy. There will be times when you load a shotshell and realize that you used the wrong wad or dropped the incorrect charge or wrong kind of powder. Regardless of the reason, it is nice to save the components, especially if you're thrifty. After all, you'd certainly bend down and pick a dime off the floor, wouldn't you? The Kirdoc shell dismantler is a clever device that allows the operator to safely and easily cut a tough plastic hull in half, exposing the internal components. This gadget will pay for itself in a short time because we all run into occasional problems.

After cutting a salvaged shell in half, it's easy to dump the powder into one container, the shot into another and put the wad into its original bag. What about the primer, you ask? I do not recommend removing a live primer from any shell or cartridge regardless of the situation. If you hesitate to throw away the cut hull with a live primer, put the hull into a shotgun and fire it. Then the hull is completely inert and safe to handle or throw into the trash. Primers are like mini hand grenades — they are explosive devices and if they explode out of their normally-protective environment (inside a primer pocket and inside a gun's chamber), they can cause excessive damage. *Do not attempt to remove a live primer.* Accept the 2 cent loss and write it off.

Specific information concerning loading data can be obtained from publications issued by companies that produce components or from manufacturers of reloading equipment. Instructions included with each press will give a new reloader step-by-step directions which, if followed, will result in a perfectly-loaded shotshell. Additionally, there are reloading books available from DBI Books, Inc. and others with useful information.

If, after an introduction to the whys and wherefores of reloading and a brief look at some of the equipment available, a shooter wants to jump into reloading on his own, good luck and good shooting. Reloaders may not save a lot of money, but they'll have a lot of fun and derive a great deal of satisfaction doing something constructive to support their hobbies.

14

Know Your Shotgun for Better Scores

A COUPLE OF YEARS AGO I surveyed trap and Skeet shooters about patterning their favorite competition guns. Nearly all of the 75 said they had taped a piece of paper to a pattern board frame, stepped back 40 yards and fired their shotguns. Then they visually inspected the pattern, nodded their heads in silent approval, slid the shotgun back into its case and closed up shop for the day.

Less than 10 (eight to be exact) took the time and trouble to do the job properly. As you will discover, patterning a shotgun takes time and patience and results are not gotten any other way.

Point of Impact

One of the more critical aspects of trap and Skeet shooting is a three-word phrase that is often misunderstood or misinterpreted — point of impact. It's well accepted that the shotgun's point of impact is not always in line with the shooter's point of sight. So, if a shooter looks at a target in a certain way and the gun throws its shot charge differently, the obvious result is a lost target.

Surprisingly, the vast majority of shooters will go along with this great self-imposed handicap by adjusting their shooting styles to conform to the shotgun's point of aim. A few talented shooters make necessary mental calculations to correct this problem, but the majority cannot. I seriously doubt that any of today's topnotch golfers would use a club with the "sweet spot" anywhere else but dead center on the club's face. Ditto for tennis players and their very expensive racquets.

I can guarantee that today's "hot hammers" in both trap and Skeet tailor their guns to print a pattern exactly where they are looking. Even though humans are supposed to be smarter and wiser than a piece of machinery, some stubborn shooters can't stand the thought of altering their prized shootin' irons just for the sake of performance. To those unyielding individuals, I offer sympathy and thanks — sympathy for being such good losers and thanks for contributing entrance fees for my winning share of the purse!

For any shooter who has ever missed a single target — and how many of you maintain a 100 percent average — it will behoove you to stop what you're doing and carefully analyze your gun's point of impact.

Ascertaining exactly where your shotgun shoots will require a great deal of time and shooting. To perform this task properly, you'll need a lot of ammunition, at least 20 sheets of pattern paper and much patience because there are no shortcuts to the process.

First, let me state that the regulation 40-yard patterning distance is not relevant for this test. If you're testing your Skeet gun, use 25 yards. If it's a trap gun for 16-yard targets, 32 yards is proper. For Handicap shooting, add 16 yards to your assigned yardage — 38 yards for a 22-yard shooter, 40 yards for a 24-yard shooter, etc. — to get your optimum test yardage.

You'll need about 40 square inches of clean pattern paper to contain the entire shot swarm. A sighting dot, at least 4 inches in diameter, must be placed dead center in the pattern sheet because that will be the spot at which you'll point the gun's front sight. After the pattern paper is tacked to a backing or pattern board, step back to the measured yardage and fire at least 10 separate patterns on 10 separate sheets of paper. On the corner of each sheet mark the firing sequence, the load used and the distance at which the shot was fired.

Human nature being what it is, shooters will probably perform this test using different ammunition than they use in tournaments. That is a mistake — only shoot the same brand, dram equivalent and shot size that you'd use in a registered event. If you use your reloads for 16-yard shooting, use them for these point-of-impact tests. But, if you only use factory shells for Handicap events, use duplicate ammo for conclusive results. Shotguns are somewhat like rifles and handguns as they will perform differently with various brands, types and loads.

It is important that you assume a shooting stance exactly like you would in a competitive event. Don't shoot from a sitting or braced position, but from one which closely duplicates your natural stance. "Bench-

PATTERN PAPER FRAME

Clip pattern paper

Slide the spring clips to adjust for pattern paper width

32"

Space holes 1 inch apart

Select a hole to match length of the pattern paper

Feed the wire through the hole in the spring clip— bend it around

There're a number of ways to build a pattern board. This simplistic approach is fine if the wind isn't blowing too strongly, but a better method is to tape the pattern paper onto a nonflexible backing which will hold up in the wind. Solid steel pattern boards are worthless for accurate testing as counting pellet hits is virtually impossible. (Courtesy *Shotgun Sports*)

If you have any doubts or misgivings about a certain barrel's performance, there's only one sure test — a long session on the pattern board.

resting" a shotgun is not duplicating your usual shooting position, so stand up on your "back legs" as you normally would. Shooting from the "benchrest" position requires that the forend be placed over a board, sandbag or similar object, which places stress on the barrel and actually causes it to bend — ever so slightly, granted — and influence the point of impact.

Don't sight down the barrel like a rifleman; point like a shotgunner. If you're a two-eyed shooter, aim at the center spot with both eyes open. Many shooters/testers close their "off" eyes to draw a finer "bead" on the aiming spot. Wrong! Fire the test shots like you would on a flying clay for accurate test results.

This is an excellent opportunity for your children, if old enough, to help you with the grunt work. If possible, have your helper change the paper, which saves a lot of leg work and more importantly, prevents you from looking at the targets until you're finished. Humans being who they are, if you sneak preview your first few shots, you'll have a tendency to try and correct or compensate for any of the gun's point-of-impact failings. Don't fall into that trap. This important test is *not* to determine your ability to correct where your shotgun is shooting, but to determine its point of impact in relation to your line of sight!

If you have the benefit of a helper, ask him to "call" your shot for you. After mounting your shotgun in your natural stance, let him holler "pull, shoot" or any other command. Place the gun's front sight on the target and pull the trigger. If you feel you "pulled the shot" in one direction or another, ask your helper to mark your predictions on the test pattern. If, on the other hand, you believe your sight picture was correct, don't say anything and assume the shot was "zeroed."

As suggested earlier, you should fire a minimum of 10 shots on 10 separate clean sheets of paper to average out any sighting errors. If you only shoot at two or three targets and inadvertently pull off the target spot, you'll initially tend to incorrectly blame the gun, when you were actually at fault for a poorly-aimed shot. With this 10-shot rule, both good and bad sightings will even out so that a true picture can be analyzed from the results.

Let's assume that you've fired your 10 pattern sheets and now it's time to make that most eagerly-sought discovery. The most important determination is whether your shotgun shoots high or low and left or right of dead center, but simply eyeballing the pattern sheet is not good enough. For proper evaluation, fold the pattern sheet in quarters from the center spot and count the pellet hits in each square. If the upper left square has more pellet holes than the upper right, your gun places its main shot charge left of center. Optimally, all four squares should have an equal pellet count, but this is nearly impossible because a shotgun never produces

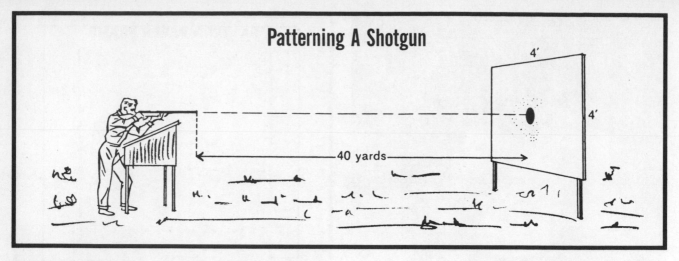

Patterning A Shotgun

4'

4'

←——————— 40 yards ———————→

Checking the Patterns

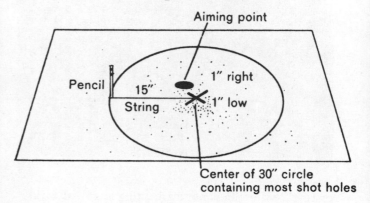

Aiming point

Pencil

15"

1" right

String

1" low

Center of 30" circle
containing most shot holes

Competitive shooters must know exactly where their pet shotgun prints its pattern. If the shotgun does not shoot where the shooter is looking, then the result will be lost targets. It is rare that a factory-new shotgun barrel will be bent, but it could happen during shipping or mishandling. It's best to visually inspect new and used barrels from time to time to insure their straightness.

identical patterns from shot to shot regardless of the type of ammunition. The ultimate method to determine the gun's point of impact is to count each square on all 10 pattern sheets, calculate the average and then examine the results on each sheet. For example, let's assume the total pellet count for the upper left square on the 10 test targets is 1500 hits. Divided by 10, each target averages 150 hits in this square. Reviewing each target, it is easy to determine whether or not that particular pattern sheet falls within this calculated standard.

Squaring the target paper into four separate sections allows the tester to determine both "windage" and "elevation" results of his test gun. A similar structured evaluation can be made to determine how high — or low — the shotgun's point of impact is. If more than half of the shot swarm is above the center line, the shotgun shoots high. If more than half of the pellets are printed on the lower half of the target paper, the shotgun obviously shoots low.

Common terms used by many shooters and gun writers to describe where a shotgun's pattern prints in relation to the center of the pattern sheet are 70/30, 50/50, 65/35, etc. They have been bandied about and with few exceptions, there have been very few explanations of

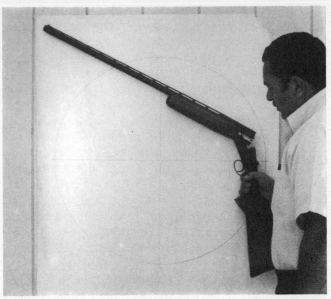

To accurately determine the results of a shotgun's barrel performance, a minimum of 10 test shots should be averaged for accuracy. Standard shotgun test procedures fired at 40 yards are not valid tests for trap and Skeet guns because of both longer (Handicap trap) and shorter (Skeet and short-yardage trap) distances. Most shots fired at Skeet targets are about 21 yards downrange, and for trap the yardage is plus 17 yards.

While patterning a shotgun barrel, you are checking for two things—the number of pellets (concentration) on the pattern paper and location of the main shot swarm (location). Combining and understanding these two facets will enable you to determine the density of the pattern and whether or not the pattern is in line to where you are looking.

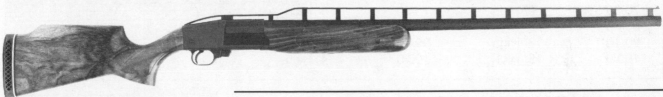

This Ljutic Olympic model features a very high profile ventilated rib. Combined with the exceptionally high-combed stock, this design works best for shooters who keep their heads in a very erect position. Shooters who "crawl" a stock and lean into the stock will find this design very difficult to get used to.

Approximate Number of Pellets in a Given Charge

Shot Size	1/2 oz.	3/4 oz.	7/8 oz.	1 oz.	1 1/8 oz.
#7 1/2	175	262	306	350	393
#8	205	308	359	410	462
#9	292	439	512	585	658

Note: Only the above loads and shot sizes conform to both ATA and NSSA rules.

what these numbers mean. Simply, these percentages relate to the amount of shot that hits the paper above and below a predetermined sighting point. A 12-gauge shotshell loaded with 1 1/8 ounces of No. 7 1/2 shot contains about 393 pellets. If, for example, 235 pellets are found above the center line and 158 below, simple arithmetic (235 divided by 393 and 158 divided by 393) calculates a pattern of 60/40. The accompanying chart gives approximate pellet count for a given charge. Determining the exact point of impact from these results is not a science, but a calculated estimate. Unlike rifle shooting in which a single projectile is used for simpler evaluation and measurement, the shot charge has hundreds of projectiles, each subjected to deformation, which alters flight characteristics. The problem is compounded further because each pellet is not exactly the same as its brethren.

Continuing this scenario, after scrutinizing the results of your tests, let's assume that windage is right on and (if it's not, how to make corrections is explained later in this chapter) concentrate on elevation. Only in the last decade or so have trap and Skeet guns been designed by the factory to shoot high; many old-time scatterguns produced 50/50 or 40/60 patterns. Shooting at fast-rising trap targets requires a "higher" shooting gun. Similarly, most of today's "hot shot" Skeeters advocate a 6 o'clock hold, which enables the shooter to see the target at all times. Although most trap and Skeet shooters rarely admit it, the majority of targets are "lost" because they were shot low. Yes, even missed low-house Skeet targets fall in this shooting hazard. Measuring or calculating a shotgun's barrel (in percentages) can be accomplished by actual pellet count, as previously mentioned, or by carefully measuring where the exact center of the pattern impacts the pattern sheet. The accompanying chart will help you "classify" your shotgun barrel's performance.

We've demonstrated a proper technique to evaluate and accurately judge a shotgun's point of impact. Let's

commercially-made lace-on or slip-on pad can be used to increase the width of the comb. When the shooter lays his cheek against the buttstock, the cast-off will have been artificially reduced. The third method is to have the stock "bent," which is a delicate job that can only be undertaken by a skilled stockmaker. The buttstock is immersed in hot oil — near boiling temperature — for a predetermined time (known only to the "immerser") until the wood is pliable enough to accept a bend at the wrist. Sometimes a stock breaks, but the customer is informed ahead of time of this possibility. In that event, the customer loses a stock and the stockmaker loses a job. If the operation goes as planned, after slowly cooling, the stock retains a "set" and the cast alteration is complete.

This same technique can also be used to raise or lower the stock. A last resort, because it is the most expensive method, is to employ a stockmaker to slice off part of the comb, shim and reglue it, or replace it

Point of Impact Relationship at Known Yardages

| 30" Pattern Test at 42 Yards | | 30" Pattern Test at 32 Yards | | 30" Pattern Test at 22 Yards | |
Pattern	Distance	Pattern	Distance	Pattern	Distance
0/100	15" Low	0/100	14" Low	0/100	13" Low
10/90	12" Low	10/90	11" Low	10/90	10" Low
20/80	9" Low	20/80	8" Low	20/80	7" Low
30/70	6" Low	30/70	5" Low	30/70	4" Low
40/60	3" Low	40/60	2" Low	40/60	1" Low
50/50	Center	50/50	Center	50/50	Center
60/40	3" High	60/40	2 "High	60/40	1" High
70/30	6" High	70/30	5" High	70/30	4" High
80/20	9" High	80/20	8" High	80/20	7" High
90/10	12" High	90/10	11" High	90/10	10" High
100/0	15" High	100/0	14" High	100/0	13" High

assume we now have a windage problem to solve. After the 10-target shooting test is performed, the 10 different pattern sheets viewed and calculated, it is obvious the shotgun produced a pattern that strongly leaned to the left of the aiming point. The horizontal ratio is calculated as 60/40. (To avoid confusing this issue, we'll leave out the vertical ratio at this time.)

There are three methods to re-zero the shot swarm and put it in dead center to the line of sight. First, the front sight can be moved by a gunsmith slightly to the left, because the old screw hole must be filled and the front sight remounted in a newly drilled and tapped hole. This is not impractical for a shotgun with a ventilated rib on top of the barrel, as most trap and Skeet guns today have. The second method is to alter the cast on the buttstock, which can be done a couple of ways. If the amount of cast-off (for a right-handed shooter) has to be reduced, which means the angle of the buttstock in relation to the line of the barrel must be reduced, a

with another piece of wood which closely duplicates the existing stock's grain structure.

Some of you have probably heard about the barrel-bending technique and may be wondering why I haven't offered this method to adjust and change an incorrect point of impact to line of sight. I oppose this method for two reasons. First, any time metal is bent "cold" it places stress and fatigue where the bend was made. Second, "cold bending" is not permanent and after an unknown number of shots, the barrel will revert to its original position due to the memory of the steel. While this reversal process takes place, the barrel's point of impact gradually returns to where it originally was and the shooter will slowly "bleed to death" by missing targets and not realizing the cause. At best, this "fix" is only good for a couple of hundred shots, depending on the metallurgy of the barrel. As the ventilated rib barrel is bent it creates a sharp line of near breakage on the top of the rib, which weakens the rib at worst and creates a

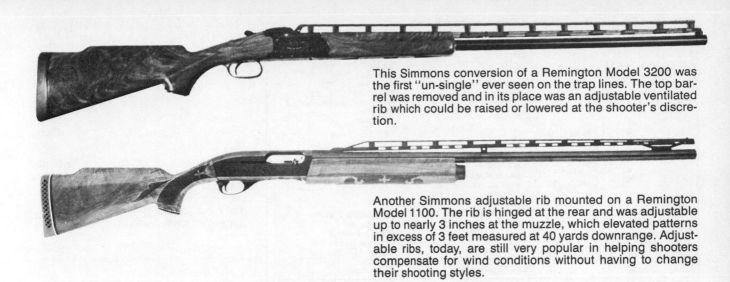

This Simmons conversion of a Remington Model 3200 was the first "un-single" ever seen on the trap lines. The top barrel was removed and in its place was an adjustable ventilated rib which could be raised or lowered at the shooter's discretion.

Another Simmons adjustable rib mounted on a Remington Model 1100. The rib is hinged at the rear and was adjustable up to nearly 3 inches at the muzzle, which elevated patterns in excess of 3 feet measured at 40 yards downrange. Adjustable ribs, today, are still very popular in helping shooters compensate for wind conditions without having to change their shooting styles.

Changing a stock will indeed change point of impact to line of sight for most shotguns. This thumbhole-type stock with its higher comb raised the original point of impact a half pattern high. Always test a new gun or stock on pattern paper to make certain you know where the gun is shooting.

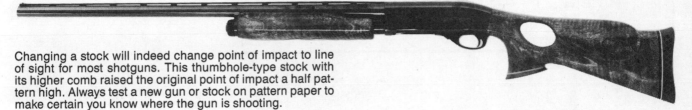

Sighting flat down rib gives true P.O.I. of the barrel.

Figure 8 is preferred by most shooters.

Sight picture seen after bending barrel or raising comb.

Unquestionably, the most important test for shooter and shotgun is to determine the shotgun's point of impact. Without knowing exactly where the shot swarm will strike downrange, shooting is being done by luck and guesswork — neither of which is conducive to breaking many targets. (Courtesy *Shotgun Sports*)

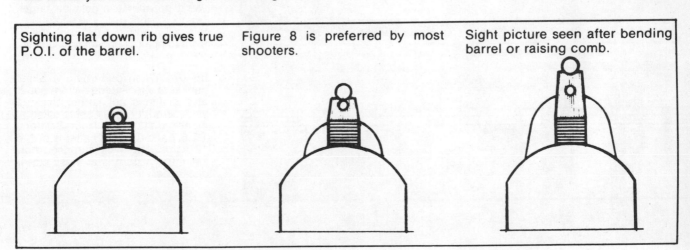

O Line of sight   X Shot path

#1 Standard setup, flat shooting. #2 Rib built to change line-of-sight. #3 Barrel bent and reribbed to change point-of-impact.

Shotguns may be mechanically corrected to change the line of sight to correspond to the point of impact by altering the position of the rib, but the author does not agree with the "barrel-bending" theory. (Courtesy *Shotgun Sports*)

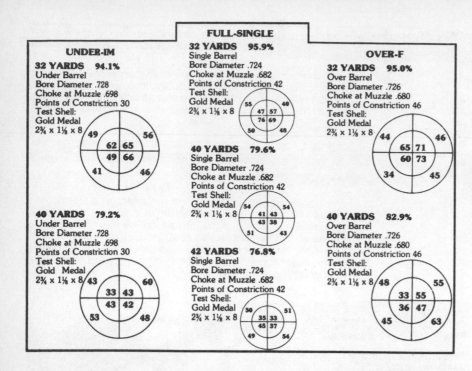

FULL-SINGLE

32 YARDS   95.9%
Single Barrel
Bore Diameter .724
Choke at Muzzle .682
Points of Constriction 42
Test Shell:
Gold Medal
2¾ x 1⅛ x 8

```
     55      40
       47 57
       76 69
     50      48
```

UNDER-IM

32 YARDS   94.1%
Under Barrel
Bore Diameter .728
Choke at Muzzle .698
Points of Constriction 30
Test Shell:
Gold Medal
2¾ x 1⅛ x 8

```
   49         56
     62 65
     49 66
   41         46
```

OVER-F

32 YARDS   95.0%
Over Barrel
Bore Diameter .726
Choke at Muzzle .680
Points of Constriction 46
Test Shell:
Gold Medal
2¾ x 1⅛ x 8

```
   44         46
     65 71
     60 73
   34         45
```

40 YARDS   79.6%
Single Barrel
Bore Diameter .724
Choke at Muzzle .682
Points of Constriction 42
Test Shell:
Gold Medal
2¾ x 1⅛ x 8

```
   54       54
      41 43
      43 38
   51       43
```

40 YARDS   79.2%
Under Barrel
Bore Diameter .728
Choke at Muzzle .698
Points of Constriction 30
Test Shell:
Gold Medal
2¾ x 1⅛ x 8

```
   43         60
     33 43
     43 42
   53         48
```

40 YARDS   82.9%
Over Barrel
Bore Diameter .726
Choke at Muzzle .680
Points of Constriction 46
Test Shell:
Gold Medal
2¾ x 1⅛ x 8

```
   48         55
     33 55
     36 47
   45         63
```

42 YARDS   76.8%
Single Barrel
Bore Diameter .724
Choke at Muzzle .682
Points of Constriction 42
Test Shell:
Gold Medal
2¾ x 1⅛ x 8

```
   50         51
      35 33
      45 37
   49         54
```

These series of shotgun patterning tests are more valid and informative than using the 40-yard standard which, over the years, has proven to be more pertinent for hunting and field shotguns. (Courtesy *Shotgun Sports*)

(Left) When shooting at a pattern board, mount and fire the shotgun exactly in the same manner at which you'd go after a regulation target. Do not "benchrest" the shotgun as this will produce a different line-of-sight to point-of-impact relationship.

(Below) When patterning a Skeet gun, spot shoot at the pattern paper at a distance not farther than 21 yards. And for those shots taken at closer distances, from Stations 1,2,6,7 and 8, shoot patterns at 7 to 12 yards. You'll be surprised how small the pattern is at these closer distances.

distorted sight picture at best.

The correct method, in my opinion, and to save wear and tear on an expensive gun barrel, is to alter the vertical point of impact by working on the stock, a relatively easy task. If the pattern is too high for a particular shooter's style, the top of the comb can be lowered by physically removing a small dimension of wood — no more than 1/16-inch at a time. A light rasp or coarse-grade sandpaper can be used to "lower" the comb and test shots should be fired and evaluated before the stock is completely refinished. Conversely, if the pattern prints too low for a particular shooter, a reverse process can be applied to raise the comb again, only in increments of 1/16-inch at a time.

There are also various types of artificial combs on the market. One of the more popular is from Meadow

Industries, Dept. 50S, Forest, VA 24551. Dubbed "Convert-A-Stock," this kit has interchangeable spacers and is held securely in place by Velcro fasteners. Six to 11 different comb heights are available to raise the height of the comb from $1/16$-inch to $5/8$-inch.

Another thrifty fix for the "do-it-yourselfer," is simple moleskin — the type used for foot protection — which can be laid on top of the comb until the desired height is obtained. Ultimately, though, most shooters only use these methods as a measuring system and either have a new stock made or alter the existing chunk of wood for a permanent fix.

If shooting a pump or autoloading shotgun, another way to raise the comb height is to have a competent stockmaker reshape the inletting at the junction of the stock to the back of the receiver. Some "smithys" do an excellent job at this intricate task and some don't. If this seemingly easy, yet difficult to properly perform task is not done with precise mating of the entire inletted surface to the receiver, the stock will undoubtedly crack or even shatter because of recoil after a few shots are fired. Take heed if you opt for this frangible process. When the Winchester Model 12 was "King" of the trap and Skeet fields, this was the prescribed method.

The importance of proper stock fit cannot be underestimated. Unfortunately, a great majority of trap and Skeet shooters use shotguns that do not fit them and there are all kinds of rationales — "What's the big deal, I'm only shooting for fun!" or "I can't afford to have that done." But, wouldn't you have more fun if you broke more targets? And if you blew a tire on your automobile, wouldn't you buy a new one?

Like any sport you participate in, there are certain "costs" required to become a top-flight trap or Skeet shooter — the first and most important being stock fit. Besides, your first "big win" will probably give you a giant dollar or equally-valuable intrinsic return on your stock-altering investment.

Patterning

Why should trap and Skeet shooters pattern their shotguns? I've known many shooters who absolutely refuse to shoot a pattern on paper, yet they do reasonably well with their shotguns on the score sheet.

It seems that a competition shooter will only pattern his pet scattergun when he is in a shooting slump. No doubt he is grasping for straws, hoping that his favorite shotgun, for some inexplicable reason, has failed him. Hey, whatever it takes to get the shooter to the pattern board. In fact, proving that "old Betsy" still puts her shot swarm right down the pike will help the shooter get out of his slump that much faster. There are numerous stories — probably all true — about competitive shooters who read an interesting article in a gun magazine about how and why they should pattern their shotguns. The typical reader will suddenly become enthusiastic

about this testing procedure and go through the mechanics of locating a place to conduct these semi-exhaustive tests, scrounge up pattern paper, etc. Unfortunately, these tests are usually based on the "40-yard" standard. Shotgun makers and ammunition manufacturers closely adhere to the standards set down by the Sporting Arms and Manufacturers Institute. For many years, SAAMI has set the "standard" shotgun patterning range at 40 yards. For hunting or field guns that is fine, but, unfortunately, trap and Skeet shooters rarely fire at a target always 40 yards downrange. Therefore, trap and Skeet gun pattern evaluation distances must use a different "standard" for optimum results.

When patterning Skeet guns, the standard distance is no farther than 25 yards. Most of the time, Skeeters fire at targets closer than 25 yards and many shots are taken at 10 to 15 yards, especially second shots on Doubles and those at Station Eight. Some Skeet shooters prefer to set "their" standards at 21 yards, exactly halfway between the high and low houses. A fast Skeet gunner generally shoots at his targets at ranges less than 20 yards, therefore his standard should be reduced to mimic his shooting style. The advantages of "standards" is that there are so many of them, if you get the point. If not, read on.

Remember that you are patterning your shotgun to improve your performance. Just because you read an article or hear someone explain how he patterns his shotgun doesn't necessarily mean that that "standard" is correct for everyone — not by a long shot. (Pardon the pun!) Every shooter, trap or Skeet, has different timing, and therefore, should pattern his shotgun at the range he normally shoots at a target. Novices, or newcomers to the Skeet field, are considered "slow shooters" as a rule and fire at outgoing targets well past the center stake. Remember, the center stake is located 21 yards between the two houses. So, if a newcomer shoots at a target 5 to 6 yards beyond the stake, he should set his standard for 26 to 27 yards for outgoing targets. Conversely, the same shooter will probably shoot at incoming targets a bit too late and at ranges 7 to 10 yards out from the muzzle. Then we have a Catch 22 situation. Does the tyro set his standard for 26 yards to predict results on outgoing targets or 10 yards for incoming targets at 10 yards? Neither. Skeet newcomers should not fret about patterns until they are accustomed to this unique shooting game, develop a serious attitude and more importantly, establish a predictable style and timing.

The most important thing to remember is that Skeet is a fun game. Becoming too technically involved can quickly dilute a new shooter's enjoyment. Shoot it for a few months without worrying about the subtle idiosyncrasies. Then, and only then, if you wish to pursue it further, learn all about its finer points. Until that time comes — just shoot and enjoy!

After a few months of shooting, you will be able to

Always run pattern tests with the exact ammunition you plan on using during a tournament. Strangely, many shooters will pattern their shotguns with handloads, and then go out and shoot the tournament with factory ammunition. The reason? Cost of reloaded ammunition versus factory.

establish your own personal "standard." Now it's time for some serious pattern work. Earlier in this chapter we discussed the point of impact and how to test it and evaluate the results. The Skeet shooter can also use the POI test to determine pattern percentages and scan the pattern sheet for "holes," or areas on the pattern sheet which are presumably large enough for a target to slip through unscathed. Even though there may appear to be many of these voids, in the real shooting world this is only remotely possible and not worthy of consideration. One of the major drawbacks of "reading" a pattern sheet is that the flat piece of paper does not relate to the length of shot string. As stated earlier, shotgun patterning is still an unsolved mystery due to its many variables. All we can do at this point is evaluate the evidence on hand and attempt to make an accurate judgement, which at best is merely a logical assumption, but a guide and reference point nonetheless.

Don't be alarmed if a pattern sheet graphically indicates "black holes" of infinity — especially if you and your shotgun are consistently breaking targets. The crux of these pattern tests is to imbed in your mind the actual diameter of your shotgun's pattern at a given distance, along with the percentage of shot contained within a 30-inch diameter circle. If you can visualize what your shotgun pattern looks like at 21 yards, it will help in your quest to consistently break 100 straights.

Learning and memorizing what a shotgun pattern looks like is often a two-edged sword. Some shooters, after discovering their guns produce a nicely-rounded pattern of nearly 30 inches in diameter become sloppy in their pointing techniques, rationalize, and think all they have to do is be "close enough" to break any target. Wrong! Instead, pretend that the pattern is only the size of a pie plate. That way if the shooter misjudges the lead of the target, the ring of shot outside this imaginary 10-inch circle will become the insurance policy and hopefully "chip" the bird to record a "dead" target on the score sheet.

Occassionally even experienced Skeet shooters unintentionally aim instead of point the shotgun because they want to become too fine and careful in their shooting styles. Shotguns, as stated earlier, are always pointed, never aimed. Aiming a shotgun is a sure way to stop the learned swing and acquired mandatory methods to hit a flying object, especially one as small as a clay target. Often, you'll hear shooters complaining to one another that they are aiming at targets and their scores are plummeting to new depths. The aiming syndrome often arises when a Skeeter is mired deep in a shooting slump. Good things happen one at a time — problems crop up in bunches!

Another important reason for patterning a Skeet or trap gun is to verify that it is choked as marked on the

The "clay" target only measures 3.5 inches across, and does not present a very large target, especially in the silhouette view. Knowing this, the shooter must determine if his pattern is dense enough to hit every target. Shooting a shotgun with a too-open choke will allow the target to slip through the pattern unscathed.

Maker: Beretta

On the upper barrel of most over-unders, the choke markings are usually marked "F/M" for "Full and Modified" with the upper letter indicating the top barrel and the lower letter for the bottom barrel. Thus, S/S equals "Skeet and Skeet," "IC/M" equals "Improved Cylinder and Modified," etc.

Maker: Perazzi

This company marks their shotguns in two manners for the European and American markets. U.S. barrels are clearly marked "Full," "Modified," etc. For guns used in Europe, Perazzi uses a series of "zeros" to indicate chokes as follows:

00	= Full
000	= Improved Modified
0000	= Modified
00000	= Improved Cylinder

Maker: Winchester

Many Model 101s are double marked with both a series of asterisks and abbreviations as follows:

*(Full)	= Full
**(Imp. Mod.)	= Improved Modified
***(Mod.)	= Modified
****(Imp.Cyl.)	= Improved Cylinder

---

barrel, as is the case with over/under barrels. Some manufacturers use ambiguous marking methods, some use abbreviations and letters, while other makers clearly mark the barrel Full, Improved Modified, Modified, Improved Cylinder, Skeet, or Cylinder. The accompanying tables will help decipher the manner in which some of the shotgun makers mark their barrels with regard to choke.

Shotgun manufacturers have good intentions, yet occasionally a barrel won't produce the pattern as marked, regardless of the various loads and shot sizes used. On these rare occurrences, we must prove the barrel's performance and determine if, in fact, it throws a pattern close to what the barrel is marked. Choke markings should not be taken for granted. As-

Identification of Ambiguous Choke Marking Terms

Maker: Browning

Marking Symbol	Choke	Percentage
*	Full	65-75%
*_	Improved Modified	55-65%
**	Modifed	45-55%
**_	Improved Cylinder	35-45%
**S	Skeet	30-35%
***	Cylinder	25-35%

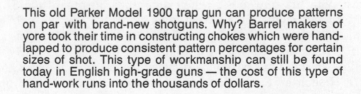

This old Parker Model 1900 trap gun can produce patterns on par with brand-new shotguns. Why? Barrel makers of yore took their time in constructing chokes which were hand-lapped to produce consistent pattern percentages for certain sizes of shot. This type of workmanship can still be found today in English high-grade guns — the cost of this type of hand-work runs into the thousands of dollars.

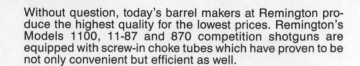

Without question, today's barrel makers at Remington produce the highest quality for the lowest prices. Remington's Models 1100, 11-87 and 870 competition shotguns are equipped with screw-in choke tubes which have proven to be not only convenient but efficient as well.

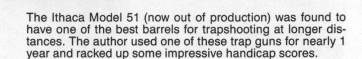

The Ithaca Model 51 (now out of production) was found to have one of the best barrels for trapshooting at longer distances. The author used one of these trap guns for nearly 1 year and racked up some impressive handicap scores.

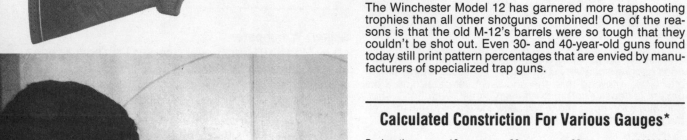

The Winchester Model 12 has garnered more trapshooting trophies than all other shotguns combined! One of the reasons is that the old M-12's barrels were so tough that they couldn't be shot out. Even 30- and 40-year-old guns found today still print pattern percentages that are envied by manufacturers of specialized trap guns.

Calculated Constriction For Various Gauges*

Designation	12 ga.	20 ga.	28 ga.	.410** bore
Full	.040	.034	.030	.020
Imp. Mod.	.030	.025	.023	.018
Modified	.020	.017	.015	.010
Skeet	.015	.012	.011	.006
Imp. Cyl.	.010	.008	.008	.002

* These numbers are intended to be used only as a guide as virtually every shotgun manufacturer will develop a constriction factor which works best in their own particular product.

**In reality, there have been instances where certain .410 shotguns have produced near-Full choke patterns even when the barrel was clearly marked "Skeet."

Trap guns are designed to place their main shot swarm slightly above the line of sight as the target is generally rising while the shooter is making the shot. Skeet guns, on the other hand, should print a 50/50 pattern to compensate for erratic flight of the target.

suming that a barrel marked "**S" or "Skt" always produces Skeet patterns is a pitfall shooters can prevent from happening by actually testing and evaluating the results after a session on the pattern board.

The trapman should always perform this same important confirmation test with his trap guns, which are more difficult to pattern and regulate than Skeet guns because of the varying distances to the target. If all the targets are shot at a precise and consistent distance, trapshooters can "tailor" a shotgun's barrel to produce a "perfect" (if there is such an entity) pattern for a known range. But, alas, target distances vary from shot to shot and again a compromising "standard" must be established.

The trapshooter, like the Skeet shooter, to properly evaluate the patterning performance of his shotgun, must disregard the SAAMI 40-yard patterning standard. For Singles or 16-yard shooting, the average trapshooter breaks targets approximately 15 to 17 yards out of the trap house. By adding the distance the shooter stands from the trap house (16 yards) to the "breaking site" of the target, up to 32 yards, the trapshooter

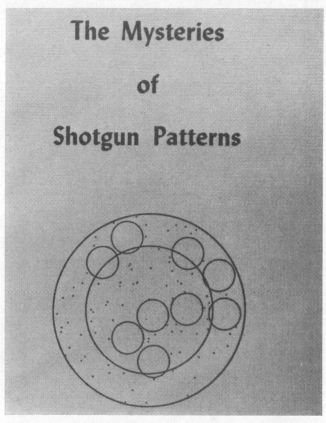

The Mysteries of Shotgun Patterns

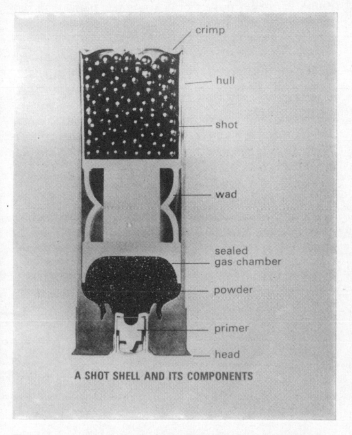

crimp
hull
shot
wad
sealed gas chamber
powder
primer
head

A SHOT SHELL AND ITS COMPONENTS

This is the title of a famous book dedicated to attacking the problems involving shotgun patterning. Unlike rifle and handgun ammunition which has a single projectile, shotshells have multiple missiles which make predictions virtually impossible.

The contents of a typical shotshell loaded by either the factory or the handloader. The quality of components, i.e., hard versus soft shot, use of the correct type of wad, all bear greatly on the results at the pattern board.

should fire on a string of 10 pattern targets from 32 yards to evaluate his gun's performance. For the Handicap (not handicapped) trapshooter, adding 16 yards to his yardage (i.e., 22 + 16 = 38 yards, 26 + 16 = 42 yards, etc.) should determine the proper patterning "standard." Again, like any pattern testing, at least 10 shots should be fired on clean pattern paper for accurate determination and evaluation of the results.

More knowledgeable shooters go one step further and place their trust in bore "constriction." Constriction is merely the result of actually measuring the shot-

gun bore in two locations and subtracting the smaller number from the large. For example, if — and most are — a 12-gauge shotgun's bore measures .729-inch at its widest point inside the barrel (not including the chamber area), and the measurement at its narrowest point (at the end of the choke area) is .689-inch, subtracting the latter from the former determines the amount of constriction, which, in this case is .040-inch.

Measuring inside barrel diameters can only be accomplished with an accurate set of inside calipers or by using a bore gauge. These precision instruments are

213

usually available at a qualified gunsmith or gun dealer. These measurements are an excellent guide to determine whether or not a barrel has been altered, but again, not an "absolute" as to the type of pattern it produces. See the accompanying table for more detailed information on shotgun bore constrictions.

Finally, the size and hardness of the shot pellet influences pattern performance. Three rules prove themselves every time a shotgun is patterned. **(1)** Hard shot, which contains at least 5 percent antimony produces a tighter pattern than soft shot, which contains a lower percentage of antimony. Hard shot has higher percentages because the pellets are not as badly disfigured and distorted after leaving the barrel. Therefore, a round(er) pellet travels on a straighter plane than one flattened on one side or badly misshaped, which causes it to fly erratically. **(2)** The velocity of the shot swarm leaving the barrel has a calculable effect on the pattern. As a rule, higher velocities tend to open up a pattern more than lower velocities. A 12-gauge shotshell loaded to a 3-dram equivalent and containing $1^1/8$ ounces of No. 8 shot produces a more open or larger pattern than its counterpart loaded to a $2^3/4$-dram equivalent. **(3)** Larger size shot tends to produce tighter patterns than smaller sizes. A gun shooting No. $7^1/2$s produces slightly smaller (tighter) patterns than No. 8 shot. The disparity is negligible because the difference in shot diameters is rather miniscule as indicated in the chart below.

This is a cut-away drawing of the famous "shot tower." Patterns are dependent on shot size, roundness, hardness and deformation, plus many other variables we haven't even thought of yet! No, shotgun patterning is far from an exact science.

#7$^1/2$ shot	= .095-inch in diameter
#8 shot	= .090-inch in diameter
#9 shot	= .080-inch in diameter

By now, you must be wondering if patterning a shotgun is important. Yes, it really is, but there are few *absolute* conclusions that can be drawn from these lengthy tests. After years of testing and evaluating shotgun patterns and reading and studying other tomes written on this controversial subject, I can positively state that patterning is not the perfect evaluation of a gun's presentation of pellets to the target, but it is currently the best method we have to offer and work with until somebody comes up with something better. Can you?

15

Accessories for Guns and Gunners

A SHOTGUNNER absolutely needs only two things to participate in trap or Skeet competition — a shotgun and a good supply of shells. (Plus a fair amount of money for other expenses, of course.) This is unquestionably a true statement, as far as it goes. However, an aspiring scattergun champion will soon find there are several other equipment items he either needs or wants, in addition to the basic necessities.

By carefully observing veteran claybird shooters in action and by talking to them after a shoot, a newcomer to the sport will quickly learn what extra gear is essential. Not everyone agrees when it comes to choosing accessories, of course, and personal opinions and experiences influence auxiliary equipment selections. Experience has shown, however, that certain items not only help improve scores, but make life on clay pigeon fields safer and more convenient.

Personal safety should be a shooter's prime concern, not gun-handling safety — that's another subject. Shooting glasses are necessity No. 1. The possibility of being struck in the eye by a flying particle is great when operating any firearm, but a shotgun is perhaps the most potentially dangerous. Stray bits of unburned powder, ricocheting shot, fragments of broken targets — all and more could cause a serious eye injury. Accidents of this nature don't happen often, but a little forethought could prevent a lot of misery if an unexpected mishap occurs.

Shooting glasses should be large enough to cover the entire eye area so there is ample protection above, below, and to both sides of the eyes. It is particularly important that lenses extend above the eyebrows, since proper shooting stance forces shooters to look well above their normal line of sight through the glasses. Glass lenses should be chemically hardened or heat treated to resist breakage. Plastic lenses are highly impervious to breakage without additional treatment but there is no such thing as a completely unbreakable lense. All lenses can break if hit hard enough, and a blow of such intensity won't be stopped by glasses alone anyway. If a corrective lens is needed to ameliorate a visual problem, shooting glasses may be ground.

Hy-Wyd glasses by Decot have long been a favorite of shotgunners all over the world. Hy-Wyd lenses are made of scratch-resistant CR-39 plastic, available in orange, purple, bronze, vermilion, gold, flesh tone, green, brown, yellow, gray, and photogray (glass only). Available in three sizes, Hy-Wyds fit almost any face. Decot Hy-Wyds can be furnished in either single-vision or bifocal prescription form, as well as regular plano (no power).

There's recently been tremendous interest in the development of a new type of shooting glasses dubbed **"Blue-Blockers."** These lenses effectively prevent virtually all of the ultra-violet rays from reaching the shooter's eyes. By eliminating the blue hue, contrast against a blue background (sky) is dramatically increased. Three shades of Blue-Blockers are available — dark, medium and light.

Many serious competitors have at least three different shades or colors of shooting glasses to create optimum visual conditions during various types of weather ranging from light yellow through dark gray. Since the introduction of Decot Blue-Blockers, however, these knowledgeable shooters have gone strictly with a light- or medium-shade Blue-Blocker in all lighting conditions with amazingly excellent results.

Literally thousands of trap and Skeet shooters think they are forced to shoot with one eye. They are doing themselves an injustice because there are methods and devices available which let them use both eyes, even if their master eyes are not the same as their master hands. **Magic Dot** makes a series of pressure-sensitive backed, 1/2-inch diameter colored dots that are applied to the shooting glasses and allow the "off" eye to be dominant by temporarily blocking the master eye's pinpoint vision while retaining depth perception and peripheral vision. A wide range of colors are available and an alignment dot and four colored dots sell for less than $2. A real bargain.

Silencio, of the hearing protector fame, entered the very competitive shooting glasses business with four new models of eye protection. They make a **Tri-Lens** ensemble with three different tinted plastic lenses —

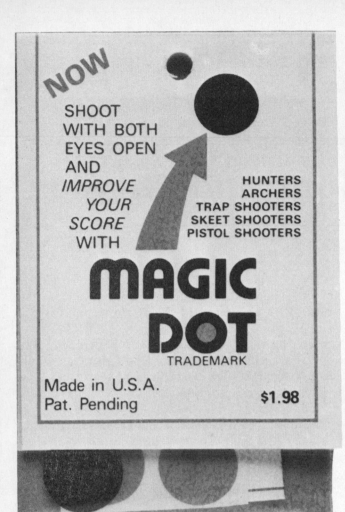
Some shooters must shoot with one eye because of incorrect master eye dominance. This Magic Dot system allows those with this affliction to use both eyes by placing a translucent colored dot directly on the shooter's glasses which will allow the shooter peripheral vision and depth perception without closing the "off-eye."

smoke, yellow and vermilion. These three colors seem to satisfy the majority of trap and Skeet shooters under a wide range of lighting conditions. They also offer a line of traditional styles in aviator and thin-bridge along with a lightweight shield-type, which is excellent for beginning shooters because it provides more protection than traditional-type lenses.

Jim Sheffield of Oak Lawn Optical makes **High-Shooter glasses** similar in appearance to Decot Hy-Wyds. Using Armorlite plastic lenses, High-Shooters come in all popular colors, both in plano and prescription form. A case is included and there is a warranty on both frame and lenses.

Another shooting glass which has maintained its popularity over the years is made by **Bausch & Lomb.** B&L shooting glasses are available in most good gun shops and sporting goods stores in non-prescription form. Any optometrist should be able to provide prescription lenses if a visual correction is necessary.

Standard lense colors are gray, brown, yellow (kalichrome), photogray and photobrown.

Tasco makes a very nice non-prescription shooting glass, available in a variety of tints including a polarized lense that eliminates bright-spot glares. **Zeiss** also produces high-quality shooting glasses, but not in prescription form. Zeiss' colors are yellow, gray, green and vermilion. Both Zeiss and Tasco glasses should be available through gun shops and sporting goods stores.

Good shooting glasses may be obtained from other sources as well, but care should be taken that lenses are of first quality, and that the frames are sturdy enough to withstand the rigors of active use. There is nothing as annoyingly uncomfortable as a spectacle frame that will not stay in adjustment.

Shooting glasses are not only a must, but at many gun clubs are mandatory and shooters not wearing them may be banned from competition. There are countless styles, colors and manufacturers of shooting glasses. Note that the shooting glasses sit high on the bridge of the nose so that when the shooter places his head on the stock, he is looking through the center of the lense.

Some shooters are bothered by distractions in the peripheral visual field. Blinders attached to the temple pieces of shooting glasses block vision to the side, which may be helpful in such cases. However, these cardboard pieces become soggy from perspiration and have to be changed frequently. The slickest way to solve the peripheral distraction is by using a unique new product called **ShootKap.** A product from Laurence & Laurence, Inc., the bill of the cap is relatively short—2 inches — but bends at the corners to form integral "blinders." The cap itself is first rate and attention is paid to important details like a mesh back for ventilation, a non-reflecting cloth under the bill and a padded sweatband. It is adjustable to fit virtually all shooters.

L&L also makes the famous **ShootBoot,** which I believe is the best shooting shoe ever devised. Ever notice how many shooters wear cowboy boots? The raised

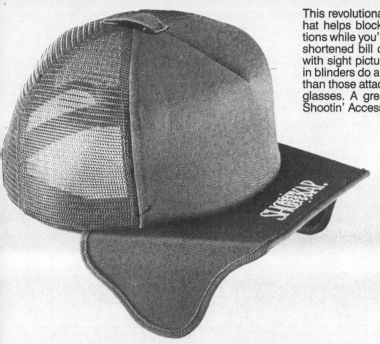

This revolutionary new shootin' hat helps block out all distractions while you're shooting. The shortened bill doesn't interfere with sight picture and the built-in blinders do a much better job than those attached to shooting glasses. A great product from Shootin' Accessories, Ltd.

Many trap and Skeet shooters prefer a waist-level pouch (right) to the traditional shooting vest or jacket. Pouches eliminate weight and bulkiness.

heel keeps the shooter's weight forward — the most desirable position. The ShootBoot lifts the shooter's heels nearly 2 inches and provides an extra layer of cushioning. Other features include speed laces, heel loops, foam insole, fiberglass arch support, foam-padded ankle collar and Vibram soles. Shooters often rest their gun muzzles on the toes of their shoes, which quickly blackens shoes or boots with muzzle soot. ShootBoot eliminates this problem because the top of each toe is covered with a plastic-type material that is impervious to dirt and grime and restored to "as new" with the wipe of a damp cloth. The ShootBoot's greatest asset is

that they are extremely comfortable.

Finally, there's the L&L **ShootPowch,** a twin-pouch shell carrier with two zippered pockets to carry "onboard" accessories. Made from DuPont Cordura nylon, this all-black duo-pouch system is fully adjustable for 28- to 50-inch waists and easily accommodates 100 shotgun shells — empty or full. This, too, is a high-quality product that should last a shooter a lifetime.

All shooters should wear some form of hearing protector. Shotguns don't have quite as loud a muzzle blast as big-bore pistols or high-powered rifles, but constant exposure to shotgun discharges will inevitably cause

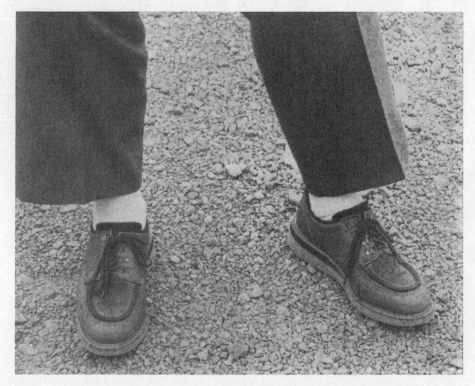

There's an old adage, "When your feet hurt, you hurt all over." These ShootBoots from Laurence & Laurence should be of prime consideration for competitive shooters. Rugged, yet reasonably fashionable, these specially-designed shooting boots provide maximum comfort and stability. They have a built-in "forward lean" to keep the shooter in proper balance. Quite possibly the most important shooting accessory a shooter needs.

some degree of hearing loss. Only a fool will play the "tough guy" who feels that hearing protectors are for sissies. Ask any old-timer in the shooting game (in a loud voice, of course) about the subject, and he will, without a doubt, say that he who does not use a noise-reducing device while shooting is an idiot.

Ear muffs, like the type produced by **Safety Direct Inc.,** are one of the most effective ways to reduce harmful noises. Ear muffs from Safety Direct bear the **Silencio** label and are made in two models — one has plain vinyl cushions and a headband that may be worn behind the head, over the head, or under the chin and another, similar in appearance, has ear cushions filled with liquid for maximum protection with minimum discomfort.

from silicone rubber, these are a bit more comfortable to wear and they form a somewhat-tighter seal in the ear canal.

The Norton Co. makes an ear plug with a small valve that closes against loud noises, yet allows normal conversation to be carried on with practically no interference. The **Norton Sonic II** is an updated version of the **Lee Sonic** ear valve that was on the market for many years. The Sonic II is an excellent choice for shooters who object to ear muffs. The Norton Co. also makes an ear muff called the **Gun Muffler,** which quite effectively reduces shotgun muzzle blast.

David Clark Co. is a pioneering firm in the hearing protection field. Clark offers a full line of audio-suppression equipment, including newly-designed **Flow**

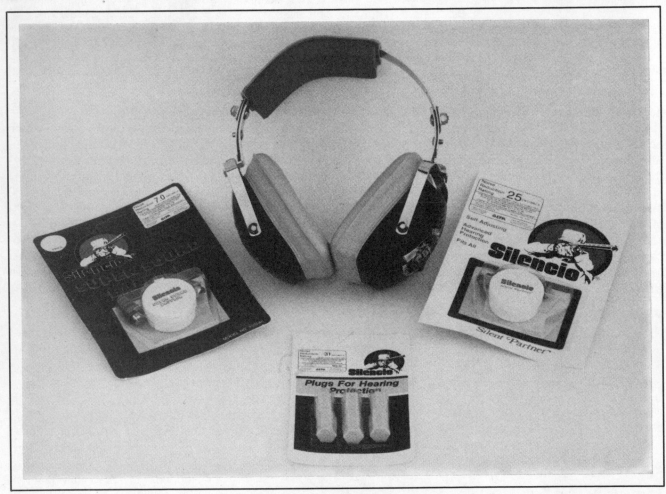

Some shooters find that ear muffs interfere with mounting the stock firmly against their cheeks. If muffs ride too heavily on the gunstock, scores can be adversely affected. For those who find the muffs annoying, ear plugs are perhaps a better choice and these vary in design from simple foam plastic cylinders that may be discarded after each use to custom-fitted units individually contoured. Silencio "SDI" plugs are made of soft air-filled plastic that mould themselves to the ear's shape and sharply limit noise input. A slightly better design is the Silencio **Silent Partner** plug. Made

Silencio makes hearing protectors to fit every budget and shooter's preference. The soft foam ear inserts work fairly well, but the more advanced ear plugs reduce the decibel level further. The best protection are ear muffs that completely cover the entire ear.

Fit Ear Seals for their top-of-the-line muffs. Clark protectors have been a favorite with shooters for decades.

Once the budding clay bird buster is equipped with adequate eye and ear protection, he will find he desperately needs at least one other piece of personal gear —

Nylon pouches and bags are quickly replacing vinyl and leather due to their light weight and durability. These bags are available from Shootin' Accessories, Ltd.

This shell pouch from Bob Allen is particularly useful to the lead-off man in a trap squad. All too often, it is easy to lose one's place when concentrating on breaking targets. Merely looking or feeling into the box of shells will tell the shooter how many shots are left at a given station.

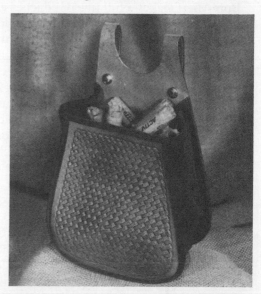

If you prefer leather over nylon or expanded vinyl, this lineup from Shootin' Accessories, Ltd. will satisfy the most discriminating trap and Skeet shooter. (Left, right, below)

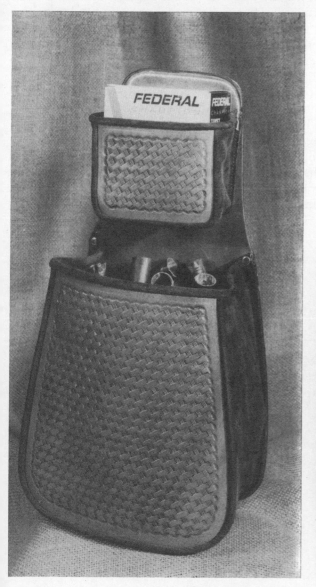

something to carry ammunition in. Pants and jacket pockets are awkward places to store shells, and 25 take up more space than is usually available in clothing not designed for that purpose.

A better solution is a shell pouch that hangs from the belt designed to hold a full box of shells. Either the regular trouser belt may be used or a special one for the pouch worn over outer clothing. With a full box of ammo handy, there should be no more fumbling that experienced shooters find bothersome. If empty shells are to be kept for reloading, a second pouch into which fired shells may be easily dropped may be hung below the one holding fresh ammo. Instead of carrying two pouches, some shooters prefer a larger divided pouch that holds live rounds in one compartment and empties in another.

Bob Allen makes a full line of pouches and shell carriers in both vinyl and nylon that should satisfy the needs of any clay target shooter. **The Hunter Corp.**, makers of holsters and other fine leather goods, offers several leather pouches and carriers for shooters who prefer leather over plastic. **The Maverick Leather Company** also makes a handsome oil-tanned leather shell pouch with matching belt to hold 50 loaded rounds and 50 empties in two separate compartments. Pachmayr's **Mark 5 Shooter's Bag** attaches to a special belt loop with Velcro fasteners. There is room for a full box of shells in an inner pouch, along with a larger outer pouch for empties. Loops for five extra shells are also provided.

Shooting vests or coats with pockets large enough to hold both loaded and empty shells are another solution. Vests are made in many styles and weights for either summer or winter wear. Most have shoulder pads and some are equipped with an "International-style" pad that extends from shoulder to waist to ease the motion of mounting a gun held at hip level for Olympic-type events. Left-handed shooters are not left out in the cold, since padded left shoulders are offered by almost all clothing manufacturers. The theory behind wearing a vest instead of a full jacket is that the arms are left free of restraint, except for a light, loose shirt. Speaking of shirts, **Bob Kraft Trap & Skeet Accessories** makes a full line of light to heavyweight shooting sweatshirts, with and without hoods. Padded shoulders and slightly over-sized for ample movement, these shooting shirts are just the ticket for warmth without bulk. They're also available in left-handed models and for a nice touch, names can be applied for personalization.

In extremely cold winter weather, there is no choice but to wear a coat of some sort, but it must allow maximum freedom of movement of both arms and shoulders. Whereas a rifleman can use a coat as a recoil-absorbing device on the target range, a shotgunner can't tolerate any restriction of his upper body. An ordinary winter jacket may be fine for warmth, but a trap or Skeet shooter should have a coat designed specifically for the purpose. **Bob Allen,** among others, makes a complete line of coats and vests that should satisfy any reasonable need.

A hat of some variety is worn by most serious clay target shooters. Though some prefer to shoot bareheaded, there is considerable merit to having some protection against sun glare and weather. On a windy day, shots can be spoiled by hair blowing in the eyes and a proper hat can prevent this sort of interference. A shooting hat should cover the head, protect the eyes from glare, yet not interfere with mounting the gun or sighting. For these reasons, a simple, billed cap is usu-

When the weather turns frigid, shooters need maximum protection against the conditions. This Bob Allen down-filled jacket (far left) is lightweight, yet warm and supple. Remember though, whenever wearing a heavyweight jacket the shotgun stock is lengthened, thus making a different swing and sight picture.

This (left) is probably the finest all-around shooting vest available from Bob Allen. The large, over-sized pockets are expandable thus providing easy entry to shells. The gabardine material is easily cleaned. There's an inner belt to help suspend the loaded pockets from resting on the shooter's shoulders. This quarter-century old design has satisfied many shooters' needs.

ally seen on trap or Skeet fields. Hats of all kinds are available everywhere and style and fit are individual, since comfort and convenience are more important than appearance. In really cold weather, a cap with ear flaps can provide warmth and comfort without interfering unduly with one's shooting stance. Unless a hat has a heavy sweatband, perspiration can be a problem on hot summer days. Nothing is quite as disconcerting as having drops of sweat suddenly appear on shooting glasses to blur your vision at a critical moment. A cotton sweatband, of the type commonly worn by athletes, can keep those annoying droplets out of your eyes.

If there is no way to resist braving wintry blasts for a

Shootin' caps are fun to collect. There are those who have collections ranging in the 100s of different types of advertising.

round or two of trap or Skeet, gloves are an absolute necessity. Frozen fingers do not make for good shooting. Gloves worn should be designed specifically for shooters because regular ones don't allow enough freedom for the trigger finger or for loading shells. Incidentally, some shooters wear lightweight gloves even in the summer, for much the same reasons race car drivers wear them — to absorb perspiration and improve grip.

Trousers are a matter of personal choice. The only thing to be aware of is that they must be loose enough so they don't bind when swinging on a target. Special pants are made for shooters, but it is really not necessary to go to this extreme to be correctly dressed for trap or Skeet.

A minor item, but a welcome one on hot summer days, is a towel for wiping perspiration off hands and gun. **Bob Allen** makes a neat towel with an elastic strap that clips on the belt so it is out of the way, but always ready when needed. Any old rag will do, of course, but it's nice to have equipment with that little extra touch of class.

As trap or Skeet shooting becomes more or less a way of life, clay bird shooters will find that they habitually carry a rather large number of small items like cleaning materials, gun oil, small tools, extra shells, a couple of candy bars, or maybe a bottle of aspirin. A bag of some kind to carry all these items is almost a must. A brown paper bag will serve the purpose but, face it, that's tacky. A utility bag for shooters is the answer here.

Bob Allen, who has carefully researched the special needs of shotgunners, makes an excellent utility bag that holds practically everything a shooter requires at the range. **Dan Titus Shooting Specialties** supplies a handsome top-grain cowhide case with room for eight boxes of shells plus space for accessories. The **Case-Gard Model S-175**, from MTM Molded Products Company, is a sturdy, plastic case that holds up to seven

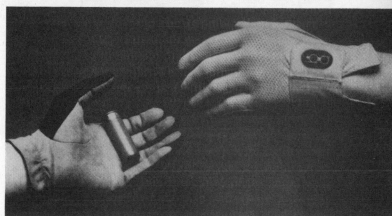

There are many good reasons why shooters should wear shooting gloves like this lightweight model available from Bob Allen. In extremely hot weather most shooters' hands perspire profusely — a pair of gloves absorbs perspiration which prevents rusting of the gun. Also, gloves provide a surer grip on the gunstock and forend.

boxes of 12-gauge shells, with room leftover for storage of other items. A handy shoulder strap leaves the shooter's hands free. **Ed Scherer Custom Leather Craft** makes carrying bags, shell pouches and belts in either plain leather or beautifully hand-tooled finishes. Scherer's leather goods are among the best. There is no need to be ashamed of your luggage if all your gear is lodged in a smartly-designed carry-all. It isn't essential for good shooting, but it's neat.

A good gun case, however, is another story. Not only does it protect a valuable gun from miscellaneous dings and scratches, but other shooters, and spectators, feel more comfortable when a gun is carried on and off the shooting line in a case. A soft, padded, zippered case is probably the most convenient type, although if traveling a long distance or by public transportation, a substantial, solid case might be preferred.

If guns are to be transported by common carrier such as an airline or railroad, a hard case with good locks is absolutely necessary. A big, heavy case not only protects a valuable firearm, but discourages petty thievery

This shooter's bag holds a raft of ammo and supplies. The interior will easily accommodate 200 shells, either empty or loaded. The side pocket will hold extra shooting glasses, emergency cleaning equipment, spare gun parts or almost anything a shooter needs while on the line.

Trap and Skeet shooters have thousands of dollars invested in their guns and related equipment. Taking them to a registered shoot is easy, protecting them from non-shooters can often be more difficult. This gentleman built a special sliding drawer made of steel with a locking steel top for the back of his pickup truck. Not only are the guns and equipment out of sight, they are secured as best possible.

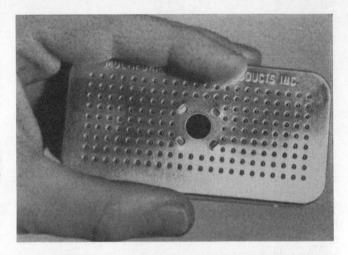

If you live where there's humidity, this neat little gadget (right) absorbs excess moisture which prevents guns from rusting in gun cabinets or cases. A must-have product from Shootin' Accessories, Ltd.

— at least as much as it possibly can.

There are so many fine gun cases on the market it is impossible to mention them all. **Woodstream Corporation** makes a comprehensive line of hard gun cases. Moulded from high-impact polypropolene with tight-fitting, weather-resistant tongue and groove flanges to prevent moisture from getting inside, these cases meet airline specifications. Full-length single or two-gun cases are available, along with extra barrel sets. Woodstream also offers a **Hunter's Seat,** easily converted to a trap and Skeet shooters' seat. This field chair has a hollow interior and outboard pockets made of heavy-duty canvas. There's ample room to carry 100 loaded shells, and 100 empties can be dumped inside. More importantly, it allows the shooter to sit while waiting to shoot because not all gun clubs provide chairs or benches. Woodstream also offers a **Shooter's Accessory Case** which holds up to eight boxes of 12-gauge shells or four boxes with space for 100 plus empties. For good measure there is still enough space for cleaning articles, shooting glasses, gun parts and all those other

Personalized gun cases are available from Bob Allen and help organize the trunk of a car or van. Allen offers a "name" case for virtually every popular shotgun manufacturer in a wide variety of colors and lengths.

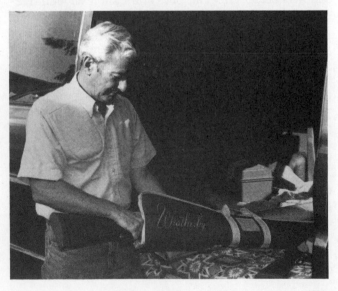

things shooters must take with them down the line. Woodstream also offers shooting glasses and shotgun shell cases. Keep your eyes peeled for Woodstream products — they offer quality products at reasonable prices.

Michaels of Oregon, better known as Uncle Mike's of sling swivel fame, has brought out a couple new products designed for the trap and Skeet shooter. **Side-Kick** nylon gun cases have thick foam padding and a soft nylon lining that won't hang up on a shotgun's front bead. They are available in black, tan, camouflage and green.

All better sporting goods stores and gunshops display a selection of cases to fit every need and budget. It usually pays in the long run to buy a case that is as well made as you can afford. It is false economy to house a gun that costs several hundreds, or thousands, of dollars in an inadequate, ill-fitting case.

Judging by the number of gun accessories on the market, few shooters are satisfied for long with a shotgun just the way it comes from the factory. All claybirders seem to have their own ideas about what it takes to make a good gun better. Some after-market add ons are of dubious value, while others are unquestionably helpful in one way or another. Shooters would be wise to discuss planned additions or alterations with others who are familiar with a particular product or service.

The most sought-after shotgun accessory is a device that will reduce recoil, or at least diminish its effect on the shooter. An adequate recoil-absorbing butt pad is a virtual necessity on a trap and Skeet shotgun. Without some degree of protection, shoulders can quickly become uncomfortably bruised. Though many guns today are fitted with butt pads at the factory, a shooter may find that a different thickness or contour is more to his liking. The easiest pad to install is a slip-on, such as the ones supplied by **Supreme Products** and **Michaels of Oregon.** These are made from neoprene and come in different sizes, one of which will fit almost any shotgun. Supreme also makes a variety of screw-on pads in several thicknesses. Pachymayr Gun Works has been a major source of recoil pads for over 4 decades, and they make pads in various sizes and ribbing styles to suit all

This Action Cheek Saver is a boon to those shooters who suffer cheek chafing. A soft covering of suede over a pad of Akton recoil absorbing material helps reduce recoil and also provides a soft, comfortable place to cheek the stock.

shotgun applications. Their newest creation, the **Decelerator,** is available for both trap and Skeet guns in varying thickness, colors and faces. Michaels of Oregon currently offers a good lineup of **Open Cushion Recoil Pads** ranging in thickness from 1 to .85 inch. They're offered in brown or black with many different pad faces. They also offer a slip-on version which enables the shooter to temporarily fix a too-short stock.

New space-age material infiltrating the trap and Skeet fields is under the official name of Sorbothane. This cushioning material is used in recoil pads — both on the gun and inside shooting vests and shirts. I.N.C., Inc. markets their shotgun recoil pads under the trade name **KickEez** and claim to be the best recoil-absorbing material ever devised. There have been many industrial-type products made from Sorbothane to absorb recoil such as acoustical dampening and vibration isolation items. KickEez recoil pads are available in a

Recoil pads are available in a wide variety of shapes, designs and thicknesses. Make sure that your shotgun is equipped with the proper recoil pad for the type of shooting you're doing. If you're not certain what type of pad is installed on your trap or Skeet gun, take it to a qualified gunsmith and ask questions. An incorrect pad will cost you targets!

host of configurations, sizes and colors.

Morgan's adjustable recoil pad allows a shooter to quickly alter drop, pitch and recoil absorption as conditions dictate. A good-looking accessory, these pads are made by **Morgan Adjustable Recoil Pad Co.**

Many other makes of available butt pads are also entirely satisfactory. Whatever the choice, a butt pad must be properly installed — usually a job for a competent gunsmith. Remember, too, that a pad that is thicker or thinner than the original will change the length of pull (the distance from trigger to butt). It may be necessary to cut off the stock or add spacers to achieve a pull that is right for a particular shooter.

Accessory cheekpieces are used by some shooters, not only to reduce recoil effects against the face, but to alter the height of the comb. Cheekpieces are not normally attached permanently, but are fitted in place with laces or Velcro fasteners. Leather is the material most commonly used, although some modern plastics are equally satisfactory. Meadow Industries makes the **Convert-A-Stock** pad that attaches with Velcro fasteners and allows the shooter to select up to 11 different heights for better control of pattern impact through cheekpiece adjustment. A new device that does a superb job of relieving recoil shock to the face is the **Action Cheek Saver** by Action Products. Made of a thin layer of Akton, a shock-absorbing plastic material, it is covered with a soft suede outer layer that is remarkably comfortable. **Action Products** also make an Akton pad that may be fitted into a shooting shirt or coat and has a pocket built into the shoulder pad. Impact absorption of Akton is little short of miraculous and it must be experienced to be believed. This space-age material should have a whole host of applications in all shooting sports.

Over the years, shooters and tinkerers have dreamed

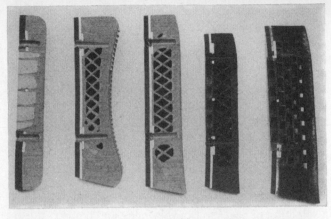

These five pads have been cut in half to illustrate the different types of air chambers that help absorb the shotgun's recoil. From left to right, the first pad has a smooth face and is solid core, thus providing little recoil absorbing qualities. The next pad (second from left) is designed for the trap-shooter as the curved face fits into the shooter's shoulder precisely. The middle pad is a Skeet model with an almost straight face and ample air chamber. The fourth pad is also a Skeet model, but in a smaller size. The pad on the right is composed of many air chambers and does the best job of absorbing recoil, but does not provide enough sideways strength and deflects easily during shooting.

up all types of gadgets to be attached to shotguns (and rifles) to defeat basic laws of physics as applied to recoil. A majority of these devices proved totally useless, but some actually reduce felt recoil to a great extent. Most recoil-reducing attachments spread the reaction of gun discharge over a longer period of time, changing a sharp shock into more of a pushing sensation.

The earliest successful recoil-reduction system, the **Hydro-Coil,** was devised in the early 1950s by Los Angeles shooter Ralph Hoge and is discussed in a previous chapter. Shooters have attempted to thwart recoil for many years. Numerous patents have been granted

Master stock maker, Ed Sowers of Hydro-Coil fame, still installs and makes Hydro-Coils the old-fashioned way — by hand! Invented in the early 1950s, these shock-absorber type of recoil-reducing mechanisms have proven to be the most effective devices to reduce felt recoil on the shooter. Tests have conclusively proven that recoil has harmful effects on the shooter's pulmonary and nervous systems.

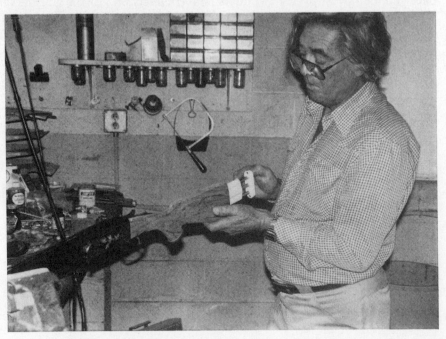

for energy-absorbing apparatuses attached to rifles and shotguns dating back to the turn of the century. An 1892 patent was issued for an **"Extension Gun Stock and Cushion Plate,"** which used springs to help reduce felt recoil and correctly position itself against the shooter's shoulder for added comfort. J.R. Winter's **"Recoil Pad for Guns"** of 1896 was based on a single cell fitted to the shotgun buttstock and filled with air with a small hand pump. By 1906, a two-piece telescoping, spring-actuated, buttstock was devised by Buikard Behr of Hamburg, Germany. Similar ideas showed up in 1909, 1948, and 1963 (Hydro-Coil) and J.M. Ahern's **"Hydraulic Recoil Absorber"** was introduced in 1966.

Rod Brakhage, of Stillwater, Oklahoma, makes a device called the **Counter-Coil,** which consists of a hydraulic unit that replaces a gun's regular buttplate. It is adjustable for various gauges and loads so shooters may take full advantage of its effect. The Counter-Coil cuts the level of felt recoil by about 50 percent. It should be installed by the factory or a good gunsmith, although templates are supplied if a gun owner wishes to do the job himself. Some wood must be trimmed from the buttstock to retain the desired length of pull. Counter-Coil adds from 4 to 8 ounces to a gun's overall weight, not enough in most cases to make any appreciable difference in balance. Counter-Coil is available from MBM Enterprises.

SoftTouch is an oil-filled recoil device from Shooter's Emporium and boasts an adjustable comb. The existing stock may be converted to accept this recoil device. Another product, from Allison & Carey Gun Works, is the **Carey Comb.** This device uses the shotgun's existing stock but is greatly altered by cutting the stock in two and adding a hydraulic shock absorber between the two parts. This split comb is also adjustable.

The **Air-Cushioned Gunstock** by Joe Shiozaki is a near duplicate of the original Hydro-Coil, although a bit heavier due to its all-aluminum construction. One of its unique features is the ability to adjust the length of the stock without using spacers. A full, wrap-around stock comb may be ordered with custom dimensions.

"Recoil reducers" are also installed inside the buttstock, in the lower barrel of over/unders or in the magazine tube of pumps and autoloaders.

Perhaps the best-known recoil reducer was developed by Jesse Edwards of Alton, Illinois. Simply called the **Edwards Recoil Reducer,** it consists of a tube about 1-inch in diameter in which a weighted piston is suspended between two springs. Weight, spring tension and length (from 3½ to 4½ inches) are varied for best results with different guns and loads. A 1-inch hole is drilled in the rear of the buttstock for installation. Additional absorption of recoil may be gained by using two units placed one above the other. A claimed advantage of Edwards' system is that muzzle jump is tamed so that second shots at Doubles are more easily made.

Many leading trap and Skeet shooters endorse the Edwards Recoil Reducer and it is used by shotgunners worldwide. Standard Edwards reducers retail for about $45, plus installation.

Another method of recoil reduction using a movable weight is found in the **Mercury Recoil Suppressor** made by C & H Research. This is a hollow steel tube, ⅞-inch in diameter, partially filled with mercury and permanently sealed. Instantaneous movement of liquid mercury is said to absorb much of the shock of recoil. The overall weight is 11 ounces, including 6 ounces of mercury. The units are made for buttstock installation or insertion in a magazine tube. A third type may be fitted into the unused chamber of a double-barreled gun and all models sell for about $47.50.

The **Staub Mercury Inertia system** offers five different sizes and models of their recoil control system and is available for virtually every shotgun and rifle on today's market. Weights range from approximately 5 through 12 ounces depending on the installation.

Okie Manufacturing makes the **Shootin-Cushin** recoil reducer available in a wide range of models for both stock or magazine installation. Weights range from 5 to 10 ounces, depending on the model.

A different approach to the recoil problem is taken by the **Griggs Recoil Redirector.** It operates on the principle of changing the force of recoil from a backward thrust to a downward motion through a sliding buttplate mechanism. On firing, the buttstock moves down and away from the face as well as to the rear. Springs within the unit return it to its original position almost immediately. The Griggs sliding buttplate weighs little more than the pad it replaces.

Reduction of felt recoil may also be achieved by adding a muzzle brake or porting the barrel near the muzzle to vent propellant gases upward. Muzzle brakes enjoyed a certain popularity in times past, but the current consensus seems to be that they do not work sufficiently and have an adverse effect on shot patterns. Barrel porting, on the other hand, accomplishes the same thing without any of the problems connected with muzzle brakes. Although porting is now done by many gunsmiths, the method originated with Larry Kelly of **Pro-Port, Ltd.** After almost 25 years of research, Kelly devised a way to cut 11 compound ellipsoidal ports into each side of a barrel using electrical discharge machining. This type of "drilling" leaves no tool marks or damage to surrounding metal. The upward venting of gases counteracts muzzle lift and lowers perceived recoil by 20 percent.

Len Evans, of **Evans Tool and Die,** drills a series of small round holes on each side of a barrel near the muzzle that direct gases up and to the sides for recoil reduction. Although the exact number of vent holes varies with gun and gauge, a sample **Precision Porting** job on a Krieghoff had a total of 76 holes in each barrel. Porting is done by many gunsmiths, but care should be taken that no burrs are left around the holes or that barrel contours are not altered, or patterns may be adversely affected.

Variable choke devices, such as the venerable **Cutts Compensator** used widespread many years ago have gone out of fashion. Add-on adjustable chokes have been superseded by screw-in interchangeable choke tubes. Many gun makers, such as Winchester (now Classic Doubles) with their **WinChoke** system, offer screw-in chokes as standard equipment. Gun owners lacking such modern conveniences who would like to experiment with different chokes will have to rely on various specialty shops as a source of this item. **Briley Manufacturing, Inc.** has added screw-in chokes to their line of products. Once known primarily as a

Screw-in chokes are best installed with a specially supplied wrench. They should be quite snug, but not overly tight otherwise they will be virtually impossible to remove after a days shooting. These choke tubes are becoming more and more popular as they are now available in a wide selection of choke degrees and are reliable.

maker of insert tubes for Skeet guns, Briley has become the dominant supplier of screw-in choke conversions for trap and Skeet guns. Available in all gauges from 8 through 410 bore, these ultra-light, 2½-inch screw-in choke tubes are available in eight bore constrictions from X-Full through Skeet. Briley also offers a new product dubbed the **"Excentrix"** choke which is a non-adjustable, screw-in choke that changes or cor-

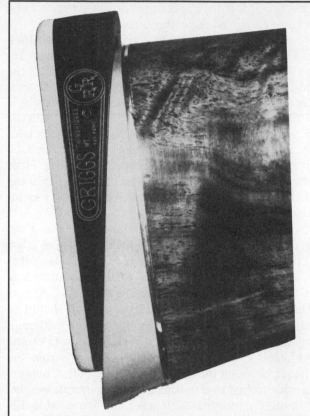

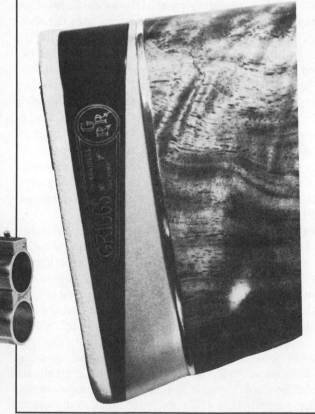

The Griggs Recoil Redirector is a clever accessory that actually pulls the buttstock away from the shooter's face during recoil thus preventing the stock from slapping a shooter's face. The device is spring actuated and recovery time between shots on doubles targets is more than adequate.

Pro-port vents are directed upward and outward at an angle of 45 degrees on the upper barrel of this over/under shotgun. For added stability and effectiveness, ports on the lower barrel are angled at 60 degrees from vertical.

rects the point of impact of your shotgun up to 11 inches in any direction of a 360-degree circle at 40 yards. These choke tubes not only correct point of impact problems, but give the competitive shooter the ability to adjust to different wind conditions, different stock or comb heights and different shooting sports. For example, if these tubes are installed in an over/under shotgun and the shooting game is trap Doubles or even Flyers, the shooter will want to have the under, or first barrel, deliberately shoot high to compensate for the fast-rising target or boxed pigeon. **D&M Enterprises** specializes in this sort of work. **Stan Baker,** one of the first to make screw-in choke conversions, has equipped the guns of many of the nation's top shooters with chokes of his design. Stan has a free booklet describing his work. There are numerous custom gunsmiths who do choke work, and any good gunshop should be able to direct a scattergunner to a specialist for this critical modification.

Another of the better-known screw-in choke systems is made by Mike Bruce of **Pro-Choke, Inc.** Pro-Choke bores out muzzles to exact concentricity with the gun's barrel. Then muzzles are threaded to accept a choke tube installed with a supplied special wrench. Only 1/4-inch extends beyond the original muzzle, so the general appearance of the gun is not changed to any appreciable extent.

Skeet, of course, is shot with guns in four different gauges, but what about using the same gun for all four events? It's definitely possible if you use an over/under 12-bore with insert tubes for the smaller gauges. Many years ago, **Claude Purbaugh** made up a set of inserts in 20-, 28-, and 410 gauge for a 12-gauge Browning that met with considerable success. Since then, tubes have been improved to the point that they are being used by Skeet shooters everywhere. Purbaugh tubes, the choice of many champion shooters, are available from **Multi-Gauge Enterprises.**

Claude Purbaugh, inventor of the Purbaugh Tube System for Skeet guns, first came out with this innovative device in the mid-1950s. These insert tubes allow the shooter to change gauges quickly and easily thus keeping the gun's balance consistent from one gauge to another. The insert tube concept's greatest attribute is cost reduction. Three tube sets are quite a bit less expensive than three more guns or even three more barrel sets.

For those who wheel and deal in shotguns, this Stan Baker Universal bore and choke gauge set is a necessary accessory. It will accurately read the inside of the bore and choke area for six sizes — 10, 12, 16, 20, 28 gauges and 410 bore. Contact Shootin' Accessories, Ltd.

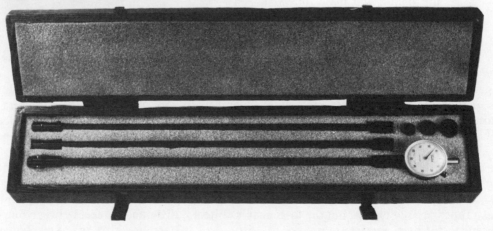

After the initial acceptance of Purbaugh's invention, **Larry Kolar** of New York began making his own version using titanium chambers in 28-gauge, which equalized weights of 410-, 28- and 20-gauge installations. Kolar later sold his business to Don Mainland of Racine, Wisconsin, who operates the **Target Arms**

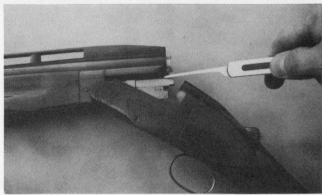

A special tool for removing "stuck" shells in a gun's chamber should be carried in a shooter's pocket at all times. There are times when a shell's base will expand to the point where the gun's ejector cannot kick out the empty hull. Simply placing a hooked-type blade between the shell's rim and chamber and a smart tug will dislodge a swollen shell.

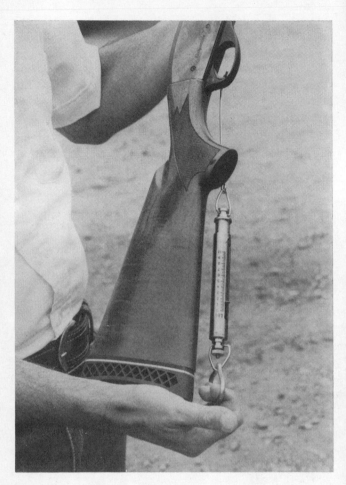

The trigger scale is an invaluable accessory for the competitive shooter. All too often a shooter will go into a slump without knowing why and accept it as part of the game. Too many times, a shotgun's trigger mechanism will go slightly "south," and destroy a shooter's rhythm and timing.

company. Today's Kolar tubes are made in combinations of titanium and stainless steel, with integral extractors that fit over the regular 12-gauge extractors. A weight is added to the gun when in 12-gauge configuration to equalize overall weights of all four gauges so there is no difference in feel, balance or trigger action when changing from one gauge to another. Target Arms offers several possible combinations of tubes at varying prices. Tubes are not cheap, but the total cost is quite a bit less than for four separate guns.

Jess Briley of Houston, Texas also makes matched sets of tubes with extractors that compete favorably with Kolar tubes. Briley's tube sets come in a custom-fitted case that make a very handsome piece of equipment.

For those who would rather have complete interchangeable barrels, several gunmakers offer this option. All barrels in a set weigh the same so there is no difference in feel between one gauge and another. Four-barrel sets are made by **Browning** for their Citori and

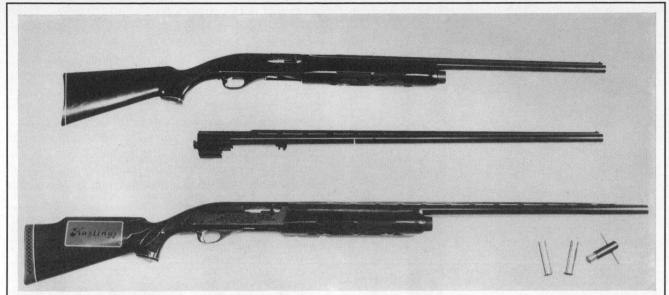

Hastings makes a wide variety of barrels for popular shotguns (bottom). The Leo Harrison Signature Trap barrel features a high rib for the Remington Model 1100. Perazzi TM-1 (center) replacement barrels are available in either 34- or 35-inch lengths, with or without Briley screw-in choke systems. Note, however, that these barrels must be fitted by a competent gunsmith. A Sousa Skeet special (top) features a 26-inch, rifled barrel that is said to drastically improve shot patterns at Skeet ranges. All of these Hastings barrels appear to be made from high-quality steel.

Superposed models, by **Shotguns of Ulm** for the K-80, and **Perazzi.** Prices range from around $2500 for the Citori to $10,000 or so for the Perazzi. Barrel sets are also produced by various custom barrel makers on individual order. Gunsmiths who specialize in shotguns are the best source for this kind of work.

the better makers of trigger groups for regular-production shotguns is **Allen Timney,** who makes replacement units for Remington 1100s and 870s. Timney triggers have enjoyed an enviable reputation among both shotgunners and riflemen for many years.

Some shooters prefer a release trigger over a conven-

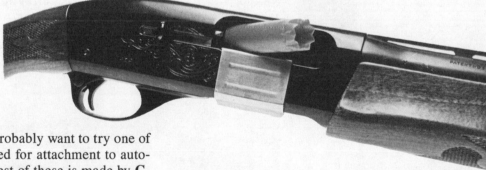

This shell catcher from T&S is super simple, yet works perfectly every time. It merely snaps in place and is immediately removable for shooting Doubles.

Shooters who reload will probably want to try one of several shell catchers designed for attachment to autoloading shotguns. The simplest of these is made by **C. C. Petersen.** It is a wire spring that fits over the ejection port, doesn't interfere with loading, and may be turned down out of the way when shooting Doubles. Two models are available to fit most self-loaders. It fastens to the side of the receiver with two-sided adhesive tape. T&S Industries make a shell catcher that clips onto a receiver below the ejection port. Instant installation and removal adds to the utility of the **T&S Shell Catcher.**

Standard factory triggers are notorious for their poor actions because the pulls are often gritty, over-long and heavy. A bit of judicious gunsmithing can frequently clean up a factory trigger to acceptable levels, but for those who want the best trigger possible, it is sometimes necessary to install a custom assembly. One of

tional "pull" type. Release triggers are noted for their function as a last-ditch cure for inveterate flinchers, but that is not by any means their only attribute, since many claybirders simply shoot better scores with them. **M. L. Schwab** specializes in release triggers for several of the most popular shotgun models used on trap and Skeet fields.

Shotgun firing pins are surprisingly fragile and nothing does them more harm than dry firing. To avoid damage that could be caused by dropping a hammer on an empty chamber, snap caps are the answer. Snap caps are dummy shells that take up the impact on a firing pin so that inertia loads don't overstress it to the point of breakage. **Pachmayr** supplies an exceedingly sturdy snap cap, as does **Shootin' Accessories, Ltd.** A minor

Above is a stout, short-bladed pocketknife fashioned after a 12-gauge shotgun shell that features a locking back for safe use.

This clever-looking knife (left) initially appears to be a 12-gauge shotgun shell, when in reality it is a combination blade with screwdriver. A nice pocket piece from Shootin' Accessories, Ltd.

investment in one or two of these little firing pin savers could eliminate a potential problem that plagues all shotgunners.

An excellent source of miscellaneous small accessory items for shotgunners is **Shootin' Accessories, Ltd.** A screwdriver set with sizes to fit most gun screws is something every shooter needs. And how many times does a shooter wonder if his trigger pull has changed? A trigger-pull gauge like gunsmiths use will tell the tale. Owners of Remington 1100s or 870s will definitely want a punch that fits the pin holding the trigger assembly — a wooden-handled punch is available

Pachmayr "Snap Caps" allow the gun owner to safely lower the shotgun's firing pin without cause for breakage.

that matches the pin precisely and virtually eliminates scratched receivers. A small, leak-proof oiler takes up little space in a shooter's utility bag, yet provides the critical drop or two of oil needed to make things run smoothly. Lastly, a handy folding knife in the shape of a shotshell could be a clever addition to any shooting kit.

After a day's shooting, guns must be cleaned. Cleaning equipment is available at all gunshops and sporting goods stores, as well as by mail order from many firms. A good, solid cleaning rod especially for shotguns is needed, plus proper brushes, swabs, patches and solvents. Excellent materials are available from **Outers** and **Hoppes,** specialists in this field. A new cleaning

Some of the items available from Shooting Accessories include a full-length gun sock to prevent wear of the gun's metal surfaces, a leak-proof oiler, a brush to clean those hard-to-reach places inside a gun's action, wooden handled punches to knock out trigger pins and a small pocketknife in the shape of a shotshell.

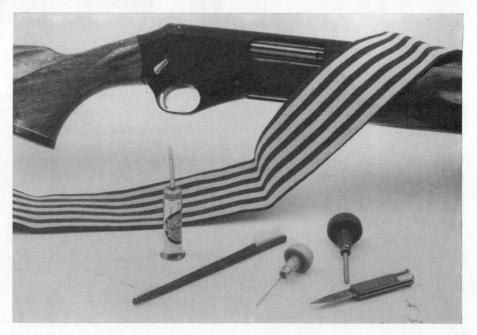

Shootin' Accessories, Ltd. has so many neat little products that we don't have space to show them all—but each one has been thoroughly tested to be sure they work as advertised and really fill a need for the shotgunner. These are brushes for cleaning a gun's chamber.

A new product from Hornady, "One Shot" is a combination cleaning agent and dry lubricant. It is "oilless" and odorless, yet does the job as advertised.

The famous Tico shotgun barrel cleaners are the best ways to maintain the bore of your pet shotgun. They are available in all sizes from Shootin' Accessories, Ltd.

Snap caps are an inexpensive insurance against premature breaking of firing pins. Even though some gun manufacturers state that it's OK to dry fire, for a low cost, snap caps will eliminate any possibility of firing pin breakage.

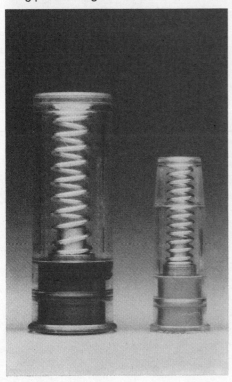

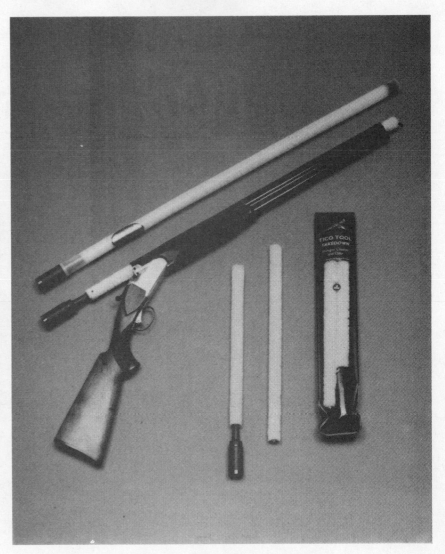

system that originated in Germany is now marketed by **Beeman.** Beeman's unit consists of a sturdy rod plus scrubbing and oiling patches made to precisely fit the bore. A rod guide prevents damage to the muzzle or chamber mouth when removing deposits from the barrel. The Beeman kit is perfect for those meticulous shooters who wish to give their highly-valued guns the best care. **RIG Products** manufactures a handy cleaning rod made in sections small enough to be carried in a pocket or shell carrier without taking up a great deal of space. RIG also makes an excellent line of cleaning solvents and gun oils.

The past few years have brought a host of new products to help teach the trap and Skeet shooter more about his favorite shooting sport without having to leave the comfort of his easy chair. A wave of video and audio tapes have come down the pike, some good, some not so good, others very good. Nearly all of these instructional devices are authored by a well-known shooter. I have viewed most of all these videos and have listened to at least a dozen or so tapes. The quality of reproduction ranges from very poor to acceptable and only a very few are considered broadcast quality. None of the

Some sportsmen prefer aerosol spray cans over liquid applications — Birchwood Casey offers all of their cleaning products in both versions. (above, below) BC's bore cleaner is an exceptionally fine product along with their dry film lubricant which is designed to work inside the gun's action and trigger group.

This bore cleaner (right) is designed to melt away the plastic buildup in barrels caused by today's plastic wads. It also works very well on lead, copper and powder residue.

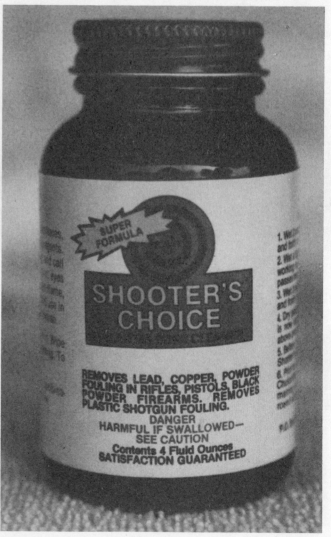

232

The competition shooter should carry with him at all times a good assortment of cleaning equipment and supplies (left). The majority of gun failures and malfunctions can be traced directly to dirt and grime which prevents the shotgun from performing properly. There's no rule stating that the shooter cannot clean his or her guns between events instead of standing around "chewing the fat" with the boys.

Birchwood Casey, an old-line company, has been making and offering a wide range of cleaning supplies for decades (below). Their Presto Gun Blue Pen (far right) is a handy item to touch up light scratches and dings to a gun's metal finish. The silicon impregnated cloths help prevent rust and their use is encouraged to help keep firearms in best condition.

All-weather grease by Venco is packaged in a convenient plastic syringe for easy application in tight spots.

video tapes I saw had outstanding graphics due to the cost of ultra-high-speed video cameras. Most were produced by home-style cameras and unless professional editing was employed, these tapes were fraught with technical errors. On the positive side, however, the language was of the greatest value. Frank Little's trio of tapes, **16 Yard/Handicap, Doubles** and **One-Eye Shooting** were, in my opinion, the best of the bunch, simply because he presented the subject matter concisely. Again, the graphics weren't great but they did illustrate Little's method of teaching trapshooting. I recommend previewing these tapes before purchasing them. Most sell for $60 to $70 a copy and unless a group gets together to purchase one, that is a bit expensive.

Inner Psych, owned by Phil Kiner, perennial trapshooting All-American, offers a wide selection of subliminal audio tapes on both trap and Skeet shooting for about $30 each. The theory behind subliminal listening is that the listener hears below the level of conscious awareness. All he consciously hears is the sound of the ocean, seagulls and crickets while positive suggestions are subliminally transmitted. There are those who swear that these tapes not only "turned around their shooting," but helped them in everyday life as well.

For those who prefer to use cleaning patches for slick shotgun barrels, Shootin' Specialties offers large bags of 200 count soft, absorbent patches just right for the job at hand.

Just a few of the many publications that are most helpful to clay bird shooters. Reference books like these are a ready source of information when needed.

Video instructional tapes are very popular forms of going to school without leaving the comfort of your own home — sort of like armchair traveling. The best of all are those presented by Frank Little.

Since the advent of pocket-size cassette players, a crop of self-teaching, subliminal cassettes ranging in subject matter from "Winning at Shootin' " through "Shootin' Fundamentals" are available.

Three "MUST HAVE" magazines for the competition shooter are *Skeet Shooting Review*, *Trap & Field* and *Shotgun Sports*. The first two are dedicated to Skeet and trapshootin', while *Shotgun Sports* caters to both plus Sporting Clays.

While mired in a deep shooting slump, I purchased a Sony Walkman portable cassette player and listened to Kiner's tape on trapshooting for almost a month. I did emerge from the slump eventually, but am not sure the tape was the influencing factor because I didn't have anything to compare it to. But, like a big bowl of chicken soup when you've got a cold — it can't hurt!

Another type of listening tape is offered by **Mental Ministries Unlimited.** These tapes basically teach self-hypnosis and are available on a wide variety of subjects from smoking and weight control to trap and Skeet shooting. They all seem to be strictly confidence builders with positive thoughts presented in a dreamy

World and *The American Rifleman* frequently contain information of great interest to scattergunners. Other periodicals catering exclusively to shotgun sports are *Skeet Shooting Review, Shotgun Sports* and *Trap and Field.* All these shotgun magazines are slanted toward clay target shooting and anyone interested in these activities should take time to peruse them. Brochures and catalogs are another source of information.

Literally dozens of books have been written about shotgunning, many advertised in current magazines. For hardcover books that are either out of print or hard to find, **Ray Riling Arms Books** is undoubtedly the country's leading dealer in firearms books. The names

Who says there's nothing new under the sun. Eyerobics is a unique visual aids training program that increases seeing skills and improves physical and mental performance while reducing visual fatigue. It is from Shootin' Accessories, Ltd.

manner. I made numerous attempts to hypnotize myself unsuccessfully, but at only $12.50 per subject, they're worth a listen.

Though not accessories in the generally-accepted sense, books, periodicals and other printed material can be invaluable to shooters to keep them abreast of developments as well as improve their shooting abilities. Most of the top shooters have extensive libraries and avidly read periodical publications to gain more information about their beloved sport. Magazines such as *Sports Afield, Outdoor Life* and *Field and Stream* regularly run articles of interest to shotgunners. Strictly gun magazines, including *Shooting Times, Guns, Gun*

of other dealers and publishers of gun books can be found in the directory section of *Gun Digest,* published by DBI Books, Inc.

The accessory items mentioned have only scratched the surface of what is available to shotgunners. A complete and comprehensive listing of all makers and products is more than we have room for in this book, but hopefully we have given the reader an idea of what kinds of things a shooter might need or want to make life easier on trap or Skeet fields. The addresses of the suppliers mentioned in this chapter plus several additional sources are listed in the Appendix in the back of the book under "Manufacturers' Directory."

16

Questions and Answers

Question *When was the fabled Winchester Model 12 introduced in 12-gauge configuration?*

Answer Winchester brought out the 12-gauge version in the fall of 1914. The 20-gauge was the initial offering.

Question *Did Winchester ever make a plastic shotgun?*

Answer Not exactly, but they did make a fiberglass barrel for their Model 50 dubbed the Model 59. The barrel was an engineering marvel. Nearly 500 miles of glass fiber was wrapped around a thin steel tube, covered with fiberglass cloth and a traditional blue finish. When tested, these barrels withstood pressures many times greater than normal steel barrels, and were about half the weight. Some barrels were made with "screw-in" chokes. Unfortunately, the Model 59 was discontinued in 1965.

Question *What year did Parker introduce their Single-Barrel trap model?*

Answer In 1917, with a price tag of $173.

Question *What manufacturer had the first successful slide-action shotgun?*

Answer A U.S. patent was issued to Spencer Arms Company in 1885 which signaled the start of slide-action shotguns. Eventually, this particular shotgun design became the Winchester Model 1893.

Question *What is the difference in weight between No. 7½ and No. 8 size shot?*

Answer 18 grains.

Question *Can you give me any information about the venerable Remington Model 32?*

Answer The Remington Model 32 over/under was made for approximately 10 years from 1932 until the early stages of WW II. It was made only in 12-gauge, but in four barrel lengths and three versions — 26, 28, 30, 32 inch, and Skeet, trap and field, respectively. Only 5053 guns were manufactured. Immediately following WW II, Remington sold all the tooling to the West German firm of Krieghoff. By the mid-1950s, Krieghoff was producing and selling a near-duplicate dubbed the Krieghoff Model 32. Today's Shotgun's of Ulm are look-a-likes for the Model 32 except for major interior upgrades. The Remington Model 3200 is a completely different shotgun and only slightly resembles the older Model 32s.

Question *How much recoil is generated from a 12-gauge shotgun?*

Answer Shooting a trap or Skeet gun that weighs 8½ pounds and shooting a 3-dram 1⅛-ounce shot load, free recoil would be 21½ fpe. A "light," or 2¾-dram load, also loaded with 1⅛ ounces of shot would produce 19 fpe of free recoil.

Question *When did Browning introduce their Superposed in 20-gauge.*

Answer In 1949, with 28-inch barrels choked Full and Modified. By mid-1950, 26-inch barrels and open choke configurations were available along with a Skeet-grade 20-gauge.

Question *How many Model 24s did Winchester make?*

Answer The Winchester Model 24 was a medium-priced side-by-side shotgun and production records indicate 116,280 were made between 1940 and 1957. Available in 12-, 16- and 20-gauge, it boasted double triggers, a raised matted rib and above-average quality furniture.

Question *I own a Winchester Model 37 single shot shotgun. The gun is in near-perfect condition, yet I cannot find any evidence of a serial number. Why?*

Answer Prior to the GCA of 1968, gun manufacturers were not required by federal law to mark firearms with serial numbers. It was the manufacturers' option and many companies chose not to do so to reduce manufacturing costs.

Question *I own a very old Browning Superposed in 12-gauge with an unusual set of double triggers. Can you give me more information on this relic?*

Answer You probably have an early model with what Browning dubbed "Single-Double Triggers" (Twin Single Trigger). Because this model did not have a trigger-selection system, pulling the front trigger twice fired the bottom barrel and then the top barrel; pulling the back trigger twice reversed the firing procedure. The 12-gauge Browning O/U hit the market in late 1930, even though the original patent claim was dated October 15, 1923 with the patent grant awarded March 30, 1926. It took Browning more than 4 more years to finalize the product and eliminate all the bugs. The basic design hasn't changed in 65 years.

Question *What was Remington's first gas-operated autoloading shotgun?*

Answer The first was the Model 58 Sportsman introduced in 1956. This gun boasted a "Dial-A-Matic" knob located on the magazine cap screw that was adjustable for light to heavy loads. Later, in 1959, the Model 878 Automaster hit the scene featuring a power-compensation system that eliminated the need for hand adjustment of power levels. In 1963, the "King"— Model 1100—was introduced, forcing all previous Remington gas guns into early retirement.

Question *Who invented the shotgun choke?*

Answer Most accounts point to the great market hunter Fred Kimball of Illinois in the 1860s. Kimball worked with single-barreled muzzle loaders which eventually were able to throw all of their 1¼-ounce shot charges into a 30-inch circle at 40 yards.

Question *Are the screw-in choke tubes for the Perazzi MT-6 interchangeable with the Winchester Win-Choke system?*

Answer No. They look the same, but the choke tubes for the MT-6 are made by Perazzi in Italy, even though Winchester was the importer, and though the choke tubes appeared the same, they are definitely not interchangeable.

Question *Many years ago I heard about a recoil-absorbing device called Hydro-Coil. Any information on this gunstock?*

Answer The Hydro-Coil is alive and well. Ed Sowers still makes custom Hydro-Coil gunstocks for Skeet, trap and field shooters. His address is: Ed Sowers, 8331 DeCelis Place, Sepulveda, CA 91343 (818) 893-1233.

Question *I've seen steel pattern boards with some sort of thick white paint used to define the shotshell's pattern. What is that substance?*

Answer It is usually a mixture of white lead and lard oil. Depending on the geographical area, the mix should be thick enough to allow it to "stick" on the plate, yet thin enough to be smoothed over with a paint brush for subsequent shots. While this system is fine for "one-time-only" shots, plain 40×40-inch paper sheets are more desirable because they are easily handled and stored for future reference.

Question *Who holds the record High All Around score at a registered trapshoot?*

Answer Dan Orlich broke a perfect 400x400 at the P.I.T.A. Grand in Reno, Nevada in the early 1960s. There have been quite a few 399x400s in ATA competition with Roger Smith missing only one Doubles target at the 1980 Grand American Tournament.

Question *How many loads per pound of powder will I get when loading 18 grains of 700X.*

Answer Three hundred and eighty-eight. There are 7000 grains in a pound, and dividing 18 into 7000 equals 388. To save you the trouble of figuring out other powder drops, here's a convenient chart:

Drop Charge	Loads per Pound
15	466
16	437
17	411
18	388
19	368
20	350
21	333
22	318

Question *Is there that much difference between "light" and "heavy" target loads? If so, how do you determine which is best?*

Answer If you are super-technically minded, the scientific differences between the two loads are listed below. With this information you can decide which is best for you; however, your selection might not be best for your shotgun.

Target Load Differences

Load	Muzzle velocity	40-yard velocity	40-yard energy	Time flight to 40 yds	Drop @ 40 yds
2³/₄ - 1¹/₈ - 8	1150 fps	640 fps	0.96 ft lbs	.1458 sec.	4.1″
2³/₄ - 1¹/₈ - 7¹/₂	1150 fps	655 fps	1.19 ft lbs	.1437 sec.	4.0″
3 - 1¹/₈ - 8	1200 fps	660 fps	1.02 ft lbs	.1410 sec.	3.8″
3 - 1¹/₈ - 7¹/₂	1200 fps	675 fps	1.26 ft lbs	.1389 sec.	3.7″

Question *How much does it cost to shoot the entire Grand American Tournament.*

Answer Totaling all the events from the 1988 program, it would set you back $2,277, including shells.

Question *When was the first 100x100 shot with the 410 in the world championships?*

Answer Not until 1960 by William Brown, Jr., Lynnhaven, Virginia.

Question *Who was the first to shoot a perfect 550x550 during the world championships?*

Answer Charlie Parks in 1976 in San Antonio, Texas.

Question *Who was the first 27-yard trapshooter to win the Grand American Handicap?*

Answer Reggie Jachimoski won it in 1978 with a perfect 100x100.

Question *How late did Winchester offer sold ribs on their venerable Model 12?*

Answer Until its "first" demise in 1964. As many Winchester advocates know, the Model 12 was resurrected in the late 1970s as public interest demanded. However, the company had to charge such a high price that they eventually buried the 12-gauge version once and for all. A side note: Browning has introduced a Model 12 replica in 20-gauge that is a direct knock-off of the original Winchester version and is a real beauty.

Question *Why are shotgun bore diameters called gauges, except for the 410 bore?*

Answer The origin of gauging a firearm dates back to smoothbore muskets. The bore size was classified by the size of the round ball it shot and how many of those round balls it took to make 1-pound. Therefore, if it took 12 balls to make 1-pound, the gun was classified as a 12-gauge. In those days, there were many "gauges" used with known examples for 4, 8, 10, 12, 14, 16, 20, 24, 28, 32, and 36. The 410 was developed much later and was named for its bore diameter—.410-inch. Converting it to a gauge, the 410 would be dubbed the 67.5 gauge—or thereabouts.

Question *Please define the phrase, "in the white?"*

Answer There's no way to determine where or when the phrase "in the white" originated, but it seems only to be relevant to the firearms industry. When a gun is "in the white," the complete firearm or its various parts are completed mechanically and ready for final finish, meaning blueing, browning, case-color hardening, etc. The "white" refers to the natural state of the steel after machining and polishing and before the final finish is applied.

Question *I'm confused about the choke markings on my Belgian Browning Superposed. Can you set me straight on what the asterisks mean?*

Answer Sure. Full=*, Improved Modified=*-, Modified=**, Improved Cylinder=**-, Skeet=**S, Cylinder=***. These choke markings also apply to all Browning shotguns, including the Japanese-made Citoris.

Question *My dad still shoots an occasional round of trap with an old Ithaca single-barrel trap gun. Can you tell me about it?*

Answer This venerable veteran of trapshooting wars dates back to the Flues models made from 1908 until 1921. All the Flues models had serial numbers under 400,000. The Knick model dates from 1922 until around 1938, and includes the Victory model. The Model 7E was in the Ithaca line until 1964 and the 4E until 1976. Since then, very few guns have been produced, something less than 10 per year, and all on a custom, special-order basis.

Question *Will repeatedly firing a shotgun without cleaning the barrel thoroughly tighten up the choke with lead fouling?*

Answer Absolutely. The average choke will tighten up from 2 to 3 thousands of an inch in approximately 5000 rounds of shooting without a regular cleaning program to remove lead and/or plastic buildup.

Question *When did Remington introduce their Model 870 Competition?*

Answer In mid-1980 for $549.95. This single shot, pump-action trap gun was equipped with a specially-designed gas-operated recoil reduction system which spread the effect of recoil over a longer period of time. The Competition model was designed with a new long-style forend and straight comb stock that had a great deal of downpitch for shooting comfort. Remington discontinued the Competition model in 1985.

Question *What is Circassian walnut?*

Answer Walnut from the Circassian mountains in Eastern Europe down through Turkey. This beautiful wood is reknown for its deep color range of red through black with many shades of brown and orange. It is probably the most expensive walnut in the world due to its limited access. There are many American walnuts almost as magnificent, especially Bastogne (French for bastard), which is a mix of English and California Claro walnuts. Like Circassian, it tends to be dark and is brilliantly colored in various hues of reds, browns and blacks.

Question *Have you ever heard of a Remington Model 878?*

Answer Yup. This unique autoloader was a transition gun between the Models 58 and 1100. It was only in the Remington lineup for a brief time—from 1959 until 1962. The next year, Remington brought out their fabulous Model 1100 and it was sayonara for the 878.

Question *How long and how many Remington Model 31s were made?*

Answer This super-slick pump was introduced in 1931 and discontinued in 1949 with a total production run of 189,243 in three gauges—12, 16 and 20.

Question *Who holds the record for the highest 16-Yard Singles average for one year?*

Answer The "King of Trapshooting," Dan Orlich. In 1968, Orlich missed just five out of 2850 targets for an unequalled percentage of .9982 percent.

Question *What is the difference between "station" and "post?"*

Answer None. Station is the correct term used to designate one of the five trapshooting positions. "Post" originated from early-day trapshooting when a post was set into the ground with a platform perched on top of it to hold a box of shells for the shooter. With the advent of shooting vests and pouches, the posts were left to deteriorate and never replaced.

Question *Can you give me a thumbnail sketch of the Winchester Model 21?*

Answer The Winchester Model 21 was a side-by-side introduced in 1931 and available in 12-, 16-, 20-, 28-gauge and 410 bore. Barrel lengths ranged from 26-inch Skeet models through 32-inch Duck guns. Single-selective triggers and automatic ejectors were standard equipment. A trap grade was first available in 1932 with either 30- or 32-inch ventilated rib barrels. As many of these guns were "custom" ordered, there are many variations of each version.

Question *I recently saw a Model 32 that wasn't named Krieghoff. What gives?*

Answer What you saw was the original Remington Model 32 over/under, the forerunner to the German-built Krieghoff. Remington introduced the Model 32 in 1932 in 12-gauge. During its short 9-plus year reign (production stopped during WW II) six different grades were available: 32A—Standard Grade; 32TC—Target Grade; 32S—Trap Special; 32D—Tournament Grade; 32E—Expert Grade and 32F—Premier Grade. Less than 6000 (5053 to be exact) 32s rolled off the Remington production line. At the end of WW II, Remington sold the tooling for the Model 32 to Krieghoff and by the mid-1950s, a few Krieghoff Model 32s started to cross the pond and penetrate our shores.

Question *When did the pipsqueak 410 come on the shooting scene?*

Answer Tough question. Nobody seems to know for certain, but early accounts go back to 1896 in W.W. Greener's Book, *The Breechloader and How to Use It*. The European designation is 12mm. If converted to a "gauge," the 410 would rank approximately as a 67-gauge, or it would take 67 round lead balls to make 1-pound.

Question *How far will shot travel?*

Answer It depends on the size, load and angle of trajectory. The following table is based on standard factory loads fired at a 45-degree angle.

Shot Size	Maximum Distance
BB	386 yards
#2	336 yards
#3	320 yards
#4	303 yards
#5	290 yards
#6	273 yards
#7½	243 yards
#8	240 yards
#8½	232 yards
#9	223 yards

And for those who are still curious, here's what the big stuff will do:

Shot Size	Maximum Distance
Rifled Slugs	817 yards
00 Buck	610 yards
0 Buck	590 yards
1 Buck	567 yards
3 Buck	497 yards
4 Buck	480 yards

Question Question *I own a Mini-Model 12 in 410-gauge, tell me about it?*

Answer First, it's not a 410-gauge, but a 410-caliber. Second, although it does have a distinct Model 12 look to it, it's actually a Model 42. It was introduced by Winchester in 1933 and expired in 1963 after 159,353 guns were produced. It was available in two barrel lengths—26 or 28 inches—three chokings—Full, Modified and Skeet—and two chamberings—2½ and 3 inches—with plain, solid matted and ventilated rib barrels. It's a fine little gun, although it has a bad reputation for malfunctioning during ejection.

Question *I've been shooting my Model 12 for more than 2 years with reasonable success. Lately my scores have plummeted to the point that I fear I will have to give up trapshooting? Any suggestions?*

Answer I, too, was the victim of a similar set of circumstances many years ago. The problem was a broken firing pin that upset my timing. A Model 12 firing pin is prone to breakage, yet will still function, albeit a few milliseconds slower, which will raise havoc and cause all kinds of timing and lead problems. To check, open the action, and making sure the gun is unloaded, turn the butt to the sky and peer into the bolt face. If the firing pin is broken, it will protrude past the firing pin hole. If the hole is clear, the pin is OK and you'll have to read the rest of the chapters in this book to hopefully solve your shooting slump.

Question *I've experienced a few "hangfires" from my reloads, what should I do?*

Answer First, check to see if your loading machine is functioning properly and dropping the correct powder charge. Second, visually inspect your reloaded shells not only at the crimp, but also at the primer. Check for proper seating depth of the primer to make sure it is flush with the base and not set too deep. Many shotguns, especially over/unders, and the older Browning Superposed in particular, have "short" firing pins for the bottom barrel due to space limitations and the angle at which the pin strikes the primer. Deeply-seated primers are often the result of "hangfires."

Question *The Winchester Model 12 was America's first successful hammerless shotgun, right?*

Answer Wrong. Credit must go to the Stevens Model 520 introduced 8 years before the Model 12—in 1904. It was in production until 1930. Incidentally, the Stevens 520 was invented by . . . you guessed it, John Moses Browning.

Appendices

Amateur Trapshooting Association
Rules and Guidelines

I
Organization Of The
Amateur Trapshooting Association

The following is an informative summary of the organization of the Amateur Trapshooting Association. Complete details are contained in the Articles of incorporation and the By-Laws of the Corporation which are contained in a separate booklet. The Official Trapshooting Rules of the Amateur Trapshooting Association govern the shooting of registered targets, the conduct of shooters and the duties of shoot management. The Amateur Trapshooting Association has the responsibility for the formulation, regulation and enforcement of these Rules. The Rules are contained in this article.

The Amateur Trapshooting Association reserves the right to make alteration in, or amendments to these rules at any time, whenever it deems it to be in the best interest of the Amateur Trapshooting Association.

A. Purpose of the A.T.A.

The purpose of the Amateur Trapshooting Association is to promote and govern the sport of amateur trapshooting throughout the world.

B. Membership

Membership is divided into two classes, both of which have full shooting rights and privileges. The membership year runs from October 1 through September 30.

Life Members. Only Life Members may hold office in the A.T.A. Life memberships are issued at a charge of $150.00 but pay no annual dues.

Annual Members. Annual members pay annual dues of $10.00. They are entitled to vote for State Delegates to the A.T.A. but may not hold that office, or any other offices in the A.T.A.

C. State Organizations And A.T.A. Delegate Elections

Shooters in the various states and provinces are organized into state and provincial associations which control shooting in their own territories and conduct state and provincial championship tournaments. Such associations receive aid from the A.T.A. in the form of trophies and cash refunds. This aid is covered in a detailed set of written rules elsewhere in this article.

At each annual state or provincial championship tournament sanctioned by the A.T.A., a business meeting must be held on a date and time specified in the program for the tournament. The date of the meeting must be no earlier than

8:00 A.M. and no later than 9:00 P.M., except that if the meeting is held on the last day of the tournament, then the meeting must commence no later than 12 Noon. All members of the A.T.A. residing in that state or province who are present in person at the meeting and who are also members of their state organization, are entitled to vote for the state or provincial delegate to the A.T.A. and for not more than two alternate A.T.A. delegates. The criteria for election as a State Delegate or Alternate Delegate shall be actual physical residence within the boundaries of the state of representation, in receipt of life membership certificate from the Amateur Trapshooting Association and member in good standing of the State Association of the state of representation. In the event the elected State Delegate becomes no longer an actual physical resident of the state of representation, either temporarily or permanently, that person's state as State Delegate shall terminate, and the duties of the State Delegate shall transfer to the duly elected Alternate Delegate. Selection of the state or provincial delegate and alternate delegate(s) should be given the utmost consideration. As delegates, in a properly called meeting, constitute the Board of Directors of the Amateur Trapshooting Association and as such have the responsibility of overseeing the operation of the Association, only those persons who are responsible, dedicated individuals should be considered.

D. Zones

The zones are comprised of the following territories:
CENTRAL: Illinois, Indiana, Michigan, Iowa, Minnesota, Nebraska, North Dakota, Ohio, South Dakota, Wisconsin, and the Provinces of Manitoba and Saskatchewan in Canada.
EASTERN: Connecticut, Delaware, Maine, Maryland, Massachusetts, New Hampshire, New York, Pennsylvania, Rhode Island, Vermont, New Jersey, and the provinces of Ontario and Quebec, Canada and the provinces in Canada lying east thereof.
SOUTHERN: Alabama, Florida, Georgia, Kentucky, Mississippi, North Carolina, South Carolina, Tennessee, Virginia, West Virginia and the Canal Zone.
SOUTHWESTERN: Arkansas, Colorado, Kansas, Louisiana, Missouri, New Mexico, Oklahoma and Texas.
WESTERN: Alaska, Arizona, California, Hawaii, Idaho, Montana, Nevada, Oregon, Utah, Washington, Wyoming, and the Provinces of Alberta and British Columbia.

E. Executive Committee And A.T.A. Manager

1. The Executive Committee consists of a representative from each of the five zones elected each year to the Executive Committee at the annual meeting of the Board of Directors. One member of the Executive Committee is designated President and the other four are designated Vice-Presidents.

2. The Board of Directors has delegated direction of the affairs of the A.T.A. between annual meetings to the Executive Committee.

3. The Executive Committee employs a manager to handle the daily affairs of the A.T.A. under its supervision. The A.T.A. Manager implements the policy set forth by the Board of Directors and/or the Executive Committee and follows their directions.

4. The main office and records of the A.T.A. are located at Vandalia, Ohio.

F. Board Of Directors

The Corporate Powers of the A.T.A. under Delaware law are vested in the Board of Directors which consists of a delegate from each state or province. The Board of Directors meets annually during the Grand American Tournament.

G. Constitution And By-Laws

The A.T.A. is organized under the Corporate Laws of the State of Delaware and has a Delaware charter and corporate by-laws formulated in accordance with Delaware laws.

H. Jurisdiction

The A.T.A. has jurisdiction over all affiliated associations regardless of location.

II
Information For New Shooters

A. Procedure For Joining A.T.A.
1. Annual Members

Application for annual membership may be made at any registered shoot by filling out an application which requires two life members' signatures and the payment of $10 dues to the A.T.A. A temporary receipt will be given to the shooter, upon receipt of a proper application. The temporary receipt should be retained as evidence of payment and be used in lieu of a membership card until the membership card is received. The A.T.A. will issue an annual membership card in the usual course of business. This card will be marked to indicate the shooter's handicap yardage.

Annual members have all the shooting rights and privileges of Life Members, but may hold no office in the A.T.A. Annual Members are entitled to vote for the state delegate and alternates to represent their state, or province, at a meeting of the Board of Directors of the A.T.A. Annual memberships are renewable by mail on or before October 1st. Send your complete name, address, including zip code, and $10 to A.T.A., Vandalia, Ohio 45377, to renew, if you do not receive a renewal form from the A.T.A.

2. Life Memberships

Life Memberships are obtained by the submission of a proper application and the payment of $150. Upon approval of the application, the A.T.A. will issue a Life Membership Certificate.

PLEASE NOTE: If you pay dues at a shoot, retain your receipt until you receive your A.T.A. membership card. Unless you can show evidence of membership fee payment, you may have to pay again. Be sure you record all scores you have shot before you receive your A.T.A. card and then transfer these scores to your new card.

If you do not receive your A.T.A. card within four weeks, send a letter to the A.T.A., 601 West National Road, Vandalia, Ohio 45377, advising the A.T.A. that you made application on certain date and give A.T.A. the name of the gun club where you made your application.

From the $10 annual membership, $2 is returned to the state organization.

From the $150 life membership, $75 is returned to the state organization over a ten (10) year period and part is retained in a special A.T.A. emergency fund.

From the $1 daily fee you pay, twenty percent (20%) is returned to the state organization.

B. Target And Membership Year

The target year and Membership year runs from October 1st to September 30th; however, scores shot at any tournament ending after September 30, regardless of starting date, will be included in the following year's averages.

C. Handicap Yardage For A New A.T.A. Shooter
1. New Lady Shooter

New lady shooters will be assigned a Handicap of 18.0 yards.

2. New Sub-Junior Shooter

A shooter who has not reached his or her 15th birthday will be classified as a sub-junior and will be assigned a handicap of 18.0 yards.

3. New Male Junior Shooter

All male shooters between the age of 15 and 18 will be assigned a handicap of 19.0 yards.

4. New Male Shooter

A new male shooter, 18 years of age or older, will be assigned a handicap of 20.0 yards.

5. A new member who had previously been a member of another trapshooting association (prior to current and previous years, see rule III, Q) must shoot their last assigned yardage in that association unless he has received an A.T.A. 1000 target review and been granted a reduction.

It will be the responsibility of the new member to notify the handicap committee of his last assigned yardage in that association.

D. Classification Of A New Shooter In 16 Yards And Doubles Events

A new shooter may be assigned to any class in 16 yards and doubles events until the shooter establishes his known ability.

E. Rules Of Conduct Of An A.T.A. Shooter

Each member will be furnished a copy of these Official Trapshooting Rules, and it is assumed that the member will read and understand each rule. Members are strongly encouraged to know these rules and abide by them, both for their own benefit and for the benefit of other shooters.

1. By entering the competition, every person agrees to accept all official decisions and to abide by these rules.

2. It is the duty of each A.T.A. member to have his or her Average Card punched is yardage is earned. The Average Card must be punched to the correct earned yardage on the day the yardage is earned and before leaving the tournament grounds. If a member is required to leave the tournament grounds prior to the completion of a handicap event, it is the member's duty to determine if his or her score qualified for a yardage increase and to have his or her Average Card punched to the correct yardage prior to entering any other tournament. All 16 yard, handicap and doubles scores are required to be correctly and legibly entered on each member's Average Card in the spaces provided at the completion of each tournament event. 16 yards and doubles averages are required to be kept current on the Average card in the columns provided for that purpose for use by classification committees. Failure of any member to strictly comply with this rule may lead to penalty classification, disqualification and/or suspension from membership in the A.T.A.

3. When making your entry at any registered shoot, produce your plastic identification card and your average card so that your name, address, and membership number are properly noted and errors in records prevented. Shooters not having a plastic card should always list their entire name and address on the event cards.

The score card is intended for the purpose of providing the classification committees at the shoots with up to date data on your shooting ability. Shooters not having their cards up to date may be put in a higher class or otherwise penalized.

Failure to accurately record scores, or the falsification of scores, can lead to suspension from the A.T.A.

4. Veterans are defined as male or female shooters 65 years of age or older. Senior Veterans are 70 years of age or older. Sub-Juniors, Juniors and veterans will be required to change their status on the date of their birthday, e.g., on the day a sub-junior turns 15 any event shot on that day will be shot as a junior. When a junior reaches 18, on that day he or she must shoot as an adult. Veterans will qualify for veterans' races on their 65th birthday. The only exceptions are as follows:

   a. When considering High-Overall or All-Around when there is a sub-junior, junior or veterans' trophy the contestants age on the first day that qualifies him for said award must be utilized.

   b. In the Grand American, when qualification for sub-junior or junior is determined at the state level, he may be able to participate in the Champion of Champion event based on his age at the state shoot.

5. A contestant is duly notified to compete when his name is called by the scorer, or other person authorized to do so by the management. If a squad hustler is furnished, it is a matter of courtesy only and does not relieve the contestant from his responsibility of reporting when his name is called by his referee, scorer or other person authorized to do so. Shooters not responding when duly notified may be disqualified by the management.

6. A contestant may hold his gun in any position when it is his turn to shoot. He must in no manner interfere with the preceding shooter by raising his gun to point or otherwise create a distraction.

7. It is the duty of the contestant to see that his score as determined by the referee is correctly recorded. In case of error, it shall be the duty of the contestant to have that error corrected before he has fired the first shot at the succeeding position or before he leaves the trap if the target concerned was within the last five targets of that sub-event. Otherwise the score must stand as shown on the score sheet.

F. Renewing Membership In The A.T.A.

Any shooter reapplying for membership in the A.T.A., who had been assigned a previous handicap yardage, shall resume shooting at that yardage. The only exception is if he was assigned a yardage based on age; because of present age he may be required to shoot at a longer yardage. Failure of a shooter to shoot his previously assigned yardage will result in disqualification and the winning scores and prizes forfeited.

III
Official Rules Of A.T.A. Tournaments

In these rules the word "State" is intended to include province or other similar territory having an affiliated association.

A. Registered Shoots

The A.T.A. governs the conduct of all shoots registered with it. Only clubs affiliated with their state association will be permitted to hold registered shoots.

To constitute a registered shoot at least five (5) or more persons must compete and compete each event, and provided that they first become members of the A.T.A. and pay the registration fee of $1 for each day of competition at each shooting location, and such other state association fees and dues may be charged.

No daily fee charges shall be permitted except those assessed by the A.T.A., the Zone, or the State in which the tournament is being held.

B. Who May Participate

Only members in good standing who have paid their annual dues or are Life Members may participate in a registered A.T.A. Shoot.

C. Events And How Shot

In official A.T.A. usage a sub-event is any number of

targets shot on any one field at one time, with one full rotation on all five stations by each shooter, such as 25 singles or handicap targets or in doubles 25 pairs, 15 pairs or 10 pairs. An event is the total targets of a specific type (16 yard, handicap, or doubles) such as 200 16-yard targets, 100 handicap targets, etc. for which separate entry is made. Therefore, an "event" consists of two or more "sub-events." It is not necessary to change traps after each sub-event. Events of less than 50 targets may not be registered.

1. 16 Yard Singles

This event must be shot 5 shots at each post from 16 yards (14.6m) with each shooter in order shooting at one target until all have shot five times, and then rotating in a clockwise manner to the next station.

2. Handicap Targets

This event must be shot 5 shots at each post from 17 to 27 yards (15.5-24.7m) with each shooter in order shooting at one target until all have shot five times, then rotating in a clockwise manner to the next station.

A contestant must stand on the highest whole yardage punched on his or her card. For example, if a card is punched at 20.5 yards, the shooter will stand on 20.0 yards. However, if one half yard is then earned, the card must be punched to 21.0 yards and the shooter must stand on the 21.0 yard line.

A shooter may not stand on a higher yardage than he is punched, unless assigned penalty yardage by the shoot handicap committee.

If there is a 200 target race, the second handicap event must not begin prior to the awarding of earned yardage based on the first 100 target event.

It is not permitted to have more than 50 and/or 75 target handicap event in a registered tournament in any one day.

3. Doubles

This event must be shot from 16 yards (14.6m), with each shooter in order shooting at two targets thrown simultaneously from the trap house until all have shot the specified number of times, then rotating in a clockwise manner to the next station. (A doubles event will be shot by having each squad shoot successive alternating 15 pair and 10 pair sub-events on the trap or traps be utilized, or a club may elect to throw Doubles in sub-events of 25-pairs.)

D. Classification, Handicapping, And Special Designation

1. For 16 yard targets and Doubles, shooters should be placed in 3 or more classes, according to their known ability.

a. To arrive at "known ability" the following should be taken into account as far as such information can be made available.

(1) Official registered targets (Abnormally low scores should be disregarded.) Averages of all registered shooters are compiled and published annually.

(2) Non-registered scores including shoot-off scores, non-registered events, practice scores, etc.

(3) Any other information bearing on a shooter's ability to shoot and break targets.

b. For 16-yard events the following systems are suggested:

Five Classes

97% and over	AA
94% and under 97%	A
91% and under 94%	B
88% and under 91%	C
Under 88%	D

Four Classes

95% and over	A
92% and under 95%	B
89% and under 92%	C
Under 89%	D

Three Classes

95% and over	A
91% and under 95%	B
Under 91%	C

c. For Doubles events the following systems are suggested:

Five Classes

93% and up	AA
89 % and under 93%	A
85% and under 89%	B
78% and under 85%	C
Under 78%	D

Four Classes

90% and up	A
85% and under 90%	B
78% and under 85%	C
Under 78%	D

Three Classes

89% and up	A
83% and under 89%	B
Under 83%	C

d. Any club desiring to use a different classification may do so by printing the desired classification in the program of the shoot.

e. For better classification of shooters it is suggested that the following method be used.

(1) If the shooter has less than 500 targets on current year's score card, use the previous year average and known ability.

(2) If the shooter has between 500 and 1,000 targets (inclusive) on his current year's score card, use the current average and known ability or the previous year's average and known ability, whichever is the higher.

2. Recommended 16 Yard Punch System

a. This system is to be utilized for classification at only the Grand American, A.T.A. Zone Championships, State Championships, Golden West Grand, Spring Grand, Midwestern Grand, and Southern Grand Tournaments. Cards shall not be punched at any other than the above shoots.

b. Classification at all shoots shall be decided by the club shoot classification and handicap committee.

c. All scores equaling or exceeding those of champions, runner-ups, and the respective class winners will receive one punch. This will apply only to the singles championships when at the above mentioned shoots.

d. The shooter's average card will be printed providing for two punches in each of the five A.T.A. classes. When a shooter has one punch it indicates he has one that class at one of the above shoots. A shooter with two punches in a class should be advanced.

e. It will be the shooter's responsibility to see that his card is properly punched prior to entering any of the above listed tournaments.

f. The intent of the system is to inform classification and handicap committees of prior wins. Punches indicating these wins may be disregarded by the classification committee if they so choose.

3. A shooter will be handicapped between 17 and 27 yards at the highest yardage punched on this card, unless he is required to shoot at Penalty yardage. (Section 5.)

4. Penalty Classification

The management of registered shoots may establish penalty yardage, and penalty classification for 16 yard targets and doubles, if said conditions are printed in the program. In no event shall any shooter be assigned a handicap of less than the minimum yardage appearing on his handicap card.

5. Special Categories

Ladies, Juniors, Sub-Juniors, Veterans, Sr. Veterans and Industry shooters shall be so designated.

a. All female shooters shall be designated as Ladies, though because of age they may also be designated as Juniors, Sub-Juniors, Veterans or Sr. Veterans.

b. A shooter who has not reached his or her 15th birthday will be designated as a Sub-Junior.

c. A male shooter upon reaching age 15 ,must shoot from a minimum handicap average of 19 yards unless he has already earned greater yardage.

d. A shooter who is 15 but has not reached his or her 18th birthday will be designated as a Junior.

e. A male shooter upon reaching age 18 must shoot from a minimum handicap yardage of 20 yards unless he has already earned greater yardage.

f. A male or female shooter who is 65 years or older will be designated as a Veteran.

g. A male or female shooter who is 70 years or older will be designated a Sr. Veteran.

h. Industry personnel shall be so designated and may shoot for only those championships and trophies so designated.

i. All ladies, sub-juniors, veterans, senior veterans and industry shooters must declare their special category at the time of their entry in any registered event. Without such declaration at the time of their entry, the shooter will not be allowed to compete for the applicable special category trophies. No exceptions to this rule to be allowed.

E. Squadding

1. In all A.T.A. events contestants shall shoot in squads of five except:

a. When there are less than five contestants available for the last squad of any program.

b. When yardage differences in handicap events make it impossible or unsafe.

c. When there are withdrawals from a squad after the competition has begun and squads are scheduled.

d. When in the opinion of shoot management, the harmony of the shoot may be enhanced by squadding less than five contestants.

2. It is illegal for more than five shooters to be in a squad.

3. The squadding of practice shooters with those shooting registered events shall not be allowed, no shall anyone be allowed to shoot registered events on a non-registered basis.

4. The shooter in position 1 is the SQUAD LEADER and should:

a. Ascertain that all members of the squad are ready before commencing the event or sub-event.

b. Initial the score sheet at the end of each sub-event.

c. The Squad Leader ONLY may call for one target before starting his squad to shoot in a regular or shootoff event.

5. If a broken or irregular target is thrown, the Squad Leader may ask to see another target; if there is a delay due to trap or gun trouble the contestant in turn, may ask to see another target. If during a sub-event a contestant is consecutively thrown two illegal or broken targets, the contestant shall have the right to see a legal target before he resumes shooting.

F. Official Scoring

1. Procedure

a. The official score is the record kept by the scorer on the sheet furnished him by the management for said purpose and shall show in detail the scores made in the event or sub-event for which furnished. It is recommended that the score sheet shall not be smaller than 10 inches by 28 inches and the box provided for each score not smaller than 3/4 by 3/4 of an inch. Score sheets on which more than one sub-event is recorded may be carried from trap to trap by the squad leader. Such score sheets must be left at the last trap to be handled by club personnel from that point.

b. The scorer shall keep an accurate record of each score of each contestant. If he calls dead or lost, the scorer shall promptly mark 1 for dead and zero for lost. His record of the competition shall be official and shall govern all awards and records of the competition to which it relates.

c. The scorer shall call all targets, or only the lost targets, as directed by the management.

d. Should more targets be fired in a sub-event than the event calls for, then the excess targets of the sub-event will not be scored.

e. It is the duty of the referee to see that the shooters change firing points at the proper time; however, any targets shot after failure to move at the proper time shall be scored.

f. The official score must be kept on a score sheet in plain view of the contestants. If contestant's view of the score sheet is obscured for any reason, he may refuse to shoot until he has an unobscured view of the score sheet.

g. It is an error if the scorer fails to properly mark the results of any shot in the section of the score sheet where the results should have been recorded. In such cases it is the duty of the contestant to have any error corrected before he has fired the first shot at the succeeding position or in the case of his last post before he leaves the trap. Failing to do so he shall be held to the score as recorded (see Rule C.3).

h. Every contestant in a squad shall be permitted to examine his score before the sheet is sent to the bulletin board or to the cashier's office. The score sheet should be initialed by the squad leader.

i. Errors in the details of the official score can only be corrected in strict accordance with the aforementioned rules, but an error made in totaling said details shall be corrected whenever same is discovered.

j. The referee shall distinctly announce "lost" when the target is missed and "no target" when a target is thrown broken.

2. Broken Or Dead Target

A broken target (called dead) is one that has a visible broken piece from it; or one that is completely reduced to dust. The referee shall declare such target dead when it is so broken in the air. A "Dusted Target," is a target from which there is a puff of dust, but no perceptible piece is seen; it is not a broken target.

3. Lost Target

The referee shall call "lost":

a. When the contestant shoots and fails to break the target whether missed completely or when only dust falls from it.

b. When the contestant flinches and does not shoot.

c. When the shell is defective but no part of the over powder wads or shot remains in the barrel.

d. When a whole target appears promptly after a contestant's recognizable command and is within legal limits of flight and the contestant does not shoot.

e. When the contestant after calling "pull" fails to shoot because his gun was unloaded, uncocked, not properly closed, because the safety was on, or was faulty, or jarred back, whether from his oversight or not, *except* that some vital part of the gun has suddenly broken so that it cannot possibly be made to function without repairs, or that he has an allowable misfire.

f. When an illegal target, or a freak target is shot and missed. Contestant may refuse illegal targets, but if he shoots, the results must be scored.

g. If a contestant has more than two (2) misfires in any sub-event of 25 targets (or other number in case of doubles) and did not change guns or change to the other barrel of a double barrel gun, or change shells as outlined. If these changes are not made, any misfires shall be called lost.

h. When a contestant voluntarily withdraws from, or is disqualified, and takes no further part in a sub-event after having shot at one or more targets called for by said sub-event and thereby does not shoot at the total number of targets called for by such sub-event, the referee shall declare all targets which the contestant did not shoot at in the sub-event to be lost targets and they shall be scored accordingly.

i. When a score sheet shall come into the office with one or more targets that are not scored at all, they shall be scored as lost targets by the management.

j. If a contestant uses a shell after it has misfired, he shall abide by the result obtained through the use of that shell.

k. If after an apparent dud shell or misfire the contestant opens his gun before the referee come to him to make a decision, the target shall be called "lost."

4. No Target

a. To better apply the following rules, these definitions are given:

(1) Misfire (Dud Shell); failure of a shell to fire when the primer is struck with the firing pin or when evidence is present that the hammer did fall even though the primer shows no indention, or a shell which lacks a live primer or one in which the primer fires, but through failure of the shell or lack of components, and which consequently leaves part of or all the charge of shot or wad in the gun. A soft load, in which the shot and wad leave the barrel, is not a misfire.

(2) Malfunction of a gun; failure of the gun to function, or work as it was designed to. Malfunction of a gun applies only to a second shot of doubles.

(3) Broken gun; a gun in which some vital parts has broken so that the gun cannot be made to fire without repairs.

b. It is a "no target" and the referee shall allow another target under the following conditions:

(1) When the target is thrown broken, regardless of the results of any shots fired.

(2) When a contestant shoots out of turn.

(3) When two contestants, or a contestant and non-contestant shoot at the same target.

(4) When the trap is sprung without any call of pull, or when it is sprung at any material interval of time, before or after the call of the shooter, provided the contestant does not shoot. If the shooter shoots, the result must be scored, unless the shot is fired after the target has struck the ground.

(5) When in single shooting two targets are thrown at the same time, regardless of whether the shooter fires.

(6) When an "illegal" target is thrown, a target that is more than twenty-five degrees outside of the prescribed limits of the angles in single-target shooting, or what is known as a "flipper" or "freak" target that may have slipped out of the carrier of the trap or one not properly placed on the trap provided the contestant does not shoot at it. If he shoots, the result must be scored.

(7) When a target, whose color is markedly different from that of the others, is thrown and the contestant does not shoot. If he shoots, the result must be scored.

(8) When firing, the contestant's feet must be behind the firing mark assigned to him. He must stand with at least one foot on the imaginary line drawn through the trap and firing point, or have one foot on each side of the line. Exceptions to this rule contained in the second sentence of this paragraph may be granted by the referee due to inequalities in the shooting platform. Should a shooter fail to observe this rule the referee shall call any target shot at and

broken a "no target," but if shot at and missed, the result shall be scored accordingly.

c. When the contestant has a misfire shell, or apparent misfire, he, without opening his gun or removing the shell or shells, must forthwith allow the referee to inspect his gun before making his decision. If the shooter opens his gun before the referees come to him to make a decision, the target shall be called "lost." The referees shall not be required to handle firearms in any manner whatsoever in the performance of their duties.

d. If a contestant has a second misfire in the same sub-event of 25 targets (or other number in case of doubles) he shall be warned by the referee. The shooter must at that time demonstrate to the referee that he is either (1) changing guns or changing to the other barrel of a double barreled gun , or (2) that he is changing shells. If he fails to do one of these things, all succeeding misfires in that sub-event will be called "lost."

e. If, after the change of guns or shells, the shooter has another misfire in the same sub-event, he must make the other change of the option for the remainder of the sub-event or be disqualified for interfering with the harmony of the shoot. Management shall also disqualify him on the same grounds of interference if he persists in using the same gun or guns, or shells on succeeding sub-events with resultant misfires. To avoid disqualification he may withdraw from the sub-event, have the gun repaired or shells replaced, and finish the sub-events as directed by the management.

f. In addition, in Doubles shooting, the referee shall declare "no target" under the following conditions:

(1) When only one target is thrown.

(2) When more than two targets are thrown.

(3) When both targets are broken by one shot.

(4) When there is an allowable misfire on either shot.

(5) When the gun breaks down so either shot cannot be fired.

(6) When there is a maximum of one (1) gun malfunction for the second shot on any one trap per sub-event, whether the sub-event consists of 10 or 15 pairs. In sub-events of 25 pairs two (2) gun malfunctions are allowed. If the shooter changes guns, he will be allowed another malfunction per sub-event. However, if the shooter does not change guns, any subsequent malfunction shall be called "lost." Misfires are not considered malfunctions.

(7) When one or both targets are thrown broken even though the shooter fires at one or both targets.

(8) If one or both targets are not within prescribed angle or height limits and the shooter does not fire either shot. If the shooter shoots at an illegal first target and the second target is legal, he must also shoot at the second target. However, a shooter is not required to shoot an illegal second target even though he shot at the first target which may have been either legal or illegal.

(9) Both targets shall be called "lost" if the shooter deliberately shoots at the same target twice. This rule is not applicable to a gun "doubling" or "machine-gunning," these are malfunctions and are not deliberate second shots.

G. Shoot-Offs

The management of a tournament may rule that ties shall be carried over the first (or more if needed) sub-event of the next like event. However, when there are ties in a handicap event and any tying shooter earns yardage and consequently will be shooting farther back in the subsequent handicap event, all tying shooters must agree to the carry-over.

All ties whenever possible shall be shot off and in such a manner as the management of the competition shall designate. Unless otherwise specified by the management, ties on singles events shall be shot off in 25 target events and doubles of 10 pair events.

Ties for All-Around championships shall be shot off on 20 singles, 10 handicap, and 5 pair of doubles. Ties for High-Overall shall be shot off in such a manner that the shoot represents as closely as possible the same proportion of singles, handicap and doubles targets as the High-Overall program contains but keeping the shoot off to 50 targets or less.

The singles, handicap and doubles portion of the shoot-off shall be in order that the event occurred in the program.

When squadding shooters for shoot-offs for High-Overall and All-Around the shooting order shall be in the order in which they shot in the last event involved except where such order would be inadvisable or dangerous because of yardage differences, and this order shall remain through subsequent shoot-offs. In subsequent shoot-offs the position shall be rotated in a clockwise manner, with the shooter from position 1 advancing to position 2 and the shooter from position 5 rotating to position 1 or to the position dictated by the number of shooters remaining, but always in a clockwise rotation.

The following method shall be used for rotation of shooters: Starting firing points to be used shall be as follows except where handicap yardage makes it unsafe.

If one shooter—firing point number 2.

If two shooters—firing points 2 and 4.

If three shooters—firing points 2, 3 and 4.

If four shooters—firing points 2, 3, 4 and 5.

If five shooters—firing points 1, 2, 3, 4 and 5.

If more than five shooters are involved in the tie, they shall be divided as equally as possible into two or more squads as directed by the management.

H. Safety

1. It is the shooter's responsibility and the shoot management's responsibility to conduct a shoot in a safe manner.

2. It is the shoot management's responsibility to remove and competitor who is conducting himself in an unsafe manner (repeat violators should be reported to the Executive Committee for further action.)

3. It is the shoot management's responsibility to instruct the trap help in the proper and safe conduct of their respective duties.

4. All trap help must have a flag or other warning device to warn of the trap boy's exit from the trap house.

5. Trap personnel should be totally instructed in the potential danger of the trap (particularly the target throwing arm).

6. Movement and exposure on adjacent traps should be kept to the minimum.

7. The practice of tracking targets behind a shooting squad is unsafe, disconcerting to the shooter and is not permitted.

8. Alcohol impairs judgment and the A.T.A. rules pertaining to alcohol must be enforced by club management. This rule shall be strictly complied with and shall apply to practice shooting as well as regular events.

9. In singles and handicap shooting, only one shell may be inserted in the gun at one time; in doubles only two shells may be inserted in a gun at anytime.

10. In handicap there shall be no more than two (2) yards difference between adjacent shooters in the squad, *and no more that a total difference of three (3) yards in a squad.* When squadding 17, 18 and 19 yardages, there shall be no more than one yard difference between adjacent shooters in the squad, and no more than a total difference of two yards in a squad.

11. In case of failure to fire, where referee is needed, shooters must remain in position with the gun pointed toward the target area and the referee must go to the shooter.

12. A gun may be loaded only when the shooter is on the firing station and the gun must be empty when shooter is moving from station to station.

13. All guns must be unloaded with the action open at all times except on the firing line or in a gun rack. Violators subject themselves to immediate disqualification, without recourse, with dismissal from the grounds. Repeat violators will be notified of a 30-day suspension upon second violation, third violation will receive a 90-day suspension and continuing violators will be reviewed by the Executive Committee for further disciplinary action.

14. As a safety precaution test shots will not be permitted.

15. A contestant shall load his gun only when at firing point facing THE TRAPS. *In singles shooting he may place only one shell in his gun at a time and must remove it or the empty case before moving from one position to another. In changing from one post to another, the shooter should not walk in front of the other competitors.* All guns used by contestants must be so equipped and so used as not to eject empty shells in a manner to substantially disturb or interfere with other contestants. The management may disqualify a contestant for violation of these rules.

I. Guns And Ammunition

A contestant cannot use:

1. A gun whose chamber is larger than 12 gauge. Only 12 gauge shotguns and ammunition may be used at the Grand American Tournament; guns of smaller gauges are permissible in other registered shooting, but no consideration shall be given to the fact in handicap and classification.

2. Any load other than lead shot. This includes tracers, copper and nickel coated shot.

3. Any load heavier than 3 drams equivalent of powder or $1\frac{1}{8}$ ounces of shot by standard measure struck, or any load containing shot larger than number $7\frac{1}{2}$.

4. Any shell loaded with black powder.

Any shooter violating any of these rules shall be barred

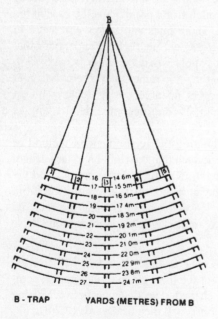

B - TRAP   **YARDS (METRES) FROM B**

Diagram I
Trap and Firing Positions

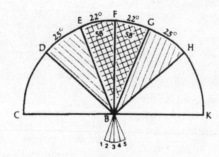

Diagram II
Legal Target Flight Area for 16 Yards and Handicap Shooting
1 to 5—Firing Points spaced 3 yards (2.7m) apart.
B—Trap.
CDEFGHK—Fifty yards (46m) from trap.
BDEFGHB Shaded—Area of Legitimate Target.
BEFGB—Cross Hatched—Most desirable area in which to throw target.
3BF—Imaginary straight line through Trap and No. 3 Firing Position.
CBK—Imaginary straight line through Trap at right angles to 3BF.
EF,FG—The distance between these two points shall be a straight line 58 feet (17.7m) long.
Target elevation 8 to 12 feet (2.4 to 3.7m) above number 3 firing point at point M 30 feet (9m) in front of trap. Target distance 48 to 52 yards (44 to 48m).

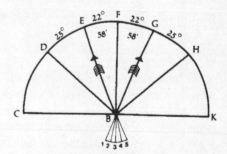

Diagram III
Double Target Shooting
1 to 5 Firing Points spaced 3 yards (2.7m) apart.
B—Trap, 16 yards (14.6m) from Firing Points.
CDEFGHK—Fifty yards (46m) from Trap.
3BF—Imaginary straight line through Trap and No. 3 Firing Position.
CBK—Imaginary straight line through Trap at right angles at 3BF.
Arrows indicated recommended flight of target.
Distance of Targets' Flight—48 to 52 yards (44 to 48m).
EF,FG—The distance between these points shall be a straight line 58 feet (17.7m) long.
Elevation of target 8 to 12 feet (2.4 to 3.7m) above number three firing point at a distance of 30 feet (9m) in front of the trap.

from competition. Any such violator shall be referred to the Executive Committee for possible further disciplinary action.

J. Firing Position And Shooting Order

1. There shall be 5 firing points, numbered 1 to 5, left to right, spaced 3 yards apart, and sixteen yards from B (Diagram II). At all positions the contestant's feet must be behind the firing mark assigned to him, and he must stand with at least one foot on the imaginary line drawn through the trap and the firing point or have one foot on each side of the line.

The 16 yard (16.6m) position shall be 16 yards behind the center of the trap in the traphouse. The distance that the target shall be thrown shall also be measured from this point.

2. All contestants must shoot in regular order or sequence according to his or her position on the squad. A contestant who does not shoot in regular order is "out of turn" and the results are not scored.

3. When the referee calls no target for any contestant, the next contestant is not in order until the preceding shooter has shot and the referee has ruled dead or lost.

4. The referee shall not throw a target unless all contestants are in the correct positions.

5. To preserve the harmony of the competition, no member of a squad shall move toward the next firing point until the last shot of the inning has been fired.

6. An any registered trapshooting competition, no person shall be permitted to "shoot up" that is, enter and take a part in any completed or partially completed event or events after Squad no. 1 shall have completed sub-event no. 1 of any new event to be shot on Trap no. 1.

7. At tournaments which are shot "section system" with several squads, starting at the same time on several traps, such procedure shall be construed for purposes of this rule to be the same as if all squads started on Trap no. 1.

K. Trap Machine

An automatic trap machine which throws targets at an unknown angle shall be used. All trap machines used to throw A.T.A. registered targets shall be so manufactured, modified, or equipped as to interrupt irregularly the oscillation of the trap or otherwise assure the unpredictability of the flight of substantially all targets thrown.

L. Traphouses

Traphouses must adequately protect the trap loaders and shall not be higher than necessary for the purpose. Traphouses constructed after January 1, 1956 shall conform to the following specifications:

Length not less than 7 feet, 6 inches (2.3m), nor more than 8 feet, 6 inches (2,6m).

Width not less than 7 feet, 6 inches (2.3m), nor more than 8 feet, 6 inches (2.6m).

Height not less than 2 feet, 2 inches (.7m). nor more than 2 feet, 10 inches (.9m), the height to be measured from the plane of the number 3 shooting position.

Firing Points. The firing points shall be three yards (2.7m)

apart on the circumference of a circle whose radius is 16 yards (14.6m).

M. Targets

No target shall measure more than four and five-sixteenths (4⁵/₁₆) inches (10.94 cm) in diameter, not more than one and one-eighth (1¹/₈) inches (28.58mm) in height, and shall weigh 3.5 ounces (99.23g) with an allowable variation of five percent from this figure.

N. Flights And Angles

Targets, whether singles or doubles, shall be thrown not less than 48 yards (44m) measured on level ground in still air. The recommended distances for the throwing of any target shall be 50 yards (46m).

Targets, whether single or double, shall be between 8 (2.4m) and 12 feet (3.7m) high, when ten yards from the trap. *The recommended height is nine feet.* The height at a point ten yards (9m) from the trap is to be understood to mean height above an imaginary horizontal straight line drawn through the firing point and the trap. (See Diagram II.)

In singles shooting the trap shall be so adjusted that within the normal distribution of angles as thrown by the trap, the right angle shall not be less than a straight-away from firing point 1 and the left angle shall not be less than a straight-away from firing point 5. To help in determining legal angles, stakes should be placed on the arc of a circle whose radius is 50 yards (46m) and whose center is the trap. One stake should be placed where a line is drawn through firing point 1 and the base of the trap intersects this arc and another stake placed where a line drawn through firing point 5 and the base of the trap intersects the arc. These lines and stakes will assist in determining the required angles, but it is to be understood that the angle specifications apply when the target is from 15 to 20 yards (14-18m) from the trap rather than where the target strikes the ground. However, no target is to be declared illegal unless it is more than 25 degrees outside the angles prescribed.

In doubles target shooting the recommended method of throwing targets shall be such that the right hand target shall be approximately straight-away from firing point 1 and the left hand target shall be an approximate straight-away from firing point number 5. However, no target shall be declared illegal unless it varies more than 25 degrees from these recommended angles.

Distance Handicaps. The distance handicaps when used shall be prolongations of the lines given in Diagram I, commonly known as fan shaped. The distance between firing points at 16 yards (14.6m) shall then be 3 yards (2.7m).

A common misconception is that once the first squad of an event has shot over a trap the trap cannot be reset unless it is throwing illegal targets. This is not true. Should, for some reason, a trap be throwing targets that, though not necessarily illegal, are so poorly thrown that it will appreciably affect the shooter's score, any shooter may request that the management reset the trap. It will be the management's responsibility to decide if the trap(s) should be reset.

O. Trophies, Aids And Requirements For States And Zones.

1. Residence

No person, amateur or industry representative, may compete for A.T.A. Trophies or Titles in State or Zone tournaments, unless he or she, for the immediately preceding six (6) months, has been a bona fide resident of said State or Zone, and a member in good standing of the State Association of that person's residence. No person may compete for any such A.T.A. Trophies or Titles in more than one (1) State or Zone each target year. However, nothing shall preclude such person from returning to the former State or Zone residence and competing for trophies in the event he or she has not been a bona fide resident of another State or Zone for the immediate preceding six (6) month period prior to such competition.

In case there is a dispute with respect to the residence of a shooter attending a State or Zone tournament, it shall be the duty of the State Association or the Zone Officials in which the shoot is being held to rule as to said shooter's right to compete as a resident shooter. The ruling of the State Association or Zone Officials shall be final.

2. Targets Only

At all state and zone championship events in which A.T.A. trophies are donated, contestants who are residents of that state or zone must be allowed to shoot for targets only, plus payment of A.T.A. and state registration and/or zone fees in those events and be eligible to win A.T.A. trophies and the respective championships.

3. At all shoots where A.T.A. trophies are furnished a line referee must be provided by the host club or State Association.

4. Compulsory Purses

No compulsory purse and/or option shall be permitted at the Grand American and/or championship events at the State, Zone or Provincial tournaments.

5. State Aids

The A.T.A. in its program of building strong state associations aids them financially from the $10 annual membership, $2 is returned to the state organization. From the $150 life membership, $75 is returned to the state organization over a ten (10) year period and part is retained in a special A.T.A. emergency fund from the $1 daily fee you pay, twenty percent (20%) is returned to the state organization.

These are made to the state association ten days prior to the State Tournament, provided such tournament is held and provided the state turns in to the A.T.A. at least $200 annual membership dues and registration fees. From this refund, there will be deducted an amount equal to that which is represented by "unpaid cards" of shooters from that state who shot in registered shoots without payment of annual membership dues, and any fines because of late shoot reports. On or before January 1 of each year the A.T.A. shall inform the secretary of each state of the approximate amount of refund to be paid to that State and this information must be printed in the program for that annual State Tournament.

6. State A.T.A. Trophies

The A.T.A. will also donate to each state and provincial association trophies for the winners of the championships in singles, doubles, handicap, All-around and five (5) classes in either the Class or Singles Championships.

The A.T.A. will also donate trophies to the winners of the Ladies, Juniors, Sub-Juniors, Veterans, Senior Veterans Championship 16 yard events. With the sole exception of the A.T.A. State or Provincial Championship trophy, nothing shall prevent a lady, junior, sub-junior, veteran or senior veteran from winning their category trophy and any other A.T.A. State or Provincial Championship Class Trophy in the same or another event if their scores qualify them for such win. The A.T.A. State or Provincial Championship Trophy will be awarded to the Champion of the event and no other A.T.A. State or Provincial Championship Class or Special Category Trophy shall be awarded to the Champion. *However, when there are both junior and sub-junior A.T.A. trophies, the junior must take the junior trophy, and the sub-junior must take the sub-junior trophy regardless of the high score between the two of them. This rule also applies to veterans and senior veterans.* These rules should not be construed as governing trophies from other sources.

7. Championship Events At State Tournaments

The four state championships mentioned above shall be determined on the following:

Singles—200 targets
Doubles—50 pair
Handicap—100 targets
All-Around—the sum of the above, 400 targets.

Ladies, Junior, Veterans, Sub-Junior, Senior Veterans, and any other championships, not included in the five mentioned above may be determined on a lesser number of targets at the discretion of the state shoot management.

8. Zone Aids

Zone officials may determine the division of the A.T.A. added money for zone tournaments in the singles and doubles class championships and in the championship events of singles, handicap, and doubles. It shall be made available to all A.T.A. registered shooters regardless of the location unless the money is specifically restricted to zone residents at the discretion of the various A.T.A. zones and it must be so stated in the zone programs.

9. Zone A.T.A. Trophies

The A.T.A. will donate trophies to the winners of the championships in Singles, Doubles, Handicap and All-Around. The A.T.A. will also provide 5 Class trophies for Class Day and 5 Class Doubles for the Doubles Championships, and to the winners of each five classes in the Singles Championship events at each of the five A.T.A. Zone Tournaments. Trophies will be presented to lady, junior, sub-junior, veteran and senior veteran zone championships in the Singles championship event.

Nothing shall prevent a lady, junior, sub-junior, veteran, or senior veteran from winning other Championship trophies in the same event. *However, when there are both junior and sub-junior A.T.A. trophies, the junior must take the junior trophy and the sub-junior must take the sub-junior trophy regardless of the high score between them. This rule also applies to veterans and senior veterans.* Winners of Championship trophies are not eligible for class trophies in the same event.

10. Championship Events At Zone Tournaments

Zone championships shall be determined on the following:

Singles—200 targets
Doubles—50 pair
Handicap—100 targets
All-Around—the sum of the above, 400 targets

Class championships—a minimum of 100 targets (not to be shot concurrently with the Singles Championship).

Zone tournament programs shall call for a minimum of 600 registered targets.

P. Grand American Qualification

No shooter shall shoot Handicap events at the Grand American Tournament (except Veteran. Sr. Veterans. Ladies, Juniors, and Sub-Juniors) at less than 25.0 yards unless he has a minimum of 1,500 registered handicap targets recorded for that year and/or the previous two years, of which at least 500 handicap targets have been shot since October 1 of the previous year and not later than the Friday preceding the first regular day of the Grand American of the current year.

Senior Veterans, Veterans, Ladies, Juniors, and Sub-Juniors who have not met the minimum target requirements above may shoot in any Grand American Handicap event from their assigned yardage provided they forfeit all rights to trophies, options and purses.

No shooter shall shoot 16 yard events at the Grand American Tournament in less than Class A unless he has a minimum of 1,500 registered 16 yard targets recorded for that year and/or the previous two years of which at least 500 have been shot since October 1 of the previous year and not later than the Friday preceding the first regular day of the Grand American of the current year.

No shooter shall shoot doubles events at the Grand American Tournament in doubles classification less than Class A unless he has a minimum of 1,000 registered doubles targets recorded for that year and/or the previous two years, of which 500 have been shot since October 1 of the previous year and not later than the Friday preceding the first regular day of the Grand American of the current year.

It shall be the shooter's responsibility to inform the Handicap Committee as to his or her target eligibility.

Yardage earned for high score and all ties in any Grand American handicap event in the regular program (does not include preliminary events) may not be removed in part or whole by any committee action prior to the end of the Grand American Tournament the following year.

Q. Special Rules For Members Of Other Shooting Organizations

If a shooter is a member of any other trapshooting association or was a member of such association the preceding year *and* shot targets in such association in the current or preceding A.T.A. target year, he or she will shoot from the handicap yardage of whichever association shows the greater yardage.

A member who, at any time has previously been a member of another trapshooting association must shoot their last assigned yardage in that association (if it is greater) unless they have received an A.T.A. 1,000 target review and receive a yardage reduction and have not shot that associations targets for the period of time prescribed in the above paragraph.

It will be the responsibility of the shooter to notify the shoot handicap committee if he or she holds or has held a card of another trapshooting association. Failure to notify the shoot handicap committee of another trapshooting association card may cause for penalty action resulting in forfeiture of entry fees and all monies and possible suspension from all A.T.A. shoots for one year.

R. OPTIONS AND MONEY DIVISIONS

1. Added Money. No tournament promoter or other person responsible shall in any advertisement or program mention any purse or money in excess of the money actually added or guaranteed. Examples of money divisions may be included provided it is clearly stated that the amounts listed are examples and not guaranteed amounts. The word "example" must be included. Failure to observe the above provisions shall be grounds for disciplinary action by the state association and/or by the executive committee.

The A.T.A. does not guarantee and is not responsible for actual payment of added money, guaranteed money and prizes advertised or offered at any shoot except the money, prizes and trophies directly supplied by A.T.A.

2. At every registered tournament the cashier, or other official in charge, is required to post on an outside bulletin board the name of all contestants who have entered any purse, options or any other monies, with each type of entry by each contestant noted. Purses, options, etc., may be entered by and for contestants only. *Any club or cashier may deduct up to one-half (1/2) of one percent of the gross amount of purse and options to help defray costs of computations, breakage accumulated by rounding off is to be considered part of the one-half (1/2) of one percent.* All monies collected from purses, options, Lewis Class purses, guaranteed purses, or other wise shall be returned to the shooters in the same event collected with the sole exception of the one-half (1/2) of one percent mentioned immediately above and Hall of Fame contribution awards. This Rule shall not apply to any monies collected above the actual costs of any merchandise or other such prizes, *for which a separate fee is charged, and any excess monies of that type shall not be required to be returned to the shooters provided specific notification* of non-return of such monies shall be conspicuously inserted into each program where such monies will be collected.

The cashier shall have posted on the bulletin board the amount to be paid each purse or option winner. In the event payment is made by check after the shoot is over and the contestants have left the grounds, a payoff sheet for unposted events must accompany each check showing the amount paid for each individual event or option included in the payment.

Any reasonable request to inspect the cashier sheets must be honored by the shoot management. A shooter or a gun club must file a written complaint or contest any payoff or trophy award within 60 days after the competition or forfeit the right to do so.

Failure to comply strictly with this rule shall result in disciplinary action by the State Association and/or the Executive Committee.

3. Calcuttas

The A.T.A. does not condone or encourage calcuttas at any registered A.T.A. Trapshoot.

S. Payment And Overpayments

Anyone who presents a check at any shoot for fees and targets, or has or allows his or her fees and targets to be paid by such check, that is returned or dishonored for insufficient funds or any other reason, may not compete in any registered shoot until full payment has been made to the individuals or club to which it was presented; further, the provisions of Rule III,V,I,d, shall apply. Clubs receiving such a check shall report the name and address of the shooter or individual issuing the check to the A.T.A. along with a copy and a statement that the check was for registered targets and/or fees. After having been reimbursed the club MUST immediately inform the A.T.A. so that reinstatement proceedings may be initiated.

Any A.T.A. member who has been suspended for presenting a check that is returned for insufficient funds or other causes and thereafter becomes eligible for reinstatement shall be required to pay the sum of $25 to the A.T.A. as a reinstatement fee.

Any club which conducts a registered tournament should make payment of all added money, purses, optionals, and other moneys to the shooters as promptly as possible. Failure to do so within 15 days may result in the cancellation of registration privileges of that club for the remainder of the year, and no further registration shall be granted to that club until all moneys due to shooters, the A.T.A. and state organizations have been paid. The persons responsible, and/or officers of such delinquent clubs, shall be barred from shooting registered targets until such payments have been made.

Any competitor at a registered shoot, who, through error, has been overpaid on any purse, added money, optional, or other awards, and who is notified of the overpayment by registered mail, must return the overpayment within 15 days. Failure to do so shall result in disbarment from all registered shoots until payment is made.

T. Challenge And Protest

Any contestant may challenge the load of any other contestant. On receipt of a challenge the management shall obtain a shell or shells from the challenged party, and if after examination, the management finds the contestant violated the A.T.A. rule, he may be disqualified.

A protest concerning a score or scores must be made before or immediately after the close of the competition to which such scores relate. A protest may be made by a contestant.

U. Disqualification

1. A shooter may be disqualified for an event or for a whole tournament by the management.

   a. If in the opinion of the management he is disrupting the harmony of the shoot;

   b. if he shoots at any place other than the regular firing line;

   c. if he fails to shoot at the yardage assigned to him;

   d. if he fails to have his card punched for earned yardage at a prior shoot;

   e. if he behaves in an ungentlemanly or disorderly manner, such as physical or verbal abuse of shoot personnel;

   f. if he interferes with the management's procedures in conducting the shoot;

   g. if he does not respond and report to the firing line when his squad is called to shoot;

   h. if he does not abide by the rules of the A.T.A. and by the rules set out by the management and/or in the official program.

2. It is the required duty of any registered shoot management to immediately remove and disqualify any contestant who consumes alcoholic beverages while participating in any event or who is under the obvious influence of alcohol or drugs before starting any event, or who handles a gun dangerously on or off the firing line by deliberately or carelessly violating gun safety precautions thereby endangering contestants, spectators, or gun club personnel.

3. Disqualification for a single event does not prevent a contestant from participating in other events in the same tournament, and scores shot in other events are not affected.

4. If the infraction is severe the management may disqualify the contestant for the entire tournament and require him to leave the grounds.

5. Disqualification for a tournament does not prevent a shooter from participating in other tournaments.

6. All entrance monies in events not competed in as a result of disqualification are to be returned in full. Events which have been started do not qualify for refunds due to disqualification.

7. Scores shot in an event or a tournament for which a shooter is disqualified will not be registered, and any trophies or monies which the contestant has received for an event for which he is disqualified MUST be returned.

V. Suspensions, Expulsions, And Reinstatement

1. The Executive Committee may at any time at its discretion suspend any member or discipline shoot management who:

   a. Presents a check at any shoot for fees and targets, or has or allows his fees and targets to be paid by such check, that is returned or dishonored for insufficient funds or any other reason; further any person who presents such a check, more than two (2) times shall be automatically suspended for a period of one (1) year;

b. falsifies his scores;

c. fails to have his handicap card properly punched for earned yardage;

d. fails to return any overpayment after proper notification;

e. is convicted of any gun or firearms violation;

f. willfully, deliberately, or repeatedly violates the rules of the A.T.A. as contained in the Official Rules Book;

g. whose behavior constitutes causes for suspension in the opinion of the Executive Committee.

2. A member who is suspended is barred from shooting A.T.A. targets or otherwise participating in A.T.A. activities for the period of his suspension.

3. If the Executive Committee feels the violations warrant suspension for longer than one year, or expulsion, the member shall have the right of appeal if he complies with the terms and provisions of the By-Laws.

4. The procedure for suspension or disciplinary action is as follows:

a. All complaints of violations of A.T.A. rules by individuals and/or gun clubs, whether made to the A.T.A. headquarters or to any A.T.A. official, shall be immediately called to the attention of the A.T.A. state or provincial delegate representing the state in which the alleged violation occurred.

b. The delegate will then proceed to obtain such complaint in writing, specifying the exact rule(s) violated along with full details. The delegate shall make an immediate investigation and confirm, to the best of his ability, the details of the incident in question.

c. Within ten (10) days of the first notice of the complaint, and after complying with paragraph (b), above, the delegate shall serve written notice of the complaint upon the alleged violator, by certified mail, receipt requested, and require a written reply within ten (10) days of receipt. A copy of such notice of complaint shall at the same time be sent to the zone vice-president, along with a copy of the supporting file.

d. Upon receipt of any answer from the alleged violator, or if no such answer is received within ten days, the delegate shall confer with such state officers as he deems necessary, and recommend appropriate action to the zone vice-president within seven (7) days.

e. The zone vice-president, upon receipt of the delegate's recommendation(s) shall review the entire file and write his own recommendations, with supporting facts, to all members of the Executive Committee within ten (10) days.

f. All other members of the Executive Committee will, within seven (7) days, advise the A.T.A. president and their agreement or disagreement with the recommendations of the zone vice-president.

g. The A.T.A. president will then immediately cause appropriate action to be taken in accordance with the majority vote of the Executive Committee. Suspensions and/or expulsions made under this section shall conform to the applicable provisions pertaining thereto as fully set forth in the Articles of Incorporation and By-Laws of the Amateur Trapshooting Association of America.

5. Reinstatement

Any A.T.A. member who has been suspended for any cause must pay a $25 reinstatement fee when his period of suspension is completed or when, in the case of returned checks, he has reimbursed the club where the check was written.

W. Industry Personnel

Any person who (a) receives compensation for shooting or for the display or sale of the products or merchandise of any firm, company, corporation, or individual engaged in the manufacture, fabrications, importation, distribution, sale or servicing of arms, parts, ammunition, components, clay targets, or other products or services related to trapshooting or (b) received any allowance, remuneration (whether partial or total), or other consideration for attending, shooting at, or otherwise participating in trapshooting events, shall be deemed an Industry Representative upon receipt by the A.T.A. of his or her written declaration setting forth such relationship and expressing the intention to be designated an Industry Representative. No Industry Representative shall compete for money or trophies in registered events, except those events especially provided for Industry Representatives. An exception to this rule is--tournaments sponsored by Indian, fraternal or similar organization and those events clearly designated as open to both Amateurs and Industry Representatives. An Industry Representative may regain amateur standing after termination of the relationship which qualified him for designation as an Industry Representative by furnishing written certification thereof to the A.T.A. via registered or Certified Mail postpaid to the Manager, Vandalia, Ohio 45377. When he receives his new amateur card from the A.T.A., he will then be classified as an amateur.

X. Amateurs

Unless a shooter qualifies as an "industry personnel," that shooter is considered as an amateur and shall be entitled to all rights as set forth in these rules.

Y. All-America Team Requirements

	16's	HD	DBLS
Men	3000	2000	1000
Women, Juniors	2500	1500	750
Sub-Juniors, Veterans	2000	1000	500
Sr. Veterans, Industry	2000	1000	500

1. Men must have competed in at least three different states; other categories in at least two states.

2. A person's age on Monday of the Grand American determines category.

3. The proper form for team consideration may be submitted to the A.T.A. office before October 31st. This form is available at the Grand or by request from the A.T.A. office or Trap & Field.

IV
THE A.T.A. HANDICAP SYSTEM

The A.T.A. handicap system is the method whereby shooters whose ability to win has been demonstrated and shooters whose ability is unknown are handicapped by shooting a greater distance from the trap house. The minimum handicap is 17.0 yards and the maximum is 27.0 yards. A shooter's yardage is determined by rules governing new shooters, by yardage earned, or by his established handicap yardage which is based on known ability and 1,000 target reviews.

At each State or Provincial shoot the handicapping and classifying shall be the responsibility of a committee appointed by the state association with the A.T.A. delegate as chairman.

A. Central Handicap Committee

1. The Central Handicap Committee, made up of a chairman and 5 or more members, is appointed by the Executive Committee.

2. It is the responsibility of the Central Handicap Committee to control yardage of all members of the A.T.A. Any Central Handicap Committee member may increase a shooter's yardage at his discretion when applying the known ability rule. The only others authorized to increase a shooter's yardage are members of the Executive Committee.

B. Known Ability

Handicap and 16 yard averages and/or scores in both registered and non-registered shoots may be used as the basis for determining known ability. Scores abnormally low in relation to the remainder of the scores shot may be disregarded at the discretion of the handicap committee.

C. Earned Yardage

1. Yardage will be automatically earned by shooters of high scores in all A.T.A. registered events, according to the table following. This additional yardage is indicated by punches on the shooter's handicap card.

Earned Yardage Table
High Scores (and all ties)

Number of shooters	1st	2nd	3rd	4th	5th
15-24	$1/2$-yd.				
25-49	1 yd.	$1/2$-yd.			
50-124	1 yd.	$1/2$-yd.	$1/2$-yd.		
125-249	1 yd.	1 yd.	$1/2$-yd.		
250-499	$1^1/2$ yd.	1 yd.	$1/2$-yd.	$1/2$-yd.	
500-1499	2 yd.	$1^1/2$ yd.	1 yd.	$1/2$ yd.	
1500 and up	$2^1/2$ yd.	2 yd.	$1^1/2$ yd.	1 yd.	$1/2$-yd.

2. Any score of 96 will automatically earn $1/2$ yard provided it does not earn at least that much under the earned yardage table. Any score of 50x50 or 75x75 in events of that length will automatically earn $1/2$ yard provided it does not earn at least that much under the earned yardage table.

3. The State Handicap Champion will automatically earn 1 yard.

4. Any score of 97, 98 and 99 will automatically earn 1 yard, a score of 100 will automatically earn $1^1/2$ yard provided these scores do not earn at least that much under the earned yardage table.

5. The earned yardage table applies to events of 50, 75, or 100 handicap targets.

6. In case of handicap events of more than 100 targets, each 100 targets (or remaining part of 100 targets) shall constitute a separate event for earned yardage purposes and shall be reported as a separate event on the shoot report form.

7. A shooter's card will be punched from the yardage actually shot. *It is the shooter's responsibility to see that this handicap card is properly punched before shooting another handicap event. Failure to do so will make him subject to disqualification or suspension.*

8. Industry shooters or their scores shall not be counted when determining the number of shooters in an event for earned yardage purposes or in applying the earned yardage table. The number of amateurs starting the event will be the number used for the earned yardage table.

9. Any industry shooter whose score equals or exceeds that of an amateur earning yardage under the earned yardage table shall earn a like increase in yardage.

D. Penalty Yardage

The management of registered shoots may establish penalty yardage, if said conditions are printed in the program. In no event shall any shooter be assigned a handicap of less than the minimum yardage appearing on his handicap card.

E. Special Handicap Rules

1. A shooter must continue to shoot from the last yardage assigned or earned until he receives a target review, regardless of the length of time that has elapsed since that yardage was assigned or earned.

2. A shooter's handicap yardage may be reduced only as a result of 1000 target review or a special review. No reduction may be made in the field.

3. A shooter's handicap yardage may be increased at any time during the year including immediately before and during the Grand American Tournament.

   a. Because of earned yardage or;

   b. as a result of a review or;

   c. at the discretion of a member of the Central Handicap or Executive Committee.

4. A shooter at all times shall have the right to appeal any committee action to the Executive Committee.

5. Yardage earned for the high score and ties in any Grand American handicap event in the regular program (does not include preliminary events) may not be removed in part or whole by any committee action prior to the end of the Grand

American Tournament in the following year.

6. If a shooter earns increased yardage while a reduction is in process the reduction shall automatically be void.

7. When multiple 100 target handicap events (marathon) are shot in the same day, only two 100 targets events may be considered as a maximum per day towards reduction. The two events considered out of the marathon must be those two in which the two highest scores are registered.

F. Reviews

1. 1000 Target Review

The shooting record of each member will be automatically reviewed for possible yardage changes after each successive 1000 registered handicap targets shot in the current and previous year if no yardage was earned.

a. A shooter with a low purified handicap average accompanied by a relative 16 yard average will, with the approval of his state delegate, receive a one yard reduction, *except*

(1) No shooter will be reduced more than two yards in any target year.

(2) No male shooter eighteen (18) years of age or older will be handicapped below 20 yards without a special review; exceptions to this policy may be Sub-Juniors, Juniors, Veterans, Senior Veterans and ladies.

(3) The known ability rule will be used in assessing a shooter's record.

b. A shooter with a high purified handicap average will receive a "Special Review" for possible yardage increase.

c. If a yardage change is made, the shooter will receive by mail a new membership card with the new assigned yardage.

2. Special Review

A "Special Review" is an evaluation by the Central Handicap Committee generated by a high purified average on a 1000 target review or initiated by a shooter through his state delegate or the Central Handicap Committeeman. The results of a Special Review shall be agreed upon by the Central Handicap Committee and the shooter's state delegate. If after a reasonable communication, a disagreement in yardage assignment exists between the state delegate and the Central Handicap Committee, the matter may be directed to the Executive Committee. A Special Review may be used:

a. To determine possible yardage increases for shooters showing high purified handicap averages on a 1000 target review.

b. To determine possible yardage reduction for a shooter because of advancing age or physical disability. The review may be initiated by a shooter through his state delegate.

3. Assigned Yardage Increase

a. To consider appeals from increased yardage by assignment, a member may appeal an assigned yardage increase by writing to the A.T.A. office after having shot 500 targets at the assigned yardage. However, for any further reduction, 1000 additional handicap targets must be shot.

b. There will be no yardage increase by shooter request.

c. The only persons authorized to decrease or increase a member's handicap yardage are the members of the central handicap committee and the executive committee.

V
Requirements And Recommendations For Conducting A Registered Shoot

A. Application

Proper blanks, obtained from the A.T.A. (or local state secretaries) should be filled out and mailed to the state secretary for approval. If there are club dues or other obligations in your state, these must be enclosed with applications.

If the application is in order, your state secretary will approve and forward it to the A.T.A. for certification of registration.

Upon receipt of the approved application blank, the A.T.A. will issue the registration certificate, provided all conditions of application have been met and that the date requested will not conflict with the dates of a tournament granted to another club or association in close proximity. The question of close proximity is left to the judgment of the officials of the state. A record of the issuance of this certificate of registration will be kept on file in the office of the A.T.A., prior to the holding of the tournament, necessary office supplies for the proper recording of scores will be sent to the club or association. Each gun club that throws A.T.A. registered targets must have on file in the A.T.A. office a signed affidavit that the traps used meet the specifications listed in section K. The state A.T.A. Delegate is responsible for the enforcement of this rule.

B. Preparation And Programs

1. Programs should be sent to an up-to-date list of shooters. It is recommended that the total amounts of money spent on trophies be included in the program.

It is required that A.T.A. shoot programs indicate the specific amount collected on behalf of the A.T.A. and it is further required that such fees be set apart as a separate fee from all other fees and charges made by shoot management. No tournament promoter shall in any advertisement or program mention any purse or money in excess of the money actually added or guaranteed. Examples of money divisions may be included provided it is clearly stated that the amounts listed are examples and not guaranteed amounts. The word "example" must be included. Failure to observe the above provisions shall be grounds for disciplinary action by the state association and/or the Executive Committee.

The A.T.A. does not guarantee and is not responsible for actual payments of added money, guaranteed money and prizes advertised or offered at any shoot except the money, prizes and trophies directly supplied by the A.T.A.

2. The management should ascertain that the gun club facilities are in good condition prior to the shoot and that an adequate supply of such things as shells, targets, bulletin sheets, squad sheets, scoring crayons, thumb tacks, average books, change, and spare trap parts is on hand. Adequate toilet facilities should be provided for, as well as drinking water and lunch.

C. Checklist For The Shoot

1. The management should arrange for;

a. Capable classifying and handicapping committee.

b. Competent cashiers who will figure purses and options correctly and pay off as many events as possible before the close of the shoot.

c. Squadding personnel. (Note—At small shoots, all three of the above may be done by the same person or persons.)

d. Sufficient and trained trappers who are provided with a safety flag or other warning device to indicate when they are exiting from the trap house.

e. Referees who know the A.T.A. rules and whose decision on whether a target is dead or lost is final, subject to review only by the shoot committee or other governing body.

f. Scorers who have been adequately trained to call all targets, or only the lost targets as directed, and to record the scores correctly on the sheets provided.

g. Pullers who must be provided with an unobstructed view of shooters. It is illegal at an A.T.A. shoot for shooters to supply their own pullers. (Note—One person may serve as puller, scorer, and referee. If the person or persons serving in these capacities is negligent or inefficient, the management shall remove him or them.)

h. Any additional help needed to conduct the tournament efficiently, such as squad hustler, score board recorder, score sheet runners, and enough personnel to properly operate a shooting facility.

2. The management of any registered tournament, at its discretion, may reject any entry, or refund any entry. In all cases except as may be otherwise provided in these rules, the authority of the management of a registered shoot is supreme and all contestants must abide by its rulings.

3. The management shall appoint a judge or judges to be called upon for ruling on official complaints when the occasion arises. If a judge has not been appointed, the president of the club, or in his absence, the secretary shall act as judge. The scorer must call upon a judge to settle and controversy regarding a score or when he has made an error by being ahead or behind in his scoring.

The official of the A.T.A. will not change the decisions of these persons made in accordance with these rules, or change the report of any shoot held in accordance with these rules.

4. At every registered tournament all targets on the official program shall be registered. Registered scores which have been made by any contestant as a result of duplicating any portion of the regularly advertised program will not be recorded. Special events may be held and the scores registered provided that shooters have been notified of such special events by shoot management, that the special event is announced and posted, and that at least five entries shoot and compete the special event.

5. The sponsors of registered tournaments are responsible for the payment of all added money, guaranteed money, purses and/or prizes advertised or offered in their shoot programs. If the management of a registered shoot does not meet the above obligations, the A.T.A. is not responsible for such payments and will not be liable.

6. The management shall see that the cards of any shooters earning yardage are punched. If for any reason a card is not punched at the shoot, the gun club should immediately inform the A.T.A., the shooter, and the shooter's State Delegate in writing.

D. Follow Up Duties

Following the conclusion of a tournament the management is responsible or should delegate the responsibility for;

1. Completing and sending to the A.T.A. office:

a. The A.T.A. report form with complete names, addresses, A.T.A. card numbers and accurate scores of all shooters.

b. The earned yardage report.

c. Names and addresses of those paying A.T.A. dues at the shoot.

d. A check for A.T.A. daily fees collected at the shoot.

e. One copy of the official shoot program.

This must be done within 15 days following the last day of the registered shoot to avoid a $25 late shoot report fine which will be deducted from the rebate to the state in which the shoot is held.

2. Sending State fees collected to the State Association.

3. Sending a copy of the shoot report to Trap & Field.

4. Reporting shoot results to the local radio and TV stations and the local newspapers.

5. Making sure that scores are reported on any sub-events of 25 targets which is completed. In case the shooter is prevented by reasons beyond his control from completing a 25 target sub-event, the scores for that partial sub-event shall not be reported. Example, a shooter has shot 61 targets of a 100 target event when a storm permanently stops shooting. The management should report his scores on the first 50 targets only.

E. Keeping Shoot Records

The tournament management is responsible for keeping the records from all registered shoots for at least one year.

NATIONAL SKEET SHOOTING ASSOCIATION OFFICIAL RULES

SECTION I - EQUIPMENT

A. Targets

Standard targets of good quality measuring no more than four and five-sixteenth ($4^5/_{16}$) inches in diameter nor more than one and one-eighth ($1^1/_8$) inches in height shall be used.

B. Ammunition

1. Gauge Specifications—Lead shot only.

Shells commercially manufactured by reputable companies, which are clearly labeled and guaranteed as to lead shot sizes and weight are recommended for use in registered Skeet shoots. However, the National Skeet Shooting Association will accept results of shoots and register scores where reloads have been sanctioned by member clubs subject to state or regional association approval. Any shooter who will use reloads in a registered event must signify his intention to do so at time of entry. The National Skeet Shooting Association assumes no responsibility in connection with the use of reloads.

2. Checking Reloads

a. It shall be permissible for the shoot management to appoint a person, usually the chief referee, to pick a shell at random any time during each shooting event from each contestant using reloads. This shell is to be tagged with the shooter's name, witnessed by the shooter, and the shot load is to be weighed by management. If the load exceeds the maximum load permissible, as described below, the shooter's score will be disqualified. This table makes ample allowance for manufacturing purposes, but the use of a proper shot bar is cautioned (a 12- gauge bar designed for 7 1/2 shot will weigh approximately 11 grains heavy when No. 9 shot is used). Shooters are to replace shells at their own cost. No refunds will be made when a score is disqualified.

Gauge	Ounce Lead	Grains Standard	Grains Maximum
12	$1^1/_8$	492.2	507
20	$^7/_8$	382.8	394
28	$^3/_4$	328.1	338
410	$^1/_2$	218.8	229

To minimize interference with a squad, shooters should be asked to display their shells by a handful from each pocket. Further the shell selection should be made as the entire squad progresses from any station to the next station.

b. Any shooter may elect to have his shells weighed by management before entering an event. The shooter must submit all shells to be used in said event. After one shell is selected, weighed and approved by these standards, the balance of the shells shall be stamped, approved and sealed by some suitable method and not be opened until on the field where the event is to be shot in the presence of the field referee. Failure to have the field referee witness the breaking of the sealed boxes of containers on their respective fields shall necessitate the shooter using factory ammunition or having his score disqualified. Any shooter using approved and sealed ammunition shall be immune from further checking.

3. Checking Factory Loads

Any shooter found to be deliberately using commercial loads heavier than the maximum grains permissible as listed in 1-B-2a, shall have his score disqualified for that event.

4. Challenge Rule

At shoots where shells have not been checked any contestant may, upon formal challenge presented to the shoot management, have the chief referee, who shall use timely discretion, select a shell from another contestant and have said shell checked as per Section 1-B-2 or 1-B-3. To prevent abuse of a shooter with this rule, shoot management shall make known the challenger and the individual challenged. Entire groups or squads cannot be challenged for purposes of anonymity.

5. Shooters using reloads shall be required to furnish their own spares for defective ammunition.

C. Field Layout

A Skeet field shall consist of eight shooting stations arranged on a segment of a circle of twenty-one (21) yards radius, with a base chord exactly one hundred twenty (120) feet, nine (9) inches long, drawn six (6) yards from the center of the circle. The center of the circle is known as the target-crossing point and is marked by a stake. Station 1 is located at the left end of the base while standing on the periphery of the segment. Stations 2 to 6 inclusive, are relocated on the periphery at points equidistant from each other. The exact distance between Stations 1 and 2, 2 and 3, etc., is twenty-six (26) feet, eight and three-eighths ($8^3/_8$) inches. Station 8 is located at the center of the base chord.

Shooting Stations 1 and 7, each a square area, three (3) feet on a side, shall have two sides parallel to the base chord. Shooting Stations 2 to 6, inclusive, each a square area, three (3) feet on a side, shall have two sides parallel to the base chord.

Shooting Stations 2 and 6, each a square area, three (3) feet on a side, shall have two sides parallel to a radius of the circle drawn through the station marker. Shooting Station 8 is rectangular area three (3) feet wide by six (6) feet long, with the long sides parallel to the base chord. The marker for shooting station 8 is on the center point of the base chord. The location of each shooting station shall be accurately designated. The marker for shooting stations 1-7, inclusive is on the center of the side nearest the target crossing point. At Station 8 the shooter will stand on the most distant half of the 3-foot rectangular pad from the respective high or low house.

A shield should be installed at the target opening of each Skeethouse so that the Skeet operator is not visible to the shooter when he is firing at Station 8. This precaution is desirable as a safety factor for the protection of the Skeet boy from possible injury from direct or ricocheting shot. As a safety precaution there will be a barrier (wire, chain or rope) located between the shooting stations and the spectators. No spectators shall be allowed within this barrier and the referee shall be responsible for the enforcement of this rule. This barrier shall be mandatory at all state, regional and world championship shoots.

One target should emerge from a Skeethouse (called high house) at a point three (3) feet beyond the Station Marker 1 (measured along the base chord extended), and ten (10) feet above the ground level. The other should emerge from a Skeethouse (called low house) at a point three (3) feet beyond Station Marker 7 (measured along the base chord extended), and two and one-half (2 1/2) feet from the base chord extended (measure on side of the target-crossing point), and three and one-half (3 1/2) feet above the ground.

Suitable markers shall be placed at points forty-four (44) yards and sixty (60) yards from both the high house and the low house to indicate the shooting boundary limit (44 yards). These distances shall be measured along a line and the flight of a regular target (60 yards) from the opening (where target emerges) in Skeethouse through the target-crossing point. It is recommended that the 60-yard distance markers be suitably marked to indicate Station 8 ground level where possible.

The target-crossing point must be marked in a visible manner where physically possible. It is recommended to remove posts or box stands tangent to the front of the stations interfering with the shooter. Each Skeet mount at world championship sites must be approved by the Skeet manufacturers and by a NSSA appointed representative. Unusual or undesirable field variations must be corrected before contract negotiations are completed.

It is recommended and desirable that the side of the Skeethouse, from the bottom of the chute to the top of the house, be a very light color or painted white where feasible.

Mandatory Positions for Referees

For shooting Station 1 (1R), stand six feet to the right and three feet back of the front of Station 1 where possible.

For shooting Station 2 (2R), stand six feet back and three feet to the right of Station 2.

For shooting Station 3, 4, 5 and 6 (3-4-5-6R), stand six feet back and three feet to the left of the respective station.

For shooting Station 7 (7R), stand six feet to the left and three feet back of the Station 7 where possible.

For shooting Station 8 (8R) stand on center line of field, not less than 6 feet from shooter (and not more than 10 feet).

During "Doubles" shooting, as shooters are coming back around the circle, referees should stand six feet back and three feet to the right of station 5, 4, and 3.

Exception: A shooter may request the referee to move behind the station at station 3 or 5.

Recommended Positions for Shooters

It is recommended for courtesy to team members that shooters do not advance more than one-third of the way to the next shooting station until all shooters on the squad have completed the station. Furthermore, shooters should stand a minimum of six feet outside the shooting circle while waiting to shoot.

Recommended Procedure for Setting Distance on Targets

It is recommended to adjust the Skeet machine spring to a tension that will just reach the 60-yard stake, passing near dead center on the target setting hoop, under a "no wind" condition. Once this setting is made, it is unnecessary to change the spring tension during a tournament unless the spring becomes defective. The prevailing wind during a shoot may cause the targets to fall short or long, but they are legal targets providing they pass through the setting hoop.

Clubs encountering too much target breakage may set the target as short as 55 yards under "no wind" conditions and they are still legal. Weakened springs should be replaced because over-tightening can result in spring and housing breakage.

SECTION II—REGISTERED SHOOTS

A. GENERAL

1. Identification of eligible shooters

Members shall receive a new classification card as soon as possible after October 31.

a. This card will be of high quality paper and is to be used throughout the shooting year. Classification cards will be a different color each year for ease of identification. Replacement cards can be obtained from NSSA home office if lost or accidentally destroyed.

b. Presentation of a classification card, indicating a member's shooting record and paid-up membership status, and plastic NSSA membership card is required for entry in a registered shoot.

c. Classification for the beginning of the year shall be indicated in the appropriate place on each classification-shoot record card.

d. These cards also shall contain columns in which the holders are to keep their up-to-date running averages posted for each gun.

2. Qualifications and Responsibilities

a. Club

(1) Only clubs affiliated with the NSSA with affiliation fees currently paid up for the year concerned shall be eligible to conduct registered shoots. Evidence of club's status in this regard must be displayed in the form of official

NSSA membership certificate for the appropriate year. Only clubs also affiliated and in good standing with their state or territorial association will be permitted to hold registered shoots in areas where such associations are active.

(2) Where state territorial associations exist, application for a registered shoot must be made through those bodies, which in turn, after giving approval, will submit application to the NSSA, which will issue proper certification and supplies on which to report scores, winners and make financial report. Where an area association does not exist, clubs will make application directly to the NSSA. The application form furnished by the NSSA shall include the number of targets in each event and may not be altered without 10 days notice. Shoot applications, properly sanctioned, must be postmarked or received by NSSA at least 10 days prior to the shoot date. Open shoots should be advertised to a majority of local contestants, and closed club shoots posted a minimum of seven days prior to the shoot date. Failure to advertise may result in a disqualification of shoot scores. Exception may, however, be granted by the Executive Director on merit.

(3) It shall be the responsibility of the management of the club, association or other organization granted a certificate of registration, to see that each shoot is conducted in accordance with the official rules of the NSSA.

(4) The group or club sponsoring the shoot shall check the NSSA membership of each shooter before accepting his entry and shall be responsible for the annual dues if they allow a participant to shoot when said participant's membership in NSSA has expired. All individual shooters in all registered shoots must be members in good standing of the NSSA. It shall be the responsibility of the club holding registered shoot to check cards of all participants and enforce this rule rigidly. Management will be billed by NSSA in all cases where expired members are allowed to shoot. Management may seek reimbursement from said shooters.

(5) Management shall check the shooter's classification card to ascertain the proper classification in which he should compete and enter the shooter's classification card the classification in which it is entering him in each gun.

(6) Class winners must be reported if they are to be reported in the magazine.

(7) Scores shot in shoots on which complete records are not made by shoot management will not be recorded and the national association shall not be liable to refund fees received in such cases.

(8) It is the shoot management's responsibility to appoint a chief referee.

(9) Registered shooting at night is permissible. Applications for night registered shoots by clubs must designate on the face of the application that it will be night shoot and all promotion by club shall clearly indicate that it is a night shoot. All scores for night registered shoots will receive the same treatment as any other registered shoot. Participants in night registered shoots must accept the conditions at the club where the shoot is held and no protest concerning shooting conditions, i.e., light conditions, natural or artificial, etc., will be allowed. At night registered shoots, white targets must be used.

(10) In the interest in safety, interference and time, only the club management's personnel shall be permitted to pick up empty shells from the grounds during a registered shoot, and extreme care must be exercised to prevent interference with other squads shooting.

(11) Shoot management shall determine the number of targets to be shot on a field. When shooting background is fairly uniform, it saves time to shoot 50 or 100 on the same field.

(12) Shoot management has the right to determine the rotation and shooting sequence of events, in their program, as well as shooting mixed guns in squads, unless their state association rules otherwise.

(13) All two-man and five-man events must be limited to club teams unless management exercises their prerogative of holding open or state team events duly announced in the program, or posted prior to acceptance of the first entry.

b. Individuals

(1) Residents of a state or territory must be members in good standing of their own state or territorial association before they can register targets shot in that state.

(2) It shall be the sole responsibility of the shooters to see that they entered into all the events desired. The official cashier sheet/entry form must be used. Once entered, clerical errors are the responsibility of shoot management.

(3) Each shooter must verify his score and initial the official score sheet before leaving each field or accept it as the record. It shall be the responsibility of every shooter to enter in his proper class or classes at each shoot, including advancing himself in class when required by the rules based on averages at the completion of the regular string.

(4) A shooter who fails to keep all of his correct scores posted on his card and shoots in a lower class than the one in which his record places him shall forfeit any winnings earned while shooting in the wrong class for the first offense, and for the second offense shall forfeit all winnings and also be disbarred from registered competition for one year.

A shooter winning trophies or money by shooting in a lower class than the one in which he was entitled to shoot must return his winnings within 15 days after notification by NSSA headquarters that said winnings must be returned. Failure to comply within this 15-day period shall subject the shooter to suspension as an NSSA member and permanent disbarment from registered competition.

A shooter who enters, or allows himself to be entered in an event or class lower than the class in which he was entitled to shoot forfeits all rights to any trophies or purses he would have earned shooting in his proper class unless the mistake is corrected prior to the distribution of such trophies or purse money.

(5) It is the responsibility of the shooter to see that his safety is off and his gun is properly loaded with unfired shells of proper size and load before calling for a target (for safety purposes).

3. *Shooting Order*

The management shall determine the shooting order of the individuals in each squad at the beginning of the round, and the shooters shall adhere to this order.

If the order is changed during any succeeding round of the same event, each squad member shall be responsible that his name be in the proper order on the respective score sheet, and that the change be plainly indicated for the attention of the final recorder.

Each squad shall report to the field at its appointed time. Upon failure of a shooter to appear at the appointed time, where a regular schedule has been posted in advance, or after proper call, the squad shall proceed without the absent shooter and the offender be dropped to the first vacancy in the schedule, or if there is no vacancy, to the bottom of the list. Weather conditions shall not be deemed sufficient excuse for delay in taking the field or proceeding with the round, unless all shooting has been officially suspended at the discretion of the management.

4. *Squadding Restrictions*

The squadding or practice shooting in a registered event shall not be allowed. Violations of this rule shall be sufficient cause for non-registration of all scores in the squad.

Exception: If there should be a single entry in the last squad of any event, shoot management may allow no more than two additional shooters to shoot for practice, but only if requested to do so by the lone entry and said last squad. Pacer for lone participant on a field in shootoff shall not be permitted.

5. *Checks—Payments, over-payments*

Anyone who presents a check at any shoot that is returned for insufficient funds or other causes, may not compete in any registered shoot until full payment has been made to the individual or club to which it was presented. Any club receiving such a check shall report name and address of the shooter issuing the check to the NSSA and to its own state, territorial or district association.

Any competitor at a registered shoot who, through error, has been overpaid on any purse, added money, optional or other prize money and who is notified of the over-payment by registered mail, must return the over-payment within fifteen days. Failure to do so shall result in disbarment from all registered shoots until repayment is made.

B. Standard Event Specification

For the purpose of uniformity in records, averages, etc., the following provisions shall apply to all shoots registered or sanctioned by the NSSA.

1. *Gauge Specifications*

12 gauge events shall be open to all guns of 12 gauge or smaller, using shot loads not exceeding one and one-eighth ($1^1/_8$) ounces. Twenty gauge events shall be open to all guns of 20 gauge or smaller, using shot loads not exceeding seven-eighths ($7/_8$) of an ounce. Twenty-eight gauge events shall be open to all guns of 28 gauge or smaller, using shot loads not exceeding three-quarters ($3/_4$) of an ounce and .410 gauge guns using shot loads not exceeding one-half ($1/_2$) ounce. A gun of larger gauge, which has been converted to take a smaller gauge shell may be used in an event for which it has been converted providing that the shell itself complies with the rules requirements for that event. No shot smaller than No. 9 (2mm) shall be used in any load.

2. *Concurrent Events*

a. Events designated for veterans, seniors, sub-seniors, sub-sub seniors, women, juniors, sub-juniors, military service, two-man team or five-man team, may be shot concurrently with the corresponding event on the regular program, or separately, at the discretion of the management.

b. No junior, sub-junior or collegiate shall be required to pay any part of entry fee that is to be returned to the shooters in the form of money, including open purses and concurrent purses, but not to include team events if the involved junior, sub-junior or collegiate is shooting as part of an open team.

3. *All-around Titles*

All-around titles must be an aggregate of all gauges offered in that registered tournament (special events such as preliminary events, Champion of Champions, etc., not to be included) and will officially be recognized by the NSSA only when they include championships, or title events in at least three of the four standard gauges and load divisions defined in paragraph No. 1 above and a total of at least 200 targets. Provided that the foregoing shall not be deemed to forbid local awards of special prizes for events of combinations not recognized.

4. *Minimum Number of Targets*

No event of less than fifty (50) targets shall be designated as a championship or title event.

5. *Open Shoot Registration*

The term "open," as it may appear in any application for registration or sanction, or in the shoot program, if any, shall be deemed to mean "open to NSSA members without regard to residence."

6. *Method of Breaking Ties*

In all registered NSSA tournaments, ties shall be decided in a uniform manner as prescribed in the following paragraph unless the shoot management gives due notice of any deviation in its published shoot programs, or unless in the absence of a shoot program the shoot management post conspicuous notice of deviation at the place of registration, thus informing all shooters of deviation, before accepting entry fees.

a. All ties for championship titles, such as event champion, two-man and five-man teams, veterans, seniors, sub-seniors, women, juniors, junior women, military, or any other concurrent title designated by the management , must be shot off by "miss-and-out" (sudden death). Where the same individuals are tied for concurrent titles, such as event champion and senior champion, only one shootoff will be held to determine both titles, unless the shoot management announced in advance of the first shootoff that separate shootoffs will be held. Management may combine other shootoffs only by approval of all the individuals involved in same.

b. After determining the position of all persons involved in shootoffs, all other awards shall be decided on the basis of the longest run in the event, forward beginning with the first target shot at or backward beginning with the last target shot at (whichever is longest). If long runs are tied, the long run from the opposite end shall be used to break the tie. If long runs are still tied, "miss-and-out" shootoffs must decide.

c. Long runs for team scores shall be the total of targets broken by the members of the team combined up to the first miss by any member of the team; or the total number of targets broken by all members of the team after the last miss by any member of the team, whichever run is longest.

d. All ties for all-around championship must be decided by a miss-and-out shootoff commencing with the smallest gauge gun of which the all-around score is comprised. If a tie remains after this round, then the next larger gauge shall be employed for the next round. If a tie remains after all gauges have been employed, the shootoff shall revert back to the smallest gauge.

e. All other ties for all-around awards shall be decided on the basis of the longest run from front or rear (whichever is longest) in the smallest gauge event. If this also results in a tie, the same method shall be applied to the next larger gauge until the tie is broken.

f. Shootoffs take precedence over long runs, so all persons competing in a shootoff must continue to shoot off for all places beneath the event championship for which they may be tied.

7. *NSSA Rules for Procedure for Shootoffs*
NSSA rules shall apply subject to the following:

a. Shoot management may elect to use regular Skeet or a doubles event and shall follow NSSA rules for whichever event elected.

b. In employing doubles for shootoffs a fifty (50) target event is not required. Further, shoot management may elect "miss-and-out" or full round total score for doubles shootoffs.

c. In shooting using total score of a complete round, the shooter with the highest score shall be determined the winner. Tied high scores must continue to shoot complete rounds until the tie is broken and the winners determined. Lesser place winners shall be decided by the highest scores and if a tie exists, long run from the front shall determine these winners, if still tied, continue to shoot until the tie is broken.

d. In "miss-and-out" shootoffs, long run from the front shall determine the winners. Ties shall continue to shoot the round until the tie is broken.

e. For Two and Five-Man Team Shootoff management may combine or separate teams for shootoffs; and

(1) If "miss-and-out," team winners shall be determined by the full team shooting until the first miss and comparing this long run with other squads involved. Any squads tied with long runs shall continue to shoot their rounds until the tie is broken.

(2) If "total score," the total of the team scores shall determine the winner.

f. Shoot management shall post notice of time of shootoff as soon as possible during each event and shall also announce same by public address system if possible.

g. Contestants involved in shootoffs forfeit all rights to the shootoff if absent or if they do not report within five minutes of the time the shootoff is called. However, any such person shall be entitled to any award he would have won by finishing last in the shootoff. It shall be the shooter's sole responsibility to determine the time of the shootoff before leaving the grounds. Shootoffs may not be held prior to the completion of an event (registration for the event has closed and no possible ties or winners left on the field) or of events of that day unless all parties involved agree.

h. If completion of a shootoff is prevented by darkness, as defined in Section IV-C, the management and the contestants concerned shall determine the champion by a mutually agreeable method, but if no mutually agreeable method can be decided upon, then the shoot management shall determine in what manner the ties shall be decided. Management should make every effort to schedule the last squad of the day early enough to permit normal shootoffs.

i. If shooters involved in a shootoff offer management a mutually agreed upon method of determining the places, management may accept. If management does not accept, shootoffs must continue and any shooter or shooters who refuse to continue forfeit as in paragraph "g" above.

Declaring of event co-champions at the world championships shall not be permitted. Contestants must continue to shoot or forfeit.

j. The shooting order for shootoffs shall be the sequence of finishing the event, where possible, and each lead-off man shall be dropped to last position on subsequent rounds.

k. Where shootoffs are held under lights it shall be compulsory to use white targets.

l. A shooter involved in a shootoff with a broken gun shall be allowed a ten minute time limit to repair or replace a broken gun, and then continue in the shootoff.

8. *Concurrent Event Awards*
Any shooter charged an entry fee for a regular event and an additional entry fee for a concurrent event shall be eligible to win in both events unless clearly stipulated in the written program.

9. *High Gun System*
In explanation of the high gun system: If, for example, in a class, three shooters should tie for high score and two tie for a second high score, the top three scorers would divide the monies for first, second and third places, and the two tying

for second high score would divide the monies for fourth and fifth places.

C. Eligibility

1. Individuals

a. Before participating in any events for money prizes, all shooters are warned of the following official rules:

The United States Olympic Association and the Amateur athletic Union both consider everyone who shoots for any money a professional and ineligible for all forms of athletic competition under their jurisdiction. The National Athletic Association has ruled that shooting for money does not impair eligibility of the shooter to participant in other sports conducted under its jurisdiction. Under the rules of the National Federation of State High School Associations, the problem is left up to the individual member state association, some of which will permit shooting for money. (Parents of prep school students are urged to ascertain the position of their own state association.) Entries of minors in money events will be accepted only with the written consent of their parents or guardians. This written consent must be given to the NSSA and the scoreboard must carry the signatures of compliance.

b. No junior, sub-junior or collegiate shall be required to pay any part of any entry fee that is to be returned to the shooter in the form of money.

c. All competitors must be members of NSSA in good standing, with current dues paid up.

d. A sub-junior is any boy or girl who has not reached his or her fourteenth (14) birthday.

e. A junior is any boy or girl who has not reached his or her eighteenth (18) birthday.

f. A collegiate shooter shall be defined as a full-time undergraduate student in an accredited degree oriented learning institution up to a maximum of four (4) years eligibility. A shooter is eligible to compete as a collegiate shooter prior to his freshman year as long as he produces a letter of acceptance from a degree oriented learning institution for one time only.

g. A sub-sub-senior is any man or woman who has reached his or her fortieth (40) birthday.

h. A sub-senior is any man or woman who has reached his or her fiftieth (50) birthday.

i. A senior is any man or woman who has reached his or her sixtieth (60) birthday.

j. A veteran is any man or woman who has reached his or her seventieth (70) birthday.

k. Any employee of an arms, target and/or ammunition company who services registered shoots in his assigned area at the direction of his superiors and whose job is to further the sales of his company's products and who is compensated for his shooting, traveling and entertaining expenses by his company, shall be considered a professional and not eligible for amateur competition. Questionable cases shall be decided by management of the company involved.

Ex-professionals are eligible to enter registered competition as amateurs 90 days after applying to NSSA with proof of job separation, provided such application is approved by the Executive Committee.

l. No contestant shall be eligible for more than one concurrent event based on age.

m. Where shoot programs offer special concurrent events based upon age, shooters entering such special events must shoot in the one for which they are qualifies by age, if such a class is available. Example: Seniors cannot enter as sub-seniors if a senior event is offered. A shooter's age at the start of a program shall determine his eligibility to enter events based on age for the entire program.

n. In parent and child events, unless specifically stated otherwise in the shoot program, the child must be of junior or sub-junior eligibility age.

o. Neither state champions nor provincial champions will be recognized by NSSA unless sanctioned by state organization, or provincial organization, recognized with proper by-laws on record at NSSA.

p. An individual must be a bonafide resident (permanent abode) of a state to be eligible for state championships or to shoot as a state team member. Persons with residence in more than one state must declare their eligibility by writing their state and club affiliation on the face of their current year membership. Servicemen, by the same act, may choose their home state or the state in which they are permanently assigned for duty.

Persons who change their official abode shall become immediately eligible to shoot as individuals in the state shoot. They should contact NSSA for new membership cards reflecting change of address and present same before entering shoot.

q. No person shall be eligible for state competition in more than one state in the current year (from November 1 of one year through October 31 of the following year).

r. Shooters entering AAA class at the world championship must have earned that distinction by average, and are not permitted to declare into the class.

2. Five-Man and Two-Man Club Teams (definition)

a. A five-man team shall consist of five (5) individuals.

b. Team members must have been fully paid members of the club they represent for a period of at least ninety (90) days prior to the date of the shoot (honorary, inactive, non-resident members, or members whose dues or assessments are in arrears are not eligible).

Such team members shall be accredited by the NSSA to the state in which they reside, but irrespective of residence, they may shoot as a five-man team for one club and one club only. They shall not be eligible to shoot for any state championships except in the state in which they reside. Such team members must be certified by the management of such club as having been active shooters at the club for a minimum period of ninety (90) days before they are eligible to shoot for that club. A shooter who shoots on one club team, either two-man or five-man, shall by that act elect that club as the only club he shall represent in club team events during the current year.

No person shall reside more than 100 miles from the club he represents unless he resides in the same state in which the club he represents is located.

Exception: Privately operated clubs, which require no paid membership, may with the approval of the NSSA be represented by either two-man or five-man teams if the members of such teams meet all the other requirements except those applying to club dues and club membership. This rule shall apply to two-man competition.

c. Team members must not have represented any other club in a team event in any NSSA registered shoot at any time during the current year.

Exception: Service personnel who have, within this period, shot on teams sponsored by military organizations, such as division teams representing specific departments of the same branch of service, and have been required to do so as a duty assignment, may immediately shoot on teams representing individual military clubs, providing that said former teams have been definitely disbanded and also providing that they have been members in good standing of the clubs they are about to represent for a period of at least 90 days prior to the shoot.

d. Be members in good standing of the NSSA with current dues paid up.

e. The club represented must be affiliated and in good standing with the NSSA with dues currently paid up.

f. State Championship Team Events. Any out of state team whose membership complies with state residence requirements and Rule II-C-2b, may enter club team events but may be subject to a surcharge at the discretion of the state association.

3. State Five-Man and Two-Man Teams (definition)

a. A state team shall consist of five (5) individuals, each of whom is a member in good standing of the NSSA. Each member of a state team must be domiciled in the same state for at least three (3) months immediately prior to the date of the shoot.

b. State teams may shoot in national competition, or in state shoots if approved by the state organization.

4. Open Five-Man and Two-Man Teams (definition)

An open team is one which is composed of members with no restriction as to club or domicile. Records established by open teams shall not be accepted to establish official records.

5. Team Representation

a. No individual may shoot on more than one team representing the same or any other club in any one event.The members of a team must be designated before the team begins the event.

b. Each five-man club team and state team shall designate a team captain who shall be the team representative.

c. At the completion of each round, the shooters shall view their respective scores and initial them.However, in the case of team shooting, the captain of the team may assume the responsibility for the shooters and sign for his entire squad.

6. Two-Man Teams (definition)

a. All the foregoing eligibility provisions of individual, five-man club teams, state teams and open team representative shall govern in two-man competition.

b. No individual may shoot on or be a member of more than one team in any two-man event, except in re-entry events, where the program states that it is permissible.

7. NSSA World Championship Five-Man Teams

a. In the NSSA World Championships all members of a five-man team will shoot in the same squad through that particular event. If any team member fails to finish with his proper squad for any reason whatsoever, the team shall be disqualified as such but not the members as individual contestants.

b. Under no circumstances, however will the provisions on broken gun and shooting up affect the requirement of shooting shoulder-to-shoulder throughout five-man team competition at the NSSA World Championships.

c. In shoots other than the NSSA Championships, the management may deviate from this rule if they deem it to be advisable to conduct five-man teams in more than one squad. For convenience in tabulating team scores, it is more desirable to keep a five-man team in one squad.

8. Exceptions to Domicile and Club Membership Team Requirements.

The provisions of domicile and club membership of individuals on two-man teams and five-man (club) teams do not apply to:

a. Shooters who have affected a bonafide change in place of domicile with resultant change in club membership affiliation.

b. Clubs organized within less than 90 days prior to the date of the shoot, provided that members representing such clubs comply with Section II-C-2c.

c. New members of any club who have never previously fired in a team event in an NSSA registered shoot.

d. Former members of college teams and school teams and school teams who have become members of senior clubs after their graduation.

9. Armed Forces Team Representation

For team representation the domicile of members on active duty with the Army, Navy, Air Force and other military establishments shall be defined as the place at which they are stationed by reason of proper orders. Retired, reserve, or National Guard personnel are not eligible for service team membership unless on active duty for a period in excess of 90 days.

10. Two-Man and Five-Man Team Squadding

Two-man teams may shoot in separate squads, but five-man club teams and five-man state teams must shoot shoulder-to-shoulder, unless management published otherwise in their program or same is posted prior to accepting the first entry.

11. The spirit and intent of these rules shall be taken to be, to include all bonafide teams properly organized in pursuance of club and/or domicile requirements, and to exclude all teams of makeshift or pick-up character, organized on the grounds and seeking to take advantage of technicalities either herein or in program stipulations or omissions.

D. Protests

1. *A shooter may protest:*

a. If in his opinion the rules as herein stated have been improperly applied.

b. The conditions under which another shooter has been permitted to shoot.

c. Where he feels an error has been made in the compilation of a score.

2. *How to protest*

A protest shall be initiated immediately when it is possible to do so upon the occurrence of the protested incident. No protest may be initiated by the shooter involved after thirty (30) minutes shall have elapsed after the occurrence of the incident for which a protest is desired to be made. Failure to comply with the following procedure will automatically void the protest.

A protest involving the scoring of a target, if filed immediately on the station, second shot, or shots will be fired and the results recorded and noted as a protest. The protest shall proceed in the prescribed manner.

a. State the complaint verbally to the chief referee. If not satisfied with his decision, then:

b. File with the shoot management a protest in writing, stating all the facts in the case. Such protest must be filed within 12 hours after the occurrence of the protested incident. If not satisfied with the decision of the shoot management, then:

c. File with the NSSA a written appeal, stating all the facts. Such appeal must be filed within 12 hours after the decision of the shoot management has been made known to the shooter. Protests in team events must be made by the team captain. Team members who believe that have reason to protest will state the facts to their team captain, who will make the protest if he feels such action justified by the facts. The shoot management may appoint a shoot judge to handle protests to it which have been handled in the manner stated above.

E. Disqualification and Expulsion

The shoot management shall upon proper evidence:

1. Disqualify any shooter for the remainder of the shoot program for willful or repeated violation of gun safety precautions which endanger the safety of shooters, field personnel and/or spectators.

2. Elect to refuse the entry or cause the withdrawal of any contestant whose conduct in the opinion of the shoot management is unsportsmanlike or whose participation is in any way detrimental to the best interests of the shoot.

3. Any shooter may be disqualified from a shoot for misrepresentation of his status under the eligibility rules.

4. Expel any shooter physically assaulting a referee or any shooter using extreme, abusive language to a referee upon adequate evidence presented by the chief referee.

5. The shoot management shall report to the NSSA all cases of disqualification and expulsion and the reasons for same. Subsequent action by the Executive Committee could result in being expelled and barred from further membership in the NSSA.

F. Official Scores

1. All scores of records, to be recognized as official, must be shot under the official NSSA rules.

2. All scores shall be recorded as having been shot with the gun in which event they are shot, i.e., scores shot with a 20 gauge gun in a 12 gauge event must be recorded as 12 gauge scores. Such scores may not be included as part of a 20 gauge long run or average.

3. Only the scores shot on scheduled dates, approved by NSSA, shall be registered. Scores made in shoot-offs shall not be registered, however, all NSSA rules shall apply in shoot-offs.

4. No shooter will be permitted to enter an event more than once, even though his score has been disqualified.

5. The scores of any shooter who takes part in a registered shoot shall be considered official, and shall be registered with the NSSA even though the shooter had given notice that it was not his intention to have his score recorded.

6. While the management may refund the entry fees and permit withdrawal of shooters who would be required to compete under drastically changed and clearly intolerable weather conditions or darkness not confronted by a majority of participants in an event, scores of all shooters who do participate must be recorded. In the event of extreme weather conditions, power failure, trap failure, or unusually early darkness, the shoot management may elect to continue the event some other time (i.e.,the next morning or the following weekend), but must immediately notify NSSA, with full explanation, who will sanction the change, provided it is deemed in the best interest of Skeet.

7. When a contestant stops or withdraws without finishing an event in which he has started, his partial scores shall be reported to the NSSA along with the other scores of the event.

8. If a contestant stops or withdraws voluntarily, or after disqualification by the management, his partial score for the round in which he is shooting shall be entered as his score of targets broken for that full round of twenty-five (25) targets. He shall not be penalized, however, for any of the remaining full rounds of that particular event. Where such withdrawal is the result of sickness or injury, the shooter withdrawing shall be charged only with the targets actually fired upon in compiling and reporting his score.

9. Reporting Requirements

a. It is the duty of each club or association holding a registered shoot to promptly:

(1) Make payments of all money, purses and optionals to the shooters; and

(2) Submit fees and reports due to its state association;

(3) Send all required reports and fees, along with membership applications and dues, to the NSSA.

b. The above reports must be postmarked no later than fifteen (15) days following the last day of the shoot. Failure to fulfill these obligations shall carry the following penalties.

(1) Cancellation of all subsequent shoot dates for the offending club or association.

(2) Denial of right to apply or re-apply for any further registered shoot dates for a period of thirty (30) days in the case of first offense, or ninety (90) days in the case of second or subsequent offense or until obligations have been met.

(3) Officers of any delinquent club or association shall be barred from shooting registered targets until all required obligations of said club or association are met to the shooters, to the state association and NSSA.

10. *Shoot/Financial Reports*

All shoot reports must be made on standard forms furnished by NSSA. Financial report must include:

a. NSSA daily fees collected at two (2) cents per target shot, and

b. NSSA dues collected. Duplicate copies of all membership receipts of all types sold must be attached to financial report and must be completely and legibly filled out, including full name and complete accurate mailing address of purchaser. (Shooter buying membership receives original receipt.)

11. Official entry form/cashier sheet must contain legible full names or initials corresponding to their NSSA membership cards, the city and state of their residence and their complete scores. NSSA membership numbers of all participants must be given. This is all included on membership card. All trophy winners with full names, towns and scores must be listed in appropriate spaces on individual form.

12. The shoot management is responsible to see that each squad's scores are posted on the score board, preferably by the referee, when feasible, or by an official score man, within 30 minutes of the time the squad finishes shooting.

G. High Average Leaders

1. Minimum requirements

a. For the purpose of determining yearly champions on the basis of average alone, leaders will be recognized if they have shot the following minimum requirements of registered targets:

	.410	28	20	12
	700	700	800	1200
sub-junior	400	400	500	700

b. Candidates for All-American selection must have shot the above minimum targets.

2. Long Runs

a. Long runs in an event shall be figured forward from beginning with the first target shot at, or backwards beginning with the last target shot at, whichever is longest, and the optional shot shall be counted in the proper sequence where it was fired.

b. Only scores shot in registered events shall be included in official long runs. Scores shot with a smaller gun than the one for which the event is scheduled shall not be accredited as part of a long run with the smaller gun.

c. Shoot-off targets and other non-registered targets shall be not counted as part of a long run.

d. All long runs shall be compiled in the order in which the scoring appears on the official score sheets except the optional shot shall be counted in the proper sequence where it was fired. The sequence in which the official score sheets are posted must coincide with the sequence in which the scores were broken.

3. High All-Around Averages

For purposes of determining the yearly all-around averages, the following formula should be used:

.410 gauge average X 25% = _____%
28 gauge average X 25% = _____%
20 gauge average X 25% = _____%
12 gauge average X 25% = _____%

4. Average for age groups

A shooter's age on May 1 (halfway mark of the 12-month Skeet year) shall determine his eligibility for high average consideration on all targets shot that season in any category based on age. Example: If a shooter is still a junior on May 1, his whole average for that season shall be considered his average as a junior. However, the day he is age 18, he loses his eligibility to compete in junior events. Likewise, a shooter becomes eligible for sub-junior competition on the date he attains 40; a sub-senior, 50; a senior, 60; a veteran, 70.

H. Registered Shoot Reports

Two reports must be made on all registered shoots. Use forms provided by NSSA.

1. Financial report

List number of targets shot each day of shoot and remit to NSSA a daily registration fee of .02 per target.

Remittance and copies of receipts of all types of NSSA memberships sold must be attached.

2. Registered target official report

An individual entry form score sheet must be submitted on every shooter. This report must include number of targets shot at, broke, and class shot in or declared in. Complete information on N/C shooters must be included.

Regardless of what method was used in making awards, winners must be determined and reported under NSSA classification system. This applies even if no awards are made. Do not list winners above class champions unless such awards were made.

3. Clubs are required to deliver or mail a copy of the official shoot reports to the shooter. They are however, required to retain copies of the scoreboard and/or field score sheets on file for 90 days after the end of the applicable shooting year.

SECTION III—SHOOTING PROCEDURE

A. Definitions

1. Shooting Position
Standing with any part of both feet within the boundaries of the shooting station.

2. Gun Position
Any position which is safe and comfortable to the shooter.

3. No Bird
Any target thrown for which no score is recorded, or failure of a target to be thrown with the prescribed time limit of one second. This permits the throwing of instant targets, but gives a short time period in order to prevent a contestant from refusing a target which does not appear immediately after his call. If a shooter fires upon a target which appears after one second has elapsed his call and the emergence of the target, and also before the referee calls "no bird" provided he, in his sole judgment, decides that they delay the exceeded one second time allowance. The pull is not required to be instantaneous.

4. Interference
a. Any circumstance beyond the shooter's control which unduly affects opportunity to break any particular target.
b. The sun shall not be considered as interference. It must be accepted as a normal hazard.

5. Regular Target
A regular target is one that appears after the shooter's call and within a period not to exceed one (1) second and which passes within a three-foot circle centered at a point fifteen (15) feet above the target crossing point. The target crossing point shall be measured from the level of Station 8. (This target, in still air, must carry to a distance equivalent, on level ground, to fifty-five (55) yards, from the Skeet house, but must not exceed sixty-five (65) yards.)

6. Irregular Target
a. An unbroken target that has not conformed to the definition of a regular target.
b. Two targets thrown simultaneously in singles.
c. Target thrown broken. Under no circumstances shall the result of firing upon a broken target shall be scored.

7. Regular Double
A regular target thrown from each Skeet house simultaneously.

8. Irregular Double
Either of both targets of a thrown double as irregular targets or only one target is thrown.

9. Proof Double
A repeat of a double.

10. Shooting Bounds
For Stations 1 to 7, inclusive, an area of forty-four (44) yards in front of the Skeet house from which the target is thrown. For Station 8, the distance from the Skeet house to a point directly over a line with Station 4, 8, and the target crossing point.

11. Balk
Failure to shoot at a regular target or double.

12. Malfunction of Gun
Failure of gun to operate or function through no fault of the shooter.

13. Defective Ammunition
Failure of ammunition to fire or function properly, i.e., failure to fire, provided firing pin indentation is clearly noticeable or firing of the primer only, where powder charge has been omitted or not ignited, which is characterized by a very weak report and absence of any noticeable recoil. Components of the load remaining in barrel shall be considered as evidence of but not a requirement. Wrong size shells, empty shells and bloopers shall not be considered defective ammunition.

14. Blooper
Term used to describe an unusual burning of powder when a shell is fired, and is distinguished by a louder then normal booming report. Usually occurs in reloads and caused by tilting of the over-powder wad, incorrect pressures, or overload of powder. This cannot be considered defective ammunition.

15. Dead Target
A target from which in the sole judgment of the referee a visible piece is broken as a result of having been fired upon.

16. Lost Target
A target from which in the sole judgment of the referee no visible piece is broken as a result of having been fired upon.

17. Optional Shot
The shot fired after the first 24 targets have been scored dead in any one round (Station 8 low house only); or fired following the shooter's first lost target. In the latter instance it must be fired from the same station and at the same house as the first one missed.

18. Skeet Squad
a. A normal Skeet squad is composed of five shooters.
b. Any five (5) shooters may designate themselves as a squad. All other shooters shall be formed into squads of five (5) shooters each, as nearly as possible. Less than five (5) is permissible for expediency, but more than six (6) should not be squadded for safety reasons.

19. Round of Skeet
A round of Skeet for one person consists of twenty-five (25) shots, the object being to score the greatest number of dead targets. Twenty-four shots are fired as described in III-B-1. The first shot scored lost in any round will be repeated immediately and the result scored as the twenty-fifth shot. Should the first shot "lost" occur in a double, the lost target shall be repeated as a single with the result of this shot scored as the twenty- fifth (25) shot.

If the first shot "lost" should be the first target of an irregular double, then a proof double shall be fired upon to determine the result of the second shot, and then the first target scored "lost" shall be repeated as a single and scored as the twenty-fifth (25) target.

Should the first twenty-four (24) targets of a round be scored "dead," the shooter shall take his optional target at low house eight only.

20. Shooting Up

The procedure of a late shooter shooting out of turn to catch up with his squad. (III-B-6)

B. General

1. Squad shooting procedure for a round of Skeet.

A squad shall start shooting at Station 1 in the order in which the names appear on the score sheet. The first shooter shall start shooting singles at Station 1, shooting the high house target first and the low house target second. The first shot scored lost in the round shall be repeated immediately as his optional shot. Then, loading two shells, he shall proceed to shoot doubles shooting the first shot at the target from the nearest Skeet house and the second shot at the target from the farthest Skeet house before leaving the station. The second shooter shall then proceed likewise followed by the other members of the squad in their turn. Then the squad shall proceed to Station 2 and repeat the same sequence as on Station 1. The squad shall then proceed to Station 3 where each shooter will shoot at a high house single target first and low house single target before leaving the shooting station. The same procedure shall be followed at Stations 4 and 5.

Upon advancing to Station 6 the lead-off shooter will shoot singles in the same sequence as at the previous stations. Then, loading two shells he shall shoot doubles by shooting at the low house target first and the high house target second before leaving the station. The other shooters will follow in their turn.

The same procedure will be followed on Station 7.

The squad will then advance to Station 8 where each shooter shall shoot at a target from the high house before any member of the squad shoots at a target from the low house. The squad shall then turn to Station 8 low house and the lead-off shooter will shoot at the low house target. The shooter shall repeat the low house for his optional shot before leaving the station, provided he is still straight (no lost targets in the round), the other shooters will follow in turn. At this time the shooter should verify his own score.

2. Rules and Procedures for Doubles Events

a. No less than a fifty (50) target event.

b. Shooting commences at Station 1 and continues through 7 backwards from 6 through 5, 4, 3, and 2. Rounds two and four will end with doubles on Station 1 using the 25th shell from rounds one and three. That is, rounds one and three will consist of 24 shots ending with doubles at Station One.

c. When shooting doubles at Station Four, the shooter must shoot first at the high house target going around the stations from one through seven and shoot at the low house four target first when coming back around the stations from seven through two (or one).

d. "No bird" shall be declared unless a regular pair of targets is thrown.

3. Shooters Right To Observe Targets

At the beginning of each round the squad shall be entitled to observe two (2) regular targets from each Skeet house and shall have the option of observing one regular target after each irregular target.

Shoot management, State Association, State Chief Referee and/or Zone Chief Referee shall have the right, where topographically possible, to make it mandatory to use a hoop or other suitable devices whenever a target adjustment is necessary.

4. Progress from Station to Station

a. No member of a squad shall advance to the shooting station until it is his turn to shoot, and until the previous shooter has left the shooting station. No shooter shall order any target or shoot at ant target except when it is his turn. The penalty for shooting out of turn without permission of the referee shall be to score all target so fired upon as "lost."

b. No member of a squad, having shot from one station, shall proceed toward the next station in such a way as to interfere with another shooter. The penalty for willful interference in this manner shall be disqualification from the event.

c. No shooter shall unduly delay a squad with good and sufficient reason in the judgment of the referee on charge of his squad. A shooter who persists in deliberately causing inexcusable delays after receiving a first warning from the referee shall be subject to disqualification from the event.

5. Broken Gun

When a gun breaks in such a manner so as to render it unusable, the shooter has the option of using another gun if such gun can be secured without delay, or dropping out of the squad until the gun is repaired and finishing the event at a later time when a vacancy occurs or after all other contestants have finished the event. Nothing shall prohibit the shooter from missing one round because of a broken gun, having the gun repaired and then rejoining the squad for all later rounds that the squad has not started. In that case the shooter will finish any or all rounds, starting with the shot where the breakdown occurred, that were not shot because of a broken gun, on the proper fields and in the first vacancy that may occur, or after the event has been finished by all other contestants.

6. Shooting Up

a. Where a shooter has registered in but does not show up to start an event with his squad, he will not be permitted to shoot up after the first man in the squad has fired a shot at Station 2. He may join the squad for all later rounds, but the round missed because of lateness must be shot on the proper field in the first vacancy, or after all other contestants have finished.

b. In the interest of conserving time the shoot management may modify this rule to meet special conditions, if it so desires.

7. Slow Squads

It is suggested that shoot management use substitute fields when breakdowns or unusually slow-shooting squads are disrupting the normal sequence of squads. Under normal conditions, a squad should complete a round in 20 minutes. Squads desiring more time should not object to being transferred to a substitute field.

C. Scoring

1. The score in any one round shall be the total number of dead targets.

2. Targets declared "no bird" shall not be scored.

3. One "lost" target shall be scored on:

    a. A balk or failure of gun to fire due to fault of shooter. Should this include both targets of a regular double, it shall be scored as first target lost, and a proof double shall be thrown to determine the result of the second shot only.

    If a balk should occur, or his gun fail to fire because of the shooter's fault, when a proof double is thrown and the result of the first shot has already been scored, the second target shall be scored as "lost."

    b. Each successive malfunction or malfunctions of gun.

    c. Doubles fired upon in reverse order.

    d. Target broken after it is outside the shooting bounds.

    e. Each target fired at when shooter fires out of turn without permission of referee.

    f. Each target fired upon and allegedly missed because the shooter's gun had a bent barrel, or a bent compensator, or any other bent tube or accessory.

    g. Each successive time balk. It shall be considered a time balk if a shooter deliberately delays more than 15 seconds for each shot on a station and the referee shall warn him once each round without penalty.

4. A shot shall be repeated for each instance of defective ammunition. If a shell having once misfired is used again, and fails to fire, the result shall be considered a fault on the part of the shooter and scored "lost."

5. No claim of irregularity shall be allowed, either on singles or doubles, where the target or targets were actually fired upon and alleged irregularity consists of deviation from the prescribed line of flight, or because of an alleged "quick pull," unless the referee has distinctively called "no bird" prior to the firing of the shot in the event of the "quick pull," or prior to the emergency of the target from the Skeet house in event of a "slow pull." Otherwise, if the shooter fires, the result shall be scored. The referee shall have final say as to whether he called "no bird" before the shooter fired.

6. If the brass pulls off a hull between shots on doubles, score as defective ammunition but do not score it as a gun malfunction.

7. If the brass pulls off a hull, or if defective ammunition occurs between shots on doubles, the referee shall rule that if the first target was a "dead bird," nothing is established, and a proof double shall be fired upon to determine the result of both birds. However, if the first target was "lost," it shall be so established and a proof double shot to establish the second shot result.

D. Malfunctions

1. A target shall be repeated for each allowable malfunction.

2. Only two malfunctions of any one gun in the same round shall be allowable. The third and all subsequent malfunctions of the same gun shall be excessive. However, when more than one person is using the same gun in the same round, this rule shall apply to each of said persons separately.

3. During the shooting of single targets, a shooter may load two shells except at Station 8 high house, or unless forbidden by club rules, and if the gun jams or malfunctions between shots, it shall be scored as a malfunction and the shooter permitted to shoot the target over. However, the shooter is still restricted to two allowable malfunctions with one gun in one round.

4. Malfunction on Singles or First Shot Doubles

    a. If the gun is handed to the referee in the same condition as at the time the shooter attempted to fire it, referee will exercise caution not to jiggle or attempt to further close the action, and will apply normal pressure to the trigger and the result will be declared a lost bird if the gun fires or a "malfunction" if it doesn't fire.

    b. If however, the shooter is holding the trigger pulled and doesn't want to give the gun to the referee, the referee will place his finger over the shooter's and apply pressure as above after seeing the gun is pointed in a safe direction. The result shall be scored a "lost bird," if the gun fires, or a "malfunction" if it does not fire.

    c. After exercising "a" or "b" above, the referee shall examine the gun for ammunition, etc. (Shooter's responsibility).

5. Malfunction Between Shots on Doubles

If an apparent malfunction occurs between the first and second shot on doubles:

    a. The referee shall apply the same procedures as listed under malfunction on singles (a, b and c, above) to determine if an allowable malfunction has occurred.

    b. If an allowable malfunction has occurred, the referee shall rule that if the first target was a "dead bird," nothing is established, and a proof double shall be fired upon to determine the result of both birds. However, if the first target was "lost" then both birds shall be scored "lost."

6. If a gun "doubles" or "fan-fires" while shooting singles or doubles the referee shall rule a malfunction, and if the first target was a dead bird," nothing established, and a proof single or double shall be fired upon to determine the results. However, if the first target was "lost," it shall be established and a proof double shot to establish the second shot result.

E. Doubles or Proof Doubles

1. If the first target of a double is thrown irregular as to deviate from the prescribed line of flight and is not shot at, a proof double shall determine the score for both shots, whether the second target is fired upon or not. The referee shall be the sole judge of irregularity.

2. If the first target emerges broken, the double shall, in all cases, be declared "no bird" and a proof double shall be thrown to determine the result of both shots.

3. If the first target of a double is thrown irregular as to deviation from the prescribed line of flight, and is shot at, the result shall be scored for the first shot in accordance with III-C-5 and the following rules pertaining to the second shot shall apply: In shooting doubles, if the shooter is deprived of a normal second shot because:

a. The second the is thrown broken, or

b. The second target is thrown irregular as to deviation from the prescribed line of flight and is not shot at, or

c. The second target is not thrown at all, or

d. The second target is not thrown simultaneously, the result of the first shot shall be scored, and the second target only shall be declared "no bird" and a proof double shall be fired to determine the result of the second shot. If the shooter fires at the irregular target described in (b) above the result shall be scored unless the referee calls "no bird."

4. If a double is thrown but the targets collide, before the result of the first bird is determined, it shall be declared "no bird," and the result of a proof double shall determine the score of both shots.

5. If a double is thrown but the shooter is deprived of a normal second shot for any of the following reasons, the result of the first shot shall be scored, and the second target only shall be declared "no bird" and a proof double shall be fired to determine the result of the second shot only.

a. Both targets are broken with the first shot.

b. The wrong target is broken with the first shot. (For proof double ruling see paragraph 8 below.)

c. The first shot is lost and a collision occurs before the result of the second shot is determined.

d. The second target collides with fragments of the first target, properly broken, before the result of the second target is determined.

e. The result of the first shot is determined, and interference occurs before the second shot is fired.

6. If a double is thrown and an allowable malfunction occurs on the first shot, it shall be declared "no bird," and the result of a proof double shall determine the score of both shots. If such malfunction is excessive, (not allowable), the proof double shall be thrown to determine the result of the second shot only.

7. The shall be no penalty for withholding the first shot when either target of a double is irregular. A proof double shall determine the score of both shots thereafter.

8. In shooting a proof double after the first target (of a double) is "lost," if the shooter fires at, or breaks the wrong target first, said proof double shall be scored as both targets "lost." If, in such a proof double after the first target (of a double) is "dead," the shooter fires at, or breaks, the wrong target first, it shall be scored as first target "dead" and second target "lost."

F. Interference

1. Any circumstance beyond the shooter's control which unduly affects his opportunity to break any particular target is interference.

a. If a shooter fires his shot, the appearance of a target, or a piece of target, from an adjoining field shall not be ruled as interference, unless such target, or piece of target strikes or threatens to strike the shooter or his gun. It shall be the final judgment of the referee to consider the evidence and determine whether a target or piece of target strikes or threatens to strike shooter or his gun.

b. If a shooter withholds his shot due to what he considers to be an interference, and if the cause is observed and ruled interference by the referee, the interference may be allowed.

c. If a shooter still holds a shot for safety purposes, the referee may give the shooter the benefit of the doubt and rule interference, providing he agrees safety was involved.

2. If the shooter shoots at a target, he accepts it. He must abide by the result unless the referee considers that there was legal interference. Following are a few illustrations of what may be considered legal interference.

a. A target box being thrown out the door in the shooter's line of vision between the time of the shooter's call and the firing of his shot.

b. Opening the Skeet house door unexpectedly or suddenly under the same circumstances.

c. Any sudden disturbance or exceptionally loud noise, except an announcement over the loud speaker.

d. A bird flying directly across the target's line of flight just before it is fired upon.

e. A child or any other person or animal running out on the field suddenly in the shooter's line of vision.

f. A thrown object, or wind-blown object, blown through the air so as to cause a conflict (a piece of paper being merely blown along the ground shall not qualify in this category).

g. All of these, and of course, a number of other occurrences can be allowed as interference if the referee, in his own judgment, feels there was sufficient interference to justify such a thing.

h. The sun shall not be considered as interference. It must be accepted as a normal hazard.

G. Safety Precautions

The safety of competitors, field personnel and spectators requires continuous attention by all to the careful handling of guns, and caution in moving about the field and club grounds. Self-discipline is necessary on the part of the shooters, field personnel and spectators.

Where such self-discipline is lacking it is the duty of the field personnel to enforce discipline and the duty of the competitors to assist in such enforcement. Team captains shall be held strictly to account for discipline within their respective teams.

1. No gun shall be loaded until the shooter is on the shooting station. Loading is considered as putting any part of a loaded shell in any part of the gun.

2. The loaded gun shall be kept pointed in a direction that will not endanger the lives of shooters, field personnel or spectators.

3. When not on the shooting station, the gun shall be carried with breech open. Pumps and automatics will have the bolt open. Fixed breech (double barrels including over and unders and side-by-sides) will be broken open.

4. When the shooter is on the shooting station and ready to shoot and a delay occurs, such as equipment breakdown, the gun shall be opened and all shells extracted.

5. During the shooting of singles targets, the management may permit the loading of two shells at all stations except Station 8 high house. However, the management cannot compel the loading of two shells in the shooting of singles.

6. The loading of more than two shells in the gun shall not be allowed at any time.

7. Shooter will not be permitted to use a gun with a "release-type" trigger unless the referee and the other members of the squad are notified. Extra caution must be exercised if the gun is given to a referee who is unfamiliar with its operation.

8. Any shooter whose gun accidentally discharges twice within one round for mechanical reasons shall be required to change guns or, if time permits, have his gun repaired, before continuing to shoot the round or subsequent rounds.

9. When a shooter intentionally fires a second time at a missed target, he shall be warned by the field referee. The second time the shooter intentionally fires a second shot at a missed target in any round, the penalty shall be automatic disqualification from the event.

SECTION IV—REFEREES

A. Licensed Referee

1. NSSA-licensed referees shall pass prescribed written examinations with the aid of a rule book given by their state associations or NSSA affiliated clubs, and also eye examinations, using glasses if necessary. A visual card system will suffice and save cost of a professional eye examination. Applications for official NSSA referee cards and emblems shall be approved by the applicant's state association, where one exists, or by NSSA affiliated club where there is no state or district association. It is recommended that all state organizations adopt the policy of using only NSSA licensed referees as chief referees. All world championship shoot referees must be so licensed. All applicants for referee licenses must be paid up regular members of the NSSA.

2. Plan of approval of referees for NSSA World Championship shoots.

    a. All applicants must be registered NSSA referees for current year.

    b. Each applicant must be recommended in writing by two presiding officers of his state association or by one NSSA director from his state or zone.

B. Associate Referee

1. NSSA Associate Referees must meet all eligibility requirements specified for NSSA licensed referees (IV-A-1), with the exception of paid up membership in the NSSA.

    a. An Associate Referee is eligible for an associate referee patch.

    b. Application for an Associate Referee status must be approved by applicants state and/or Zone Chief Referee.

    c. An Associate Referee is not eligible to referee the World Championships.

    d. In no event can this designation be conferred upon an individual for more than five years.

C. Chief Referee

The shoot management shall designate a qualified chief referee, approved by NSSA, who shall have general supervision over all other referees and who shall be present throughout the shooting. It is recommended that chief referees also have the responsibility of instructing all other referees and being certain they are acquainted with the rules and approved interpretations.

It shall be the chief referee and/or shoot management's responsibility to stop a shoot or shootoff when darkness or other conditions prevents a fair chance to shoot. This action must be carried out simultaneously on all fields. Example: Use of public address system or the shutting off of power; or a suitable signal, the significance of which is known to all referees. Use of the referee's eye test card—$5/16$" dot at 21 yards—is mandatory.

It is mandatory that each state association appoint a chief referee for its state where practical. It is suggested that this chief referee be placed in charge of all referees in the state and that he conduct training courses to develop better referees, and that he represents his state association at all registered shoots from within the state. His scale of pay should be established by the state association and the cost should be borne by the state association and/or by the club holding the registered shoot.

D. Field Referee

The field referee is responsible for the conduct of shooting on the field to which he has been assigned. He shall have jurisdiction on the field to which assigned and in the area in rear of the field used by other shooters and spectators. He shall be completely familiar with the shoot program and with the NSSA rules. He must be constantly alert, impartial and courteous though firm in the handling of shooters.

Upon protest, the referee shall rule upon the occurrence and then proceed with the round, without delay, as if nothing has happened. At the completion of the round, he shall notify the chief referee.

It is better for a referee to continue to officiate at the same field.

The referee shall:

1. Announce distinctly "lost" or "no bird," as the case may be.

2. See that each shooter has a fair opportunity to shoot in his turn, and if in his sole opinion a shooter has been unduly interfered with while shooting, he shall declare "no bird" and allow the shooter another shot. Claims of interference may be allowed when a target or a piece of target , from an adjoining field strikes or threatens to strike a shooter or his gun, provided that such interference occurs after the shooter has called for his target and before he fires upon it.

3. Declare "no bird" as soon as possible when:

  a. The shooter's position is not according to rule. The shooter shall be warned by the referee of his illegal shooter's position, but if he continues to violate the position, he shall be penalized by the loss of one target for each subsequent violation in that round.

  b. Target does not emerge within the allowed time after the shooter's call.

  c. Target emerges before shooter's call.

  d. An irregular target is thrown in singles, doubles or proof doubles.

It shall be the referee's first duty after releasing the target to declare "no bird" as quickly as possible when he determines that an irregular target has been thrown.

  (1) If the shooter fires before the "no bird" call, the result of the shot shall be scored.

  (2) In the case of doubles or proof doubles, if the referee's call of "no bird" occurs after the firing of the first shot (and said first shot was fired at a regular target) the result of the first shot shall be scored and a proof double shall be thrown to determine the result of the second shot only.

No Result of Firing On a Broken Target Shall Be Scored.

4. In any instance the result of shooting at a target after it has been declare "no bird" shall not be scored and the shot will be repeated.

5. Declare as "lost" dusted targets or perforated targets that are retrieved after landing.

6. Declare as "lost target" the third shot fired when gun has been loaded with more than two shells.

7. Suspend shooting when the targets thrown from any machine are reportedly irregular and order the machine adjusted or repaired. (He may, at any time allow a shooter making such request, to see a target, providing the request is reasonable and not excessive.)

8. Grant a shooter permission to shoot out of his regular turn where it is justified.

9. Disqualify, for the event, a shooter who in his opinion has willfully interfered with another shooter while the latter is shooting.

10. Disqualify, for the event, a shooter for repeated violation of any of the safety precautions listed in Section III or for any act that in the referee's opinion endangers the safety of shooters, field personnel or spectators.

11. It shall also be his responsibility to supervise the keeping of correct scores and to see that all scores are verified by the respective shooters before the score sheet is taken from the field. The referee's responsibility in seeing that shooters verify their scores is to announce after each round "Please check your scores." If an error in score-keeping is discovered on the field, the field referee shall remedy it promptly at the time of discovery. In the event there is any question as to the correctness of any score any scoresheet leaves the field, the chief referee or shoot committee chairman shall order the score corrected after checking with the field referee and the score sheet.

12. The referee shall be the SOLE judge of decision of fact.

For example, his decision as to whether target is dead or lost shall be irrevocable, regardless of the opinion of spectators or other members of the squad.

13. Relief referees shall not take over the fields until the shooters have completed the round, except in cases of emergency, such as illness, etc.

14. No NSSA licensed referee may be disqualified in the middle of a round but he may choose to disqualify himself.

15. No member of a shooting squad may score or referee for other members of that squad.

E. Referee's Digest

(A summarization of suggestions and interpretations for the purpose of improving and standardizing Skeet officiating universally.)

Referees shall at all times be courteous and impartial. Your alertness and fairness are prime factors in the success of any shoot. Your conduct will reflect on the NSSA and you should always bear in mind that the shooters make the association possible. Whenever possible, the referees should meet before the shoot and discuss any problems which might arise and familiarize themselves with the schedule for the shoot.

There should be a chief referee appointed by the shoot management before the shoot and he shall be in complete charge of and responsible for all other referees. It shall be the responsibility of the chief referee to appoint the necessary assistant chief referees and all other referees must meet with his approval. The chief referee shall designate and assign the referees the fields and shall be held responsible for their conduct at all times during the shoot.

At all world championship shoots there shall be not less than one relief referee for each four shooting fields.

When assistant chief referees are used, they shall be held responsible for their assigned referees and any misconduct or irregularities shall be reported to the chief referee immediately.

Each referee shall be in charge of his field and shall see that all safety rules are complied with. He shall have jurisdiction over the spectator area of his field and allow none but authorized personnel on the shooting field during the shooting. The field referee shall notify the chief or assistant chief referee as soon as possible of any protest, irregularity or violation. Before the start of the shooting, the referee shall be supplied with a squad sheet showing the shooting line-up and shall assemble the shooters at Station 1. He shall ascertain that each shooter is aware of his or her squad position and shall not change any squad's shooting order until approved by the chief or assistant chief referee after notification that the change or changes have been made in the office.

The referee should ascertain that the shooter is shooting a proper gauge gun for the event in which he is entered. (Shooter's responsibility)

In cases where management rules on the loading of one or two shells during the shooting of singles (NO EXCEPTION to be made at Station 8 high house, where it is NEVER permissible to load more than one shell) the referee should inform the shooters of the ruling.

The referee should, as a courtesy, inquire of the squad if there are any questions of rules or regulations not clear before starting to shoot. He may request that they check their guns to make certain that their safeties are off.

The referee shall inform the squad that they are entitled to view two regular birds from the high house and two regular birds from the low house prior to the starting of the squad, and the first shooter shall decide which one he wishes to see first.

The referee shall, at the command of the shooter to pull or mark the bird, respond to the call within one second, and if delayed or in doubt as to the call, shall declare "no bird" immediately.

When a call is given by the shooter and the bird emerges from the Skeet house and is fired upon, the referee shall declare, in a distinct and audible voice, "lost" or no bird if applicable.

The referee, at all times, shall see that the shooter is given a fair opportunity to shoot and if in the opinion of the referee, the shooter has been interfered with or caused by some condition beyond the shooter's control to interrupt the shooter, he, the referee, may declare "no bird." Be uniform, it is up to the referee to use good judgment in calling interference.

Every target declared "no bird" shall be repeated. Every regular bird scored on shall be shown on the score pad and the marking "X" shall signify "dead" and the marking "O" shall signify "lost." In the case of a malfunction of the shooter's gun, a small "m" shall be marked in the scoring book showing the station at which the malfunction occurred, thus assisting the referee in complying with the rule governing malfunction (Sec. III-D-2).

The position of the referee during the shoot is of vital importance both to the shooter and the referee. For required position, see field layout.

If the referee observes a shooter violating an of the rules on his field, he should, as a courtesy, inform him of the violation personally, but not as a reprimand before the squad. If the shooter fails or refuses to heed the referee's request, the chief or assistant chief referee should be summoned and the problem taken up with higher authority. Any call for the bird to be "pilled" or "marked" shall be executed only when given by the shooter on the station.

If a shooter should advance to the next station and call for a bird prior to completion of shooting by the entire squad at the previous station, the referee shall not pull the bird, if operating the traps, or if the birds are released from a pull house, the referee shall declare "no bird." If, in the referee's opinion, there is a reasonable doubt as to his correct decision, the ruling should be in favor of the shooter.

The referee shall see that no shell is loaded or dropped into any part of any gun until the shooter is on the shooting station.

F. Interpretations

Any regular bird thrown after the shooter calls shall be scored as follows: If any visible piece of the bird is observed by the official referee broken as a result of the shooter having shot, it will be scored "dead bird." Any bird thrown that emerges from the trap house broken shall be declared "no bird" and shall be repeated. If the referee knows that a chip is broken off the target, it should be called "no bird" even if the shooter hits it before the referee calls "no bird." If the shooter misses it, it also must be called no bird. In singles, if the bird emerges from the wrong house, it shall be declared "no bird" and another bird shall be thrown from the proper house. However, in the shooting of singles, if by error or for mechanical reasons doubles are shown, and the shooter shoots and breaks or misses the correct bird, it shall be scored as in singles, it shall be the shooter's prerogative to elect to shoot or withhold his shot when doubles are thrown in the calling of singles. If, however, the referee declared "no bird" prior to the shot, the bird shall be repeated. If, in the shooting of doubles, only one regular bird emerges and the shooter elects to shoot it, it shall be scored "dead" or "lost" and a proof double shall be thrown. If, however, the referee calls "no bird" prior to the firing of the shot, it shall be repeated.

When a shooter misses his first bird, he shall immediately, when shooting singles, repeat the shot, this being his "optional." If in the shooting of doubles, the shooter misses the first bird and a proof double is required the shooter shall complete the shooting of the doubles at that station and then take his "optional." If the shooter completes the round without a miss, he shall shoot his "optional" at Station 8 low house.

If more than one second elapses between the time the shooter calls for his bird and its release, "no bird" should be called and the shooter should not be penalized, PROVIDED HE HAS NOT FIRED ON THE TARGET BEFORE THE REFEREE'S CALL OF "NO BIRD."

There is a concrete block of designated shooting platform at each station of the Skeet field. The shooter must stand with any part of both feet within the boundaries of this platform. Any shooter with one or both feet definitely off the shooting station should first be made to shoot over and, if he persists in standing off the station, he shall be penalized by loss of the target for each subsequent violation in that round.

However, if the shooter missed the target while committing the first violation of shooting position, the result shall be scored "lost."

The shooter must not be considered at fault if he has complied with the manufacturer's operating instructions for loading the gun, and the gun does not fire. In the case of the gun going into battery (locking closed) for the first shot on doubles or any shot on singles, if the shooter has closed the action in accordance with the manufacturer's instructions, and if the bolt appears visually to be closed, the failure of a gun to fire shall be scored as a malfunction.

Automatics

1. On an automatic the shooter is not required to push forward or strike the breech bolt lever to insure locking the gun. This is a normal gun function.

2. The shooter must load the shell or shells into the gun and see that the action appears closed. If he loads 2 shells on singles or doubles, and if the second shell fails to go into the chamber or is thrown out of the gun, it shall be scored a malfunction.

Pump guns

1. The shooter is required to pump the gun, as recommended by the manufacturer, on doubles and to close the action completely forward (visually) on singles.

2. If the shooter "short-shucks" the gun, the hammer will not be cocked, a fault of the shooter.

3. If the lifter throws the second shell out of the gun it shall be a malfunction.

4. It shall be a malfunction if between shots on singles or doubles the gun returns the empty shell to the chamber provided the hammer is cocked.

5. The referee shall check for a malfunction as instructed under that title and shall then apply forward pressure on the forearm to see if the shell is lodged (a malfunction). However, if the gun closes smoothly, without jiggling, it is not a malfunction.

Double-barreled guns

1. The shooter is responsible for loading a shell in the proper barrel, or two shells for doubles.

2. The shooter must close the action in accordance with manufacturer's recommendations.

Shell catching devices

Where any device is attached to a shotgun which must be adjusted or removed to permit shooting doubles, it shall be the shooter responsibility to perform such adjustment or removal. Failure to fire a second shot on doubles, due to such device, shall not be an allowable malfunction, and the bird shall be scored lost.

SECTION V—NSSA CLASSIFICATION

A. Definitions

1. NSSA Shooting Year

The NSSA shooting year shall be any twelve month period running from November 1 through the following October 31.

2. Current Year

The twelve month period November 1 through October 31 of the year for which classification is being determined.

3. Previous Year

The twelve month period immediately preceding the current shooting year, i.e., November 1 - October 31.

4. Initial String

The required minimum number of registered targets in each gauge necessary for an Initial Classification is 200.

5. Regular String

The required minimum number of registered targets in each gauge necessary for RECLASSIFICATION of a classified shooter is 300.

6. The first classification of a newly classified shooter based on his INITIAL STRING of registered targets shot during the CURRENT year, or during the PREVIOUS year and the CURRENT year combined.

7. Regular Classification

a. The classification of a classified shooter at the beginning of the CURRENT year in each gauge will be based on all registered targets shot during the previous year, providing at least 200 targets were shot.

b. The reclassification of a classified shooter based on his average for totals of all REGULAR STRINGS of registered targets shot during the CURRENT YEAR.

8. Class Attained

The class in which a shooter would be required to shoot were he to compete in a subsequent shoot during the CURRENT year, whether or not he has ever shot in that class.

9. Classification/Shoot Record Cards

a. As soon as possible after October 31 of each year, each PAID UP member will receive from NSSA a classification/shoot record card.

b. This classification/shoot record card shall include provisions for club designation, targets shot, targets broke, running average in each gauge and shall be imprinted with:

(1) Member's name, address, membership expiration date and membership number.

(2) Shooter's class for the start of the current year in each gauge in which he is a classified shooter, or NC if he is a non-classified shooter.

(3) The number of targets shot at and broken in each gauge during the previous year, if any.

(4) The highest class in which shooter shot during the previous year.

c. Any errors on shooter's new classification card, including those caused by failure of shoot reports to be received at NSSA headquarters in time to be included on new card, should be promptly reported to NSSA by the shooter so that a corrected card can be supplied to insure proper inclusion in permanent record.

10. Classified Shooter

a. One who has fired at least the required INITIAL STRING of registered targets, or more, during the PREVIOUS year, or

b. One who has fired at least the required initial string of registered targets, or more, during the current year, or

c. One who has fired at least the required initial string of registered targets, or more, during the previous year and the CURRENT year combined.

11. Non-Classified Shooter

A new shooter, or one whose record does not conform with any of the preceding requirements for classified shooters.

a. NC must be offered in all registered events and will not be combined with any other class.

b. Awards and/or purses for the NC shooters may be optional with shoot management, BUT NOT MANDATORY.

c. NC shooters will not be eligible for awards other than NC category except for teams and other concurrent events. For classifying NC shooters on concurrent events see Section V-D-1.

d. For classification procedures see below.

B. Procedures

1. Maintaining Shoot Record Card

a. Each shooter will bear the responsibility of promptly and accurately entering his own score with the date, etc., in the proper gauge division at the conclusion of each registered event in which he participates. Where a single event extends more than one day he should enter the total, not day-to-day scores.

b. Shooter shall have his classification changed in reclassification spaces on his classification/shoot record card promptly whenever they have changed by averages on regular strings or cumulative strings.

c. The shooter is required to carry his card to each registered shoot and present it at registration.

(1) A shooter failing to present his classification card, for any reason, may be assigned Class AA at the discretion of shoot management.

(2) In the case of a lost card, or accidentally forgetting a card, the shooter may sign an affidavit attesting to his classification, subject to specified penalties. Such affidavit must be attached to the shoot report when it is forwarded to NSSA for tabulation.

Note: Replacement for a lost card (including reported scores to date) may be obtained from NSSA upon request. If the original card is later found, the shooter should carefully consolidate the record, then destroy the extra card.

d. In the space provided for club on his classification/shoot record card, each member shall designate, not later than his first competition in such events, the club he has elected to represent in club two-man and five-man team competition.

e. A shooter falsifying any entries or improperly using more than one card shall be disqualified and reported to NSSA for action according to Section II-A-2-b(4).

2. Classification/Reclassification of Classified Shooter

a. Using the Universal Classification Tables, a classified shooter's class for the state of the current year shall be figured on the basis of his average on the total number of registered targets shot during the previous year, however, such class shall be no lower than one class below the highest class in which he shot during the previous year.

b. A shooter shall maintain throughout each shoot his classes and running averages as they at the time of entry. A classified shooter shall not be subject to changes in classification during a shoot for any reason nor have his classification changed for a consolation event held after the regular shoot.

(1) The only exception to the above is: A NC shooter who completes an initial string of targets, even at the end of a preliminary event becomes classified for all remaining events of that gauge.

(2) The total number of targets scheduled for an event are to be used in determining strings for classification and reclassification.

Examples:

(a) A non-classified shooter has shot 150 registered 12 gauge targets and enters a 100 target, 12 gauge event. He shall be classified on the total 250 targets and not after shooting the first 50 targets of the event, which would total 200 targets.

(b) A classified shooter has shot 550 registered 20 gauge targets and enters a 100 target 20 gauge event. He shall be reclassified on the total 650 targets and not after shooting the first 50 targets of the event, which would total 600.

(c) A shooter who is classified at the beginning of the year on totals of targets shot during previous year will reclassify at the end of his first regular string and at the end of all succeeding regular strings shot during the current year.

Example:

	Shot	Broke	Average	Class
Current year	100	xx		C
	100	xx		C
	100	xx		C
Reclassify at	300	xxx	.xxxx	A
	100	xx		A
	100	xx		A
Reclassify on	600	xxx	.xxxx	A
and again on	900 etc.			

(d) Shooters must, however, always reclassify at the end of each regular string even though the correct number of targets for reclassification comes between the preliminary and the main event. Reclassification is not effective until after the shoot, but must be accomplished on the correct number of targets.

Example:

	Shot	Broke	Average	Class
Current year	100	xx		C
	100	xx		C
	100	xx		C
	300	xxx	.xxxx	A
	100	xx		A
	100	xx		A
Preliminary	100*	xx		A
	600	xxx		AA
Main Event of Above Shoot	100*	xx		A
	100	xx		AA
	100	xx		AA
	900	xxx		AA

*Note that shooter must reclassify at end of regular string even though he does not change class until after shoot.

(e) A shooter who becomes a classified shooter on combination of targets shot during the previous year and current year shall be reclassified on each succeeding regular string of registered targets shot during the current year. (Also see "Reclassification Limitation.")

Example:

	Shot	Broke	Average	Class
Previous Year	100	xx		NC
Current Year	100	xx		NC
Classify On	200	xxx	.xxxx	D
	100	xx		D
	100	xx		D
	100	xx		D
Reclassify on 400 shot in current year	400	xxx	.xxxx	B
	100	xx		B
	100	xx		B
	100	xx		B
Reclassify on 700 shot in current year	700	xxx	.xxxx	B

NOTE: After Initial Classification, targets shot in previous year are not used in calculating averages.

(f) A classified shooter who wishes to voluntarily declare himself up in class may do so. When he so elects, he must (at a registered shoot) have his card marked for which he is declaring himself. His card shall be marked with the new classification by self-declaration in the class where he declared himself, and be entered on the Official Entry Form with notation "self-declared."

3. Classification of a Non-Classified Shooter

A new shooter or one who has not attained a classification during the previous year will be entered as non-classified (NC) in each individual gauge until he has shot at Initial String of 200 targets in each gauge.

a. Upon completing an Initial String, in each individual gauge, the shooter will be given a classification based on average.

Note: A NC shooter who completes an initial string of targets, even at the end of a preliminary event becomes classified for all remaining events of the gauge.

b. After this initial classification, a shooter will reclassify after each succeeding regular string, using the total number of targets shot during the current year and will follow procedures as outlined in items b. through f. of Classification/Reclassification of Classified Shooters.

c. A Non-classified shooter who voluntarily wishes to declare himself classified may do so provided he declares himself in Class AA.

When he so elects, he must have his card marked (at a registered shoot) in AA before competing in the event for which he is declaring himself and Class AA must be entered on the Official Entry Form with notation "self declared."

C. Universal Classification Tables

1. Use of the Universal Classification Tables shall be required for all registered shoots and shall be in accordance with the following tables of averages:

For Open Individual

Class	12 Gauge	20 gauge
*AAA	98.5% and over	
AA	97.5% to 98.49%	96% and over
A	95% to 97.49%	93% to 95.99%
B	93% to 94.99%	90% to 92.99%
C	90% to 92.99%	86% to 89.99%
D	86% to 89.99%	Under 86%
E	Under 86%	Only 5 Classes

*Class AAA attained only by average based on last reclassification.

Class	28 gauge	.410 Gauge
AA	95% and over	93.5% and over
A	92% to 94.99%	89.5% to 93.49%
B	89% to 91.99%	84.5% to 89.49%
C	85% to 88.99%	81% to 84.49%
D	Under 85%	Under 81%

Class Double

Class	Doubles
*AAA	97% and over
AA	95% to 96.99%
A	91% to 94.99%
B	85% to 90.99%
C	80% to 84.99%
D	Under 80%

a. Shooter's correct class and average shall be posted on his shoot entry form.

b. Classification in each gauge gun is independent and shall be treated without regard to classification in any other gauge.

2. High Overall

Shoot management may establish the method of determining a shooter's class for high overall events in any manner they desire, i.e., 12 gauge classification, 4 gun average, or any other appropriate method. The method must be properly posted or published in the program.

3. Compulsory Classes

a. A class for Non-Classified shooters must be offered in all registered shoots for all events.

b. Only Classes AA, A, B, C, D, and NC (also E in 12 gauge) shall be compulsory. Class AAA shall be optional and when AAA is not offered, Class AA shall include all shooters who would be in Class AAA if it were offered.

(1) It shall be the sole responsibility of shoot management to determine whether Class AAA shall be offered and its decision shall be published in the shoot program or posted before the shoot.

(2) Class AAA could be offered where the number of entries eligible for that class justifies doing so.

D. Team and Other Concurrent Events

1. The average for a non-classified shooter competing in a team or other concurrent event shall be considered the highest percentage in "B" class of the gauge entered.

2. Division of two-man, five-man team, women and junior

events into classes is not mandatory. In cases where shoot management should desire to establish classes in these events, they may do so.

When such classes are established, they should be designated by number rather than letter, i.e., Class 1 (or I) XX—and over, Class 2 (or II) under XX—.

3. Classification for TEAM EVENTS shall be combined average of team member's scores, carried to the fourth decimal place at their initial or last classification. (i.e. .9525).

E. Limitations for Reclassification

1. During the current year a shooter is subject to reclassification upward only.

2. Each shooter classified at the beginning of the Skeet year will shoot in that class or a higher class as determined by average. Reclassification down will only be accomplished by NSSA headquarters at the beginning of the next Skeet year.

3. Any Skeet shooter who believes he is entitled to compete in a lower class due to illness, accident, age, etc., may appeal to the classification committee of NSSA after prior approval of his request by his state association. In the absence of a state association in the shooter's state, his appeal made by made directly to the classification committee.

4. Reclassification in all cases shall be subject to the restrictions and qualifications set out in this section and in the sections headed "Classifications."

SECTION VI—INTERNATIONAL CLASSIFICATION

The NRA and the National Skeet Shooting Association (NSSA) have common goals concerning the support and growth of International skeet. The major goal, after joint compliance with UIT rules and procedures, is one of congruent classification rules and procedures. Achievement of that goal is reflected in joint application of the following classification procedures by the NRA and NSSA. Paragraph numbers coincide with NRA rules.

19.1 Classified Competitors—Are all individuals who are officially classified by the NRA and NSSA for International Skeet competitions, or who have a record of scores fired over courses of fire used for classification (See Rule 19.4) which has been recorded in a Score Record Book or NSSA Classification Card.

19.2 Unclassified Competitor—is a competitor who does not have a current NRA or NSSA classification, either regular or temporary by Score Record Book (Rule 19.4). Such a competitor shall compete in the Master Class.

19.4 Scores Used for Individual Classification—Scores to be used for classification and reclassification will be as follows:

1) Those fired in individual and team matches in both NRA and NSSA competition (except Postal Matches).

2) Scores from Registered Leagues may be recorded during the league firing season in score books but will only be used by the NRA Headquarters Office at the end of the league firing season for issue of Official Classification Cards.

19.7 Lack of Classification Evidence—It is the Competitor's responsibility to have his NRA Official Classification card, NSSA Classification Card, or Score Record Book with required scores for temporary classification (Rules 19.1 and 19.4) and to present classification evidence when required. Any competitor who cannot present such evidence will fire in the Master Class. A competitor's classification will not change during a tournament. A competitor will enter a tournament under his correct classification and fire the entire event in that class. Should it be discovered that a competitor has entered in a class lower than his current rating, the tournament records will be corrected to show the correct classification for the entire tournament.

19.8 Competing in a Higher Class—Any individual or team may elect, before firing, to compete in a higher classification than the one in which classified. Such individual or team must fire in such higher class throughout the tournament and not revert to earned classification for any event in that tournament.

When there are insufficient entries in any class to warrant an award in that class according to the match's program conditions, the individual or team concerned may be moved by the Tournament Executive Officer (NSSA Shoot Management) to a higher class provided this change is made prior to the individual or team concerned having commenced firing in the tournament.

19.9 Obsolete Classifications and Scores—All classifications and scores (including temporary, Rule 19.14) except Master, shall become obsolete if the competitor does not fire in NRA or NSSA competition at least once during 3 successive calendar years. Master classifications and scores shall become obsolete if the competitor does not fire in NRA or NSSA competition at least once during 5 successive calendar years. NRA Lifetime Master classifications will not become obsolete.

19.10 Appeals—Any competitor having reason to believe he is improperly classified may file an appeal with the NRA or NSSA starting all essential facts. Such appeal will be reviewed by the NRA Protest Committee or NSSA Executive Director.

19.11 Protests—Any person who believes that another competitor has been improperly classified may file a protest with the NRA or NSSA stating all essential facts. Such protests will be reviewed by the NRA Protest Committee or NSSA Executive Director.

19.12 Team Classification—Teams are classified by computing the "Team Average" based on the classification of each firing member of the team. To compute the team average the key in Table No. 1 for the different classes will be used and the team total divided by the number of firing members of the team. Any fractional figure in the team average of one half or more will place the team in the next higher class. The "team average" will establish classification of team as a unit but will not affect in any way the individual classification of team members.

Table No.1—Team

Class	Key
AA-Master	5
A	4
B	3
C	2
D	1

19.13 Reporting Scores—NSSA COMPETITIONS—Clubs registering shoots with NSSA will report scores and winners to NSSA on official shoot report forms as required by Rule II-f.

NRA COMPETITIONS—Sponsors of NRA registered shoots will report to the NRA all individual and fired team match scores fired over the courses stated in Rule 19.4. Scores will be reported as aggregate totals for all matches completed by a competitor. Scores will be reported to each NRA Registered League at the competition of the league schedule. NRA and NSSA will exchange all the reported scores above and utilize them in International classification.

19.14 Score Record Book—(Temporary Classification)—At NRA registered matches a Score Record Book will be obtained by each unclassified competitor from the Official Referee, Supervisor, or tournament Statistical Office at the time competitor competes in his first tournament or from the Secretary of Registered League. He will record all scores fired by himself in all NRA or NSSA competition (except Postal Matches) until such time as he receives his Official NRA or NSSA Classification Card. Competitor will total all scores and divide that total by the number of registered targets shot. The average so obtained will determine the competitor's NRA or NSSA Classification at that time (see Rule 19.15 for average score for each classification).

Individual and team scores fired by the competitor during at least one tournament (Rule 1.13.1) or from the most recent league match (Rule 1.7) must be posted in the Score Record Book to establish a temporary classification. The Score Record Book will be presented by the holder of all NRA or NSSA competition entered until the competitor's Official NRA or NSSA Classification Card becomes effective.

Note: It is the competitor's responsibility to obtain the Score Record Book, enter scores and present it at each tournament until his official NRA or NSSA Classification Card becomes effective. When the NRA or NSSA Classification Card becomes effective the Score Record Book becomes obsolete.

19.15 Individual Class Averages—Competitors will be classified as follows and NRA Classification Cards issued accordingly:

International Skeet

AA Master	95.00 - 100.00
A	87.00 - 94.99
B	81.00 - 86.99
C	75.00 - 80.99
D	0 - 74.99

19.16 Establishing Classification—A competitor will be officially classified by the NRA or NSSA when the total score for a minimum of 200 targets has been reported. However, classification averages will be computed only after the total score for a tournament or league has been posted and, therefore, the average may be based on a greater number of targets, but will not be based on a lesser number. Total scores so reported to the NRA or NSSA will be posted to the Classification Record for the competitor concerned. When the scores for the stated minimum number of targets (or more if this minimum is reached during the scores of any tournament or league) have been so posted the average score will be computed. The competitor will be sent an Official NRA or NSSA Classification Card based on the average so computed and according to the table in Rule 19.15 which classification will become effective the date shown on the card issued by the NRA or NSSA.

19.17 Reclassification—A competitor who has been classified by the NRA or NSSA will be reclassified as follows:

a. A record of all completed (see Rule 19.9) NRA or NSSA Competition (except Postal Match) scores fired by a classified competitor will be maintained in the NRA Headquarters and/or NSSA Headquarters.

b. When additional scores of 300 targets have been posted, the competitors average will be established by dividing the total score by the number of targets represented. This average will be computed as outlined in Rule 19.16 at the end of the tournament or league in which the minimum number of targets, or more have been posted.

When a competitor's new average places him in a higher class, he will be reclassified accordingly and notified by Headquarters. (Note: This paragraph applies to NRA only.)

c. A competitor who believes his classification is too high may file a request with the NRA Protest Committee or NSSA Executive Director that his classification be lowered. Such a competitor must remain in the class concerned until at least 600 targets have been posted to his classification record. When the average of such shots places the competitor in a lower class he will be reclassified accordingly. When a competitor has been so classified downward, and by scores fired in NRA or NSSA competition (except NRA Postal Matches) has again earned his former classification, such classification shall become final and the competitor shall retain the earned classification and reclassified into a higher class as outlined in paragraph (b).

d. A reclassified competitor shall be sent a new NRA classification card which will become effective on the date shown on the card issued by the NRA. NSSA members are responsible for keeping up-to-date records and moving to a higher class when required.

United States Sporting Clays Association Rules and Regulations

1.0 DEFINITION OF TERMS

1.1 Shoot Promoter

Individual(s) or entity which provides for the facilities and organization of the competition. Shoot Promoters may also act as Shoot Official(s).

1.2 Shoot Officials

Individual(s) appointed by the Shoot Promoter and responsible for course layout, target selection, and appointment of Field Judges. Shoot Official(s) shall be responsible for both layout and testing of the course. Shoot officials are responsible for ensuring that competitors are not allowed to test or preview the course prior to the competition.

1.3 Field Judge

Person over 18 years of age assigned by the Shoot Official(s) to score targets and enforce the rules.

1.4 Station, Stand or Butt

A shooting position from which one or more targets are attempted.

1.5 Field

A field contains a station or group of stations from which targets are attempted sequentially. One a squad or individual checks into a "field," all "stations" and/or all targets on the "field" are attempted before moving to another "field." The shoot official(s) will provide direction for execution of shooting at each field.

1.6 Report Pair/On Sound of Gun

Two sequential targets where the second target is launched at the sound of the gun firing at the first target.

1.7 Following Pair

Two sequential targets where the second target is launched behind the first target at the official's discretion after the first target has been launched.

1.8 Simultaneous Pair

Two targets launched simultaneously, also called "True Pair."

2.0 EQUIPMENT

2.1 Targets

Targets thrown in any event may include any or all of the following:

2.1.1 Regulation sporting clay targets as specified by the USSCA or FITASC will be 110 millimeter plus or minus 2 millimeters in diameter and 105 grams plus or minus five grams in weight. Targets must be approved by the USSCA for performance.

2.1.2 Mini (60mm), midi (90mm), batue rocket, or rabbit targets as specified by FITASC.

2.1.3 Propeller mounted ZZ-Pigeon targets.

2.1.4 Any sporting target approved by shooting official(s).

2.1.5 "Poison Bird" targets of a separate and clearly discernible appearance may be included at random. Shooters attempting shots at these targets shall be scored a "miss" or "lost bird." Shooters correctly refraining from attempting the "poison bird" (protected pieces) will be scored as a "hit" or "dead bird." Poison bird targets are not thrown as a "hit" or "dead bird." Poison bird targets are not thrown as a simultaneous or True Pair.

2.1.6 Target number and selection for any competition shall be at the discretion of the Shoot Official(s). No more than 30 of the total number of targets shall be other than targets described in 2.1.1. Target number shall be the same for all shooters.

2.2 SHOTGUNS

2.2.1 Shotguns of 12 gauge or smaller gauges, in safe working order, and capable of firing two shots are to be used in attempting all targets.

2.2.2 Shotguns with interchangeable or adjustable chokes are permitted at the shooter's discretion. Chokes can be changed only between fields or as otherwise directed by the Shoot Official(s).

2.2.3 Shotguns fitted for multiple barrels (of various chokes and/or lengths) are permitted. The shooter is allowed to change barrels only between fields or as otherwise directed by the Shoot Official(s).

2.2.4 Competitors may enter a shoot with various guns and attempt targets at various stations with different guns, or the gun of another competitor. Guns may be changed only between fields or as otherwise directed by the Shoot Official(s).

2.3 AMMUNITION

2.3.1 All shotgun shells (cartridges) are to be commercially manufactured and clearly factory marked to denote the characteristics of the load.

2.3.2 Loads for 12 gauge guns shall not exceed $1^1/_8$ ounces of shot charge.

2.3.3 Maximum shot charge may not exceed $3^1/_4$ dram equiv. for any given competition, but may be further limited by the Shoot Official(s).

2.3.4 Shot size shall not exceed U.S. # $7^1/_2$ (diameter 0.095"; wt. 1.07 grains).

2.3.5 Shot shall be normal production shot. Plated shot is permitted.

2.4 THE COURSE

2.4.1 The course will provide for a predetermined number of shooting fields from which each competitor will attempt various targets. The number of "stations" and the number and characteristics of targets from each station, on each field, will be determined by the Shoot Official(s), and will be the same for all competitors.

2.4.2 Targets will be propelled by, and launched from, any of a number of commercially produced, modified, or hand-made devices which will propel an approved target in a manner to approach the characteristics (in the opinion of the Shoot Official(s)) of a game bird or animal typically taken with a sporting shotgun.

2.4.3 Launching devices which provide for targets traveling at varying angles and distances to the competitors are acceptable (i.e. wobble traps). No more than 20% of the targets shall be presented from such devices. No less than 80% of all targets in a shoot shall be presented with a reasonably consistent trajectory, distance and velocity to all shooters.

2.4.4 Devices which provide for propelling multiple targets are permitted.

2.4.5 Devices propelling targets of more than one type and devices capable of providing targets at varying angles and distances, shall be employed only as the varying aspects of these devices will be the same for all shooters and will be free of all human element of selection.

2.4.6 Field Judges will be required at each station in sufficient numbers to competently enforce all "rules for the shooter," as well as, to score the attempts accurately. Numbers and positions for Field Judges shall be determined by the Shoot Official(s).

3.0 EXECUTION OF THE SHOOT

3.1 Shooting Order Contestants shall proceed through the course and competition in one of the following formats:

3.1.1 European Rotation. Individual competitors or groups of 2 through 5 competitors will proceed to the various stations. Groups may shoot in any order selected by the shooters. The squad or group shooting the stations of any field may be changed from field to field.

3.1.2 Squadding. At the discretion of the Shoot Official(s), groups of 3 to 5 shooters will be formed to proceed from field to field in a fixed sequence.

3.1.3 In European rotation, a shoot start and shoot end time will be established. It will be the responsibility of each shooter to complete the entire event between these times.

3.1.4 In squadding sequence, squads will be assigned to a start time and it is the responsibility of each shooter to be ready on time, or within no more than 5 minutes of that time.

3.1.5 In either the case of shots not attempted by the "shoot end time" (European Rotation), or shots not attempted by a shooter joining his squad after they have begun (squadding), those targets not attempted will be scored as "lost."

The Shoot Official(s) shall have the right to provide for make up targets if sufficient justification can be presented. Make up targets are provided solely at the discretion of the Shoot Official(s).

3.1.6 Rotation of Order. In squads of shooters, rotation of shooting order is permitted between stations. Rotation may be formatted by Shoot Official(s), to be followed by all squads. If not prescribed by Shoot Official(s), order will be determined by the shooters.

3.1.7 Shooters Viewing Targets. The first shooters on a given field shall be allowed to view targets.

3.2 Attempting Targets. Targets will be presented for attempt at each station in one or more of the following formats:

3.2.1 Single Target/Single Shot

3.2.2 Single Target/Two Shots. The target will be scored "hit" or "dead" if successfully attempted on either shot.

3.2.3 Doubles/Two Shots. Doubles may be presented as report, following, or simultaneous pairs. In simultaneous pairs the shooter has the right to either of the targets first. If the shooter has misses the first target he may fire the second cartridge at the same target. When shooting report or following pairs, the shooter will have the right if missing the first target to fire the second cartridge at the same target (the result being scored on the first target and the second target being scored as lost). Should the shooter break both targets with either the first or the second shot then the result will be scored as two "kills."

3.2.4 Multiple Targets/Two Shots. Two shots with no limit on dead birds.

3.2.5 Stations at which the shooter is walking are permitted.

3.2.6 Time Reloads. Targets presented with set time periods for the shooter to reload prior to the presentation of the subsequent targets are permitted. Five seconds is the normal reload time but other intervals may be used at the discretion of the Shoot Official(s).

4.0 RULES FOR THE SHOOTER

4.1 Low Gun. Gun stock must be visible below the shooter's armpit. This does not mean partially visible, but the whole butt of the stock must be visible below the armpit not in front otherwise.

4.2 Call for Target. Target will be launched immediately or with a delay of up to 3 seconds.

4.3 Mounting of Gun. Shooter is to keep from mounting his gun until target is visible. If in the judgment of the Field Judge, the shooter moves to mount his gun prior to seeing the target, the target will be a "no bird" and the sequence and call will begin again. No penalty will be assessed the shooter. Excessive "no birds" (3 per day) can be construed as cause for scoring targets as lost.

4.4 Shooter's Responsibility. It will be the responsibility of each shooter to be familiar with these rules. Ignorance of the rules will not be a cause to "re-attempt" targets lost because of rule violations.

5.0 SCORING

5.1 Targets shall be scored as "hit" or "Killed" or "dead" and designated on score cards by an (X) when in the opinion of the Field Judge, a visible piece has been broken from the target. Targets not broken by the shooter's shot shall be called "lost" or "missed" and designated on score cards by a (0).

5.2 The call of "lost" or "dead," "hit" or "miss" shall be announced by the Field Judge prior to recording the score on every target.

5.3 If the shooter disagrees with the Field Judge's call, he must protest before firing at another set of targets or before leaving that station. The Field Judge may poll the spectators and may reverse his original call. In all cases the final decision of the Field Judge will stand.

5.4 Each shooter will be assigned a score card to be presented to the Field Judges at the various stations or fields. Field Judges will score each shooter's attempts on the individual's score card. The total shall be tallied and the scores written in ink and initialed by the Field Judge.

5.4.1 Each shooter is responsible for his score card from assignment, at the start of the shoot, until the card is filed with the Shoot Official(s) at the end of each day's shooting.

5.4.2 Shooters are responsible for checking the Field Judge's totals of "hits and misses" at each station and/or field.

6.0 MALFUNCTIONS

6.0.1 No gun malfunctions.

6.0.2 No ammunition or cartridge malfunction.

6.0.3 Targets shall be scored as lost if the shooter is unable to fire for any reason.

6.2 Target Malfunction

6.2.1 A target which breaks at launching shall be called a "no bird" and shooter will be provided a new target.

6.2.2 A target which is launched in an obviously different trajectory shall be called a "no bird" and the shooter will be provided a new target.

6.2.3 If a bad target or "no bird" is thrown on the second target of a double, and if the shooter has already attempted the first target prior to the Field Judge's call, the attempt on the first target will be recorded as fired. The complete double will be repeated, however, the first target of the pair will remain as scored and the "proof double" will be thrown only to record the attempt of both targets. Failure to make a legitimate attempt on the first target shall be cause for scoring the second target as "lost."

6.2.4 If a bad target or "no bird" is thrown during a time reload sequence, the shooter will repeat the sequence beginning with the last target established. As in the proof double described in 6.2.3 the shooter must make an attempt at the established target before proceeding with the remaining sequence. If the last established target occurred before the time reload, the shooter shall begin the sequence accordingly and proceed through the reloading again. The Field Judge shall enforce his judgment (either by implementing a suitable penalty, or allowing a repeat of the reloading sequence) to prevent a "no bird" or "bad target" thrown after either a successful or an unsuccessful reloading attempt from changing the results of the initial sequence.

6.2.5 At a station of multiple targets, at least two good targets must be presented or a "no bird" will be called and the multiple targets will be attempted again. Multiple targets shall be shot as "fair in the air," two new shots will be attempted and scored, no scores from previous "no bird" attempts will stand.

6.2.6 Any target broken by another target, or pieces from another target, will be called "no bird" and treated as per paragraph 6.2.3.

7.0 MISCELLANEOUS

7.1 Shooters must have the direct permission of a Field Judge to test fire any gun. Other than on such permitted test firings, guns will be discharged only in attempt at competition targets.

7.2 Field Judges may be assisted by markers to record scores on the shooter's score cards.

7.3 It is the sole responsibility of the shooter to begin any event, station, and/or field with sufficient equipment and ammunition. Failure to do so, which in the opinion of the Field Judges will delay the shoot, will result in the loss of all targets as required to keep the shoot moving. Make up targets will be provided only at the discretion of the Shoot Official(s).

8.0 DISPUTES

8.1 A shooter may protest if in his opinion the rules as stated herein are improperly applied.

8.2 There will be no protests concerning calls or scoring of hits, or misses. The Field Judges final decision will stand.

8.3 Protests shall be made immediately upon completion of the shooting at a given field. Protest shall be made to the Shoot Official(s).

8.4 The Shoot Official(s) shall convene a predetermined "jury" of 3 to 5 Field Judges or competitors who are known to be representative of the shooters present, and knowledgeable about these rules. The jury will decide on the validity of the protest and the resolution or award bonuses as they determine to be fair and in the spirit of the competition.

Appendix D

U.S. Registered Gun Clubs

Trap, Skeet, Sporting Clays

TRAP AND SKEET SHOOTING

Below is a listing by state of gun clubs that hold registered ATA and/or NSSA competition events.

ALABAMA

Dixie Trap Club, 4514 Lowell Rd., Montgomery, AL 36105/205-288-5427

Muscle Shoals Skeet & Trap, P.O. Box 334, Florence, AL 35631/205-764-1502

ARIZONA

Beeline Trap & Skeet, 16644 N. Boxcar Dr., Fountain Hills, AZ 85268/602-947-1111

Black Canyon Trap & Skeet Range, 12416 N. 28th Dr., Phoenix, AZ 85029/602-582-5296

Bullhead City Gun Club, P.O. Box 1026, Bullhead City, AZ 86430/602-768-3543

Casa Grande Trap Club, P.O. Box 952, Casa Grande, AZ 85222/602-836-8300

Flagstaff Trap & Skeet Club, P.O. Box 3259, Flagstaff, AZ 86004/602-526-1265

Garden Canyon (Sierra Vista) Gun Club, P.O. Box 777, Ft. Huachuca, AZ 85613/602-538-2761

Prescott Gun Club, P.O. Box 1881, Prescott, AZ 86302/602-772-9539

Show Low Elks Gun Club, P.O. Box 21, Lakeside, AZ 85929/602-537-5590

Tucson Trap & Skeet Club, 7800 W. Old Ajo Way, Tucson, AZ 85732/602-883-6426

ARKANSAS

Remington Gun Club, I-40 Highway, Lonoke, AR 72086/501-676-2677

CALIFORNIA

Escondido Fish & Game, P.O. Box 506, Escondido, CA 92025/619-749-3277

Eubanks Redlands Trap & Skeet Range, 2125 N. Orange Blvd., Redlands, CA 92373/714-792-5780

Fresno Trap & Skeet Club, Hwy 99 & Shaw Ave., Fresno, CA 93779/209-846-8750

International Trap & Skeet Range, 831 No. Rosemead Blvd., El Monte, CA 91733/818-443-1518

Kern County Gun Club, China Grade Loop, Bakersfield, CA 93302/805-871-9977

Kingsburg Gun Club, Hwy 99 & Ave 384, Kingsburg, CA 93631/209-897-2160

Livermore Rod & Gun Club, Inter. 580 & Livermore Ave., Livermore, CA 94550

Martinez Gun Club, P.O. Box 910, Martinez, CA 94553/415-272-9599

Merced Fish & Game, Hwy 59 & Dickinson Ferry Rd., Merced, CA 95341/209-723-5852

Miramar Gun Club, 9400 Miramar Gun Club Rd., San Diego, CA 92138/619-278-3173

Newman Swamp Rats, 806 Orestimba, Newman, CA 95360/209-862-2142

Novato Trap Club, P.O. Box 482, Novato, CA 94948/415-897-9712

Oak Tree Gun Club, 23121 N. Coltrane, Newhall, CA 91322/805-259-7441

Pacific Rod & Gun Club, 520 John Muir, San Francisco, CA 94132/415-239-9613

Palm Springs Regional Trap & Skeet, 84-245 Indio Springs Dr., Indio, CA 92201/714-347-4811

Palmdale Fin & Feather, 600 East Avenue South, Palmdale, CA 93550/805-273-9879

Peninsula Sportsman's Club, P.O. Box 696, Menlo Park, CA 94025/415-322-4882

Sacramento Trap Club, 3701 Fulton Ave., Sacramento, CA 95821/916-484-9889

San Jose Trap & Skeet, 645 Cochran Rd., Morgan Hill, CA 95037/408-779-9710

Santa Lucia Sportsman's Club, 10400 Santa Clara Rd., Atascadero, CA 93422/805-544-1598

Santa Maria Gun Club, 3150 Telephone Rd., Santa Maria, CA 93456/805-925-6673

Stockton-Waterloo Gun Club, 4343 N. Ashley Lane, Stockton, CA 95205

Tri-County Gun Club, 17501 Pomona Rincon Rd., Chino, CA 91710

Tulare Trap Club, 8601 W. Roosevelt, Visalia, CA 93291/209-651-2525

COLORADO

Aurora (Denver) Gun Club, 301 Gun Club Rd., Aurora, CO 80017/303-366-9030

Cortez Trap Club, P.O. Box 48, Cortez, CO 81321/303-565-7396

R.F. Clement Trap Range, 4000 S. Carr St., Denver, CO 80235/303-986-8857

CONNECTICUT

Hartford Gun Club, 157 South Main, East Granby, CT 06026/203-658-1614

Remington Gun Club, 1207 Prospect Dr., Stratford, CT 06497/203-375-2526

FLORIDA

Gator Skeet & Trap Club, 5204 N.E. 46th Avenue, Gainesville, FL 32609/904-372-1044

Orange County Trap & Skeet Club, 10955 Smith-Bennett Rd., Orlando, FL 32819/305-351-1230

Palm Beach Trap & Skeet Club, 2950 Pierson Rd., West Palm Beach, FL 33414/305-793-8787

Sarasota Trap & Skeet Club, Knight Trail Park, Rustic Road, Sarasota, FL 33578/813-924-3210

Silver Dollar Trap & Golf Club, 17000 Patterson Rd., Odessa, FL 33556/813-920-3231

Skyway Trap & Skeet Club, 3200 74th Ave., St. Petersburg, FL 33702/813-526-8993

GEORGIA

Forest City Gun Club, 9203 Ferguson Ave., Savannah, GA 31406/912-354-0210

South River Gun Club, 5202 Highway 212 North, Covington, GA 30209/404-787-5279

HAWAII

Big Isle Gun Club, 320 KaManelo Place, Hilo, HI 96720

ILLINOIS

Darnall's Skeet & Trap Club, RR #3, Bloomington, IL 61701/309-379-4331

Decatur Gun Club, Faries Park, Decatur, IL 62525/217-423-6831

Frankfort Sportsman's Club, Mokena, IL 60448/815-469-9887

Highland Pistol & Rifle Club, P.O. Box 2, Highland, IL 62249/618-654-5971

Land O'Sports, RR #4, Springfield, IL 62707/217-546-0871

Northbrook Sports Club, P.O. Box 766, Grays Lake, IL 60030/312-223-5700

Peoria Skeet & Trap Club, RR #1, Spring Bay Rd., East Peoria, IL 61611/309-822-8146

X-Line Gun Club, Grinnell Rd., Kankakee, IL 60901/815-939-9211

INDIANA

Chain O'Lakes Gun Club, 55959 Country Club Rd., South Bend, IN 46619/219-287-8520

Columbus Gun Club, US 11 & Ind 46 Jct., Columbus, IN 47210/812-376-7005

Deer Creek Conservation Club, P.O. Box 210, Gas City, Marion, IN 46933/317-674-8670

Elkhart Shooting Center, 53049 Paul Dr., Elkhart, IN 46514/219-262-2406

Evansville Gun Club, RR #2, Haubstadt, Evansville, IN 47639/812-768-6370

Fulton County Conversation Club, RR #3, Box 91, Rochester, IN 46975/219-223-2072

Henry County Conservation Club, P.O. Box 35, New Castle, IN 47362/317-533-6602

Indiana Gun Club, RR 1, Box 190A, Fortville, IN 46040/317-485-6540

Kingen Gun Club, RR #1, Box 77, McCordsville, IN 46055/317-335-3781

Kossuth Gun Club, St. Road 135 North, Salem, IN 47167/812-358-3392

Roachdale Gun Club, RR 2, Ladoga, Roachdale, IN 47954/317-942-2054

IOWA

B&M Gun Club, P.O. Box 72, McCausland, IA 52758/319-225-2311

New Pioneer Gun Club, RR #2, Box 9, Des Moines, IA 50263/515-987-4415

Otter Creek Sportsman Club, P.O. Box 31, Cedar Rapids, IA/319-393-5814

Quail Ridge Gun Club, P.O. Box 168, Tiffin, IA 52340/319-645-2519

KANSAS

Kansas Trapshooters Assn. Trap Park, 117 St. North & Hillside, Wichita, KS 67147/316-755-9140

Liberal Gun Club, P.O. Box 1733, Liberal, KS 67901/316-624-5810

Tuttle Creek Trap Park, 1712 Ranser, Manhatten, KS 66502/913-539-4392

KENTUCKY

Jefferson Gun Club, Box 53, South Park Rd., Louisville, KY 40109/502-957-4661

LOUISIANA

Shreveport Gun Club, 44435 Meriweather Rd., Shreveport, LA 71109/318-686-9810

MANITOBA (CANADA)

Brandon Gun Club, P.O. Box 1104, Brandon, Manitoba, Can. R7A 6A3/204-728-4744

MARYLAND

Synepuxent Rod & Gun Club, P.O. Box 742, Libertytown, MD 21811/301-641-1312

MASSACHUSETTS

Holbrook Sportsman's Club, P.O. Box 275, Holbrook, MA 02343/617-767-4971

Minute Man Sportsman's Club, Francis Wyman Road, Burlington (Billerica), MA 01803/617-272-7169

Royalston Fish & Game Club, Main Road, Phillipston (Royalston), MA 01368/617-249-3004

Shirley Rod & Gun Club, Kittredege Road, Shirley, MA 01464/617-425-4701

Singletary Rod & Gun Club, Qunicy Street, Leicester (Oxford), MA 01524/617-987-8783

Walpole Sportsman's Assn., Lincoln Road, Walpole, MA 02081/617-668-6919

MICHIGAN

Barry County Conservation Club, 1180 South Cook Rd., Hastings, MI 49058/616-945-9058

Battle Creek Gun Club, Helmer Road, Battle Creek, MI 49017/616-964-1425

Berrien County Sportsman's Club, 2985 Linco Rd., Berrien Springs, MI 49103/616-429-3792

Michigan Trapshooting Assn., 1534 West Service Rd., Mason, MI 48854/517-676-2295

Seaway Gun Club, 3400 West Bard Rd., North Muskegon, MI 49445/616-766-3428

MINNESOTA

Central Minnesota Gun Club, Del-Tone Road, St. Cloud, MN 56301/612-251-9873

Fort Thunder Public Shooting Center, Route 3, Box 30, Perham, MN 57573/218-346-6083

Metro Gun Club, 10601 Naples Street N.E., Blaine, MN 55434/612-786-5880

Minneapolis Gun Club, 20006 Judicial Rd., Prior Lake (Minn.), MN 55372/612-469-4386

MISSOURI

Hi Point Hunting Club, RR 1, Box 28, Breckenridge, MO 64625/816-644-5708

KCTA Public Shooting Park, Route 2, Box 129A, Smithville (Kansas City), MO 64089/816-532-4427

Missouri Trapshooter's Assn. Gun Club, Rt. #1, Box 396, Linn Creek, MO 65052/314-346-2449

Wright City Gun Club, 57 Huck Finn, St. Charles (Wright City), MO 63303/314-724-3964

MONTANA

Missoula Trap & Skeet Club, P.O. Box 5365, Missoula, MT 59806/406-549-4815

NEBRASKA

Beatrice Gun Club, Rt #2, Beatrice, NE 68310/402-228-4368

NEVADA

Las Vegas Gun Club, 9200 Tule Springs Rd., Las Vegas, NV 89131/702-645-5606

Spring Creek Trap & Skeet Club, 451 E. Spring Creek Pkwy, Elko, NV 89801/702-753-6295

NEW JERSEY

Farmingdale Gun Club, Yellowbrook Road, Farmingdale, NJ 07727/201-938-2189

Pine Belt Sportsman's Club, Route #541, Indian Mills, NJ 08088/609-268-0237

Pine Valley Gun Club, New Freedom Road, Pine Hill, NJ 08021/609-267-7661

Thunder Mountain Trap & Skeet, Ringwood State Park, Ringwood, NJ 07456/201-962-6377

NEW MEXICO

Albuquerque Trap Club, P.O. Box 3746, Albuquerque, NM 87110/505-877-2688

Truth or Consequences Trap Club, 600 Broadway, Truth or Consequences, NM 87901/505-894-6860

NEW YORK

Bridgeport Rod & Gun Club, Bull Street & Eastwood Road, Bridgeport, NY 13030/315-699-3313

Falcon Trap & Game Club, Lime Rock Road, Mumford, NY 14467/716-538-9972

Mid-Hudson Gun Club, North Ohioville Road, New Paltz, NY 12550/914-255-7460

Ontario Rod & Gun Club, 2523 Trimble Rd., Ontario, NY 14519/315-524-7717

Suffolk Trap & Skeet Range, 52 Gerard Rd., Yaphank, NY 11980/516-924-4490

Taconic Trap Club, Route #82, Salt Point, NY 12578/914-266-3788

NORTH CAROLINA

Pinehurst Gun Club, P.O. Box 4000, Pinehurst, NC 28374/919-295-6811

Tar Heel Gun Club, Route #4, Box 101, Advance, NC 27006/919-998-4259

NORTH DAKOTA

Grand Forks Gun Club, Highway 2 West, Grand Forks, ND 58201/701-772-1551

Minot Gun Club, RR #1, Box 56, Minot, ND 58701/701-838-7472

OHIO

Crystal Lake Gun Club, 1900 Lake Rd., Medway, OH 45341/513-849-6649

Dover Bay Gun Club, 27954 Lake Rd., Bay Village, OH 44140/216-871-6222

Fairfield Sportsmen's Association, 6501 River Rd., Cincinnati, OH 45030/513-738-9915

Fisher-Jaqua Gun Club, 900 East Bigelow Ave., Findlay, OH 45840/419-422-0912

Great Eastern Gun Club, P.O. Box 210, Walnut Creek, OH 44610/216-893-2930

Jefferson County Sportsman, 3130 Sunset Blvd., Bloomingdale, OH 43952/614-944-1881

Logan County Fish & Game Club, 4494 Company Rd., Bellefontaine, OH 43311

Middletown Sportsmen's Club, 6945 Michael Rd., Middletown, OH 45042/513-422-5112

Sportsmen's Shooting Center, 1232 Chelmsford St. N.W., Canton, OH 44720/216-875-8081

Toledo Trap & Skeet, 3150 North Berkey Southern, Toledo, OH 43504/419-829-5101

OKLAHOMA

Enid Elks Gun Club, P.O. Box 3791, Enid, OK 73702/405-874-2551

Ota Shooting Park, Rt #2, Box 162AA, El Reno, OK 73036/405-262-9011

Shawnee Twin Lakes Trap Range, 5509 South Monte Dr., Oklahoma City, OK 73119/405-685-2712

Tahlequah Gun Club, Route #3, Box 235, Tahlequah, OK 74464/918-456-4749

ONTARIO (CANADA)

Quinte Trap & Gun Club, RR #5, Belleville, Ontario, Canada/613-962-3852

St. Thomas Gun Club, Cowan Park, St. George North, Ontario, Canada/519-633-2550

PENNSYLVANIA

Bradford Gun Club, Rt #770, Bradford, PA 16701/814-368-6245

Clairton Sportsmen's Club, 412 Coal Valley Rd., Clairton, PA 15025/412-233-4411

Langhorne Rod & Gun Club, Stoneyford Road, Holland, PA 18966/215-968-9973

Lappawinzo Fish & Game Club, Rd #2, Northampton, PA 18067/215-262-9904

North End Rod & Gun Club, Rd #2, Allentown, PA 18066/215-298-2555

Northumberland Point Township Sportsmen's Association, Rd #2, Northumberland, PA 17857/717-473-3272

South End Gun Club, Lorane Road, Reading, PA 19606/215-582-4289

Valley Gun & Country Club, P.O. Box 327, Elysburg, PA 17824/717-672-3130

Western Pennsylvania Sportsmen's Club, 5730 Saltsburg Rd., Murrysville, PA 15668/412-327-9918

SOUTH CAROLINA

J&W Trap & Skeet, P.O. Box 1627, Easley, SC 29641/803-859-2954

SOUTH DAKOTA

Crook's Gun Club, P.O. Box 427, Sioux Falls, SD 57101/605-543-5481

Sioux Falls Gun Club, 1500 South Norton, Sioux Falls, SD 57105/605-332-9558

TENNESSEE

Bend of the River Public Shooting Center, Rt #1, Box 218, Cookeville, TN 38501/615-528-2010

Kettlefoot Rod & Gun Club, P.O. Box 384, Bristol, TN 37621/615-878-3057

Montlake Public Shooting Center, 2009 Mowbray Pike, Soddy Daisy, TN 37319/615-332-1195

Tennessee State Trapshooting Association, 3912 Hillshire Dr., Chapel Hill, TN 37013/615-748-4116

TEXAS

Creekwood Gun Club, Highway 105 West, Conroe, TX 77305/409-588-1452

Ft. Worth Gun & Skeet Club, Rt #17, Box 283-B, Ft. Worth, TX 76126/817-244-9878

Greater Houston Gun Club, 6700 FM 2234, Missouri City, TX 77459/713-437-6025

Midland Shooters Association, P.O. Box 6354, Midland, TX 79711/915-563-4479

UTAH

Golden Spike Trap Club, 1400 West, 300 South, Brigham City, UT 84302/801-723-3427

WEST VIRGINIA

Brooke County Sportsmen & Farmers' Association, P.O. Box 3, Wellsburg, WV 26070/304-737-1504

WISCONSIN

Janesville Conservation Club, Read Road, Janesville, WI 53547/608-752-9107

St. Croix Valley Rod & Gun Club, P.O. Box 83, Hudson, WI 54016/715-386-9955

Waukesha Gun Club, 4040 N. 71st St., Milwaukee, WI 53216/414-547-9785

WYOMING

Jackson Hole Trap Club, Box V, Jackson, WY 83001/307-733-5067

Laramie Trap Club, P.O. Box 669, Laramie, WY 82070/307-745-9901

Rocky Mountain Gun Club, P.O. Box 1386, Casper, WY 82602/307-235-8067

SPORTING CLAYS

ARKANSAS

Mid America Sporting Clays, Crowley Ridge Shooting Resort, Route 1, Box 350, Forrest City, AR 72335/501-633-3352. Contact: Dale Horton

CALIFORNIA

Antelope Valley Sportsmen's Club, 45408 160th St. West, Lancaster, CA 93536. Contact: David Whiteside

Fowls Fare Gamebird Farm & Hunt Club, P.O. Box 3016, Gonzales, CA 93926/408-675-2473. Contact: Bruce Barsotti

Pachmayr Hunt School, 1875 South Mountain Ave., Monrovia, CA 91016/818-357-7771. Contact: R. J. Giordana

Raahauge's Pheasant Hunting Club, 5800 Bluff St., Norco, CA 91760/714-735-2361. Contact: Mike Raahauge

Sacramento Sporting Clays Gun Club, 1047 Shetland Ct., Roseville, CA 95661/916-786-0987. Contact: Curt Zolliner

Winchester Canyon Gun Club, P.O. Box 3306, Santa Barbara, CA 93130/805-965-9890. Contact: Jim Metcalf

CANADA

Club Roue Du Roy, 882 Quest Rd., Hemmingford, Quebec, Canada J0L 1H0/514-247-2882. Contact: R. Longtin

COLORADO

Buck Point Club, 9495 Country Rd. 115, Glenwood Springs, CO 81601/303-945-7610. Contact: Dr. Russell Scott

Front Range Sporting Clays, Heil Valley Ranch, Left Hand Canyon, Boulder, CO 80302/303-444-5243

Glenarm Sporting Clays, 68202 Trout Rd., Montrose, CO 81401/303-249-6498

High Country Game Birds, 33300 Road 25, Elizabeth, CO 80107/303-646-3315. Contact: Jim Pederson

Rocky Mountain Roosters, 21171 Road 78, Route 1, Calhan, CO 80808. Contact: Brett Axton

Western Colorado Sporting Clays, 2929 Beechwood St., Grand Junction, CO 81506/303-241-9480. Contact: Jeanie Kruger

CONNECTICUT

Bristol Game & Fish Association, P.O. Box 783, Bristol, CT 06010/203-582-3910

DELAWARE

Ommelanden Shooting Grounds, 1205 River Rd., New Castle, DE 19720/302-328-2256. Contact: George Long

DOMINICAN REPUBLIC

Casa De Campo, P.O. Box 140, La Romana, Dominican Republic/809-523-3333. Contact Bill Massarda

FLORIDA

Indian River Trap & Skeet, 389 Island Creek Dr., Vero Beach, FL 32963/407-569-5311

Rocky Comfort Hunting Preserve, Route 4, Box 373, Quincy, FL 32351. Contact: Jesse Beasley

GEORGIA

Bear Sports Center, Inc., P.O. Box 1698, Thomasville, GA 31792. Contact: John H. Flowers

South River Gun Club, 5203 Highway 212, Covington, GA 30209/404-786-9456. Contact: Jerry English

ILLINOIS

Midwest Shooting Sports, Ltd., Route 1, Thompsonville, IL 62890/618-982-2906. Contact: Jim McCuan

Trout & Grouse Shooting Grounds, 1147 Wilmette, Wilmette, IL 60091/312-251-8090. Contact: Andrew J. Burrows

INDIANA

Tippecanoe Sporting Clays, 1340 Fawn Ridge, West Lafayette, IN 47906/317-743-1809. Contact: Mart Maassen

IOWA

Lazy H Hunting Club, Route 2, Woodbine, IA 51579/712-647-2877. Contact: Murray Hubbard

North Iowa Sporting Clays, Route 1, Box 213, St. Ansgar, IA 50472/515-736-4893. Contact: Jon Kruger

Outpost Clays Range & Hunting Preserve, P.O. Box 385, Missouri Valley, IA 51555

Triple H Ranch Hunting Preserve, Route 2, Box 165, Burlington, IA 52601/319-985-2253. Contact: Keith Hoelzman

KENTUCKY

Mashomack Fish & Game Preserve, P.O. Box 308, Pine Plains, KY 12567/212-249-4638. Contact: Daniel Daly

MARYLAND

Beretta Prince George Trap & Skeet Range, P.O. Box 421, Glenn Dale, MD 20769/301-577-1477. Contact: Phil Murray

Hopkins Game Farm, Route 298, Kennedyville, MD 21645/301-348-5287. Contact: George B. Hopkins

MINNESOTA

Crookston Gun Club, Inc., P.O. Box 259, Crookston, MN 56716/218-281-5143

Game Pointe Hunt Club, Route 3, Goodhue, MN 55027/612-923-4775. Contact: David L. Anderson

Minnesota Horse & Hunt Club, P.O. Box 482, Prior Lake, MN 55372/612-447-2272. Contact: Terry Correll

MISSISSIPPI

Quail Wood Plantation, P.O. Box 1296, Oxford, MS 38655/601-357-2660. Contact: Wayne Hale

Wilderness West, 5455 Kaywood Dr., Jackson, MS 39211/601-956-4762. Contact: John H. Allen

MISSOURI

Blackhawk Valley Hunting Preserve, Route 1, Box 118, Old Monroe, MO 63369/314-665-5459

Game Hill Hunting Club, Route 2, Box 194A, Weston, MO 64098/816-431-5057. Contact: Gary Norris

Malinmor Sporting Estate, Highway WW, Eolia, MO 63344/314-324-3366. Contact: Rick Merritt

MONTANA

Mallards Rest Sporting Clays, 1819 Avenue D, Billings, MT 59102/406-259-2888. Contact: Tom Jordan

NEVADA

Flying M Hunting Club, 70 Pine Grove Rd., Yerington, NV 89447. Contact: Jack Hedger

Topaz Sportsmen's Center, c/o Sleeping Elephant Ranch, 3851 Highway 208, Wellington, NV 89444/701-266-3512. Contact: Evan Allred

NEW HAMPSHIRE

Skat/Eastern Shotgun Sports, P.O. Box 137, New Ipswich, NH 30371/603-878-1257. Contact: Tony Haigh III

NEW JERSEY

Buckshorn Sportsmen Club, 507 Friendship Rd., Salem, NJ 08079/609-935-4659

West Creek Gunning Club, Stipson Island Road, Eldora, NJ 08270/609-861-2760. Contact: George Campbell

NEW YORK

Dutchess Valley Rod & Gun Club, Inc., Route 1, Aikendale Rd. Box 378, Pawling, NY 12564/914-855-5014. Contact: Harold N. Howard

Mid-Hudson Gun Club, 411 No. Ohioville Rd., New Paultz, NY 12561/914-255-7460. Contact: Hugh Davis

Morris Creek Fish & Game Preserve, Route 1, Box 122, South New Berlin, NY 13843. Contact: Lee Harden

Pawling Mountain Club, P.O. Box 573, Pawling, NY 12564/914-855-3825. Contact: Charles Schneible

Rochester-Brooks Gun Club, 926 Honeoye Fall Road 16, Rush, NY 14543/716-533-9913. Contact: Ronald E. Conner

NORTH CAROLINA

Beaver Dam Sporting Clay Range, Inc., Route 4, Box 97M, Greenville, NC 27834/919-758-2266. Contact: Rick Spivey

OKLAHOMA

Southern Ranch Lodge & Hunting Club, Route 2, Box 75, Chandler, OK 74834/405-258-0000/918-377-4226.

USA Clays, 5900 S.E. 48th St., Oklahoma City, OK 73135/405-793-7308. Contact: Craig Danks

OREGON

Treo Corporation, Route 1, Box 3171, Heppner, OR 97836/503-676-5840. Contact: Philip Carlson

SOUTH CAROLINA

Brays Island Plantation, P.O. Box 1539, Beaufort, SC 29901/803-525-6303. Contact: George Flint

Charleston Sporting Clays, P.O. Box 773, Mount Pleasant, SC 29464

The Oaks Gun Club, Ltd., Route 2, Box 196-A, Georgetown, SC 29440/803-527-1861. Contact: Herbert J. Butler

River Bend Sportsman's Resort, Inc., P.O. Box 625, Inman, SC 29349/803-583-2048. Contact: Ralph Barnwell

SOUTH DAKOTA

Valley West Trap & Sporting Clay Range, P.O. Box 88045, Route 3, Highway 17, Sioux Falls, SD 57105/605-361-3173

TENNESSEE

Nashville Gun Club, 6801 Holt Rd., Nashville TN 32711

Stones River Gun Club, P.O. Box 900, Murfreesboro, TN 37130/615-893-1975. Contact: Clyde Craddock

TEXAS

Champion Lake Shooting Club, 5617 Hiltonview, Houston, TX 77086/713-893-5868. Contact: Danny McMillan

Clear Creek Gun Range, 306 Crystal, League City, TX 77573/713-337-1722. Contact: Earnest L. Randall

Greater Houston Gun Club, P.O. Box 97, Missouri City, TX 77459/713-437-6025. Contact: William Poole

Highland Bend Shooting School, P.O. Box 580, Fulshear, TX 77441/713-341-0032. Contact: Jay Herbert

Honey Creek Sporting Clays, Route 3, Box 174, Hico, TX 76457/817-796-2148. Contact: Mike Mize

LaPaloma Sporting Club, Inc., P.O. Box 160516, San Antonio, TX 78280/512-438-4424. Contact: Henry Burns

Love's Shooting Range, P.O. Box 6452, Midland, TX 79711/915-563-4479. Contact: Gene Love

Spanish Dagger Hunting Resort, P.O. Box 478, Campwood, TX 78833/512-278-2998. Contact: George T. Cooper

Upland Bird Company, P.O. Box 1110, Corsicana, TX 75110/214-872-5663. Contact: Steven Stroube

VIRGINIA

Atlantic Coast Gun Club, 2431 Chainbridge Rd., Vienna, VA 22180/703-938-5636. Contact: Dallas Berry

WASHINGTON

The Washington Hunt Club, 1111 Third Avenue, Suite 1580, Seattle, WA 98101/901-258-6600. Contact: T. Featherly III

WASHINGTON D.C.

Dr. Ronald S. Godwin, 3600 New York Ave., N.E., Washington, DC 20002

WEST VIRGINIA

Foxy Pheasant Hunting Preserve, Route 1, Box 437, Kearneysville, WV/304-725-4963. Contact: Gene Abelow

WISCONSIN

River Wildlife, 444 Highland Dr., Kohler, WI 53044/414-457-0134. Contact: Mark Grube

Top Gun Sporting Clays, P.O. Box 44, Woodland, WI 53099/414-625-3908. Contact: Dave Fiedler

Manufacturers' Directory

AMMUNITION (Commercial Shotshell)

Activ Industries, Inc., P.O. Box F, Kearneysville, WV 25430/304-725-0451 (shotshells only)

Dynamit Nobel-RWS, Inc., 105 Stonehurst Court, Northvale, NJ 07647/201-767-1995

Estate Cartridge Co., P.O. Box 3702, Conroe, TX 77305/409-856-7277

Federal Cartridge Co., 900 Ehlen Dr., Anoka, MN 55303/612-422-2840

Fiocchi of America, Inc., Rt #2, Box 90-8, Ozark, MO 65721/417-725-4118

Remington Arms Co., 1007 Market St., Wilmington, DE 19898/302-773-5291

Winchester, 427 N. Shamrock St., East Alton, IL 62024/618-258-2000

CHOKE DEVICES, RECOIL ABSORBERS & RECOIL PADS

Action Products Inc., 22 N. Mulberry St., Hagerstown, MD 21740/800-228-7763 (rec. shock eliminator)

Allison & Carey Gun Works, 10218 S.E. Powell Blvd., Portland, OR 97266/503-760-3388

Bob Allen Companies, 214 S.W. Jackson St., Des Moines, IA 50315/515-283-2191

Armsport, Inc., 3590 N.W. 49th St., Miami, FL 33142/305-635-7850 (choke devices)

Stan Baker, 10000 Lake City Way, Seattle, WA 98125/206-522-4575 (shotgun)

Briley Mfg. Co., 1085-B Gessner, Houston, TX 77055/713-932-6995 (choke tubes)

C&H Research, 115 Sunnyside Dr., Lewis, KS 67552/316-324-5445 (Mercury recoil suppressor)

Clinton River Gun Serv. Inc., 30016 S. River Rd., Mt. Clemens, MI 48045 (Reed Choke)

D&M Enterprises, Box 118, Soda Springs, ID 83276

Dahl Gun Shop, 6947 King Ave. West, Billings, MT 59106/406-652-3909

Edwards Recoil Reducer, 269 Herbert St., Alton, IL 62002/618-462-3257

Emsco Variable Shotgun Chokes, 101 Second Ave., S.E., Waseca, MN 56093/507-835-1779

Griggs Recreational Prods. Inc., 270 S. Main St., Suite 103, Bountiful, UT 84010

I.N.C., Inc., P.O. Box 12767, Wichita, KS 67277/316-721-9570

Joe Shiozaki, 938 East Alosta Ave., Azusa, CA 91702

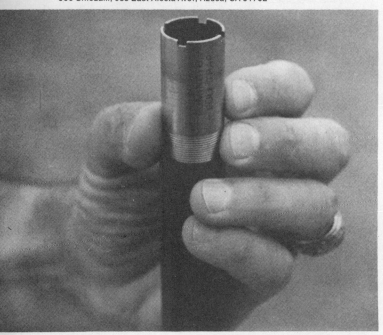

With the wide popularity of screw-in chokes for today's competition shotguns, shooters often forget to either change or check these choke tubes for type and installation. It is wise to take full advantage of the different choke constrictions especially in trapshooting. Singles or 16-yard targets do not require the tight constriction of Handicap shooting, yet all too often, a shooter will use a modified choke for the Singles events and then forget to swap choke tubes for the Handicap event.

Lyman Products Corp., Rte. 147, Middlefield, CT 06455 (Cutts Comp.)

MBM Enterprises, 715 East 46th St., Stillwater, OK 74074

Mag-na-port International, Inc., 41302 Executive Drive, Mt. Clemens, MI 48045/313-469-6727 (muzzle-brake system)

Mag-na-port of Canada, 1861 Burrows Ave., Winnipeg, Manitoba R2X 2V6, Canada

Morgan Adjustable Recoil Pad Co., 4746 South Ave., Youngstown, OH 44512

Multi-Gauge Enterprises, 433 W. Foothill Blvd., Monrovia, CA 91016/818-357-6117/358-4549 (screw-in chokes)

Okie Manfacturing, Rt. 1, Box 155, Hendrix, OK 74741

Pachmayr Gun Works, Inc., 1875 S. Mountain Ave., Monrovia, CA 91016

P.A.S.T. Corp., 210 Park Ave., P.O. Box 7372, Columbia, MO 65205/314-449-7278 (recoil reducer shield)

Poly-Choke Div., Marble Arms, 420 Industrial Park, Gladstone, MI 49837/906-428-3710

Precision Porting, 157 North Salem Rd., Conyers, GA 30208/404-922-3480

Pro-Choke, Inc., 2760 NE 7th Ave., Pompano Beach, FL 33064

Pro-Port Ltd., 41302 Executive Dr., Mt. Clemens, MI 48045/313-469-7323

Purbaugh, See: Multi-Gauge Enterprises

Shooters Emporium, 10125 N.E. Glisan, Portland, OR 97220/503-257-0524

Shotgun Machine, 7630 Miramar Rd., San Diego, CA 92126/619-695-1620

Ed Sowers, 8331 DeCelis Place, Sepulveda, CA 91343/818-893-1233

Sportsman's Haven, 14695 E. Pike Road, Cambridge, OH 43725/614-432-7243

Staub Gun Specialties, 261 Herbert, Alton, IL 62002/618-465-6286

Supreme Products Co., 1830 S. California Ave., Monrovia, CA 91016/800-423-7159/818-357-5395 (recoil pads)

Target Arms, 1951 S. Memorial Dr., Racine, WI 53403

CLEANING & REFINISHING SUPPLIES

American Gas & Chemical Co., Ltd., 220 Pegasus Ave., Northvale, NJ 07647/201-767-7300 (TSI gun lube)

Anderson Mfg. Co., P.O. Box 4218, Federal Way, WA 98063/203-838-4299 (stock finishers)

Armite Labs., 1845 Randolph St., Los Angeles, CA 90001/213-587-7744 (pen oiler)

Armoloy Co. of Ft. Worth, 204 E. Daggett St., Ft. Worth, TX 76104/817-461-0051

Belltown Ltd., 11 Camps Rd., Kent, CT 06757/203-354-5750 (gun clg. cloth kit)

Birchwood-Casey, 7900 Fuller Rd., Eden Prairie, MN 55344/612-927-7933

Blacksmith Corp., P.O. Box 1752, Chino Valley, AZ 86323/602-636-4456 (Arctic Friction Free gun clg. equip.)

Blue and Gray Prods., Inc., R.D. #6, Box 362, Wellsboro, PA 16901/717-724-1383

Break-Free, a div. of San/Bar Corp., P.O. Box 25020, Santa Ana, CA 92799/714-953-1900 (lubricants)

Browning Arms, Rt. 4, Box 624-B, Arnold, MO 63010

J.M. Bucheimer Co., P.O. Box 280, Airport Rd., Frederick, MD 21701/301-662-5101

Chem-Pak, Inc., 11 Oates Ave., P.O. Box 1685, Winchester, VA 22601/703-667-1341 (Gun-Savr. protect & lubricant)

Chopie Mfg. Inc., 700 Copeland Ave., La Crosse, WI 54601/608-784-0926 (Black-Solve)

Clenzoil Corp., Box 1226, Sta. C, Canton, OH 44708/216-833-9758

The Dutchman's Firearms Inc., 4143 Taylor Blvd., Louisville, KY 40215/502-366-0555

Forster Products, 82 E. Lanark Ave., Lanark, IL 61046/815-493-6360

Forty-Five Ranch Enterpr., 119 S. Main St., Miami, OK 74354/918-542-9307

Fountain Prods., 492 Prospect Ave., W. Springfield, MA 01089/413-781-4651

Frank C. Hoppe Division, Penguin Ind., Inc., Airport Industrial Mall, Coatesville, PA 19320/215-384-6000

Ken Jantz Supply, 222 E. Main, Davis, OK 73030/405-369-2316

Jet-Aer Corp., 100 Sixth Ave., Paterson, NJ 07524 (blues & oils)

Kleen-Bore, Inc., 20 Ladd Ave., Northampton, MA 01060/413-586-7240 (Rust-Guardit)

Terry K. Kopp, 1301 Franklin, Lexington, MO 64067/816-259-2636 (stock rubbing compound; rust preventative grease)

LPS Chemical Prods., Holt Lloyd Corp., 4647 Hugh Howell Rd., Tucker, GA 30084/404-934-7800

Mark Lee, 9901 Francis Ct., Lakeville, MN 55044/612-461-2114 (rust blue solution)

Lynx Line Gun Prods., div. of Williams Shootin' Iron Service, Rte. 1 Box 151 A, Bennett Hill Rd., Central Lake, MI 49622/616-544-6615

MP Research, P.O. Box 1348, Victorville, CA 92393/800-248-5823

Marble Arms Co., 420 Industrial Park, Gladstone, MI 49837/906-428-3710

Old World Oil Products, 3827 Queen Ave. N., Minneapolis, MN 55412/612-522-5037

Omark Industries, Box 856, Lewiston, ID 83501/208-746-2351

Original Mink Oil, Inc., P.O. Box 20191, 11021 N.E. Beech St., Portland, OR 97220/503-255-2814

RBS Industries Corp., 1312 Washington Ave., St. Louis, MO 63103/314-241-8564 (Miracle All Purpose polishing cloth)

Reardon Prod., 103 W. Market St., Morrison, IL 61270 (Dry-Lube)

Rice Protective Gun Coatings, 235-30th St., West Palm Beach, FL 33407/407-848-7771

Richards Classic Oil Finish, John Richards, Rt. 2, Box 325, Bedford, KY 40006/
502-255-7222 (gunstock oils, wax)
Rig Products, 87 Coney Island Dr., Sparks, NV 89431/702-331-5666
Rusteprfe Labs, 1319 Jefferson Ave., Sparta, WI 54656/608-269-4144
Rust-Guardit, See: Kleen-Bore, Inc.
San/Bar Corp., Break-Free Div., P.O. Box 25020, Santa Ana, CA 92799/714-953-
1900 (lubricants)
Saunders Sptg. Gds., 338 Somerset, N. Plainfield, NJ 07060 (Sav-Bore)
TDP Industries, Inc., 603 Airport Blvd., Doylestown, PA 18901/215-345-8687
Texas Platers Supply Co., 2453 W. Five Mile Parkway, Dallas, TX 75233 (plating
kit)
Totally Dependable Products, See: TDP
C.S. Van Gorden, 1815 Main St., Bloomer, WI 54724/715-568-2612 (Van's Instant
Blue)
Venco Industries, 16770 Hilltop Park Place, Chagrin Falls, OH 44022/216-543-
8808
WD-40 Co., P.O. Box 80607, San Diego, CA 92138-9021/619-275-1400
Williams Gun Sight, 7389 Lapeer Rd., Davison, MI 48423 (finish kit)
Woodstream Corp., P.O. Box 327, Lititz, PA 17543 (mask)
Z-Coat Co., 3915 U.S. Hwy. 98 So., Lakeland, FL 33801/813-665-1734 (Teflon
coatings)
Zip Aerosol Prods.,: See Rig

EYEWEAR

Bausch & Lomb, 42 East Ave., Rochester, NY 14603
Bilsom Intl., Inc., 109 Carpenter Dr., Sterling, VA 22170
Decot, P.O. Box 15830, Phoenix, AZ 85060
Doctor Yochem, 21783 Highway 18, Apple Valley, CA 92307
Lehman Optical, 3125 North 34th Place, Pheonix, AZ 85018
Magic Dot, 10228 West Burleigh St., Wauwatosa, WI 53222
Oak Lawn Optical, 100-C One Turtle Creek Village, Dallas, TX 75219
Opti-Sport, Inc., 2350 Bowen Road, Elma, NY 14059
Silencio, 23 Snider Way, Sparks, NV 89431
Tasco, 7600 NW 26th St., Miami, Fla. 33122
Willson Safety Prods. Division, P.O. Box 622, Reading, PA 19603
Zeiss, Box 2010, 1015 Commerce St., Petersburg, VA 23803

GUNS (Foreign)

Armes de Chasse, P.O. Box 827, Chadds Ford, PA 19317/215-783-6133 (Merkel)
Armsport, Inc., 3590 N.W. 49th St., Miami, FL 33142/305-635-7850
Benelli Armi, See: Heckler & Koch (shotguns)
Beretta U.S.A., 17601 Beretta Dr., Accokeek, MD 20607/301-283-2191
Bretton, 19, rue Victor, Grignard, Z.I. Montreynaud, 42-St. Etienne, France
Browning (gen. Offices), Rt. 1, Morgan, UT 84050/801-876-2711
Browning, (parts & service), Rt. 4, Box 624-B, Arnold, MO 63010/314-287-6800
Classic Doubles, 1982 Innerbelt Business Center Dr., St. Louis, MO 63114/314-
423-6191
Connecticut Valley Arms Co., 5988 Peachtree Corners East, Norcross, GA 30092/
404-449-4687 (CVA)
Charles Daly, See: Outdoor Sports HQ
Dixie Gun Works, Inc., Hwy. 51, South, Union City, TN 38261/901-885-0561 (ML)
Dynamit Nobel-RWS, 105 Stonehurst Court, Northvale, NJ 07647/201-767-1995
(Rottweil)
Euroarms of American, Inc., P.O. Box 3277, 1501 Lenoir Dr., Winchester, VA
22601/703-661-1863 (ML)
J. Fanzoj, P.O. Box 25, Ferlach, Austria 9170
Armi FERLIB di Libero Ferraglio, 46 Via Costa, 25063 Gardone VT. (Brescia), Italy
Firearms Imp. & Exp. Corp., (F.I.E.), P.O. Box 4866, Hialeah Lakes, Hialeah, FL
33014/305-685-5966
Auguste Francotte & Cie, S.A., rue de Trois Juin 109, 4400 Herstal-Liege, Belgium
Frigon Guns, 627 W. Crawford, Clay Center, KS 67432/913-632-5607
Armas Garbi, Urki #12, Eibar (Guipuzcoa) Spain (shotguns, See W.L. Moore)
Griffin & Howe, 589 Broadway, New York, NY 10012/212-966-5323 (Purdey, Hol-
land & Holland)
Heckler & Koch Inc., 21480 Pacific Blvd., Sterling, VA 22170/703-450-1900

Incor, Inc., P.O. Box 132, Addison, TX 75001/214-931-3500 (Cosmi auto shotg.)
Interarms, 10 Prince St., Alexandria, VA 22313
Paul Jaeger Inc., P.O. Box 449, 1 Madison Ave., Grand Junction, TN 38039 (Heym)
Kassnar Imports, P.O. Box 6097, Harrisburg, PA 17112/717-652-6101
Krieghoff International, P.O. Box 549, Ottsville, PA 18942/215-847-5173
Midwest Gun Sport, 1108 Herbert Dr., Zebulon, NC 27597/919-269-5570 (E. Du-
moulin)
Wm. Larkin Moore & Co., 31360 Via Colinas, Suite 109, Westlake Village, CA
91361/818-889-4160 (Garbi, Ferlib, Piotti, Perugini-Visini)
Navy Arms Co., 689 Bergen Blvd., Ridgefield, NJ 07657
Outdoor Sports Headquarters, Inc., 967 Watertower Lane, Dayton, OH 45449/513-
865-5855 (Charles Daly shotguns)
Parker Reproductions, 124 River Rd., Middlesex, NJ 08846/201-469-0100
Perazzi USA, 1207 S. Shamrock Ave., Monrovia, CA 91016/818-303-0068
Precision Sports, P.O. Box 708, 3736 Kellogg Rd., Cortland, NY 13045/607-756-
2851 (Parker-Hale side-by-side shotgun)
Quality Arms, Inc., Box 19477, Houston, TX 77224/713-870-8377 (Bernardelli
shotguns)
Rahn Gun Works, Inc., 3700 Anders Rd., Hastings, MI 49058-616-945-9894 (Garbi
shotguns)
Ravizza Carlo Caccia Pesca, s.r.l., Via Melegnano 6, 20122 Milano, Italy
Rottweil, (See Dynamit Nobel-RWS)
SKB Gun Co., RD #8 Box 145, Manheim, PA 17545/717-664-4040
Savage Industries, Inc., Springdale Rd., Westfield, MA 01085/413-562-2361
Thad Scott, P.O. Box 412; Hwy 82 West, Indianola, MS 38751/601-887-5929 (Peru-
gini-Visini; Bertuzzi s/s dble.; Marlo Beschi shotguns)
Sigarms, Inc., 470 Spring Park Pl., Unit 900, Herndon, VA 22070/703-481-6660
33054
Stoeger Industries, 55 Ruta Ct., S. Hackensack, NJ 07606/201-440-2700
Tradewinds, Inc., P.O. Box 1191, Tacoma, WA 98401
Ignacio Ugartechea, Apartado 21, Eibar, Spain
Valmet, See: Stoeger Industries
Verney-Carron, B.P. 72, 54 Boulevard Thiers, 42002 St. Etienne Cedex, France
Perugini-Visini & Co. s.r.l., Via Camprelle, 126, 25080 Nuvolera (Bs.), Italy
Weatherby's, 2781 Firestone Blvd., So. Gate, CA 90280/213-569-7186
Italy
Antonio Zoli U.S.A. Inc., P.O. Box 6190, Fort Wayne, IN 46896

GUNS (U.S.)

Firearms Imp. & Exp. Corp., P.O. Box 4866, Hialeah Lakes, Hialeah, FL 33014/
305-685-5966 (F.I.E)
Ithaca Gun Co., Route 34B, King Ferry, NY 13081
Ljutic Ind., Inc., P.O. Box 2117, 918 N. 5th Ave., Yakima, WA 98902/509-248-0476
Marlin Firearms Co., 100 Kenna Drive, New Haven, CT 06473
O.F. Mossberg & Sons, Inc., 7 Grasso St., No. Haven, CT 06473
Navy Arms Co., 689 Bergen Blvd., Ridgefield, NJ 07657
Remington Arms Co., 1007 Market St., Wilmington, DE 19898
Ruger, See: Sturm, Ruger & Co.
Savage Industries, Inc., Springdale Rd., Westfield, MA 01085/413-562-2361
Sporting Arms, Inc. Mfg., P.O. Box 191, Littlefield, TX 79339/806-385-5665 (Snake
Charmer II shotgun)
Sturm, Ruger & Co., Southport, CT 06490
Thompson Center Arms, P.O. Box 5002, Rochester, NH 03867/603-332-2394
Trail Guns Armory, 1422 E. Main St., League City, TX 77573/713-332-5833
U.S. Repeating Arms Co., P.O. Box 30-300, New Haven, CT 06511/203-789-5000
Winchester, See: U.S. Repeating Arms

HEARING PROTECTORS

AO Safety Prods., Div. of American Optical Corp., 14 Mechanic St., Southbridge,
MA 01550/617-765-9711 (ear valves, ear mffs)
Bausch & Lomb, 42 East Ave., Rochester, NY 14603
Bilsom Interntl., Inc., 109 Carpenter Dr., Sterling, VA 22170/703-834-1070 (ear
plugs, mffs)
David Clark Co., Inc., 360 Franklin St., Worcester, MA 01604
Insta-Mold, P.O. Box 2146, Boulder, CO 80306/303-447-2619

Some form of hearing protector is an absolute necessity for all shooters, but trap and Skeet competitors really need them because of the high volume of shooting involved.

Marble Arms Corp., 420 Industrial Park, Gladstone, MI 49837/906-428-3710
North Consumer Prods. Div., 2664-B Saturn St., Brea, CA 92621/714-524-1655 (Lee Sonic ear valves)
Safety Direct, 56 Coney Island Dr., Sparks, NV 89431/702-354-4451 (Silencio)
Smith & Wesson, 2100 Roosevelt Ave., Springfield, MA 01101
Willson Safety Products Div., P.O. Box 622, Reading, PA 19603 (Ray-O-Vac)

MAGAZINES, PERIODICALS, & VIDEO TAPES

The American Rifleman, 1600 Rhode Island Ave., NW, Washington, D.C. 20036
Field & Stream, 1515 Broadway, New York, NY 10036
Frank Little, P.O. Box 1336, Mechanicsburg, PA 17055/717-432-4129
Guns, P.O. Box 85201, San Diego, CA 92138
Gun List, 700 E. State St., Iola, WI 54990
Gun World, 34249 Camino Capistrano, Capistrano Beach, CA 92624
Inner Psych Unlimited, 3113 White Cloud, Cheyenne, WY 82001
Kay Ohye, 600 Holly Lane, North Brunswick, NJ 08092
Mental Ministries Unlimited, 11720 Windmill Road, Colorado Springs, CO 80908
Outdoor Life, 380 Madison Ave., New York, NY 10017
Shooting Times, P.O. Box 1790, Peoria, IL 61656
Shotgun Sports, P.O. Box 6810, Auburn, CA 95604
Skeet Shooting Review, P.O. Box 680007, San Antonio, TX 78268/800-531-7928
Sports Afield, 250 W 55th St., New York, NY 10019
Trap & Field, 1000 Waterway Boulevard, Indianapolis. IN 46202/317-633-2075

MICELLANEOUS

Custom stockmaker, Artifact Arms, RD #2, Rt. 53, Brandon, VT 05733/802-247-6119
Custom stockmaker, Larry Scheetz, 2427 Liberty St., Allentown, PA 18104/215-432-9618
Custom stockmaker, Paul D. Hillmer, Anton Custom Gunstocks, 7251 Hudson Heights, Hudson, IA 50643/319-988-3941
Custom stockmaker, Reinhart Fajen, Inc., P.O. Box 338, Warsaw, MO 65355/816-438-5111
Safes, Fort Knox, 1051 N. Industrial Park Rd., Orem, UT 84057/800-821-5216
Shootin' Accessories, P.O. Box 6810, Auburn, CA 95604
Shooting accessories, Bill Thurwanger, P.O. Box 72, McCausland, IA 52758/319-225-2311
Shooting clothes, Back Fence Sportswear, P.O. Box 432, Welda, KS 66091/913-448-6467
Shooting clothes, Bob Allen, 214 S.W. Jackson, Des Moines, IA 50315/800-247-8048
Shooting clothes, Bob Kraft, P.O. Box 80, Iselin, NJ 08830/201-634-7261
Shooting clothes, Chimere, Inc., 4406 Exchange Ave., Metro Park #119, Naples, FL 33942/813-643-4222
Shooting clothes, Laurence & Laurence, P.O. Box 261, Skokie, IL 60076
Shooting clothes, R.E.J. Enterprises, 111 Barbara Ann St., West Monroe, LA 71291/318-325-4862
Shooting coats, 10-X Products Group, 2828 Forest Lane, Suite 1107, Dallas, TX 75234/214-243-4016
Shotgun barrel repairs, William J. Nittler, 290 Moore Dr., Boulder Creek, CA 95006/408-338-3376
Shotgun bore, Custom Shootg. Prods., 8505 K St., Omaha, NE 68127
Shotgun choke specialist, Wm. J. Nittler, 290 Moore Dr., Boulder Creek, CA 95006
Shotgun competition choking, Ken Eyster Heritage Gunsmiths, Inc., 6441 Bishop Rd., Centerburg, OH 43011/614-625-6131
Shotgun ribs, Poly-Choke Div., Marble Arms Corp., 420 Industrial Park, Gladstone, MI 49837/906-428-3710
Shotgun sight, bi-ocular, Trius Prod., Box 25, Cleves, OH 45002
Shotgun specialist, Moneymaker Guncraft, 1420 Military Ave., Omaha, NE 68131/402-556-0226 (ventilated, free-floating ribs)
Shotshell adapter, PC Co., 5942 Secor Rd., Toledo, OH 43623/419-472-6222 (Plummer 410 converter)
Shotshell adapter, Jesse Ramos, Box 7105, La Puente, CA 91744 (12 ga./410 converter)
Trophies, Creative Casting, Inc., 400 West Coffin St., Denison, TX 75020/800-338-2252
Trophies, Kirk Stieff, 800 Wyman Park Dr., Baltimore, MD 21211/301-338-6000

RELOADING TOOLS, COMPONENTS AND ACCESSORIES

ACTIV Industries, Inc., P.O. Box 238, Kearneysville, WV 25430/304-725-0451 (plastic hulls, wads)
American Wad Co., P&P Tool, 14729 Spring Valley Rd., Morrison, IL 61270/815-772-3336 (12-ga. shot wad)
Ballistic Research Industries (BRI), 2825 S. Rodeo Gulch Rd., #8, Soquel, CA 95073/408-476-7981 (shotgun slug)
Bonanza Sports, See: Forster Products
C-H Tool & Die Corp., 106 N. Harding St., Owen, WI 54460/715-229-2146
Camdex, Inc., 2330 Alger, Troy, MI 48083/313-518-2300
CRW Products, Box 2123, Des Moines, IA 50310
Division Lead Co., 7742 W. 61st Pl., Summit, IL 60502
Eldora Plastics, Inc., P.O. Box 127, Eldora, IA 50627/515-848-2634 (Lage Uniwad)
Flambeau Prods. Corp., 15981 Valplast Rd., Middlefield, OH 44062/216-632-1631

Forster Products Inc., 82 E. Lanark Ave., Lanark, IL 61046/815-493-6360
Francis Tool Co., P.O. Box 7861, Eugene, OR 97401/503-345-7457 (powder measure)
Hollywood Loading Tools by M&M Engineering, 10642 Arminta St., Sun Valley, CA 91352/818-842-8376
Hornady Mfg. Co., P.O. Drawer 1848, Grand Island, NE 68802/308-382-1390
Huntington, P.O. Box 991, Oroville, CA 95965/916-534-1210 (Compac Press)
Lage Uniwad Co., 1814 21st. St., Eldora, IA 50627 (Universal Shotshell Wad)
Lee Precision, Inc., 4275 Hwy. U, Hartford, WI 53027/414-673-3075
Ljutic Industries, P.O. Box 2117, 732 N. 16th St., Yakima, WA 98907/509-248-0476 (plastic wads)
Lock's Phila. Gun Exch., 6700 Rowland, Philadelphia, PA 19149/215-332-6225
Lyman Products Corp., 147 West St., Middlefield, CT 06455
MEC, Inc., See: Mayville Eng. Co.
Mayville Eng. Co., 715 South St., Mayville, WI 53050/414-387-4500 (shotshell loader)
Ohaus Scale, See: RCBS
P&P Tool Co., 14729 Spring Valley Rd., Morrison, IL 61270/815-772-7618 (12-ga. shot wad)
Pacific Tool Co., See: Hornady
Pattern Control, 114 N. 3rd St., Garland, TX 75040 (plastic wads)
Ponsness/Warren, South 763 Highway 41, Rathdrum, ID 83858/208-687-2231
RCBS, Inc., Box 1919, Oroville, CA 95965/916-533-5191
Redding Inc., 1089 Starr Rd., Cortland, NY 13045
Stalwart Co., P.O. Box 357, Pocatello, ID 83204/208-232-7899
Trico Plastics, 590 S. Vincent Ave., Azusa, CA 91702
W.T.W., 750 West Hampden Ave., Suite 170, Englewood, CO 80110/303-781-6329 (plastic wads)
Webster Scale Mfg. Co., P.O. Box 188, Sebring, FL 33870/813-385-6362

TRAP & SKEET SHOOTERS EQUIP.

Bob Allen Companies, 214 S.W. Jackson, Des Moines, IA 50315/515-283-2191
The American Import Co., 1453 Mission St., San Francisco, CA 94103/415-863-1506 (Target thrower)
Americase, P.O. Box 271, Waxahachie, TX 75165/800-972-2737 (gun case)
Black Sheep, P.O. Box 210019, Dallas, TX 75211/800-527-6762 (gun case)
D&H Prods. Co., Inc., 465 Denny Rd., Valencia, PA 16059/412-898-2840 (snap shell)
Frigon Guns, 627 W. Crawford, Clay Center, KS 67432/913-632-5607
Hastings Barrels, 4th & Court St., Clay Center, KS 67432
Hoppe Division, Penguin Inds. Inc., Airport Mall, Coatesville, PA 19320/215-384-6000 (Monte Carlo pad)
Hunter Co., Inc., 3300 W. 71st Ave., Westminster, CO 80030/303-427-4626
Littleton Shotmaker, 22 Service St., Oroville, CA 95966/916-533-6084
MTM Molded Products Co., P.O. Box 14117, Dayton, OH 45414/513-890-7461
The Maverick Leather Co., P.O. Box 12305, El Paso, TX 79912
Meadow Industries, P.O. Box 450, Marlton, NJ 08053/609-953-0922 (stock pad, variable; muzzle rest)
Michaels of Oregon, P.O. Box 13010, Portland, OR 97213
NASCO Aluminum, 14232 McCallum Ave. N.E., Alliance, OH 44601/216-821-4621 (gun cases)
Outers Laboratories, Div. of Omark Industries, Route 2, Onalaska, WI 54650/608-783-1515 (trap, claybird)
C.C. Peterson, 2221 Ashland Ave., Racine, WI 53403
Remington Arms Co., 1007 Market St., Wilmington, DE 19898/302-774-5048 (trap, claybird)
Ed Scherer Leathercraft, P.O. Box 603, Elm Grove, WI 53122/414-968-4788 (shell carrier)
M.L. Schwab, 4910 N. Alicia, Tucson, AZ
Shamrock Leathers, 10125 N.E. Glisan, Portland, OR 97220/503-257-0524 (shell carriers/pouches)
T&S Shell Catcher, 1027 Skyview Dr., West Carrollton, OH 45449
TSA Manfacturing, 106 W. Fillmore Ave., St. Paul, MN 55107/612-297-9977 (shell carriers/pouches)
Timney Mfg. Inc., 3065 W. Fairmount Ave., Phoenix, AZ 85017/602-274-2999 (custom triggers)
Daniel Titus, Shooting Specialists, 872 Penn St., Bryn Mawr, PA 19010/215-525-8829 (hullbag)
Trius Products, Box 25, Cleves, OH 45002/513-941-5682 (can thrower; trap, claybird)
Winchester, div. of Olin Corp., Shamrock St., East Alton, IL 62024 (trap, claybird)

CLAYBIRD TRAPS

Electro Ballistic Lab., 616 Junipero Serva Blvd., Stanford, CA 94305 (Electronic Trap Boy)
Outers Laboratories, Div. of Omark Industries, Rte. 2, Onalaska, WI 54650/608-783-1515 (claybird traps)
Remington Arms Co., Bridgeport, CT 06602 (claybird traps)
Trius Prod., Box 25, Cleves, OH 45002/513-914-5682 (claybird, can thrower)
U.S. Repeating Arms Co., P.O. Box 30-300, New Haven, CT 06511/203-789-5000 (claybird traps)
Winchester, div. of Olin Corp., Shamrock St., East Alton, IL 62024